HANDBOOK OF INTERPERSONAL PSYCHOTHERAPY

(PGPS · 101)

Pergamon Titles of Related Interest

Brenner   *THE EFFECTIVE PSYCHOTHERAPIST: Conclusions from Practice and Research*
Gurman/Razin   *EFFECTIVE PSYCHOTHERAPY: A Handbook of Research*
Kanfer/Goldstein   *HELPING PEOPLE CHANGE: A Textbook of Methods, 2nd Edition*
Karoly/Kanfer   *SELF-MANAGEMENT AND BEHAVIOUR CHANGE: From Theory to Practice*
Marsella/Pedersen   *CROSS-CULTURAL COUNSELING AND PSYCHOTHERAPY*
Rachman/Wilson   *THE EFFECTS OF PSYCHOLOGICAL THERAPY, 2nd Edition*
Walker   *CLINICAL PRACTICE OF PSYCHOLOGY: A Guide for Mental Health Professionals*

Related Journals*

ADVANCES IN BEHAVIOUR RESEARCH AND THERAPY
CLINICAL PSYCHOLOGY REVIEW
JOURNAL OF PSYCHIATRIC RESEARCH
JOURNAL OF PSYCHIATRIC TREATMENT AND EVALUATION
PERSONALITY AND INDIVIDUAL DIFFERENCES

*Free specimen copies available upon request.

HANDBOOK OF INTERPERSONAL PSYCHOTHERAPY

Edited by
Jack C. Anchin
State University of New York
College at Buffalo

Donald J. Kiesler
Virginia Commonwealth University

Pergamon Press
New York   Oxford   Toronto   Sydney   Paris   Frankfurt

Pergamon Press Offices:

U.S.A.	Pergamon Press Inc., Maxwell House, Fairview Park, Elmsford, New York 10523, U.S.A.
U.K.	Pergamon Press Ltd., Headington Hill Hall, Oxford OX3 0BW, England
CANADA	Pergamon Press Canada Ltd., Suite 104, 150 Consumers Road, Willowdale, Ontario M2J 1P9, Canada
AUSTRALIA	Pergamon Press (Aust.) Pty. Ltd., P.O. Box 544, Potts Point, NSW 2011, Australia
FRANCE	Pergamon Press SARL, 24 rue des Ecoles, 75240 Paris, Cedex 05, France
FEDERAL REPUBLIC OF GERMANY	Pergamon Press GmbH, Hammerweg 6, 6242 Kronberg/Taunus, Federal Republic of Germany

Library of Congress Cataloging in Publication Data
Main entry under title:

Handbook of interpersonal psychotherapy.

    (Pergamon general psychology series ; v. 101)
    Includes bibliographical references.
    1. Psychotherapist and patient. 2. Psycho-
therapy. I. Anchin, Jack. C. (Jack Charles),
1951-   . II. Kiesler, Donald J. III. Series.
[DNLM: 1. Physician-patient relations. 2. Psychotherapy. WM 420 H2316]
RC480.8.H36   1981   616.89'14   81-8499
ISBN 0-08-025959-6   AACR2

Printed in the United States of America

To Our Parents:

Anita and Edward Anchin

Mildred and John Kiesler

Contents

PART IV. SUMMARY AND CONCLUSIONS

Foreword
Hans H. Strupp

The central theme of this volume is the redefinition of the psychotherapeutic relationship as a two-person system. At first glance, this revision of what used to be seen as a subject-object relationship may not seem radical. As the authors represented in this forward-looking volume demonstrate, however, we stand on the threshold of a revolution in psychotherapy that will predictably have incisive consequences for practice, training, and research in the years to come. Many of the ideas have been with us for several decades but, like all scientific and social developments, they have taken time to mature and therapeutic practice, for the most part, has remained relatively unaffected. Sullivan, for example, ranks as one of the major contributors to the new trend, yet his writings went relatively unappreciated for many years. The authors of this volume have chosen different approaches to this redefinition, and their languages differ. The implications, however, are clear. They demand a new role for the therapist, new concepts that are interactional rather than unidirectional, and new approaches to research that have barely begun to be implemented. To quote Kiesler: "The therapeutic relationship . . . is the momentary and cumulative reciprocal emotional and other engagements occurring between client and therapist—the continually evolving reciprocal effects of messages sent to and received by the client and the therapist."

In simplest terms, psychotherapy is now seen as a truly interpersonal process. Fundamentally, it is no different from anything that goes on between two people in any other situation, that is, the same interpersonal dynamics govern psychotherapy that govern any other human relationship. What differs is the therapist's role as an observing participant in the process and the experiences of the patient that result from this specialized interaction. In contrast to the traditional psychoanalytic view, the "therapeutic situation" is not the patient's relationship *to* the therapist nor is the therapist the passive recipient of the patient's transference distortions.

Carson states: "[P]atently maladaptive behavior persists over lengthy time periods because it is based on perceptions, expectations, or constructions of the characteristics of other people that tend to be confirmed by the interpersonal consequences of the behavior emitted." The cogency of this observation was brought home to me in a dramatic sequence. A young woman whom I had been seeing in therapy for some time increasingly attempted to engage me in a power struggle. The basic issue, as I eventually came to see, was whether she could succeed in recreating a father-daughter relationship with me, thereby resurrecting her father who had died several years ago, and with whom she had what would previously have been called a sadomasochistic relationship. As the storm mounted and became all encompassing, she enacted the following intense scenario: "I offer myself on the altar of total devotion and loyalty. In return, I expect the same from you. I will never leave you, and you must never leave me. If you reject my offer or otherwise disappoint me, I shall be enraged and fight any change." I steadfastly adhered to the therapist role, as the patient became more belligerent, whining, and seemingly helpless. She became contemptuous and sought to provoke me. Concomitantly—this occurred to me after a matter of weeks—she had fallen behind in her payments for treatment and a substantial balance had accumulated. In short, a vicious circle was in progress. I must confess that for a time I experienced considerable counteranger, fueled by a sense of pervasive impotence. Eventually the issue became clear to me and I was able to take corrective action. It consisted of telling the patient in simple terms that if she wanted me to be her therapist and if she wanted my help in working out her problems, I was willing to help her. At the same time, I left no doubt that I could not and would not play any other role and that there was no prospect of such an occurrence. To underscore my point, I insisted that my fee be paid on an hour-by-hour basis and that I expected liquidation of the remaining balance in a reasonable period of time. Perhaps it should occasion no surprise that the patient showed immediate "improvement" and began to treat me—as well as herself—as an adult.

The incident may be read on many levels and it had far-reaching implications for this patient's therapy, which I shall not pursue. The important point is the unmistakable enactment of an old interpersonal scenario with the therapist as a co-actor in the present. As Levenson (1972) beautifully put it:

whatever goes on in the family will be replayed in therapy. Moreover, it will not be a *distortion* or transference but an actual isomorphic replay in which the therapist participates. The therapist cannot avoid it by being "well-analyzed" or perceptive. It is not the therapist's uncoding of the dynamics that makes the therapy, not his "interpretations" of meaning and purpose, but, rather, his extended participation with the patient. It is not his ability to resist distortion by the patient (transference) or to resist his own temptation to interact irrationally with the patient (countertransference) but, rather, his ability to be trapped, immersed, and participating in the system and then to work his way out. This is [the new] version of "working through": not constant reinterpretation of distortion but the gradual changing of the patient's entire field by resisting transformation—which is a process of boring from within.

In a certain sense, the therapist of course does not resist participation in the enactment of the patient's self-defeating scenario but in another sense, he can only help the patient by becoming a participant in the patient's game. In my opinion, this is precisely the nature of the therapist's skill: It is not his or her knowledge of psychodynamics, his understanding of the antecedents of neurotic behavior, or an ability to make astute interpretations. What is critical is his ability *partially* to participate in and redirect the scenarios being played out by the patient. It is the context of such an experience, as Robert Carson points out in Chapter 4, that the critical structural tranformations of the patient's "perceptions, expectations, or constructions of the characteristics of other people" occur. That is the crux of therapeutic learning, and it delineates the essential therapuetic skill that I have previously called the therapeutic management of a human relationship.

The thrust of contemporary developments, exemplified by the authors of this volume, is not merely a redefinition of such terms as transference, countertransference, or resistance, which had their roots in Freud's nineteenth-century view of therapy as a treatment administered by a physician to a patient afflicted by a "neurotic illness." Rather, we are in the midst of a paradigm shift in Kuhn's sense. The clinical phenomena, of course, have not changed nor are the contemporary developments a discredit to Freud's seminal insights which themselves set the stage. What is changing is the therapist's behavior and his understanding of the process and goal of therapy. Countervailing trends are the deeply entrenched metapsychology and the anachronistic "remedicalization" of psychotherapy, as it is currently being choreographed by psychotherapists who seek reimbursement from the government and insurance companies under the banner of physical health.

To reiterate, the proper study of psychotherapy is the study of the *interpersonal transactions* between patient and therapist and the intrapsychic consequences of these transactions. The latter encompass the "therapeutic learning" whose nature has remained the central problem for psychotherapists as well as the cognitive psychologists. Therapists have learned a great deal about how to instrument therapeutic change but as yet we know little about the nature of the structural transformations that are registered by the patient and clinical observers as "improvements."

In the light of contemporary developments, it is difficult to see how classical analysts could have been oblivious to the *total context* of the patient-therapist relationship. Yet, the single-minded emphasis on the *content* of the interpretations rather than the *manner* in which they were made and how the patient heard them (e.g., as a criticism, exhortation, punishment, or as a helpful tool in his struggle for independence and autonomy) reveals an astonishing disregard for what every human being intuitively understands: *what* is said matters less than *how* it is said (see Levenson, p. 184). In some respects, the latter-day emphasis on the "therapeutic alliance" is a rediscovery of factors that should never have been obscured in the first place.

When all is said and done, we will gain a new appreciation for what may stand as Freud's most brilliant and lasting contribution—his discovery of the universal human tendency to enact and to reenact patterns of past relationship with significant persons in the present. The full elaboration and exploration of this insight is still in progress, and the present volume is a signpost in this continuing quest.

REFERENCE

Levenson, E. A. *The fallacy of understanding: An inquiry into the changing structure of psychoanalysis.* New York: Basic Books, 1972.

Introduction
Jack C. Anchin and Donald J. Kiesler

Psychotherapeutic practice is in a state of transition. There has been a distinct shift in the model used to conceptualize the process. Today the individual person is no longer viewed as a fixed entity. Instead he is seen as an integral part of the physical and interpersonal world in which he exists. Thus, boundaries between the individual and his overall environment are always in a state of complex interpenetration or ecological balance.

    This point of view is in sharp contrast to the former view of the individual patient as primary object of therapeutic exploration and intervention. [G. Chrzanowski, Chapter 2.]

Unfortunately, over the years, schools of psychotherapy have tended to evolve into scientist and practitioner "establishments," whose polemicists articulate theoretical and clinical dogmas, and who also sporadically launch propaganda assaults and counterassaults against opposing theoretical camps. In offering this volume on interpersonal psychotherapy to the field, we would like to head off anything like this kind of consequence. Hence, we state immediately that this volume *does not* offer a new school of individual psychotherapy.

    Instead, this book presents interpersonal/transactional viewpoints regarding the events of individual psychotherapy. These interpersonal perspectives reflect what we see as a gradually emerging new paradigm for explaining the events of psychotherapy in particular, and of human behavior more generally.

    The major thrust of the interpersonal paradigm is stated succinctly in the above quote from Chrzanowski's chapter. Kiesler makes the same point in Chapter 1: *"Interpersonal study focuses on human transactions, not on the behavior of individuals. . . . That human activity to be understood and explained is interpersonal or social, which necessitates focus on at least a dyad or two-person group."* Peterson echoes the same theme when he states in Chapter 8 that there is "increasing realization among psychotherapists that most if not all human disturbances are linked in their origins to the relationships people have with one another, and that the relief of human distress can be accomplished most powerfully if problems are approached from an interpersonal as well as an individual viewpoint."

    A key implication of this basic assumption for therapeutic intervention regards the pivotal priority of the therapist-client relationship. As Kiesler states in Chapter 1, "Despite its unique characteristics, the client-therapist interaction has major similarities to other human transactions. . . . [T]he therapist experiences 'live' in the sessions the client's distinctive interpersonal problems." Further, the therapist's inner engagements or interpersonal "impacts" while interacting with the client are central for both therapeutic assessment and intervention. Cashdan, in Chapter 11, reiterates: "It is the client-therapist relationship, particularly the contempoary here-and-now nature of it, that in my opinion lies at the bottom of meaningful psychotherapeutic change." And Carson similarly asserts that the "special power of the interpersonal approach to therapy . . . is that the therapeutic relationship itself, in all of its immediacy to observation and its possibility of permitting controlled input to the client, becomes the arena in which the major corrective experiences occur" (Chapter 4). Coyne and Segal, in Chapter 13, likewise assert that "for the purposes of intervention, the interpersonal context is sufficient as its own explanation." In the same vein, Chrzanowski, in Chapter 2, describes what so frequently and unfortunately results in therapy cases when relationship issues are downplayed or ignored: "Some therapeutic situations come to unsatisfactory ends because no direct effort was made by therapist and patient to explore the personal relationship in its own right. In other situations a therapeutic marathon ensues with two tired and inherently uninvolved parties. Often neither party can let go or break through, which leads to a sad clinch between two hapless parties." Generally, then, a recurrent theme of the chapters of this volume is that the client needs to experience dramatically different consequences for his or her intepersonal transactions, especially from his or her therapist, if he or she is to begin to let go of constricted and crippling maladaptive styles of dealing with other persons.

If this interpersonal paradigm is valid, it will be able to encompass and integrate the learnings of the past, including the interventional principles and procedures from other therapeutic approaches whose validity has been empirically and/or intuitively established. For now, it is merely our *belief* that the interpersonal model of human personality and individual psychotherapy presented in this volume can accomplish this theoretical expansion and consolidation. Much empirical research remains to be done before this belief can be confirmed or negated.

Further, it is incumbent on all of us to remember that, as has so often been the case in the short history of psychology, that which seems "new" typically has solid historical underpinnings. More precisely, then, our "new" paradigm is simply one that has been gradually forgotten, ignored, or given mere lip service in more recent theoretical and empirical approaches to individual therapy.

Actually, the interpersonal perspective is well established in the therapeutic endeavors of marital and family therapy, where transactional and systems principles underlie by far the majority of therapeutic approaches. In contrast, the field of individual psychotherapy and behavior change, which is the major focus of this volume, has yet to mine the rich interpersonal ore systematically. One purpose of this volume, then, is to titillate the prevailing establishments regarding individual psychotherapy, to stimulate their members to consider seriously the validity and therapeutic implications of the interpersonal paradigm.

To our psychoanalytic colleagues, we suggest that this volume can provide the directions for the next expansions of contemporary object relations theory and more recent formulations of therapeutic countertransference. Although we find these recent developments exciting, with few exceptions, they continue to miss the essential Sullivanian conceptual revolution which moves beyond exclusively intrapsychic events to interpersonal ones—to transactions that not only originate developmentally in interpersonal encounters, but which are also maintained by present-day interpersonal systems. What this volume offers our psychoanalytic colleagues, therefore, is not a mere linguistic translation of transference and countertransference formulations, but an inherently different methodology and fundamental redefinition of these therapeutic phenomena.

To our behavioral colleagues, whose theoretical and clinical approaches increasingly incorporate cognitive components of human functioning, we offer our interpersonal principles and interventions as their next step of systematic evolution and development. As Peterson emphasizes in Chapter 8, the next crucial step for behavioral assessment is to extend the "functional analysis" of human behavior to encompass the essential stochastic

nature of interpersonal transactions. Kiesler, Bernstein, and Anchin (1976) earlier docu-
mented that the behavior therapies need to incorporate explicitly into their therapeutic
approaches both the methodology of nonverbal communication and the interpersonal
theory of relationship. A central message to our behavioral colleagues, then, is that
relationship in psychotherapy concerns much more than mere facilitative conditions.
Indeed, relationship patterns are the essence of the client's psychopathology, and their
targeting in the client-therapist relationship is a powerful intervention priority for effective
psychotherapeutic applications.

This volume brings together the contemporary work of interpersonal theorists/
therapists who are studying individual psychotherapy from the interpersonal perspective.
Even our contributing authors have not been totally aware of each other's clinical and
empirical work. The need has emerged to pull this work together in one place, both for our
own benefit and, it is hoped, for the field at large. A common characteristic of all our
contributors is that they are scientist-professionals of varying mixtures. As second generation Sullivanians, this commonality is appropriate and necessary. Our chapters, thus, offer
different corresponding mixtures of (1) clinical case studies and examples, (2) theoretical
discussions, and (3) empirical data and measures.

Further, we consider this volume the next systematic expansion of interpersonal
theory for individual psychotherapy, next in succession to three previous, classic, interpersonal publications: Sullivan's (1953) *Interpersonal Theory of Psychiatry* and related
volumes, Leary's (1957) *Interpersonal Diagnosis of Personality*, and Carson's (1969) *Interaction Concepts of Personality*. We heartily recommend all these works to the reader
who wants intimate exposure to the interpersonal tradition for individual psychotherapy.

ORGANIZATION OF THE VOLUME

This volume is organized into four sections. Part I provides a theoretical overview as well
as more general interpersonal statements for personality, psychopathology, and psychotherapy. Part II presents chapters which deal directly with the assessment of interpersonal
behavior and/or with the diagnosis of maladaptive behavior defined in interpersonal terms.
Part III's contributors focus either on specific process models of interpersonal therapy or
on specific interpersonal interventions. Finally, Part IV offers a summary/conclusions
chapter which projects evolving themes and future directions for developments in interpersonal theory, research, and therapeutic practice.

Part I

In Chapter 1, Kiesler provides an historical overview of interpersonal psychotherapy. He
first develops six central interpersonal assumptions for human personality, followed by six
key assumptions for psychopathology and psychotherapy. Since the basic themes that are
developed by Kiesler recur in various forms throughout the volume, his chapter will
provide the reader with an overview of the essential underpinnings of interpersonal psychotherapy.

In Chapter 2, Chrzanowski, a recognized authority of Sullivanian psychotherapy,
details his long-term immersion in interpersonal therapy and presents his own contemporary model which extends Sullivan's notions in creative and challenging directions. For
some time Chrzanowski's writing has functioned in part as a gadfly to his psychoanalytic
colleagues. In this chapter, he continues to argue cogently that the revolutionary ecological/

systems nature of Sullivanian concepts offers not merely a translation of Freudian theory, but rather a dramatically contrasting paradigm for understanding personality and psychotherapy.

In Chapter 3, Wachtel further amplifies some basic conceptual and procedural differences between psychoanalytic and interpersonal approaches to psychotherapy. Continuing the incisive analysis of his important 1977 volume, Wachtel develops the theme that in following the Freudian premise of technical neutrality, analysts have failed to recognize that all behavior, including wishes and fantasies, must be understood in relation to its present interpersonal context. That is, far from being "locked-in remnants" from that past, "unconscious wishes and fantasies are as much a consequence of the neurosis as a cause," are brought about in the present both by a patient's own behavior as well as by the behavior he or she evokes in others. In contrast to analytic neutrality, Wachtel argues that an interpersonal perspective dictates a much more explicitly active stance by the therapist, "that efforts to intervene in a variety of ways in the vicious circles that characterize neurosis are often necessary in order to be maximally helpful to the patient." Throughout his chapter, he demonstrates (1) how direct efforts at change in the patient's present patterns of living may help to resolve what at first appear to be "deeper" conflicts which "underlie" the manifest patterns, and (2) how simultaneous focus on unconscious conflicts and manifest interaction patterns has a "synergistic effect" in which actions and feedback continually affect the patient's understanding while his or her understanding continually generates some kind of effort at action. Wachtel's final section then focuses on an interpersonal reanalysis of behavioral assertiveness training as "a multifaceted approach to bring about new, more effective interpersonal behavior," and argues for incorporation of these redefined action-oriented techniques into traditional therapeutic approaches.

In Chapter 4, Carson continues to develop the themes he presented in his important 1969 volume. As one of the foremost "cognitive" interpersonal theorists, he developed the thesis that "with rare exception, patently maladaptive behavior persists over lengthy time periods because it is based on perceptions, expectations, or constructions of the characteristics of people that tend to be confirmed by the interpersonal consequences of the behavior emitted." He argues that, as a result, the essential task of the interpersonal therapist is to detect and turn to therapeutic advantage, within the context of the client-therapist transactions, the client's misconceptions or misconstruals of what is going on interpersonally around him or her. For Carson, then, interpersonal therapy essentially restructures "the errant cognitive system underlying the maintenance of the client's maladaptive, self-defeating interpersonal behavior."

In Chapter 5, Duke and Nowicki offer some promising integrations of Rotter's social learning theory with interpersonal formulations. They focus their analysis on three major interpersonal communication constructs: "complementarity," "congruence," and what they refer to as "multiphasic human relationships." They provide stimulating theoretical extensions of each of these interpersonal concepts, as well as related research translations. They argue throughout for the centrality of situational factors in interpersonal theory and research. Addressing the fact that most interpersonal theorists have not specified situations beyond the general category of "signifcant others," they present an initial taxonomy of situations that has guided their research program. They conclude by describing their multilevel model of "human interaction constellations" which systematically incorporates relational (complementarity), communicational (congruence), and situational factors. Duke and Nowicki's theoretical and research efforts are rich in heuristic value, offering a challenging stimulus for future interpersonal research on both normal and abnormal populations.

In Chapter 6, Anchin offers the hypothesis that an interpersonal perspective represents not only a viable and perhaps particularly efficient therapeutic approach in its own right, but more importantly, that it may serve as a "bridge" facilitating systematic integrations among different psychotherapy systems in treating clinical problems. This proposal is based upon several arguments to the effect that "interpersonal factors—i.e., covert and overt processes in relation to self and classes of others—are centrally involved in inducing, eliciting, and maintaining human distress; that enduring clinical change is intimately associated with modifications in these factors; and that self/other phenomena serve directly or indirectly as common treatment targets across different therapeutic approaches." It is suggested, however, that efforts to explore and optimize this "integrational potential" will be facilitated through first clarifying the referents of concepts emphasized by interpersonal theorists, which in turn enables more precise designation of entry points for other concepts and procedures in facilitating assessment and modification of dysfunctional interpersonal behavior. Anchin concretizes these ideas by first defining three pivotal interpersonal concepts: interaction sequences, interpersonal patterns, and interpersonal styles. Specific therapeutic implications of these concepts are subsequently discussed, with emphasis placed upon a synthesis between interpersonal communication and cognitive-behavioral perspectives. These implications are presented in terms of three broad, related sets of clinical operations, referred to as Descriptive, Reflective, and Enactive Interventions. Anchin concludes by calling attention to Goldfried's (1980) recent call for more concerted efforts at working toward therapeutic rapprochement and consensus, suggesting that an interpersonal direction may offer one productive avenue in pursuing this important objective.

Lakoff, in Chapter 7, provides an in-depth linguistic analysis of the crucial but subtle differences between "psychotherapeutic discourse" (PD) and "ordinary conversation" (OC). Her premise is that if we can clearly differentiate the two types of conversation, "we will be better able to see what is intrinsic to all therapeutic styles that makes them effective, and thereby be better able in the future to develop models of therapeutic intervention that are apt to be effective in general as well as, perhaps, specific types that may prove particularly useful for specific purposes." The paradox she addresses is that "viewed superficially, most (though not all) forms of therapeutic discourse resemble ordinary conversation, yet all PD is engaged in explicitly with different intentions from OC." Her central thesis is that although the surface structures of PD and OC are similar, the abstract or deep structures are not. An important contrast she develops is that in therapeutic discourse the reciprocity rule which governs ordinary conversation is paradoxically "amalgamated" with essential nonreciprocity rules. As Lakoff states, at the deep structure level, the principle of reciprocity "is utilized, or not utilized, in an idiosyncratic way in the therapeutic encounter. . . . What is strikingly different about PD is that it is in fact underlyingly nonreciprocal in nature, but has a superficial veneer . . . of reciprocity discourse." She concludes that any psychotherapeutic situation essentially "forces the patient to confront new conventions, new possibilities of understanding, multiple meanings in the simplest exchanges, and by being exposed to these frightening possibilities in safe surroundings, to become willing to discover that all of the conventions we are used to can be altered or terminated if they become stagnating."

Part II

Part II deals explicitly with the assessment of interpersonal behavior and/or with the diagnosis of maladaptive behavior defined in interpersonal terms. Pointing out in Chapter

8 that "Assessment, like treatment, must proceed from a conception of the phenomena under study," Peterson first presents an integrative "guiding conception" for the study of interpersonal relations; this is followed by a stimulating overview of methodologies for assessing interpersonal relationships. He argues that the basic assessment model of behavioral therapies, "functional analysis," needs to be expanded to deal with the patterned sequence of interpersonal transactions more directly. As he states, "the functional analysis of interpersonal behavior has only begun in clinical practice." As one exciting attempt in this direction, Peterson describes and exemplifies his own innovation, the "Interaction Record," as one move toward filling in this assessment void.

In Chapter 9, Horowitz and his colleagues present their systematic work in developing a model for, and measures of, interpersonal "problems" and "complaints." Their chapter describes their progress in exploring the important issue of the precise relationships that exist between clinical symptoms and interpersonal problems. Drawing from contemporary cognitive psychology, they introduce their central, "integrating concept" of the "prototype," which permits a logical and empirical hierarchical categorization of the multiple covert and overt behavioral components of any given psychopathological complaint or symptom. To enliven their methodology, they apply their prototype analysis to the particular complaint of "depression," emphasizing its specific interpersonal aspects. Their methodology is exciting as well as promising, and offers an important conceptual-empirical bridge between clinical symptoms and maladaptive interpersonal styles.

The final assessment chapter, Chapter 10, is that of Benjamin, who has been immersed since 1968 in the study of interpersonal diagnosis as an alternative to the traditional DSM psychiatric nosology. Her empirical approach to interpersonal assessment and psychotherapy, "Structural Analysis of Social Behavior" (SASB) is comprehensive and, as McLemore and Hart observe in Chapter 12, "by far, to date, the most scientifically rigorous and clinically astute model published." Benjamin briefly summarizes her SASB model, but addresses most of her attention to an illustration of its concrete applications to a single clinical use. Her SASB system, in its sixth version, is a far-reaching methodology "for systematically describing social and intrapsychic behavior in a manner which has both etiological and treatment implications."

Although not their primary focus, Kiesler's Chapter 1 and McLemore and Hart's Chapter 12 also contain brief overviews of interpersonal assessment.

Part III

Part III brings together the contributors whose chapters focus either on specific process models of interpersonal therapy or on specific interpersonal interventions. Most of these chapters present explicit psychotherapy process models as defined in detail earlier in the important work of Cashdan (1973). For Cashdan, a psychotherapy process is "essentially a miniature theory that specifies how therapist operations are sequenced [and which] predicts what changes can be expected in the patient as therapy progresses" (pp. 3–4). Process, thus, represents a series of "stages," each of which is composed of a set of "rules" for the therapist, as well as associated behavioral shifts for the patient. Rules for a given stage are principles which guide the therapist's "technique," that is, guide the concrete responses of the therapist. Accordingly, most of the chapters in Part III present interpersonal process models which articulate the distinct stages of intervention that prevail sequentially over the therapy sessions.

Appropriately, this section begins with Cashdan's Chapter 11, which updates the earlier presentation of his "Interactional Psychotherapy" with additional clinical examples.

His therapy system encompasses five sequential stages: (1) Hooking, (2) Maladaptive Strategies, (3) Stripping, (4) Adaptive Strategies, and (5) Unhooking (Termination). Cashdan emphasizes throughout his presentation that his theory is "a systematic way in which maladaptive strategies are dealt with in the context of the therapist-client relationship." Cashdan then extends his analysis by turning to the question of why strategies are employed: "Why do people resort to these maneuvers in the first place? What function do they play in the lives of human beings?" For Cashdan, "The answer has to do with something called the 'self,' " and in elaborating on this perspective, he offers a creative integration of object relations and symbolic interactionist positions.

In Chapter 12, McLemore and Hart detail their "Relational Psychotherapy" approach. They outline their theoretical tradition and assumptions and describe their standard interpersonal assessment battery, with accompanying clinical material to illustrate their therapeutic procedure. The heart of their presentation is their psychotherapy process model which consists of five distinct stages: (1) Inquiry, (2) Stabilization, (3) Assimilation, (4) Confrontation, and (5) Transition. As a key part of stage 4, they describe their distinctive intervention referred to as "The Disclosure," which involves bringing, at the same time, the client and one or more significant others into the therapy session. This focal point of their interpersonal procedure has the purpose of assisting the patient "at the appropriate time, and in the appropriate manner, to inform his or her significant other(s) of what the patient thinks and feels about some private 'something.' " Central to this approach is the assumption that psychotherapy "largely consists of intimacy training. It teaches the client how to attain and perpetuate emotional closeness with others." And "Until intimacy is established with one's significant other(s), at least mentally, intimacy in other relationships will be hindered by unresolved introjected material."

Coyne and Segal, in Chapter 13, extend and systematize Watzlawick and colleagues' "Brief Strategic Therapy" developed at the Palo Alto Mental Research Institute. Offering many clinical examples, they first provide a description of five basic maladaptive interpersonal patterns—what they refer to as "five basic metapatterns of interpersonal solutions." They describe five process stages in the sequence of brief strategic therapy: (1) Pretreatment Considerations, (2) Obtaining a Problem Description, (3) Describing Attempted Solutions, (4) Eliciting a Goal Statement, and (5) Strategic Planning and Interventions. A central emphasis of their approach is that therapeutic interventions should focus on the "attempted solutions," the characteristic problem-solving efforts of patients and their significant others, rather than on the presented difficulties themselves. This follows from their belief that "the vicious cycle of interaction between the problem and attempted solutions is a self-perpetuating system."

In Chapter 14, Young and Beier expand on Beier's (1966) earlier presentation regarding the "asocial response" as the central therapeutic intervention of his system of interpersonal psychotherapy. In presenting this "Communications Analytic" approach, they argue that "therapeutic communications are messages which are effective because they interrupt the client's communications, they consequently help to extinguish the expected pattern of social interaction prompted by the client's style of behavior. : . . When the customary, preferred, or expected response is withheld in the therapy session, the client experiences a sense of 'beneficial uncertainty.'" As a result, the client is put into the position of having to discover new styles of communicating and relating since the therapist has shifted to the client responsibility for his or her conduct, and "preferred styles . . . no longer produce the familiar responses that have been a mainstay of the client's psychological diet." Young and Beier go on to discuss a number of "disengagement techniques," reanalyzing other, more traditional therapeutic interventions as examples of the asocial response, and conclude that "the efficacy of these tools is based on their asocial qualities within the interaction rather than on other theoretical considerations."

In Chapter 15, Kiesler presents his model of effective use in therapy sessions of the therapist's inner reactions or "impacts" for confronting the client's maladaptive interpersonal patterns. He first defines and illustrates the cognitive, affective, fantasy, and action-tendency components of the therapist's impacts or "complementary response." He then presents a general, two-stage process model for therapist impacts: (1) the Engaged or Hooked stage, and (2) the Disengaged or "Squirmed-Loose" stage. Kiesler subsequently defines and illustrates eight interventional principles that can guide the therapist's "meta-communication" with his or her client about the therapist's internal engagements experienced live in the therapy sessions. He concludes that it should be abundantly clear "that a therapist can be nothing other than a *participant* observer with his clients; that a therapist's humanity enters the room with his clients; that therapy with the client is to some degree inevitably therapy for the therapist; that *every* aspect of the therapist's experience—feelings, thoughts, fantasies, action tendencies—is engaged in his therapy encounters, and cannot *not* be impacted."

In Chapter 16, Weissman, Klerman, and colleagues discuss their "Short-term Interpersonal Psychotherapy" (IPT), developed specifically for treatment of "ambulatory, nonbipolar, nonpsychotic, depressed patients." At present their system is being empirically contrasted on large samples of depressed patients with both Beck's (1976; Beck et al., 1979) cognitive therapeutic approach and with tricyclic antidepressant medication in a research project funded by the National Institute of Mental Health. For both methodologic and training purposes, the authors have developed a procedural manual, still in revision, which attempts to operationalize the concepts, techniques, and strategies of their interpersonal psychotherapy. In this chapter, Weissman, Klerman, and their colleagues briefly summarize their therapy model and outline its goals and major foci. In applications of their system, they differentiate four subareas of depressive interpersonal problems, and present differential therapeutic strategies for each, as follows: (1) Abnormal Grief Reactions, (2) Interpersonal Role Disputes, (3) Role Transitions, and (4) Interpersonal Deficits. Their final section summarizes the data they have collected since 1967 which offer support for the efficacy of their treatment approach. They conclude that the strength of their approach rests with two important methodological advances: "(1) operationalized and defined diagnostic criteria to allow for relatively homogeneous patient groups, and (2) operationalized and defined psychotherapeutic procedures to assure comparability of treatment condition."

Part IV

Part IV offers a summary/conclusions chapter which projects evolving themes and future directions for developments in interpersonal theory, research, and therapeutic practice. In Chapter 17, Anchin observes that across interpersonal perspectives presented in previous chapters, "diversity exists with regard to how interpersonal maladjustment is conceptualized, specific targets and operations comprising one's assessment methodology, and the nature and sequencing of treatment interventions." From this diversity, he extracts four broad themes characterizing the interpersonal paradigm: (1) Ecological/Reciprocal Deterministic Emphasis, (2) Development and Expansion of Sullivanian theory, (3) Circumplex Models of Interpersonal Behavior, and (4) Procedural Variability Among Interpersonal Theorists. Within this framework, he fleshes out a number of points of convergence across contemporary interpersonal models of personality and psychotherapy, and translates these into recommendations for future developments in interpersonal theory, research, and practice. In concluding, Anchin cites a consensus among interpersonalists that "the theory, practice, and scientific study of individual psychotherapy and behavior change have yet to incorporate fully and systematically the knowledge and measurement methodologies associated with this rich and productive interpersonal tradition." From previous chapters, however, it is evident that "the interpersonal paradigm is steadily maturing, and that more concerted attention to its evolving constructs, methodologies, and treatment procedures can considerably enrich the science and practice of individual psychotherapy."

REFERENCES

Beck, A. T. *Cognitive therapy and the emotional disorders.* New York: International Universities Press, 1976.

Beck, A. T., Rush, A. J., Shaw, B. F., & Emery, G. *Cognitive therapy of depression.* New York: Guilford Press, 1979.

Beier, E. G. *The silent language of psychotherapy: Social reinforcement of unconscious processes.* Chicago: Aldine, 1966.

Cashdan, S. *Interactional psychotherapy: Stages and strategies in behavioral change.* New York: Grune & Stratton, 1973.

Goldfried, M. R. Toward the delineation of therapeutic change principles. *American Psychologist,* 1980, 35, 991–999.

Kiesler, D. J., Bernstein, A. J., & Anchin, J. C. *Interpersonal communication, relationship and the behavior therapies.* Richmond: Virginia Commonwealth University, 1976.

Leary, T. *Interpersonal diagnosis of personality: A functional theory and methodology for personality evaluation.* New York: Ronald Press, 1957.

Sullivan, H. S. *The interpersonal theory of psychiatry.* New York: Norton, 1953.

Wachtel, P. L. *Psychoanalysis and behavior therapy: Toward an integration.* New York: Basic Books, 1977.

Part I:

Overview and General Interpersonal Formulations

Chapter 1
Interpersonal Theory for Personality and Psychotherapy
Donald J. Kiesler

The aim of this chapter is to present the essential underpinnings of interpersonal approaches to personality and psychotherapy. In the first section, interpersonal explanations of human personality are delineated. In the second section, the focus is narrowed to a discussion of interpersonal principles for effective individual psychotherapy.

Before proceeding, however, a few words are necessary to place this discussion in historical perspective. The reader who wants more detail is referred to the excellent works of Carson (1969) and Swensen (1973). I lean on both authors' summaries and analyses throughout this chapter, although they are not accountable for my interpretations and emphases.

SOME HISTORY

The interpersonal movement embraces interpersonal psychiatary, interpersonal communication, interpersonal relations, interpersonal approaches to personality, transactional analysis, psychology of encounter, as well as others. Its diverse disciplinary roots include, among others, psychiatry, sociology, personality psychology, social psychology, psycholinguistics, communication theory, and nonverbal communication. Strength in this diversity comes from converging agreement as to the importance of some common principles for studying, understanding, and changing human behavior.

Unquestionably, the first systematic articulation of interpersonal theory was presented by H. S. Sullivan (1953a, 1953b, 1954, 1956, 1962, 1964). What Sullivan offered was an interpersonal alternative to the intrapsychic or intrapersonal emphasis that prevailed in psychoanalytic theory. The major interpersonal themes developed by Sullivan were:

1. Human personality is "the relatively enduring pattern of recurrent interpersonal situations which characterize a human life" (1953b, pp. 110–111).
2. A person's self-system is above all interpersonal in both its development and its current and evolving contents.
3. Deviant human behavior is the consequence of disordered interpersonal relations and is manifested in disordered interpersonal communication.
4. Disordered communication includes both the verbal and nonverbal ("gestural") channels.

5. Disordered communication reflects a person's "parataxic distortions" which, in the therapy context, take the form of generalizing to the therapist as a present-day partner earlier experiences in interpersonal relatedness.
6. Interpersonal transactions are characterized by continuous negotiation of complementary needs through reciprocal patterns of activity among participants (theorem of reciprocal emotion).
7. It is necessary to develop a science of psychiatry which rests on operational definitions for psychiatric concepts.

Subsequent to Sullivan, intepersonal theory fragmented, with various persons elaborating aspects of Sullivan's theory which were only implicit or minimally stipulated. The first important line of this development was that of Bateson and his colleagues (Bateson, 1958; Bateson et al, 1956; Haley, 1959a, 1959b; Jackson, 1959, 1968; Ruesch & Bateson, 1951; Watzlawick, Beavin, & Jackson, 1967) who attempted to characterize the communication matrix for families of schizophrenic patients. The result was their "double-bind" theory. Important spin-offs from this work were family therapy approaches applying communication and systems principles (Aponte, 1974; Bandler & Grinder, 1975; Bowen, 1960, 1961; Grinder & Bandler, 1976; Haley, 1962; Jackson, 1959, 1968; Jackson, Riskin, & Satir, 1961; Lederer & Jackson, 1968; Minuchin, 1974; Satir, 1967, 1972), marital therapy paradigms (Jackson, 1965; Lederer & Jackson, 1968; Tharp, 1963; Winch, 1958), transactional analysis (Berne, 1961, 1964, 1966; Harris, 1967), and Laing's interpersonal perception methodology (Laing, 1962, 1967, 1969; Laing, Phillipson, & Lee, 1966).

The analysis of family communication patterns stimulated and developed along with a second line of interpersonal study—nonverbal communication. The pioneering work of Birdwhistell (1952) in kinesics; Trager (1958) in paralanguage; Ekman and Friesen in human facial emotion (Ekman, 1965; Ekman & Friesen, 1967; Ekman, Friesen, & Ellsworth, 1972); Hall (1959, 1966) in proxemics; Frank (1957) and Montagu (1971) in touch; Mehrabian (1971, 1972) in relationship; and Dittmann (1962; Dittmann & Wynne, 1961), Scheflen (1964, 1966), and Pittenger and Smith (1957) in psychiatry and psychotherapy led to the currently well-established area of nonverbal communication (Argyle, 1975; Danziger, 1976; Harper, Wiens, & Matarazzo, 1978; Harrison, 1974; Kiesler, Bernstein, & Anchin, 1976; Knapp, 1978; LaFrance & Mayo, 1978; Siegman & Feldstein, 1978; Waxer, 1978).

A third line of development from Sullivan included the work of Leary (1957), Foa (1961, 1965, 1966; Foa & Foa, 1969) and Schutz (1958) which has been excellently reviewed and extended by Carson (1969). This branch provided theoretical and empirical delineation of two to three central dimensions of interpersonal behavior: control (dominance-submission), affiliation (love-hate), and inclusion. Various interpersonal assessment instruments (outlined below) evolved from this tradition.

A fourth branch developed in social psychology among theorists of person perception, interpersonal attraction, small group process, and game thoery. Carson (1969) was among the first theorists to integrate these social psychological contributions into the mainstream of interpersonal theory. These contributions include exchange theory as proposed by Thibaut and Kelley (1959) and by the sociologist Homans (1961); Heider's (1958) balance theory, and Newcomb's (1953, 1956, 1961) and Secord and Bachman's (1961, 1964, 1965) refinements; the attribution theory of Heider (1958) and Kelley (1967, 1971); the social reinforcement theory of Byrne (1961, 1969; Byrne & Lamberth, 1971; Clore & Byrne, 1973); game theory (Buchler & Nutini, 1969; Von Neumann & Morgenstern, 1947) especially as modified by Rapoport (1966, 1969); and role theory (Biddle &

Thomas, 1966; Parsons & Bales, 1955; Sarbin & Allen, 1968). Related work in sociology was that of Goffman (1959, 1961, 1963, 1967) specifying rules governing encounters among people.

The direct and indirect offshoots from Sullivan depicted in these four branches represent rather strange outgrowths. The amount of theory and research generated by these investigators is enormous. The crucial question addressed in what follows is: what are the commonalities which pull together these multifaceted approaches? That is, what are the assumptions common to these interpersonal approaches to personality and psychotherapy?

INTERPERSONAL ASSUMPTIONS FOR HUMAN PERSONALITY

In the remainder of this chapter I attempt to abstract from the interpersonal literature what I consider the basic theoretical assumptions of any interpersonal approach. A given theorist may take exception to a particular assumption, but my guess is that almost all would concur with the majority. In this first section I will develop six fundamental assumptions regarding human personality.

1. *Interpersonal study focuses on human transactions, not on the behavior of individuals.* What needs to be studied is not conceptually isolated "human behavior," but rather the behavior of persons relating to and interacting in a system with other persons. That human activity to be understood and explained is interpersonal or social, which necessitates focus on at least a dyad or two-person group.

Most of our previous theoretical attempts have focused on intrapsychic, intrapersonal, or overt behavioral events by studying the individual person. As a result, they have tended to ignore the most pervasive and essential feature of human activity, namely its embeddedness in dyadic and other transactions. Goffman (1961) calls this basic interpersonal unit the "encounter," a face-to-face interaction between two or more people.

Insistence on studying transactions is deeply rooted in Sullivanian theory and expresses the revolutionary differentiation of his system from analytic and other predecessors. Sullivan's Individuality Corollary reveals the extent to which he wanted to draw this contrast. He felt that the concept of the individual apart from other persons is a myth peculiar to our culture, that personality is manifest in interpersonal situations only. The study of psychology, personality, or psychotherapy is concerned with what individuals do when they are solitary, isolated, or not engaged in transactions only insofar as these situations have interpersonal components—which is indeed the typical case. Even when we are physically alone, we carry other persons with us and engage these others symbolically so that, as Carson (1969) states, "the mere physical absence of others does not preclude their having an influence on the actor" (p. 10).

Another way of making this point is to assert that we need to study persons in social situations rather than in impersonal environmental contexts, and that even impersonal situations have interpersonal components in the form of imagined or otherwise symbolized presences. It is rare for us, even when alone, not to "interact" with others, not to be influenced even in our solitary activity by the presence of these fantasized persons. Our most "personal" moments, our self-reflected appraisals, are interpersonal. Our anxiety-laden moments of existential crisis are dominated by our awareness of separation from others—a profoundly interpersonal event. Once we are thrown at birth into the human game, we cannot extract ourselves from a basic level of our reality which is interlaced with other persons.

Hence, the essential interpersonal thrust is that personality is "inconceivable other than in the context of interpersonal relations" (Carson, 1969, p. 25). Older constructs such as "instinct," "habit," or "trait," as traditionally defined, do not adequately represent the transactional feature of human behavior. Instead, we need explanatory concepts such as "interpersonal style," "transactional positions," "interactional synchrony," and the like, which reflect the embeddedness of human activity in a social, interpersonal context. As Laing (1964) observes, to understand human transactions we need to study them at the level of the dyad, and not at the level of the individual person within the dyad. The dyad is a system, a two-person process, not one person at a time interacting with another.

Carson (1969) summarizes these points well when he redefines Sullivan's notion of personality as "nothing more (or less) than the patterned regularities that may be observed in an individual's relations with other persons, who may be real in the sense of actually being present, real but absent and hence 'personified' or illusory" (p. 26). One must take care not to endorse this transactional position lightly, since its adoption can lead to permanent abandonment of some familiar ways of thinking.

2. *In interpersonal explanations the construct of self occupies a central theoretical position. This self is social, interpersonal, transactional in its development and functioning throughout life.* It is not a biologically, physiologically, or intrapsychically restricted notion.

Sullivan's self-system develops entirely out of interactions with others, and its symbolic contents consist of experiences with other persons. Its functioning is tied to recurrent experiences of anxiety in transactions with important persons, with "significant others." Sullivan was influenced by Cooley (1956), who felt that all human phenomenological experience was an internal dialogue or communication with other persons, whether imaginary or real; and that a person's self has no existence apart from relationship with other persons. Mead (1934), another progenitor, similarly defined self in exclusively social terms: "It is the social process of influencing others in a social act and then taking the attitude of the others aroused by the stimulus, and then reacting in turn to this response, which constitutes the self" (p. 17). Swensen (1973) paraphrases these notions: "Literally to exist as a person, to have a self, to be a personality, one must have others to interact with. If there is no one around to interact with, no self, no personality, no human being, as we usually think of the concept, can exist" (p. 6). What we think of ourselves is inextricably interwoven with what we think others think of us.

The interpersonal self-system has as its content a conglomerate of attributes about "I" or "me" resulting from "reflected appraisals" from the important, significant persons in one's life. Once developed, new reflected appraisals are admitted only to the extent that they are consistent with the existing appraisal system. Experiences inconsistent with the self-system tend to arouse anxiety and become suitable targets for selective inattention.

One of the system's major functions involves the self-presentations we make to others. A pervasive feature of our transactions is our presentation to others of the basic ways we perceive ourselves in relation to them. This presentation is accomplished by messages (primarily nonverbal) sent to interactants about our emotional states and our "claim" regarding the reciprocal responses we want from them. This claim pulls others into the kind of dyadic system-state that is most comfortable, least threatening, in terms of our conceptions of who we are.

Leary (1957) was the first to describe the functioning of this presentational self in detail. For him, the purpose of interpersonal behavior is to induce reactions from the other person that are "complementary" to the behavior presented. From a similar perspective, Goffman (1967) stated that the important risk in social transactions concerns the self. In every encounter a person risks that the self might be confirmed or disconfirmed, that one's face might be "saved" or not. The person uses various personal performances to create certain effects in the "audience" of interactional participants.

Beier (1966) elaborated these notions by observing that a person makes these relationship claims with greater or lesser degrees of intent, awareness, or attention. The more aware the person, the more the relationship message can be called "persuasive"; the less aware, the more the claim can be described as an "evoking" message. The goal of either is "to impose a condition on the respondent under which he behaves as the sender wishes without being aware that he has been led to that particular choice with a certain message. . . . The sender increases the probability of the occurrence of a specific response by constricting the respondent's response activity" (Beier, 1966, p. 11). By this process a person, with more or less intent, helps to create environmental reponses which confirm his or her view of self and of the world.

To understand ourselves or others, it is essential to identify the dyadic system-states that we as individuals recurrently seek, shape, evoke, and ensure in our interactions with others. As Wachtel (1977) observes, "the signals we emit to other people constitute a powerful force field. The shy person does many . . . things to make it difficult for another person to stay open to him very long. Even a well-intentioned person is likely eventually to help confirm his view that others aren't really very interested" (p. 52). States we experience as euphoria, contentment, anger, disgust, or anxiety result from our degree of success in producing consequences isomorphic to the interpersonal dimensions of our selves—the self as how-we-want-ourselves-to-be-with-others, and how-we-want-ourselves-to-be-seen-by-others. For Sullivan, anxiety is our natural response to some level of awareness that an incongruence exists between a current experience of interpersonal feedback and our current self-definition—an awareness of some degree of consensual invalidation.

A major set of cues for identifying the recurrent interpersonal climate a person produces are the distinct covert and overt responses the person elicits or "pulls" from others. The best clues to a person's private conceptions of self are these covert engagements produced in others. Kiesler (1973, 1979; Kiesler, Bernstein, & Anchin, 1976; Kiesler et al., 1975, 1976; Perkins et al., 1979) refers to these covert engagements as the "Impact" message, the interpersonal consequences of a person's use of Beier's evoking message. If we use these concepts, Sullivan's "personality" can be defined more precisely as the "relatively enduring pattern of recurrent evoking and impact messages which characterize a human life." Personality, acting as it does in the social environment, is in the impact or engagement of the beholder.

3. The third assumption of interpersonal theorists is that *a person's recurrent pattern of interpersonal situations (or evoking and impact messages) represents distinct combinations of two to three basic dimensions of interpersonal behavior: control, affiliation and inclusion.* To concretize these dimensions, Leary (1957) developed an Interpersonal Circle around the axes of dominance-submission and love-hate, subsuming eight octants or sixteen interpersonal behavior clusters on the periphery.

Empirical developments evolved from Leary's work as attempts to measure behavior categories of the circle. Leary and his colleagues' (LaForge & Suczek, 1955; Leary, 1957; Leary & Coffey, 1955) Interpersonal Check List provides 16 category scores from subjects' self-reported (adjective checklist) descriptions of their own interpersonal behaviors. Lorr and McNair (1963, 1965, 1966, 1967; Lorr, Bishop, & McNair, 1965) translated the Interpersonal Check List adjectives into concrete descriptions of overt interpersonal behaviors. The result was their Interpersonal Behavior Inventory used by observers to rate another person's interpersonal behaviors.

Kiesler and his colleagues (Kiesler et al., 1975, 1976; Perkins et al., 1979) derived from Lorr and McNair's device a measure of the complementary response to a person's interpersonal behavior—a measure of the self-reported engagements elicited or pulled from interactants in the presence of the person. Their Impact Message Inventory yields 15 scores complementary to Lorr and McNair's 15 categories. Benjamin (1974, 1977, 1978, 1979) developed an interpersonal model called Structural Analysis of Social Behavior. Organized around the axes of affiliation and interdependence, it contains three isomorphic surfaces: the parentlike and the childlike for interpersonal behaviors, and the introject or intrapsychic for intrapersonal behaviors or attitudes. A series of three questionnaires, designed for each of the surfaces, measures a person's ratings of another person, of himself in relation to that other person, and of himself as he habitually relates to others more generally.

Schutz (1958) developed the Fundamental Interpersonal Relations Orientation questionnaire (FIRO-B) to measure the basic human needs of control, affection, and inclusion. The FIRO-B also provides two subscores for each of these dimensions: a measure of the wanted or wished aspect of a particular need, and a measure of the expressed aspect.

With the availability of these measures, we can take the next step in refining Sullivan's notion of personality. As Carson (1969) states, "an interpersonal act represents, in part, a prompt or 'bid' to elicit response behaviors falling within a certain range of the interpersonal circle" (p. 115). "Recurrent interpersonal situations," thus, can be redefined as recurrent evoking and impact messages which fall in a restricted range of the interpersonal circle, reflecting in turn the basic relationship dimensions of control, affiliation, and inclusion.

4. It should be apparent by now that *interpersonal theory takes an interactionist position in which a person's social behaviors are a function of both his or her predispositions toward transactions and situational/environmental events.* In line with Lewin (1935), $B = f(P,E)$. Surprisingly, it has taken the fields of psychology and psychotherapy (Kiesler, 1966, 1971) some time to begin to apply this principle seriously in research and clinical practice.

Interpersonal theorists tend to insist on two important refinements of the interactionist (Endler & Magnusson, 1976) position. The first is a phenomenological restatement asserting that *situational factors relevant to a person's behavior are environmental events as perceived by the person.* This restatement addresses a perennial issue in personality theory, namely, the relative importance of the objective versus subjective environment, or as Murray (1938) stated it, of "alpha" versus "beta" "press." Since Sullivan, interpersonal theorists have argued for the primacy of the subjective environment, of beta press, as the determinant of human transactions.

Emphasis on the subjective environment represents a clear phenomenological/existential stance. Human activity is a function of a person's internal, covert experience. A person's perception of a given environment is all he knows, the only experience to which he can react. An individual's experience of an "identical" objective environment may be (and typically is) divergent from the experience of a second person. In most instances, however, there is overlap—that is,a positive correlation exists between the subjective and objective environments. But for persons in any given context, the total range of intercorrelation is possible. In line with Murray (1938), interpersonal theorists maintain that it is vital to consider both the subjective and the objective environments, the former through self-report, the latter from observations by external judges.

Selective attention and inattention are important processes in the person's experiential world and influence perception of the objective environment at any given moment. A person tends to filter out or selectively ignore or delegate to the "ground" feedback from the interpersonal world that does not confirm his or her self-system; and tends to focus on or selectively attend to or make "figure" of feedback components that are interpreted as confirmatory. If attended to, nonconfirmatory feedback is threatening, signals anxiety, and, as a result, is selectively ignored. The degree of consistency between the self-system and environmental feedback determines, through selective attention, the resulting perception by the persons of his or her environment, that is, it determines the subjective environment.

A second refinement of the interactionist position has been emphasized by Kiesler, Bernstein, and Anchin (1976), among others. *The most important class of situations for human behavior is that of other persons, in contrast to impersonal situations.* Major determinants of our social behavior are the behaviors of persons interacting with us, as perceived by us.

Surprisingly, situational taxonomies are wanting in the psychological literature. In line, however, with the elaborations of Leary (1957) and others of Sullivan's notions of complementarity, the best candidate for an interpersonal taxonomy seems to be the Interpersonal Circle itself. Interpersonal situations, thus, can be classified into the categories of interpersonal behavior on the Circle, as perceived by a given person in transaction.

Somewhat paradoxically, then, Lewin's equation, $B = f(P,S)$, is translated by interpersonal theorists into $B = (P,S = P)$. And to the extent that the Interpersonal Circle validly reflects our human social reality, we can use isomorphic assessment devices for both persons and situations (other persons).

5. In attempting to understand and explain human transactions, *interpersonal theorists adopt a notion of "circular" rather than linear causality.* Rather than viewing a person's behavior as a direct effect of situational events and intrapersonal motives, the focus instead is on two-person mutual influence, on bidirectional causality. Human social behavior is embedded in a feedback network wherein the "effect" influences or alters the "cause," where the person both affects and is affected by the environment, where independent and dependent variables are arbitrary and interchangeable. As Wachtel (1977) observes, "the events that *happen to* us are in large measure brought about by us, and can be seen as consequences of the behavior generated by our cognitions and motives" (pp. 74–75). Bateson (1958) incorporates circularity into his definition of social psychology as "the study of the reactions of individuals to the reactions of other individuals" (p. 175).

For any given transaction, it is arbitrary to designate the behavior of one participant (A) as cause, and the reaction of the other (B) as effect. This stop-action snapshot is an arbitrary slicing of reality which easily loses track of B's prior and simultaneous input into the behavior of A. To assert that B becomes angry in response to A's critical remarks is a stop-action description expressing a linear causal notion. The circular expansion is that B's prior request for affection, as well as B's provocative posture and gaze during the time A was making his critical comments, also determined A's critical comments. Danziger (1976) notes, in his excellent contrast of circular and linear notions, this feedback inherent in human transactions inevitably implies that "two individuals in interaction are simultaneously the causes and the effects of each other's behavior" (p. 184).

In addition to feedback, Danziger lists two other essential features of circular systems: redundancy and nonsummativity. Redundancy refers to the fact that human transactions show consistencies and regularities over time, that dyads show an "orderliness in the sequence of interaction" (p. 184). The spin-out of exchanges between two persons includes a series of reciprocal behaviors that shows a significant deviation from chance ordering—that is, the series manifests a patterned order. The third feature, nonsummativity, refers to the notion that the time sequence in human transactions can modify the meaning of an "identical" bit of behavior by an interactant. A smile which follows an outburst of anger has different meaning from the "identical" smile which appears after an outpouring of fear. It is often naive simply to count the frequency of a given behavioral event (such as the number of smiles) and sum over a period of time as a valid index of a transactional phenomenon. As Danziger (1976) notes, "elements occurring at one point in a communication sequence cannot be summed with elements occurring at a different place in the sequence" (p. 185).

The contrast of circular versus linear causality is not a sterile, esoteric exercise. Recognition of the pervasive circularity in human transactions prompts important shifts in one's thinking about human behavior. My colleagues and I (Kiesler, Bernstein, & Anchin, 1976) have spelled out these implications in detail. Suffice it to say here that our traditional experimental design strategy in psychological research (isolation of separate and linearly related independent and dependent variables) ignores all three aspects of circularity: feedback, redundancy, and nonsummativity. We need design alternatives which can directly address the essential features of circular transactions, all of which require study of larger temporal slices of human transactions to isolate sequential redundancies.

Fortunately, this new methodology is emerging. The generic name is stochastic analysis (Parzen, 1962), and one relatively primitive tool is called finite Markov-chain analysis (Hertel, 1972; Kemeny & Snell, 1960; Rausch, 1972). The basic features of stochastic analysis are analysis of larger units of transaction between interactants representing longer temporal sequences, and statistical procedures which can identify redundant patterns that deviate from chance orderings.

Since Sullivan's theorem of reciprocal emotion, the notion of redundancy has been firmly established in the interpersonal literature. The key concept, which has its own evolving tradition, is "complementarity." According to Sullivan (1954), "integration in an interpersonal situation is a process in which (1) complementary needs are resolved (or aggravated); (2) reciprocal patterns of activity are developed (or disintegrated); and (3) foresight of satisfaction (or rebuff) of similar needs is facilitated" (p. 129). It was left to subsequent theorists to begin to fill in the void of specificity which Sullivan left in regard to this theorem. The continuing general notion of complementarity is that the behaviors of participants are redundantly interrelated, have patterned regularity, in some manner over the sequence of a transaction.

For Leary (1957), complementarity or redundancy in a dyad occurred on the basis of "reciprocity" for the dominance-submission axis (dominance in A evokes submissiveness in B, and vice versa), and on the basis of "correspondence" for the love-hate axis (expressions of love by A evoke expressions of love from B, and hate evokes hate).

In defining complementarity, other theorists have concentrated on the various types of Leary's reciprocity possible on the control dimension. Bateson (1958) was the first to use the terms "complementary" and "symmetrical" to describe dissimilar and similar control behaviors occurring in transactions. A complementary relationship is characterized by a fixed pattern over time of unequal control (A dominant, B submissive). In contrast, a symmetrical relationship refers to a more equal distribution of control wherein A and B struggle to maintain at least an equal power equilibrium. Lederer and Jackson (1968) added a third type of reciprocity with the concept of "parallel" relationship where control not only tends to have an equal distribution, but also flows easily and alternatingly from A to B to A as the situation changes and dictates. In other words, A is dominant at some times, B at others, and both agree on the appropriateness of the shifts.

Other modifications of Leary's reciprocal control pattern have been proposed (Berne, 1964; Goffman, 1967; Laing, 1962; Schutz, 1958; Winch, 1958). Yet we have little systematic knowledge regarding the range of transactional redundancies which characterize the myriad transactions among human participants. It is imperative that, through increased stochastic study of human interactions, we discover the important governing parameters.

6. My final interpersonal principle is that *the vehicle for human transactions is communication, including linguistic and nonverbal messages.* Communication refers to messages sent by an encoder to a decoder participant, and the decoder's reciprocal response. It consists of a complex stimulus pattern that includes messages sent simultaneously along the linguistic and nonverbal channels. Messages within a given pattern can be consistent with each other or congruent, or can exhibit inconsistency, contradiction, or incongruency. Interpersonal communication is inherently circular, incorporating the features of feedback, redundancy, and nonsummativity.

Once we shift our focus to human communication we come face to face with the centrality of nonverbal messages in the transactional process. Scientific study of nonverbal communication has grown exponentially during the last two decades. An overwhelming conclusion from this body of evidence is that nonverbal communication is the language of emotion and relationship. How we feel about ourselves and about each other, and the kinds of claims we place on each other are communicated primarily through nonverbal messages. Our most pervasive human activities, then, consist of analogic messages, most of which occur as "ground" around the "figure" of our transactions, the latter being the sentences we say to each other.

There are two levels of communication (Ruesch & Bateson, 1951), two levels of simultaneous messages sent between interactants. One level is that where our attention is usually focused, namely the "report" (Watzlawick, Beavin, & Jackson, 1967), "representational" (Danziger, 1976) or "denotative" (Kiesler, 1973; Kiesler, Bernstein, & Anchin, 1976) level—the manifest content of speech, information coded symbolically on the linguistic channel. The second level is usually out of focus, serves as "ground," and is referred to respectively as the "command," "presentational," or "connotative-relationship" level—the emotional and self-presentational messages we send to others primarily through nonverbal signals. To the extent that transactions are the proper unit of study for human behavior, it becomes necessary to study the relationship level of nonverbal communication.

This stance has important implications for the study and conduct of psychotherapy. As I have stated elsewhere (Kiesler, 1980), therapists and process researchers can no longer ignore the nonverbal behavior of either therapist or client. Exclusive focus on the linguistic messages between client and therapist can result only in the observer missing most of the action. Restricted study of only one of the multiple channels of communication can produce only incomplete, misleading, inconclusive, or invalid results. Investigators must move beyond typescripts (beyond content analysis), beyond audiotape recordings (linguistics and paralanguage) to either live observation or audio-video recordings of psychotherapy sessions. Only video representations can capture the important visual channels including kinesic, proxemic, and touch behaviors. And it is precisely these visual channel messages which nonverbal research points to as crucial for communicating emotional and relationship messages.

Summary: The Interpersonal Manifesto, Part I

1. For the interpersonal theorist the crucial targets, the proper units, for psychological study are the transactions that occur between human participants at least at the level of the dyad. Study of persons encompasses interpersonal situations, and even impersonal contexts have symbolized interpersonal components. We need transactional explanatory constructs such as "complementarity" and "interactional synchrony" which reflect this basic embeddedness of human activity in the social, interpersonal context.

2. A social, interpersonal conception of self serves a central role in interpersonal theory. What we think and feel about ourselves is inextricably plaited with what we think others think of us. Our transactions have as a pervasive feature the presentation to others of the basic ways in which we view ourselves, as well as our claims regarding the kind of relationship we want with others. Hence, to understand ourselves or others, it is essential to identify the dyadic system-states, the interpersonal climates that we recurrently seek, shape, evoke, and ensure in our interactions with others.

3. Recurrent patterns of interpersonal behavior, repetitive dyadic system-states, can be validly characterized as falling on the Interpersonal Circle. Attempts at empirical assessment adopt various versions of the Circle to characterize a person's bids to elicit responses from others as falling within a certain range of the Circle—thereby isolating the recurrent evoking and impact messages which distinguish a person's life.

4. Interpersonal theory cannot not adopt an interactionist position in which both person and situation factors interactively determine a person's transactions. The interpersonal stance, however, is phenomenological, emphasizing the psychological environment, the situation as perceived by the person. Further, the most important class of situations is that of other persons, especially significant others. Major determinants of our interpersonal behavior, thus, are our experience of self and our perceptions of the interpersonal behaviors of others.

5. Interpersonal transactions reflect a reality of circular rather than linear causality. Dyadic transactions consist of two-person mutual influence, bidirectional simultaneous causality. Human social behavior is embedded in a feedback network where the effect influences or alters the cause, where the person both shapes and is shaped by the environment. New empirical methodologies are necessary to measure the basic circular aspects of human transactions: feedback, redundancy, and nonsummativity. At present, the best guess is that transactional redundancy or complementarity occurs by reciprocity for the control dimension, and by correspondence for the affiliation dimension.

6. The vehicle for human transactions is communication, including messages on both the linguistic and nonverbal channels. Since nonverbal messages predominate in the transmission of emotional and relationship communication, study of nonverbal behavior is crucial in understanding human living. The focus of interpersonal study is on the command, in contrast to report, level of human communication.

INTERPERSONAL ASSUMPTIONS FOR PSYCHOTHERAPY

In this second section, I summarize how the principles articulated above apply to the problems of abnormal behavior and psychotherapy. For purposes of consistency and emphasis, instead of the phrase, abnormal behavior, throughout I will use more interpersonal terms such as problems in living or disturbed interpersonal relations. This section is heavily saturated with my own thinking, and is based in part on Kiesler (1973, 1979) and Kiesler, Bernstein, and Anchin (1976).

Disturbed Interpersonal Relations

Problems in living reside in the recurrent transactions of a person with others, especially significant others, in his life. Problems in living are defined as disordered, inappropriate, or inadequate interpersonal communications. They result originally and cumulatively from a person's not attending to and not correcting the self-defeating, interpersonally unsuccessful aspects of his communications. Largely by nonverbal messages, the disturbed person consistently communicates a rigid and extreme self-presentation, and simultaneously pulls for a rigid and constricted relationship from others. The individual imposes a rigid program on transactions, a program he is unwilling or unable to modify despite the initially varying interpersonal stances of others. Sullivan called this transactional rigidity "parataxic distortion." For Leary (1957), the disordered person "tends to overdevelop a narrow range of one or two interpersonal responses. They are expressed intensely and often, whether appropriate to the situation or not. . . . The more extreme and rigid the person, the greater his interpersonal 'pull'—the stronger his ability to shape the relationship with others" (p. 126).

In contrast, as Carson (1969) describes, the more normal individual has a sufficiently broad style of interacting, reflecting a more flexible definition of himself and others. The normal person enacts varied sets of actions appropriately tuned to the interactant. In each instance he negotiates a mutually agreed upon definition of self and other, responding to the unique aspects of the particular situation. For the abnormal person, however, this ability to modify his definition of both himself and others in line with situational factors seems strikingly absent.

What the disordered person attends to are some aspects of his claim as to how he defines himself in important relationships. What he does not attend to are some aspects of his communication style and the aversive interpersonal consequences he himself produces unintentionally. For example, many obsessive individuals take pride in presenting themselves as very rational, logical, and self-controlled persons. Part of the obsessive's communication pattern is a very careful and cautious use of words, frequent qualifications of opinions and feelings, a monotonous voice tone, and minimal range in his body movements and other nonverbal behaviors. As a direct result of this style, persons interacting with an obsessive individual gradually experience complementary impact responses such as boredom, impatience, being evaluated by the obsessive, caution themselves in expressing opinions and feelings, and so on. Because of the predominantly negative tone of these engagements, others tend to withdraw from the obsessive person or countercommunicate in similarly unclear, cautious, and incongruent ways. The overall result is that the obsessive increasingly feels isolated from others, lonely, experiences few if any intimate relationships, and gradually experiences the accumulated anxiety and depression of the disordered person. Moreover, he has little understanding of how he had come to or is responsible for this miserable state of affairs.

Kaiser (Fierman, 1965) describes the commonality of disordered behavior as the "universal symptom of duplicity." During his therapy sessions he observed that patients

did not talk straight. They were never completely, never wholeheartedly behind their words. Listening to them required a very special effort. . . . Listening to them caused some inner struggles, almost as if one has to listen to two speakers talking simultaneously. There was a strange duplicity about their communications. There were words and sentences and whole stories which were quite understandable and made sense in themselves; but the accompaniment of the tone of voice, facial expressions and gestures interfered subtly and sometimes grossly with the total communication effect. [Pp. 36–37.]

Moreover, "patients seemed never to be aware of their own universal symptom . . . seemed completely blind to (their) own duplicity" (p. 61). For Kaiser, indirect, confusing, and ambiguous communication is the universal symptom shown by patients in psychotherapy. By various duplicitous patterns a patient avoids an open, direct, and clear relationship with other persons, including the therapist.

The culprit in disordered behavior, therefore, is duplicitous communication. This duplicity results from a selective inattention which ignores aspects of messages to and from others that are inconsistent with the disordered person's constricted self-definition. The person ignores the "ground" of his experience, continual avoidance of which prevents both a holistic and integrated experience of self and a consensually validated perception of self in relation to others. Fragmented and constricted experience of self leads to fragmented and constricted (duplicitous) communications to others.

For interpersonal theorists, individual differences in disordered communication represent the range of constricted and extreme styles on the interpersonal circle around the axes of control, affiliation, and inclusion. The disordered person tenaciously holds to a restricted "slice" of the Circle for self-definition and for expressing claims on others through his evoking messages. Problems in living are directly but duplicitously expressed through a person's distinct evoking and impact messages. These constricted, extreme, and rigid evoking and impact messages are the problem!

McLemore and Benjamin (1979) argue that interpersonal behavior may be the most useful basis for a classification system for abnormal behavior which eventually can function as an alternative to the present DSM-III. Available interpersonal classification systems, cited in detail above, provide both the theoretical and empirical basis for "translating traditional diagnostic categories into psychosocial terms, consistent with the assumptions and procedures of behavioral science" (McLemore & Benjamin, 1979, p. 32). Kiesler and Federman (1978) make an initial translation within this framework by demonstrating that the obsessive personality exhibits a triad of Hostile, Mistrustful, and Detached Circle behaviors, while the hysteric personality clusters at the Affiliation, Sociability, and Exhibitionism categories.

In sum, problems in living are manifest in disordered transactions through duplicitous, self-defeating messages sent to others, through the recurrently ambiguous and negative pattern of evoking and impact messages. This duplicitous communication reflects a constricted and incomplete experience of self, and a rigid and extreme style of self-presentation. The range of possibilities for disordered self-presentation is the range of the Interpersonal Circle, with the disordered person expressing rigidly and extremely a distinct cluster of Circle behaviors. This constricted self-presentation pushes others into rigid complementary roles to ensure that only confirmatory feedback of the constricted self-system can be obtained. This command of others eventually elicits from them ambiguous or negative consequences which are baffling to the disordered person since he does not see his responsibility for these consequences at all. Until this rigid transactional style is disrupted, and flexibility and choice substituted, the disordered person can only continue to engage others in his overprogrammed, self-defeating manner.

Interpersonal Psychotherapy

1. The rock-bottom assumption of interpersonal psychotherapy is that *the client-therapist interaction, despite its unique characteristics, is similar in major ways to any other human transaction.* The therapist is just as much a participant as the client despite

the one-sided linguistic focus. In Sullivan's terms, the therapist can be nothing other than a *participant* observer.

It follows that the proper units for studying psychotherapy are the transactions between client and therapist, which incorporate all the features of circularity spelled out earlier. The nonverbal messages of the participants are of central focus, since they constitute the primary vehicle for communicating emotion and relationship between client and therapist. From initiation and throughout therapy, the therapist becomes perceived by the client as a significant other.

It also follows from this transactional assumption that the client will communicate to the therapist in the same duplicitous, self-defeating way that he communicates with other important persons in his life, that he will send the same rigid and extreme evoking messages to the therapist he sends to others. As a result, the therapist will experience "live" in the sessions the client's distinctive interpersonal problems. The therapist, at his or her end of the feedback loop, registers the client's distinctive style with the impact messages he or she experiences with the client—impacts complementary to a distinctive cluster of the interpersonal circle.

In contrast to other theorists, Kaiser (Fierman, 1965) emphasizes that the therapist will experience complementarity primarily on the control axis, with affiliation-inclusion representing for him expressions of the universal human motive. The universal human conflict is existential in Kaiser's system. We are separate and alone and, no matter how close we may get to someone, we cannot fuse with them. For Kaiser, the basic strategy of the disordered person is to attempt to fuse (chasing the "illusion of fusion") by surrendering his autonomy. The vehicle for this surrender is duplicitous communication: "What drives [the neurotic] into the office of the psychiatrist is not so much the realistic hope of getting cured as the wish to step out of his isolation. . . . As his adult intellect does not allow him to maintain an illusion of unity he does something which is a compromise between fusion and mature relationship: Namely, he behaves either submissively or domineeringly" (p. xix).

2. *The first important task of the interpersonal therapist is to attend to, identify, and assess the client's distinctive evoking style as it unfolds in the client-therapist transactions. A major component of this assessment includes the therapist's own emotional and other felt engagements or "pulls" experienced during these transactions.*

I have spelled out in detail elsewhere (Kiesler, 1979; Kiesler, Bernstein, & Anchin, 1976) the multiple components of relationship assessment. The point to be emphasized here is that the therapist's prepotent assessment tool involves his or her own internal responses to the client. The therapist must attend to the "ground" of the communication process more than to the "figure" of linguistic content. The ground subsumes the client's and therapist's nonverbal messages as well as the therapist's covert experiences or engagements. Attending to this ground can be threatening to the therapist as well as to the client. This is so since, because of its negative, rejecting or antitherapeutic tones, the ground is inconsistent with one of the major ways the therapist defines himself or herself— namely, as a nurturant, understanding, accepting, and competent helper.

3. *The goal of interpersonal therapy is for the therapist and client to identify, clarify, and establish alternatives to the rigid and self-defeating evoking style of the client. Their task is to replace constricted, extreme transactions with more flexible and clear communications adaptive to the changing realities of specific encounters.*

The therapist's priority task is to stop responding in kind, in complementary fashion, to the client's duplicitous communication—i.e., not to respond in the same ways as have others in the client's life. Instead, as Kaiser (Fierman, 1965) emphasizes, the therapist offers a spontaneous, genuine, direct, clearly communicative relationship. In Leary's (1957) and Carson's (1969) terms, the therapist must avoid adoption of an interpersonal position complementary to and confirming of the client's rigid and extreme self-presentation. In Halpern's (1965) terms, the therapist must avoid ensnarement in the "disturbance-perpetuating maneuvers of his patient." As Beier (1966) stresses, the therapist instead must provide the "asocial" response, by refusing to make the response the client forcefully evokes in her. And as I have emphasized (1973, 1979; Kiesler, Bernstein, & Anchin, 1976) the therapist must break the vicious transactional circle by not continuing to be hooked or trapped by the client's engagement or pull so that he or she can usefully "metacommunicate" with the client about the self-defeating cycle itself. Accordingly, improvement in therapy is seen first as a change in the baseline of client-therapist communication within the therapy sessions themselves.

In my system, the other crucial intervention of the interpersonal therapist is to metacommunicate with the client about the client's evoking style and its self-defeating consequences. The client's duplicitous communication patterns need to be altered as they operate in important contexts, with the crucial situations encompassing important others in the client's life, including the therapist.

Within the client-therapist transaction the client affects the therapist as much (if not more, especially early in the transaction) as the therapist affects the client. The therapist cannot not be hooked by the client. The therapist's first task is to attend to and identify this hooking so that he or she can disengage from the emotional climate engulfing him or her. The therapist's error is to continue to provide the complementary response. His or her second task is to metacommunicate with the client by talking about the transactions occurring between them, by discussing openly with the client the evoking-impact cycles which characterize the client's disordered encounters.

It should be evident by now that interpersonal therapy focuses on events referred to by Freud as transference and countertransference. Interpersonal definitions of these events, however, suggest fundamental differences and emphases.

a. In contrast to analytic therapy, the emphasis of both interpersonal assessment and *intervention* is on the therapist's emotional, cognitive, fantasy, and behavioral engagements experienced in his or her sessions with the client. The priority interventions are to provide the asocial response and to metacommunicate with the client about his or her self-defeating evoking messages.

b. Interpersonal theorists do not use psychoanalytic theory to derive the centrality of transactional events in human behavior and in psychotherapy. As Wachtel (1977) observes, "Freud was not . . . a student of interaction sequences. When the patient's overt interpersonal behavior was the focus of his inquiry, it tended to be of interest as a further vehicle for expressing the underlying dynamics. Rarely was it examined for its *consequences*. . . . The framework provided by Freud did not emphasize examining how the patient's behavior was a response to the current behavior of others, and it emphasized still less how the behavior of others could itself be seen as a function of one's own acts" (pp. 48–49).

c. The interpersonal theorist is locked into Sullivan's rather than Freud's tradition when he asserts that evoking responses, self-presentations, are aspects of all human transactions. Thus, transference-like events are not exclusive by-products of the psychotherapy transaction, and are not all restricted to erotically tinged Oedipal events.

d. Sullivan's notions are being extended when it is asserted that human as well as psychotherapy transactions obey a reciprocal-circular causal model, rather than a Freudian predetermined, intrapsychic, unidirection-linear model. As Chrzanowski (1973) observes, Sullivan's notions that humans perpetuate more or less enduring interpersonal patterns "changes the concept of transference by viewing it as a two-way phenomenon in a field, rather than as an intrapsychic, self-generated form of behavior . . . transference is not merely a carryover from the past; it incorporates in its manifestations the other person's response to the distortion" (pp. 135–136).

e. Interpersonal theorists operationalize relationship-transactional events in the verbal and especially nonverbal messages of the client and therapist, and also in the self-reportable, covert engagements of each.

f. Interpersonal analysis parallels recent psychoanalytic emphases that the therapist's countertransference reactions, far from being a hindrance to the therapy transaction, rather contain important message value and, if carefully examined, can shed important light on the patient's defenses and their dynamics. It goes farther than most analysts, however, in asserting that one of the therapist's priority tasks is to metacommunicate with the client regarding these transference-countertransference engagements.

g. Interpersonal theory redefines countertransference to include recent analytic emphasis on *all* the therapist's emotional, cognitive, and fantasy engagements experienced from the client. Therapist impact responses are by no means restricted to irrational responses. Rather, impacts experienced by the therapist are shared by others in the client's life, serve as important cues to the client's unsuccessful style, and are important feedback to the client in resolving his interpersonal problems. In short, the client's maladaptive evoking style *is* the problem, and the therapist's strategy is to address that problem directly.

4. Another proposition of interpersonal therapy is that *statements offered by therapist or client to clarify the client's living patterns are at best hypotheses or guesses which vary in their usefulness to facilitate changes for the client.* As Sullivan emphasized, the linguistic transactions of therapy have features identical to the propositions of science. More or less useful hypotheses are suggested by either the client or therapist regarding the thematic aspects of the client's disordered patterns of living. Validation of these hypotheses comes from changes in the client's pattern of communication both with the therapist and with others. These changes can be mediated by any combination of interventions targeting the client's emotional experience, cognitive expectancies or beliefs, or overt verbal and nonverbal behaviors. But the priority intervention targets the evoking-impact themes manifest within and outside the therapy transaction. The client needs new, more consensually validated hypotheses about living, new and more consensually validated communication strategies.

An interpersonal perspective challenges any compartmentalization of the "process" and the "outcome" of psychotherapy. If the client brings his basic interpersonal problems into sessions with the therapist, client-therapist transactions should be simultaneously relevant to outcome as well as to process. If the client shows adaptive changes, these should be evident in more adaptive transactions with the therapist in their sessions. Further, these client changes of necessity imply changes in the dyadic system, so that both therapist and client should change away from the transactional baseline of their earlier sessions.

The point that hypotheses are the best we can do in verbal therapy transactions follows from the phenomenological stance of interpersonal theory. The stimulus for our communications is the psychological environment, the objective environment as we perceive it. Useful therapy transactions are those which facilitate changes in the client's experiential-perceptual world. Since a therapist or anyone else cannot directly apprehend or intuit another's private world, inferences are all that remain. Similarly, we cannot directly apprehend changes in the client's psychological environment. Validation of our hypotheses, therefore, comes from the therapist's and others' perceptual experience of changes in the client's transactional patterns.

A therapist, thus, speaks most validly when reporting his or her own impacts as a basis for clarification and understanding of the client's interactional patterns. The therapist is the only valid reporter of his or her own internal states as he or she experiences them. In contrast, the therapist speaks least validly when presenting, through a nonverbal attitude, inferences about the client as having a truth-value which cannot be questioned. Certainty—if it applies at all, which is doubtful—applies only to the therapist's internal responses as he or she experiences them. Everything else appropriately takes on a tentative, "let's explore the usefulness of this statement" flavor. Most of the therapist's interventions are based on tentative formulation; and this hypothetical quality, if communicated clearly, leads to participatory exploration with the client of the value of any given intervention.

5. *Interpersonal theorists emphasize the necessity of translating general therapy principles for the wide range of abnormal behavior patterns. General propositions for assessment and therapy need to be translated as they apply to different groups of clients or client problems in living.*

As with any theory of personality and psychotherapy, it is crucial to incorporate explicit statements regarding individual differences. Empirical anchoring of "core" theory (Maddi, 1976), which attempts to explain what is common to humans, occurs primarily at the "periphery" where individual differences are rampant. Therefore, the crucial question of psychotherapy theory, research, and practice is: what therapist intereventions are effective with which groups of clients producing what specific client improvements? (Kiesler, 1966, 1971; Paul, 1967).

Although he made considerable efforts to delineate communication patterns for traditional groups of psychiatric patients, Sullivan's (1956) theory, like most others, is deficient in terms of peripheral elaboration. For more contemporary interpersonal theorists, empirical anchoring of distinctive disordered interpersonal patterns involves refinements and extensions of the interpersonal circle. Some evidence (Benjamin, 1978; Kiesler & Federman, 1978; Lorr, Bishop, & McNair, 1965) supports the validity of interpersonal translations.

The purpose of interpersonal peripheral theory is to define the specific content of general propositions as they apply to separate groups of homogeneous clients. For example, for the traditionally labeled obsessive personality (Kiesler, 1973, 1977; Kiesler & Federman, 1978), it is necessary to articulate the specific verbal and nonverbal transactions that define his evoking style. The exact cluster of categories on the Interpersonal Circle needs to be established, as well as the distinctive impacts the obsessive elicits from others. It is necessary to isolate the salient components of interpersonal situations which trigger relatively intense expressions of the obsessive's evoking style, as well as the degree of cross-situational consistency that is evident. Most importantly, all these peripheral propositions need to be translated into corresponding therapeutic rules, techniques, and phasings, thereby outlining the most efficient and effective facilitation of improvement in the obsessive's transactions.

In addition to conceptualizations for the clinical obsessive personality, other interpersonal peripheral conceptualizations are beginning to appear (Coyne, 1976a, 1976b; Lemert, 1962; Wiessman, this volume). It is obvious that we have a long way to go before we can accumulate scientifically solid answers regarding the validity of interpersonal approaches to psychotherapy. But since validity must ultimately be established at the periphery where individual differences abound, interpersonal therapy must be tested by applications to specific homogeneous groups of clients.

Summary: The Interpersonal Manifesto, Part II

1. Problems in living are defined as disordered transactions, resulting originally and cumulatively from a person's neither attending to nor correcting the self-defeating aspects of his communications to others. The disturbed person consistently communicates, largely by nonverbal messages, a rigid and extreme self-presentation, and simultaneously pulls for a rigid and constricted response from others. He imposes a rigid program on his transactions which he is either unwilling or unable to change despite the varying interpersonal stances that others offer. The culprit in disordered transactions is duplicitous communication which results from selective inattention, whereby the person ignores those aspects of his own and others' messages that are inconsistent with his self-definition and self-presentation. Individual differences in disordered communication reflect the range of styles on the Interpersonal Circle around the axes of control, affiliation, and inclusion.

2. Despite its unique characteristics, the client-therapist interaction has major similarities to other human transactions. The client communicates to the therapist, sends the same rigid and extreme evoking messages, in the same duplicitous way that he communicates with important others in his life. As a result, the therapist experiences "live" in the sessions the client's distinctive interpersonal problems.

3. The central assessment task of the interpersonal therapist is to attend to and identify the client's evoking style as it unfolds over the therapy session. Central to this assessment are the therapist's own emotional and other engagements experienced with the client.

4. The therapist's priority interventions are first to stop responding in kind, in a complementary fashion, to the client's duplicitous communications. The therapist breaks the vicious transactional cycle by not continuing to be hooked or trapped by the client's engagements or pulls. Second, the therapist metacommunicates with the client about the client's evoking style and its self-defeating consequences both with the therapist and with others outside therapy. The goal of interpersonal therapy is for the client and therapist to discover more adaptive options, to replace constricted and extreme transactions with more flexible and congruent communications adaptive to the changing realities of specific encounters.

5. Statements offered to clarify the client's disordered transactions are more or less useful hypotheses or guesses at best. To attain more adjustive living, the client needs more consensually validated hypotheses about relating to others. Validation of these hypotheses comes from changes in the client's pattern of communication with both the therapist and others. Certainty for the therapist is approximated only with internal responses as he or she experiences them. Most of the therapist's interventions are based on tentative formulations, and this hypothetical quality, if communicated clearly to the client, facilitates participatory exploration with the client to the validity of any given statement.

6. General propositions of interpersonal assessment and therapy need to be translated as they apply to distinct groups of clients or to distinct problems in living. Interpersonal peripheral statements define the specific content of general propositions as they apply to concrete groups of homogeneous clients. Validation of interpersonal psychotherapy ultimately results only from these concrete clinical and research applications.

REFERENCES

Aponte, H. J. Organizing treatment around the family problems and structural bases. *Psychiatric Quarterly*, 1974 **48**, 209–222.

Argyle, M. *Bodily communication*. New York: International Universities Press, 1975.

Bandler, R. & Grinder, J. *The structure of magic: I*. Palo Alto: Science and Behavior Books, 1975.

Bateson, G. *Naven*. Stanford: Stanford University Press, 1958.

Bateson, G., Jackson, D. D., Haley, J., & Weakland, J. Toward a theory of schizophrenia. *Behavioral Science*, 1956, **1**, 251–264.

Beier, E. G. *The silent language of psychotherapy: Social reinforcement of unconscious processes*. Chicago: Aldine, 1966.

Benjamin, L. S. Structural analysis of social behavior. *Psychological Review*, 1974, **81**, 392–425.

Benjamin, L. S. Structural analysis of a family in therapy. *Journal of Consulting and Clinical Psychology*, 1977, **45**, 391–406.

Benjamin, L. S. Relation of interpersonal behavior to some diagnostic categories as presented in DSM-III. Unpublished manuscript, 1978.

Benjamin, L. S. Structural analysis of differentiation failure. *Psychiatry*, 1979, **42**, 1–23.

Berne, E. *Transactional analysis in psychotherapy*. New York: Grove Press, 1961.

Berne, E. *Games people play*. New York: Grove Press, 1964.

Berne, E. *Principles of group treatment*. New York: Oxford University Press, 1966.

Biddle, B. J. & Thomas, E. J. *Role theory: Concepts and research*. New York: Wiley, 1966.

Birdwhistell, R. L. *Introduction to kinesics*. Louisville: University of Louisville Press, 1952.

Bowen, M. A family concept of schizophrenia. In D. D. Jackson (Ed.), *The etiology of schizophrenia*. New York: Basic Books, 1960.

Bowen, M. The family as the unit of study and treatment. *American Journal of Orthopsychiatry*, 1961, **31**, 4–60.

Buchler, I. B. & Nutini, H. G. (Eds.) *Game theory in the behavioral sciences*. Pittsburgh: University of Pittsburgh Press, 1969.

Byrne, D. Interpersonal attraction and attitude similarity. *Journal of Abnormal and Social Psychology*, 1961, **62**, 713–715.

Byrne, D. Attitudes and attraction. In L. Berkowitz (Ed.), *Advances in experimental social psychology*, Vol. 4. New York: Academic Press, 1969.

Byrne, D. & Lamberth, J. Cognitive and reinforcement theories as complementary approaches to the study of attraction. In B. Murstein (Ed.), *Theories of attraction and love*. New York: Springer, 1971.

Carson, R. C. *Interaction concepts of personality*. Chicago: Aldine, 1969.

Chrzanowski, G. Implications of interpersonal theory. In E. G. Witenberg (Ed.), *Interpersonal explorations in psychoanalysis*. New York: Basic Books, 1973.

Clore, G. L. & Byrne, D. The process of personality interaction. In R. B. Cattell & R. M. Dreger (Eds.), *Handbook of modern personality theory*. New York: Appleton-Century-Crofts, 1973.

Cooley, C. H. *Human nature and the social order*. Glencoe, Ill.: Free Press, 1956.

Coyne, J. C. Toward an interactional description of depression. *Psychiatry*, 1976, **39**, 28–40. (a)

Coyne, J. C. Depression and the response of others. *Journal of Abnormal Psychology*, 1976, **85**, 186–193. (b)

Danziger, K. *Interpersonal communication*. New York: Pergamon, 1976.

DiMascio, A., Weissman, M., Neu, C., Prusoff, B., Klerman, G. F., & Rounsaville, B. *Manual for short term interpersonal psychotherapy (IPT) of depression*. Unpublished manuscript. New Haven-Boston Collaborative Depression Project, 1978.

Dittmann, A. T. The relationship between body movements and mood in interviews. *Journal of Consulting Psychology*, 1962, **26**, 480.

Dittmann, A. T. & Wynne, L. C. Linguistic techniques and the analysis of emotionality in interviews. *Journal of Abnormal and Social Psychology*, 1961, **63**, 201–204.

Ekman, P. The differential communication of affect by head and body cues. *Journal of Personality and Social Psychology*, 1965, **2**, 726–735.

Ekman, P. & Friesen, W. V. Head and body cues in the judgment of emotion: A reformulation. *Conceptual and Motor Skills*, 1967, **24**, 711–724.

Ekman, P., Friesen, W. V., & Ellsworth, P. C. *Emotion in the human face*. New York: Pergamon, 1972.

Endler, N. S. & Magnusson, D. (Eds.) *Interactional psychology and personality*. Washington, D.C.: Hemisphere, 1976.

Fierman, L. B. (Ed.) *Effective psychotherapy: The contribution of Hellmuth Kaiser*. New York: Free Press, 1965.

Foa, U. G. Convergence in the analysis of the structure of interpersonal behavior. *Psychological Review*, 1961, **68**, 341–353.

Foa, U. G. New developments in facet design and analysis. *Psychological Review*, 1965, **72**, 262–274.

Foa, U. G. Perception of behavior in reciprocal roles: The ringex model. *Psychological Monographs*, 1966, **80**, (Whole No. 623).

Foa, U. G. & Foa, E. Resource exchange: Toward a structured theory of interpersonal communication. In A. W. Siegman & B. Pope (Eds.), *Studies in dyadic communication*. New York: Pergamon, 1969.

Frank, L. K. Tactile communication. *Genetic Psychology Monographs*, 1957, **56**, 204–255.

Goffman, E. *The presentation of self in everyday life*. Garden City, N.Y.: Doubleday Anchor, 1959.

Goffman, E. *Encounters*. Indianapolis: Bobbs-Merrill, 1961.

Goffman, E. *Behavior in public places*. New York: Free Press, 1963.

Goffman, E. *Interaction ritual*. Garden City, N.Y.: Doubleday Anchor, 1967.

Grinder, J. & Bandler, R. The structure of magic: II. Palo Alto: Science and Behavior Books, 1976.

Haley, J. The family of the schizophrenic: A model system. *Journal of Nervous and Mental Disease*, 1959, **129**, 357–374. (a)

Haley, J. An interactional description of schizophrenia. *Psychiatry*, 1959, **22**, 321–332.

Haley, J. Family experiments: A new type of experiment. *Family Process*, 1962, **1**, 265–293.

Hall, E. T. *The silent language*. New York: Fawcett, 1959.

Hall, E. T. *The hidden dimension*. New York: Doubleday, 1966.

Halpern, H. M. An essential ingredient in successful psychotherapy. *Psychotherapy*, 1965, **2**, 177–180.

Harper, R. G., Wiens, A. N., & Matarazzo, J. D. *Nonverbal communication: The state of the art*. New York: Wiley, 1978.

Harris, T. A. *I'm OK—You're OK: A practical guide to transactional analysis*. New York: Harper & Row, 1967.

Harrison, R. P. *Beyond words: An introduction to nonverbal communication*. Englewood Cliffs, N.J.: Prentice-Hall, 1974.

Heider, F. *The psychology of interpersonal relations*. New York: Wiley, 1958.

Hertel, R. K. Application of stochastic process analysis to the study of psychotherapeutic processes. *Psychological Bulletin*, 1972, **77**, 421–430.

Homans, G. C. *Social behavior: Its elementary form*. New York: Harcourt, Brace, 1961.

Jackson, D. D. Family interaction, family homeostasis and some implications for conjoint family psychotherapy. In J. H. Masserman (Ed.), *Individual and familial dynamics*. New York: Grune & Stratton, 1959.

Jackson, D. D. The marital quid pro quo. *Archives of General Psychiatry*, 1965, **12**, 589.

Jackson, D. D. (Ed.) *Communications, family and marriage*. Palo Alto, Calif.: Science and Behavior Books, 1968.

Jackson, D. D., Riskin, J., & Satir, V. A method of analysis of a family interview. *Archives of General Psychiatry*, 1961, **5**, 321–386.

Kelley, H. H. Attribution theory in social psychology. In D. Levine (Ed.), *Nebraska symposium on motivation*. Lincoln: University of Nebraska Press, 1967.

Kelley, H. H. *Attribution in social interaction*. New York: General Learning Press, 1971.

Kemeny, J. G. & Snell, J. L. *Finite Markov chains*. Princeton, N.J.: Van Nostrand, 1960.

Kiesler, D. J. Some myths of psychotherapy research and the search for a paradigm. *Psychological Bulletin*, 1966, **65**, 110–136.

Kiesler, D. J. Experimental designs in psychotherapy research. In A.E. Bergin & S. L. Garfield (Eds.), *Handbook of psychotherapy and behavior change.* New York: Wiley, 1971.

Kiesler, D. J. *A communications approach to modification of the "obsessive personality:" An intitial formulation.* Unpublished manuscript. Emory University, Atlanta, 1973.

Kiesler, D. J. *Communications assessment of interview behavior of the "obsessive personality."* Unpublished manuscript. Virginia Commonwealth University, Richmond, 1977.

Kiesler, D. J. An interpersonal communication analysis of relationship in psychotherapy. *Psychiatry,* 1979, **42**, 299–311.

Kiesler, D. J. Psychotherapy process research: Viability and directions in the 1980s. In W. DeMoor & H. R. Wijngaarden (Eds.), *Proceedings of the XI International Congress of Psychotherapy.* Amsterdam: Elsevier/North Holland Biomedical Press, 1980.

Kiesler, D. J., Anchin, J. C., Perkins, M. J., Chirico, B. M., Kyle, E. M., & Federman, E. J. *The Impact Message Inventory.* Richmond: Virginia Commonwealth University, 1975, 1976.

Kiesler, D. J., Bernstein, A. B., & Anchin, J. C. *Interpersonal communication, relationship and the behavior therapies.* Richmond: Virginia Commonwealth University, 1976.

Kiesler, D. J. & Federman, E. J. *Anchoring obsessive and hysteric personalities to the interpersonal circle.* Unpublished manuscript. Virginia Commonwealth University, Richmond, 1978.

Knapp, M. L. *Nonverbal communication in human interaction.* New York: Holt, Rinehart & Winston, 1978.

LaForge, R. & Suczek, R. F. The interpersonal dimension of personality III: An interpersonal checklist. *Journal of Personality,* 1955, **24**, 94–112.

LaFrance, M. & Mayo, C. *Moving bodies: Nonverbal communication in social relationships.* Monterey, Calif.: Brooks/Cole, 1978.

Laing, R. D. *The self and others.* Chicago: Quadrangle Press, 1962.

Laing, R. D. *Reason and violence.* New York: Humanities Press, 1964.

Laing, R. D. *The politics of experience.* New York: Pantheon Books, 1967.

Laing, R. D. *The divided self.* New York: Pantheon Books, 1969.

Laing, R. D., Phillipson, H., & Lee, A. R. *Interpersonal perception.* New York: Springer, 1966.

Leary, T. *Interpersonal diagnosis of personaltiy.* New York: Ronald, 1957.

Leary, T. & Coffey, H. S. Interpersonal diagnosis: Some problems of methodology and validation. *Journal of Abnormal and Social Psychology,* 1955, **50**, 110–124.

Lederer, W. J. & Jackson, D. D. *The mirages of marriage.* New York: Norton, 1968.

Lemert, E. M. Paranoia and the dynamics of exclusion. *Sociometry,* 1962, **25**, 2–20.

Lewin, K. *A dynamic theory of personality.* New York: McGraw-Hill, 1935.

Lorr, M., Bishop, P. F., & McNair, D. M. Interpersonal types among psychiatric patients. *Journal of Abnormal Psychology,* 1965, **70**, 468–472.

Lorr, M. & McNair, D. M. An interpersonal behavior circle. *Journal of Abnormal and Social Psychology,* 1963, **67**, 68–75.

Lorr, M. & McNair, D. M. Expansion of the interpersonal behavior circle. *Journal of Personality and Social Psychology,* 1965, **2**, 823–830.

Lorr, M. & McNair, D. M. Methods relating to evaluation of therapuetic outcome. In L. A. Gottschalk & A. H. Auerbach (Eds.), *Methods of research in psychotherapy.* New York: Appleton-Century-Crofts, 1966.

Lorr, M. & McNair, D. M. *The Interpersonal Behavior Inventory,* Form 4. Unpublished manuscript. Washington, D.C.: Catholic University of America, 1967.

Maddi, S. L. *Personality theories: A comparative analysis.* Homewood, Ill.: Dorsey, 1976.

McLemore, C. W. & Benjamin, L. S. Whatever happened to interpersonal diagnosis? A psychosocial alternative to DSM-III. *American Psychologist,* 1979, **34**, 17–34.

Mead, G. H. *Mind, self and society.* Chicago: University of Chicago Press, 1934.

Mehrabian, A. *Silent messages.* New York: Wadsworth, 1971.

Mehrabian, A. *Nonverbal communication.* Chicago: Aldine, 1972.

Minuchin, S. *Families and family therapy.* Cambridge, Mass.: Harvard University Press, 1974.

Montagu, A. *Touching: The human significance of the skin.* New York: Columbia University Press, 1971.

Murray, H. A. *Explorations in personality*. New York: Oxford University Press, 1938.

Newcomb, T. M. An approach to the study of communicative acts. *Psychological Review*, 1953, **60**, 393–404.

Newcomb, T. M. The prediction of interpersonal attraction. *American Psychologist*, 1956, **11**, 577.

Newcomb, T. M. *The acquaintance process*. New York: Holt, Rinehart, & Winston, 1961.

Parsons, T. & Bales, R. F. *Family, socialization and interaction process*. New York: Free Press, 1955.

Parzen, E. *Stochastic processes*. San Francisco: Holden-Day, 1962.

Paul, G. L. Strategy of outcome research in psychotherapy. *Journal of Consulting Psychology*, 1967, **31**, 109–118.

Perkins, M. J., Kiesler, D. J., Anchin, J. C., Chirico, B. M., Kyle, E. M., & Federman, E. J. The Impact Message Inventory: A new measure of relationship in counseling/psychotherapy and other dyads. *Journal of Counseling Psychology*, 1979, **26**, 363–367.

Pittenger, R. E. & Smith, H. L., Jr. A basis for some contributions of linguistics to psychiatry. *Psychiatry*, 1957, **20**, 61–78.

Rapoport, A. *Two-person game theory: The essential ideas*. Ann Arbor: University of Michigan Press, 1966.

Rapoport, A. Games as tools of psychological research. In I. B. Buchler & H. G. Nutini (Eds.), *Game theory in the behavioral sciences*. Pittsburgh: University of Pittsburgh Press, 1969.

Rausch, H. L. Process and change—a Markov model of interaction. *Family Process*, 1972, **11**, 275–298.

Ruesch, J. & Bateson, G. *Communication: The social matrix of psychiatry*. New York: Norton, 1951.

Sarbin, T. R. & Allen, V. L. Role theory. In G. Lindzey & E. Aronson (Eds.), *The handbook of social psychology*, Vol. 1. Reading, Mass.: Addison-Wesley, 1968.

Satir, V. *Conjoint family therapy*. Palo Alto: Science and Behavior Books, 1967.

Satir, V. *Peoplemaking*. Palo Alto: Science and Behavior Books, 1972.

Scheflin, A. E. The significance of posture in communication systems. *Psychiatry*, 1964, **27**, 316–331.

Scheflin, A. E. Natural history method in psychotherapy: Communicational research. In L. A. Gottschalk & A. H. Auerbach (Eds.), *Methods of research in psychotherapy*. New York: Meredith, 1966.

Schutz, W. C. *FIRO: A three-dimensional theory of interpersonal behavior*. New York: Holt, Rinehart, & Winston, 1958.

Secord, P. F. & Backman, C. W. Personality theory and the problem of stability and change in individual behavior: An interpersonal approach. *Psychological Review*, 1961, **68**, 21–32.

Secord, P. F. & Backman. C. W. *Social psychology*. New York: McGraw-Hill, 1964.

Secord, P. F. & Backman, C. W. An interpersonal approach to personality. In B. A. Maher (Ed.), *Progress in experimental personality research*, Vol. 2. New York: Academic Press, 1965.

Siegman, A. W. & Feldstein, S. (Eds.) *Nonverbal behavior and communication*. Hillsdale, N.J.: Lawrence Erlbaum, 1978.

Sullivan, H. S. *Conceptions of modern psychiatry*. New York: Norton, 1953. (a)

Sullivan, H. S. *The interpersonal theory of psychiatry*. New York: Norton, 1953. (b)

Sullivan, H. S. *The psychiatric interview*. New York: Norton, 1954.

Sullivan, H. S. *Clinical studies in psychiatry*. New York: Norton, 1956.

Sullivan, H. S. *Schizophrenia as a human process*. New York: Norton, 1962.

Sullivan, H. S. *The fusion of psychiatry and social science*. New York: Norton, 1964.

Swensen, C. H., Jr. *Introduction to interpersonal relations*. Glenview, Ill.: Scott Foresman, 1973.

Tharp, R. G. Psychological patterning in marriage. *Psychological Bulletin*, 1963, **60**, 97–117.

Thibaut, J. W. & Kelley, H. H. *The social psychology of groups*. New York: Wiley, 1959.

Trager, G. L. Paralanguage: A first approximation. *Studies in Linguistics*, 1958, **13**, 1–12.

Von Neumann, J. & Morgenstern, O. *Theory of games and economic behavior*. Princeton: Princeton University Press, 1947.

Wachtel, P. L. *Psychoanalysis and behavior therapy: Toward an integration*. New York: Basic Books, 1977.

Watzlawick, P., Beavin, J. H., & Jackson, D. D. *Pragmatics of human communication.* New York: Norton, 1967.
Waxer, P. H. *Nonverbal aspects of psychotherapy.* New York: Praeger, 1978.
Winch, R. F. *Mate-selection: A study of complementary needs.* New York: Harper & Row, 1958.

Chapter 2
Interpersonal Formulations of Psychotherapy: A Contemporary Model
Gerard Chrzanowski

CHANGING CONCEPTIONS OF PSYCHOTHERAPY

Psychotherapeutic practice is in a state of transition. There has been a distinct shift in the model used to conceptualize the process. Today the individual person is no longer viewed as a fixed entity. Instead he is seen as an integral part of the physical and interpersonal world in which he exists. Thus, boundaries between the individual and his overall environment are always in a state of complex interpenetration or ecological balance.

This point of view is in sharp contrast to the former view of the individual patient as primary object of therapeutic exploration and intervention. Significantly, it dislodges neurosis, psychosis, and other psychopathologies from their stellar positions in the psychotherapies. The therapist today deals with person-to-person relations in terms of recurrent interpersonal patterning and past and present integrations with other people. The elaboration of personal experience moves to the foreground of our interest, replacing our former predominant search for intrapsychic conflicts as manifestations of Id and Ego forces. Metapsychological constructs as explanatory props recede into the background and give way to a less parentifying ambience in the therapeutic situation. This goes hand in hand with a more collaborative procedure in a more egalitarian setting. The therapist is no longer characterized by anonymity and neutrality, but has become an integral part of the teamwork between two responsible individuals. In this fashion the new model emerges, which is more specifically anchored in relational participation, open-ended communication including the freedom of appropriate interchanges pertaining to reciprocal impressions, feelings, and observations within the context of the therapeutic situation. Insight and interpretation assume a different meaning in this new context which addresses itself to varying degrees to formative and ongoing experiences derivative of the particular relationship which evolves in a given therapeutic situation.

In this chapter I address myself further to this new interpersonal model of psychotherapy. It is my aim to allude briefly to Sullivan's theory of therapy and then to expand certain concepts as they have evolved in clinical practice since Sullivan's death in 1949. In our present state of knowledge we have reliable data that point strongly in the direction of a dynamic transaction and potential interpenetration between genetically preformed attributes and acquired patterns representing an interface of native endowment and adaptation. No new evidence has been presented that permits us logically to declare nature or nurture as the key factor in explaining human thought and action. A distinction needs to be made between adaptation as a biopsychosocial requirement on the one hand and conformity on the other. Adaptation, as I use the term, refers to a process akin to building up immunities, pigmentation, socialization, and security in response to prevailing conditions. This is in contrast to "I will be as you and the environment expect me to be." Sullivan addressed himself to those unfortunate inroads on emerging personality trends made by excessively "playing the rules of the social game" and following the complexities and irrationalities of societal prescriptions. His construct of the self-system accounts for maladaptations, yet at the same time permits the self to develop and grow despite faulty environmental integrations which have been mediated by significant people. For Sullivan, the self-system accomplishes its tasks by employing the medium of selective inattention, i.e., "look the other way" in the presence of anxiety. It should be noted in this connection that Sullivan's interpersonal schema includes the social dimension of human existence as an essential complement to the biological dimension. This leitmotif in Sullivan's psychological thinking includes his concept of human personality as a reasonably stable configuration which is bound to a recurrent patterning of interpersonal situations that assume a characteristic lifestyle. In turn, interpersonal situations are a reflection of societal and other environmental circumstances.

THE INTERPERSONAL SCHEMA OF HARRY STACK SULLIVAN

The interpersonal point of view was introduced by Harry Stack Sullivan as a novel clinical dimension and variant methodology about 50 years ago. Sullivan was a maverick whose initial approach to mental disorders was based on the classical constructs of psychoanalysis. His own observations about person-to-person transactions in daily life and in the practice of psychiatry led him to modify certain of these tenets and to explore new arrangements in the existing scheme of psychotherapeutic approaches. Sullivan's technical innovations were based on a number of considerations. In particular he retained the classical developmental approach based on the concept of sequentially evolving stages or epochs but he suggested that these serve as way stations for interpersonal integrations. At certain intervals, new capacities come to the fore which intimately interact with the human surroundings and lead to an unfolding or truncating of inherent potentials. Early relational patterns with significant people form the matrix for future self-esteem and the esteem one is capable of attributing to others. The interference of anxiety leads to cognitive distortions which Sullivan defined as an experience that stems exclusively from situations fraught with interpersonal tension. Another key consideration of Sullivan centers on an operational transactional model within the construct of field theory. In essence it means that person-to-person involvements create a dynamic field of their own which transcends the particular personalities of the participants.

The interpersonal scheme devised by Sullivan is a relational model which attempts to bridge biological, sociocultural, physiochemical, and psychological dimensions of human existence. What emerges is an open-ended, dynamic construct of an interpersonal self that is conceptually emancipated from intrapsychic domination. The interpersonal self emerges as a predominantly experience-based manifestation that lends itself to checking and verification. Experience in this frame of reference becomes a broad term which covers all events that impinge on the human organism and which includes conscious as well as unconscious phenomena, verbal-nonverbal communications, actions, thoughts, and biologic events. Experience invariably mediates a person's relatedness to the physical and interpersonal world in which the individual has his existence. The actual event and its symbolic representation may differ in many instances. The Cartesian dichotomy of intrapsychic versus interpersonal yields to a more ecological construct in which the dividing line between what is inside and outside is mainly timebound.

There is increasing evidence today that the human organism creatively engages the environment from very early on while the environment impinges on the organism, in a number of ways. Intrapsychic phenomena are a combination of endopsychic and interpersonal events. The human organism is not capable of living in a setting of an interpersonal vacuum or in total sensory deprivation while maintaining its specifically human characteristics. An ecological model of human existence points to an ongoing interpenetration of intrapsychic and interpersonal processes. Logically we cannot have something which is alive but at the same time cut off from the network required for its existence. According to the principles of ecology, inside and outside processes do not exist behind impermeable walls. The walls are permeable in either direction. Therefore, we cannot maintain the notion of intrapsychic and interpersonal processes as separate, independent manifestations.

Sullivan's interpersonal conceptions center on:

1. A biological underpinning of the human organism that is on a *morphological structure*;
2. Its mode of functioning or *its particular physiology*; and culminate
3. In the dynamic interpenetration of the human organism with its interpersonal and physiochemical environment which constitutes the *ecological dimension*.

This cursory description of Sullivan's far-reaching interpersonal formulations requires a more detailed presentation. Space does not permit an elaboration of the basic tenets, conceptions, and implications of his point of view. The reader is referred to Sullivan's (1953/1956) *Collected Papers* and to Chrzanowski (1977a, 1978) and other publications for more information.

I now offer an abbreviated outline of Sullivan's interpersonal conceptions as they pertain to psychotherapy. This will be followed by what I consider to be my present-day model of psychotherapy.

SULLIVAN'S INTERPERSONAL MODEL OF PSYCHOTHERAPY

Participant Observation and Expert-Client Relationship

The method of participant observation, introduced by Sullivan, placed the therapeutic situation in a novel light. Patient and therapist form a dynamic transactional field. The therapist as the observer and the patient as the observed are both intrinsic parts of a common process. A complex interaction evolves within the respective expert-client roles of the therapeutic situation. I have addressed this particular topic elsewhere (Chrzanowski, 1977b, pp. 351–352; see also 1977a).

The patient's verbal, emotional and non-verbal communications are expertly monitored by the analyst who must include his personal impact on the field of observation as part of the unfolding data within the therapeutic field. The method of observation centers around the appreciation of the fact that the analyst hears what he hears and observes what he observes by never experiencing himself outside the field of his observation. His participant observation is an expression of an ever-present reminder of his intricate involvement in modifying the patient's mode of revealing himself within the analytic relationship.

Participant observation in contrast to direct participation presents a potential fail-safe barrier against being party to the patient's neurosis or psychosis. All effective forms of psychotherapy require a measure of distance from the patient's area of disturbance (pp. 351–352).

In the same text I pointed to the twofold change in the therapeutic situation, with reference to participant observation. The method relies on an ongoing interchange between therapist and patient, and at the same time, the model of the therapist as participant observer reduces the prescriptive use of insight as a therapeutic modality (see Chrzanowski, 1980a). Participant observation is based on the idea that the instrument and the object of observation impinge upon each other to a certain degree. The process of observing constitutes one form of intervention which modifies the object of observation in one form or another (Heisenberg, 1958).

Sullivan casts the therapist in the role of the participant observer whose primary activity is centered in his expert method of observing. The role model suggested by Sullivan transcends the notion of a therapeutic catalyst who remains an objective observer in an allegedly neutral position. Sullivan was intensely concerned with the therapist's function as an expert vis-à-vis the patient. To him the expert was not a person who knew answers. He conceived of an expert as a professional person who is well versed in the study of interpersonal relations and sensitive to human malintegrations or difficulties of living in their common and variegated manifestations.

The expert's skill consists in applying the method of participant observation as a primary tool in obtaining relevant data in the face-to-face, person-to-person psychotherapeutic situation. Communication in psychotherapy is not merely a matter of exchanging verbal contexts. It is the intricate process of an exquisitely complex pattern of person-to-person, transactional, communicative phenomena which imply significant conclusions about the participants concerned. The observationally participant therapist is an integral part of the field processes that bring personal data into focus. In particular, it is of critical importance that the participant observer be free to observe and to subject the multitude of his own performances to analysis as a dynamic center in the emerging integrational patterns that characterize the therapeutic situation.

Consensual Validation

Consensual validation is basically a procedure of checking and verification. Its purpose is to avoid collusion to truth or falsehood and to establish a workable platform for exploration and communication. The principle of consensual validation is based on the observation that, everything else being equal, two pairs of eyes are capable of less distorted perceptions than is one pair alone. It may be rightfully argued that consensual validation contains the potential risk of a *folie à deux*. The occasional occurrence, however, of a shared perceptual distortion is a small handicap compared to the large-scale opportunity for calibrating experiential data in the therapeutic process. In essence, consensual validation addresses itself specifically to cognitive phenomena.

Sullivan paid much attention to cognitive processes and to the act of perceiving with particular reference to the "inner" elaboration of events. He conceived of all experience as occurring in three modes which he named prototaxic, parataxic, and syntaxic modes of experience. Prototaxic refers to the most rudimentary form of prehension of "cosmic-like" sensations, without an awareness of space, time, or self. This is developmentally followed by the parataxic mode which, through the manifestation of parataxic distortions, constitutes the major area of psychotherapeutic exploration. Experience in the parataxic mode contains the bulk of symbolic integrations which took place at a time when the awareness of sequential processes and logical consistency was inadequate. Dreams, myths, and "illusory others" fall in this particular category.

Sullivan considered it unrealistic to expect communication to take place at a higher developmental level than the actual level at which the experience occurred. This point of view represents a sharp deviation from conventional psychotherapeutic tenets. The prevailing psychoanalytic and psychotherapeutic hypothesis is that the analysis of repressed and unconscious material as well as a potential reliving of early experiences represents a major therapeutic tool which paves the way toward insight and eventual recovery from conflict. By contrast, Sullivan's cognitive scheme emphasizes the unique quality of experience embedded in its mode of perception. This means that a prototaxic or parataxic operation is a phenomenon *sui generis* with a particular frame of reference that cannot be consensually validated. Syntaxic modes of experience have transcended more rudimentary and primitive referential processes and have lost contact with mental operations of a different kind. This concept bears some resemblance to the pioneering work about memory of Ernest Schachtel. Schachtel pointed out that a person's adult way of viewing the world and a child's perception of the world cannot use the same frame of reference. There is no specific mediation available between what is experienced at the time of childhood and how it is reviewed in adult life.

According to Sullivan, dreams, myths, obsessional thoughts, schizophrenic content, and similar phenomena are relatively valid parataxic operations for the relief of insoluble problems of living. Thus, they represent referential processes in the nonsyntaxic mode which defy all efforts to turn them into syntaxic or consensually validated data. That they are not syntaxic in no sense alters their validity and importance in intensive psychotherapeutic work. It only means that they cannot be transposed into a syntaxic mode of experience. Reported dreams, schizophrenic, obsessional, or other parataxic operations are viewed as communicative efforts at seeking validation with someone else. All spoken words, including the reporting of dreams, fantasies, obsessional, or schizophrenic verbalizations, undergo a measure of embroidery in the process of communicating about them with another person. Stripped of this decoration, the dream, myth, or preoccupation of warped thought content confronts the dreamer with some aspects of his life problems that have been kept out of awareness by security operations.

The following illustrates this point: A young schizophrenic man reported experiences which had taken place while he was away from home in college. He spoke of hallucinatory phenomena when he looked out of his college dorm window combined with frightening images of perceiving the buildings in his field of vision in a highly distorted fashion. These perceptual distortions were "explained" by him as a result of having taken LSD on a bicycle trip in Europe several years earlier. My therapeutically geared listening stance may best be compared with a game called "Hot and Cold" whereby the audience indicates that a person designated to find a hidden object is close to or far from the object. In the situation related here, my response was clearly on the "cold" side as far as the LSD connection is concerned. The patient recalled next that he had felt extremely isolated in college, which had been a repetition of his high school years in a small community where he had been the bright oddball. His parents were loners who had always kept themselves aloof from the community which they chose as their home.

In other words, the schizophrenic content led to the patient's acute awareness of his lifelong isolation from his fellow human beings. This led to an expression of anguish on his part in speaking about the futility of ever making contact with others. He expressed an ambivalence of wanting to live in lonely splendor, never wishing to have anything to do with people, and at the same time feeling ostracized and humiliated. He looked at people defensively with a feeling of superiority in regard to their general motives, attitudes, and behavior. He also related outright paranoid content. It was his conviction that everybody stared at him, that old ladies whom he passed in the street looked at him as a violent mugger. He had a morbid fear of speaking to people and would suffer the pains of hell when he had to go to a store to buy groceries and other essentials.

While this patient reported the above data to me, I responded to only a few particulars. For instance, I expressed surprise that people paid that much personal attention to a young man of nonconspicuous appearance. I remarked that in my experience people tend to be rather self-occupied and do not ordinarily focus excessively on inconspicuous others. I added that there was one aspect about him that caught my attention. His facial expression struck me as not particularly relaxed and it may well have been that his expression did not necessarily invite a friendly smile from a passerby. He did not reply to my comment but angrily slammed the door to my office on his way out.

At the time of his next visit, he reported a nightmare he had had while spending a night alone in his parents' house while they were away on vacation. He dreamt about a man who lived across the street from his parents. It turned out that there were bad feelings between this man and his parents that had led to litigation and a court battle. In the dream, this man came crashing through a skylight in his parents' house and was intent on killing the patient. He woke up trembling and could not fall asleep for the rest of the night, afraid that some mysterious bodily harm would come to him. (There actually was no skylight in the house). In talking about the dream, the patient emphasized that he had the nightmare because he had a cup of coffee just before going to bed. Then he spoke of how he had feared his father's towering rage in his early years, particularly when wild battles took place between the parents. He told me that his father's rage had been "tamed" by many years of psychoanalysis and that the father was now much quieter and more submissive to the mother. I inquired at this point whether he feared that the same fate was in store for him if he committed himself to the therapeutic process. He blushed, smiled faintly, and made it clear that this was exactly what he feared—that I would turn him into a hapless character who would no longer stand up for his rights.

This illustration addresses itself to dealing with data which indicate schizophrenic content and include a reported dream by the patient. In the first instance, no effort was made to analyze the content of the communication or to speculate on the nature of the patient's hallucinations or delusions. Instead, my nonverbal attitude disclaimed interest in his blaming a one-time LSD experience as the causative factor in his predicament. Reporting the schizophrenic content brought the patient in touch with his profound xenophobia, isolation, and loneliness, as well as with some of his security operations, including his fear that therapy might turn him into a piece of clay. My comment evoked anxious anger on the part of the patient but opened the therapeutic inquiry to a highly significant topic. In a somewhat different way, the dream served as a platform for responding to the patient's need for some validation from me. It should be understood that the basic therapeutic appeal to problem solving invariably concerns itself with immediate situations. There obviously cannot be any problem solving as such regarding past events. The past serves as a valuable guide to the appreciation of certain attitudes, anticipations, and cognitive distortions. Nevertheless, problem solving must always be applied in the here and now since the past cannot be changed.

The technique advocated here essentially discourages a content analysis and addresses itself to covert communicative efforts on the patient's part. Content serves primarily as a means to an end, that is, to serve as a medium for patient-therapist rapport. It frequently enables the patient to get in touch with problems that were not represented as such in his mind. Cognitive distortions obscured the nature of the problem which the patient then has a chance to check and verify in the therapeutic situation. In other words, reports in a nonsyntaxic mode are used to establish or reinforce consensual validation. Stripped of verbal encumbrances and stated in oversimplified language, the patient speaks in "Tibetan," which neither he nor the listener can understand. Content reported in "Tibetan" camouflages a series of experiences which appear to be beyond the scope of problem solving. A therapeutic listener is interested in the underlying communication and applies himself to encouraging the emergence of data that lead to problem solving. It all goes to show that experiences in different cognitive modes are not interchangeable and cannot be transposed to a common denominator. The basic problem lies in the inherent dissimilarity of the experience rather than in the verbal overlay. Meaningful contact between patient and therapist can take place only in areas of a common experiential range.

The syntaxic mode of experience is a form of consensual validation with an element of commonality. It refers to an open field of communication in which information can be interchanged without major parataxic distortions since both parties communicate with each other in the same experiential mode. Otherwise, the patient may express himself in an experiential mode that is basically alien to the therapist since a specific anxiety-laden interaction is the prerequisite of all parataxic manifestations. Therapists cannot pretend to have undergone the type of anxiety-fraught interpersonal situations which the patient has encountered in his particular life situation. Basically, we can see, hear, feel, and directly deal only with experiences that are in our "self." Potential blind spots, distortions, and warps occur when we deal with experiences that are out of context with our own. For most events we can acquire familiarity with something on a dual scale. We may learn about a foreign country by visiting the country and studying it in situ. Or we may learn about the country from books, maps, reports, or personal acquaintances. In the realm of emotions, only the personal visit provides experience of a valuable kind. It is for this reason that communication about events that took place under the impact of anxiety are not in the "self" since one has not been capable of looking at and observing what was going on at such a time. The result is the occurrence of parataxic distortions which in turn preclude consensual validation. Suppose a patient tells me that he saw a monster with fiery eyes which from out of nowhere appeared in the middle of his living room. It is of no significant therapeutic value if I say "How very scary! Could this phantom conceivably have been your mother?" The patient may say yes or no to my comment without much emotional resonance unless he has already made that association himself. In either case, we are not necessarily speaking about an actual person who is the patient's mother rather than the patient's anxiety-laden experience of some aspects of the mother. The therapist could not know the quality of the morbid mother-child interaction even if he had met the mother in person. Be that as it may, the actual experience as such cannot be recalled by the patient or adequately reconstructed by the therapist. Accordingly, communication in this nonsyntaxic mode is a dead end. What lends itself to discussion and potential avenues of problem solving is the patient's ability to verbalize some of the consequences of events and life problems without undue emphasis on particular causative factors. It offers the patient an opportunity to get some validation from the therapist about some of the anxiety-induced scars, blind spots, and distortions. It should be understood that there may occasionally be a dream or a parataxic operation that is a thinly disguised communication. Under such circumstances a more direct response seems appropriate without changing the basic principle described.

The role of anxiety in the manifestation of security operations and parataxic distortions is a topic in its own right. It will suffice here to state that anxiety vis-à-vis another person, real or imaginary, is the exclusive trigger mechanism which brings transference-countertransference into play. The intervention of anxiety may be the result of anticipatory, anxious structuring of the situation by one partner or the other, or by both; it may also take place because of a potential relational miscarriage in the here and now, resulting from varying degrees of mutual security operations.

Be that as it may, in the scheme outlined here, the underlying parataxic distortion acts like an allergy. It leaves a person vulnerable to human contact and integrations which take place under the impact of anxiety.

The developmental sequence of prototaxic and parataxic modes of experience proposed by Sullivan covers in some fashion elements of Freud's primary process model while the syntaxic mode is a more distant relative of secondary process. Sullivan did not delineate the maturational shift from the prototaxic to the parataxic experiential scheme with clarity. There is a question in my mind how significant such a line of demarcation would be for therapeutic purposes which I will allude to in a later part of this chapter.

Sullivan's parataxic model changes some basic therapeutic considerations. It implies that transference-countertransference manifestations are not phenomena *sui generis*, but interpersonal manifestations in the presence of the experience of anxiety.

Interchange of Information

Information is invariably supplied by the patient in the therapeutic process. It is the task of the therapist to report what he has heard to the patient. This summarizing reply by the therapist has a double purpose. It allows the patient to modify data that may have given an erroneous impression. It also provides the patient with an opportunity to get a feeling for the way the therapist has listened and the areas that may have struck him as being of therapeutic significance. The initial act of information gathering is loosely structured by the therapist during the first interview.

The interchange of information does not merely consist of obtaining a history or of eliciting relevant clinical data and subjecting them to checking and verification; it also forms the basis for a particular network of verbal, nonverbal, emotional, and personally geared communication. As such, it aids in the evolution of the therapeutic field in which the patient—his inner conflict and his particular psychopathology—recedes as the focal psychotherapeutic target. The emphasis of both participants moves in the direction of interpersonal integration within the expert-client patterning while informational interchanges enhance the element of commonality between the participating parties. Significant differences are clearly acknowledged and identified without a need to place the differences in the foreground. This point will be further discussed in connection with Sullivan's "one genus postulate."

Enlarging the Observation and Communicative Faculties

A major goal of the therapeutic process is to widen the patient's observational horizon and to help him feel more at ease articulating personal experiences. The promotion of this process leads to greater sensitivity about integrating tendencies of conjunctive or disjunctive proportions. It aids in a better recognition of parataxic distortions and promotes an appreciation of viable and workable alliances versus hostile integrations. Observation is closely linked to self-awareness, which in turn enables a person to observe the self with greater clarity. Sullivan considers the self and anxiety at opposite poles whereby the field of observation is circumscribed by the self-image that is the reflected appraisal of one's self in the eyes of others. Anxiety beclouds the self-image by profoundly lowering self-esteem. It is for this reason that Sullivan designates the self as the primary center for the awareness of anxiety, which means the experience of lacking elementary approval by significant other people. The level of self-esteem is inculcated early in life as a result of anxiety-fraught interpersonal relations with key people in one's formative years. The relatively durable scar of self-esteem is a lifelong cross to bear. Psychotherapy cannot undo past experiences. Its task in this respect is to broaden the scope of observations and communicative faculties which in a way means to stabilize the self by enlarging self-perception and the capacity to talk in personal terms about oneself. In Sullivan's own words, a significant aspect of psychotherapy is viewed as follows: "Every constructive effort of the psychiatrist, today, is a strategy of interpersonal field operations which 1) seeks to map the areas of disjunctive force that block the efficient collaboration of the patient and others, and 2) seeks to expand the patient's awareness so that this unnecessary blockage can be brought to an end" (Sullivan, 1953, p. 376). He also stated categorically that "what anyone can observe and analyze becomes ultimately a matter of tension and energy transformations, many of the latter being obvious actions, but many others of which are obscure activities that go on, as we say, in the mind" (Sullivan, 1953, p. 368).

Anxiety as a Strictly Interpersonal Phenomenon

Anxiety in contrast to fear is a strictly interpersonal phenomenon. In Sullivan's formulation, anxiety is a purely psychological manifestation which in itself does not have any neuroanatomic underpinning. The experience of anxiety which is exclusively evoked by malintegrations between people represents a disjunctive tension. In Sullivan's schema, tensions lead to action by inducing energy transformations. This type of energy is not psychic in nature, but refers to a physical force capable of producing action. Anxiety is the one and only tension that does not lead to the transformation of energy, but, on the contrary, leads to a state of paralysis.

Sullivan postulated the existence of basic integrating tendencies such as the desire to seek person-to-person intimacy. In one statement he writes: "Integrating tendencies pertain to the very tissue of life" (Sullivan, 1956, p. 9) while in another statement he says: "Integrating tendencies. . . . [are] reflected in all those situations in which two or more people tend to understand each other better, to come to a clearer grasp of their particular little differences of views, impulses, and so on" (Sullivan, 1956, pp. 7–8). Anxiety in this frame of reference disrupts communication, precludes intimacy, interferes with constructive or creative thought processes, and leads to profound miscarriages and malfunctioning in human integrations. Anxiety permeates the field of person-to-person contact and obscures a clear appreciation of the factors involved in recognizing precursors of the evolving interpersonal tensions. Anger, resentment, sterile bickering, as-if performances, and so forth are frequently veneers for the intervention of anxiety. In the presence of anxiety there may also be a complex feeling tone of embarrassment, humiliation, shame, guilt, and chagrin. Sullivan thought that anxiety is an interpersonal umbrella that covers every aspect of human existence. At the same time, he felt strongly that the human capacity to cope with this manmade tension is not adequate. In Sullivan's view it is a major task of psychotherapy to educate patients to the presence of anxiety so that they can learn, like sailors, to observe the ripples in the water before the full blown gust of wind hits. Sullivan did not believe that anxiety as such can be minimized since it is an experience which takes place outside of a person's awareness and outside the realm of recall.

Developmental Approach

Sullivan advocated a longitudinal, developmental approach. His aim was to gain a mutual understanding with the patient of how the patient came to be who he is at the time he enters psychotherapy.

Interpersonal theory conceives of every step in the developmental ladder as a stepping stone to the next level of development. A biologically ordained serial maturation of capabilities is the underlying frame of reference for the stages of infancy, childhood, the juvenile era and preadolescence, early and late adolescence, to maturity. Experience of a valuable kind can occur only when maturation of capacities has occurred. In turn, the experience depends on the prevailing interpersonal situations which promote, truncate, or oppose appropriate integrations. If experience runs counter to providing competence for living with others at a particular developmental threshold, the possibility for future satisfactory relations are definitely reduced with particular reference to the developmental epoch that was of negative value. Each developmental epoch is important in its own right as a platform for a person's repertoire in interpersonal relations in the lifespace extending from birth toward mature competence in a fully human world.

Preadolescence brings the developmental epochs of basic dependency on the home to an end. Up to that time, the capacity to be closely attuned to the needs of another person in a spirit of genuine reciprocity of sharing, of nondependent, nonpossessive concern, is greatly limited. It is only in preadolescence that the basic need for an intimate exchange with a fellow human being, a chum, a friend, a loved one, emerges in full force.

In Sullivan's developmental scheme, preadolescence is a way station at which major conjunctive experiences can undo many disjunctive integrations preceding it: "I believe that for a great majority of our people, preadolescence is the nearest that they come to untroubled human life—that from then on the stresses of life distort them to inferior caricatures of what they might have been" (Sullivan, 1940, p. 56).

Anticipation and Foresight

Experience, according to Sullivan, is invariably permeated by events that pertain to the near past, the more distant past, and by elements of the near future, i.e., anticipation, expectation and foresight. The role of foresight, aspiration, and anticipation to a large degree determines the adequacy and appropriateness of overt and covert activity to the actual demands of the situation in which a person finds himself involved with significant others. In other words, the near future becomes a tangible dimension which plays a distinct part in explaining many human events. Except for unforeseen interference of circumstances, human beings live with their past, the present, and the neighboring future as relevant components in explaining their thoughts and actions. The phenomenon of foresight represents another important field of study in the therapeutic process.

The One Genus Postulate

The "One Genus Postulate" is a key concept of Sullivan's interpersonal psychiatry. It emphasizes his basic conviction and probably his most widely quoted phrase, "We are all much more simply human than otherwise, be we happy and successful, contented and detached, miserable and mentally disordered or whatever" (Sullivan, 1940, p. 16). Inherent in this formulation is the assumption that even in the most severe instances of mental disorder we find some common aspects of every human being's experience. What differs mainly is the timing, duration, and particular circumstances under which thought and action take place. In the study of interpersonal relations and in the practice of psychotherapy, the multitude of individual differences matters far less than the potential similarities. The basic assumption in this schema is that deviant interpersonal situations, with the exception of differences in language or custom, are a function of differences in the relative maturity of the person concerned. The ubiquitously human will invariably be more pronounced than anything else in human personality. In the therapeutic process we approach the patient on the basis of our common humanity rather than on his anomalous, aberrant, interpersonal integrations. We aim to get in touch with the patient's syntaxic mode of experience, while appreciating the existence of interpersonal miscarriages and concomitant parataxic distortions.

The eight points mentioned above are a sketchy and incomplete outline of certain therapeutic principles embedded in Sullivan's interpersonal theory. What follows is a contemporary model of interpersonal psychotherapy.

More than 50 years have elapsed since Sullivan outlined his pioneering point of view. An additional 30 years have passed since his death. The reification, dogmatization, and premature systematization of Freud's brilliant inventions and discoveries have been an impediment to the evolution of the overall field of psychotherapy. Sullivan's formulations were intentionally open-ended and incomplete in many respects. Theoretical models need to be brought in tune with new discoveries as well as with changes in the Zeitgeist (Kohut, 1978.). An increasing need presents itself to incorporate the growing body of empirical data in the overall structure of the therapeutic process. It is only by becoming thoroughly familiar with major theories of therapy and by testing their clinical applicability that progress can be made. The task of transcending the tyranny of longstanding dogma is formidable. In this connection, we should take great care not merely to discard older formulations but to transform them, if possible, in the light of clinical experience.

Sullivan has made far-reaching contributions to the field of psychological as well as psychoanalytic theory and practice. His work has inspired many aspects of group and family therapy, milieu therapy, social, and transcultural considerations. Sullivan's interpersonal revision of the mirror-analyst model has gained considerable acceptance among most psychotherapeutic schools of thought that have not usually credited Sullivan with the innovation. The same holds true in other respects where his formulations and technical advances have greatly enlarged the horizon of psychotherapeutic procedures. In my opinion much is to be gained by studying Sullivan's body of conceptualizations in detail in spite of the fact that many of his ideas have unwittingly become the common heritage of present-day psychotherapy. It should be appreciated at the same time that not all of Sullivan's tenets and principles have stood the test of time. In my presentation of a contemporary model pertaining to interpersonal psychotherapy, I refer to some modifications, changes, extensions, and innovations pertaining to the therapeutic study of interpersonal relations. My primary concern is on enlarging the scope of the clinical application of certain interpersonal constructs. In my endeavors, particular consideration is given to the fuller application of the ecological principle with reference to individual personality. Emphasis is shifted to a more epigenetic, open-ended point of view with greater attention paid to the modification of relational patterns of ongoing, significant, interpersonal situations. The longitudinal, developmental approach is maintained without excessive concern for formative fixations. In this connection, the experiential role of the self, self-system, and self-esteem is viewed in a somewhat different therapeutic light. *Relational participation* and *collaborative inquiry* are suggested as methods of choice in place of participant observation. A playing down of the expert-client model has given rise to a basically more egalitarian ambience in the process of psychotherapy. Personal affirmation has been added as an additional dimension legitimately buttressing a patient's self-esteem. The preponderance of observing parataxic distortions has yielded to increasing scrutiny of characteristic nonneurotic, nonpsychotic, nonprescriptive relational manifestations between two responsible parties in the therapeutic endeavor. My emphasis is that the contextual interaction of patient and therapist constitutes a major therapeutic dimension in its own right, a dimension which unfolds outside the realm of transference-countertransference implications and requires special attention as an observational and communicative medium *sui generis* (Chrzanowski, 1980b).

I would like to add to this outline a modification of Sullivan's pan-anxiety model and a transcending of his energetic preoccupations which hark back to older mechanistic models. What follows is a contemporaneous version of a psychotherapeutic model which is based on an interpersonal point of view.

A CONTEMPORARY MODEL OF INTERPERSONAL PSYCHOTHERAPY

Relational Participation and Collaborative Inquiry

Participant observation as a methodology represented a milestone in the theory and practice of psychotherapy. It transcended the original construct of the mirror analyst, who allegedly without interaction with the patient, reflected everything back to him. Inherent in this concept is the assumption that such an attitude places the therapist in a supposedly objective, instrumental position. It also casts the therapist in a role that is characterized by neutrality and anonymity which is actually impossible. This runs counter to the current scientific view which emphasizes that observer and observed constitute an interacting indivisible unit.

Formerly, my clinical work proceeded quite well when I assumed the role of the participant observer. With the passage of time, however, thoughts came to mind which encouraged me to modify my method. First, I realized that participant observation is a potential tautology since the term observation as used here includes the element of participation with the observer as an integral part of what he observes. My attention then shifted to the particular therapeutic area of participation or observation. I concluded that the therapist's participation in the process centers on the nature, quality, and mode of the personal relationship between the participants. Accordingly, it seemed appropriate to me to speak of *relational participation* rather than *participant observation*. My aim in making the change was to open the door for a systematic study of how patient and therapist interact outside of the expert-client role, independently of distortions imposed by transference-countertransference phenomena.

The concept of relational participation led me to the concomitant principle of *collaborative inquiry*. I have elaborated on this topic elsewhere (Chrzanowski, 1980a). Collaboration, a term coined by Sullivan, is a developmental manifestation of preadolescence. It signals the capacity for a special kind of relationship characterized by validation and intimacy. With certain modifications, some of the basic principles of collaboration apply to the relational patterning of psychotherapy. The main difference lies in the goal of the therapeutic collaboration or teamwork which excludes the emergence of mutual admiration. In psychotherapy the primary focus is on the patient's welfare. Another advantage of relational participation and collaborative inquiry is a legitimately affirmative response to the patient. By legitimate, I mean that the therapist must be genuinely able to discover something of personal worth in the patient. It does not necessarily mean that he has to like him.

In a more generous mood, it has probably occurred to some of us that every viable method of competing psychotherapies has some legitimate claim of success. The common denominator in this great wilderness is the personalities of the respective practitioners.

There have also been a number of studies, such as Whitehorn and Betz (1975, pp. 270–280), which clearly point to the therapist's personality as a significant factor in the rate of successful versus unsuccessful therapeutic endeavors.

The notion that patients experience therapists mainly as devoted "healers" strikes me as an unfortunate distortion. By the same token, it is not realistic to view therapists predominantly as therapeutic instruments rather than as individuals in their own right whose personalities participate decisively in the therapeutic process. Relational participation is not to be confused with a buddy-buddy attitude or with the need to fill gaps in personal satisfaction with something that is derived mainly from the patient. Collaboration as discussed here differs from the model of the working alliance which places a distinctly larger burden to be cooperative on the patient (Chrzanowski, 1979a).

Melanie Klein, Bion, Sullivan, and the existentialists each deal with the therapeutic situation in their own right without reference to a working alliance (Chrzanowski, 1979a). The term "working alliance" appears perfectly innocuous at first glance. On closer inspection the term includes a number of implicit and explicit covenants. According to Ralph Greenson, who coined the term, the capacity to form a working alliance requires the capacity for a transference neurosis as a sine qua non for successful therapy. Greenson (1967) distinguishes the transference neurosis from the neurotic defenses and resistances. He clarifies his position by stating, "In the course of analysis the patient is expected to be able to regress to the more primitive and irrational transference reactions which are under the primary process." Greenson is of the opinion that the analyst must deprive and frustrate the patient up to the patient's capacity to take it while, at the same time, he also must induce collaboration (i.e., the working alliance).

I personally consider the "shrinking" and regression of the patient an unfortunate procedure and recommend a more egalitarian approach. I have always wondered why it would be reasonable to inflict one neurosis on a patient in order to cure him of another. The role of an antithetical attitude on the analyst's part as recommended by Greenson also strikes me as artificial. I do not believe that the necessity to set limits and to promote a mutually respectful, professional atmosphere needs to be split off from the collaborative ambience.

There is also an implicit assumption in Greenson's approach that the patient's irrational parental introject will be replaced by the introject of the rational analyst. It seems to me that the amelioration of cognitive distortion is facilitated by the way in which the patient's and the analyst's personalities integrate. The therapeutic principle lies more in the increasing capacity to rely on one's undistorted observational acumen and the possibility for some checking and verification with another person. I very much doubt that the infantile neurosis in all of its epigenetic vicissitudes is predominantly resolved by reliving the past as a means of clearing the way for new experiences.

The Individual Personality and the Interpersonal Self

The individual personality

The myth of individual personality becomes one of the more controversial landmarks of interpersonal theory and practice. Individual personality represents a symbolic component which has been endowed with a certain mythology that makes it sacrilegious to speak out against a so-called God-given, indivisible core of "man." Sullivan rejected the notion of individual personality as an atomistic construct and insisted that such a notion is basically a metaphor that cannot be subjected to checking and verification. The main thrust of psychological study in the interpersonal frame of reference centers on the integrating tendencies between two or more individuals within the field of their transactions under the prevailing conditions.

In my opinion, the concept of a real or authentic personality is illusory and misleading if it refers to an inherently independent entity. The image of an "authentic" self, immaculately embedded somewhere in the human mind, defies the principle of interacting facets of human personality and interdependency.

Up to this point, interpersonal formulations stand on sound epistemological principles. Difficulty arises, however, when the interdependence of human personality is used as an argument against basically stable, individual patterns which assume certain characteristics in a particular personality. Qualities such as integrity, compassion, courage, temperament, leadership, and others cannot be considered to be transactional phenomena rather than individual personality endowments. There is also a risk in focusing exclusively on processes without devoting adequate attention to structure. An emphasis on human similarities and commonalities over the multitude of differences in people in psychotherapy is probably the most important innovation made so far in the conceptualization of a therapeutic model. Once we assimilate this giant in our clinical practice, however, the necessity to focus on structural components becomes a requirement. Unique aspects of individual personality come to the fore once we make the relational field a primary focus of our attention. A characteristic "Me" emerges most clearly opposite a characteristic "You." I consider it more useful to think of a constellation pertaining to individual personality in preference to a static, "authentic" core. Furthermore, clinical evidence points to an active as well as a reactive part of human personality which is never rigidly fixed. There are inherent temperamental differences to the degree to which individual personality traits actively engage the environment. Yet, we do find clearly marked differences in the circumstances which mobilize potential activity or passivity in the personality structure. A sensitive appreciation of this phenomenon is a significant dimension in the therapeutic situation. The therapist's mode of listening, his expectations, his affirmative attitudes, his sensitivities, his potential areas of anxiety all contribute to highlighting or downplaying personality trends in both participants.

The interpersonal self

The formulation of an interpersonal self harks back to the field of social psychology and specifically to George Herbert Mead's conceptualization in *Mind, Self and Society* (1934). Mead's ingenious model of "the generalized other" played a distinct part in Sullivan's model of a reflected appraisal of oneself in the eyes of others as the primary area of one's self-image or self-awareness. In the presence of severe anxiety there is no self since this most sensitive observational "camera" then operates in a field of darkness. The resulting operational paralysis of self does not permit the representation of anxiety-fraught integrations with others. It means that the self ceases to operate when a severe threat to self-esteem is anticipated and/or evolves.

I have discussed the growing interest in a psychology of the self elsewhere (Chrzanowski, 1978). In this connection I made a reference to the now well-known contributions of Heinz Kohut. In *The Analysis of the Self* (1971), Kohut considers the self as a psychic structure which in keeping with the construct of libido theory is imbued with instinctual energy. At the same time Kohut conceives of the self as a structure of the mind with continuity in time. This formulation gives the self a more independent status than Kohut's earlier model in which he views the self as a content of the mental apparatus, but none of its constituents.

In *The Restoration of the Self* (1978), Kohut presents poignant arguments against classical metapsychology and winds up by adding a new psychological dimension without transcending the older dogma. Kohut speaks of the necessity of two approaches—that is, a psychology in which the self is seen as the center of the psychological universe on the one hand while on the other hand he adheres to a psychology in which the self is a metapsychological construct. Kohut's psychology of self coexists with the abstractions of Id, Ego, and Superego as the structural underpinning of all experience. As such, his formulation leaves much to be desired. There is a major distinction between Kohut's formulations of a psychology of the self and the psychology of the self advocated in this chapter and in some of my previous writings. I only wish to reiterate that classical theoreticians look at the self as a potential surface phenomenon, that is, as a thin, social or interpersonal shield that conceals the inherent basic human stuff. Classical analysts accord the id, ego, and superego an excessively concrete, reified status in contrast to the self, which is not considered by them to be an *integral* part of the psychic apparatus. The classical self is thus depicted as a poor relation of the ego which is recognized as the more respectable part of the psychic establishment.

I personally prefer the term "self" because terms such as "ego," "personality," "identity," and others have assumed a distinctly biased meaning reflecting dogma, while the construct "self" has a potentially open-ended stance. In addition, the use of deterministic verbal tools has a coercive impact on our mental processes and observations.

It should be evident from the material presented so far that a psychology of self must stand on its own merit. There is no room for a self with a Janus head, that is, a single head with two faces pointing in opposite directions. A psychology of self can open the door to novel psychological territory if it transcends the pitfalls of ego psychology, the structural model of agencies of the mind, and the psychology of the drives. Such a psychology also needs to rise above any concretization of a self. By the same token it must deal with individual style and remove itself from energic considerations.

One major consideration in beginning to forge a psychology of the self is the acquisition of valid information pertaining to the ways and means of maintaining as well as enhancing self-esteem.

In interpersonal formulations the exclusively experiential foundation of the self is a major advance in theory as well as clinical practice. It has great potential for widening the scope of therapeutic inquiry and promotes consensual validation. The construct of a self-system which permits a measure of learning and of constructive integrations despite profound restrictions in self activity buttresses the scheme under discussion. The main difficulty with Sullivan's interpersonal model of a self is its total dependence on anxiety and its resulting lack of continuity as a structure in one form or another. Sullivan's self is a looking-glass, akin to an optical instrument which relies predominantly on the reflected appraisal or reproduction of the outside image in a given individual. In my opinion, this model conceives of the individual as having practically no clarity of vision of his own. The viewer depends almost entirely on the image reflected in his eyes and is potentially blurred by cognitive distortions caused by the interference of anxiety. Another flaw of an exclusively anxiety-bound self is its basic anonymity. The self as an empirical, observational medium in an operational system would be expected to have some sort of structure since as an observing instrument it becomes an integral part of what it observes. In other words, the self cannot be a participant observer unless it has something relatively tangible which enters the observational field and interpenetrates with it. In therapy the interpersonal self emerges as a focal exploratory area since it reflects significant aspects of the way in which the therapist's and patient's personalities integrate in the therapeutic process. If all goes well, the respective interpersonal selves of the participating parties in the therapeutic process provide a communicative channel for relatively undistorted exchanges.

Some patients tend to bring a good deal of anticipatory anxiety into the therapeutic situation. Each therapist has varying degrees of sensitivity to the anxiety which is "injected" into the process of therapy. Profoundly distressing experiences in the therapist's present and past life situations will also cause the therapist occasionally to infuse the therapeutic situation with his own anxiety. In both situations I have found it helpful to address the situation at hand directly. For instance, when I feel unduly sleepy with a patient after having enjoyed a good night's rest, I will say words to the effect that I have difficulty holding my head up and difficulty in not falling asleep in spite of having slept well the preceding night. I will say something like, "I wonder whether something about me is making you uncomfortable or something about you is evoking discomfort on my part?" "Are you by any chance depressed, anxious, burdened by bad fantasies or by some other headaches?" More often than not, I get some worthwhile information in response to my query. Even if there is no response from the patient, my sleepiness tends to wane and my alertness returns when I take this kind of initiative. I may also get some notion of what may have numbed my mind and blocked communication. Instead of sleepiness, I may inform the patient that contrary to my usual habit, I had looked at my clock excessively since time just did not seem to move, or my mind had started to wander off and seemed to obsess about extraneous things when I ordinarily have little difficulty listening without undue distractions. In some instances the patient tells me that I have been unusually fidgety, moved around in my chair excessively or seem distracted. It is my habit to acknowledge the patient's observation if I can find any confirmation for it and, where appropriate, to give some factual information that I do not feel rested, that I had a difficult day, had encountered some aggravation and related happenings. There is no need to go into detail, to unburden myself or explain what happened to me explicitly. The main point is to affirm for the patient the validity of his observations where it applies. These comments illustrate a distinct shift of therapeutic focus. A dimension is added by demonstrating the patient's impact on the therapist rather than pointing predominantly to the patient's anxiety or general psychopathology. It brings to the patient's attention how the therapist participates in the process and the impact the patient can have on him. By the same token, the patient's observations about the therapist are carefully considered and discussed. In my opinion, a more detailed and structured formulation of the self aids in this respect.

Parataxis, Countertransference and Personal Relationship

Freud observed a particular phenomenon in his clinical work which he called transference. By this term he referred to an emotionally charged reaction to the therapist as if he were like a familiar figure of the past. The manifestations of positive and negative transference became one of the key areas of therapeutic exploration. The interpretation of transference became a mjaor factor in overcoming resistances. The classical therapeutic model relies heavily on free association as the patient's required modus operandi while interpretation constitutes a primary response on the part of the therapist. Inherent in this assumption is the added expectation that transferential regression will clarify unrecognized aspects of the past and will free the patient from neurotic conflicts. The patient, in experiencing his past by means of interpretation, becomes conscious of his infantile impulses, of his compulsive need to repeat unresolved conflicted acts, and eventually gains emotional and intellectual mastery over his psychic functions.

Countertransference—as will be discussed after an elaboration of the concept of parataxis—has come a long way from its definition as the mere reciprocal of transference (Chrzanowski, 1979b).

The term "parataxis," which Sullivan borrowed from Don Thomas Vernon Moore, was intended to emphasize the dynamic operation of a transactional field process. In the old model, transference was an intrapsychic process which unfolded without the therapist's participation in the event. Countertransference, then, was a reverse manifestation whereby the therapist's unresolved inner conflicts become manifest. By contrast, all aspects of parataxis are interpersonal in origin and come into existence as a result of anxiety-fraught integrations with significant others. Parataxic concomitance or parataxic distortion refers to cognitive phenomena that occur in a great variety of interpersonal situations. Involved in the process are relatively primitive symbol operations that persist through life. It is not that parataxis refers to a different content from transference; it refers to a different way of viewing the same data. The concept of parataxis, therefore, is an attempt to bring about a dynamic fusion of transference and countertransference phenomena in an interactional field that transcends static intrapsychic or endopsychic conceptualizations.

In its modern usage, countertransference has enlarged the scope of psychotherapy (Epstein & Feiner, 1979). In particular, the sophisticated application of self-monitoring and the judicious sharing of personal observation and experience with the patient represents a therapeutic dimension of major significance. To some degree the modern concept of countertransference has transcended the predominantly intrapsychic model and has moved closer to experiential, interactional constructs. There is much to be said in favor of refining, clarifying, and technically expanding the modern version of countertransference. This does not change the fact that the construct has some drawbacks and limitations. For one, it is historically and therefore inextricably tied up with the concept of transference and overfocuses on the therapist's role in the therapeutic process. The central consideration of a transactional field is not included in the term and the connotations of countertransference as the other side of transference is not adequately dismissed. I believe that parataxis, despite its odd-sounding name, is a more dynamic construct anchored in an interpersonal frame of reference. Countertransference has much appeal since it addresses the therapist's creative potential, but it does not sufficiently credit the patient as a required collaborator. In a similar vein, parataxis focuses excessively on the expert as having the know-how to observe malintegrations and distortions. It minimizes the nonparataxic components in the respective personalities of patient and therapist. In my clinical experience, I find much evidence that important therapeutic work takes place in this area of contact parallel to or independently from cognitive distortions, conflicts, ambivalences, and other neurotic manifestations.

Thus, my emphasis is on the personal, nontechnical relationship between two responsible parties in the therapeutic process as a dimension *sui generis*. The concept of a personal relationship should not be confused with pseudo-intimacy in its numerous disguises. It should not be viewed as the equivalent of friendship, chumship, or related interpersonal structures; nor is personal relationship an occult, mythical, pseudo-romantic encounter between individuals, nor the meeting of two authentic selves making beautiful music together. Personal relationship as discussed here is the complex interaction of the patient's and the therapist's personalities. The nature of the personal relationship tends to enhance mutual self-awareness in a fashion that promotes an experiential mode of communication and widens the field of collaborative inquiry. Under such circumstances, an increased opportunity presents itself for checking and verification, as to the emergence of constructive, disruptive, or ineffectual interpersonal patterns inside and outside the therapeutic situation. In particular, communicative miscarriages, mutual mishearing, misunderstanding, and miscommunication are revealed more clearly in contrast to the emergence of communicative bridges that may assist the patient in the task of problem solving. I do not find that opening communicative channels in the therapeutic situation is a burden that rests predominantly on the therapist's shoulders. Nor do I find person-to-person communication largely obstructed by the ebb and flow of transferential and countertransferential data. There are a number of nontechnical, nonprescriptive transactions between therapist and patient that deserve to be monitored carefully, explored in detail, systematized, and clinically applied.

Some therapeutic situations come to unsatisfactory ends because no direct effort was made by therapist and patient to explore the personal relationship in its own right. In other situations a therapeutic marathon ensues with two tired and inherently uninvolved parties. Often neither party can let go or break through, which leads to a sad clinch between two hapless parties.

It means that a sterile integration has taken place in the therapeutic partnership. Frequently it indicates that a point of diminishing productivity has been reached without a mutual effort to explore the relational miscarriage that interfered with therapeutic progress. This cul de sac is often encountered at a time when major problems presented by the patient have been discussed from many angles and fresh material suitable for therapeutic exploration is not immediately available. At the same time, symptoms have assumed a measure of chronicity which is unwittingly accepted as status quo.

Another problem centers on the wisdom of a therapeutic repertoire that is specifically geared to the patient's prevailing psychopathology. Certain theories of therapy tend to be more successful in dealing with particular mental disorders. Such a point of view has much appeal but overemphasizes psychopathology without adequate regard for the respective personalities of therapist and patient. The therapeutic ambience actually changes, depending on the nature and severity of the clinical syndrome presented by the patient. An acutely paranoid patient, for instance, will contribute to a type of relationship that differs significantly from the transactions with a patient in whom blaming, suspiciousness, and projection are mainly peripheral manifestations. The presence of a severe disorder often calls for a respectfully restrained area of person-to-person contact without calling for a basically different "therapeutic hat." There is no need for a wardrobe of hats carefully chosen to match the patient's particular mode of malintegration. One therapeutic headgear suffices if it can be tilted slightly when the occasion calls for it. Some patients require more distance while others can tolerate more contact; some therapists need considerable "elbow room" and run into difficulty when communicative and relational aspects improve markedly. It is not unusual for therapists as well as patients to hide behind their carefully elaborated respective roles when more personal interactions come into play. The interpersonal method of psychotherapy repetitively refocuses on processes which characterize integrational patterns between the participants in the therapeutic situation. This does not minimize the significance of experiential and developmental events in their formative patterning of current relational manifestations. Nor does it negate in any way the inner elaboration of interpersonal experiences, that is, intrapsychic processes, symbol operations including dreamwork, "illusory others," etc. What gives the interpersonal methodology its particular stamp is the endeavor to bring as much of what is "locked into a person" as possible into that interrelational field which characterizes the therapeutic situation. In other words, the actual relationship between therapist and patient turns into a screen on which ongoing conjunctive and disjunctive interactions are reflected and subjected to mutual inquiry. Patterns of relational accommodations, hostile integrations, distance-making operations or contact-enhancing communications are transposed into a contextual setting which invariably includes the therapist as a relational participant. In this frame of reference, communication is not divided into the sender versus the recipient. Donald Kiesler (1979) formulates six statements of how relationship operates in psychotherapy as a therapeutic agent. He defines one of two therapeutic priority tasks: "To decode and identify the predominant self-defeating evoking style of the client as it shows up in interactions during psychotherapy—through identification of the predominant impact responses being pulled from the therapist by his client" (p. 307). In my opinion, the emergence of competent and adequate lifestyles should be viewed as being of equal importance to the identification of self-defeating operations. Furthermore, my model of collaborative inquiry and relational participation stresses the contextual aspects of the therapeutic situation by viewing the therapist as an integral part of the here and now psychopathology. The second area of holding a different view centers on Kiesler's statement that "relationship occurs primarily through nonverbal messages by which a person invokes a claim on the interactant to accept the person's self-presentation" (p. 310). The verbal component in terms of words, serving the purpose of concealing rather than revealing, is just as important as the nonverbal aspects of relationship. I also believe that the interactant contributes to and modifies the person's self-presentation within the context of a relationship.

Generally speaking, in the model outlined in this chapter, the act of decoding assumes a more collaborative pattern in which the therapist is not necessarily the person who is familiar with the key to the code. The primary supplier of information is invariably the patient while the processing of the data becomes a mutual process which involves the exploration of how the emerging data manifest themselves in the patient-therapist interaction. Transference-countertransference and a host of neurotic or psychotic manifestations are explored genetically, experientially, as well as in their particular impact on the therapeutic setting. Whatever problems a patient may have, it is always important to learn something about their origin. In a number of situations it may not be possible to trace the specific source of a specific problem with clarity. Not infrequently we may be compelled to use conjecture as an explanatory hypothesis. Next comes an attempt by patient and therapist to appreciate how the problem manifests itself in a variety of interpersonal settings, in personal, domestic, and professional life. This part of the inquiry includes the awareness of anticipatory factors, of the intervention of anxiety, of parataxic distortions, and of a host of security operations. In this connection much attention is paid to characteristic integrational patterns. Sooner or later the problem under discussion is explored in the way in which it manifests itself in the patient-therapist relationship. The problem then is no longer an internal malperception, malintegration, or self-perpetuating personal psychopathology rather than a phenomenological event that involves both therapist and patient each in his or her own way.

CONCLUSION

Throughout this presentation I have spoken exclusively of psychotherapy without making any references to psychoanalysis or psychoanalytic psychotherapy. The distinction between psychotherapy and psychoanalysis has merit in my opinion despite our finding it most difficult to draw a clear line between the two. For the purpose of this presentation, I will simplify the differentiation and address myself mainly to differences in degree rather than in substance. To my way of thinking, psychotherapy is a basic modus operandi which applies to every form of psychological therapeutic intervention including psychoanalysis. Historically, psychoanalysis is rooted in a theory of therapy which is in many ways no longer attuned to a host of clinical practices. In my personal use of the term, psychoanalysis is an intense form of psychotherapy which centers on an interpersonal approach, whether it refers to object relations, ego-psychology, classical psychoanalysis, or what have you. The intense aspect of psychoanalysis heightens the person-to-person relationship. Psychoanalysis is also a basic ideology which affirms individuality as a vital component of all interpersonal relations.

An interpersonal model of psychotherapy, as sketchily outlined in this chapter, is offered as an open-ended transactional model. It does not represent itself as a specific formula for psychotherapeutic application. The birds-eye view described here is intended to serve as a common denominator which applies to all psychological models of psychotherapy and includes the clinical side of psychoanalysis. The method of relational participation, the principle of collaborative inquiry and the myth of neutrality are conceptualizations of an interactional therapeutic process between two responsible and contributing partners. They reflect the interpenetration or ecological aspect of the mutual personality factors within the context of the therapeutic situation. I have said relatively little in this chapter about technical aspects and addressed myself more specifically to the interpersonal process per se. The literature has emphasized the prescriptive, technical dimension of psychotherapy without so far focusing on what I consider another equally significant dimension, that is, the part played by the respective personalities of therapist and patient in their actual person-to-person relationship which takes place independently from therapeutic strategy. It is hoped that this outline of an interpersonal model of psychotherapy will broaden the basis for therapeutic exploration and promote a greater measure of checking and verification which will in turn encourage problem-solving thoughts and activities on the patient's part.

REFERENCES

Chrzanowski, G. Implications of interpersonal theory. In E. Witenberg (Ed.), *Interpersonal explorations of psychoanalysis*. New York: Basic Books, 1973.

Chrzanowski, G. *Interpersonal approach to psychoanalysis: A contemporary view of Harry Stack Sullivan*. New York: Gardner Press, 1977. (a)

Chrzanowski, G. Participant observation. *Contemporary Psychoanalysis*, 1977, **13**, 351–355. (b)

Chrzanowski, G. From ego psychology to a psychology of self. In E. Witenberg (Ed.), *Interpersonal psychoanalysis*. New York: Gardner Press, 1978.

Chrzanowski, G. Participant observation and the working alliance. *Journal of the American Academy of Psychoanalysis*, 1979, **7**, 259–269. (a)

Chrzanowski, G. The transference-countertransference transaction. *Contemporary Psychoanalysis*, 1979, **15**, 458–471. (b)

Chrzanowski, G. Collaborative inquiry, affirmation and neutrality in the psychoanalytic situation. *Contemporary Psychoanalysis*, 1980, **16**, 348–366. (a)

Chrzanowski, G. Reciprocal aspects of psychoanalytic listening. *Contemporary Psychoanalysis*, 1980, **16**, 145–156. (b)

Epstein, L. & Feiner, A (Eds.) *Countertransference*. New York: Jason Aronson, 1979.

Greenson, R. R. *The technique and practice of psychoanalysis*, Vol. 1. New York: International Universities Press, 1967.

Heisenberg, W. Physics and philosophy. In R. N. Anshen (Ed.), *World perspectives*, Vol. 19. New York: Harper and Bros., 1958.

Kiesler, D. J. An interpersonal communication analysis of relationship in psychotherapy. *Psychiatry*, 1979, **42**, 299–311.

Kohut, H. *The analysis of the self*. New York: International Universities Press, 1971.

Kohut, H. *The restoration of the self*. New York: International Universities Press, 1978.

Mead, G. H. *Mind, self and society*. Chicago: The University of Chicago Press, 1934.

Sullivan. H. S. *Conceptions of modern psychiatry*. New York: Norton, 1940.

Sullivan, H. S. *The interpersonal theory of psychiatry*. New York: Norton, 1953.

Sullivan, H. S. *The psychiatric interview*. New York: Norton, 1954.

Sullivan, H. S. *Clinical studies in psychiatry*. New York: Norton, 1956.

Sullivan, H. S. *The collected papers of Harry Stack Sullivan*, Vols. 1 & 2. New York: Norton, 1953/1956.

Whitehorn, J. & Betz, B. *Effective psychotherapy with the schizophrenic patient*. New York: Jason Aronson, 1975.

Chapter 3
Interpersonal Therapy and Active Intervention*
Paul L. Wachtel

A central hallmark of Freudian psychoanalysis, especially as it has evolved in America, has been an attempt to minimize and restrict the activities of the analyst so as not to interfere with either the unfolding of the transference or the evolution of the patient's autonomy. I will argue in this chapter that an interpersonal perspective on the observations garnered by psychoanalysts suggests instead that a much more explicitly active stance by the therapist is advisable, that efforts to intervene in a variety of ways in the vicious circles that characterize neurosis are often necessary in order to be maximally helpful to the patient. Therapists of an interpersonal persuasion have all too often followed in essence the Freudian premise of technical neutrality. In doing so, they have failed to appreciate the full implications of the view of the therapist as participant-observer or of the recognition that all behavior must be understood in relation to its interpersonal context.

Elsewhere (Wachtel, 1977, chs. 2 & 3) I have tried to show that the psychoanalyst's emphasis on a stance of neutrality and nonintervention rests centrally on a theoretical conception in which aspects of psychological life are cut off from further influence by events in the person's life because of early repressions. I would like to raise here the question of whether it is possible to account for the seemingly childlike fantasies and wishes often evidenced by neurotic patients in another way—one that does not assume that these wishes and fantasies are locked-in remnants of the past but considers instead how they relate to the actual way the person is presently living his or her life. In so doing, I try to show how direct efforts at change in the person's present patterns of living may help to resolve what at first appear to be "deeper" conflicts which "underlie" the manifest patterns, and how simultaneous focus on unconscious conflicts and manifest interaction patterns can have a synergistic effect.

If one looks closely at an instance of persisting psychological conflict, it is usually possible to see how the desires and conflicts which dominate the person's life can be understood as *following from*, as well as causing, the way he or she lives that life. By resisting the temptation to explain the longing or fantasy quickly as a simple perpetuation of the past, we may see how it is brought about in the present, both by the patient's own behavior and by the behavior he evokes in others. Consider, for example, the patient whose excessive niceness and gentleness is seen as a defense against extreme rage and vengeful desires. If, in the traditional fashion, we look back into his history, we may well

* Sections from: *Psychoanalysis and Behavior Therapy* by Paul L. Wachtel. © 1977 by Paul L. Wachtel. Published by Basic Books, Inc., New York. Reprinted by permission.

seem to find sufficient justification and understanding of his situation from that direction. We may uncover in his history the presence of violent death wishes toward a parent, which he desperately attempted to cover up; and we may be able to see a continuity in this pattern which seems to suggest that he is still defending against those same childhood wishes. We may even find images and events in his dreams that point to continuing violent urges toward the parent and may discern many other indicators of warded-off rage toward that figure. If we look in detail at his day-to-day interactions, however, we see a good deal more. We may find that his meekness has led him to occupy a job that is not up to his real potential and that he silently and resentfully bears. On the job and in his other social interactions as well, he is likely to be unable to ask for what is his due, and may even volunteer to do things for others that he really doesn't want to do. One can see this excessively unassertive and self-abnegating behavior as motivated by the need to cover up his strong aggressive urges, and this would be correct as far as it goes. But it is equally the case that such a lifestyle *generates* rage. Disavowed anger may be a continuing feature of his life from childhood, but the angry thoughts that disturb his dreams tonight can be understood by what he let happen to himself today.

Such a person is caught in a vicious circle. Having learned early to fear his angry feelings, he has built up overt patterns of behavior designed to squelch and hide them. Even the smallest assertion seems dangerous, because he senses an enormous reservoir of violence behind it. Yet it is just such excessive restrictions upon his assertiveness that create the conditions for further violent urges. Ironically, his impulses are in large measure a product of the defense against them.

Such a perspective is not entirely lacking in the modern Freudian perspective, which pays considerable attention to the environmental events which trigger patient's reactions, to the feeling evoked in the therapist by the patient's behavior, and to certain kinds of vicious circles. But as I have tried to show elsewhere (e.g., Wachtel, 1977, pp. 42–43, 47–50, 60–63), these considerations are not carried through in the same way and are contravened by other emphases in the Freudian approach, which point to very different methods both of garnerning clinical observations and of providing therapeutic assistance (Wachtel, 1977, pp. 35–40).

The view presented here places considerably greater emphasis than most psychodynamic approaches on the role of present factors in generating maladaptive patterns. From the perspective of the approach described here, patients' problems may indeed have their *origin* in early childhood, but the effective causes today are seen as residing in their present interactions with others (and in the meaning such interactions have for the person and the new fantasies and wishes that are generated as a consequence). It thus seems considerably less important from this point of view for the patient to gain a detailed understanding of the history of his difficulties. Such understanding is therapeutically useful *at times* (see Wachtel, 1977), and is certainly important as a concern for the researcher. But I do not take it as a defining feature of the aim or the method of psychodynamic psychotherapy.

Such an approach to the role of the past and the present in the person's life is at times criticized as lacking a developmental point of view. This is, I believe, an error. A major focus on how the patient's current way of living perpetuates his problems does not imply that there are no continuities between present reactions and those of the past. The similarities are very clear. So too is the great importance of childhood in shaping the way of life that will be evident in the adult.

But if connections or continuities are discovered, the question remains: how are these continuities mediated? The more traditional developmental view in psychoanalysis is one that stresses the layering of residues of past patterns in hierarchical fashion. The imagery is archaeological. The focus is on the early structuring of the personality; the personality patterns attained by the end of the Oedipal period are seen as set and relatively unresponsive to changing conditions.

A somewhat different view can also account for the tendency for early patterns to be maintained, but in addition it readily handles instances where change is instead rather striking. (More importantly, as we shall see, this view points to a wider range of ways in which change can be brought about.) This view emphasizes that the kind of experiences we have early in life, and our way of dealing with these experiences, strongly influences what further experiences we will encounter, as well as how we perceive those experiences and how we deal with them.

For example, the two-year-old who has developed an engaging and playful manner is far more likely to evoke friendly interest and attention on the part of adults than is the child who is rather quiet and withdrawn. The latter will typically encounter a less rich interpersonal environment, which will further decrease the likelihood that he will drastically change. Similarly, the former is likely to continually learn that other people are fun and are eager to interact with him; and his pattern, too, is likely to become more firmly fixed as he grows. Further, not only will the two children tend to evoke different behavior from others, they will also interpret differently the same reaction from another person. Thus, the playful child may experience a silent or grumpy response from another as a kind of game and may continue to interact until perhaps he does elicit an appreciative response. The quieter child, not used to much interaction, will readily accept the initial response as a signal to back off.

If we look at the two children as adults, we may perhaps find the difference between them still evident: one outgoing, cheerful, and expecting the best of people; the other rather shy, and unsure that anyone is interested. A childhood pattern has persisted into adulthood. Yet we really don't understand the developmental process unless we see how, successively, teacher, playmates, girlfriends, and colleagues have been drawn in as "accomplices" in maintaining the persistent pattern. And, I would suggest, we don't understand the possibilities for change unless we realize that even now there are such "accomplices," and that if they stopped playing their role in the process, it would be likely eventually to alter.

It is important to recognize, however, that it is not that easy to get the accomplices to change. The signals we emit to other people constitute a powerful force field. The shy person does many (sometimes almost invisible) things to make it difficult for another person to stay open to him very long. Even a well-intentioned person is likely eventually to help confirm his view that others aren't really very interested.

Thus, from this perspective, the early pattern persists, not in spite of changing conditions but because the person's pattern of experiencing and interacting with others tends continually to recreate the old conditions again and again. In many cases, the effects are subtle and not readily apparent without careful scrutiny. But on close inspection, each person may be seen rather regularly to produce a particular skewing of responses from others that defines his idiosyncratic, interpersonal world. Even in seemingly similar situations, we are each likely to encounter slightly different interpersonal cues that may render the texture of the experience critically different. We then act (again) in a way that seems appropriate to this particular state of affairs, and create the conditions for others to again react to us in the same fashion and thus again set the stage for the pattern to be repeated. Rather than having been locked in, in the past, by an intrapsychic structuring, the pattern seems from this perspective to be continually being formed, but generally in a way that keeps it quite consistent through the years. It may appear inappropriate because it is not well correlated with the adult's "average expectable environment," but it is quite a bit more closely attuned to the person's idiosyncratically skewed version of that environment.

Emphasis on such a cyclical recreation of interpersonal events, and on the real behavior of "accomplices" in perpetuating characterological patterns, does not imply that the person is perceiving every situation "objectively." Most clinicians have seen abundant examples of patients' distortions of what is going on, particularly in transference phenomena. Such aspects of psychological functioning must be included in any tenable account of how neurotic patterns are perpetuated. But rather than relying on the metaphors that analysts have traditionally employed in conceptualizing such phenomena, I prefer to think in terms of the Piagetian notion of "schema." Such a notion implies that not only do we assimilate new experiences to older, more familiar ways of viewing things (as is implicit in the concept of transference), we also do eventually accommodate to what is actually going on.

Thus, as in transference phenomena, new people and new relationships tend to be approached in terms of their similarity to earlier ones; and frequently, particularly in the special conditions of the psychoanalytic situation, one sees what appear to be quite arbitrary assumptions and perceptions occurring. But in principle, I would suggest, accommodation is always proceeding apace and would, with nonreactive sources of stimulation, eventually lead to a fairly accurate picture of what one is encountering. The problem is that other people are not nonreactive. How they behave toward us is very much influenced by how we behave toward them, and hence by how we initially perceive them. Thus, our initial (in a sense distorted) picture of another person can end up being a fairly accurate predictor of how he or she will act toward us; because, based on our expectation that that person will be hostile, or accepting, or sexual, we are likely to act in such a way as to eventually draw such behavior from the person and thus have our (initially inaccurate) perception "confirmed." Our tendency to enter the next relationship with the same assumption and perceptual bias is then strengthened, and the whole process likely to be repeated again. [See Wachtel, in press, (a) for a more detailed discussion of how this Piagetian notion can illuminate the psychoanalytic idea of transference.]

TIES TO "EARLY OBJECTS"

In describing this view of development, there is one more important issue for us to consider at this point. Frequently, psychoanalytic exploration reveals that, without awareness, the person remains tied in fantasy life and in secret strivings to figures from his or her early past. Typically, discovery of such a tie is viewed as accounting for the inhibitions and symptoms of the adult. The pull from the past is regarded as the causal influence. We shall now consider an alternative way of understanding this common observation.

As but one example, let us consider still another set of interlocked influences that our two-year-old might encounter and then perpetuate. Suppose that he is not encouraged by his family to develop the skills that can help gain greater independence from them. This need not take the form of outright prohibition or interference. Indeed, the knot is often tighter when not readily visible, as when an ambivalent parent gives explicit encouragement to the child's budding independence but in subtle ways undermines it. Perhaps the mother, without noticing it, is more frequently warm and attentive when the child sweetly says "I love you, mommy" than when he shows her something he has put together. Perhaps she cuddles him when he stands apart from the other children ("to make him feel better, so he won't be afraid to play") instead of helping him to initiate play, or instead of joining in with the group of children until her child is comfortable there. There are many ways in which, through ignorance or unacknowledged intent, a parent can bind and cripple a child while thinking he or she is encouranging independence.

When such is the case, there is likely to be a point at which the child's fearful clinging is recognized as distinguishing him from his age peers. Not infrequently, the parental reaction is likely to be a nagging, complaining, or insulting one, motivated by parental anxiety, embarrassment, guilt, or desperation. Even if the parent does not come out with "What's wrong with you? Why can't you be like the other kids?" or some similar assault, the simple act of continuing to encourage participation in age-appropriate activities (when not accompanied by effective efforts to help the child accomplish the transition) can be experienced as punishment and cause the child considerable pain.

A child caught in such a developmental tangle is likely to remain more tied to his parents than most children his age. Having fewer alternative sources of gratification and security, he is likely to feel more than most the need to be mommy's or daddy's little boy. Not only is this likely to further impede the exploration and assertion needed to develop the skills that would get him out of this dilemma, it is also likely to make him quite fearful of expressing anger or disagreement toward his parents—and this in circumstances more likely than usual to arouse his anger. So we see an unhappy little child, afraid to venture forth, clinging to mother in a way that angers her (even as it also may gratify her), feeling frustrated and irritated and perhaps even sensing a grasping intent in the mother's harmful cloistering. Yet he desperately tries to be loyal and to be a "good boy" in order to at least maintain the security of his tie to mother. In so doing, he continues to prevent himself from develping the independence and expansiveness necessary for him to dare to loosen his hold on his mother or to feel able to cope with the complexity of his feelings for her.

In many instances, despite being confronted with such a dilemma, the child continues to grow. There are enough countervailing forces in innate developmental processes, as well as in the expectations and reward structure of the larger social order—and even in other aspects of their own parents' behavior—to allow millions of children with such a history to grow up and become taxpayers, spouses, and parents—that is, in a very general way, functioning adults. It takes a rather extraordinary effort to inhibit cognitive and personality growth so completely that these rather minimal stigmata of "normality" are not achieved.

But the situation I have described takes its toll. Such a person does not "make it" without pain and struggle, and usually he does not make it without paying a psychological price. In many respects he may advance along the way more slowly than his age peers, getting there eventually but always feeling a bit behind or a little "out of it," venturing less, mastering less, and thus again venturing less, and so on.

THE INTERPERSONAL RATIONALE FOR ACTIVE INTERVENTION

In a number of places, Sullivan cautioned against trying to "cure" the patient and against giving advice or doing anything other than "clearing the brush" so that the patient could himself see clearly enough to decide what to do. His conception of the therapist as a participant-observer, however, provides a rationale for considering a substantially broader range of interventions than most dynamic therapists—including most Sullivanians—are willing to consider. The idea that by not doing anything conspicuous one sees the patient (and the patient sees himself) as he is really is, with his inner workings not disguised by any misleading reference to external causes of his behavior, appears from this perspective to be an illusory one. The therapist can never really be a "blank screen," nor can one ever see "the patient" in any abstract or isolated sense. One always sees the person *in a context*, and in psychotherapy the therapist is part of that context. He is as much a part of the context if he is silent and invisible as he is if he is face to face with the patient and overtly and discernibly responding to him. One doesn't elude the limits of participant observation or, so to speak, undo the Heisenberg principle, by remaining silent or with-holding one's opinions. One merely limits one's direct observations about the patient to his way of dealing with only a restricted range of situations.

It is also important to recognize that from an interpersonal perspective the therapist need not worry that by acting in such a way as to prevent a full therapeutic regression and the emergence of archaic desires, he will leave the underlying cause of the patient's problems untouched and still able to generate symptoms or distort the patient's character. From an interpersonal perspective, such desires are viewed as existing in such primitive and intense form only because a self-defeating cyclical neurotic process is going on. These unconscious urges and fantasies are as much a consequence of the neurosis as a cause. By intervening directly in the way the patient overtly interacts with others, one may never get to see the archaic manifestations observed by analysts in a regressive transference neurosis. But according to the view presented here, this would be the case not because the therapist has failed to discover what is really there, but because what has been done by the therapist has *changed* what is there.

Finally, an interpersonal perspective suggests that a substantial price is paid when the therapist does *not* intervene. If the neurotic process is largely maintained by a cyclical reconfirming of neurotic assumptions by the consequences they bring about, then there should be many points at which the vicious circles are appropriately interrupted. Interpre-tive efforts, aimed at insight into origins or even current motives, are but one of many ways of disrupting the destructive circle of events. Often such interpretive efforts may be undermined if they are not combined with efforts aimed more directly at bringing about new behavior in day-to-day situations.

FACILITATING ACTION IN THE REAL WORLD

It has been traditional in accounts of psychotherapy to suggest that when the patient fully understands, he will then be able to change his behavior. In some cases, changes in overt behavior are an important explicit final goal; in others, where the patient's chief complaint is about his sense of himself or some other more exclusively subjective phenomenon, overt behavioral changes are often treated as relatively unimportant. In either case, how-ever, there tends to be, in traditional conceptions, little emphasis on *direct* efforts to change overt actions. Such changes are viewed as a *by-product* of new understanding, and it is the understanding that is directly of concern to the therapist.

Not infrequently there is a substantial ethical component in the reluctance of tradi-tional therapists to try to directly influence the patient's actions. One frequently hears cited such contentions as: action on his understanding is the patient's responsibility; the patient must be free to choose not to change; the therapist has no right to tell the patient what to do; and so on. These kinds of issues have been discussed in some detail elsewhere (Wachtel, 1977, ch. 12). Here I wish to focus on some of the ways in which the therapist *can* facilitate action based on the patient's new understanding, and why I believe it is often a practical necessity to do so if enduring change is to occur. This discussion of the practical realities is, for me, a necessary prelude to consideration of the ethical issues, for a sensible system of ethics must be based on some conception of the anticipated consequences of alternative choices of action (or inaction).

One of the reasons why the traditional view has been maintained for so long is that sometimes patients do change, after a point, simply from better understanding their own desires and their life situation. A clearer view of what one faces, or a perceptual-cognitive reorganization that suggests a whole different range of alternatives, can be a very powerful force for change.

Frequently, however, understanding is not followed by a changed way of living. I have discussed elsewhere (Wachtel, 1977, ch. 6) some of the limitations of the explanation that understanding did not lead to change, in some cases, because it was intellectual rather than emotional. Here it may be added that even if this were an adequate conceptualization, one could in such instances still ask why, if one grants the value of emotional insight, the therapy has gone on for years and years and has not been able to bring change about. It is not an adequate answer to say the patient was resistant. If he was resistant to what the therapist was doing, then the therapist should have been doing something different.

The interpersonal perspective described here suggests that one of the things the therapist must do differently in many cases is to make more direct efforts to instigate and guide new behavior patterns than is traditionally done in dynamic therapies. A number of considerations all point in this direction. First of all, as I have discussed, actions sustain structures. The persistent modes of thinking and perceiving and related motivational tendencies which analysts have observed in great detail are not preserved simply by the configuration of forces in a hypothetical psychic apparatus. They are kept going in important ways by the consequences of patients' day-to-day actions in living. These consequences include both the responses evoked in others by the patient's behavior (for example, the hostility evoked by a paranoid attitude, which confirms the patient's suspiciousness and perpetuates the cycle) and the relatively direct effect of the patient's actions upon how he experiences his own motives, his self-worth, and so on. (For example, the patient may not ask for things, out of a fear of being too "demanding" or "voracious." This may lead to considerable deprivation and the build-up of intense desires, which in turn confirms the sense of himself as dangerously overdemanding and starts the whole cycle going again.)[1]

Through such processes, the work of the analytic session can readily be undermined by the neurotic living that goes on between sessions and, so to speak, repairs the neurotic structures that were partly dismantled in the session. Formulations that regard change in neurotic patterns of interaction as a by-product of changes in self-perception and motivational states, and therefore not the direct responsibility of the therapist, fail to consider sufficiently the degree to which change in either one of these poles of human experience (that is, either self-perceptions *or* overt action patterns) is part and parcel of the process of change in the other. If the analysis presented in this chapter is correct, then even where therapeutic efforts that spurn direct intervention in the patient's day-to-day behavior *are* successful, they probably take longer than they should and achieve somewhat less than they might. Further, it is likely that when they do work, they do so because the patient's environment is very encouraging of those new interaction efforts that do get instigated by the interpretive work of the sessions; thus, even here, new actions are aiding intrapsychic change as well as vice versa. As will be discussed shortly, however, there are likely to be many aspects of the patient's life context that hinder rather than foster such changes.

A second, and related, consideration that points to the importance of therapist efforts to directly monitor and guide new interaction patterns by the patient involves the constraints upon insight brought about by desperate clinging to old modes and old relationships. When the patient has closed off many options in his daily living and has come to seek his gratifications from very few people and in highly stereotyped ways, he may be frightened to question and reflect upon his feelings about these relationships. If he can begin to take small steps to live his life differently, he can begin to examine and reflect somewhat more freely.[2]

IMPEDIMENTS TO CHANGE IN DAILY LIFE

For a number of reasons, reactions from others that are counter to the patient's growth and change may be more common than is generally suggested in psychoanalytic writings. Not infrequently, those who become involved with the patient on a long-term basis do so to satisfy rigid neurotic needs of their own, and have a stake in keeping the patient involved in the same interaction pattern. This phenomenon in itself is not new to traditional therapists (though the arguments in this chapter, that such current sources of feedback are probably a more potent source of resistance than the traditionally emphasized intrapsychic ones, are likely to be quite controversial in some circles). Students of neurosis and/or marriage have long been familiar with such classic pairings as the know-it-all husband and the take-care-of-me wife, the pair of fearful people who reassure each other that others' more adventurous lives are superficial, the "busy" pair whose mutual fear of sharing and intimacy comfortably mesh, the hostile overbearing wife whose husband's identity is that of an abused martyr, and numerous other combinations equally (and equally sadly) familiar. Not only in marriage, but in any long-term relationship of some degree of importance and some degree of voluntarism in whether it is continued, one must ask if those who complement the patient's neurotic behavior patterns do so at least in part out of a need to participate in such an interaction (or, in other language, whether something about an interaction which would seem to be aversive might actually be reinforcing).

Induced Development of Complementary Needs in Partners

Less frequently noted in the psychodynamic literature is that even where the other person enters into a relationship with the patient because of its *nonneurotic* aspects and *in spite of* the neurotic ones, it is important to consider the likelihood that human adaptational flexibility may interact virulently with human neurotic rigidity. By this I mean that the individual who is attracted to a partner largely for the partner's nonneurotic qualities may at first try to change the neurotic patterns but, finding them inflexible and still being interested in the relationship, he may begin to adapt to these patterns, perhaps even to find ways in which he can derive some pleasure or benefit from them. Over a period of time, if he is really good at making a virtue of a necessity, he may increasingly bring a certain side of himself to this relationship and fulfill needs here that other relationships don't as readily permit to be gratified. Thus, after a while, the partner's adaptational efforts may lead him to construct a relationship with our patient such that he does begin to have a stake in keeping things going as they are. His adaptive resolution of the problem of how to get the most out of a relationship that is gratifying but marked by neurotic annoyances may help keep the other person locked into neurotic patterns of living.

Needless to say, I am not suggesting that all of the above efforts, adaptations, and gratifications need be in awareness. Nor am I suggesting that the partner, even where he has strong needs to perpetuate the neurotic features of the relationship, does not suffer in some way for his participating in this mess, and would not benefit from a change in the interaction pattern if one could be arranged. I am merely emphasizing that the partner may be motivated by short-term considerations to resist the changes in the patient and may—again, not necessarily consciously—try all sorts of ways to undo them.

Involuntary Confirmation by Partners of Patients' Neurotic Patterns

The various contingencies just described are in contrast to a substantial number of other cases in which the clinical evidence does not justify any emphasis on the partner's *needing* the patient to be neurotic, yet in which the partner is nonetheless, perhaps unwittingly or even unwillingly, an accomplice in perpetuating the patient's neurotic pattern. In such instances, the partner experiences largely pain and frustration in response to the patient's neurotic behavior, yet is induced to behave in ways that help keep it going.

The sexual partner of a patient who is strongly conflicted about sexuality, for example, is likely to respond to the patient's tentative, anxiety-ridden advances with a good deal of tension and discomfort of his or her own. The partner may be quite capable of responding fluidly and sensually with other partners, but with our patient sex is stiff, clumsy, and not really much fun. The partner may genuinely desire that the patient be freer and more expressive sexually, yet be unable to respond to the patient's awkwardness other than in ways that, by making their sexual encounter largely tense and joyless, actually keep the patient's anxieties going and make him again unable to give, or receive, sexual pleasure.

Similarly, someone involved with an aggressive, suspicious individual may genuinely wish he would drop his guard and be more loving and trusting. Yet the constant assault of suspicion and hostility may make it hard for the partner not to react with anger or withdrawal, and hence strengthen the patient's view that others can't be trusted or relied on.

In another kind of situation, the overly dependent individual may elicit behavior from others in which they assume what should be his responsibilities and thereby do not allow him to develop his own resources sufficiently so that his dependency can begin to diminish. Though in this latter type of process the "giver" is often satisfying his or her own needs (viz., the classic picture of the overprotective mother), the dependent person's demands are often a genuine pain in the neck instead; yet the person who is entangled with him may be strongly pushed toward just the behavior that will keep the annoying dependency going.

Failure to Notice Change

In still other instances, those who interact with the patient help keep old patterns going when they fail to notice the initial changes that occur. Frequently our expectations guide our perceptions to such a degree that we continue our old way of categorizing and responding to others' behavior even in the face of fairly considerable change in that behavior. Once we have labeled someone as "shy" or "insincere" or "uninteresting," a great many behaviors that would in other circumstances be viewed differently are likely to be seen as consistent with our ongoing picture of the person. Eventually, if the patient's changed behavior persists, the change is likely to get through to those who interact with him. But often the lack of initial response from others can be discouraging, and the changed behavior does *not* persist. The patient goes back to his old ways, others' perception of him remains unchanged or even strengthened, and the conservative effects of perceptual expectations keep the repetitive cycles from changing. In those instances, it is important to help the patient persist through the early stages until others do begin to provide different feedback.

Deficits in Social Skills

Perhaps the most important reason for needing special techniques to guide the patient's overt behavior—important both because it is so pervasive and because it is so rarely discussed in traditional accounts of therapy—is that the conflicts and inhibitions that typically are at the core of the patient's problems lead very regularly to specific deficits in the learning of social skills. When the conflicts and inhibitions are reduced and the patient begins to try to put into practice his new understanding, the deficit remains, and his first efforts to act differently are often crude and ineffective. Instead of encountering newer and more positive responses from others, he may instead experience rebuff or disdain. Thus punished instead of rewarded, he may be discouraged about trying again or even have his earlier fears and "unrealistic" fantasies strengthened.

Many writers on therapy explicitly disavow concern with this problem. They assume that the patient knows what to do and how, but does not do so because of inhibition and conflict—or that if for some reason he does not know, he can easily and quickly learn. Thus the patient who complains that he does not know what to say to people at parties, or how to put his foot down in a way that does not get dismissed, or how to approach a girl without seeming overly aggressive or excessively awkward, is viewed as manifesting a kind of resistance, and it is expected that he will rapidly discover he is able to do these things effectively once his conflicts are resolved.

Such a view, I would contend, fails to take sufficiently into account just how complex and prolonged is the process whereby we learn to achieve the interpersonal behaviors appropriate to an adult in our culture. It is easy to overlook this long and difficult process because it is so gradual and because, once achieved and exercised daily, its manifestations seem inherently "obvious." Yet if one looks at the social behavior of children and adolescents, one is struck by the succession of forms that social actions take and the inappropriateness of any of these earlier forms for an adult.

Thus, adults, like children, can feel left out of a conversation and wish to have the conversation directed to them or be about them. But whereas at age two my son could count on a positive response when he said to us, "Don't talk to Daddy, Mommy, talk to Kenny" or "Talk about me," an adult wanting the same thing would be ill advised to express it in quite the same way. Children must go through a long process of learning how to effectively channel and express their feelings. Their initial crude efforts would be readily discouraged were adult standards of moderation, articulate expression, or subtlety applied to them. Fortunately, the expectations brought to bear in evaluating the child's response are usually geared to his developmental stage, so that he can achieve satisfying interactions throughout the many years in which his behavior gradually evolves into its adult form.

But where neurotic inhibitions have interfered with this gradual learning process and kept it from proceeding in normal fashion, the adult who in the course of therapy begins to express a need he has largely inhibited for years is likely to do so in a way that lacks the fine tuning of typical adult behaviors and resembles to some degree the cruder efforts of children. As therapists, when we are faced with unmodulated and inappropriate anger in a patient who had previously been defending against such feelings, or unrealistic demands for attention and devotion from someone who had been compulsively independent, we are likely to be pleased that *some* change is occurring and not to be put off by the less than optimal form these early expressions take. The set we adopt as therapists enables us to respond empathically and encouragingly to behavior in our patients which we often would not tolerate in our friends. And our unusually understanding and growth-oriented way of experiencing things in this unique kind of situation can easily lead us to overlook how others, engaged in a different kind of relationship, might respond to this kind of behavior.

When the poignant struggle we observe in our sessions does not lead to the progress in the patient's way of living that we hope for, it is probably often because other figures in the patient's life are not nearly as encouraging of these first crude efforts as we are. In addition to having a stake in old ways, as discussed above, these figures also (not really inappropriately) employ different standards than we do in reacting to the patient's behavior; and in their reactions, they may again teach the patient that expression of what he is feeling is dangerous. Sometimes the negative reaction comes from an explicit aversion to the crudity or lack of modulation of the patient's behavior, as when a sexual advance does not conform to the cultural rituals that the other person is accustomed to. At other times, the disappointing and inhibition-strengthening reaction is a result of insufficient skill, intensity, or persistence, as when a previously meek person risks speaking up and asserting himself, but once having stuck his neck out does not know how to handle the other's reaction and retreats in acute humiliation.

Such kinds of failure experiences can result either from explicit ridicule or put-down or from the shame that comes when others don't even notice one's efforts to reach out or speak up. Thus, the person who tries to be a more active participant at parties by sharing in a joke-swapping session, instead of just listening and feeling impotent as he had previously done, may stumble or mess up the punch line. He may even fail to complete the first sentence, since getting the floor when several people are eager to be "on" next requires a sense of timing and a kind of assertive persistence if two people start talking at once and it is rightly your turn. If the patient stops after three words and the other person who began simultaneously keeps talking, or if he starts while people are still laughing at the last joke and thus isn't heard, or if he waits until someone else has already begun the next joke, he may feel as humiliated by not having managed to get the attention of the group as he would by having gotten the floor, muffed the joke, and been explicitly ridiculed.

Because all of these varied kinds of discouraging consequences of unskillful social behavior can feed back to undermine therapeutic change, it is important not only to monitor the patient's efforts to apply his new understanding in his daily life (I would contend that in *every* case one should pay a good deal of attention to such efforts and their consequences) but also in many cases to focus with the patient on training social skills and developing an explicit program of practicing and applying them. A useful model for doing this is provided by the method behavior therapists call assertive training, and by applications and extensions of its various components.

ASSERTIVE TRAINING

By assertive training I am referring here to a multifaceted approach to bringing about new, more effective interpersonal behavior. It tends to include such (not necessarily mutually exclusive) methods as role-playing anticipated real-life interactions in the sessions, practicing desired behaviors in the session (perhaps with successive approximations to some appropriate criterion), modeling by the therapist of effective ways of dealing with particular situations, and setting up a graded series of real-life tasks for the patient to perform in shaping his interpersonal skills and altering his ongoing relationships. "Assertive training" is by now a misnomer, and at times a misleading one; the methods that were originally developed to facilitate the ability to stand up for one's rights have been (or can be) extended to apply to almost every kind of inhibition in effective transactional behavior (for example, meeting members of the opposite sex, expressing feelings of love, requesting help, engaging in easier or more genuine conversation with friends, and so on).

Clinical Rationale for Assertive Training

In Wolpe's (1958) early writings on this topic, assertive training was conceived of as primarily a way of getting the patient to emit behavior incompatible with anxiety. Thus, within the reciprocal inhibition model, assertive behavior played a role similar to that of muscular relaxation, and assertive training could in a sense be viewed as a variant of systematic desensitization. Certainly one of the consequences of successful assertive training is that the patient is less anxious. The reduction of anxiety, however, now tends to be seen as part of a complex set of interacting processes and not only a result of direct deconditioning. Wolpe's pioneering efforts in this area have led to considerable further developments, both by him and by others, that have led to new understanding of the possible ways of using assertive training and related methods. It is now recognized that as the patient learns to interact with others more appropriately, skillfully, and effectively, he receives quite different feedback from others, which contributes to more positive feelings about himself and to reduction of anxiety; it also helps create a context in which adaptive behavior is made increasingly likely. Additionally, as will be discussed below, the assertive training procedures can also be an important aid in facilitating insight. When the process goes well, the anxiety reduction, better feedback, clearer understanding, and more adaptive behavior all enhance each other in a positive version of the kind of spiralling emphasized in this chapter.

As the framework for conceptualizing assertive training has broadened and become more sophisticated, so too has its clinical practice. At one time it may perhaps have been justified to object to the assertive training approach as overly mechanical, or as an inappropriate effort to teach the patient to react as the *therapist* would, in accordance with *his* values and personal style rather than the patient's. This is, however, not at all an accurate description of assertive training as it is practiced today by sensitive clinicians who understand the complexities of how the development of adaptive interpersonal behavior may be either impaired or facilitated.

In fact, far from imposing the therapist's values or preferences upon the patient, skillful use of assertive training can have as one of its valuable consequences the facilitation of the patient's own self-understanding and ability to act in terms of his own inclinations rather than others' wishes. One of the things that most struck me when I first observed behavior therapists using assertive training in complex cases, was that in some instances what they were doing could readily be seen, in the language of dynamic therapists, as facilitating the expression of what the patient was preconsciously leaning toward. I have, for example, observed several instances of patients being aided by behavior therapists in dealing with an overbearing, intrusive, hypercritical mother. Some therapists tended simply to tell the patient what to do ("You ought to say to her . . ."). Others, however, in dealing with very similar clinical problems, were more likely to say to the patient things like, "It sounds like you'd like to tell her in no uncertain terms to stop opening your mail, but something keeps you from doing so. You shrink back from it at the last minute and tell yourself it's not important." Such comments were often followed by patient statements such as, "Yeah, I guess I really would like to tell her off, maybe more than I realized. But you don't know my mother! That's easier said than done."

This combination of a kind of insight (which, as in dynamic therapies, is much more likely to be gradual and almost obvious by the time it is expressed and genuinely experienced, rather than sudden and dramatic) with an expression of the difficulty of putting it into practice is a very common one, seen by both dynamic and behavioral clinicians, and is often the consequence (in either case) of what is essentially the interpretation of a conflicted action tendency. Effective behavior therapists, no less than analysts, address themselves to just such tendencies; and like analysts, their impact tends to be greatest when their focus is on those tendencies that the patient is just beginning to acknowledge but is still also motivated to retreat from or deny. The behavior therapist doesn't tend to talk about interpretations or insights, and certainly doesn't refer to preconscious urges, but in practice the skilled practitioner does in fact pick up what the patient is himself inclined to do but may be only scarcely aware of until it is voiced. Further, not only does he address himself to the patient's incipient actions, but focusing on such tendencies frequently makes it possible in later sessions to discern still other conflicted action tendencies that had previously been associated with even more intense anxiety and the avoidance of which had strongly influenced the person's style of life. (The psychoanalytic reader will recognize this as similar to the familiar sequence whereby continued interpretation of that which has become preconscious leads to progressively "deeper" trends that had once been unconscious and defended against.)

Thus, the sensitive application of assertive training procedures can begin with efforts to clarify the patient's conflicts using probes and statements not always distinguishable from what many dynamic therapists would try. Where the assertive training model begins to lead in a somewhat different direction is in its way of dealing with the patient's demur in the above illustration ("But you don't know my mother! That's easier said than done."). Even here, the two approaches at first tend to be rather similar. Most therapists, of whatever persuasion, would want to know what the patient anticipates the mother would do. But whereas many dynamic therapists would seek, through a series of interpretations, to expose highly unrealistic repressed infantile fantasies (which they would view as the most influential factor in maintaining the patient's inhibitions), the therapist utilizing the assertive training model would take a different course. Rather than restricting himself to interpretations, and assuming that appropriate action will eventually follow adequate understanding, he would make an early effort to foster the occurrence of real-life actions, and would expect new understanding to follow—not just as an epiphenomenon, but as part of a synergistic process in which actions and feedback continually effect understanding and one's understanding continually generates some kind of effort at action. Such is certainly the view of action and understanding underlying the use of assertive training within the active interpersonal approach propounded in this chapter, and it is what I take to be the view of many more strictly behavioral clinicians as well.

Within the assertive training model, the new real-life actions are fostered both by events within the session and by planned experiences outside the session. Usually both are used, but not necessarily; occasionally, real-life actions are planned without any special preparation in the sessions; at other times, within-session work leads to "spontaneous" effective actions by the patient that were not explicitly programmed but that are effective enough for such explicit planning to become unnecessary.[3]

IN-SESSION ASPECTS OF ASSERTIVE TRAINING

Assertive training, as has been noted, usually consists both of planned actions in the patient's everyday situation and specific experiences within the therapeutic session. The latter most often relies on various aspects of role playing to achieve its effects. The simulation, within the session, of situations encountered in the patient's day-to-day activities has a number of functions in the therapeutic effort. It deals with the problem of the patient's vulnerability to others' responses by letting the patient first try out new behaviors in the safe context of the therapeutic relationship, where the therapist is in a position to assure that they will be met with a positive response. It enables the therapist to see more clearly and vividly just what the patient actually does in the situations which give him trouble. It enables the *patient* to gain a new perspective on his behavior, especially if audio or video tapes are available. It facilitates *behavior rehearsal*, the systematic practicing and development of new adaptive patterns of interaction. And it permits *role reversal* (that is, the therapist playing the part of the patient and the patient the part of someone he interacts with) and thereby both the possibility of the patient's gaining understanding of what it feels like for someone to interact with him (if the therapist plays the role in the way the patient usually does) or of alternative ways of dealing with situations that give him trouble (if the therapist, in the patient's role, *models* alternative behavior).

Let us consider first the provision of a safe place to try out new behaviors. The value of such a haven for experimentation should be obvious from the discussions earlier in this chapter. The difference between the therapist's set to accept and encourage new and more adaptive behavior, however crude, and the set of people not in the therapeutic role to expect appropriate adult behavior is crucial to recognize. The therapeutic setting provides a unique opportunity to try out new ways of being without the dangers usually inherent in such efforts.

Even for the therapist, it is not always easy to respond in a way that encourages the patient's gropings toward a lifestyle that is more rewarding and expressive of his convictions and inclinations. Wolf (1966) has lucidly described how the therapist can be drawn into the patient's neurotic patterns and confirm or strengthen them rather than working against them—or in the terms introduced earlier in this chapter how the therapist can become an "accomplice" in the patient's neurosis. An important part of the therapist's training involves sensitizing him to the subtleties of nonverbal communication, so that cues can be identified and articulated instead of leading to automatic responses. This disengagement from the kind of automatic reciprocity that keeps neurotic patterns going is also facilitated by the way the therapist structures the relationship with the patient so as to be able to listen and reflect.

Because the therapist's training and his stance of participant-*observer* enable him to respond (it is to be hoped) is a more growth-facilitating way, some of what is achieved in assertive training by way of providing a place to safely try out new ways of living is provided in traditional therapeutic efforts as well. The patient can try things with the therapist he wouldn't dare try outside; this is encouraged both by the atmosphere of acceptance that the therapist tries to create and by his interpretations, which demonstrate a readiness on his part to notice and deal with incipient behaviors that the patient might otherwise brush aside and that others in relation to him might be unlikely to pick up on. This can be very helpful, but its value is often limited in traditional approaches by a reluctance on the part of the therapist to directly address the problem of transfer or accommodation to the conditions in the patient's daily world. Without explicit efforts to bridge the gap between the nurturant therapy relationship and the more demanding world outside, there is a good chance that the patient will learn to discriminate and act one way with the therapist and another with everyone else. The therapist then has the conviction—correct as far as his (within-session) direct experience of the patient is concerned—that the patient has become freer, more open, more healthy and genuine; yet in the patient's day-to-day living, change is far less extensive. If this occurs frequently, it accounts for why therapists can be sincerely convinced that they are having a major impact, whereas research confirmation of their effect remains more equivocal—patients may *really* change a great deal with the therapist, but not nearly so much in other contexts.

Some traditional therapists are well aware of this problem and do pay a good deal of attention to what actually goes on in the patient's daily life. In many instances, this kind of informal monitoring may be quite sufficient. The patient has gained enough clarification of issues, or reduction of anxiety, or understanding of the necessity for changed behavior to go and try the change, and has enough sense of what he has to do to have a fair chance of succeeding. Certainly not *every* patient needs formal assertive training.

For many patients, however, more explicit and detailed attention to building new interaction patterns is needed; and even where it is not essential, it would lead them to faster or more extensive change. It is not only a matter of the patient not *knowing* the most appropriate or effective way to deal with the situation. I do think that this is often the case—that for the reasons discussed above, the patient's conflicts and inhibitions have frequently limited the possibility of his observing and assimilating how people behave in various situations. But even where the patient does in a certain sense "know" what do do, this knowledge may not be available or usable in a way that enables him to act effectively. The patient may be able to describe what is called for, but not to put it into practice. Or he may be able to manifest assertive behavior with his wife but not with his boss, or vice versa.

Gradually structuring real-life efforts and playing out some of these interactions in the session may enable anxiety about taking action in particular settings to be desensitized and may facilitate the translation of implicit action patterns into manifest actions in new settings or contexts. The effect of assertive training in such instances may be less one of teaching something new than of acting as a kind of *releaser* of knowledge that has been stored somehow, but not in a way that is readily translatable into behavior. The person who has difficulty saying goodbye, for example, has certainly had a good deal of opportunity to observe others saying goodbye. But he may continue to experience himself as not knowing how to do so, until an opportunity to rehearse in nonthreatening circumstances gives him a chance to integrate the representations of his observations with action patterns and interpersonal cues. He may then "learn" much more quickly than the person who has to master a kind of interaction about which he has really picked up very little, even in a strictly passive-observer mode. Thus, while not necessary in all cases, role playing and behavior rehearsal may, for a variety of reasons, be important in enabling the patient to take effective action.

Role playing procedures are also of value in giving the therapist a picture of the patient's style in a way which no amount of description of the "So then I said that I didn't like what he was doing" variety can convey. The value of this kind of direct observation is, of course, one of the reasons the therapist is trained to be attentive to just what the patient does with him, including the style and inexplicit communications that accompany and sometimes modify or even reverse the explicit messages the patient thinks he is conveying (for example, the glint of pleasure or triumphant stubbornness in the patient's report that he has "tried" to do what the therapist suggested but finds that he "can't"). But as I have noted, it is essential that the therapist also have a vivid picture of how the patient is with others (especially since some kinds of interactions of importance in the patient's life may *not* be replicated in his relationship with the therapist.[4] And for this, role playing is an invaluable therapeutic aid. Detailed inquiry into an exact sequence of events, especially if the patient has been asked to keep actual written records made as soon after the event as is feasible, are of course also of great value in this respect, and at times quite sufficient. In many instances, however, one discovers something in seeing the patient actually play out just what he said and how he said it that is masked in the patient's reporting of the event.

The difference between reporting and acting is sometimes vividly illustrated in the patient's hesitancy to role-play. On several occasions patients have protested to me that they did not want to role-play because it was too "artificial," and in each instance they came rather quickly to recognize that what they feared was in fact precisely the opposite—that playing out what occurred (or could have occurred—see below) made it *too real*. In fact, one must at times be cautious in role playing precisely because of this. The patient can feel exposed and stripped naked when his "I told her off" or "I told her to stop doing it" is revealed, when finally played out, as a rather ineffectual statement, undermined by tone of voice, frequent "uhs" and hesitations, an obsequious posture, and so on, or when he says "I told her I really loved her," and in role playing the interaction it becomes clear that genuinely affectionate statements stick in his craw, and in response to the question "Tom, do you really care for me" he literally cannot say "Yes, I really love you" without making a face or tensing up as if a punch were about to be thrown at him.

For this reason, patients will frequently, when role playing is introduced, slip away from it at first. Elaborating the above illustration to include its early vicissitudes, the therapist after explaining role playing, and indicating that he is playing the part of the patient's wife, says "Tom, do you really care for me?" Tom says "I would say to her that I do, but she'd complain." Therapist: "Don't tell me what you *would* do. I'm Jane. Talk to me. Tom, do you really care for me?" Tom (turning away, looking slightly disgusted): "Yes." Therapist (still as Jane): "You don't say it like you mean it." Tom: "Yeah, that's what she says, and I usually—" Therapist (interrupting): "You're again telling me *about* what you'd say. I'm Jane. Tom, you don't say it like you mean it." Tom: "It's very hard for me to answer her when she says that." Therapist: "How do you feel when she says it?" Tom: "Angry, pushed." Therapist: "OK, I'm Jane. Tell me how you feel." Tom: "Jane, when you do that it really turns me off. Maybe if you didn't ask me so often I'd be able to say it spontaneously without feeling like a puppet. . . . (then, in a tone that indicates he is now talking to the therapist as therapist) Gee, I wonder what would happen if I really said that to her." Therapist: "Let's play it out a little further and see how it would feel. How do you picture her reaction?"

As the last part of the interchange indicates, the role-playing procedure can be a way of increasing the *patient's* understanding as well as the therapist's. The exploration, observation, and rehearsal aspects of the role-playing procedures are not sharply differentiated in practice, and the same sequence in the session can be viewed from several perspectives. Not only can the patient gain understanding from observing his behavior in role, under circumstances more favorable to self-observation than the often pressure-filled real encounters (especially where audio or video tape recording permits detailed retrospective examination); he can also gain considerable insight into those he must deal with, and into his impact on others, by engaging in *role-reversal* procedures.

Behavior therapy writings do not tend to stress this aspect of role reversal. Behavior therapists tend to introduce role reversal for other reasons, such as to enable the therapist to gain a clearer picture of the behavior of significant others by having the patient act it out, or to provide the therapist with an opportunity to model more effective behavior in the course of playing the patient's role, or perhaps to enable a shy patient to ease his way into role playing by playing the role of someone else instead of acting his own part.[5] Role reversal can, however, be a very useful way of facilitating certain kinds of understanding on the part of the patient.

CONCLUSION

Many other uses of active intervention flow as well from the considerations presented here. Insight, for example, and the hoary clinical issue of intellectual versus emotional insight, can be approached in terms of the consequences of exposure to previously avoided experiences. When it is, the methods which behavior therapists have developed to facilitate such exposure can be brought into play as very useful therapeutic adjuncts. In the process, one's understanding of those methods is in turn modified (see Wachtel, 1977, chs. 6–8). When one abandons the quest for neutrality, and bases one's therapeutic stance instead on the inevitability of being a participant as well as an observer in the patient's life, a number of important technical considerations are clarified with regard to the wording of comments to patients and regarding as well the role of reinforcement considerations in psychodynamic therapies (see Wachtel, 1977, ch. 11, 1979, 1980). These considerations inevitably confront the therapist with important ethical questions, which cannot be addressed here but which I have discussed elsewhere (Wachtel, 1977, ch. 12, in press, b). I believe that full consideration of the issues raised in this chapter points not only to a more effective kind of therapy but one that is also more humane and more respectful of the interdependency among us which the interpersonal perspective highlights.

NOTES

1. Short-cut terms like "build-up of desires" should not be taken as an endorsement of hydraulic or energic models. One can account for the same phenomena in largely cognitive terms, such as emphasizing how memories of past slights and deprivations, comparisons with what others have, and other factors can intensify (not necessarily consciously) one's current longings, increase what would be needed to feel satisfied and have one's just deserts, and so on (see Klein, 1967).

2. These first steps are almost certain to be gross and sporadic. It is difficult to accomplish finely tuned interpersonal accommodations, or to be prepared to deal in a persistently progressive way with all the possible setbacks, unless clearer understanding of the issues in one's life is also developing. Considerable blurring of the realities of one's transactions with others and experience of self is almost always a feature of neurotic patterns of living. This has been emphasized, in somewhat different terms, by many behavior therapists in the cognitive or broad-spectrum wing of the behavior therapy movement; and even among the neo-Skinnerians, there are fewer and fewer who insist on focusing solely on overt behavior, without regard for cognitive set, attention, or other organismic variables.

3. Sometimes, of course, valuable real-life change occurs with *no* explicit focus by the therapist on how the patient might handle his current life situation. The traditional psychoanalytic model of therapy emphasizes such instances, viewing overt behavioral change as a by-product of therapy not directly addressed by the analyst. My guess is that in most instances where psychoanalysis is helpful, one important factor has been the analyst's not quite explicit (perhaps even covert and guilty) efforts to guide the patient in taking adaptive action in addition to helping him understand; and my interest in assertive training reflects my belief that this is done better when it is explicit and systematically followed through.

4. As I have argued elsewhere (Wachtel, 1973), the generalizability of emotional interaction styles is probably greater than many social learning theorists would expect from their experiments, but not so great that it can automatically be *assumed* that everything of importance in the patient's life will necessarily become evident in the transference.

5. This may seem to some readers counterintuitive. One might expect the patient to be more self-conscious having to portray another person than just himself. In my experience, however, patients do at times find it easier to begin role playing via role reversal and feel less that they are "laying themselves on the line."

REFERENCES

Klein, G. S. Peremptory ideation: Structure and force in motivated ideas. *Psychological Issues*, **5**, 2–3 (No. 18–19), 80–128. New York: International Universities Press, 1967.

Schafer, R. Internalization: Process or fantasy? *Psychoanalytic Study of the Child*, 1972, **27**, 411–436.

Sullivan, H. S. *The psychiatric interview.* New York: Norton, 1954.

Wachtel, P. L. Psychodynamics, behavior therapy, and the implacable experimenter. *Journal of Abnormal Psychology*, 1973, **82**, 324–334.

Wachtel, P. L. *Psychoanalysis and behavior therapy: Toward an integration.* New York: Basic Books, 1977.

Wachtel, P. L. Contingent and non-contingent therapist response. *Psychotherapy: Theory, Research and Practice*, 1979, **16**, 30–35.

Wachtel, P. L. What should we say to our patients?: On the wording of therapists' comments. *Psychotherapy: Theory, Research and Practice*, 1980, **17**, 183–188.

Wachtel, P. L. Transference, schema, and assimilation: The relevance of a Piagetian concept for some problems in psychoanalytic theory. *The Annual of Psychoanalysis*, in press. (a)

Wachtel, P. L. The philosophic and the therapeutic: On the value assumptions of psychoanalysis. In R. Stern & K. D. Irani (Eds.), *Science and Psychoanalysis*, vol. 4. New York: Haven Press, in press. (b)

Wolf, E. Learning theory and psychoanalysis. *British Journal of Medical Psychology*, 1966, **39**, 1–10.

Wolpe, J. *Psychotherapy by reciprocal inhibition.* Stanford, Calif.: Stanford University Press, 1958.

Chapter 4

Self-Fulfilling Prophecy, Maladaptive Behavior, and Psychotherapy*

Robert C. Carson

Several years ago the author received a telephone call from a never-married woman in her late twenties with whom he had had a brief previous acquaintance; in rather direct fashion she requested that he take her on as a psychotherapy client. There appeared to be no emergency, and he felt compelled owing to a heavy schedule to suggest referral to another therapist. The woman declined, but phoned again approximately a year later with the same request. Again, and for the same reason, he attempted to divert the client to another therapist, but she was adamant and requested to be put on his "waiting list." Intrigued, and admittedly somewhat flattered, he thereupon relented and psychotherapy commenced.

One of the peculiarities of the author's therapeutic style is to address questions explicitly and immediately as they arise, and the first question here, obviously, was, "Why me?" The client unabashedly responded with two comments: (1) she thought he would be in some way especially likely to be of help to her, and (2) he reminded her of her father. Only over the course of the subsequent year was he able to gain a full appreciation of how unpropitious a beginning this was.

The client immediately adopted an extremely hostile and suspicious attitude, refused virtually all therapeutic suggestions, and was generally uncooperative and abrasive. She repeatedly gave vent to her perception of the therapist as vain, arrogant, power-driven, Machiavellian, manipulative, and incapable of normal human sensitivities to others' suffering. Every gesture of warmth on the part of the therapist was interpreted as merely additional evidence of the above attributes. In short, it *seemed* that she was doing everything possible to provoke an exasperated unilateral termination of the relationship. She might have succeeded in doing so, had the therapist not learned long before *not* to do in therapy precisely those things he felt most impelled to do. Instead, he implacably but calmly insisted on a thorough examination of the evidential bases of the characteristics assigned to him, and repeatedly asserted his willingness to be put to *fair* tests, having *explicit* criteria, concerning his personal attitudes and commitments.

*The author gratefully acknowledges the help of Tracey Potts Carson, who contributed numerous helpful suggestions in the writing of this chapter.

This client had had a marked affectional attachment to her father, whom she idealized. As is often the case, however, the father was quite unprepared to handle his daughter's maturation into a physically adult female, and he reacted with strong signals of rejection to any "femininity" she displayed; his almost phobic reaction to female sexuality was voiced crudely and often. On the other hand, he demanded that his daughter be "successful" in the conventional terms of education and the attainment of professional status, a demand the client interpreted as being wholly narcissistically motivated, and which she therefore deviously managed not to fulfill, although giving the appearance of (and in some sense "honestly") trying. He uniformly rebuffed her attempts to become acceptable on any other grounds.

The client's only other important relationship with a male had occurred several years prior to her therapy and involved a young man who also reminded her of her father. While the relationship had begun somewhat idyllically, it ended in the client's being rather cruelly exploited and rejected. She had remained celibate since, and indeed had developed a style of dealing with men that was virtually certain to drive them away in the first minutes of an encounter. She was also lonely and miserable much of the time.

Even with such a brief recounting the reader will probably have little difficulty in reconstructing this young woman's perceptions and beliefs about the characteristics of men, and of what she might reasonably expect from them. In a word, she regarded them as exclusively concerned with the satisfaction of their own needs and as contemptuous and exploitative toward women, particularly but not exclusively in their sexual aspect; in fact, concerning the latter, she had largely bought into her father's definition that a sexual woman must necessarily be a "cunt." Somewhat paradoxically—given her father's pronounced overt aversion to sexuality—she regarded nearly all other men as wishing to convert her to that status. After the affair mentioned above, she relentlessly deprived herself of any opportunity to disprove this hypothesis.

My main point in recounting this vignette, in fact, is to illustrate how the client had organized her life in such a manner as to be virtually certain to fail to disconfirm the principal hypotheses guiding it, and indeed to run a considerable risk of having certain of them actively and positively supported by empirical events. Many men in her acquaintance *were* driven to excessive displays of "macho" and self-aggrandizing behaviors in the face of her withering, unremitting, and obviously conveyed contempt of them, dismissing her as unworthy of the serious attention she secretly craved; others indicated in varying ways that they would be willing to put up with her only as long as it would take to satisfy themselves sexually. Not surprisingly, she brought the same attitudes into her therapy, although, as has already been implied, she somehow intuitively sensed that it might come out differently. After a very long time, in fact, the client came to see the relationship with the therapist as the most honest and rewarding she had ever experienced, and therapy proceeded to a very satisfactory conclusion—the first such outcome this client had ever enjoyed with a male person.

"Might come out differently," is the operative phrase here, because, as already noted, the test of the therapist was a *severe* one. In fact, at a midway point in therapy, the client explicitly expressed her intention *not* to be influenced by therapy because such an eventuality would indicate, among other things, that: (1) the therapist would be entitled to a "feather in his cap"; (2) he would thereby win a victory in the "obvious" battle of wills between them; and (3) he would gloat unmercifully at the successful conclusion of this alleged contest. She gave no quarter on the point that a successful conclusion might enhance the satisfaction of the therapist out of concern for her and her future happiness. The latter was to come much later, and then at first only grudgingly; but it did come, more or less concurrently with the gradual emergence of the client from the personal hell she had been living.

The central thesis of this chapter is that, with rare exception, patently maladaptive behavior persists over lengthy time periods because it is based on perceptions, expectations, or constructions of the characteristics of other people that tend to be confirmed by the interpersonal consequences of the behavior emitted. In effect, what is proposed is an unbroken causal loop between social perception, behavioral enactment, and environmental reaction. The term "self-fulfilling prophecy" suggests a primacy in the first-mentioned of these components, but in fact this is merely a convenient starting place for analysis, one that lends itself to integration with certain classic psychotherapeutic concepts. In truth, assuming the reality of such loops, we have little compelling knowledge of how they may have begun. In any event, a principal corollary of this central thesis is that the psychotherapist must be primarily concerned with interrupting and altering this self-perpetuating cycle. The remainder of this chapter is an attempt to analyze the problems to be addressed in any such undertaking.

PERSONIFICATION AND PARATAXIC DISTORTION

Among all of the rich outpourings of Sullivan's (1953) fertile mind, there is probably none more important than the related concepts of personification and parataxic distortion. While obviously strongly influenced by the psychoanalytic notion of transference, Sullivan added a distinctively cognitive, information-processing perspective to earlier formulations of the manner in which one's past influences one's present in his carefully rendered account of these dual constructs. And thus—as in so many other instances—he anticipated what was to become a major thrust of contemporary psychological science.

Sullivan's basic idea is remarkably similar to our present, largely empirically and experimentally derived understanding of the structure and functioning of human memory, and of the manner in which the latter determines our ongoing interpretations of reality and of the behavioral choices we make. In brief, we process current experience in the light of a richly structured and interconnected network of schematic elements derived in large part from extant constructions of past experience (Bower, 1975). While the empirical underpinnings of this conception have involved work mainly with rather simple stimuli, there is growing evidence that our cognitions relating to *persons* are formed and operate in essentially the same manner (Cantor & Mischel, 1977, 1979a, 1979b; Hastie et al., 1980). According to this general view, then, the Sullivanian "personification," which is said to develop originally out of our primitively organized (i.e., parataxic) attempts to structure our experience of ourselves or of significant other persons, functions thereafter as a cognitive template or prototype that in part determines the manner in which new person information will be processed. Presumably, such templates are accessed or activated upon any presentation of relevant stimulus configurations.

Sullivan made clear that the relationship between any real person and the relevant personification that the child develops concerning that person will inevitably be, at best, a very loose fit, largely because very imprecise cognitive operations are involved in the construction of the personification. It is of some interest to note in this connection that the categories and schemata appearing generally to underlie memorial and cognitive functioning at the adult level also seem to have "fuzzy" boundaries (Rosch, 1975; Zadeh et al., 1975), and both Wiggins (in press) and Cantor and Mischel (1977, 1979a, 1979b) have noted that cognizing about persons does indeed seem to involve the employment of similarly loosely defined sets. To put it another way, people seem to think about people in prototypic terms, rather than in terms of specific behavioral attributes. One important implication of this "analogic" (as opposed to "digital") process, as Sullivan saw so well in his parataxic distortion concept, is that persons will often be seen as having certain characteristics for which there is in fact little or no evidence in their behavioral output. The only requirement for such distortion to occur would seem to be that the perceived person emit some signal—for example, one associated with his or her gender—that acts to prime a given important person-schema in the perceiver's cognitive apparatus.

We have little reason to suppose that, in general, persons are aware of their internal-ized prototypes or of the manner in which these function in selectively organizing sensory input. There is no intent here to raise the specter of the unconscious mind, as traditionally conceived. On the contrary, it is the author's conviction that the conscious-unconscious dichotomy is a false one and should be replaced by the concept of a gradient of awareness. It is clear, nevertheless, that much mental processing occurs outside of conscious aware-ness. Nisbett and Wilson (1977), for example, have discussed a plethora of instances in which experimental subjects have been: (1) unaware of the existence of a stimulus that actually strongly influenced their responses; (2) unaware that their responses had actually occurred; and (3) unaware that a particular stimulus had in any way affected responses that were made. These authors contend that persons routinely formulate the causes of their own behavior in stylized, conventional, plausible terms, and that such formulations are accurate, in general, only by accident or by virtue of exceedingly salient stimulus conditions. While it is not essential for purposes of the present argument to entertain an extremist position in respect to such matters, Nisbett and Wilson convincingly document the limitations on persons' abilities to observe their own cognitive processes directly. One practical implication of this state of affairs is that a client's important "personifications" will usually have to be inferred from indirect sources of information; "insight" is unlikely to be of help, except in retrospect.

The view being developed here depicts the typical psychotherapy client as primarily engaged with demons relating to his or her past that have, at most, only a metaphorical connection with the real people populating that past or indeed with the client's current complement of relationships, and usually (assuming the therapist is competent) an even more remote connection with the "real" behavior and other characteristics of the thera-pist. Moreover, the interpersonal psychotherapist generally assumes this to be the case independent of the particular complaint or problem that is stated to be the reason for the client's seeking help. For example, the client who complains of multiple phobias not infrequently turns out to be a person who believes himself or herself to be helpless and who fervently maintains the corollary belief that there are others in the world who are, or who might become, constant and unconditional devotees to the maintenance of one's own security—the main fly in the ointment being the question of how to find such a relation-ship, or how to retain at least the illusion of its persisting indefinitely. Alas, there probably are no such Mr. Goodbars, not even among therapists, and these mistaken conceptions and their accompanying strategy, should they remain unexamined, almost inevitably doom the client to a life of both childishness and misery.

The foregoing discussion is intended to lay the groundwork for making a general statement about the conduct of psychotherapy. It may be phrased as follows: a major task of the psychotherapist is that of explicit identification of the client's habitual, disorder-related, parataxic distortions of social cognition, an examination of their sources, and a comprehensive analysis of the manner in which they affect the client's behavior, particular-ly in its maladaptive aspects. In the typical instance, much of the task can be accomplished through a detailed analysis of events that occur *within* the therapeutic relationship. It must be admitted that, so stated, this principle sounds eerily akin to certain classic Freudian notions, such as "transference neurosis" and "working through." Doubtless, there *is* a kinship; the differences will become apparent in the following discussion.

NONCOGNITIVE PROCESSES

The reader will perhaps have noticed that, thus far, our analysis has focused almost exclusively on the aberrant cognitive processes that appear to underlie maladaptive behavior; it has been essentially amotivational. Does the author really believe that motivational and emotional processes (needs, drives, impulses, feelings, etc.) are irrelevant to an understanding of maladaptive behavior? No indeed, but these issues do require a careful examination.

It should first be noted that our penchant for making a sharp conceptual distinction between affective and cognitive processes, while intellectually convenient in certain ways, is rarely useful in understanding the concrete behavior of real persons; that is, it may be for the most part a convenient fiction. With possible rare exceptions in severe psychopathology, the conative, affective, and cognitive states of persons at any given point in time represent an integrated, coherent, internally consistent unit, such that a change in any element is associated with a reorganization of the whole. This is, of course, one of the dicta of gestalt theory, but it is so commonplace in our everyday observations that we tend to lose sight of its significance.

One implication of the above is that a reorganization of a person's current internal state of affairs may conceivably be accomplished by any one of several qualitatively differing forms of input to the system. And to be included here are inputs that more or less directly alter overt *behavior*, since that too, as we have learned from work on dissonance, attribution, and self-perception, is but another integrated aspect of the whole. Looked at from this perspective, it should not be surprising that we have a superabundance of differing types of psychotherapy and psychotherapists—all of them claiming, probably mostly with justification, to be effective in ameliorating people's difficulties. Thus, we have therapies manifestly intended to change people's motivations (e.g., psychoanalysis), people's affects (e.g., relaxation training), people's cognitions (e.g., RET), and people's behavior (e.g., operant learning), when in fact it is inconceivable (and would be undesirable) that a change in any one subsystem would not produce corresponding changes in the others. The interpersonal psychotherapist's tendency to focus centrally on *cognition* may have the appearance, therefore, of arbitrary choice.

Several considerations, however, suggest that the cognitive choice may be other than completely arbitrary. There is first the demonstrated power of an altered cognitive "fix" to have widespread ramifications in behavior generally. Bandura (1977), for example, has summarized much evidence pointing to the conclusion that an essential common ingredient in all effective forms of therapeutic intervention is the client's enhanced *belief* in his or her own efficacy. Similarly impressive has been the pronounced shift in recent years of many behavioristically oriented therapists to a predominantly cognitive format (Mahoney & Arnkoff, 1978). And the demonstrated effectiveness of Beck's (Beck et al., 1979) cognitive approach to the treatment of depression, formerly considered a fundamentally *affective* disorder, represents perhaps one of the most important discoveries made in the field of psychopathology in decades.

Also to be noted is the fact that human beings seem to have evolved as predominantly cognitive animals, and many organismically more "basic" processes have come under the control of the higher mental functions. Sexuality, than which few things are more basic in our biological heritage, is a case in point: there is so much of the cognitive in our arousal patterns, our preferred activities, and the likelihood of our achieving consummation that biological procreation seems to have little essential place in the scheme of things. A similar point could be made concerning cognitive control of the functioning of organ systems or the effect of cognitive states on physical health (Jones, 1977).

And finally, it may simply be the case that a client's cognitive processes are easier to observe and more subject to planned and subtle forms of direct external influence than are his or her affects and motivations, and possibly even behaviors.

In the author's opinion, however, there is a more intrinsic reason for the interpersonal therapist's preoccupation with the cognitive processes of clients. It concerns the interpersonalist's focus upon the transactions that occur between the client and his or her environment, particularly the social environment. The focus, in other words, is upon input and output, and the central agency here is the client—or more particularly the information-processing system that *is* the client. The *relationships* between input and output can be understood only insofar as we can understand the partially unique set of transformations that occur within the "black box." Sullivan's invention of the concepts of personification and parataxic distortion is doubtless a product of his having achieved this fundamental insight.

Before taking leave of the issue of the relative significance of cognitive and noncognitive processes in personality and psychotherapy, it will be well to remind ourselves of another of Sullivan's profound observations: "We are all much more simply human than otherwise." That is, the profiles of basic needs and capacities for pain and hurt probably do not vary substantially from one person to another. Some merely have a harder time than others in working it all out.

THE ROLE OF EXPECTANCY

A number of years ago, Bolles (1972), in an important paper, summarized the by then quite overwhelming evidence that the "simple" forms of learning known as conditioning could not be accounted for without reference to a cognitive factor, not even in lower animals. This is, of course, an idea that Tolman (1932) had voiced many years before. The cognitive factor identified as central in the process was called "expectancy." Certain stimuli acquired, through conditioning, the property of eliciting an expectancy that other stimuli would more or less immediately follow; in the operant case, what was learned was the expectancy that certain stimuli would occur promptly following the enactment of a particular behavior. Apparently influenced by Bolles, Mischel (1973) subsequently incorporated this reformulation of conditioning into his well-known "reconceptualization of personality," billed as a "cognitive social learning" approach. Since then, as has already been suggested, many former strict behaviorists have come to see the error of their ways, although this statement should be taken in the context of an acknowledgment of the very real contributions the behavioral perspective has made to clinical psychology in the past two decades.

If expectancy is an important element in the production and maintenance of "simple" organismic responses, we should anticipate its being no less so in the case of complex, molar behavior, particularly human social behavior. This is clearly the case; indeed, it is difficult to imagine a human society existing in the absence of a complex set of expectancies, more or less shared among its members, concerning the behavior that others will enact in particular situations. By and large, of course, these expectancies are fulfilled, and when they are not we tend to seek extraordinary explanations for the discrepancy, as by postulating unusually strong contrary traits in the behaving person—including, in extreme cases, the "trait" of mental disorder.

The above paragraph contains the crux of another central theme in this chapter. That is, that much of what we regard as "abnormal" in human behavior is in essence nothing more (nor less) than violation of our conventionalized propriety expectancies, and that these to-be-expected expectancies may not be shared by the abnormally behaving person. At one level, the latter is merely a restatement of the old aphorism about some people marching to a different drummer. The problem for the psychotherapist, however, is that of getting to know, as intimately as possible, the principal drummers to which his or her client is marching, including the drummer conventionally termed the "self." Moreover, the unusualness or even uniqueness of these drummers is important not for what it may tell us of the client's past—although that may be interesting—but rather for what it presages in the client's present and future. In the view of the writer, in other words, the drummers are in fact the client's *expectancies*, particularly his or her expectancies about the nature of the interpersonal environment and the characteristics of those who populate it. For the typical client, such expectancies are heavily infused with elements that derive from his or her parataxically imposed cognitive person-schemata, or personifications.

CONFIRMING AUTISTIC EXPECTANCIES

One of the most fundamental yet routinely neglected problems in psychopathology and psychotherapy generally is that of the intractable persistence of patently maladaptive behaviors. Given what we know about the manner in which hedonically relevant outcomes determine the directional flow of behavior, how is it that our clients repeatedly enact behaviors whose consequences are at best unsatisfying and at worst disastrous? Historically, there have been two main answers to this question, neither of them very satisfactory.

Freud was the first to confront the question in a systematic manner, having been literally forced to do so because of the challenge such behavior presented to his fundamental "pleasure principle" construct. As is well known, his response was to invent the concept of the *repetition compulsion*, according to which neurotic persons are allegedly forced to relive their childhood conflicts in adult life. It is readily apparent, however, that this "explanation" is in fact no explanation at all; at best, it merely provides a colorful label, somewhat tinged with magical thinking, for the observed self-defeating behavior.

A more widely accepted account, at least among psychologists, derives from the psychology of simple learning. The operative construct here is that of the *gradient of reinforcement*, according to which reinforcing events occurring more proximal in time to the behavior in question are said to be more potent in maintaining it than those more temporally remote. Thus, if a particular behavior has the immediate effect of reducing anxiety it will tend to be strengthened irrespective of any long-range negative consequences. The major problem with this explanation is that it derives from observations of lower animals, where the effect is by no means uniformly present, and has often been uncritically accepted as characteristic of the functioning of persons. In fact, a myriad of seemingly contradictory examples of human behavior can be produced by virtually anyone with but a moment's reflection. Furthermore, attempts to salvage the gradient of reinforcement in the face of such contradictory evidence normally employ strikingly cognitive redefinitions of "reinforcement," as in the idea of "self-reinforcement" via fantasy. Thus, it is proposed that the student repeatedly attends a boring class on the basis of the immediacy of the self-stimulation he produces in invoking thoughts about graduation day. The fantasy of graduation might indeed be a powerful incentive under such circumstances, but its reinforcement value, in the traditional sense of that term, is a contrived one at best. Instead, graduation appears to function as an outcome to be *expected*, contingent on the performance of certain behaviors. The distinction between these two versions of what is happening is far from trivial in a number of respects, of which the most important here is the very equivocal status of the reinforcement gradient conception.

The position taken in this chapter, as suggested at the outset, is that by far the most important cause of persistently maladaptive behavior is the tendency of the interpersonal environment to confirm the expectancies mediating its enactment. In simplest terms, if a client expects the world to be a hostile place, he or she will tend to behave in a manner that conforms to that expectation, and will thereby induce others, sooner or later, to enact behaviors confirming the "reality" of the original expectancy. The other side of the coin is that such a client will tend to have minimal corrective experience of the type that suggests that *some* people in the world are *not* necessarily hostile, inasmuch as the patience of most of us is not inexhaustible when confronted with unremitting prickliness in the other. The corollary contents of the client's self will contain the highly accessible category of "potential victim."

The author has elsewhere (Carson, 1979) made a beginning attempt, largely on theoretical grounds, to specify the types of experience deficit regarding others' behavior that would be expected to accompany varying types of constricted behavioral styles, considered from the standpoint of the principal quadrants of the Leary (1957) Circle. Thus, for example, Hostile-Dominant types should experience little love in their fellow humans and should observe that, as a class, they divide up into winners and losers—which is presumably the expectation with which they started. "Started" is used loosely here, however, because of the perplexities already alluded to above; we do not know, in the final analysis, how such things start, and the expectancy choice is thus partly a choice of convenience. It does have the advantage of accounting for the frequently observed tendency of clients to convert many or most new relationships into replicas of past ones. Seen in this light, a crucial task of the therapist is to "give the client a new experience," as described by Young and Beier elsewhere in this volume (Chapter 14). As most interpersonal therapists will readily acknowledge, however, that task is far from easy to accomplish.

The difficulty of the task stems not so much from client perversity as from the expertise most clients will have developed in the art of surviving in phenomenal worlds populated by perverse others. After all, the client can hardly be expected to understand at the outset either that he or she sets up unnecessarily constrained forms of engagement with other people, or that these constrained engagements virtually ensure the frustration of at least some apparently universal human needs. And so the client will typically have a history of grim but very extended practice in living in the world in which he or she lives. Comparatively, the typical therapist is a novice, an amateur; and one of the ironies of the psychotherapeutic trade is that few therapists fully appreciate the disadvantaged status with which they enter their relationships with most clients. The "turf" on which the client plays may be substantially autistic, but it is the client's turf. The number of therapeutic relationships in which therapists have (often belatedly) discovered themselves to be under the control of their clients is unknown, but it is undoubtedly legion.

The directional trends of such client control of events that transpire in therapy will normally, as we have seen, have the effect of recreating past relationship failures, unless they are successfully identified and turned aside. Nor need we assume, contrary to an earlier position taken by the writer (Carson, 1969), that the client is necessarily *motivated* to make it come out that way. The corruption of normal information-exchange processes may be a danger inherent in virtually all client-therapist relationships. The often glaring deficits in the manifest behavioral repertoires of clients (e.g., in affectional gestures), usually seen in conjunction with a pronounced exaggeration of "opposite" behavior (e.g., hostile gestures), do indeed create powerful instigations for the therapist to react with insufficient thoughtfulness concerning strategic issues in the relationship. Seen in this light, the client's failure to change may merely be an inadvertent by-product of the therapist's inability to fashion inputs that correctively modify the dysfunctional expectancies guiding the client's behavior.

In this connection, one is reminded of Colby's (1973) artificially paranoid client, PERRY, a computer program that could rapidly produce a deteriorating relationship between itself and "interviewing" psychiatrists. PERRY was programmed to have a marked tendency to detect threat in the remarks of his interaction partners, a sensitivity that in fact increased with increases in "affect." Psychiatrist-subjects could not discriminate between PERRY and genuine paranoid clients, nor were they very helpful in reassuring "him."

DIFFERENTIAL "GENERALIZED OTHERS"

To this point, largely for convenience of presentation, a somewhat oversimplified picture has been drawn. It is typically *not* the case that a psychotherapy client will react in essentially the same manner to all interaction partners, or by implication to different psychotherapists he or she might engage. To hold that view would be to indulge in a special type of "uniformity myth" (Kiesler, 1966). In reality, the client will typically manifest maximum difficulties only in relating to *certain* others, although these others might well occupy central roles (e.g., spouse) in his or her life. Other persons, or other *classes* of persons, might find little or nothing remarkable in relating to the client, nor he or she in relating to them. Of course, the more severe the client's disorder, the more pervasive are relationship difficulties likely to be; in fact, the latter statement may be something of a tautology.

While it is conceivable that, like PERRY, a person might have a set of expectancies largely undifferentiated with respect to the stimulus characteristics of differing interaction partners, it is probably much more frequently the case that cognitive organizations relating to "other people" are at least to some extent more complex. Thus, a client may access his or her more problematic or parataxically rich person-schemata only when confronted with particular stimulus configurations emanating from the other person, as the client described at the beginning of the chapter did in relation to men; her relationships with women were entirely unremarkable. To put it another way, as the Sullivanian concept of personification implies, a person will normally have several internal "generalized others," not all (or perhaps any) of whom would necessarily be a source of difficulty. A corollary observation is that a person might have several respectively complementary "selves," a notion suggested by Sullivan for which there is considerable empirical support (Gergen, 1971). Parenthetically, it may be noted that we are here making close contact with the English, object-relations school (e.g., Guntrip, 1971), and with certain contemporary trends in American psychoanalysis (e.g., Kernberg, 1975).

An important implication of the pluralistic character of an individual's person-schemata and self-organization is that the particular stimulus configuration the therapist presents to the client, whether inadvertently or by design, will have profound effects on the nature and course of the transactions that occur between the two. That is, what happens in the relationship should be determined to an important degree by the kinds of person-memories the person of the therapist activates in the client's cognitive system. A further implication is that therapy should proceed efficiently or less so depending on the quality and degree of connectedness between the therapist's "real" characteristics and the person-structures contained in the client's cognitive apparatus. Obviously, we are touching here on the question of therapist-client matching (see, for example, Carson, 1973), an issue about which we know virtually nothing. Our ignorance notwithstanding, however, experience suggests that it is in fact a consideration of very great importance. Again referring to the client of the earliest pages, a person of considerable psychological sophistication, one suspects that her choice of therapist was neither accidental nor inconsequential in terms of outcome. Clearly, this is an area highly deserving of research attention, especially in the light of known instances of therapeutic casualty (Bergin & Lambert, 1978).

ADDITIONAL THERAPEUTIC IMPLICATIONS

This is obviously not the place to attempt a comprehensive, how-to manual of interpersonal psychotherapy as the author sees it. Rather, what follows is an attempt to sketch out certain general issues of psychotherapy and psychotherapeutic strategy that would seem to be more or less directly implied by the foregoing discussion.

To take the last-mentioned problem first, there is little reason to suppose that any therapist will be equally effective with all clients, quite aside from issues of competence. While we do not yet know how to match clients with therapists to achieve predictions substantially above chance in regard to outcome, it is likely that every therapist has experienced or will experience the client who does not seem to move in response to the best that he or she can offer in psychotherapeutic dedication. Too often under such circumstances, the therapist—presumably to avoid unpleasant self-attributions—declares the client untreatable, usually in the process discovering a new and graver diagnosis for the client, of which the current favorite seems to be "borderline." We often fail to recognize that, whereas one physician's prescription is like all other physicians' prescriptions containing the same labeled compound, psychotherapists are *not* interchangeable, not even those belonging to the same "school." Much pain for both clients and therapists could be avoided by an acceptance of the idea that poor, unefficacious matches do inadvertently occur, and quite naturally so. Clearly, an unprejudiced referral to a therapist colleague is the proper—not to say ethical—course when it becomes clear that a client is not benefiting from the ministrations of the current therapist.

Moving into the realm of psychotherapeutic strategy itself, the author would contend that one essential element in the therapist's role stands out above all others in importance: namely, the ability to detect and to turn to therapeutic advantage the client's misconceptions or misconstruals of what is going on around him or her. In the final analysis, it is the nature of these misunderstandings that reveals to us both the character of the distorting influences in the client's information-processing system, and the directions in which we shall have to move in order to render the latter more functional for the client's welfare.

In the typical instance, the client at the outset may be observed to misconstrue systematically a variety of interpersonal events external to the therapeutic relationship itself, and an appreciation and analysis of these will normally prove to be helpful throughout the course of therapy. At best, however, the therapist is but a distant spectator in regard to these extramural relationship events. The special power of the interpersonal approach to therapy, in the author's opinion, is that the therapeutic relationship itself, in all of its immediacy to observation and its possibility of permitting controlled input to the client, becomes the arena in which the major corrective experiences occur. But, of course, they will not occur in the absence of the therapist's having a firm grasp of what it is that he/she is trying to correct, and such awareness is most unlikely should the therapist become enmeshed in providing "proof" of the client's way of construing things.

Let us take, for example, the commonly occurring case of a young and somewhat insecure therapist who manages to get paired with a skillfully competitive client, one who is reasonably convinced that life with at least a fair proportion of humankind is a constant struggle to avoid the "one down" position, and that the best way of accomplishing this objective is to go on the offensive. Such a client, not surprisingly, will typically have many realistic complaints about an absence of normal human satisfactions in his or her life. But in a sympathetic attempt to "find an answer" in collaboration with the client, the therapist notices that his or her own life is less satisfying than it once was; in extreme cases, he or she may even come to dread the next appointment, perhaps feeling guilty for having that reaction. He or she has perhaps also noticed how uncomfortable it was when the client "innocently" inquired about the therapist's professional credentials, and there is also the fairly constant anxiety that the client will already have thought of, and dismissed, any new idea the therapist might come up with. The scenario is not promising, unless, of course, the therapist can detach himself or herself sufficiently to realize that the battle is the crux of the issue, and that to engage the client in the battle, as opposed to examining what it is all about, is to risk an unproductive relationship, or worse. In any event, it is a battle the therapist is almost certain to "lose."

As suggested above, effective examination of a client's distorted way of viewing interpersonal relations presupposes at a minimum that the therapist is aware that such distortions are occurring. This in turn requires that the therapist have a more or less secure and accurate sense of reality, including the reality of his or her own person. In the absence of accuracy, discrepancies from reality in the productions of the client will be difficult to detect; and, in the absence of a reasonable level of confidence in his or her own judgments on the part of the therapist, the client's blandishments in this regard are likely often to be persuasive. Consider again the example of the young therapist and the competitive client. The therapist is "inexperienced," and this is a reality to be squarely faced. This does not necessarily make him or her a poor therapist for this client, and—of even greater importance—the business of the therapy is not to establish who is top dog. A main reality in this example is that the client lives in a psychological jungle, thereby depriving himself or herself of a whole range of human satisfactions other than that of secretly being top dog. And another main reality is that it is the therapist's responsibility to fashion an approach to the client that will alter, rather than extend, this state of affairs.

One could wish, from this point of view, that all therapists be undefensive, philosophically mature, appreciative of the range of human behavior and experience, perceptually sensitive and acute, and, perhaps especially, that they have a full appreciation of their own general social stimulus impact on others. It is where these qualities are minimal or absent that client misconstruals are most likely to remain uncorrected. Alas, many therapists do not meet such standards, and effective quality-control systems in the production of psychotherapists are, for a variety of reasons, practically nonexistent. We do not know the extent to which such attributes as the above are learnable by people generally, partly because, with certain exceptions, this is another neglected area in the field. Most of us who have trained therapists over the years have become convinced that *some* recruits to the field are unfortunately not educable in respect to these seemingly essential awarenesses and skills. In these instances, the best therapeutic strategy in the broad scheme of things would seem to be that of assisting the individual to choose another life work.

While forming an accurate conception of the manner in which the client processes interpersonal information is a basic requisite, it is of course only a first step in the induction of positive change. The more fundamental task is that of causing a restructuring of the errant cognitive system underlying the maintenance of the client's maladaptive, self-defeating interpersonal behavior. As has already been observed, this is most likely to be accomplished with efficiency when the therapist himself or herself is an object of centrally involved perceptual distortion on the part of the client, assuming, of course, that the therapist is prepared to confront such distortion in an appropriate manner. As we have also seen, however, there is little reason to suppose that all therapist-client relationships will necessarily be subject, in the natural course of things, to such major client distortion. The author has observed numerous instances of apparently successfully conducted therapy that involved little or no client inaccuracy in attributions made concerning the person of the therapist. In such cases, the burden of therapy is carried by an in-depth examination of other of the client's relationships, in particular the problematic ones.

The question arises as to the strategic wisdom of the therapist's attempting, by artifice as it were, to present stimulus configurations that *will* activate the client's more problematic person-schemata. Recognizing the dangers inherent in any such approach, it is the author's belief that this is sometimes justifiable and sometimes a very productive strategy. For example, in working with a client having a history of multiple suicide attempts, all of them tests of whether her current lover should be placed in the "unconditionally good" or the "unremittingly evil" categories of her cognitive system, the author virtually at the outset announced that he had a strong aversion to emergencies, and that, in the event of an irresistible urge to suicide, the client should contact her family mortician rather than the therapist. The client lived and, after a rather eventful and hectic period of therapy, went on to establish a very successful and happy life for herself; she maintains periodic and mutually affectionate contact with the author. It should be noted that there is no intent here to encourage unnecessarily risky or irresponsible therapist behavior, but only to suggest that, under some conditions, a degree of therapist "ungenuineness" may pave the way for more effective client functioning in the long run. As with all therapeutic interventions, thoughtfulness is an essential precondition.

It should also be noted in this connection that extraordinary or risky therapeutic operations, in general, ought not be attempted unless the therapist is reasonably certain that he or she will have opportunity to repair any immediate damage that ensues. Normally, this entails the prior establishment of a secure relationship—one unlikely to be abruptly terminated by the client in response to the therapist's challenge. Goldstein (1971) and Cashdan (1973), among others, have written of the importance of the client's fundamental attraction and attachment to the therapist in enabling the latter to accomplish his or her aims. In the case just mentioned, the client had not only evidenced considerable liking and respect for the therapist, but had also almost immediately announced her intention of seducing him into marriage with her! That is, he had been firmly located in her "unconditionally good" category prior to the intervention described.

As is perhaps obvious, the author favors a very active and engaged style of psychotherapy, one in which instructional, hypothesis-testing experiences are systematically prescribed or "arranged" for the client as a means of generating perturbations in extant, maladaptive cognitive schemata and restructuring them into a more functional processing system. In this respect, his therapy bears a marked kinship with Beck's (Beck et al., 1979) cognitive therapy for depression, although it is usually more centered on the immediate relationship, particularly in its early and middle phases. In later phases, very often, the focus needs to shift to the testing of newly acquired hypotheses in respect to *other* persons in the client's life. To return once again to the client of the opening pages, it is noteworthy (and pleasant to report) that she now enjoys a better relationship with her father than ever before. She is also actively seeking out adult heterosexual relationships.

As a final note, it should be acknowledged that the author is aware of the seeming harshness and "manipulativeness" of his recommended therapeutic approach as described in the foregoing. In defense, he would only point out, once again, that the therapist will normally be at a pronounced disadvantage in his or her engagement with the typical client, and that less than potent therapeutic operations are unlikely to dislodge the average client from his or her well-practiced and eminently confirmable, although maladaptive, constructions of what the world is like. The ultimate goal of an "honest" relationship is, in the author's experience, so rewarding to both parties and so functional for the client upon its accomplishment that, in contrast to most human endeavors, the end may legitimately be said to justify the means.

REFERENCES

Bandura, A. Self-efficacy: Toward a unifying theory of behavioral change. *Psychological Review*, 1977, **84,** 191–215.

Beck, A. T., Rush, A. J., Shaw, B. F., & Emery, G. *Cognitive therapy of depression.* New York: Guilford, 1979.

Bergin, A. E. & Lambert, M. J. The evaluation of therapeutic outcomes. In S. L. Garfield & A. E. Bergin (Eds.), *Handbook of psychotherapy and behavior change.* New York: Wiley, 1978.

Bolles, R. C. Reinforcement, expectancy, and learning. *Psychological Review*, 1972, **79,** 394–409.

Bower, G. H. Cognitive psychology: An introduction. In W. K. Estes (Ed.), *Handbook of learning and cognitive processes*, vol. 1. Hillsdale, N.J.: Erlbaum Associates, 1975.

Cantor, N. & Mischel, W. Traits as prototypes: Effects on recognition memory. *Journal of Personality and Social Psychology*, 1977, **35,** 38–48.

Cantor, N. & Mischel, W. Prototypicality and personality: Effects on free recall and personality impressions. *Journal of Research in Personality*, 1979, **13,** 187–205. (a)

Cantor, N. & Mischel, W. Categorization processes in the perception of people. In L. Berkowitz (Ed.), *Advances in experimental social psychology.* New York: Academic Press, 1979. (b)

Carson, R. C. *Interaction concepts of personality.* Chicago: Aldine, 1969.

Carson, R. C. A conceptual approach to the problem of therapist-client matching. In D. E. Linder (Ed.), *Psychological dimensions of social interaction.* Reading, Mass.: Addison-Wesley, 1973.

Carson, R. C. Personality and exchange in developing relationships. In R. L. Burgess & T. L. Huston (Eds.), *Social exchange in developing relationships.* New York: Academic Press, 1979.

Cashdan, S. *Interactional psychotherapy.* New York: Grune & Stratton, 1973.

Colby, K. M. Simulations of belief systems. In R. C. Schank & K. M. Colby (Eds.), *Computer models of thought and language.* San Francisco: Freeman, 1973.

Gergen, K. J. *The concept of self.* New York: Holt, 1971.

Goldstein, A. P. *Psychotherapeutic attraction.* New York: Pergamon, 1971.

Guntrip, H. *Psychoanalytic theory, therapy, and the self.* New York: Basic Books, 1971.

Hastie, R., Ostrom, T. M., Ebbesen, E. B., Wyer, R. S., Hamilton, D. L., & Carlston, D. E. *Person memory: The cognitive basis of social perception.* Hillsdale, N.J.: Erlbaum Associates, 1980.

Jones, R. A. *Self-fulfilling prophecies.* Hillsdale, N.J.: Erlbaum Associates, 1977.

Kernberg, O. *Borderline conditions and pathological narcissism*. New York: Jason Aronson, 1975.

Kiesler, D. J. Some myths of psychotherapy research and the search for a paradigm. *Psychological Bulletin*, 1966, **65,** 110–136.

Leary, T. *Interpersonal diagnosis of personality*. New York: Ronald, 1957.

Mahoney, M. J. & Arnkoff, D. Cognitive and self-control therapies. In S. L. Garfield & A. E. Bergin (Eds.), *Handbook of psychotherapy and behavior change*. New York: Wiley, 1978.

Mischel, W. Toward a cognitive social learning re-conceptualization of personality. *Psychological Review*, 1973, **80,** 252–283.

Nisbett, R. E. & Wilson, T. D. Telling more than we can know: Verbal reports on mental processes. *Psychological Review*, 1977, **84,** 231–259.

Rosch, E. Cognitive reference points. *Cognitive Psychology*, 1975, **7,** 532–547.

Sullivan, H. S. *The interpersonal theory of psychiatry*. New York: Norton, 1953.

Tolman, E. C. *Purposive behavior in animals and man*. New York: Appleton-Century-Crofts, 1932.

Wiggins, J. S. Circumplex models of interpersonal behavior in clinical psychology. In P. C. Kendall & J. N. Butcher (Eds.), *Handbook of research methods in clinical psychology*. In press.

Zadeh, L. A., Fu, K.-S., Tanaka, K., & Shimura, M. (Eds.) *Fuzzy sets and their application to cognitive and decision processes*. New York: Academic Press, 1975.

Chapter 5

A Social Learning Theory Analysis of Interactional Theory Concepts and a Multidimensional Model of Human Interaction Constellations

Marshall P. Duke and Stephen Nowicki, Jr.

In recent years, much empirical and theoretical interest has been directed at attempting to understand the nature and importance of interpersonal communications and human relationships and their effects upon human functioning. Although basically social learning oriented, we too have been caught up in this exciting effort to identify new concepts to explain and predict behavior.

Our excitement, however, is tempered somewhat by the prominent social learning theorist. J. B. Rotter, who wrote in 1954:

In the half century or more that psychologists have been interested in predicting the behavior of human beings in complex social situations they have avoided the incontrovertible importance of the specific situation in behavior. They have assumed that if they could only produce a somewhat better schema for attempting to describe an individual's personality from a purely internal point of view they could somehow or other overcome this failure to predict. So they have gone from faculties and instincts and sentiments to traits, drives, needs and the interaction of these within the individual, producing schema for personality organization and classification of internal states, but ignoring an analysis of the psychological situations in which human beings behave [p. 247.]

As research clinicians firmly committed to the interactional approach to diagnosis and psychotherapy we do not wish to commit the errors described by Rotter.

We have found the social learning perspective quite helpful in our previous research with the constructs of interpersonal distance, academic achievement, attraction, and adjustment. We therefore want to apply this perspective to the burgeoning area of human interaction and communication. The present chapter is the result of our effort.

We have chosen to deal with three constructs of current interest in human interaction theorizing: complementarity, congruence, and multiphasic human relationships. We will provide support for our view that the role of each of these major interactional theory variables can be clarified by applying social learning theory perspectives. In addition to this presentation of our social learning focus, we also want to consider the *process* by which we have attempted to understand and predict human interaction. In this chapter, we will note that the homogeneous-appearing group of interaction researchers are really composed of several subgroups, who are much like the proverbial blind men looking at the elephant; each subgroup of researchers appears to focus on some important aspect of human interaction and then generalize that aspect. If we use the blind men analogy, we may argue that just as the foot, trunk, and tail are all parts that make up the elephant, so are complementarity, congruence, and interpersonal style all parts of human interaction. In fact, we argue that each of the many different aspects of human interaction that these constructs refer to is needed to understand fully the rich complexity of human interaction. We will close our chapter with a proposed integration of the concepts of complementarity and congruence within a social learning theory–based, multiphasic model for human interactions.

COMPLEMENTARITY/ANTICOMPLEMENTARITY AND HUMAN INTERACTION

Based upon a circumplex model of human interaction, Timothy Leary and his colleagues at the Kaiser Institute (1957) were among the first to present a complete theory on interpersonal relations. As further developed and described by Carson (1969), Leary's circumplex model of behavior may be depicted in what has become a now-familiar diagram (see Fig. 5.1.). The conceptualization encompasses the empirically and theoretically derived interaction of two orthogonal axes of Love-Hate and Dominance-Submission with the resultant formation of four major quadrants that Leary later shows can be divided into 8 and finally 16 different interpersonal styles. An individual's position relative to the major axes determines qualitative variations in behavior while distance from the center of the circle indicates the intensity level of the behavior in question. Thus, an individual whose interpersonal behaviors are described as rejecting, exploiting, punitive, boastful, and so on, would fall into the Hostile-Dominant quadrant while a friendly, responsible leader would be characterized as Friendly-Dominant. Leary's conceptualization has had a significant impact on the later works of such researchers as Lorr and McNair (1965), Carson (1969), McLemore and Benjamin (1979), Kiesler et al. (1975; 1976) and Perkins et al. (1979).

The basic concepts of complementarity and anticomplementarity emerge when Leary describes the interaction of dyads. Interpersonal styles reflecting places in the circumplex are systematically seen to be complementary, anticomplementary, and noncomplementary to others. Complementarity can be assessed according to certain rules that govern the reaction to the affiliation and status dimensions. In affiliation, the reaction is similar to the behavior shown; friendliness begets friendliness and hostility begets hostility. In status, the reaction is opposite to the behavior shown; dominance begets submission and submission begets dominance. A complementary interaction occurs when the dyad shows behaviors that are consistent with the similarity rule in affiliation and the opposite rule in

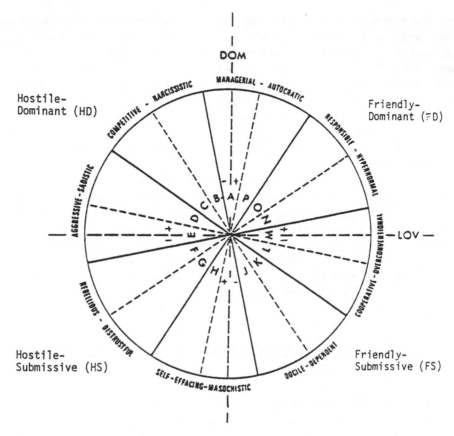

Fig. 5.1. The Interpersonal Circle. Adapted by M. P. Duke and S. Nowicki, Jr. from Timothy Leary, *Interpersonal diagnosis of personality*. Copyright © 1957, The Ronald Press.

regard to status. Therefore, the complement to Hostile-Dominance is Hostile-Submissive; to Friendly-Dominant is Friendly-Submissive.

Anticomplementarity differs from complementarity in that the reactions evoked in the anticomplementary person are counter to the rules of complementarity for *both* affiliation and status. Thus, the anticomplement of a Friendly-Dominant person would be a Hostile-Dominant person. Theoretically, individuals should be attracted to or prefer complementary others, while they should avoid or dislike anticomplementary persons.

Noncomplementarity is a third category of reaction. In these cases the dyad follows the rules for complementarity *for one* but not for the other dimension of the circumplex. Thus, the noncomplement for a Friendly-Submissive person would be a Hostile-Dominant person.

A number of studies have been done to test the relation of complementarity to effective interpersonal functioning. In that a number of these studies have been reported elsewhere in this volume, we limit ourselves to a discussion of those studies that are relevant to the perspective which we are developing.

Our review of the literature suggests that complementarity in a relationship is frequently (though not always) related to success in that relationship and that anticomplementarity is frequently (but not always) related to difficulty in relationships. While failure to find support for a hypothesized relation in every instance is not unusual in psychological research, as social learning theorists, we ask ourselves whether or not situational variables may be working systematically to account for the lack of consistency. Thus, we have attempted in our research to determine whether or not situational factors may be manipulated to affect the expected relationships between success and happiness in human interactions and the complementarity versus anticomplementarity of the persons interacting.

For example, in one study (Duke & Ekstrand, 1980), we addressed the issue of interpersonal preference as it relates to complementarity/anticomplementarity, depending on the situation. We proposed that the situational import of a competitive versus a cooperative interaction might have differential impact upon the effects of complementarity and anticomplementarity in dyadic interactions. We theorized that complementary pairs would do better on a cooperative word puzzle task than anticomplementary pairs, but that the reverse would be true if the task were competitive. Pairings were made on the basis of scores on Leary's Interpersonal Check List. Sixteen pairs of males (eight complementary and eight anticomplementary) were asked to cooperate on a task in which they tried together to "beat the record" of the number of words they could generate from the name "George Washington." An equal number of pairs were given instructions to compete against one another to determine "the winner." Using number of words generated as a measure of performance and preferred interpersonal distance as a measure of interpersonal attraction and preference, consistent with the situational perspective, we found that there was a significant interaction of situational and complementarity/anticomplementarity for number of words generated. The anticomplementary pairs produced more words in the competitive condition while the complementary pairs produced more words in the cooperative condition. In regard to interpersonal distance, complementary others were preferred significantly closer than anticomplementary others, regardless of situation. (This finding that verbal or performance measures of complementarity may differ from nonverbal measures will be discussed below when we focus on situational aspects of congruence.)

While it was only a beginning, we believe that the data from this study suggest that complementarity and anticomplementarity do not exist in a vacuum and that situational variables present a constantly changing context within which these circumplex model–based concepts must be embedded. Further research should broaden the number of situational factors altering the complementarity relationships proposed by Leary and his followers. Any effective interactional theory must be broadened to include significant situational variables.

CONGRUENCE/INCONGRUENCE AND HUMAN INTERACTION

While complementarity and its effects upon human relationships are emphasized by followers of Leary's point of view, many other researchers and theoreticians have turned their attention to the concept of communicational congruence and its effects upon human relationships. While these investigators have approached their task from the perspective of communication theory, their purpose, like Leary's, is to illuminate normal and abnormal behavior patterns and their alteration. To understand the concept of congruence/incongruence, some basic description of communication theory is necessary.

In order to elicit something from another individual, we must communicate. Kiesler et al. (1976) define communication as the transmission of messages from an encoder (sender) to a decoder (receiver) *and* the decoder's response. A message is defined as the response of an encoder which serves as a stimulus for the decoder. Encoding and decoding transpire extremely rapidly during the course of any interpersonal communication, and messages may be transmitted verbally, but are also sent via nonverbal channels such as paralanguage (vocal sounds that are not a part of language, and tone of voice), kinesics (body movements), proxemics (body distance and position), appearance, odor, and others.

Since we communicate in both verbal and nonverbal channels, Kiesler maintains two levels of message are always sent by any encoder. The most obvious level is the manifest, information content expressed through the verbal channel (defined here as words alone, not including the accompanying paralinguistics). This level is the *denotative* level, referred to by Watzlawick et al. (1967) as the *report* aspect. The other, much more subtle level of communication is the *command* or *connotative* level of communication. Thus, when two individuals interact, each may be overtly imparting concrete bits of verbal information (their words) to the other, but at the same time they may be communicating on a much different level connotatively (via nonverbal channels). Each individual in the dyad is constantly transmitting his attitudes and emotions about himself, the other person, and the relationship, attempting to define the relationship in a way that is consistent with his own self-image. What an individual may *wish* or *try* to communicate, however, may not always be what his fellow interactants receive. Kiesler et al. (1976) have suggested that such undesirable or misdirected and misunderstood communication is related to maladjustment. Expanding upon Sullivan's concept of mental disorder, Kiesler has stated:

A client-encoder can be referred to as experiencing emotional problems when as a relatively consistent consequence of his interpersonal communications (a) he experiences more or less enduring and unaccountable aversive feelings or negative self-evaluations, or (b) when over time his interpersonal communications lead to consistent and unaccountable aversive communications from significant persons in life or both (a) and (b). [Pp. 69–70.]

Kiesler (as well as Beier, 1966, and others) has stressed that disturbed individuals may not be aware of how they evoke the responses they do (or even that they evoke anything at all). One may presume that they are not using verbal channels to elicit these aversive responses from others since they would likely be aware of it if they were. If the disturbed individuals are *not* verbally transmitting self-defeating messages and *are* transmitting them nonverbally, then the two channels of communication must be incongruent. Kiesler has stated that channel incongruity is one of the major discriminative cues used by therapists to pinpoint a client's self-defeating style. Beier (1966) also stresses the incongruity of disturbed clients' communications, as does Kaiser (Fierman, 1965) in his concept of the Universal Symptom—duplicitous communication (saying one thing and meaning another). Although an individual may say one thing, nonverbal leakage is coming through with "truthful" messages and it is to these that other individuals seem to respond.

As seen in the foregoing discussion, several leading theoreticians have emphasized incongruence between the verbal and nonverbal communication channels as an earmark of interpersonal maladjustment. This emphasis, however, was typically complemented by an awareness of the potential mediating effects of situational variables (e.g. Kiesler et al., 1976, pp. 67–69). As was the case with the concept of complementarity, it has been our goal here to expand upon this previous awareness of situational factors and to examine as our primary focus the degree to which congruence/incongruence and its relationship to maladjustment may in fact be situationally embedded. We believe we will find that not only may incongruence sometimes be "normal" and appropriate, but that incongruence may actually be the prevalent mode of adult human interaction. As presented in Figure 5.2, and consistent with our social learning theory emphasis upon situational variables, we propose that an analysis of interpersonal interactions will show that there are at least four categories of dyadic congruence/incongruence situational patterns. The first of these interaction patterns, *adaptive congruence*, is typified by open, honest communication occurring in close, intimate, interpersonal relationships; in contrast, *maladaptive congruence* occurs when a person communicates "true feelings" in a situation in which such communication is not socially appropriate. An example of maladaptive congruence would be telling your best friend that you'd like to have sex with his wife. *Maladaptive incongruence* occurs when individuals do not say what they truly feel in a situation that warrants genuine communication. For example, maladaptive incongruence occurs when a wife tells her husband she loves him when she does not. Finally, *adaptive incongruence* (a pattern not described by Kiesler et al. [1976]), occurs in situations where telling the truth would be socially and interpersonally inappropriate. Examples of adaptive incongruence are often apparent in rules of social etiquette, such as teaching a young child not to tell people they're ugly. Indeed, adaptive incongruence may be a most prevalent form of day-to-day interpersonal interaction. If this contention is accurate, incongruence as a general concept needs to be reevaluated and must be viewed as associated with maladjustment only in certain situationally defined instances. In fact, we believe that it may be more accurate to say that failure to learn when, where, and with whom to be congruent or incongruent may have more to do with the development of maladjustment than with simple incongruence per se.

As in our earlier presentation of the situational perspective on complementarity, we will now present an example of a study from our laboratory which we believe has bearing upon our social learning perspective. In this study (Ladd, Nowicki, & Duke, 1979), two aspects of interpersonal situations were examined to demonstrate that degree of congru-

	CONGRUENT COMMUNICATION	INCONGRUENT COMMUNICATION
SITUATIONALLY APPROPRIATE	ADAPTIVE CONGRUENCE	ADAPTIVE INCONGRUENCE
SITUATIONALLY INAPPROPRIATE	MALADAPTIVE CONGRUENCE	MALADAPTIVE INCONGRUENCE

Fig. 5.2. The interaction between congruence/incongruence and situation.

ent communication would vary as a function of instructional set (situation). The two situational variables were: (1) the importance of the circumstance surrounding the interaction; and (2) the depth of the relationship between the interactors. The high and low importance and high and low level of relationships result in the 2 × 2 table, shown in Figure 5.3. Sixty female college students were asked to respond to a Triandis (1977)–type questionnaire in which they were asked to indicate their probable course of action in a variety of social, familial, and education situations.

Congruence was measured via a variation of the methodology described by Triandis (1977). An instrument (Social Interaction Survey) was constructed using theoretically derived assumptions concerning the independent variables of degree of acquaintance and importance of situations. Initially, ten situations were developed; five were relatively inconsequential (e.g., giving an opinion on someone's department store purchase, planning a party, etc.); the other five had more important consequences for the actors (e.g., jumping off a dangerous, high diving board, eating possibly poisonous berries, etc.). Each situation was then presented four times in the Social Interaction Survey, once for each of the following degrees of relationship: stranger, acquaintance, friend, and close relative. Thus, degree of acquaintance and importance of situation were varied systematically throughout the survey.

In the Triandis methodology, subjects are instructed to imagine feeling a certain way in response to a certain situation. For example, in one situation the subject is told that she is standing on a crowded bus and the person next to her exclaims what a wonderful day it has been and asks the subject what she thinks of the day. The subject is asked how she would respond if she were feeling that she had had a terrible day. The subject is offered four possible responses and asked to rate each. In Triandis' method of rating alternative responses, subjects are asked to rate *each* proposed alternative on a scale of 0 to 9, with 0 indicating the subjects would *never* behave as described and 9 indicating that they would *always* behave as described. The way in which they rate the alternatives reflects their

Situational Importance – Factor A

	Low	High
Low	Situation 4 Mean = 97.82	Situation 2 Mean = 136.75
High	Situation 3 Mean = 128.55	Situation 1 Mean = 143.30

Level of Relationship Factor B

Fig. 5.3. Two-factor study of the interaction of situational importance and level of interpersonal relationship in determining the level of congruent behaviors. This schematization was used in an attempt to determine the relative significance of situational importance and level of interpersonal relationship in determining the level of congruent behaviors.

expressed level of congruence in that it is possible to quantify the relationship between feelings and probable behavior. An example from the Survey follows:

You're standing in the cafeteria line with a girl you know from having a class together. Her blouse is on inside out. You most likely would:

8	a.	Cough and play with your blouse trying to give her a hint.
2	b.	Politely look away and pretend not to notice.
0	c.	Strike up a conversation like nothing was the matter.
5	d.	Tell her that her blouse is on inside out.

All subjects were exposed to all combinations of situational importance and closeness of relationship. Responses which indicated that subjects would communicate "true" feelings to their dyad partner were scored as congruent; those in which there was disagreement between feelings and verbal message were scored as incongruent. The higher the score, the more congruent the communication pattern. As shown in Figure 5.3, congruence varied with importance of the situation *and* the importance of the relationship. More congruent responses were associated with those instances in which the consequences and relationships were important. It is in such situations that incongruent responses would represent a deviation from the norm and would probably be associated with disordered functioning. At the other end of the spectrum, however, in low importance, low relationship level situations, incongruent responses are more the rule than the exception and it is here that *congruent* responses would more likely be associated with deviant behavior.

Based on the results of the above study, we suggest that congruence of messages should not be conceptualized outside their contexts and that congruence should not necessarily be seen as the sine qua non of normality. Certainly, in some very important situations it is; but in others it may not be. Seemingly then, culturally effective functioning may not always involve being congruent, and ineffective functioning may not always involve incongruence. As was our position vis-à-vis complementarity, therefore, it is our belief that congruence in a vacuum cannot serve as an (adequate) indication or explanation of maladjustment.

A SOCIAL LEARNING PERSPECTIVE ON INTERPERSONAL RELATIONSHIPS

Having examined complementarity and congruence from a situational perspective, we turn now to a third major area of concern for interactional theorists—the interpersonal relationship per se. While we are aware that there are a number of possible ways to envision the interpersonal relationship, based upon our social learning bent and our years of experience as psychotherapists, we have come to a point where we conceive of a human relationship as a series of ever-changing situations, each of which requires appropriate, yet differing responses. Specifically, we propose that an interpersonal relationship may be seen as a multiphasic sequence of varying interpersonal styles. Further, the specific type of style manifested in a particular relationship may be seen as a function not only of the basic stylistic patterns of the individuals involved—as would follow from Leary, (1957), Carson (1969), and Kiesler et al. (1976)—but of the stage of the relationship as well. In an effort to make our conceptualization clearer, we next present our basic ideas and then place them into a more formal social learning theory context.

As depicted in Figure 5.4, we propose that interpersonal relationships may be conceptualized as dynamic entities involving at least four phases—choice, beginning, deepening, and termination. We believe that each phase of a relationship demands different requirements from interpersonal styles, and failure to meet these demands may create psychological problems.

The first or *choice* phase of a relationship involves a decision whether to enter into a relationship with another. Based upon some combination of observed physical characteristics, previous experiences, and the like, a person gleans information to use in deciding whether to try to relate to a particular other.

Once a decision to pursue a relationship is made, the person enters the *beginning* phase. During this phase, persons actually attempt to establish a relationship. We believe that the success of this attempt depends on whether people have developed effective interpersonal styles that will have a favorable impact upon others. For example, if a person's opening interpersonal style results in an abrasive or inappropriate impact, then he or she will probably not be very successful in establishing relationships.

Given that a person can establish beginning relationships successfully, the onset of the next or *deepening* phase brings with it a new set of interpersonal requirements. As the interactors exhibit a wider variety of behaviors, the relationship becomes more complex and *flexibility* in interpersonal style becomes more necessary. For example, although a person may successfully use a Friendly-Submissive style to enter a relationship, some assertiveness (mild Dominance) may be necessary as the relationship progresses. If, however, a person does not have the flexibility to use different styles in different situations, and depends instead on only one style of interaction, he or she will have difficulty deepening relationships. In such cases, people may find that while they can make acquaintances they may have trouble attaining deep relationships.

A relationship may continue to deepen or may terminate. A deep relationship may terminate for a variety of reasons such as death or divorce. As is true of the first three phases, specific requirements and interpersonal skills are necessary to end relationships. In our clinical experience we have found that some people are unable to end relationships in a constructive and successful fashion. Certain interpersonal styles that may be appropriate for other phases of relationships may be maladaptive in closing out relationships. For example, people may evoke dependence from others, which, though helpful in deepening a relationship, may be maladjustive in ending one.

While the four-phase model described above may be useful heuristically, it falls somewhat short of being theoretically complete. As it is primarily a new descriptive model, based largely on our clinical experience, there is little empirical support for its assumptions. We believe, however, that it does describe well many of the relationships we as well as our clients and students have experienced. Because we believe the model is potentially useful, we wanted to tie it onto a broader body of theory with empirical support. In

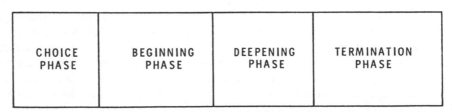

Fig. 5.4. A four-phase model for interpersonal relationships.

attempting to do this, we were faced with the choice of trying to adapt the concepts either to budding interactional theories or to a better-established framework with already developed methodologies and a rich store of empirical data. Given our long-time involvement in Rotter's social learning theory, with its emphasis on the situation and expectancies, it was our logical choice.

In order to understand fully the specific aspects and implications of a social learning theory translation of our multiphasic sequence model of human relationships, some familiarity with the basics of Rotter's theory is necessary. Therefore, prior to discussing the translation itself, we will provide a brief overview of the basic tenets of Rotter's conceptualization of behavior.

Rotter's theory (Rotter, 1975; Rotter, Chance, & Phares, 1972) explains goal-directed behavior in a specific situation by the following formula which, although formidable looking, is really quite simple:

$$BP_x, s_1, r_a = f(E_x, r_a s_{,1} \& RV_a, s_1)$$

That is, given a particular situation (*1*) and a particular reinforcement (*a*), the potential for a behavior (*x*) to occur is a function of the expectation that the particular reinforcement (*a*) will occur, given the behavior (*x*) and the specific situation (*1*) and the value of reinforcement (*a*), or the relative preference of reinforcement (*a*) in that situation (*1*). Behavior potential (*BP*), then, is a function of expectancy (*E*) and reinforcement value (*RV*).

The expectancies of individuals for situations are determined by their reinforcement history in these situations; positive reinforcements in past experiences strengthen the expectancies of positive reinforcement in future instances of a situation. The specific expectancy for a particular situation generalizes to similar situations so that both specific and generalized expectancies act in combination with reinforcement value to determine behavior.

In 1975, Rotter reemphasized the nature of the expectancy component of his formulation. In a given situation the relative importance of specific versus generalized expectancies in the determination of behavior potential may be expressed as follows (Rotter, 1975, p. 57):

$$E_{R_s} = f(E'_{s_1} + \frac{GE}{N_{s_1}})$$

This formula provides an estimate of the overall expectancy of reinforcement in situation s_1 with N representing the amount of previous experience in the situation, E' representing specific expectancies and GE representing any of a large number of generalized expectancies (such as locus of control, trust, athletic prowess, etc.) According to the formula, "the relative importance of generalized expectancy goes up as the situation is more novel or ambiguous and goes down as the individuals' experience in that situation increases" (p. 57). Duke and Nowicki (1972) and Duke (1973) have shown that this is supported in differential invocation of the generalized expectancy of locus of control as a mediating variable in interpersonal distance behavior. Specifically, they reported that when approaching people who were strangers (small amount of E'), responses were significantly correlated with the generalized expectancy of locus of control; but that when approaching people who were friends and family members (large amount of E'), the generalized expectancy of locus of control played no part in mediating responses.

Given this brief introduction to Rotter's basic concepts, we are now ready to present our social learning perspective on our four-phase model of human relationships. From the situational perspective, we propose that human behavior in a relationship may be seen as a varying series of interpersonal styles. In Rotter's terms, interpersonal styles may be translated into generalized expectancies. Thus, as depicted in Figure 5.5, our multiphasic model may now be reconceptualized as a series of situations, each of which evokes differing degrees and forms of generalized expectancies. Some examples may help explain our model. Note that Figure 5.5 is a replica of Figure 5.4 except for the replacement of interactional terms with social learning terms. According to social learning theory, on entering the choice phase a subject has few specific expectancies regarding a stranger because she or he has had few if any experiences with that person; the person therefore falls back on a generalized expectancy that is based upon her or his experiences in meeting similar people for the first time. Depending upon the person's previous experience with varieties of other people, his or her generalized expectancy will be the major determinant of whether or not to choose to begin a relationship. If the choice is made to pursue the relationship, then the person enters the beginning phase of the relationship. Here, because there are few actual experiences with the specific other, a new generalized expectancy will again determine behavior. The interpersonal style that a person may use in beginning this new relationship reflects a generalized expectancy based upon the previous success of that style; thus, this generalized expectancy is evoked in each interpersonal situation in which the person has few if any specific expectancies. It is assumed in social learning theory that as specific experiences with situations increase, the importance of generalized expectancies decrease (Rotter, 1975). Thus, we would expect that the use of a "favorite" interpersonal style will be apparent very early in relationships, but as specific experiences in interacting and communicating are amassed, normal individuals should show the potential at least to vary their interpersonal styles of behavior more as a function of specific events and experiences.

During the beginning phase the two interactants may be seen as "acquaintances"; if they mutually decide to further their relationship, the deepening phase is entered. We propose that the important transition to this third phase also is governed by generalized expectancies. This occurs because at the very least the individuals probably never have

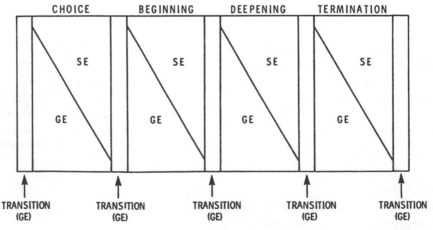

Fig. 5.5. A social learning theory conceptualization of the four-phase model.

deepened a relationship *with one another* specifically before and, at the most, they may never have progressed this far in any relationship. Individuals, therefore, must once again use interpersonal styles based on generalized expectancies learned from past experiences with people to determine behavior in the crucial passage from beginning to deepening phases. As was the case in the second phase, as the participants amass specific experiences in deepening a specific relationship, the relative importance of generalized expectancies will diminish as governors of interpersonal behavior.

The transition to termination of an ongoing relationship is also characterized by the reemergence of generalized expectancies as the most important determinant of interpersonal style. This assumption is based on the fact that few people have a great number of specific experiences in ending deep relationships. (We would assume that older people would have amassed more of these kinds of experiences than younger people.) The interpersonal style used for the final phase significantly determines successful and adaptive or unsuccessful and maladaptive interpersonal communication during this phase. For example, a person may have a maladaptive style for ending relationships; he may not like saying what is on his mind, but may use a Hostile-Submissive style of subtly picking on the other person until that person ends the relationship.

In a study reported below we have sought to begin gathering information bearing on the potential validity of our four-phase social learning reinterpretation of interpersonal processes, and our assumption that interpersonal styles may be seen as generalized expectancies. While numerous generalized expectancies exist, owing to its long research history, we have chosen to examine locus of control of reinforcement. As defined by Rotter (1966), locus of control reflects the degree to which people believe they have control over reinforcement contingencies. People who believe for the most part that reinforcements are beyond their control are termed externals while those who believe they generally have control over reinforcers are called internals. In a number of previous studies (see Lefcourt, 1976; Phares, 1976), persons with an external locus of control style show more maladjusted and anxious behavior than those with an internal locus of control. Working with a doctoral student (John Thibodeau), we sought to determine whether there were some interactional characteristics of externals which might explain in part their greater interpersonal difficulties. Within the circumplex model developed by Leary (1957) and extended by Carson (1969), we attempted to assess the degree to which externals may choose, in a maladaptive and perhaps self-defeating way, others with whom to *begin* relationships. From an initial sample of 220, forty volunteer, male college students were selected on the basis of (1) locus of control score as measured by the Adult Nowicki-Strickland Locus of Control Scale (ANSIE—Nowicki & Duke, 1974), and (2) interpersonal style as measured by the Interpersonal Check List (ICL—Leary, 1957). All subjects were shown, in counterbalanced order, two five-minute video tapes depicting a role-played "therapist" talking with a "client." In each case, the client manifested the same interpersonal style as the subject, but the style of the "therapist" was systematically varied. On one of the tapes the "therapist" was *complementary* (according to Leary's model) to the "client" (and, therefore, the subject); on the other tape, the "therapist" manifested an *anticomplementary* style.

After seeing the tapes, subjects were asked to complete measures of interpersonal comfort (the Comfortable Interpersonal Distance Scale—Duke & Nowicki, 1972) and interpersonal impact (the Impact Mesasge Inventory [IMI]—Kiesler et al., 1975, 1976; Perkins et al., 1979). These measures were designed to determine the degree of interpersonal comfort with the complementary and anticomplementary "therapists" as well as the subjects' abilities to identify correctly the interpersonal styles of the complementary versus the anticomplementary "therapists." We expected that if locus of control is a mediating variable in perception of or response to various interpersonal stimuli, some of the reasons for the well-established interpersonal difficulties among externals might be isolated. Since we were dealing with the beginning phase of a relationship, locus of control as a generalized expectancy should be significantly related to the process of the interaction. Analysis comparing CID and IMI scores of internals versus externals showed that externals chose significantly more frequently than internals to be attracted to people termed *anticomplementary* others. As we described earlier, complementarity in a dyad suggests that the interactors are likely to be secure and compatible with one another, while the opposite is true in an anticomplementary dyad. By choosing anticomplementary others, the external subjects appear to have been potentially hampering their interpersonal relationships from the very start.

While there were no differences between internals and externals in the accuracy of IMI perceptions of the actual interpersonal styles of the "therapists," it was noted that external subjects tended to misperceive *their own* interpersonal styles. Thus, externals tended to see themselves and act as if they were emitting interpersonal styles which were complementary to those persons to whom they were attracted. Externals were thus attracted to others with whom they *thought* they were complementary, but to whom they were in fact *anti*complementary. Further, informal post hoc analyses also suggested that the verbal styles of these externals were in fact complementary to those of the chosen other and should have resulted in a comfortable relationship. The *nonverbal* styles, however, were anticomplementary.

Thus, the external subjects appeared to be communicating in an incongruent fashion and their incongruence appeared to be enmeshed in some way with the complementarity dimension of their behavior. At first, this complexity puzzled us; upon pondering this interaction further, however, we were struck by our own tendencies to keep separate (as previous theorists and researchers seem to have done) the notions of complementarity and congruence. Based on our data, however, we believed that in addition to supporting our contention that measurable generalized expectancies played a role in interpersonal behavior and maladjustment, we may also have stumbled upon some systematic interaction between complementarity and congruence.

A MULTIDIMENSIONAL MODEL OF HUMAN INTERACTION

As reviewed above, Leary (1957) and Carson (1969) have used the concept of complementarity of interpersonal style or the lack of it to predict satisfaction levels of relationships. Basically, they believe that disordered individuals use a particular narrow behavior style frequently, *regardless of the situation*, to force others to respond to them in the same narrow way. But these authors do not describe *how* disordered individuals communicate these interpersonal styles. Kiesler et al. (1976), on the other hand, while they accept the circumplex as a way of describing behavior, do not wholly accept the assumption of complementarity of behavior. Instead, they focus on the incongruence between the verbal and nonverbal channels of communication as the basis for disordered behavior. Neither group of theorists appears to have taken the opportunity to assess the relative simultaneous contributions of complementarity and congruence on respondents' behavior. Elsewhere (Nowicki & Duke, 1979) we have suggested that perhaps the concurrent contributions of each of these variables needs to be included to reflect the true complexity of human behavior accurately.

Were the simultaneous contributions of congruence and complementarity both to be considered, the patterns of possible human interactions might be described by the diagram in Figure 5.6. According to this dual-factor integration, it is possible for complementary relationship behaviors to be communicated in congruent versus incongruent fashions. Thus, the impact of an anticomplementary interaction pattern might be tempered by congruent communication, or a complementary pattern's impact might be altered by incongruent communication.

The integration of congruence and complementarity into a model may resolve some of the conceptual and empirical difficulties among interactional theorists and researchers. Even though, however, potentially significant new sources of variance can be identified through this model, social learning theory suggests another source that may be equally important—the situation. The inclusion of the situational context allows for the construction of a meaningful taxonomy of interactional behaviors through a multilevel model (see Figure 5.7). In this multilevel model for the understanding and study of human interaction patterns, we have taken into account not one or two but three simultaneously acting levels of interactional information—*the relational, the communicational, and the situational.*

The relational level quite closely parallels the aspect of interactions studied by Leary (1957), Carson (1969), and most recently, Benjamin (McLemore & Benjamin, 1979). At this level, the complementarity, anticomplementarity, and/or noncomplementarity of a relationship is the focus of experience and study. For many researchers, the relational component has been viewed as the single most important aspect of interactional behaviors. We suggest that while it is important, it shares its importance with communicational and situational components in creating a *total interactional constellation.*

While the relational level focuses on how the interpersonal styles of two people fit or do not fit together, the communicational level of information deals with the degree to which there is congruence versus incongruence among various communication channels. Kiesler and his followers have been at the forefront of those who believe that the primary source of interactional maladjustment will eventually be found within the realm of congruence/incongruence. Again, we propose that communicational congruence is but one of at least three main interaction constellation factors.

The interpersonal impact, the appropriateness of a behavior, the very normality of a particular behavior, does not lie within the behavior itself. Rather, these aspects of behav-

	CONGRUENT COMMUNICATION	INCONGRUENT COMMUNICATION
COMPLEMENTARY BEHAVIOR	CONGRUENT COMPLEMENTARITY	INCONGRUENT COMPLEMENTARITY
ANTICOMPLEMENTARY BEHAVIOR	CONGRUENT ANTICOMPLEMENTARITY	INCONGRUENT ANTICOMPLEMENTARITY

Fig. 5.6. The interaction between congruence and complementarity.

iors are determined by the context in which the behavior occurs. Thus, a simple behavior such as laughing can be harmless and appropriate at a party where one has been told a joke, but grossly inappropriate in another setting such as the funeral of a friend or close relative. We believe that in addition to the relational and communicational levels of inter-action, therefore, all human interactions must be evaluated in light of their context and that the interactions between congruence and complementarity must be seen within the dimension of situational appropriateness (adaptiveness) and situational inappropriateness (maladaptiveness). This situational component, we believe is a necessary part of the total interactional constellation as it is depicted in Figure 5.7.

With the addition of the situational level, the total interactional constellation that exists between two people becomes more meaningful. Given all three components of the model, it is possible to determine in a clear and more easily agreed-upon manner such characteristics of behavior as normality, adaptiveness, consistency, adjustment, and so on. Further, with the proposed interaction of these three levels, we can generate a 12-cell taxonomy of interactional behavior (see Table 5.1). Within this taxonomy, for example, the behavior manifested by a schizophrenic person might be classed as type XII—inappropriate-incongruent-noncomplementarity—while the behavior of a couple having intercourse at McDonald's would be deemed type VII—inappropriate-congruent-complementarity. In future developments of these notions, we believe that this taxonomy

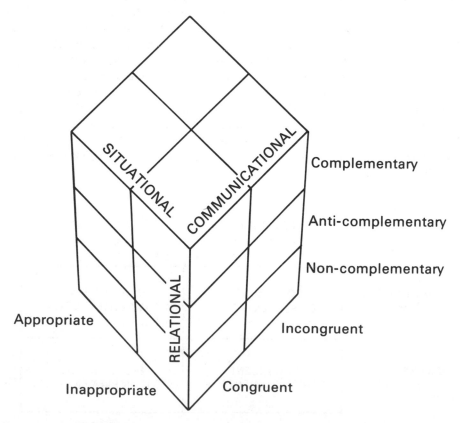

Fig. 5.7. A three-dimensional depiction of the multilevel model for the study and taxonomy of human interactional constellations.

TABLE 5.1. A TAXONOMY OF ADAPTIVE AND MALADAPTIVE INTERACTIONAL CONSTELLATIONS BASED ON THE MULTILEVEL MODEL DEPICTED IN FIGURE 5.7.

ADAPTIVE INTERACTIONAL CONSTELLATIONS	MALADAPTIVE INTERACTIONAL CONSTELLATIONS
Type I Interaction: Situation appropriate- congruent-complementarity	*Type VII Interaction:* Situation inappropriate- congruent-complementarity
Type II Interaction: Situation appropriate- congruent-anticomplementarity	*Type VIII Interaction:* Situation inappropriate- congruent-anticomplementarity
Type III Interaction: Situation appropriate- congruent-noncomplementarity	*Type IX Interaction:* Situation inappropriate- congruent-noncomplementarity
Type IV Interaction: Situation appropriate- incongruent-complementarity	*Type X Interaction:* Situation inappropriate- incongruent-complementarity
Type V Interaction: Situation appropriate- incongruent-anticomplementarity	*Type XI Interaction:* Situation inappropriate- incongruent-anticomplementarity
Type VI Interaction: Situation appropriate- incongruent-noncomplementarity	*Type XII Interaction:* Situation inappropriate- incongruent-noncomplementarity

Note: Contrary to previous theory and research, incongruence and anticomplementarity occur in both adaptive and maladaptive constellations.

will allow us to classify interactional patterns in ways not done before and with full cognizance of the primary variables identified by interactional researchers. In addition, we believe that our multilevel model allows for the extreme complexity of human behavior. This complexity is built in via the almost infinite number and forms of incongruent behavior (e.g., verbal disagreement with proxemic cues; voice tone disagreement with gestures, etc.), and via the variation in intensity and placement of individual styles in a Leary circumplex or a Benjamin structural analysis of social behavior.

The multilevel model of human interaction offers a broad perspective on human interaction, a perspective that integrates many of the foci of previous research and theory and encompasses the currently known significant sources of variation in human interactions. We suggest that this model may serve as the interactional theory parallel to the proverbial elephant of which we spoke at the beginning of this chapter. Each of the seekers of truth about the elephant knew his part of it best and assumed that his part was the whole animal. How much easier their task of generalization would have been had they "communicated" with their colleagues and accepted their colleagues' information about the beast as well as their own as valid. Surely, the true nature of the elephant would not long have remained a mystery.

To include relational (complementarity), communicational (congruence), and situational (situation) factors within one model increases the complexity of human interaction processes enormously. To do any less may shortchange the multifaceted functioning of the known organism and needlessly lead us into the trap in which the individual blind men found themselves. We hope our present model may serve as an impetus for future researchers who seek to study human interaction in all its complexity.

REFERENCES

Beier, E. G. *The silent language of psychotherapy.* Chicago: Aldine, 1966.

Carson, R. C. *Interaction concepts of personality.* Chicago: Aldine, 1969.

Duke, M. *Locus of control as a mediating variable.* Symposium paper. American Psychological Association, Montreal, 1973.

Duke, M. & Ekstrand, M. *Differential effects of dyadic complementarity/anticomplementarity in cooperative versus competitive tasks.* Unpublished manuscript. Emory University, Atlanta, 1980.

Duke, M. & Nowicki, S. A new measure and social-learning model for interpersonal distance. *Journal of Experimental Research in Personality,* 1972, **6,** 119–132.

Fierman, L. *Effective psychotherapy.* New York: Free Press, 1965.

Kiesler, D. J., Anchin, J. C., Perkins, M. J., Chirico, B. M., Kyle, E. M., & Federman, E. J. *The Impact Message Inventory.* Richmond: Virginia Commonwealth University, 1975; 1976.

Kiesler, D. J., Bernstein, A. J., & Anchin, J. C. *Interpersonal communication, relationship and the behavior therapies.* Richmond: Virginia Commonwealth University, 1976.

Ladd, M., Nowicki, S., & Duke, M. *Interpersonal congruence as a function of degree of importance of relationship and importance of situation.* Unpublished manuscript, Emory University, Atlanta, 1979.

Leary, T. *Interpersonal diagnosis of personality.* New York: Ronald, 1957.

Lefcourt, H. *Locus of control: Current trends in theory and research.* Hillsdale, N.J.: Erlbaum, 1976.

Lorr, M. & McNair, D. M. Expansion of the interpersonal behavior circle. *Journal of Personality and Social Psychology,* 1965, **2,** 823–830.

McLemore, C. W. & Benjamin, L. S. Whatever happened to interpersonal diagnosis? A psychosocial alternative to DSM-III. *American Psychologist,* 1979, **34,** 17–34.

Nowicki, S. & Duke, M. P. A locus of control scale for college as well as noncollege adults. *Journal of Personality Assessment,* 1974, **38,** 136–137.

Nowicki, S. & Duke, M. A social learning theory conceptualization of interpersonal relationships. In C. W. McLemore (Chair.), *New frontiers in interpersonal theory, research, and practice.* Symposium presented at the meeting of the American Psychological Association, New York City, September, 1979.

Perkins, M. J., Kiesler, D. J., Anchin, J. C., Chirico, B. M., Kyle, E. M., & Federman, E. J. *The Impact Message Inventory:* A new measure of relationship in counseling/psychotherapy and other dyads. *Journal of Counseling Psychology,* 1979, **26,** 363–367.

Phares, E. J. *Locus of control in personality.* Morristown, N.J.: General Learning Press, 1976.

Rotter, J. B. *Social learning theory and clinical psychology.* Englewood Cliffs, N.J.: Prentice-Hall, 1954.

Rotter, J. Generalized expectancies for internal versus external control of reinforcement. *Psychological Monographs,* 1966, **80** (Whole # 609).

Rotter, J. Some problems and misconceptions related to the construct internal versus external control of reinforcement. *Journal of Consulting and Clinical Psychology,* 1975, **43,** 56–67.

Rotter, J., Chance, J., & Phares, E. *Application of a social learning theory of personality.* New York: Holt, Rinehart & Winston, 1972.

Triandis, G. *Interpersonal Behavior.* Monterey, Calif.: Brooks/Cole, 1977.

Watzlawick, P., Beavin, J., & Jackson, D. D. *Pragmatics of human communication.* New York: Norton, 1967.

Chapter 6
Sequence, Pattern, and Style: Integration and Treatment Implications of Some Interpersonal Concepts*
Jack C. Anchin

This chapter represents an initial effort to delineate systematically the meanings of, interrelationships among, and treatment implications that stem from three concepts which figure prominently in my approach to clinical problems. These concepts are the interaction sequence, the interpersonal pattern, and the interpersonal style.

The precise rationale for this undertaking is presented in the first two sections of the chapter. In the first section I discuss several commonalities that transcend diverse therapeutic approaches, among the most important of which concerns central factors which appear to underlie enduring therapeutic change. The tentative hypothesis guiding my presentation is that an interpersonal perspective represents not only a viable and perhaps especially efficient treatment alternative in its own right, but that it can also serve as a central point of integration—a kind of bridge—for interrelating concepts and procedures defining other treatment approaches. This notion is illustrated in a later section by bringing together an interpersonal communication perspective with concepts and interventions emphasized in cognitive-behavioral approaches.

The second section briefly touches upon the importance of concepts as central mediators of psychotherapeutic practice. A central theme is that definite clarity as to the referents of and relations among concepts emphasized by interpersonal theorists, researchers, and practitioners is critical to enhancing the integrational potential of an interpersonal perspective. One chief argument in this context is that clinical concepts frequently imply a particular view of causation, and since concepts are frequently linked to technique, clinicians may unwittingly restrict their intervention options through the concepts emphasized in understanding the patient. Interpersonal approaches embrace a reciprocal deterministic view of causation, as defined by social learning theory (Bandura, 1977b). As this causal perspective is inherent in the three concepts examined here, their use may foster integration of a variety of concepts, principles, and intervention strategies in the overall effort to treat the individual patient.

* The author extends his appreciation to Dr. Edward J. Federman, Dr. Donald J. Kiesler, and Ms. Judy Glickman Zevin for their helpful comments on an earlier draft of this chapter.

Attention is turned in the third section to delineating specific referents of interaction sequences, interpersonal patterns, and the interpersonal style, particularly as these may facilitate an interpersonal understanding and treatment focus. Though necessarily discussed separately, in reality each concept provides a complementary perspective on the day-to-day interpersonal processes which are an integral part of a human life.

More specific therapeutic implications of the sequence, pattern, and style concepts are spelled out in the fourth and final section. These implications are delineated primarily in terms of descriptive, reflective, and enactive interventions—three broad, interlocking sets of clinical operations that may be systematically pursued in assessing and turning the patient's extratherapy interpersonal experiences to therapeutic advantage. A synthesis between interpersonal communication and cognitive-behavioral approaches is particularly emphasized in portions of this section.

PSYCHOTHERAPEUTIC COMMONALITIES

Despite the expanding array of psychotherapeutic approaches, a number of fundamental commonalities upon which the practice of individual therapy rests may be extracted. For example, individuals typically seek psychotherapy because they are suffering emotionally, and because their own and/or others' attempts to relieve this distress have failed. Most basically, entering treatment represents a communication by the patient that he or she is in pain and that he or she is "stuck" or rigidly entrenched in situations and behavioral patterns which bear some sensed but generally unclear relationship to this subjective distress. In entering treatment, the patient is further telling us that identifying and modifying these sources of emotional pain is a serious riddle whose solution requires professional help. Thus, while the patient's presenting complaints are usually explicitly couched in terms of specific symptoms, self-defeating thoughts, and/or interpersonal disabilities (Horowitz, 1979), the "third ear" hears the patient sending an implicit message upon which the entire psychotherapeutic enterprise rests: "I'm hurting, I'm stuck, and I need you to help me become unstuck so that my life can become a more gratifying experience."

An indeed, when all is said and done, this metamessage provides the stimulus for a given therapist's ensuing activities, irrespective of theoretical persuasion. The ultimate goal of any therapist is to help the patient move beyond his or her currently entrenched status into a position of expanded situational, behavioral, and/or experiential options. A psychotherapist's fundamental task is to provide input which, in catalytic fashion, fosters sufficient change to enable the patient to achieve, on a reasonably stable basis, more gratifying levels of functioning, including more consistently experiencing positive affective states in his or her day-to-day living.

Of course, beliefs about precisely what needs changing (targets of therapist input), specific forms this input should take (technical interventions), and what comprises meaningful and successful change (goals of treatment) vary considerably across therapists. In fact, as many obviously oversimplified summations of the targets, forms, and desired outcomes of therapist input may be formulated as there are distinct systems for conducting individual psychotherapy. Nevertheless, transcending the specifics of psychotherapists' respective working models is a shared metagoal which concerns helping the patient achieve a more gratifying and pleasurable existence. In the end, this is what psychotherapy is all about. This metagoal explains, in overarching fashion, why the analytically oriented therapist attempts to help a patient resolve longstanding conflicts concerning father, why the Gestalt therapist seeks to have the patient recontact and integrate disowned feelings of power, and why the behavior therapist works at increasing a patient's assertiveness skills. Further, were it not for the operation of this common metagoal, it would be difficult to understand the very feasibility and pragmatic value of the clear shift toward therapeutic eclecticism taking place among clinical psychologists (Garfield & Kurtz, 1976, 1977). Psychotherapists of different theoretical persuasions are ultimately motivated by the same purpose, despite their different ways of looking at, thinking about, and intervening in the patient's distress.

That certain commonalities, and not just differences, pervade the psychotherapies is vividly underscored by Bergin and Lambert's (1978) review of treatment outcome studies. They conclude that describing therapeutic operations and examining treatment outcomes from the standpoint of specific school designations is of limited value when it comes to therapy as practiced; that however therapy is practiced, it produces both internal and external changes; and that with the exception of a few behavioral methods for certain circumscribed disorders, it is thus far apparent that diverse treatment approaches are "about equally effective with the broad spectrum of outpatients to whom they are typically applied" (p. 170; see also Frank, 1979; Parloff, 1980). Integration among therapeutic approaches may proceed more speedily when explicit recognition and discussion of such convergencies occurs alongside examination of elements which differentiate treatment systems (see Goldfried, 1980b; Reisman, 1971).

A related point of convergence that emerges with particular clarity concerns the central processes underlying therapeutic changes engendered by effective treatment. Discussions and reviews by a number of clinical researchers and practitioners of diverse theoretical orientations (e.g., Bandura, 1977a; Frank, 1973; Frank et al., 1978; Goldfried, 1980a; Lazarus, 1971; Murray & Jacobson, 1978; Raimy, 1975; Strupp, 1969, 1973) point with compelling consistency to the working hypothesis that *the enduring improvements in day-to-day functioning and the sense of emotional well-being which lie at the heart of positive outcome are centrally linked to changes in three interdependent domains: the patient's customary ways of interacting with others, the attitudes he or she maintains toward others, and the beliefs he or she holds about him or herself.* This is likely to be the case even in successful treatment of circumscribed problems such as phobias (see Andrews, 1966). Indeed, perhaps differences in therapeutic operations that purport to define different therapeutic schools "are not as clear cut . . . as school designation implies" (Bergin & Lambert, 1978, p. 171), and perhaps diverse treatment approaches seem to be "about equally effective with the broad spectrum of outpatients," because in one form or another, directly or indirectly, these operations target and effect change in these three central domains.

This emerging perspective about core ingredients in therapeutic change dovetails in striking fashion with the central, explicit, and immediate foci of interpersonal approaches to psychotherapy, as reflected in chapters in this volume. As used here, interpersonal refers to "that which one person does, overtly or covertly, in relation to another person who, in some sense, is the object of this behavior" (McLemore & Benjamin, 1979, p. 19). The reference to covert activities makes explicit the important role of affective and cognitive processes as these co-occur with the overt elements of ongoing social functioning (e.g., Kiesler, Bernstein, & Anchin, 1976; Peterson, 1977). Further, it is important to bear in mind that these other persons need not be physically present (i.e., they may be cognitively represented [Carson, 1979]), and that the object of these overt and covert social behaviors may be oneself (McLemore & Benjamin, 1979). Thus, from the very outset of treatment, interpersonal therapists place the patient's covert and overt relational behaviors front and center as these occur in relation to self and other(s).

These distinctive, defining features of an interpersonal perspective signal the most recent resurgence of interest (see Wiggins, in press) in interpersonal conceptualizations and interventions to be an exciting and important development in the contemporary practice of individual psychotherapy and behavior change. Juxtaposed with previously cited discussions of the centrality of changes in self/other phenomena in enduring clinical improvement, *it may be that an interpersonal perspective represents not only a viable and perhaps particularly efficient approach to clinical problems in its own right, but more importantly, it may also serve as a bridge for integrating concepts and therapeutic procedures that characterize other treatment approaches.*

Examining the validity of this broad hypothesis is a long-term venture. Nevertheless, even an initial effort in this direction will fare poorly if one attempts to shift directly from the general assumptions about central factors involved in adaptive and maladaptive functioning upon which this hypothesis rests, to concrete efforts to assess and effect change in disordered interpersonal behavior. More specific concepts are necessary for the clinician to traverse these two poles; this mediating function is discussed next.

CLINICAL CONCEPTS, CAUSALITY, AND PSYCHOTHERAPIST BEHAVIOR

The importance of terminology in mediating clinical work is irrefutable. A principal component of any clinician's distinctive therapeutic system, however doctrinaire or eclectic, consists of the interrelated body of descriptive and explanatory concepts he or she uses for understanding adjusted and maladjusted functioning. Moreover, this matrix of concepts and propositions heavily influences the clinician's intervention options and priorities.

At the level of concrete therapist functioning, descriptive and explanatory schemata are central mediators of the therapist's perceptual, conceptual, and behavioral activities throughout the therapeutic transaction. Perceptual ramifications include the particular cognitive, affective, and/or behavioral phenomena especially attended to by the therapist as he or she listens to and observes the patient. Conceptual translations include the manner in which he or she organizes, interrelates, and interprets the patient's verbal and nonverbal (multichanneled) productions; the kinds of inferences drawn about aspects of the patient's behavior, experiences, and life situation which remain unexpressed and unobserved; and the specific treatment strategies that are planned over the course of therapy. Behaviorally, a therapist's system dictates precisely where, when, and how he or she enters the patient's stream of multichanneled productions with his or her own associations and productions.

Given these multiple effects, it behooves any therapist to work continually at making explicit to himself principal concepts and propositions which comprise the structure underlying his or her clinical understandings. Ford and Urban (1963) and Kiesler (1971) note the degree to which many therapists remain vague, even unaware, as to important elements of the conceptual systems underlying their therapeutic behavior. To the extent that the therapist can achieve this articulation, however, he or she enhances his or her capacity to function in a more systematic and in turn more effective manner with his or her patients.

Interaction sequence, interpersonal pattern, and interpersonal style are three concepts which play a particularly salient role in interpersonal approaches to understanding and modifying disordered human behavior (see, e.g., Benjamin, 1979, in press; Carson, 1969; Kiesler, Bernstein, & Anchin, 1976; Lorr, Bishop, & McNair, 1965; Lorr & McNair,

1963, 1965; McLemore & Benjamin, 1979; Peterson, 1977, 1979a, 1979b). Yet little discussion has been oriented toward systematically examining the conceptual and operational interconnections among these terms. This chapter undertakes this task, emphasizing the particular manner in which these concepts may mediate understanding and intervening in the individual's problematic extratherapy relationships, or the EO and OE meaning frames of interpersonal communication (Kiesler, Bernstein, & Anchin, 1976).

As many authors in this volume make clear, a major focus of an interpersonal therapist's attention is the patient-therapist relationship, which may provide a microcosmic representation of the self-defeating ways patients interact. It should also be recognized, however, that interpersonal therapists frequently focus upon these interpersonal issues as they manifest themselves in the patient's significant interactions with others. Among the five principal sets or foci of therapeutic operations in interpersonally oriented treatment, Sullivan (1940) specifically included "processes which clarify the action in some recent interpersonal situation, perhaps one in a relatively durable relationship with some person often discussed in the interviews" (p. 191). This focus is essential, especially from the standpoint of fostering generalization. As I will illustrate, the concepts of interaction sequence, interpersonal patterns, and interpersonal styles facilitates systematic, therapeutic handling of this extratherapy material.

It is necessary and useful to clarify these concepts for several other reasons as well. Therapists who employ them need to facilitate reliability in their usage. Without explicitness about the events to which concepts refer, "confusion will result. Different workers will not be able to employ the concepts in reliable fashion. The same term will mean different things to different people; the same concept will be used by the same person to refer to different events at different times. Communication will be poor, and reliable observations will be unlikely" (Ford & Urban, 1963, p. 38). These adverse consequences of terminological inexplicitness are certainly avoidable. My presentation of my own perspective on referential and operational relationships among these pivotal interpersonal concepts is intended to encourage the reader to examine critically his or her own definitions. The emergence of points of overlap as well as of dissimilarity is useful to the extent that this translates into definitional refinement.

Achieving clarity about these concepts also represents a necessary step in optimizing the interpersonal perspective's potential to serve the aforementioned bridging function between other therapeutic approaches. Identifying the distinctive phenomena encompassed by an interaction sequence, interpersonal pattern, and interpersonal style enables more precise designation of "entry points" for concepts and procedures from other approaches to enhance assessment, understanding, and modification of interpersonal maladjustment.

Lastly, the need to achieve explicitness about referents of particular clinical concepts is linked to the fact that usually inherent within the specific concepts emphasized by a given clinician are assumptions about the locus of fundamental causes of human behavior. Of particular importance, this causal conception has a marked impact upon the nature of and priority values assigned to the clinician's repertoire of therapeutic operations (see, e.g., Bandura, 1969, 1974, 1978; Mahoney, 1977).

Interactionist conceptions of causality (Ekehammer, 1974; Endler & Magnusson, 1976), and more specifically the reciprocal deterministic model defined by social learning theory (Bandura, 1977b; 1978), have made it abundantly clear that both internal and external variables are operative in human maladjustment. Causation from the reciprocal deterministic standpoint is represented schematically as $\overset{P}{\underset{B \longleftrightarrow E}{\diagup \diagdown}}$, with B representing an individual's overt behavior, P internal-personal (i.e., cognitive-affective) factors, and E the external environment; an interpersonal perspective emphasizes defining the latter component primarily in terms of *other persons* (see Carson, 1979; Golding, 1977; Kiesler, Bernstein, & Anchin, 1976; Peterson, 1977). Causal processes are construed as an ongoing, triadic, reciprocal interaction among these interlocking components:

> persons cannot be considered causes independent of their behavior. It is largely through their actions that people produce the environmental conditions that affect behavior in a reciprocal fashion. The experiences generated by behavior also partly determine what individuals think, expect, and can do, which in turn, affect their subsequent behavior. [Bandura, 1978, pp. 345–346.]

One important clinical implication of this view is that, considering the intricate tie between concepts and technique, therapists who persist in emphasizing either an internal or external deterministic view of chief sources of a patient's distress may unnecessarily restrict their intervention options in attempting to alleviate the distress that precipitates entering treatment. As will become apparent, however, the interaction sequence, interpersonal pattern, and interpersonal style concepts embody the reciprocal deterministic viewpoint. Their usage in clinical contexts therefore opens the way toward a synthesis of specific concepts and interventions associated with different therapeutic systems.

The next two sections are devoted to defining these three concepts and delineating their treatment implications. But before proceeding, it may be helpful to orient the reader by providing an overview of my perspective. The general conception of abnormality to which I adhere (presented in greater detail in Kiesler, Bernstein, & Anchin, 1976) assumes that the patient's distress is the momentary and cumulative result of overgeneralized, rigid, and extreme ways, or styles, of interacting with significant others in his or her daily living. The patient's rigid styles are anchored in the Interpersonal Circle (Leary, 1957; Lorr & McNair, 1965, 1966), and are reciprocally related to equally constricted ways of construing these others as well as him or herself. In conducting therapy, however, that is geared toward increasing the patient's interpersonal flexibility—i.e., expanding the range of ways the patient may comfortably interact and concomitantly the range of self- and other-construals—the interpersonal style is most accurately viewed as a summary label or a central theme which encompasses the range of more concrete, specific, self-defeating interpersonal patterns which are played out from day to day. These patterns constitute the primary targets of therapeutic interventions. They amount to recurrent and lawful, hence predictable, relationships among the individual's ongoing overt and covert processes in relation to other's multichanneled behaviors in particular settings. While all persons engage in enactment of specific, characteristic interpersonal patterns, those of the psychotherapy patient are especially rigid, extreme, and most important, sufficiently painful in their consequences to trigger the search for professional help. The regularities which define interpersonal patterns, however, are embedded within and therefore emerge through detailed examination of the live, ongoing, behavioral exchange process which characterizes the interaction sequence. It is to a more detailed discussion of these concepts that I now turn.

THREE INTERPERSONAL CONCEPTS

Interaction Sequences

The interaction sequence has consistently been identified as the fundamental unit of analysis for studying live, ongoing human interaction processes (e.g., Thibaut & Kelley,

1959; Raush, 1965; Carson, 1969; Peterson, 1968, 1977; Kiesler, Bernstein, & Anchin, 1976). This concept provides an initial way of ordering that complex process, and when applied to any interaction between two persons, can be defined as the ongoing, reciprocally interconnected series of overt multichanneled behavioral exchanges which spin out during the finite time period over which the interaction transpires. Thus, two persons come together and say things to one another, while simultaneously enacting an array of nonverbal behaviors which implicitly define the nature and quality of their relationship at that time. This mutually determinative exchange process continues for a particular duration, be it seconds, minutes, or hours, and the two interactants eventually part, perhaps coming together again at some future time to engage in another time-bound series of behavioral exchanges.

It is obvious from our experience, however, that particularly with those persons who play some significant role in our lives, any interaction entails far more than overt behavioral exchange. Indeed, the very meaning and impact of an interaction stems from the fact that, simultaneous with the flow of overt events, each interactant continuously engages in a rapidly firing, complex, yet organized array of covert affective and cognitive processes. These processes influence the perception and interpretation of the overt acts, their nature and course, and the personal and relational meanings that are derived from them. Achieving a comprehensive understanding of the relationship between what people overtly say and do vis-à-vis one another and what goes on in their respective internal-personal worlds during the pervasive human activity of social interaction necessitates capturing as much of this "inner world" data as possible.

Many perspectives have something to say about these internal processes, and none has an exclusive hold on the truth. Consequently, consideration must be devoted to how particular internal processes that are highlighted by different approaches to behavior sequentially interact with and complement one another; selected variables and constructs must not be dismissed too rapidly because of particular theoretical roots. So, for example, person perception research (Schneider, Hastorf, & Ellsworth, 1979), analyses and investigations of behavior from a social learning perspective (see, e.g., Bandura, 1977b, 1978; Mischel, 1973), writings of cognitive-behavioral therapists (see, e.g., Mahoney, 1974, 1977), analytically oriented approaches (e.g., Meissner & Nicholi, 1978), and discussions by interpersonally oriented theorists and researchers (chapters in this volume; cf. Golding, 1980) point to broad sets of affective and cognitive operations which influence live, ongoing interactive behavior to varying degrees. Though by no means exhaustive, some of the internal operations which in integrative fashion are an integral aspect of social discourse include processes of interpersonal "construal" and trait "attribution," maintenance of "expectancies" regarding momentary and cumulative outcomes of behavior emitted by self, "self-evaluative," "self-reinforcement," and "self-statement" processes, harboring of "generalized assumptions," "fantasy" activities vis-à-vis other, "mechanisms of defense" against particular behavioral inclinations, experiencing of specific affective states and reactions, "selective attention and inattention" processes, and maintaining particular conceptions and feelings about oneself.

These and certainly other cognitive-affective processes, defining the P component of the $\begin{smallmatrix} & P & \\ B & \longleftrightarrow & E \end{smallmatrix}$ schema, comprise the extremely complex network of internal activities and transformational mechanisms which regulate and in reciprocal fashion are regulated by the overt events that characterize an interpersonal exchange as this spins out over time. During a live transaction, then, the finite series of action-reaction chains (Peterson, 1977a) constituting the overt level of the sequence cannot realistically be divorced from co-occuring covert activities and transformations.

In addition to their crucial role as regulatory factors governing the nature of sequential behavioral exchanges during a specific interaction, two other reasons for the need for explicitness about internal processes as these pertain to a given sequence must be cited. First, an individual's "perception of the people and situations he encounters, the way he behaves to them and they to him, his thoughts about his feelings and his thoughts about the behavior and feelings of others, are coded by the individual and stored in symbolic form" (Hinde, 1979, p. 31). Particularly in significant relationships, these symbolically stored experiences are often retrieved at some point after the interaction and/or prior to future interactions. Through subsequent processing of these retrieved symbols, additional and/or revised cognitive and affective meanings may be derived from prior sequences, and these elaborated meanings will have implications for future behavioral exchanges, not only with this individual but probably with others as well. These "meaning-making" activities during intervals *between* interactions are often a useful focus of therapeutic investigation in the effort to establish how a patient keeps him or herself locked into rigid, hence self-defeating ways of interacting.

Second, internal processes and experiences command explicit attention because they are centrally implicated in the vital reward/cost consequences engendered through interpersonal exchanges. As Longabaugh (1963), Carson (1969), and Hinde (1979) point out, interpersonal behavior is purposive, or goal-directed, and the degree of goal attainment during a given sequence as well as across series of sequences influences for each interactant the relative reward/cost value of the relationship and the interactions of which it is comprised. Each participant may actually be pursuing several goals during an interaction each to varying degrees of awareness. For example, two persons get together with the explicit mutual goal of completing a work task, but with the less acknowledged, secondary goal of catching up on what each has been up to outside of work in recent days. Among the variety of objectives that may be pursued, however, interpersonally oriented therapy emphasizes the degree of satisfaction attained in regard to that basic human goal of maintaining and/or enhancing personal security, one's fundamental feelings of personal value and acceptability, as reflected experientially in one's sense of self-worth and esteem (Sullivan, 1953).

Carson (1969), integrating particularly the formulations of Sullivan (1953), Thibaut and Kelley (1959), and Secord and Backman (1961, 1965), has developed the compelling argument that the extent to which one effectively maintains and/or enhances feelings of personal security through an interaction is mediated by the degree to which relevant elements of the self-concept are implicitly confirmed and reinforced through feedback inherent in the behaviors enacted by the other. Further, as stressed by a number of contributors to this volume, interpersonal behavior is strongly (though usually unconsciously) shaped in a manner designed to evoke these particular, confirmatory behaviors from other. This effort to induce self-concept validating responses, it should be noted, is inseparable from attempting to define the other, and thereby to structure the relationship in a particular way. Through its security-maintaining consequences, successfully evoking responses from the other which support the self-concept is rewarding, a state of affairs which is phenomenologically reflected as positive affective states. Conversely, interpersonal response feedback disconfirming one's particular conceptions about oneself and the relationship poses a threat to personal security, phenomenologically associated with anxiety. In this regard, for Sullivan "anxiety" was a generic term which encompassed a variety of emotional states experienced in conjunction with disruptions to one's feelings of personal security; thus Sullivan subsumed guilt, shame, fear, and other forms of emotional anguish under this term (Chapman, 1978).

Some cautionary words here. Rare is it the case that persons are acutely aware that a major goal underlying their interactive behavior entails preserving and/or enhancing feelings of acceptability and self-worth, and in fact they are usually quite unaware of this covert agenda. In addition, as the literature on resource exchange suggests (see Swensen, 1973; Hinde, 1979), it would be short-sighted to contend that the momentary and cumulative reward/cost consequences incurred through interpersonal interactions have to do exclusively with the extent of self-concept and by implication relationship validation which one elicits. The range of goods and services bargained for, and therefore the sources of rewards and costs, are numerous in the interpersonal sphere. Nevertheless, outcome factors associated with preservation and/or enhancement of personal security through relationship definition and self-concept validation are the "bottom line" in a vast majority of interactions with significant others, operating "in the main at a general, metacommunicative level. . . . They are therefore largely independent of more specific rewards and costs that may be experienced as a consequence of the exchange of particular commodities" (Carson, 1969, p. 149). Especially in the case of neurotic and characterologically disordered persons seen in psychotherapy, conceptions of self and feelings of self-worth invariably emerge as mediational internal-personal factors of critical importance to understanding the relationship between characteristic interpersonal exchanges engaged in by a patient and his or her emotional suffering.

Any delineation of important aspects of interaction sequences must also recognize their embeddedness within particular settings (Peterson, 1977). Attention to the situationally bound nature of human behavior has, of course, been one of the principle contributions of social learning approaches to understanding behavior; an account of interactive behavior that overlooks the environmental conditions within which the exchange occurs is incomplete. Like the verbal and nonverbal stimulus array interactants continuously present to one another, the precise environmental setting—whether it is the work place, a dating situation, the home, or what have you—serves as input that will be decoded and construed in particular ways. In turn, these ascribed meanings will exert a degree of influence upon the nature of the interaction sequence.

To summarize, then, an interaction sequence refers to the live, ongoing process of overt behavioral exchange which transpires between interactants in a specific setting over a finite period of time. This series of overt exchanges is bound in turn to ongoing cognitive and affective processes on the part of each interactant in complex ways. In the most general sense, these covert processes govern and are governed by overt events during any given interaction. Further, through cognitive processing of an interaction as symbolically represented, persons generate additional cognitive and emotional meanings which influence the nature of future interactions. Also pointing to the critical role of covert processes throughout interaction sequences is the goal-directed nature of interpersonal behavior. A number of goals may actually be pursued by each interactant throughout a particular sequence. Nevertheless, particularly in interactions with significant others, maintaining and/or enhancing feelings of acceptability and self-worth through eliciting response feedback confirming a particular view of self represents a fundamental human goal. The degree of success one encounters in achieving this goal within and across interactions strongly influences the reward/cost consequences that accrue from important relationships. This reward/cost balance is phenomenologically reflected in one's momentary and cumulative emotional states.

In highlighting both the reciprocal relationships between A's and B's overt and covert behaviors as these spin out during the interpersonal encounter, as well as the affect-laden reward/cost consequences accruing to the interactants through the exchange, I have clearly emphasized the "process" of the interaction sequence. Issues of content are equally important. For example, what is the precise nature of an interactant's self-concept, validation of which is so central during interactions with significant others? What is the content of the self-statements he or she generates during the interaction? And in precisely what terms does he or she construe the other as the interaction proceeds? What are the expectancies into which these construals translate? Further, just what are the outcomes he or she anticipates will be forthcoming if he or she emits a particular kind of interpersonal response? And in this regard, in what terms do we characterize or describe those behaviors which are exchanged at the overt level? These are the kinds of questions which concern us when we address the issue of the content of interaction sequences when working with patients in psychotherapy.

The categories of the Interpersonal Circle, as first developed by Leary and his colleagues (Leary, 1957) and subsequently refined by Lorr and McNair (1963, 1965, 1966), provide a useful system for approaching these content issues. Of course, the actual terms in which a patient may describe during therapeutic exploration his or her views and beliefs about him or herself, how he or she construes others, and the overt behaviors enacted during an interaction, may differ considerably from the actual terminology of the Interpersonal Circle categories. Importantly, however, these descriptions are usually classifiable within Interpersonal Circle category terms. Clinically, these Interpersonal Circle translations are essential because those particular categories which are identified as most relevant to a given patient serve as individual difference dimensions, in turn facilitating development of hypotheses as to the content of other, related internal processes (e.g., assumptions, self-statements, etc.) whose descriptions and analysis may be indicated during the course of treatment. Thus, the patient whose overt behavior during sequential exchanges tends to be primarily inhibited and Detached is far more likely to hold some such assumption as "People inevitably hurt you once they get to know you well" than to believe that "It's critical that everyone accept and think highly of you." The latter assumption would more likely be maintained by the patient whose overt behavior during interaction sequences proves excessively Affiliative and Sociable.

It thus becomes apparent that comprehensive description of an interaction requires delineation of the process and content of the sequence, at both overt and covert levels. Clinically, attaining this information about a patient's actual interpersonal exchanges is vital in that interaction sequences constitute the most pervasive arenas in which day-to-day living takes place; it follows that data necessary for understanding a person's adaptive and maladaptive functioning should emerge through detailed study on his or her naturally occurring interactions (Kiesler, Bernstein, & Anchin, 1976; Wachtel, 1977).

Applying these ideas to the dyad, acquiring comprehensive characterization of a specific interaction sequence from its members would amount to gathering a detailed account of *what happened*—behaviorally, cognitively, and affectively—on the part of each participant over the course of the exchange. One would be interested in what the interactants said to each other, what they did, what each was thinking about, how each was feeling, what each thought the other meant, and so on. These, of course, are precisely the kinds of data that are targeted during the probing and exploration that transpires when examining particular interaction sequences with couples in marital treatment.

In the case of the individual patient, however, such joint examination of sequences is obviously precluded by the absence of the relevant dyadic partner(s). In the effort to understand what these difficult relationships are all about, how the patient contributes, and more specifically on particular interaction sequences, is available. But this by no means minimizes the value of undertaking detailed examination of their interactional engagements with patients. In pursuing the goal of increasing the patient's interpersonal flexibility, of expanding his or her interpersonal options so that previously avoided responses become associated with higher probabilities of occurrence in appropriate situations, it can be quite beneficial to pinpoint precisely what the patient does—and doesn't do—overtly and covertly during specific exchanges with other persons with whom he or she becomes self-defeatingly engaged.

The generic term which I use for this detailed work around patients' interaction sequences is Interactional Analysis. This procedure incorporates three broad phases or components, which I refer to as *descriptive*, *reflective*, and *enactive* interventions. While they are discussed in greater detail in the next section, the reader may benefit at this point by a brief definition of these components.

Descriptive interventions are designed to foster a reconstruction of concrete interactions with persons in the patient's extratherapy environment. An entire sequence may be reconstructed, or the patient and therapist may focus only on an especially significant portion of the interaction. The goal is to obtain a clear picture of the patient's ongoing overt and covert activities before, during, and after the interaction, particularly as these processes relate to distinctive, ongoing behaviors of his or her dyadic partner at the time. Reflective interventions entail stepping back from the sequence in order to derive still greater meaning from the interaction. Emphasis is placed upon extracting and understanding patterned relationships between the patient's and other's ongoing activities during the exchange, as well as drawing out specific implications for change. Enactive interventions subsume interventions explicitly designed to foster actual risk taking by the patient in these problematic situations. Most obviously, these risks involve experimenting with alternative overt behaviors in relation to other, but may also include having the patient experiment with modifications in covert aspects of his or her maladaptive responding.

Before we discuss these three components of interactional analysis further, it is necessary to examine several other features of interaction sequences. As will become apparent, these considerations immediately shift us to another level of analysis, that of the interpersonal pattern.

Interpersonal Patterns

The previous discussion of sequences has repeatedly emphasized the interdependency between overt and covert events on the part of A and B as these spin out and reciprocally influence one another over the course of an interaction. Implicit is the idea that in studying sequences one is less interested in isolated bits or units of behavior per se—whether this involves a statement, a nonverbal act, or a particular thought—and more concerned with the *transition, movement*, and *ordering* between consecutive events on the part of the interactants. The concept of an interpersonal pattern represents an especially meaningful way of capturing this level of information.

Following Hertel (1972), this "transition between two events . . . is labeled a contingency. The first event of a contingency is an antecedent event; the second a consequent event" (p. 424). Thus, if we break into an ongoing chain of interaction, a Dominant behavior by A could arbitrarily be considered an antecedent, and the immediately following Submissive response by B would be the consequent. Given the reciprocal relationships between behaviors during ongoing sequences, throughout the exchange an act by B which is demarcated as a consequent (the previously noted submissive response) is simultaneously an antecedent for A's subsequent response (which might be another dominant behavior), which itself then is not only a consequent but also an antecedent for B, and so on.

Stepping back and considering the sequence of overt and covert activities of the single interactant during the interpersonal exchange, it is still appropriate, and in fact quite useful, to think in terms of successive movements and transitions between the processes in which he or she engages. For example, at the outset of an interaction an individual may say to him or herself, "I know I'll make a fool out of myself"—a self-statement that is immediately followed by an overt response of silent withdrawal. This behavioral withdrawal is not only a consequent of his or her self-statement as well as an antecedent for the other's immediate next response, but importantly also acts as an automatic antecedent for the individual's own subsequent internal self-statement ("I'm safer this way. Nobody can hurt me now"). Therefore, we can also think in terms of the ongoing, successive movement among overt and covert processes on the part of a single interactant during an interpersonal exchange, though we do not want to lose sight of how they are organized around specifiable behaviors on the part of other. The utility of thinking in these terms is important to bear in mind when analyzing interaction sequences of the individual patient, since particular interest lies in highlighting relationships or successive transitions between the patient's distinctive, self-defeating, overt and covert activities in relation to particular kinds of input provided by other.

Still another feature of interaction sequences that should be explicated concerns the fact that events occuring during such sequences are seldom connected in random, hence totally unpredictable, fashion. Rather, they are typically related in a lawful, probabilistic way. There is some *meaningful organization* among processes transpiring between A and B during a sequence, though the nature of this organization and what it means about the relationship and the interactants typically becomes clear only through repeated observations.

Theoretically, the values of such interresponse probabilities can be mathematically specified. To return to Hertel (1972): "The probability with which a consequent event is expected to occur given its antecedent is labeled a contingency magnitude. The contingency magnitude indicates the likelihood that a process will move from the antecedent event in question to a given consequent" (p. 424). The contingency magnitude has also been referred to as a conditional probability (McLemore & Benjamin, 1979) and a transition probability (e.g., Raush, 1972). Representative empirical investigations of transition probabilities in interaction sequences have targeted exchanges between normal and hyperaggressive boys (Raush, 1965), dialogues between college students (Jaffe, 1968), family interchanges (Taylor, 1970), interactions in couple dyads (Gottman, Markman, & Notarius, 1977; Margolin, 1977), Rogerian and Ellisonian psychotherapy interviews (Lichtenberg & Hummel, 1976), and the interaction between a patient and a Gestalt therapist during a segment of treatment using a split-chair technique (Benjamin, 1979). As an extremely simplified example of such probabilities, in response to B's antecedent, Dominant behavior, the probability of A reciprocally responding Submissively may be quite high, reflected in a transition probability of .90, while the likelihood of a reciprocally Dominant response may be exceedingly low, reflected in a transition probability value of .10. The latter response might occur, but the likelihood is small.

The assumption here is that human behavior occurs in probabilistic, i.e., not in simple one-to-one fashion. The probability of a particular response to an immediately preceding behavior is neither 1.00 nor 0 but falls somewhere in between (Raush, 1972). Or as Bandura (1978) succinctly puts it, "events produce effects probabilistically rather than inevitably" (p. 345).

This inherent orderliness among events during interaction sequences is technically referred to as "redundancy," which designates the actual extent to which events transpiring over the sequence deviate from a random order of occurrence. The term "pattern" expresses the same idea (Danziger, 1976). Thus, in reference to a dyad, the concept of an interpersonal pattern can be defined as the distinctive, lawful relationships between the two persons' overt and covert behaviors over the course of the exchange process. The regularity to the sequence follows from the fact that to the extent that the successive series of transitions between two persons' activities are related in lawful ways, then by definition the persons reciprocally impose constraints upon the behaviors each will enact.

It is also important to bear in mind that since interaction sequences are encased within specific settings, the latter also exert influence upon the magnitude of probabilistic relationships among overt and covert behaviors exchanged and experienced. Since it is most accurate to think in terms of classes of situations, it is predictable that when specific situations within a given class arise, the essential dyadic pattern relevant to this class will tend to recur. Indeed, it is usually only when the patterned relationships between A's and B's thoughts, feelings, and actions recur over successive interactions that this patterning in all its complexity becomes evident.

Considering once again any single *individual* within the broad context of his or her daily social functioning, we may also expect to find lawful interrelationships among his or her specific cognitive, affective, and behavioral processes as these spin out vis-à-vis classes of significant others under particular circumstances. These other persons represent a complex array of stimuli and are classifiable along numerous stimulus dimensions, e.g., their own multichanneled behavioral displays (defined in terms of Interpersonal Circle categories), sex, age, physical attractiveness, and so on. For any given individual, then, it becomes important to know the salient intersecting dimensions in terms of which others are subjectively, most meaningfully "classed." The individual's characteristic interpersonal patterns refer to these distinctive and recurrent probabilistically defined transitional regularities among particular covert and overt behaviors in relation to particular classes of others.

Raush (1972) expresses a similar idea when he defines personality as "transition probabilities between recurrent antecedent events and consequent cognitive, affective, and conative responses" (p. 292). And as Raush (1972) further notes, this view of human personality is quite consistent with Sullivan's (1953) well-known definition of personality as "the relatively enduring pattern of interpersonal situations which characterize a human life" (pp. 110–111). Just as patterns characterizing a dyad emerge through study of repeated interaction sequences, however, so too do the individual's distinctive interpersonal patterns, in all their overt and covert complexity, become evident only through scrutiny of his or her recurrent sequential exchanges with the particular other(s) in question.

The range and variety of patterns enacted by any given set of individuals may vary considerably. The ever-changing demands of the interpersonal world, however, are such that more adaptive living requires a capability to enact a reasonably varied, as opposed to a restricted, set of patterns. Therefore, considered in terms of the probabilistically based regularities which define interpersonal patterns, the adjusted and maladjusted individual may be distinguished by both the range of accessible, alternative ways each has for cognizing, feeling, and acting in relation to the multichanneled stimulus configurations presented by other persons in different situations, *as well as by the relative freedom or ease of movement among these alternatives.* In connection with his previously cited definition, Raush (1972) suggests that "in a narrow sense one might define personality as probabilistic tendencies toward change in specified directions" (p. 299). Often, the maladjusted person's problem is that he or she is locked into a highly constricted range of behavioral options which he or she is exceedingly prone to shift toward in relation to particular classes of others during specific sequences. Such rigidity exists overtly and covertly. Overtly, it is reflected in marked difficulty in making a transition from behaviors anchored in a preferred portion of the Interpersonal Circle to other sections when this transition would be more appropriate and adequate to the interpersonal input at hand. Constriction at the covert level includes persistently maintaining a delimited range of beliefs and attributions—again defined in terms of Interpersonal Circle categories—about self and other(s).

Over successive interactions, as these transpire in a single relationship and/or across several relationships, this impaired transitional capacity characterizing interpersonal rigidity eventuates in accumulation of negative social experiences. For example, by inflexibly "commanding" particular responses from other, the individual implicitly disconfirms differing relationship definitions other may be attempting to propose. The individual thus locks other into particular interpersonal positions, thereby effectively precluding mutuality, which would include more equitable negotiation of need fulfillment. These excessive and rigid response demands, whatever their particular nature, recurringly experienced by other become an aversive state of affairs. In turn, these aversive feeling states are likely to be reflected in negative countercommunications in their many, often subtle, guises, engendering within the rigid interactant subjective distress. Thus, while ultimately designed to maintain and/or enhance one's characteristic level of personal security, the negative social input consequences actually elicited by interpersonal rigidity end up threatening these very same feelings of acceptability and self-worth. In the long run, the psychotherapy patient has in effect unwittingly undermined his or her own psychological well-being—and often that of his or her interpersonal partners—by virtue of a severely limited capacity to shift into alternative patterns during interaction sequences.

As a simplified illustration of this differential transitional capacity distinguishing the adjusted and maladjusted individual, consider their respective reactions upon initially meeting the same work colleague. Initially, both may be oriented toward keeping some behavioral distance from this person, thinking about him in somewhat mistrustful terms, and registering mild feelings of suspiciousness. At some point, however, as successive interactions occur and this colleague begins to let himself be known more, person A may be far more likely than person B to simultaneously revise his appraisal of the colleague in a more favorable direction, experience a greater sense of trust, and reciprocally enact more Affiliative and Sociable behaviors. In essence, the probability of shifting to alternative overt and covert behaviors is greater for person A than for person B. The latter continues to respond toward this colleague in the same mistrustful, distancing fashion during the vast majority of interactional engagements, irrespective of the particular stance adopted by this other at the time. The rigidity of this interpersonal regularity or pattern—referring here to a lawfully related set of specific construals, expectations, and overt behaviors vis-à-vis this colleague—is thus interpretable in terms of not only person B's restricted set of overt and covert options, but equally crucial, the excessively high probability associated with their interrelated occurrence during sequential exchanges with this colleague. Conversely, far smaller probabilities are associated with making transitions to other Interpersonal Circle–based attributions and overt behaviors. This mutually reinforcing overt and covert "stuckness" on the part of person B may eventually elicit such negative countercommunications as reciprocal distancing or incongruent communications (e.g., physical approach during a shared work task but accompanied by lack of eye contact, subtly angry facial expressions, and so on).

In line with this conception of interpersonal patterns, the task of increasing a patient's flexibility in problematic extratherapy relationships necessitates first extracting from the patient's recurring interpersonal experiences those distinctive regularities among precise overt and covert processes that transpire before, during, and/or after specific exchanges and which appear to be strongly linked to his or her subjective distress. Further examination of treatment implications may be pursued following discussion of one more perspective on interpersonal functioning, that enabled through the interpersonal style concept.

Interpersonal Styles

Moving from interaction sequences to interpersonal patterns entails a shift toward a higher level of abstraction. An interaction sequence refers to a time-bound series of concrete behavioral exchanges which have cognitive and affective concomitants, while the interpersonal pattern represents a regularity among these processes that may be extracted from this and other sequences. As a "higher" level of consideration about specific actions constituting sequences (Swensen, 1973), the interpersonal pattern is more inferential. As applied to pscyhotherapy, this immediately highlights the need for continual testing, modification, and refinement of one's hypotheses as to what these patterns are all about, as Sullivan (1954) continually emphasized.

The concept of interpersonal style represents still another level of abstraction, beyond that of the interpersonal pattern. Specifically, it encompasses the idea that across the range of specific self-defeating patterns that a patient plays out with significant others over the course of his or her day-to-day sequences in specific situations, there is a central theme running through a great many of these patterns. It is this common thread or theme that I refer to as a patient's maladaptive interpersonal style. It is a unifying concept, enabling one to pull together and summarize the various self-defeating patterns a patient enacts under the roof of a single interpersonal label.

This conception of an interpersonal style, in incorporating the idea that there is a general character to the normal and abnormal individual's interpersonal behavior, coincides with Carson's (1969) definition of "style" as "a discernible tendency to enact sets [of interpersonal behavior] falling preponderantly, although often subtly, within a particular range of the interpersonal behavior circle" (p. 142). Though he was operating from a quite different perspective—that of ego psychology—Shapiro (1956) similarly emphasizes frequency and generality when he defines "style" as "a form or mode of functioning—the way or manner of a given area of behavior—that is identifiable, through a range of [a person's] specific acts" (p. 1).

This emphasis on generality is not inconsistent with the importance of external input in influencing social behavior. Persons, whatever their degree of adjustment, do tend to develop particular interpersonal stances with which they are most familiar and comfortable across the range of interpersonal situations and partners encountered (see Carson, 1969). As noted earlier, however, the crucial distinction between the normal and abnormal individual lies in the relative ease of movement or shifting to other sections of the Interpersonal Circle when this would be more appropriate and adequate to the interpersonal conditions at hand. As stated elsewhere (Kiesler, Bernstein, & Anchin, 1976), relative to the functioning of the maladjusted person, "in more normal functioning it seems plausible that greater flexibility characterizes the cognitive and affective domains. There is likely to be a broader range both in the kinds of meaning the individual assigns to others, and in the emotional engagements the individual experiences, respectively. Given this greater covert flexibility, a corresponding capacity for enacting more varied overt styles would be expected" (pp. 210–211). In contrast, as we move along the continuum from mild maladjustment to more severe psychopathology, there will be greater rigidity across the cognitive, affective, and social behavioral domains, meaning decreased ability to shift to alternative styles, though this can only be decoded at the level of specific patterns that are (and are not) enacted.

This distinction between an interpersonal pattern and an interpersonal style is illustrated by considering in greater detail two of the fifteen interpersonal styles identified by the Interpersonal Behavior Inventory (IBI—Lorr & McNair, 1967). In developing the Impact Message Inventory, Kiesler and his colleagues (Perkins et al., 1979) combined items comprising each of the fifteen IBI scales to construct fifteen paragraphs describing fifteen stylistically pure individuals. In the following descriptions of the Competitive and Nurturant styles, the notion of a style as incorporating a constellation of related but distinctive patterns becomes more vivid if one thinks of the defining items as descriptive of patterns:

Competitive: C is a person who strives for symbols of status and superiority to others. As a result he seeks membership in clubs and associations which have high prestige. He is known to direct the attention of others towards his accomplishments. One means of doing this is by volunteering for jobs that gain him the attention of others. C sets difficult goals for himself and tries to achieve them. However, even in friendly situations he reacts competitively toward others. He seizes upon opportunities to rival and surpass others and always contrasts unfavorably the accomplishments of others with his own. In group situations he neglects group goals to achieve individual prominence and avoids sharing credits for achievement with others. [Kiesler, 1979, p. 4.]

Nurturant: N listens sympathetically to others and gives help or counsel to people who are having difficulty. He reassures and comforts others when they are feeling low and puts aside his own work or pleasure if someone asks for help. He lends things he values to friends and is obliging and cooperative when asked to perform little services or favors. In fact, he does favors for others without being asked and often exhausts his energies being helpful to others. [Kiesler, 1979, p. 6.]

In line with these definitions, two distinctive interpersonal patterns enacted by the Competitive person in dyadic situations include directing the other's attention toward indicators of status (e.g., his accomplishments), while in other situations attempting to rival, surpass, and outdo the other. Each of these respective patterns would give the interactions in which they are embedded a different look, of course, but the Competitive stylistic theme ties them together. Similarly, a principally Nurturant individual may enact one pattern of providing sympathetic comfort and reassurance when another feels depressed, display another pattern of lending valued possessions to friends, and still a third pattern of cooperating if asked to do a favor.

The point is that each of these specific patterns speaks to a general interpersonal style. Moreover, since each pattern incorporates equally specific thoughts and feelings it is important to keep explicit that, while an interpersonal style seems initially to be defined primarily by reference to the overt behavioral component, the notion of generality inherent in the "style" concept implies that we can also talk about central themes running through the range of an individual's specific thoughts and feelings in interpersonal situations; "characteristic interpersonal styles are complemented by and intimately linked to particular ways [i.e, styles] of cognitively appraising and affectively experiencing other persons" (Kiesler, Bernstein, & Anchin, 1976, p. 205). Accordingly, the Competitive and Nurturant overt styles described above may each be expected to be inseparably tied to general ways or styles of thinking about and feeling toward others. Benjamin (in press) and Carson (1979) have made creative starts toward specifying cognitive and affective style correlates of different overt interpersonal behavioral styles.

Defined in these terms, the interpersonal style serves as a reference point (Rosch, 1975) in relation to which an individual's distinctive interpersonal patterns vis-à-vis particular classes of persons and/or interpersonal situations may be meaningfully organized. In this sense it is a kind of prototypical interpersonal pattern. For example, construing the Nurturant style as a prototypical pattern translates roughly into taking care of and helping other, feeling warmly toward other, and construing other as needing and likely to benefit from one's aid. These are the *core* features defining this style, abstractions culled from the specific patterns that an individual who is characterized by a predominantly Nurturant style as defined above is likely to play out during concrete exchanges with a range of others. In reality, of course, persons are rarely characterizable in terms of a single style in relation to classes of others, but rather reflect a mixture of related styles—e.g., Nurturant + Sociable + Affiliative or Inhibited + Submissive + Detached. Correspondingly, an individual tending toward either of these "stylistic constellations" may well display a broad range of specific patterns when his or her actual behavior across interaction sequences is examined, but all such patterns are interrelated and able to be summarized in terms of these respective interpersonal style clusters.

Relative to the data encompassed by the concept of an interpersonal pattern, the style concept represents a more inclusive, abstract category of information. In this regard, Mischel (1979) points out that "categorizations are an inevitable, fundamental, and pervasive aspect of information processing, one that is built into our cognitive economics" (p. 744). He goes on to say that "Such categorizations can be made at different levels, with distinctive gains and losses" (p. 744), and thus at an earlier point cautions that "alternative categorizations or considerations may be gauged most wisely, not by seeking to confirm or negate their truth or reality in absolute terms, but by assessing their usefulness. And usefulness can only be judged in light of particular purposes" (p. 744). If we extrapolate these notions to the domain of psychotherapy, it is evident that the question for the clinician is not whether or not to categorize information about the patient, but rather for what purpose and therefore at what level to do so. And applying Mischel's assertions even more specifically to the concerns of the present chapter, a necessary consideration is that of distinctive purposes served by—and thus clinical utility of—employing the sequence, pattern, and style concepts in planning and conducting treatment.

At this point is may be suggested that construing the patient in terms of general interpersonal styles provides an abstract summary of the latter's interpersonal problems. This abstraction provides a useful, conceptual shorthand device for hypothesizing about the nature and directions of adaptive interpersonal change relevant to the patient (e.g, development of an increased capacity to shift from an Inhibited style to a Sociable + Affiliative style). Considering the patient from the standpoint of his or her distinctive interpersonal patterns takes the clinician to a more specific level of analysis. Overt and covert targets for change become more evident, in turn facilitating more precise selection of specific interventions than would be enabled through conceptualizing the patient solely in global, stylistic terms. And, as suggested earlier, specific patterns associated with the patient's distress become apparent through detailed examination of his or her sequential exchanges with others.

In the following section, treatment implications stemming from the sequence, pattern, and style concepts, as specifically defined in previous pages, are spelled out in greater detail. My emphasis is upon demonstrating the manner in which their application may facilitate efforts to assess and effect change in the patient's dysfunctional extratherapy interpersonal behavior. In pursuing this analysis, an attempt is made at several points to show how a synthesis between interpersonal communication and cognitive-behavioral perspectives is fostered through clinical application of these interpersonal concepts.

TREATMENT IMPLICATIONS

When persons present themselves for psychotherapy, their presenting complaints usually consist of summarizations and descriptions of cognitive, affective, and/or behavioral components of their maladaptive interpersonal patterns. One patient describes her problem as "jealousy and insecurity"; another states, "I feel different from other people. I just don't feel ordinary"; and still a third says, "I need to find myself. I just don't know who I am or what I want anymore." I assume that these respective complaints are but a small piece of each patient's "interpersonal truth," most accurately interpreted as reflections of how the patient has made sense of the more specific, self-defeating interpersonal patterns which plague him or her during daily interaction sequences. These maladaptive, patterned processes must be identified, the manner in which they eventuate in self-defeating consequences must be established, and they must be replaced with the capacity to shift toward alternative, more adaptive patterns that are linked to underemployed Interpersonal Circle–based interpersonal styles.

As briefly defined earlier, descriptive, reflective, and enactive interventions around interaction sequences provide a systematic approach to assessing and intervening in the patient's disordered ways of dealing with others. Over the long haul, the therapist shuttles among these intervention strategies. Moreover, this work around the patient's extratherapy relationships occurs in conjunction with metacommunication about in-therapy manifestations of his or her self-defeating interpersonal responding. These procedures thus complement strategies exploring in-therapy displays of problematic patterns. Insights fostered through the latter operations may be extrapolated and tested within the context of extratherapy relationships through interactional analysis procedures. On other occasions, identification of self-defeating patterns through analysis of extratherapy interactions sensitizes the therapist to cues associated with their in-therapy occurrence, thereby facilitating disengagement and matacommunication operations as the patterns emerge during sessions. Ultimately, then, metacommunications about the patient's self-defeating patterns as they occur both in and out of therapy must occur in tandem in the overall effort to increase the patient's capacity to shift to more adaptive ways of thinking, feeling, and acting during his or her significant interactions.

Descriptive Interventions

Descriptive interventions are a useful first step in the effort to identify self-defeating patterns, and involve reconstructing and labeling the actual flow of events that transpired between the patient and significant others during recent interactions which bear a connection to the patient's presenting issues and subjective distress. For example, when the patient states that her problem is "jealousy and insecurity," the therapist seeks to concretize these terms, inquiring in the process how this issue relates to a current or recent significant relationship. Eliciting a description of a recent interaction where this issue actually seemed to become manifested is often helpful in this regard. Or in later phases of treatment, when a patient opens a session with references to an interaction during the week that was associated with distress or that relates to interpersonal issues already under examination, it may be exceedingly useful to look at the interaction or significant portions of it in detail in order to turn this interpersonal experience to therapeutic benefit. By the same token, detailed reconstruction of sequences is a useful procedure for examining ramifications of adaptive changes that the patient may be attempting in his or her interactions during different points in treatment. In any of these instances, a descriptive focus on sequences is a helpful method for "entering" the patient's extratherapy interactions.

Through descriptive interventions the therapist establishes with the patient a kind of motion picture of the sequence, incorporating the setting of the interaction, and within that setting, what the patient and other said and did in relation to one another as the exchange process evolved. The inquiry, thus, takes the form of: What did you do? Say? What did he or she do next? What happened then? And so on. The extent to which the therapist asks questions of this sort depends upon a number of factors, including the amount of detail the patient supplies on his or her own, the amount of detail the therapist feels he or she and the patient need to get a solid grasp on the interaction, and the extent to which the patient needs to be kept focused as a function of tendencies toward tangentiality. As the patient provides his or her description of the behavioral aspect of the interaction, I filter my listening in terms of Interpersonal Circle categories; obviously, for any "coding" to be made with a reasonable degree of accuracy, the behavior being coded must be considered in relation to previous responses on the part of the patient and other.

This focused listening clearly requires extreme attentiveness on the part of the therapist, who must also note *how* the patient reports the interaction. As the interaction is described, I will briefly break in at points with such comments as "So you really remained pretty silent at that point," or "You acted helpless," specifically labeling and highlighting salient aspects of the patient's behavior. How these statements are made—i.e., their paralinguistic and nonverbal concomitants—is another important consideration to bear in mind.

In addition to reconstructing the overt level of the interaction, it is essential, in line with the previous discussion of interaction sequences, to assist the patient continually in identifying and labeling his or her thoughts and feelings during the exchange. As the patient describes the action, I frequently intervene with such questions as, "What was going through your head at that point?" "What were you saying to yourself?" "What were you thinking he or she would say (or do) when you said (or did) that?" "How/what were you feeling at that point?"

These questions are best posed strategically, particularly around those points of the sequence hypothesized to be "critical junctures"—points at which persistent enactment of a different kind of behavioral response by the patient might conceivably shift the course of the interaction in a direction quite different from that which it typically proceeds in, a direction whose outcomes are likely in the long run to be more beneficial to both parties. For example, as Inhibited, nonassertive patients describe their interactions with others, it becomes apparent that the resentment and hurt that they experience often stems in part from a failure to counter forthrightly statements or assertions made by others which they consider untrue or unfair. Nevertheless, they remain sullenly silent at these particular points, or at best they may offer a brief and meek statement of disagreement. By asking about the patient's thoughts and feelings around this specific phase of the sequence, the therapist and patient may develop hypotheses about specific cognitive and/or affective factors strongly governing the patient's overt behavior at those important points when a distinct behavioral shift seems essential, yet is rigidly avoided.

Often it is also useful to raise questions about the patient's covert activities before and after significant interactions. For example, with one male patient who described women as his "Achilles heel," and who experienced considerable anxiety especially around dating situations, it became apparent that at least part of this anxiety was engendered by a barrage of negative self-evaluations emitted during the process of preparing to pick up his date. Though this was by no means the sole source of his heterosexual difficulties, it was helpful for the patient to see how the negative experiences he often had on dates bore some relationship to his negative self-statements before the evening even began. In a similar vein, a severely Inhibited-obsessive patient who experienced considerable discomfort in relation to a vast array of interpersonal situations and thus preferred a posture of detachment and distancing, including minimal verbalization, came to see how his dysphoria following interactions was intricately tied to his self-critical ruminations after particular interactional episodes. These covert activities prior to and following interactions often prove to be important factors in how the patient keeps him or herself locked into self-defeating ways of interacting with others, and underscore that "interactions" continue despite the physical absence of the other in question.

Throughout these descriptive analyses of the patient's concrete interaction sequences, the importance of acquiring a solid feel for other's behavior during the exchange cannot be overemphasized. Maladaptive patterns are exquisitely intertwined with distinctive behaviors on the part of other, and therefore no pattern and any given sequence within which it is embedded is sufficiently understood without a good sense of precisely how it interconnects with the nature of other's behavior. Though the clinician is clearly removed from this other and must rely on the patient's report of the action, sensitive listening and a firm grasp of Interpersonal Circle variables facilitates development of a picture of others' characteristic styles during interactions with the patient. Like any clinical hypothesis, this formulation of characteristic behaviors and other stimulus aspects of significant others with whom the patient is self-defeatingly engaged must continually be open to modification. As will be discussed under reflective interventions, however, even in this tentative form, the therapist's formulations about these others enables him or her to raise to him or herself, and at appropriate points with the patient, questions about the patient's significant others which can enhance his or her understanding of his or her interpersonal difficulties. Only through obtaining as detailed a picture as possible of *both* the patient and his or her significant others as their interaction sequences spin out can therapist and patient arrive at consensually valid statements about the distinctive kinds of distress-inducing dyads the patient characteristically inhabits and helps produce.

Throughout descriptive interventions the therapist relies exclusively on the patient's self-report, and hence it is essential that he or she bear in mind the potential for distortions in the patient's account. As Bellack and Hersen (1977) succinctly note, "Observation, information storage, and recall are all subject to distortion" (p. 56). Indeed, even when explicit procedures are developed for enabling the patient to directly observe and record his or her behavior *in vivo*, as in behavioral self-monitoring, complete accuracy cannot by any means be assured (Nelson, 1977). Therefore, in eliciting an account of what transpired between the patient and a significant other during a recent exchange, the therapist remains alert to the inevitability that there will not be total isomorphism between what actually happened and the patient's in-therapy account. In any given instance, the patient's inaccuracy may reflect an interactive combination of the fact that human beings are imperfect observers of their own and others' behavior, that human memory is partially reconstructive in nature (Mahoney, 1974), and that distortion in accounts of interpersonal experiences may be motivated, in the sense of (usually unconsciously) attempting to evoke within one's interpersonal partner particular impressions about oneself and other. As examples of motivated distortions, the patient may be biased towards coloring him or herself as the "good guy" during interactional episodes while portraying his or her inter-personal partner in the most malevolent terms. Conversely, a patient may describe a given sequence in a way that is geared toward "confirming" to the therapist how inadequate he or she (the patient) is, despite the most well-intentioned efforts of his or her interpersonal partner.

Acknowledging that a patient's description of an interaction will inevitably entail some degree of inaccuracy need not, however, be cause for abandoning the effort. Rather, this acknowledgment can enhance the therapist's effort to foster optimal accuracy during the descriptive phase by underscoring the crucial necessity for extreme attentiveness, both to the interaction as ongoingly depicted by the patient as well as to how the patient recounts events.

For example, as the therapist listens to the patient's description of the interaction, he or she is sensitive to potential gaps in the account, as when the patient suddenly jumps from an early point in the interaction to another point without providing any picture of events in between. Events transpiring during these gaps may yield important information that can be pursued further. Consider the following exchange (P = patient; T = therapist):

P: I felt really uncomfortable, like he knew I didn't know what to say or do.
T: It sounds like you really were nervous. But what happened next?
P: Well, nothing really. The class was about to begin so we each went over to our easels and that was it.
T: But what happened before that? Did you just suddenly walk away from each other, or did anything else happen before that?
P: I suppose—it was just pretty awkward. He mentioned that we ought to talk some more about painting, and I kind of agreed. But I didn't say it with any conviction or enthusiasm; in fact I think I was looking at the floor.
T: What were you thinking?
P: I just thought he was being polite. I didn't think I had said anything during the conversation that was very meaningful. I was too concerned with thinking of things to say the whole time, and was pretty afraid that he could tell.

By pursuing additional detail about the interaction with his second question, the therapist uncovers potentially significant data that might otherwise have gone undetected had he accepted the patient's previous statement automatically. With this additional information, the therapist may pursue a number of important questions. Why does the patient so readily doubt his classmate's interest in talking at greater length with him? What is the lack of eye contact all about? And why the preoccupation with planning his statements—spontaneity must be risky, but precisely what does he fear?

The therapist may also enhance accuracy and minimize distortion by continually ensuring that the patient is in fact focusing on descriptions of what happened, and not on inferences and attributions; investigation of the latter is more appropriate to the reflective phase of interactional analysis. This distinction between description and inference, and the way the therapist shifts the patient back to the former, is illustrated in the following example:

P: It was a nice night until he started telling me that he really cared for me, that I was special to him.
T: What happened at that point?

P: I sort of jokingly told him to come off it, that I'd heard that before . . . . He's really full of it! He's like all men—as soon as you show any interest at all in them, I think they start to get ideas and try to take advantage of you.

T: I don't know if I'm ready to agree with that last part. That's an assumption you're making about Ken. At this point I really believe we need to keep looking at what happened before we can make conclusive statements like that. What happened next? What did Ken say?

P: That he really meant it, and that it hurt him a little that I didn't take him seriously. I suppose he looked taken aback, too.

T: Do you remember what you felt at that point?

P: I think sort of confused and cautious. I wasn't sure I could trust him. I remember thinking something like "I've fallen for this before, and I don't feel like getting hurt again." And yet he had been treating me well.

By steering the patient away from her global attributions and back to the interaction per se, the therapist acquires a more detailed picture of the patient's thoughts and feelings vis-à-vis this particular male. In this instance, it becomes evident that direct messages of caring and feelings of closeness from males may automatically elicit feelings of vulnerability, mistrust, and related expectations of getting hurt, a hypothesized functional relationship meriting further patient-therapist examination.

Having the patient fill in gaps in his or her account of an interaction sequence, and ensuring that the focus is on descriptions of events and not upon related inferences, are certainly not the only ways of enhancing the accuracy of information gathered during this descriptive process. The therapist has also been garnering information about the patient's general, disordered style through observing and experiencing the patient within the context of their own relationship. This in-therapy information can sensitize the therapist to predictable impediments to fully accurate accounts of interactions with others. For example, the Dominant/Competitive-obsessive, emphasizing cool-headed rationality while downplaying emotion in his interactions with the therapist, may indeed consistently draw a blank when asked about his feelings at certain points during extratherapy interactions. Directing attention to this consistency can lead to strong suggestion and encouragement that he become more attuned to his emotional reactions during interactions (an *enactive* intervention), while also leading to a necessary examination of the patient's distinctive issues around his own affective states and emotional reactions in significant relationships (a *reflective* intervention).

In a similar vein, recurring impact messages generated within the therapist sensitizes the latter to reactions the patient may attempt to evoke through the manner in which he or she characterizes him or herself and/or the other during some recent interaction. For example, where the therapist frequently feels pulled to reassure a patient as to his or her adequacy, not infrequently in discussing an outside interaction the patient will portray him or herself as totally inept and inadequate. As suggested earlier, in such an instance the patient may actually be attempting to elicit the therapist's reassurance. By sensitizing him or herself to the potential for this motivated distortion, the therapist becomes cautious lest he or she too readily accept the accuracy of the patient's description of self and other interacting.

The point to be emphasized, then, is that while the patient's descriptions of a given interaction sequence may tend toward inaccuracy to varying degrees, the therapist, by recognizing this potential, draws upon his or her unique skills as a *trained* listener, participant-observer, and interviewer to minimize distortion and to maximize accurate reconstruction of the interaction sequence.

Reflective Interventions

Reflective interventions, following upon the heels of descriptive interventions, are intended to encourage the patient to take a step back from his or her interpersonal interactions and relationships, and to appraise them from various angles. The overall aim is to help the patient expand his or her understanding of him or herself in relation to others in ways that have clear implications for change. This process is analogous to the self-reflective loop described by Yalom (1975), according to which the group "doubles back on itself . . . and examines the here-and-now behavior [among group members] which has just occurred" (p. 122). Though couched in terms of the group situation, Yalom's (1975) comments are equally relevant to the individual: "If the powerful curative factor of interpersonal learning is to be set into motion, the group must recognize, examine, and understand process. It must examine itself, it must study its own transactions, it must transcend pure experience and apply itself to the integration of that experience" (p. 122). Similarly, to understand and modify his or her self-defeating style and its component patterns, the individual in inter-personally focused treatment must be actively engaged in the self-reflective loop, with this focus including there-and-then extratherapy transactions as elaborated through descrip-tive interventions.

Although the patient's appraisal of his or her interpersonal experiences may be oriented toward various kinds of phenomena, a principal reflective focus involves extract-ing from among the processes and events that transpire those patterns, as these have been defined earlier, which in the short and/or long run engender self-defeating conse-quences. Equally important, however, the patient needs to develop an understanding as to what these dysfunctional patterns are all about, and in relation to this, to become increasing-ly cognizant of the form and substance of alternative, more adaptive ways of interacting with others in certain situations. In what follows, I will briefly touch upon these two broad aspects of reflective interventions, suggesting first some ways of introducing a reflective focus upon extratherapy interactions in the effort to extract problematic patterns, fol-lowed by a necessarily cursory discussion of several useful directions to pursue in foster-ing greater understanding about these identified patterns.

At least two strategies may be employed for shifting the patient into a reflective focus upon a previously described sequence, and these may be used independently or in tan-dem. These strategies involve open-ended questioning and the therapist verbalizing aloud his or her own impressions about the most salient, functionally related aspects of the interaction.

Open-ended questions immediately shift responsibility to the patient, while conveying that there is indeed something meaningful to be culled from the series of events compris-ing the just-described interaction. There are many ways to phrase the open-ended ques-tion: "What jumps out at you the most in that entire exchange?" "What do you make of what happened between you two during that interaction?" "In that whole series of events, is there anything in particular that stands out for you?"

Interestingly, patient's responses to these types of questions often consist of observa-tions of and/or formulations about relationships among data elicited during previous descriptive interventions, e.g., "Yeah, I was petrified of what she might say to me!"; "I guess I had to do something to make sure I was the center of attention; I was afraid that he might lose interest in me"; "I didn't think that anything I had to say was any good, so I just kept quiet."

When the patient's response to an open-ended question alludes to only a single cognitive, affective, or behavioral act—e.g., "I was just really angry!"—the therapist still has a number of response options for expanding the focus toward *connections* among events. The therapist can simply reflect the patient's response and encourage him or her to reflect further: "Yes, you really did seem to be ticked off—what do you think that anger was all about?" A follow-up question of this sort frequently leads the patient to refer to other aspects of the interaction, whether this involves other feelings or thoughts he or she experienced, behaviors he or she enacted, and/or behavior on the part of other.

An alternative procedure for expanding the focus beyond a single thought, feeling, or action involves the second reflective strategy mentioned above; the therapist echoes the patient's statement but then takes the lead in linking it to other salient elements of the sequence: "Yeah, it seemed like you really were angry at him. After all, you had been asking him to be more considerate of you, and when he wasn't, you'd had it at that point and let him know in no uncertain terms." The therapist thus links the patient's anger, identified by the latter as the most salient aspect of the interaction, specifically to previous requests made of other and the latter's failure to comply.

The therapist may choose to bypass the open-ended question format entirely in introducing a reflective focus, instead immediately initiating the processes of extracting and labeling patterns and their specific components. These observations represent the therapist's impressions, and therefore it is essential that the patient be actively engaged in collaborative examination of their validity. Folllowing are several examples of the therapist initiating this reflective shift:

You know, as I listened to that whole sequence of events I had the sense that, while you were feeling really close to Jane, you were also afraid of what she'd say if you told her this.

As you described that entire sequence, what hit me most was how nervous you were about coming across as inadequate. So you did all you could to create an impression of knowing exactly what you were doing—that you had it all under total control.

What strikes me is that whenever John seemed to you to be getting angry, you abruptly stopped talking.

The therapist can only know the extent to which the patient concurs with his or her perspective on the sequence by fostering reciprocal processing and responding. He or she invites the patient's participation particularly by paralinguistic and other nonverbal cues which convey a tentative, subtly questioning tone that implicitly says, "Here's what I think may be going on. What do you think?" Where the patient's impressions tend toward disagreement with those of the therapist, he or she should be encouraged to elaborate further; the therapist thereby capitalizes on the patient's own active processing of the sequence and the distinctive meanings he or she has derived. Alternatively, when the patient essentially concurs with the therapist's speculations about salient components and their relationships, there are numerous directions in which to proceed. This decision is best guided by the therapist's judgment as to what the patient needs most at this point, which takes into account several related questions: Within the context of what has transpired in treatment thus far, what is the patient's and therapist's current level of understanding of the former's dysfunctional style and component patterns, what about these patterns remains to be learned, and how is the patient best moved toward experimenting with alternative, more adaptive patterns in extratherapy situations?

Bearing in mind that these considerations can only be addressed on an individual basis at any given point during treatment, I will briefly sketch out three lines of inquiry which, when appropriately timed, can promote significant insight into the patient's self-defeating social behavior and can facilitate a shift toward alternative responses. These directions entail attainment of greater detail about particular components constituting patterns under consideration, establishment of the relationship between these patterns and the patient's self-concept (view of self, self-definition, self-system), and delineation of precise costs incurred through persistent enactment of these patterns.

Collaboratively pursuing greater detail around specific components of an interpersonal pattern is useful for crystallizing how the patient keeps him or herself bound in dysfunctional ways of interacting and in pointing toward specific directions for change. Therapist and patient may pursue more molecular analysis of overt, multichanneled behavioral elements of a recurring pattern, develop a sharper picture of stimulus features of other(s) which play an important role in eliciting and/or maintaining the pattern in question, or undertake closer examination of internal-personal components of the pattern. While detailed scrutiny of any one of these components is initially undertaken, it is most efficacious to explore their relationships by weaving among them during reflective interventions.

More detailed exploration of a pattern's overt behavioral component leads to a clearer picture as to how the patient actually goes about structuring his or her interactions and sending relationship messages which eventuate in self-defeating consequences. Nonverbal behaviors are emphasized at this more refined level of analysis, especially as they interact with verbal statements. In operationalizing these behavioral components, the therapist encourages the patient to specify *what he or she does* when he or she behaves in this particular self-defeating way. Thus, if a patient's dysfunctional pattern includes "pulling back" from other, how does the patient do this? Perhaps this "pulling back" is anchored primarily along the kinesic, proxemic, and verbal channels, specifically through decreased eye contact and emotional nonexpressivity in facial expression, creating greater physical distance, and saying less as the interaction proceeds. Further, what relationship messages seem implicitly to be sent through this multichanneled stimulus array? Raising this type of question explicitly is intended to heighten the patient's awareness about his or her own social stimulus value through helping him or her to become more cognizant of the messages—about self, other, and their relationship—he or she conveys through his or her multichanneled behavior.

Concretizing multichanneled elements of a pattern's overt component also translates directly into hypotheses about more adaptive behaviors and associated relationship messages which would be sent were the patient to shift behaviorally in these directions. To stay with this example, greater willingness to be more "present" in the interaction and to risk closeness would be overtly manifested in a combination of more sustained eye contact, displaying affective reactions facially, remaining in greater physical proximity to one's partner, and participating more frequently and openly along the verbal channel. Specifying the topography of underused, alternative behaviors with this degree of precision can greatly facilitate the patient's efforts to experiment with more adaptive patterns.

Just as the patient may step back from an identified pattern and concentrate upon overt behavioral components, so too may closer consideration be brought to bear upon the other in relation to whom the pattern is enacted. As noted earlier, during descriptive interventions, therapist and patient have been garnering a clearer picture as to ongoing behaviors and other stimulus features of persons with whom the patient is engaged in self-defeating fashion. Now, during the reflective phase of interactional analysis focusing more sharply upon other is geared toward attaining greater understanding as to precisely what it is about him or her that so effectively contributes to eliciting the maladaptive patterns in question. In all that other says and does in relation to the patient, what actions seem to be central in hooking the patient's self-defeating responses and/or preventing him or her from enacting alternative behaviors? For example, is there a particular facial expression on the part of other that shifts the patient into a maladaptive stance? Do the crucial discriminative stimuli lie in particular statements uttered in a certain tone of voice? In relation to these verbal and nonverbal elicitors, what implicit messages from other(s) seem to pull out and reinforce enactment of the patterns in question? Are they perceived messages of helplessness? Competition? Anger? Closeness? This, of course, gets at the issue of distinctive interpersonal styles on the part of others which are problematic for the patient. Further, are there other stimulus features of other(s) which trigger the patient's dysfunctional patterns? Is there something, for example, about other's sex, age, role, degree of physical attractiveness, and so on, which is problematic in some fashion for the patient?

In thus helping the patient to step back and acquire greater clarity about those others in relation to whom he or she enacts his or her self-defeating patterns, the therapist takes a first step toward disrupting the automatic bond, as it were, that has developed between these patterns and particular kinds of interpersonal input. The acquisition of labels for those aspects of the other which recurrently play an important role in drawing out his or her disordered patterns enables the patient to gain some cognitive distance from this other through the interceding role of symbolization. Seeing the distinctive interpersonal inputs which pose problems for him or her more clearly, the patient by this very awareness takes an initial step toward gaining control over them and reducing the automaticity of their effects.

Beyond this labeling, however, the therapist and patient use these data about the other as springboards for undertaking closer examination of critical internal-personal components of the patient's self-defeating interpersonal patterns. In this instance, the reflective focus is intended to assist the patient in understanding defects in how he or she processes these inputs and the important, ensuing cognitive and emotional meanings experienced vis-à-vis other(s). This particular domain of clinical inquiry represents a major point of interfacing between interpersonal communication and cognitive-behavioral perspectives on human behavior, emphasizing what the patient *does* internally when he or she encounters particular interpersonal stimulus configurations. So, for example, a more detailed and elaborate focus upon internal-personal elements of a particular maladaptive interpersonal pattern might target the patient's irrational assumptions and beliefs, particular self-statements, unrealistic expectancies, distorted interpretations of actions on the part of other, a faulty style of thinking, inaccurate causal attributions, or specific images and fantasies.

By thus attaining a more detailed understanding of distinctive problems in his or her internal processing of behaviors and other stimulus-input features of the other, including the resulting meanings with which these inputs are imbued, the patient may begin to reflect upon and reappraise his or her distortions and interpretive inaccuracies. The therapist plays an active part in helping the patient to correct the identified defects in his or her cognitive-interpretive system—by no means a simple task. A wide variety of specific cognitive restructuring procedures are available (see, for example, Beck, 1976; Ellis, 1973; Goldfried & Goldfried, 1980. Meichenbaum, 1977; Meichenbaum & Genest, 1980; Rathjen, Rathjen, & Hiniker, 1978), but their essential commonality lies in the goal of modifying the patient's appraisals, beliefs, and interpretive activities in the direction of greater accuracy. The emphasis in the present context is upon restructuring the patient's cognitive activities and related affective reactions as these operate before, during, and/or after the process of interpersonal exchange.

Illuminating the patient's covert processes in relation to others represents one direction of cognitive analysis in fostering understanding of characteristic interpersonal rigidities. Another entails helping the patient to achieve a fuller appreciation of the critical linkage between his or her maladaptive patterns and his beliefs and assumptions about him or herself—processes encompassed by the self-concept, or self-system. In his valuable book, *Misunderstandings of the Self*, Raimy (1975) writes:

> For years I was baffled by the problem of devising appropriate operations for applying self-concept theory to treatment; the solution, however, turned out to be more simple than I had anticipated. It now seems obvious that the self-concept is composed of the more or less organized notions, beliefs, and convictions that constitute an individual's knowledge of himself and that influence his relationships with others. Even though beliefs and convictions about others which have no self-reference are important in adjustment, I doubt that they are as central as the beliefs about the self; the conceptions which define the self in relation to others not only are long enduring but also exercise almost continuous influence upon behavior. [P. xi.]

Thus placing the self-concept in a central position in influencing human functioning, Raimy (1975) goes on to present an integrative approach to treatment based upon the specific assertion that faulty and mistaken beliefs about the self "may drastically and unrealistically limit the kinds of behavior an individual is willing to engage in, or they may relentlessly force him into unwise behavior which leads to perpetual defeat" (p. 9). Accordingly, the chief task of therapy becomes that of locating and modifying or eliminating the patient's misconceptions about him or herself. This therapeutic approach reflects most fundamentally upon the "misconception hypothesis," which posits that changing the patient's relevant, erroneous beliefs, especially those pertaining to him or herself, will lead to improved adjustment. Moreover, Raimy (1975) is quick to point out that the misconception hypothesis is by no means novel; rather, it has been a central, though implicit, theme in the history of therapy for at least a century.

As noted earlier in this chapter, rigidity in the patient's interpersonal style and the concrete patterns he or she enacts cannot possibly be divorced from his or her constricted, hence faulty, self-concept system. At the outset of treatment the patient can usually define him or herself in only a delimited number of ways without experiencing undue distress. Behavioral inclinations or actually emitted behaviors on the part of self, as well as interpersonal response feedback, perceived as inconsistent with these delimited self-conceptions engender unacceptable levels of anxiety, and therefore must be avoided. Over time, therefore, enactment of particular interpersonal styles has become associated with an exceedingly low probability of occurrence. It is as if the patient has backed him or herself and his or her interpersonal partners into an "interpersonal corner" by virtue of the constricted view of self to which he or she clings and whose reinforcement is more or less unconsciously deemed essential. To preserve a tenuous sense of security, the individual thus imposes his or her own barriers on the stylistic flexibility vital to effective interpersonal adaptation.

This was vividly illustrated by one patient, whom the author saw in treatment, whose security and feelings of acceptability were excessively contingent upon interpersonal responses, by herself and others, which supported her view of self as warm, understanding, and friendly, a person who was likable to all. Overtly, these self-conceptions were linked to an effusive Affiliative-Nurturant-Sociable style; maintaining an attractive appearance was also considered essential. While this manner of self-presentation was quite effective as a way of initiating relationships, over time excessive and rigid enactment of this interpersonal stance eventuated in a number of costly, self-defeating consequences. For example, with time she elicited a certain amount of irritation and even suspiciousness; there was a lack of genuineness to the patient precisely because this stance was so nonvariable. Moreover, it was necessary for the patient to avoid fully experiencing and clearly expressing virtually any feelings and thoughts associated with Hostile, Detached, or Mistrustful styles. For example, she proudly proclaimed at one point that "I've only gotten angry three times in my life!" The upshot, of course, was that the patient left herself quite vulnerable to being taken advantage of in her relationships, a recurrent experience that was painfully absorbed, despite efforts to dismiss it quickly with the self-effacing attitude, "Well, I understand." In the effort, then, to ensure security by eliciting responses that would confirm her narrow self-definition, this particular patient ultimately undermined it, which might be attested to by the gradually mounting feelings of anxiety and depression that led her to seek treatment.

Explicitly linking the patient's maladaptive self-concept system to his or her interpersonal difficulties often initially takes the form of the therapist hypothesizing aloud the self-definition which seems implicit in a particular recurrent pattern and/or the view of self which implicitly seems to be avoided in especially rigid fashion. The patient is then kept focused upon consideration and exploration of these all-important self-definitional issues. Thus, at one point in discussing the previous patient's characteristic pattern of so readily "understanding" and forgiving mistreatment by males with whom she began to form close relationships, I commented that "My sense is that you have this image of yourself as someone who *has* to be 'nice,' friendly, always understanding. It's as if you're not permitted somehow to make a demand, or that anger isn't allowed to enter the picture with men whom you begin to get close to." Her response was one of immediate denial, followed by a lengthy silence, which was then broken when the patient acknowledged that perhaps this was so. Over the course of this and subsequent sessions, she acquired increased recognition and undertook detailed exploration of the great discomfort she experienced when she was around anger, both on the part of others and when she sensed these feelings within herself and experienced an urge to act upon them.

Comprehensive assessment of the patient's constricted self-concept system, then, incorporates clarifying both specific self-conceptions and attributions which are rigidly maintained, as well as those particular views of self that are strongly avoided. In a very real sense the latter are experienced as alien and threatening to the patient. My therapeutic tack is subsequently to help the patient attain a clearer understanding of those specific factors which motivate excessive attachment, as it were, to a particular self-definition, but even more so, those factors which inhibit a prolonged capacity to conceive of him or herself comfortably in alternative terms. In relation to the latter, two general inhibiting factors frequently emerge. First, through the medium of early and later interpersonal developmental experiences, a strong negative valence has become associated with the avoided self-conceptions under consideration. As an active process, this valence takes the form of excessively negative self-evaluations that are emitted contingent upon perceiving oneself in the undesirable terms for an extended period of time. Second, the patient anticipates aversive outcomes in the form of particular reactions from others were he or she to enact interpersonal stylistics corresponding to the avoided self-definition.

The patient's constricted self-system becomes intelligible within the context of these two broad sets of factors. Nevertheless, as in the case of cognitive restructuring of his or her interpretive activities vis-à-vis input from others, the patient needs to learn that the negative meanings and feared consequences associated with defining him or herself in particular terms are not engraved in stone, and indeed are usually inaccurate and unrealistic. In order to correct these distortions, however, the patient, as Raimy (1975) points out, must be presented with evidence which challenges and disproves them, leading in turn to their elimination or modification. Raimy (1975) discusses at considerable length four broad procedures for presenting such evidence to the patient: self-examination, therapist explanation (e.g., interpretations, confrontations), self-demonstration (similar to enactive interventions, as discussed below), and vicariation (i.e., modeling). In the context of the present discussion, the overall aim of these procedures is to modify and expand the patient's self-definitional system in directions that increase his or her capacity to enact particular interpersonal patterns and to receive varieties of interpersonal response feedback whose chronic avoidance is centrally implicated in his or her self-defeating experiences in social interactions.

In addition to undertaking detailed exploration of specific components of his or her dysfunctional patterns and developing an appreciation of how these patterns relate to the patient's customary ways of defining him or herself, the patient's understanding of his or her interpersonal difficulties is frequently enhanced by establishing the precise costs incurred through persistent enactment of the patterns in question. The process of identifying specific self-defeating consequences incorporates, among other options, (1) underscoring the nature of others' reciprocal responding vis-à-vis the patient; (2) labeling the relationship messages implicit in these countercommunications; (3) drawing out negative implications of these countercommunications for the patient's self-definition and feelings of self-worth; (4) clarifying the manner in which his or her rigid patterns and others' characteristic countercommunications impede gratification of important human needs, wants, and desires; and (5) explicitly linking these consequences to the patient's dysphoric affective states.

Precise analysis of self-defeating consequences along these interrelated lines provides one illustration of how investigation of extratherapy interactions may dovetail with in-therapy metacommunications about the patient's maladaptive style. For example, through feeding back impact messages, the therapist may inform the patient that he or she feels distanced, kept out, and curious about what the latter is truly thinking and feeling as he or she characteristically stares at the floor while talking, all the while remaining constricted across nonverbal channels (e.g., few postural changes, minimal variations of vocal pitch, nonvariation in facial expression). Scrutiny of others' responses toward the patient may yield information that complements this feedback. A picture may emerge in which others quickly bring conversations with the patient to an end or avoid the patient completely, thereby "confirming" the patient's belief that he or she is a bore, has little to offer others, and is somehow "different." These cognitions may in turn strengthen feelings of depression and isolation. Through these procedures, an explicit hook-up is made between feelings experienced by the therapist in relation to the patient and related aversive countercommunicational consequences elicited during extratherapy interactions.

These three broad lines of work represent but a sampling of directions that may be pursued during reflective interventions. A given pattern might also be explored, for example, from the standpoint of establishing its generality, clarifying outcomes which help to explain its persistence, and/or recalling previous, rare instances when the patient succeeded in shifting out of the rigid pattern into a more adaptive mode of responding and identifying controlling variables (e.g., context, a particular mood state, or a certain other who might have been present). As is the case with any therapeutic intervention, in order to be optimally effective in moving the patient toward change, pursuit of any particular line of inquiry during the reflective phase of interactional analysis must be based on some rationale, must be linked to an open system of hypotheses about the patient, must take into account vicissitudes in the patient's anxiety level, and must consider timing and phrasing.

Enactive Interventions

Enactive interventions refer to the therapist's efforts to have the patient attempt alternative, more adaptive ways of behaving during problematic interpersonal situations. While in the broadest sense, reflective interventions encompass therapeutic efforts to enhance the patient's awareness and understanding of his or her dysfunctional interpersonal patterns and to identify the nature of more adaptive alternatives, ensuing insights remain essentially meaningless if the patient does not translate them into actual behavioral changes in those situations that have come to be associated with negative, self-defeating consequences. Enactive interventions reflect this awareness on the part of the therapist, and subsume interventions which are specifically intended to move the patient into behaving in these newer ways in relation to other persons.

Through experimenting with different stylistics during his or her day-to-day interactions, the patient garners feedback which serves to remediate faulty cognitive structures, among the most important of which are his or her self and other schemata (see Markus, 1977; Sollod & Wachtel, 1980; Wachtel, 1977; Wegner and Vallacher, 1980). Wachtel (1977, p. 212) succinctly points out that "actions sustain structures." Through consequences which ensue from persistent enactment of different interpersonal responses, the patient learns that the beliefs about and attitudes toward him or herself and others that underlie his or her interpersonal rigidities are inappropriate and outmoded. The patient in turn modifies his or her misconceptions, gradually replacing them with more accurate, realistic, and therefore adaptive beliefs about him or herself and these others. Further, if behavior sustains cognitive structures, then structures sustain actions by virtue of reciprocity. As the patient's schemata change, as he or she comes to adopt these revised beliefs and attributions on a more enduring basis, the probabilities associated with enactment of the newer stylistics undergo successive increments. The patient becomes less wedded to a constricted set of interpersonal styles, and conversely develops an increased capacity to shift to other Interpersonal Circle–based styles of behavior during exchanges with others. Through modifying and expanding his or her beliefs about self and other, then, the patient becomes capable of greater flexibility in his or her interpersonal dealings. By implication, the patient is far less dependent upon the acquisition of a delimited range of responses from his or her interpersonal partners. Greater mutuality in interactions and relationships can therefore take place. The patient is freer to meet his or her own needs and those of his or her partner(s); a greater give and take comes to characterize his or her significant relationships.

Change along these lines rarely occurs rapidly. While different patients are entrenched in their maladaptive, neurotic patterns to varying degrees of rigidity, it remains that these patterns are not readily relinquished. The effort to change a patient's customary ways of interacting with others is in large measure as effort to alter the patient's phenomenology, the way he or she has come to organize and make sense out of his or her experiences in the world. Despite their psychological costs, these self-defeating patterns and the "interpersonal cosmology" (Carson, 1977) to which they are reciprocally linked are at the same time products of a long developmental history and have come to afford the patient some measure of psychological survival, that is, predictability and safety (see Beier, 1966; Singer, 1970). Ultimately, then, in the truest sense, the patient must see and experience for him or herself the more rewarding consequences that stem from revising his or her view of self and others and from more frequently enacting interpersonal stylistics that had been avoided previously. This recognition can only come from risking new behaviors and learning that change is not only possible but is indeed desirable. These consequences of extratherapy risk taking act in concert with in-therapy input to produce enduring changes in the patient's disordered interpersonal patterns.

The identification during reflective interventions of more adaptive ways of thinking, construing, and overtly responding may lead the patient to implement these alternatives spontaneously during his or her actual extratherapy interactions; in these instances, reflective interventions have also fortuitously served an enactive purpose. The therapist, however, also *explicitly* induces an enactive set by encouraging and even urging the patient to experiment with these alternatives in relation to the relevant significant others with whom he or she is engaged in self-defeating ways. As suggested by Emery (cited in Rathjen et al., 1978), the therapist's framing of these risk-taking efforts as experiments is facilitated by raising to the patient the question of what he or she stands to gain and what he or she has to lose by trying different forms of overt and covert responding. In my experience, the power of this experimental set in fostering extratherapy risk taking is further enhanced by preceding such gain/loss considerations with references to the specific interpersonal and psychological costs incurred by continued enactment of the maladaptive pattern(s) under consideration (see Haley, 1976, ch. 2).

Beyond this exhortation to experiment with alternative stylistics, the therapist becomes optimally active in facilitating extratherapy risk taking through role playing, via behavioral rehearsal, anticipated interactions directly related to the patient's distinctive interpersonal stylistic problems, and by assigning related tasks to be performed in real-life interactional situations (see Kiesler, Bernstein, & Anchin, 1976; Wachtel, 1977). As the latter authors point out, behaviorally oriented clinicians have been instrumental in the development of these related interpersonal change strategies. Specifics regarding implementation of these procedures, as well as potential benefits to be accrued through their appropriate application, may be found in many texts and chapters on behavioral and cognitive-behavioral approaches to treatment (e.g., Flowers & Booraem, 1980; Goldfried & Davison, 1976; Kanfer, 1980; Kendall & Hollon, 1979; Nay, 1976; Rathjen et al., 1978), as well as in Wachtel (1977). As Wachtel notes, while these two therapeutic operations are frequently used conjointly, this need not necessarily always be the case. Here I will address two points in connection with these two enactive strategies.

First, behavioral rehearsal represents only one form of role playing that may be used to foster *in vivo* enactment of newer interpersonal responses. As discussed by Nay (1976), role playing, particularly within the context of individual treatment, also subsumes both cognitive/imaginal rehearsal and fixed-role therapy, as developed by Kelley (1955). In cognitive role playing, the patient enacts and rehearses the alternative interpersonal mode in his or her imagination. In addition to being used as an in-session technique, this procedure can be particularly useful when used by the patient prior to actual extratherapy interactions which have previously been overtly role-played with the therapist. Moreover, as is the case with each of these role-play methods, cognitive rehearsal can serve a useful assessment purpose. As Beck (1976) writes, "By imagining himself going through the steps involved in the specified activity, the patient is able to report the specific 'obstacles' he anticipates and the conflicts that are aroused. These blocks can then be the focus of discussion" (p. 273).

The thrust of fixed-role therapy involves the patient playing "the role of a fictitious person whose behavior is consistent with some construct system hypothesized to be more beneficial to him" (Nay, 1976, p. 196). The therapist is afforded a wide latitude of imaginativeness, detail, and specificity in portraying for the patient an alternative way of feeling, construing self and others, and overtly behaving within the fixed-role sketch; as such, this role-playing approach can be an especially powerful technique in effecting significant interpersonal risk-taking. In developing the sketch, the therapist may integrate and vividly elaborate an array of interpersonal patterns linked to specific interpersonal style clusters. Further, enlisting the patient's active participation in development of the fixed-role sketch can simultaneously engage the patient in pinpointing directions for change.

It should be apparent that use of any one of these role-playing procedures by no means excludes the use of others. Indeed, they may be integrated in creative ways for particular patients.

A second point to be addressed pertains to assignment of specific interpersonal tasks to be performed outside of treatment. An assignment may place principal emphasis upon changing overt components of the patient's responding, upon experimenting with alternative ways of cognitively responding in relation to an interpersonal situation (e.g., entering the interaction with a modified set of expectations), or it may highlight changes in both cognitive and behavioral processes (see Hollon & Kendall, 1979). Several frequently emphasized aspects of assigning extratherapy tasks may be briefly noted. A given assignment should be linked to a specific, clearly delineated, and identifiable interactional situation with other or class of others; any ambiguity about environmental situations and persons in relation to whom the task is to be enacted may interfere with its actually being carried out and/or with its successful performance. With regard to the latter, interpersonal tasks should also be graded, in the sense that any given task assigned to the patient is realistic and thus associated with a high probability of success. It is also essential to prepare the patient for enactment of the task. In addition to employing aforementioned cognitive and behavioral rehearsal as preparatory techniques, the therapist may directly inquire about the patient's fears and expectations vis-à-vis performance of the task and its outcomes. Concerns raised by the patient in this context frequently shift the therapist and patient into reflective interventions regarding factors which account for his or her interpersonal rigidities. Lastly, it is of vital importance that the therapist explicitly examine with the patient the actual process and outcomes of his or her task performance. The therapist actively collaborates with the patient in drawing out and processing feedback implications of these risk-taking efforts, an endeavor which may be facilitated by having the patient keep a written record of his or her experience. It can be especially valuable to link the process and outcomes of the experience explicitly to previously examined factors associated with the patient's maladaptive pattern in the situation under consideration. So, for example, what are the implications for particular expectations the patient maintains about his or her ability to actually perform the behavior in question (i.e., self-efficacy expectations; Bandura, 1977a), as well as for expectations about outcomes associated with this alternative form of responding? What effect did the outcomes have upon his or her feelings and attributions about him or herself during and/or subsequent to the sequence? What was the impact upon his or her affective state? Along with emphasizing the manner in which the experience disconfirms rigidly held, inaccurate, and outmoded beliefs and expectations, the patient's mastery is underscored. Kanfer (1980, pp. 358–361) and Rathjen et al. (1978) provide especially useful amplifications of points emphasized here, as well as addressing an array of other considerations to be kept in mind when implementing this particular enactive intervention.

CONCLUDING REMARKS

A principal underlying theme of this chapter has been that bringing an interpersonal perspective to bear upon human adjustment and maladjustment can facilitate a synthesis of concepts and therapeutic interventions drawn from an array of psychotherapy systems. Working hypotheses underlying this viewpoint have been that interpersonal factors—i.e., covert and overt processes in relation to self and classes of others—are centrally involved in inducing, eliciting, and maintaining human distress; that enduring clinical change is intimately associated with modifications in these factors; and that self/other phenomena serve directly or indirectly as common treatment targets across different therapeutic approaches. It was further noted that an interpersonal perspective reflects a reciprocal deterministic view of causation, as defined by social learning theory (Bandura, 1977b); in embodying this particular causal conception, an interpersonal view can enhance a therapist's efforts to *systematically* integrate treatment approaches which primarily address either internal or external contributants to maladjustment.

It was suggested, however, that in order for this integrational potential to be optimally realized, specific concepts will need to be selected and their referents clearly delineated, enabling more precise designation of entry points for different therapy systems. The interaction sequence, interpersonal pattern, and interpersonal style were chosen as three pivotal interpersonal concepts, and an effort toward spelling out salient defining features of each concept was undertaken; interrelationships among these concepts were consistently underscored. A more specific illustration of how an interpersonal viewpoint may intermesh with other concepts and interventions was subsequently presented by elucidating some treatment implications of the sequence, pattern, and style concepts. Couched within the framework of three broad sets of clinical operations—descriptive, reflective, and enactive interventions—these implications emphasized a synthesis between interpersonal communication and cognitive-behavioral approaches to therapeutic handling of extratherapy (as opposed to patient-therapist) interactional experiences.

In an important recent paper, Goldfried (1980b) has proposed that because of an emerging integrational *Zeitgeist* within the field of psychotherapy and behavior change, the time may be ripe for working in earnest toward a rapprochement among diverse therapeutic approaches. We would be wise to take heed of Goldfried's invitation; given the complexities of human maladjustment and suffering, who among us could argue against the need for and value of such systematic syntheses across orientations? In this chapter I have suggested from several different vantage points how and why an explicitly interpersonal perspective on human distress may contribute to this effort. Clearly, taken together, the ideas I have presented represent but a small, single step along this long, complex, and challenging road. But it is hoped that they will encourage other practitioners and investigators to consider seriously the extent to which pursuit of an interpersonal direction can facilitate reaching our destination of an integrated psychotherapeutic paradigm.

REFERENCES

Andrews, J. Psychotherapy of phobias. *Psychological Bulletin*, 1966, **66**, 455–480.

Bandura, A. *Principles of behavior modification*. New York: Holt, Rinehart & Winston, 1969.

Bandura, A. Behavior therapy and the models of man. *American Psychologist*, 1974, **29**, 859–869.

Bandura, A. Self-efficacy: Toward a unifying theory of behavioral change. *Psychological Review*, 1977, **84**, 191–215. (a)

Bandura, A. *Social learning theory*. Englewood Cliffs: Prentice-Hall, Inc., 1977. (b)

Bandura, A. The self-system in reciprocal determinism. *American Psychologist*, 1978, **33**, 344–358.

Beck, A. T. *Cognitive therapy and the emotional disorders*. New York: International Universities Press, 1976.

Beier, E. G. *The silent language of psychotherapy: Social reinforcement of unconscious process.* Chicago: Aldine, 1966.

Bellack, S. & Hersen, M. Self-report inventories in behavioral assessment. In J. D. Cone & R. P. Hawkins (Eds.), *Behavioral assessment: New directions in clinical psychology*. New York: Brunner/Mazel, 1977.

Benjamin, L. S. Use of structural analysis of social behavior (SASB) and Markov chains to study dyadic interactions. *Journal of Abnormal Psychology*, 1979, **88**, 303–319.

Benjamin, L. S. A psychosocial competence classification system. In J. D. Wine & M. D. Smye (Eds.), *Social competence*. New York: The Guilford Press, in press.

Bergin, A. E. & Lambert, M. J. The evaluation of therapeutic outcomes. In S. L. Garfield & A. E. Bergin (Eds.), *Handbook of psychotherapy and behavior change: An empirical analysis*. New York: Wiley, 1978.

Carson, R. C. *Interaction concepts of personality*. Chicago: Aldine, 1969.

Carson, R. C. Personality and exchange in developing relationships. In R. L. Burgess & T. L. Houston (Eds.), *Social exchange in developing relationships*. New York: Academic Press, 1979.

Carson, R. C. *Therapeutic communication in the modification of interpersonal cosmologies*. In J. C. Anchin (Chair.), Communications approaches to psychotherapy. Symposium presented at the Southeastern Psychological Association Meeting, Hollywood, Florida, May, 1977.

Chapman, A. H. *The treatment techniques of Harry Stack Sullivan*. New York: Brunner/Mazel, 1978.

Danziger, K. *Interpersonal communication*. New York: Pergamon, 1976.

Ekehammer, B. Interactionism in personality from a historical perspective. *Psychological Bulletin*, 1974, **81**, 1026–1048.

Ellis, A. *Humanistic psychotherapy*. New York: McGraw-Hill, 1973.

Endler, N. S. & Magnusson, D. (Eds.) *Interactional psychology and personality*. Washington, D.C.: Hemisphere, 1976.

Flowers, J. V. & Booraem, C. D. Simulation and role playing methods. In F. H. Kanfer & A. P. Goldstein (Eds.), *Helping people change*, 2nd ed. New York: Pergamon, 1980.

Ford, D. H. & Urban, H. B. *Systems of psychotherapy: A comparative study*. New York: Wiley, 1963.

Frank, J. D. *Persuasion and healing: A comparitive study of psychotherapy*, rev. ed. Baltimore: Johns Hopkins Press, 1973.

Frank, J. D. The present status of outcome studies. *Journal of Consulting and Clinical Psychology*, 1979, **47**, 310–316.

Frank, J. D., Hoehn-Saric, R., Imber, S. D., Liberman, B. L., & Stone, A. R. *Effective ingredients of successful psychotherapy*. New York: Brunner/Mazel, 1978.

Garfield, S. L. & Kurtz, R. Clinical psychologists in the 1970s. *American Psychologist*, 1976, **31**, 1–9.

Garfield, S. L. & Kurtz, R. A study of eclectic views. *Journal of Consulting and Clinical Psychology*. 1977, **45**, 78–83.

Goldfried, M. R. (Ed.) Some views on effective principles of psychotherapy. *Cognitive Therapy and Research*, 1980, **4**, 271–306. (a)

Goldfried, M. R. Toward the delineation of therapeutic change principles. *American Psychologist*, 1980, **35**, 991–999. (b)

Goldfried, M. R. & Davison, G. C. *Clinical behavior therapy*. New York: Holt, Rinehart & Winston, 1976.

Goldfried, M. R. & Goldfried, A. P. Cognitive change methods. In F. H. Kanfer & A. P. Goldstein (Eds.). *Helping people change*, 2nd ed. New York: Pergamon, 1980.

Golding, S. L. Individual differences in the construal of interpersonal interactions. In D. Magnusson & N. Endler (Eds.), *Personality at the crossroads: Current issues in interactional psychology.* Hillsdale, N.J.: Erlbaum, 1977.

Golding, S. L., Valone, K., & Foster, S. W. Interpersonal construal: An individual differences framework. In N. Hirschberg (Ed.), *Multivariate methods in the social sciences*. Hillsdale, N.J.: Erlbaum, 1980.

Gottman, J. M., Markman, H., & Notarius. C. The topography of marital conflict: A sequential analysis of verbal and nonverbal behavior. *Journal of Marriage and the Family*, 1977, **39**, 461–477.

Haley, J. *Problem-solving therapy*. San Francisco: Jossey-Bass, 1976.

Hertel, R. K. Application of stochastic process analysis to the study of psychotherapeutic processes. *Psychological Bulletin*, 1972, **77**, 421–430.

Hinde, R. A. *Towards understanding relationships*. New York: Academic Press, 1979.

Hollon, S. D. & Kendall, P. C. Cognitive-behavioral interventions: Theory and procedure. In P. C. Kendall & S. D. Hollon (Eds.), *Cognitive-behavioral interventions: Theory, research, and procedures*. New York: Academic Press, 1979.

Horowitz, L. M. On the cognitive structure of interpersonal problems treated in psychotherapy. *Journal of Consulting and Clinical Psychology*, 1979, **47**, 1–15.

Jaffe, J. Computer assignment of dyadic interaction rules from chronographic data. In J. M. Schlien (Eds.), *Research in psychotherapy*, vol. 3. Washington, D.C.: American Psychological Association, 1968.

Kanfer, F. H. Self-management methods. In F. H. Kanfer & A. P. Goldstein (Eds.), *Helping people change*, 2nd ed. New York: Pergamon, 1980.

Kelley, G. A. *The psychology of personal constructs*. New York: Norton, 1955.

Kendall, P. C. & Hollon, S. D. (Eds.) *Cognitive-behavioral interventions: Theory, research, and procedures*. New York: Academic Press, 1979.

Kiesler, D. J. Experimental designs in psychotherapy research. In A. E. Bergin & S. L. Garfield (Eds.), *Handbook of psychotherapy and behavior change: An empirical analysis*. New York: Wiley, 1971.

Kiesler, D. J. *Manual for the Impact Message Inventory*. Richmond: Virginia Commonwealth University, 1979.

Kiesler, D. J., Bernstein, A. J., & Anchin, J. C. *Interpersonal communication, relationship and the behavior therapies*. Richmond: Virginia Commonwealth University, 1976.

Lazarus, A. A. *Behavior therapy and beyond*. New York: McGraw-Hill, 1971.

Leary, T. *Interpersonal diagnosis of personality: A functional theory and methodology for personality evaluation*. New York: Ronald Press, 1957.

Lichtenberg, J. W. & Hummel, J. J. Counseling as stochastic process: Fitting a Markov chain model to initial counseling interviews. *Journal of Counseling Psychology*, 1976, **23**, 310–315.

Longabaugh, R. A category system for coding interpersonal behavior as social exchange. *Sociometry*, 1963, **26**, 319–343.

Lorr, M., Bishop, P. R., & McNair, D. M. Interpersonal types among psychiatric patients. *Journal of Abnormal Psychology*, 1965, **70**, 468–472.

Lorr, M. & McNair, D. M. An interpersonal behavior circle. *Journal of Abnormal and Social Psychology*, 1963, **67**, 68–75.

Lorr, M. & McNair, D. M. Expansion of the interpersonal behavior circle. *Journal of Abnormal and Social Psychology*, 1965, **2**, 823–830.

Lorr, M. & McNair, D. M. Methods relating to evaluation of therapeutic outcome. In L. A. Gottschalk & A. H. Auerbach (Eds.), *Methods of research in psychotherapy*. New York: Appleton-Century-Crofts, 1966.

Lorr, D. & McNair, D. M. *The Interpersonal Behavior Inventory*, Form 4. Washington, D.C.: Catholic University of America, 1967.

Mahoney, M. J. *Cognition and behavior modification*. Cambridge, Mass.: Ballinger, 1974.

Mahoney, M. J. Reflections on the cognitive-learning trend in psychotherapy. *American Psychologist*, 1977, **32**, 5–13.

Margolin, G. *A sequential analysis of dyadic communication*. Paper presented at the Association for the Advancement of Behavior Therapy, Atlanta, Georgia, December, 1977.

Markus, H. Self-schemata and processing information about the self. *Journal of Personality and Social Psychology*, 1977, **35**, 63–78.

McLemore, C. W. & Benjamin, L. S. Whatever happened to interpersonal diagnosis? A psychosocial alternative in DSM-III. *American Psychologist*, 1979, **34**, 17–34.

Meichenbaum, D. *Cognitive-behavior modification: An integrative approach*. New York: Plenum, 1977.

Meichenbaum, D. & Genest, M. Cognitive behavior modification: An integration of cognitive and behavioral methods. In F. H. Kanfer & A. P. Goldstein (Eds.), *Helping people change*, 2nd ed. New York: Pergamon, 1980.

Meissner, W. W. & Nicholi, A. M., Jr. The psychotherapies: Individual, family, and group. In A. M. Nicholi, Jr. (Ed.), *The Harvard guide to modern psychiatry*. Cambridge, Mass.: The Belknap Press of Harvard University Press, 1978.

Mischel, W. Toward a cognitive social learning reconceptualization of personality. *Psychological Review*, 1973, **80**, 252–283.

Mischel, W. On the interface of cognition and personality: Beyond the person-situation debate. *American Psychologist*, 1979, **34**, 740–754.

Murray, E. J. & Jacobson, L. I. Cognition and learning in traditional and behavioral psychotherapy. In S. L. Garfield & A. E. Bergin (Eds.), *Handbook of psychotherapy and behavior change: An empirical analysis*. New York: Wiley, 1978.

Nay, W. R. *Behavioral intervention: Contemporary strategies*. New York: Gardner Press, 1976.

Nelson, R. O. Methodological issues in assessment via self-monitoring. In J. D. Cone & R. P. Hawkins (Eds.), *Behavioral assessment: New directions in clinical psychology*. New York: Brunner/Mazel, 1977.

Parloff, M. B. Psychotherapy and research: An anaclitic depression. *Psychiatry*, 1980, **43**, 279–293.

Perkins, M. J., Kiesler, D. J., Anchin, J. C., Chirico, B. M, Kyle, E. M., & Federman, E. J. The Impact Message Inventory: A new measure of relationship in counseling/psychotherapy and other dyads. *Journal of Counseling Psychology*, 1979, **26** 363–367.

Peterson, D. R. *The clinical study of social behavior*. New York: Appleton-Century-Crofts, 1968.

Peterson, D. R. A functional approach to the study of person-person interactions. In D. Magnusson & N. S. Endler (Eds.), *Personality at the cross-roads: Current issues in interactional psychology*. Hillsdale, N.J.: Erlbaum, 1977.

Peterson, D. R. Assessing interpersonal relationships by means of interaction records. *Behavioral Assessment*, 1979, **1**, 221–236. (a)

Peterson, D. R. Assessing interpersonal relationships in natural settings. *New Directions for Methodology of Behavioral Science*, 1979, **2**, 33–54. (b)

Raimy, V. *Misunderstandings of the self: Cognitive psychotherapy and the misconception hypothesis*. San Francisco: Jossey-Bass, 1975.

Rathjen, D., Rathjen, E., & Hiniker, A. A cognitive analysis of social performance. In J. Foreyt & D. Rathjen (Eds.), *Cognitive behavior therapy: Research and application*. New York: Plenum Press, 1978.

Raush, H. L. Interaction sequences. *Journal of Personality and Social Psychology*, 1965, **2**, 487–499.

Raush, H. L. Process and change—A Markov model for interaction. *Family Process*, 1972, **11**, 275–298.

Reisman, J. M. *Toward the integration of psychotherapy*. New York: Wiley, 1971.

Rosch, E. Cognitive reference points. *Cognitive Psychology*, 1975, **7**, 532–547.

Schneider, D. M., Hastorf, A. H. & Ellsworth, P. C. *Person perception*, 2nd ed. Reading, Mass.: Addison-Wesley, 1979.

Secord, P. F. & Backman, C. W. Personality theory and the problem of stability and change in individual behavior: An interpersonal approach. *Psychological Review*, 1961, **68**, 21–32.

Secord, P. F. & Backman, C. W. An interpersonal approach to personality. In B. A. Maher (Ed.), *Progress in experimental personality research*, vol. 2. New York: Academic Press, 1965.

Shapiro, D. *Neurotic styles*. New York: Basic Books, 1965.

Singer, E. *Key concepts in psychotherapy*, 2nd ed. New York: Basic Books, 1970.

Sollod, R. N. & Wachtel, P. L. A structural and transactional approach to cognition in clinical problems. In M. J. Mahoney (Ed.), *Psychotherapy process: Current issues and future directions*. New York: Plenum Press, 1980.

Strupp, H. H. Towards a specification of teaching and learning in psychotherapy. *Archives of General Psychiatry*, 1969, **21**, 203–212.

Strupp, H. H. On the basic ingredients of psychotherapy. *Journal of Consulting and Clinical Psychology*, 1973, **41**, 1–8.

Sullivan, H. S. *Conceptions of modern psychiatry*. New York: Norton, 1940.

Sullivan, H. S. *The interpersonal theory of psychiatry*. New York: Norton, 1953.

Sullivan, H. S. *The psychiatric interview*. New York: Norton, 1954.

Swensen, C., Jr. *Introduction to interpersonal relations*. Glenview, Ill.: Scott, Foresman, 1973.

Taylor, W. R. Research on family interaction I: Static and dynamic models. *Family Process*, 1970, **9**, 221–232.

Thibaut, J. W. & Kelley, H. H. *The social psychology of groups*. New York: Wiley, 1959.

Wachtel, P. L. *Psychoanalysis and behavior therapy: Toward an integration*. New York: Basic Books, 1977.

Wegner, D. M. & Vallacher, R. R. (Eds.) *The self in social psychology*. New York: Oxford University Press, 1980.

Wiggins, J. S. Circumplex models of interpersonal behavior in clinical psychology. In P. C. Kendall & J. N. Butcher (Eds.), *Handbook of research methods in clinical psychology*. New York: Wiley-Interscience, *in press*.

Yalom, I. D. *The theory and practice of group psychotherapy*, 2nd ed. New York: Basic Books, 1975.

Chapter 7
The Rationale of Psychotherapeutic Discourse
Robin Tolmach Lakoff

PSYCHOTHERAPY: "FRIENDLY CONVERSATION" OR "SCIENTIFIC TECHNIQUE"?

Whether as users or observers of therapeutic procedure, we ask a lot of psychotherapeutic discourse. We have half-explicit expectations about what it is, how (or whether, or why) it "works," what "working" might entail, and how it differs from what we think of as "ordinary conversation." We want to assume it is in some intrinsic way unlike our normal mode of communication with friends and strangers. Otherwise, how can the institution be justified? Certainly everyone has heard someone say, "If I had problems, I'd talk to my friends about them, not to a therapist. That's what friends are for. Why should I pay for friendship?"[1] The important implication in such statements is that therapeutic discourse differs from friendly encouragement and advice only in the price tag attached to it.

Since this is not an inspiring point of view for psychotherapeutic practitioners—and since, incidentally, there is little evidence that ordinary friendly discourse is efficacious in solving the kinds of problems that psychotherapy is said to ameliorate about two-thirds of the time—other models for looking at the mechanisms of this type of conversational strategy have been proposed. The justifications of its methods and the arguments for one method over another are diverse, but underlying all is one important and usually, again, implicit precept: psychotherapeutic discourse is special; it is a "technique"; it is "scientific." Sometimes this is made fully explicit—as in much psychoanalytic writing—by invoking the analogy of the medical prescription: an "intervention" or "interpretation" is "timed" and its "dosage" is regulated.[2] Even when the medical model is less clearly in sight, therapeutic intervention is presented as no haphazard affair. Certain kinds of statements must be made, in certain forms, at certain times, certain intervals. There are ways to say something that guarantee efficacy. The more confident practitioner-theorists hold forth the promise that, if only neophytes will master a particular formalism, a specific formula, cures are all but in the bag. This precision in predictability, it is argued, shows beyond doubt that psychotherapy is a science, more than an art, hence respectable, and with results that are scientifically replicable, like medicine. But as research has repeatedly demonstrated, across all types of psychotherapy, regardless of method, the results are the same—two-thirds of patients demonstrate some improvement. Science demands more. In fact, if we look at the claims and disclaimers made for virtually every psychotherapeutic system that has attempted to provide a formal model for itself, we find that the instructions for the technique resemble science much less than they do other forms of human attempts to explain the universe and to account for behavior—specifically religion, or perhaps more accurately, the animism of primitive cultures.

What is characteristic of religious, and even more so animistic, discourse is its stress on the importance of form over content. In primitive rites, what is critical is that everything be said right, according to a prescribed formula that has been handed down from time immemorial. It doesn't matter if the utterance is unintelligible to its utterers—perhaps that is even better. But if one syllable is missed, if two sentences are transposed, if one synonym is substituted for another, then that's why it hasn't rained or why the crops have failed. And, of course, if it doesn't rain or the crops fail despite fervent pleas to divinities, it can be safely assumed not that the divinities don't exist or don't care, not that the means of achieving results are basically misguided, but that, unbeknownst perhaps to all participants, *something* was amiss in the observance—a syllable stumbled over, an incantation uttered too soon, or too late. Without the benfit of audio tape, of course, primitives cannot be sure that such a mischance occurred, but that is certainly the easiest explanation for the debacle.

And in fact psychotherapeutic discourse is often discussed by its practitioners in ways that, for all their appeal to a scientific paradigm, are reminiscent of this prescientific outlook. It is of course acknowledged that a large part of therapeutic efficacy lies in the delicate management of the relationship between the participants—that is, under the name of transference the role of suggestion is considered instrumental in the therapeutic process, both historically in its development and in the process of treatment. This aspect of therapeutic method seems to occasion more covert embarrassment in therapists than any other, as if it were recognized as not so far distant from other quite unscientific methods of persuasion—religion, propaganda, or commercial advertising.

Therapeutic discourse, then, has analogies to several discourse types ordinarily considered distinct, some of them held in much higher repute than others. I think this ambiguity creates difficulty in the understanding of what therapeutic discourse is, and in understanding what makes discourse therapeutic. Perhaps if we take a look at what differentiates ordinary conversation from these other types—in particular therapeutic discourse as a subtype of persuasive discourse—we will be better able to see what is intrinsic to all therapeutic styles that makes them effective, and thereby be better able in the future to develop models of therapeutic intervention that are apt to be effective in general, as well as, perhaps, specific types that may prove particularly useful for specific purposes. What I want to do at the outset is summarize some of the linguistic properties of ordinary conversation, so that we can then see which of these properties is shared by therapeutic discourse, and in what respect it differs. I want to argue that the differences that exist between the two types are more important and more widespread than the apparent similarities and that, further, similarities are in fact generally only apparent.

PSYCHOTHERAPEUTIC DISCOURSE AS RULE-GOVERNED BEHAVIOR

At the risk of courting platitude, I want to begin by remarking that *any* type of language is governed by rules, the rules of grammar. Within the field of linguistics in the past twenty odd years, there has been much dispute over the form these rules take and even the area of communicative skills they cover, but most scholars in the area would by now agree that speakers operate with such rules in at least the more "linguistic"—as opposed, perhaps, to the more broadly communicative—parts of their language-using ability, e.g., phonology (the structuring of systems of sound) and syntax (the structuring of the elements of a sentence). The assumption, as originally made explicit by Chomsky (1957), is that speakers have in their minds the internalization of a sort of template, a schema for the production of sentences. From the finite set of utterances to which young children are exposed, they construct the most efficient abstract system of rules that can be used to produce such sentences, and to prevent the production of utterances that are not recognized as "sentences of English." That is, from the relatively few examples accessible to them, children make generalizations, predictions as to what might actually occur and what might not occur. The syntactic rules formalize these predictions. It is not appropriate here to discuss the innumerable problems that are known to exist with this model, and the reader is of course aware that this discussion is almost ludicrously oversimplified. What is important for our purposes, however, is just this: the mastery of at least certain aspects of language use entails the development of an abstract system of unconsciously held and unconsciously applied rules. We recognize a deviation when we encounter it, but we do not know which rule has been broken, or how. If we are presented with a transitive active sentence—e.g., *John hit the ball*—we, as fluent speakers of English, can unhesitatingly supply its passive equivalent—*The ball was hit by John*—although we have never presumably encountered either of these variants. Hence we claim that there is a rule that governs the relation between an active sentence and its corresponding passive; that it functions as a generalization over *all* possible active and passive pairs, rather than each pair's being learned one by one as it is encountered in use; and that we use these rules without knowing their forms. (So although you can tell me, on demand, that the passive of *John hit the ball* is *The ball was hit by John*, not *John was hit by the ball*, or anything else, you cannot, without linguistic training—or, alas, at present, with it—formally state the rule used to arrive at this certainty.)

The theory invoked here also would claim that these implicit rules allow users of a language to link two distinct levels of linguistic awareness: a superficial level, that is, utterances as they emerge from the mouth (or on the page); and the deep, or abstract, or logical level which represents meanings but is not superficially accessible. To give a simple example: two sentences that have approximately the same meaning would have necessarily the same underlying structure, since that structure represents meaning; but two different surface structures. The active-passive pair *John hit the ball/The ball was hit by John* works this way. The two distinct surface structures are assumed to derive from a single underlying structure, probably resembling the active more closely than the passive variant. The rule relating active and passive mediates between underlying and surface structure, showing how an "underlying" active sentence is basic to a "surface" passive. The converse can be true as well: ambiguous sentences are those which admit more than one meaning, but have only one surface form: *Visiting relatives can be a nuisance* is one famous example, and another is *They don't know how good meat tastes*. In these cases, we have two distinct underlying structures, one representing each meaning (in the latter case, very roughly speaking, perhaps a pair equivalent to *They don't know how tasty meat is* and *They are unfamiliar with the taste of good meat*). The rule or rules involved would turn each of these, independent of the other, into a surface structure, and by more or less chance characteristics of English syntax, the two derivational paths would merge in the end into a single surface structure: *They don't know how good meat tastes*.

This is necessarily a much too brief summation of syntactic theory. In itself it is not of great interest for therapeutic purposes. What is of interest for therapeutic discourse is the form of another aspect of the grammar, the pragmatic component. As syntax regulates the relationship among items in a sentence, and semantics relates the utterance to its referent, so pragmatics relates an utterance to the participants in the discourse and the context in which that discourse is held. The reason I have spent time on the intricacies of syntactic theory is that is has become evident to many of us that the various areas of linguistic competence operate by similar principles. No area—not syntax, not phonology, not pragmatics—is autonomous, but all function with reference to one another and use the same kinds of structures, the same basic strategies and rules. The arguments that were made a generation ago by Chomsky to argue for a transformational-generative theory of syntax such as I have outlined above are equally applicable to the pragmatic sphere. The same kinds of evidence—ambiguity, paraphrase, recognition of ungrammaticality or inappropriateness—can be marshalled. In fact, the way in which we engage in therapeutic conversation stands as one piece of evidence for the proposition that pragmatics is structured according to the same tripartite system—underlying structure, surface structure, and rules relating the two—as was claimed for syntax. That is, any utterance that might occur in a therapeutic session may be, and frequently is, viewed as ambiguous— pragmatically ambiguous, the linguist would say; overdetermined, the therapist might say, meaning the same thing. A surface structure like "it's hot in here," while *syntactically* unambiguous, is *pragmatically* ambiguous in that it might interactively mean any of several things. While it has a single surface structure (explicit form) it may be related—by any of a number of rules—to any of several deeper structures. Which one is appropriate can only be determined by the context in which it is uttered—where, how, by whom, following what utterance, preceding what utterance, and so on. The therapeutic situation itself comprises a context distinct from the context of "ordinary conversation," and that distinction occasions ambiguity and attendant confusion.

The Relationship between PD and OC

So this is one way in which therapeutic discourse uses the conventions of ordinary language. In respect to the syntactic components of the grammar, for all practical purposes, the two are the same. We cannot speak of syntactic ambiguity or paraphrase relations between OC and PD. But in general, *pragmatically*, anything uttered in a "therapeutic" context must be understood as standing in a relation of ambiguity to another superficially identical statement in an "ordinary discourse" context. This is perhaps the major, the most important, and the most difficult thing a patient (or client or therapist) must learn. It is a very sophisticated concept. And yet by and large people don't have much trouble with it—indignation, sometimes, when they are confronted with the ambiguity, but no real intellectual problem. This suggests that there is a fairly clear relation between utterances in psychotherapeutic discourse (PD) and utterances in ordinary conversation (OC). What I want to do in this chapter is examine the relationship between PD and OC.

PD: DEEP AND SURFACE STRUCTURES

I am assuming that psychotherapeutic discourse uses the rules of ordinary conversation, with a few but highly important differences. This accounts for the surface similarity between PD and OC advice or encouragement from a friend. But at the same time, PD differs underlyingly—at the level of abstract understanding—from its equivalent in OC, and therefore certain things are permissibly said and understood in one but not in the other. In this sense, PD is ritualized, designed for a specific purpose—that of effecting change—and in this way it is related to religion and suggestion, though it is neither of these. To say that PD deliberately utilizes the forms of OC for a different purpose is not to say that it or its practitioners are scheming or manipulative. Rather, they are adapting a preexisting mode of interaction to a special new purpose, an act of creativity. I hope to show in this chapter both what the differences are, and how their actual form makes therapeutic change possible.

I have remarked on the seeming paradox that, viewed superficially, most (though not all) forms of therapeutic discourse resemble ordinary conversation, yet all PD is engaged in explicitly with different intentions from OC. This would imply that while the surface structures of PD and OC are similar, the abstract structures are not; we are dealing with pragmatic ambiguities. Therapist and patient—although each in somewhat different ways—both learn to adapt their knowledge of the techniques and purposes of ordinary conversation to the therapeutic encounter. What is most extraordinary of all, perhaps, is the ease with which most participants adapt to the new milieu. If PD were in fact radically different in structure from OC, we should expect something quite different: a long period of training for the patient, in which frequent gross errors were made through sheer ignorance of the communicative system, in which he had to be carefully coached and corrected time after time. One can object that this is not in fact too distorted a picture of what goes on in early parts of many therapeutic relationships; but to say this would be to misunderstand. Surely patients need to be helped to understand how to speak, what to say, what not to say, and how to understand what is said by their therapists. But they learn these new skills on the basis of the old familiar linguistic knowledge: fluency in PD is strongly based on skill in OC that has been acquired earlier. Learning PD is not nearly as difficult as, for example, learning a foreign language, and probably less complicated even than learning standard English is for a speaker of a dialect like Black English. These observations suggest that, rather than learning a new language, or a new set of rules, the neophyte speaker of PD (whether beginning therapist or new patient) is learning to recontextualize familiar skills, to apply familiar rules in a new context. The context can be viewed as a kind of metarule,[3] an injunction to understand each of the familiar rules in a particular way based on the assumption of a shared idiosyncratic situation. Once the patient accepts the reality of the special context, and internalizes the attendant need for special formulations or understanding of the old rules, PD has essentially been learned.

The Importance of Recontextualization

What is problematic about the recontextualization implicit in PD is that it is precisely the sort that a person ordinarily finds abhorrent—contrary to all the ordinary rules of conversational behavior learned since childhood, contrary to the assumptions that allow someone to enter conversations with the assurance of getting something out of them—socially if not necessarily intellectually. It is a basic principle of human interaction that we do not generally participate in any form of interpersonal behavior unless it seems likely that we will emerge from the encounter with some advantage, that there is benefit to be gained in the discourse. Sometimes the benefit is very obvious—street directions, advice, the avoidance of legal penalties, and so on. In that case, we demand no more of the discourse. Such conversations, conducted for purposes of extrinsic benefit, are usually begun, engaged in, and ended with a minimum of ritual—there is no need for rituals. We get right to the point, we say what needs to be said, we express gratitude where it is needed rather brusquely, we part company without even the barest suggestion that we are sorry to end the encounter or that we would enjoy meeting again. No one feels bad; all that anyone intended to accomplish has been accomplished.

Such encounters, however, are relatively infrequent. More often, we engage in discourse with someone else with a different benefit in mind: that of rapport, of making social contact, feeling liked and appreciated. Since this outcome is not one we can ask of another person directly, we often couch tentative rapport-oriented discourse as informational, so that if the other takes it just that way, we have not lost face. (But in fact if we approach someone else with a request for directions, or the time, with an ulterior motive, and it is treated literally, we nonetheless feel dissatisfied. We have set up an ambiguous situation, and are distressed that the other person has intentionally or otherwise misunderstood us.) The reverse, for obvious reasons, does not occur. We don't set up informational discourses with the appearance of rapport conversations. It is interesting that, in most rhetoric texts, we are urged to speak and write as if information were the coin of the conversational realm, to make our utterances as brief and to the point as possible, maximizing the effective interchange of factual data. Yet the way we act and don't act in conversations shows that we value rapport far above information, and feel much worse if an attempt to seek rapport fails than if the other person merely can't or won't inform us. We use information gathering as a stalking-horse for rapport. If the other person seems willing to give information, perhaps we can induce him to engage in rapport discourse as well. But we don't operate the other way. We tailor introductory conversation so that, whatever our deepest hopes, it looks like information exchange rather than the other way around. What is obvious here is that successful informational conversation is all right in its own way, but rapport discourse alone, properly conducted, makes us feel good and is really what most conversation is all about.

RECIPROCITY IN OC AND IN PD

What enables OC to work this way—to make its participants feel good about themselves, the conversation itself, and the others in it—is that OC is normally *reciprocal*. What one participant can do, can say, can expect, so can any other. To the extent that OC departs from this ideal, it is not rapport-oriented (as informational interchange is not) or, if clearly perceived by all parties as rapport-based, it is felt by at least one as unsuccessful and unsatisfactory. Reciprocity in this sense extends over all aspects of a discourse, from the smallest single interchange to the structure of the discourse as a whole, from concrete utterances to the abstract intentions behind them, and the uses made of all utterances by each participant. The speaker who holds the floor rather than allowing others their turns is not acting reciprocally, nor is the speaker who only responds to the questions of others, never initiating topics, or who answers only in monosyllables. The speaker who cajoles intimate revelations from another but will not make them is not behaving reciprocally, nor is the speaker who makes interpretations of the other's utterances or behavior and will not tolerate the same in return. These are just a few examples; we sense all of them as impositions, as instances of unfriendliness, and when we are subjected to them in what is ostensibly a rapport conversation, we do our best to disentangle ourselves from the conversation as soon as possible, and feel no desire to have another with the same person again.

Ordinary Reciprocal Conversation

Reciprocity is one important means of achieving rapport, giving each participant the sense that the others are engaging in the conversation for pleasure and are enjoying it, and that they consider the contributions of the other partners equal to and as worthwhile as their own. Reciprocity is the basis of all our rules of ordinary conversation.

When we look at PD with this framework in mind, we are struck at first by the apparent similarities. In general, in most types of therapeutic encounter, there is certainly the semblance of reciprocity. We must exclude classical analysis from this statement, of course; as its strictest practitioners claim to practice it, we find reciprocity of even the most superficial kind cut to the barest minimum. This is part of what is meant by the "rule of abstinence." The patient and the analyst play distinctly asymmetric conversational roles, down to the fact that eye contact is only unilateral—and only partial at that.

Reciprocity and Nonreciprocity in the Therapeutic Encounter

But if we look at even the nonanalytic therapeutic encounter more closely, we find the similarities to ordinary conversation, in terms of reciprocity, more apparent than real. This is one strong reason for the frequent invidious comparisons between psychotherapy and friendly talk, mentioned at the beginning of this chapter. If PD is like OC, and it is "reciprocal," then how can money be exchanged? Is psychotherapy, then, to friendship as prostitution is to sex? To suggest that there be payment of any kind in conversation is to destroy totally the concept of reciprocity. The implication in a presumably "friendly" discourse would be, of course, that the payer's contribution to the discourse was by itself of so little worth to the payee that only monetary advantage could make it worthwhile for the latter to continue. Such an assumption is, naturally, a contradiction of reciprocity. But it is a misconstruction of PD to see it in terms of failed reciprocity, arising from the belief—based on superficial observation of therapeutic conversation—that it functions by the same rules as does ordinary friendly discourse. Professionals tend to encourage this false belief, probably in an understandable attempt to counteract the other prevalent belief about therapy—that it is a mysterious procedure all too closely akin to its ancestor, hypnosis, in which some Svengali gets access to one's innermost thoughts and control over one's actions and feelings. To dispel *this* dangerous misapprehension, then, from their own minds as much as from their patients', therapists have tended to go to the other extreme: psychotherapeutic discourse is just a friendly chat, the participants sitting in nice comfy chairs looking for all the world like two friends in a living room. So of course there's nothing weird or dangerous about it.

The Interpretation of Nonreciprocity

The difficulty is that from childhood we have only two basic models for conversational strategy, and given the force of habit, we tend to put any new conversational situation we later encounter into one of these two convenient cubbyholes. One is reciprocal, discussed above, learned in interaction with siblings and peers. The other is nonreciprocal conversation, in which the lack of reciprocity is based on clear status distinctions, and wherein one of the participants is clearly dependent upon the other, for nurturance, knowledge, or support. Children learn this type of interaction by engaging in discourse with their parents. Later, it is extended to conversation with teachers and other obvious authority figures. In such discourse, reciprocity makes no sense; equality does not exist. The purpose of the discourse is other than simply enjoying the interaction itself—the younger participant generally needs something concrete, or anyway something not to be found within the discourse itself, from the other. In such cases, we neither need nor look for reciprocity, and our conversational expectations are different from those situations in which reciprocity must be maintained. Where nonreciprocal discourse tends to involve tension and uncertainty, reciprocal discourse tends to be much less anxiety producing and much more satisfying in itself for most children. So it is natural that we go into adulthood with two models, one loosely labelled nonreciprocal/problematic and the other reciprocal/comfortable. We have very different sets of rules for each of these, based on the assumption or nonassumption of reciprocity. If we are in a reciprocity-mode discourse, we have well-defined and understood (though implicit) rituals that we must follow to indicate how comfortable and enjoyable the situation is, and how much the other's utterances are valued. For example, such rapport-oriented conversations normally involve surprisingly elaborate entering and termination rituals. We have specific expected ways to enter into a conversation, more heavily structured and carefully orchestrated with new acquaintances, but seldom absent: hand shaking, smiling, saying, "Hello," "How are you," "Glad to meet you," are all more or less obligatory. Others may be added at the participants' will: "I've heard so much about you," "Isn't this a nice party?" and so forth. All are designed to show, however conventionally, trust, interest, and liking. And in terminating a conversation, we are more careful still, because ending is even more dangerously charged—we must be careful never to imply we find the converation distasteful, or that we would rather be doing something else. So we say, "Nice meeting you," and we break off apologetically, "I have to . . . ," never "I want to . . . ." Sometimes we resort to elaborate ruses: "Excuse me a minute—I need to freshen my drink," as the speaker heads off, never to return.

One striking feature of reciprocal discourse is its microstructural reciprocity. Whatever kinds of speech acts one participant may engage in, so may the other, and within those broad types, whatever one speaker may say or expect the other to say, the other is entitled to a symmetrical expectation. Between parents and children, this is of course not true. Parents assume that they can interrogate children about all kinds of things, and children may not return the favor; on the other hand, children can make requests of parents that parents cannot make of children. The reverse, with other kinds of requests, is also true. Parents and children generally use different kinds of imperatives or request forms to each other. Children are much more apt to use indirect or hedged forms: "I hate peas"; "All the other kids are going"; "Where's my jacket?" while adults tend to use direct forms: "Be back by 6," "Take out the garbage," "Please pick up your socks." This makes perfect sense: hedged imperatives are protective of their speakers. They allow them to pretend that they aren't asking for something so that if they do not get it, they lose less face than they would if they were to make an overt request and be ignored. Someone in an inferior position is wise to talk this way. But superiors, who assume a right to be obeyed (whether in fact they are or not), can make direct requests anticipating compliance, and if this is not forthcoming they do not lose face but rather feel righteous indignation. There is also a sense that children have the conversational right to assume that parents are interested in their needs and care about their problems, but parents normally do not expect this sort of solicitude from young children. And since children, in tending toward hedged forms, are prone to use questions and declaratives to express what really are imperatives—that is, they use other speech act types to replace the imperative—other things being equal, parents will tend to interpet children's utterances accordingly. That is, since subordinates must by virtue of their situation express themselves indirectly, using one type of speech act to stand for another, superiors have the implicit right to decide what subordinates mean by their use of any particular form. Superiors in nonreciprocal situations, partly out of necessity, reserve for themselves the right to interpret the productions of others, but the reverse is never the case. "Don't put words into my mouth," says the parent if the child attempts a role reversal, and so the child learns about this aspect of nonreciprocal discourse. This tendency to act as a child's interpreter has been cited by numerous writers as potentially schizophrenogenic[4] if abused; but it is important to realize that some amount of interpretation is necessary since so many indirect and hedged utterances are by their very nature ambiguous or otherwise unclear. What is important, though, is that through parental interpretation children tend to feel that their choices in types of speech acts are limited, whatever they say is apt to be taken as a request. Requesting, after all, is a major business of the subordinate, so it makes sense for the parent to interpret all utterances, unless there is evidence to the contrary, as requests. In any case, both restriction—in actuality or in interpretation—of speech act type and the unilateral right to overt interpretation are characteristic of nonreciprocal discourse alone.

THE REINTERPRETATION OF PD CONVENTIONS: THE THERAPEUTIC PARADOX

Psychotherapeutic theory has always correctly assumed that there were two major types of discourse but it has incorrectly defined these as "friendly" and "scientific" and further compounded the confusion by claiming on the one hand that PD worked as it did because it was special, "scientific," but in fact it really was just a form of OC, "friendly" conversation, no mystique or mumbo jumbo. In fact, most of the rules of PD are those of OC, which is what makes it possible for therapist and patient alike to learn to use PD without too long an apprenticeship, but the overarching rule of all conversation, the Principle of Reciprocity, is used, or not used, in an idiosyncratic way in the therapeutic encounter. It is this special set of assumptions that must be learned, and once this is done, individual differences may be learned automatically. What is strikingly different about PD, then, is that it is in fact basically nonreciprocal in nature but has a superficial veneer—except for the most classical forms of psychoanalysis—of reciprocity discourse. It is this amalgamation in all PD that is paradoxical and hence difficult to learn, and it is this very paradox that creates suspicion and resentment in nonprofessionals who feel that a sacred gulf is being illegitimately bridged. But it is also true that it is this very amalgamation—leading to the creation of a totally new discourse type—that makes therapy effective. It is seeing old rules operating with new meaning, old forms of discourse translated, as it were, because they occur in a totally new framework, with new associations and assumptions. A type of discourse that was purely reciprocal or purely nonreciprocal would not be effective, because no new metalearning or deuterolearning, in Bateson's (1972) sense, would be required. Even though I suggested above that orthodox psychoanalysis did not partake of this paradox, in fact that statement is not really correct. In that theory, too, there is a contradiction, an ambiguity involving reciprocity, though rather less striking than in other more seemingly egalitarian therapeutic models. In psychoanalytic discourse, at least as specified in most writings on technique, ordinary turn taking, which forms the basis of reciprocity, is missing.[5] One participant holds the floor; the other largely listens. In OC, when this happens, we are normally engaged in nonreciprocal discourse by mutual consent; a lecture or the giving of instructions or directions. In OC, non-turn-taking modes of discourse are explicitly nonegalitarian; the speaker holds the floor by virtue of a mutually agreed upon position of power usually vested in authority. What is odd about the analytic situation is that the floor holder is not in authority, not even to the extent of being responsible for the meanings of his or her own utterances. So this situation, like so many others, is unlike anything encountered in naturalistic conversational settings, and is contradictory if not actually paradoxical if viewed from the perspective of ordinary conversational structure. At a deeper and more subtle level, although it appears that both participants in the analytic encounter may produce all forms of speech acts under appropriate conditions, in fact, in terms of intended meaning or interpreted meaning—as opposed to surface form—the patient tends to be restricted to interrogatives, the analyst to declaratives. This may at first seem a grossly incorrect statement, certainly from the vantage point of superficial interaction. Probably the majority of the patient's productions are in the form of statements, and a great many of the analyst's, of questions. But in order to understand this special sort of conversation, we must go beneath the surface and ask about the *intent* of each utterance. For a speech act is in general more appropriately identified in terms of its function or its speaker's intention in the discourse than in terms of its surface form. The rhetorical question common in OC is one obvious example. Although it looks like a question, it is intended, and responded to, as a declarative utterance, an informative contribution. Another is hedged imperatives such as those discussed above, like "It's hot in here" meaning "Open the window." These have declarative form, but under proper contextual conditions function and are intended to be understood as requests. It is, of course, of interest and theoretical significance for both linguistic and psychological theory that people so often choose to express ideas in indirect ways; but we would certainly want to argue that greater insight into both linguistic behavior and human motivation is gained by understanding these utterances in terms of intended function, rather than of surface form alone. Given these facts about OC, we can see that PD in general, and psychoanalytic discourse even more particularly, uses them to particular purposes. In all forms of discourse, mismatches of speech act types lend themselves to interpretation. But PD generally, and psychoanalytic discourse even more, differs from OC in that in PD interpretation is carried on unilaterally, consciously, with greater regularity and frequency, and in much greater depth than is the case in OC. But the same guiding principle for when and how to interpret is maintained: interpret when the utterance makes no sense at face value. In determining whether an utterance "makes no sense," we don't look for total unintelligibility or utter nonsense, for that virtually never occurs in any discourse type. In fact, what we mean by "nonsense" is "an utterance that is totally uninterpretable, cannot be given meaning." To understand the relations between PD and OC better—specifically with respect to interpretability—we can define three significant levels of meaningfulness in any kind of conversation. (1) The utterance is fully meaningful at face value; the addressee need do no work to understand it; (2) the utterance is not fully intelligible on its surface; the addressee must make certain assumptions (interpretations), whether consciously and overtly or not, to derive sense from it; and (3) the utterance does not make sense and no amount of interpretation, using conventional, agreed upon (implicit) rules, will help. PD and OC treat levels (1) and (3) similarly; the crucial difference lies in level (2). One difference between (2) in OC and in PD is that in the latter, interpretation is done openly as well as unilaterally; in OC, that could signal the end of any friendship if attempted more than a few times.

I should specify further that "making no sense" in level (2) refers principally to pragmatic rather than semantic meaninglessness, where in level (3) it might be either. Level (3) occurs, though rather rarely, in psychotic discourse; level (2) occurs when someone says something that is internally coherent and rational, but whose purpose in the particular context of the discourse at hand is not immediately discernible; it is not clear how the other participants benefit from the knowledge. In the sense of Grice (1975), such interactions appear to violate one or more aspects of the Cooperative Principle, most likely the Maxim of Quantity of Relation.[6]

How interpretability works within the specialized constraints and specialized abrogation of constraints of analytic dialogue is beyond the scope of this chapter. What is relevant, though, it that superficial speech acts of one type (e.g., declaratives) from a person defined as playing a subordinate role are therefore interpretable as questions or sometimes as hedged requests; and at the same time, superficial questions from the person in authority (who, ipso facto, cannot need information from the other) are to be interpreted as statements or instructions. ("Are you thinking about your mother?" tends to mean something closer to "You are thinking about your mother.")

But since psychoanalytic discourse is a very special discourse type, it might be assumed that, while it is strikingly different from OC, other types of PD are not. Asked to decide where the sharpest differentiation exists among the three categories, OC, PD, and psychoanalytic discourse, we might intuitively make the cut between the second and the third. But I would argue that the major break comes between the first and the second, that the differences between the latter two are more apparent than real, and their similarities more significant than their differences. The argument is based on two premises: (1) the paradoxical abrogation of reciprocity paradoxically in *all* types of therapeutic discourse; and (2) a salient difference between all types of PD and OC, involving the differences required of the learner—the patient—a reorientation in terms of expectations in a discourse, in effect, to relearn the metastrategies of conversation and thereby to reexamine a form of behavior—conversation—in which the patient has been engaging for years without giving it much thought, operating according to an implicit and therefore imperceptible pattern.

Metastrategy and Metaconversation

One very important fact about a conversation is that it has a quite precise formal structure. It has a beginning, a middle, and an end, each with its own properties and its own expected forms of response. Perhaps we don't think of conversations this way—as, for instance, we think of sonnets—because we prefer for reasons of reciprocity to think of them as spontaneous, free-form events. But, as Goffman[7] and others have shown, very little human interactional behavior is truly free form; it is generally severely constrained by unconsciously applied rules. This makes sense when we think about it. Any interaction involving two or more people *must* be structured; otherwise we could not predict other participants' behavior and would not ourselves know what to do. Although it is currently fashionable in some circles to exalt spontaneity as the highest form of human achievement, in fact relatively little of our lives is truly and fully spontaneous. Nor, of course, is it true that we act entirely by rote and instinct. Rather, within strongly rule-governed structures, we are allowed considerable freedom.

Not surprisingly, then, OC divides naturally into three major parts, two of which as noted earlier are quite rigidly structured and allow relatively little spontaneity; but the middle part is preferably spontaneous, again within defined limits. As long as we observe the necessity for the structuring of the first and last parts, we have a great deal of freedom for the rest.

If we remember the importance of reciprocity, and what creates reciprocity, it will make sense that the beginnings and ends of conversations are highly ritualized, while the middles are not. For the beginnings and the ends create the most anxiety. At the beginning, participants do not know if the other person is entering the conversation freely, or whether he is enjoying it. Both participants have to act quickly in reassurance. Ritualization makes it easier; no one has to think at these tense and loaded moments of something original and creative to say—which might be the wrong thing, might fall flat or sound stupid or anxious or antagonistic. (To make all this explicit sounds rather neurotic; but in fact, however we suppress this anxiety—which of course is greater in some people than in others—some aspects of it are always there at the beginning of an encounter. If the other participant is already known to us, the anxiety is lessened; hence, the better we know someone, the shorter initial greetings tend to become.) So we go on, sometimes at some length: "Hello, How are you? How's it going?" and responses to each of these can take several minutes. Endings are ritualized even more heavily, since it must not seem that either participant is eager to get away, or is bored, or has nothing left to say. Hence we find many prescribed forms for endings: to say, "I have to go," instead of "I want to go"; we imply continuity of the relationship in "Be seeing you," and in many languages, by the idiomatic expression of leave taking—*au revoir, auf wiedersehen*, and so on.

In the middle, however, we need not repeat or reassure, at least not ritualistically. And any indication that we are following a set formula will count against us as raconteurs or conversationalists. The middle part is not threatening in the way the others are, so we can afford to give our imaginations free rein, more or less.

But therapeutic discourse does not follow these rituals in nearly the same way. It is true that "hellos" are briefly exchanged at the beginning of a session, and at the end, "goodbyes." There is, interestingly, a special valedictory ritualization on the order of "It's time to stop," "We have to stop now," reminiscent of the OC convention in that it emphasizes the necessity rather than the desirability of terminating. But all of these are curt, rather than drawn out as they might be in ordinary discourse. Moreover, they are unilateral—invariably initiated by the therapist. In part, this is because PD is not reciprocity-oriented. This fact may make the absence of the normal ritual forms tolerable. But the real reason that they do not exist is deeper, intrinsic to the nature of the therapeutic process and the efficacy of PD itself.

The "Conversation" in PD

The question is, what is the *unit* that is the "conversation"? In OC, it is the single encounter, since within that span, we must achieve satisfaction of our aims, must come out of the encounter with whatever we hoped for when we entered it. If not, we consider the interaction unsatisfactory and will not repeat it unless it is necessary for external reasons. If it is reciprocity-oriented, we require the rituals as well as other necessities that tell us that the other person is enjoying the interaction, at least until we get to know the other person well enough so that the continuance of the relationship speaks for itself. So, loosely, we can define a "conversation" for our purposes as that amount of verbal interaction within which its participants must achieve satisfaction. Then, therapeutic discourse becomes still more of an anomaly, for one participant so obviously renounces the hope of gratification within the interaction proper as to require monetary compensation. The other—stranger still—very often does not emerge from a session feeling happy, informed, or otherwise gratified. Yet, in general, the patient keeps returning for more and expresses no dissatisfaction with individual sessions. (If the patient does express dissatisfaction to the therapist, the latter is apt to accuse the former, quite correctly, of misunderstanding how therapy is supposed to work.) Rather, the success of the therapy is determined at its end, when it has run its course, usually after many sessions. Therefore, we are justified in calling the "conversation" in therapeutic discourse the whole course of treatment. For this reason, whether or not it is satisfying its purpose cannot be gauged by what happens in a single encounter any more than the degree of satisfaction of an OC can be determined on the basis of a single exchange of two utterances, one by each participant. Each exchange contributes to the whole, but is not in itself complete or intelligible.

In fact, writings on technique implicitly take this stance. Normally, a good deal of attention is paid to procedure during initial interviews, and even more to preparing for and finally bringing about the termination of therapy.[8] The latter is especially problematic, just as leave taking is in OC.

So the therapeutic treatment as a whole constitutes in one sense the conversational unit of PD, but in another sense, each session is itself an inclusive "conversation" or unit, although not in itself complete. So we have another contradictory situation, unresolvable at the superficial level, that is an essential part of the therapeutic encounter.

The claim that there are certain special and idiosyncratic linguistic behaviors characteristic of the therapeutic encounter, and intrinsic to its efficacy is far from an interesting statement. Psychotherapy has been called the "talking cure" from its inception. The usual assumption is that there is something in the "talking"—in the choice of messages exchanged by participants and in the way in which those messages are framed—that creates the "cure." And taking this belief seriously, every therapeutic school from Freud on has devised for itself a linguistic system, more or less explicity—words to say, and not to say (say "feel" not "think"; use adverbs, not nouns); sentence types to use and not to use (make "I" statements; use active, not passive, sentences).[9] Each model claims that particular linguistic choices engender particular states of mind, and changing language patterns in prescribed ways will change the mind in predictable directions. Each therefore promises that if you adopt specific new ways of talking, your mind will be altered for the better in analogous, highly specific ways. Interestingly though, although most schools of therapy concur—albeit in different vocabularies—in the ideal outcome of the process, how a healthy mind operates and is reflected in linguistic behavior, each sets its own standards for language, has its own mystique and its own heavily invested linguistic strategies for patient and therapist alike. Curiously too, although there are many diverse therapeutic systems at present, each of which claims that a particular sort of surface linguistic alteration, and only that, will produce the desired results, survey after survey (since at least 1952) has indicated that the rate of "improvement" in psychotherapy remains constant at about two-thirds.[10] If specific techniques were responsible for specific changes, we would expect one to be far more efficacious than others, for everyone, always. All therapeutic systems agree in suggesting that surface alterations of linguistic patterns create the desired behavioral changes. Yet there is no evidence that any specific surface change is linked to particular results, or indeed any results. On the other hand, if linguistic change is not relevant in psychological change, what sense does the "talking cure" make at all? Some have concluded, from this problematic situation, that psychotherapy is a hoax, or no more than simple suggestion. But the two-thirds figure is at worst superior to that of a placebo, so debunking is not the answer.[11]

The Curative Powers of Paradoxical Communication

The resolution of this confused state of understanding seems to lie in reinterpreting the role of language in psychological change. It is not particular changes in surface language forms that matter in the therapeutic result, it is the fact that language is being used, that communication is being engaged in, in a new and special way. The rules for language use and the structures they produce remain superficially the same (for most therapeutic systems); only the underlying rationale, the context that makes the application of the rules intelligible, is altered. The context is altered, and yet it remains the same; there is no reciprocity, and yet there is. The single encounter is not the conversation, and yet it is. The rules for holding ordinary conversation are not in force, and yet they are. We cannot point to a particular word or phrase or sentence-type that is necessarily altered; we could not invoke the evidence of transcripts because nothing in the transcript of any one session or even over a series of sessions of PD would be markedly different from OC. The differences would exist, if anywhere, in what was *not* found, that is, negative evidence. We would not find certain forms of questioning, certain sorts of ritualistic openings and closings. In general, it is the abstract, overarching metasystem of conversational behavior, rather than specific rules for particular conversational gambits, that is radically altered. At this abstract level there are, as we have seen, profound differences.

Gregory Bateson (1972), his co-workers, and his students have talked at length about the importance of paradoxical systems in the creation of symptoms as well as in their alleviation. It is basically a notion of homeopathy: the disease is cured by the agent that originally created it. If confusing, contradictory applications of communicative principles are—as they would argue—at the root of pathological behavior, then analogous paradoxes in controlled and secure situations such as psychotherapy can effect a cure. What happens can be seen as one form of a phenomenon called by Jay Haley (1963) "reframing"; that is, the patient must either submit totally to the paradox or rise above it to a more abstract level of communicative functioning where the particular set of strategies one has been trained to engage in is seen as only one of a large set of possible options. If one form of behavior can be seen in this light, so can all. Hence, the reinterpretation of communicative strategies leads to the reinterpretation of other nonlinguistic strategies.

The learning of new communicative possibilities in this way is facilitated, of course, by having one's conscious attention directed to the fact that one can learn new linguistic behavior. Hence, it is no doubt useful for many patients to have their attention directed to changing their use of words and syntactic patterns. But this is just a means to an end; it doesn't matter what is changed, really, or what it is changed into. It probably does help if an appealing-sounding rationale can be given. So a rationalization like "we want to take responsibility for our actions, so we will use active sentences, and I statements," will probably be better received than a directive to accept whatever happens (though this is found as well), but in principle the choice is irrelevant. What is critical in the therapeutic process is the recreation of a set of pragmatic principles, the acquisition of sensitivity toward the fact that behavior is governed by rules, that the rules that govern our linguistic behavior can be played with and changed, that there is nothing inherently logical or sensible in the way we talk, but that only convention makes it seem so. The psychotherapeutic situation forces the patient to confront new conventions, new possibilities of understanding, multiple meanings in the simplest exchanges, and by being exposed to these frightening possibilities in safe surroundings, to become willing to discover that all of the conventions we are used to can be altered or terminated if they become stagnating. Language is a window into the mind, and the rules of language are the doors that let the mind out to play. The therapist merely suggests variations in the rules of the game.

NOTES

1. For discussion from this point of view, see Schofield (1964).

2. One of the earliest and clearest expressions of these ideas, from within a psychoanalytic framework, is Strachey's (1934).

3. As discussed by Bateson (1972) and Haley (1963).

4. In, for example, Laing's (1965) concept of "mystification."

5. Here and in my later discussion of psychoanalytic discourse, I am thinking particularly of Freud (1958).

6. It seems likely that the difference between OC and psychoanalytic free association lies not in any *qualitative* differences in types of permissible utterances, but in the larger proportion in the latter of level (2) to level (1) utterances. (Level (3) is atypical in both.)

7. E.g., in Interaction Ritual (1967).

8. For example, the initial interview is discussed in great detail by Gill et al. (1954).

9. Numerous examples could easily be marshalled from diverse therapeutic schools. Exemplary are Bandler and Grinder (1975) and Schafer (1975).

10. The original survey is Eysenck's (1952); more recently, a great many such surveys have been compared by Luborsky, Singer, and Luborsky (1975).

11. Examples of this derogation of therapeutic efficacy are frequent. To cite just two examples, see Crews (1980) and Salter (1952).

REFERENCES

Bandler, R. & Grinder, J. *The structure of magic.* Palo Alto, Calif.: Science and Behavior Books, 1975.

Bateson, G. *Steps to an ecology of mind.* New York: Ballantine, 1972.

Chomsky, N. *Syntactic structures.* The Hague: Mouton & Co., 1957.

Crews, F. Analysis terminable. *Commentary,* 1980, **70**(1), 25–34.

Eysenck, H. The effects of psychotherapy: An evaluation. *Journal of Consulting Psychology,* 1952, **16,** 319–324.

Freud, S. Papers on technique. In J. Strachey (Ed.), *The standard edition of the comlete psychological works of Sigmund Freud,* vol. 12. London: Hogarth Press, 1958. Originally published 1912–1915.

Gill, M., Newman, R., & Redlich, R. R. *The initial interview in psychiatric practice.* New York: International Universities Press, 1954.

Goffman, E. *Interaction ritual.* New York: Anchor, 1967.

Grice, H. P. Logic and conversation. In P. Cole & J. Margan (Eds.), *Syntax and semantics 3: Speech acts.* New York: Academic Press, 1975.

Haley, J. *Strategies of psychotherapy.* New York: Grune & Stratton, 1963.

Laing, R. D. Mystification, confusion, and conflict. In I. Bosmorenyi-Nagy & J. L. Framo (Eds.), *Intensive family therapy: Theoretical and practical aspects.* New York: Harper & Row, 1965.

Luborsky, L., Singer, B., & Luborsky, L. Comparative studies of psychotherapies: Is it true that "everyone must win and all must have prizes"? *Archives of General Psychiatry,* 1975, **32**(8), 995–1008.

Salter, A. *The case against psychoanalysis.* New York: Harper & Row, 1952.

Schafer, R. *A new language for psychoanalysis.* New Haven: Yale University Press, 1975.

Schofield, W. *Psychotherapy: The purchase of friendship.* Englewood Cliffs, N.J.: Prentice-Hall, 1964.

Strachey, J. The nature of the therapeutic action of psychoanalysis. *International Journal of Psychoanalysis,* 1934, **15,** 127–159.

Part II:
Interpersonal Assessment

Chapter 8
Functional Analysis of Interpersonal Behavior
Donald R. Peterson

Interpersonal methods for treating psychological disorders have enjoyed a surge of popularity over the past 20 years. In the 1960s, the encounter group movement swept the country. In the 1970s, family therapy took hold. These developments, along with preceding expressions in the works of Adler, Horney, Sullivan, and others, seem to be more than fads. They witness the increasing realization among psychotherapists that most if not all human disturbances are linked in their origins to the relationships people have with one another and that the relief of human distress can be accomplished most powerfully if problems are approached from an interpersonal as well as an individual viewpoint.

With rare exceptions, however, the many interpersonal treatment methods available to practitioners have not been accompanied by methods for assessing interpersonal problems. Not all clinicicans are persuaded that encounter groups are good for everybody, or that every psychological dysfunction involves the extended family of the identified patient. Decisions must be reached about the involvement of others. In the lack of systematic assessment methods, decisions are not determined by the needs of clients but by the ideological allegiances and personal predilections of the therapists. Instead of designing a treatment strategy to suit the people they are trying to help, counselors do whatever they have come to believe in, or whatever makes them feel most comfortable. Without systematic assessment, there is no way to gauge the effects of treatment. Cases are closed. Maybe some marks are made to show whether or not the therapists thought people got better. But credible documentary evidence on the effects of treatment is seldom provided and rarely sought. Without assessment operations to define the theoretical concepts about which treatment systems are organized, the theories develop from conjecture and spread through rhetoric. Responsible professional practice must ultimately be based on a systematic body of knowledge. Some currently popular theories will hold. Others will not. If adequate methods are provided for testing the theories, facts as well as fashions may shape the conceptions on which sound practice must be founded.

This statement is concerned with the assessment of interpersonal relationships. First, a conception of interpersonal process will be outlined. Then, a set of procedures for examining interpersonal relationships will be described.

A GUIDING CONCEPTION FOR THE STUDY OF INTERPERSONAL RELATIONSHIPS

Assessment, like treatment, must proceed from a conception of the phenomena under study. Interpersonal relationships are impressively complex. All aspects of all relationships cannot be studied at once. Inquiry must be focused, and when that is done, some facets of relationships will be examined at the expense of others. If one therapist sees a patient alone, another requires participation of the nuclear family, and a third begins filling in a genogram derived from study of the three-generational extended family, different assumptions about the origins and treatment of disorders are revealed. It seems likely that penetrating methods of assessment and effective methods of treatment will develop most soundly if the main conceptual assumptions underlying inquiry and change are stated explicitly. At the present level of knowledge about interpersonal relationships, elaborate theory is premature. But a guiding conception is needed to show which way to look. General forms of the following conception have been presented before (Peterson, 1977, 1979b), and a more thoroughly developed statement has reached its third draft (Kelley et al., 1981).

Subjects of Inquiry

At least for the purposes of this discussion, an interpersonal relationship is conceived of as *a developing process of interdependent functioning characterized by recurrent patterns of interaction, the rules governing those patterns of interaction, and the relatively enduring emotional, cognitive, and behavioral dispositions of the people involved toward the people involved in the relationship.*

Interdependent functioning is the dominant defining property of any group. For a relationship to exist at all, the people in it must affect each other in reciprocally contingent ways. The actions and reactions of each person influence the actions and reactions of the others. Relationships change with time, if only by the physical maturation of the participants. The concept of relationship as a developing process expresses this fact. Over fairly long periods of time, however, most relationships show considerable stability. The same kinds of interactions occur repeatedly, the patterns of interactions that emerge in one relationship differ from those in other relationships, and the pattern of recurrent interactions defines each relationship's characteristic form. As regular patterns of interactions appear in any relationship, each party develops normative expectations about the rights and obligations of all participants. These are the rules of the relationship. In their adherence lies predictability and social order. In their violation lies disorder. As relationships continue, each person develops relatively enduring emotional attitudes, patterns of thought, and behavioral dispositions toward all the people in the relationship. The attitudes, thoughts, and behavioral dispositions are directed reflexively as well as externally. They refer not only to others but to oneself.

To understand a relationship, one must be able to describe it. To describe a relationship, one must identify the recurrent patterns of interaction that take place between the people involved in the relationship.

Two people meet for the first time. They do things to and with each other. They speak, they gesture, they may touch. In the process, each forms a conception of the other, and of self in relation to the other. Mutual feelings arise. Each affects the other in some way. The interactive process continues to an outcome. Consummatory acts of some kind are exchanged and the interaction is at an end.

The two meet again, and this time there is some variation from the previous pattern of inter-behavior. Perhaps the conditions for the encounter are different, and different outcomes occur. New information is added and the conceptions of each about the other may be changed. Different feelings may be aroused, and the relationship has taken on a richer meaning. However, then this encounter ends also and becomes part of the interbehavioral history out of which the relationship is forming. Eventually, some of the interaction sequences stabilize and in long-standing, well-developed relationships may become regular to the point of rigidity. The behavior of each party to the relationship, including the thoughts and feelings that are part of that behavior, depends on the behavior of the other. The role of each in relation to the other may often be crudely characterized by a pair of summary terms, parent-child, lover-lover, student-teacher, but in highly evolved, complex relationships these terms seldom do justice to the full richness and subtle varieties the relationship may entail. For comprehension of these, return to the original events defining the relationship is required. To understand a relationship, one must know what the people do to and with each other over time. [Peterson, 1977, pp. 306–307.]

When clients first present interpersonal problems to clinicians, they rarely describe the problems in detail. They are much more likely to summarize whatever conceptions they may have developed in trying to understand their own distress. "We can't communicate." "We are growing apart." "We fight constantly." "My son has a middle-child syndrome." "My mother-in-law is driving me crazy." The usual response of clinicians to such general statements is something like, 'Hmm, that certainly sounds like a problem. Tell me more about it." In the ensuing discussion, and as elaborated by other methods to be described below, it is important for the professional to obtain rather detailed descriptions of the interactions that exemplify the problems. Once a set of interactions has been described, some common properties can be discerned among the recurrent interactions that characterize the relationship. Sullivan called these the "characteristic patterns of living" in relation to significant others that define personality and psychopathology. The idea of "recurrent patterns of interaction" is not essentially different from Sullivan's original notion.

Important Aspects of Interactions

The view of relationships as processes of interdependent functioning and the decision to describe those processes by referring to patterns of recurrent interaction suggest a general direction for inquiry. Practical clinical assessment, however, requires more definite guides so that all functionally decisive influences that determine the patterns of interaction will be examined. Unlike pure scientists, whose investigations may be as narrow or as broad as the conditions of scientific investigation suggest, practitioners cannot afford to ignore anything important. To neglect significant aspects of the problems their clients suffer is professionally unethical. Whether or not the concepts are stated rigorously, whether or not the methods are precise, clinicians are obliged to do their best to obtain all essential information about the problems clients present to them. The following statement of important aspects of interaction is intended as a guide. Any professional who examines these aspects of interactions and relationships will not go astray, though other features of relationships may also be shown as important by further conceptual considerations and research.

Situational influences

Any interaction takes place in an environment that encourages some kinds of behavior instead of others and sets some limits on the behavior that occurs. If a drug culture is active in one school and not another, transactions related to drugs are more likely to go on in one place than the other. The patterns of interaction that take place between an Appalachian coal miner and his wife are apt to be very different from those that go on between the controlling stockholder of a major industrial conglomerate and his wife. The effects of setting conditions on interpersonal behavior are frequently massive, but there is a systematic tendency for people to underestimate their force. When people are placed in situations that create conflict, for example, they are more likely to attribute the origins of conflict to each other than to the situation of which they both are victims (Kelley, 1971). He thinks it is her fault. She thinks that it is his fault. In fact, the problems they have may be the fault of neither, but of circumstances that govern the feelings and actions of them both. Satisfactions too may often be improved by changing the situations in which interactions occur, as the following report shows.

I mentioned that I felt kind of interested in sex even though we were feeling exhausted . . . and began taking off my bra under my shirt. When the kids were put in bed we went into our bedroom. Things started off badly because I was nervous as usual and our bedroom is very cold. I finally said, "No wonder I have problems with sex . . . I always freeze to death when we come in here and undress and you don't like to get under the covers." I also complained about the bright glare from the ceiling light since our bedside lamp has been without a bulb. So Ken got up, turned up the heat . . . got a red light bulb for the bedside lamp and we had sex in a warm, red bedroom.

Personal influences

Groups are composed of individuals, and the personal dispositions that each person brings to any relationship affect the interactions that take place in the relationship. In their enthusiasm for interactional views of behavior, some practitioners and theorists ignore that fact. If one member of a family is severely paranoid, the relationships among that member and all others will inevitably reflect the suspicion, hostility, unstable arrogance, and unvalidated cognitive elaborations of the paranoid party. The other members of the family may or may not have "caused" the paranoia. The treatment of choice may or may not be an individual treatment. But the dominant functional influences on interactive behavior over a range of relationships will be centered in one person, and it is important for clinicians trying to understand families and other groups to locate the individual centers of influence in the group. Sociological, social, and individual views of behavior are not competitive but complementary. A viewpoint comprehensive enough to accommodate the common relational problems that practitioners see must include influences at all three levels.

Interactive influences

In dealing with interpersonal dysfunction, however, inquiry will usually begin and emphasis may remain on the interaction process itself. The flow of actions and reactions that go on as the clients meet, deal with each other, and then part, must be described and understood.

Consider the following exchange reported by a young married woman.

Who started the interaction? *"Phil. Phil had put the catsup bottle on the table upside down."* (She drew a sketch showing a bottle upside down on a saucer.) What happened then? *"I put my foot on the table and catsup got on the table cloth. Phil yelled at my standing on the table. I quickly informed him I was sitting down and placed my foot on the table to put my shoes on. Then he said, 'You were upright. You were standing.' I yelled the table shouldn't be loose and you shouldn't put the catsup bottle on it. Phil yelled some more. Finally I said, 'Bug off!!' After awhile we both worked to clean up the catsup and fix lunch."*

Phil had a slightly different view.

Who started the interaction? *"Helen. Helen knocked over a catsup bottle that was upside down draining the last of the catsup in a dish on the kitchen table. I said, 'Clever move, chick.' She said, 'What the hell is the bottle doing upside down?' I replied, 'What the hell were you doing standing on the table?' She had put her foot on the table to take off her sandals. We then went into a three-minute 'discussion' of the definition of 'standing on' and said some angry things to each other. I finished setting the table without comment. Helen wiped up the mess."*

A literal description of the behavior in the sequence would go roughly as follows:

1. Previous action by husband in setting catsup bottle upside down on saucer.
2. Wife places foot on table to put on sandal and knocks over bottle.
3. Husband says, "Clever move, chick."
4. Wife says, "What the hell is the bottle doing upside down?"
5. Husband says, "What the hell were you doing standing on the table?"
6. Wife says she was sitting down.
7. Husband says she was upright.
8. Wife says "Bug off!"
9. Husband sets table.
10. Wife wipes up spilled catsup.

Clinically adequate interpretation, however, requires more than literal description. The interpersonal meanings of action must also be understood. When Phil says, "Clever move, chick," he is of course not commenting on Helen's physical or mental adroitness. He is commenting critically on her behavior: "Look what you did, you clumsy boob." He is expressing his irritation. He is vindicating himself and attributing blame for the incident on his wife. When Helen says, "What the hell is the bottle doing upside down?" she is not concerned about the physical position of the bottle but about the implied stupidity of her husband, her own irritation, and the establishment of her own innocence. When Helen later wipes up the spilled catsup and her husband sets the table, not a word is spoken, but the interpersonal meanings of both actions are clear: "Well, maybe I was partly responsible. Let's get back together and go ahead with our lunch."

The distinction between two levels of meaning in social communication has become commonplace in recent years. Transactional analysts (Berne, 1964; Harris, 1967) speak of "social" and "psychological" levels of meaning. People associated at one time or another with the Mental Research Institute in Palo Alto (e.g., Watzlawick, 1974; Haley, 1976) speak variously of denotative and connotative meanings, digital and analogic meanings, communicative and metacommunicative meanings of any action. The paired terms express roughly the same distinction. Any message issued in the course of social exchange has both a literal content and an interpersonal meaning. As people talk with each other and fall silent, as they move or stay motionless, as they frown or smile, growl or groan, laugh or cry, they are not only commenting on the state of the world or even of themselves, but are constantly defining the relationship they have with one another. Clients are not always aware of the interpersonal meanings of their behavior. Scientists may ignore the meanings. Clinicians must understand them.

Although the full range of meanings that people can convey to one another is infinitely varied, the most general kinds of meanings are closely limited. Bateson distinguished between the *report* and the *command* aspects of any interpersonal statement. The dominant interpersonal reports concern affective and cognitive experience. In their reports, people are saying, "Here is how I feel," "This is what I think." In the other interpersonal aspect of any message, people declare their expectations about the behavior of the other. "Command" is a rather strong term for the kinds of messages that actually occur in everyday social exchange (Peterson, 1979a), but reciprocal demands are often stated and at some level are always implied. "Given my thoughts and feelings on the subject, this is what I expect you to do, think, or feel."

The most general kinds of import of interpersonal messages also seem to be limited in number, though nuances of meaning can vary without limit. From Schutz's early analyses of "fundamental interpersonal relationship orientations" (Schutz, 1958) through a highly consistent array of subsequent investigations (Carson, 1969; Swensen, 1973), three basic kinds of messages have appeared. One defines *inclusion* or exclusion. "We are together in this," or we are not. A second set declares *affirmation* or disaffirmation of oneself or the other. "I'm OK—You're OK." "I approve/disapprove of you/myself." A third set asserts *control*. "I am in charge." "You take over." "Let us share responsibility for this one." Different analyses may give or take a dimension or two, but these kinds of messages seem very general over many particulars of social exchange.

Important Aspects of Relationships

As any relationship continues and the interactions in it stabilize into patterned forms, the influences that determine the regularities of interaction become more general then specific, more durable than transient, more regular than episodic. Analysis requires consideration not only of moment-by-moment events, but of the relatively enduring *causal conditions* that govern classes of events. Description pertains not only to particular *interactions*, but to the continuing *relationships* within which interactions take place.

Personal dispositions

At the individual level, emotional states may generalize over a set of recurrent interactions to appear as relatively general emotional attitudes. Feelings of affection or hostility may pervade most or all of the interactions any two people have. That relationship can then be described as "affectionate" or "hostile." Transient ideas and images that arise in cognitive experience through the course of any interaction also tend to generalize as relationships continue. People develop more or less stable beliefs about themselves and others in the relationship. They see each other as worthwhile, worthless, or something in between. They see others and themselves as nurturant or demanding, helpless or self-sufficient, trustworthy or undependable. Interpersonally directed thoughts and feelings are linked to scripts for action. A wife who regards her husband as rather shiftless and untrustworthy, but loves him all the same, will treat him differently from one whose views of her husband's undependability are accompanied by a brooding anger. To survive in either relationship, each wife must have some agenda for control of at least certain aspects of her own experience. In cases like these, the agendas are likely to be at least partially concealed, and the scripts for the action less than perfectly clear even to the actor. But in these cases and in all other close and continuing relationships, the relatively enduring cognitive, emotional, and behavioral dispositions of the people involved operate as causal conditions governing patterns of interactions over quite wide ranges of time and setting. Collaboratively, they are the object relations schemata (see Raush et al., 1974) that the people in the relationship carry with them from one interaction to another. They form part of the network of determining influences that give relationships their regularity. New experiences are assimilated, and the emotional attitudes, cognitive beliefs, and behavioral dispositions that make up the schemata may be elaborated and reinforced. Some new experiences may require accommodation, i.e., a structural change in attitudes, beliefs, or behavioral dispositions. If that happens, a discontinuous, "second-order" change in the relationship (see Watzlawick, 1974, 1978) may be seen.

Relational rules

At the interpersonal level, interactions are governed by rules, that is, the normative expectations members hold for the behavior of those involved in the relationships. Rules define the rights and obligations of all concerned. Every "distressed" relationship betrays a perceived rule violation. This is true by tautology. According to the standards of at least one party, at least one person in the relationship is failing to do what he or she "ought" to do, or is doing something that he or she "ought not" to do. If everybody understands what the rules are, and all agree about the implications of the rules as to sanctions and benefits, the interactions that make up the relationship can proceed without contention and with almost perfectly predictable order.

These conditions are most obviously met where behavior is governed by culturally ascribed roles. I am a tenured professor at Rutgers University. I am scheduled to meet a group of students in room 105 of the psychology building at nine o'clock next Monday morning. Unless I am deterred by an act of God, you can bet anything you own that I will be there. Once I arrive, you can absolutely count on me to behave in a very closely prescribed manner, as related to the full range of behavior in my repertoire. I shall talk, not sing. I shall not disrobe. Similarly, when I greet my wife after a day's work, I kiss her. If I do not, she wonders about our relationship. If I kiss my barber the next time he finishes cutting my hair, he will be surprised.

In continuing close relationships such as marriage, however, the rules are far less clear and are constantly changing. This is particularly true in pluralistic, culturally fluid societies like those of modern North America and Western Europe. Rules must form anyway to avoid social chaos, but the rules are often implicit and people truly do not know where they stand in regard to one another. Worse than that, they often do not recognize that rules prevail at all. In fleeing the irrational constraints of an earlier conformity, some people in present-day American society have converted to a libertarian self-indulgence. They obey an implicit rule to obey no rules. Discerning clinicians can sometimes help the people who come to see them by identifying the rules that govern their behavior. The rules are often subtle, and at least one party may have an interest in keeping them mystified. If one of the tacit rules that governs a family, for example, is that "Mother can criticize everybody else, but nobody had better criticize Mother or there will be hell to pay," the rule is bound to be concealed and its exposure is sure to be resisted. Yet these are the very cases in which practitioners may help by identifying the rules, clarifying the privileges and obligations that all parties hold for one another, and sometimes by renegotiating contracts that enforce dysfunction. This is another way in which structural, second-order change can be brought about.

Setting conditions

The rules of relationships are embedded in surrounding cultures. Opportunities for satisfaction and constraining demands are powerfully determined by the general environmental conditions within which interpersonal relationships develop. Setting conditions may or may not be subject to change. There may not be much to do about the poverty, hopelessness, and rage that pervade the lives of many inner-city black families. There may not be much to do about the frustration and despair that are written into the roles of many working-class women. But clinicians must at least understand what those conditions are. If improvement is possible, they may join with clients in attempts to change. If they are successful, the resulting structural transformations may have effects far beyond the individual or groups whose distress provoked the effort. If they fail, people will rarely be worse off than they were before. If hopes for change are unrealistic, professionals may at least help clients avoid gross attributional errors in blaming one another, and all may come to a better understanding of their common plight.

On a more modest scale, any close relationship of a kind likely to come to the attention of a practitioner is embedded in a network of other relationships. Troubled marital relationships are complicated by relationships with children. Disturbed parent-child relationships are affected by the quality of the marriage. Both marital and parental relationships may be influenced by unresolved issues concerning families of origin. The existence and force of extended relational influences form a central premise of family systems theory as expressed by such writers as Minuchin (1974) and Bowen (1976). From the present viewpoint, the linkage of any given relationship with an extended network of other relationships must be recognized if any of the relationships in the network are to be understood. Practically, a view of relationships that incorporates the larger social context also provides options for change that might not be suggested by more restrictive views. Sometimes the quarrels of a young couple can be reduced by moving them apart from parents. Sometimes a child will stop hitting his younger sister when his mother and father stop fighting. An evenly homogeneous view of family networks, however, does not seem justified by considerations either of cause or of change. It is true that any relationship may be influenced by other relationships. For any particular relationship, however, some extended relationships matter more than others. One starts with the relationship that someone has said is troubled. One examines that relationship to see what the problem is. Often other relationships influence the primary relationship in important ways. Sometimes the other relationships include all members of the nuclear family. Sometimes only some members of the nuclear family are involved, and sometimes none of the others matters much as far as the primary relational issues are concerned. Sometimes grandparents count, sometimes not. In exploring the larger social context of which any relationship is a part, one goes as far as the facts of functional interdependence require, and no further.

ASSESSMENT OF INTERPERSONAL RELATIONSHIPS

Aims of Assessment

Therapists involved in interpersonal modes of treatment are bound to spend at least some time examining the people they are trying to help, if only by observation and inquiry in the course of treatment. The outcomes of assessment can take many forms. A common form is *typological classification*. As individuals and their problems may be sorted into categories, so may groups and relationships be classified into discrete sets. The examiner may thus determine that one marriage is "harmonious" and another "conflictual." A second common outcome of assessment is *dimensional description*. As the axial designations of DSM-III complemented the categories of DSM-II, so may the descriptions of relationships refer to continuous dimensions rather than discontinuous types. Marriages then might be placed anywhere along the line from uninterrupted harmony to continuous conflict. A third outcome of assessment is *dynamic formulation*. In this more elaborate statement, an effort is made not merely to describe behavior but to account for it, usually by inferring some set of underlying determinants of manifest activity and reconstructing the historical course by which patterns of current behavior and psychopathology developed. Again, dynamic formulations may be attempted for relationships just as they are in the study of individual personality. Patterns of marital conflict may thus be explained by reference to the needs they express, and the development of particular patterns of need considered in light of the interpersonal histories of those in conflict.

The values and limitations of each of these assessment outcomes have been discussed in detail elsewhere (Peterson, 1968). The main conclusion that emerged from the previous discussion seems as clearly true today as it did when it was written, and just as germane to the assessment of interpersonal relationships as to the study of individual behavior.

The most important aim of clinical assessment is to obtain information pertinent to change.

Nobody comes to a therapist unless some change is desired, even if the only change possible is acceptance of an otherwise incorrigible state of affairs, The clinician's job in treatment is to help bring change about, as effectively as possible. The clinician's job in assessment is to help determine what kinds of changes are desirable and feasible, what conditions may produce or facilitate change, and whether, in what form, and to what degree changes have occurred.

If assessment contributes to the central aims of change, it is clinically useful. Otherwise it is not clinically useful, whatever the values may be for such other purposes as scientific investigation or meeting the demands of a political bureaucracy. Most typological classifications are not very valuable in regard to treatment. Neither are dimensional descriptions. Categories, axes—what does it matter when it comes to helping the patient? Dynamic formulations may be useful, if the dynamic inferences and historical reconstructions are dependably made and pertinent to treatment. If not, they too are apt to be a waste of professional time and public money. In recent years, several innovators have begun to develop approaches to the assessment of interpersonal behavior that hold more promise than earlier approaches (e.g., Weiss, Hops, & Patterson, 1973; Gottman, 1979; Benjamin, this volume). In appraising the clinical utility of these procedures, however, it is still important to remember that people who come for help, or those who send them, are typically in distress. What they want from clinicians is a change in that condition, if only by way of reassurance or acceptance. The work a practitioner does by way of assessment should contribute to the aims of change.

Methods for Assessing Interpersonal Relationships

Another general conclusion in the earlier statement on the clinical study of social behavior (Peterson, 1968) also seems reasonble today.

The best way to obtain information pertinent to change is to employ the full range of methods in behavioral science.

No test will do the job. Interviews alone are not enough. Neither are observations. To obtain information about interaction process and interpersonal relationships as defined in the first part of this chapter, a more broadly based methodology is needed. The full array of methods for the systematic study of human behavior is of course very large and complex, but for clinical application it is convenient to identify five broad classes of procedures. These are interviews, observations, records, analogues, and functional analyses of behavior. In a chapter as short as this, none of the methods can be thoroughly discussed, much less all of them. The following comments will therefore be devoted to brief descriptions of one or two promising forms of each procedure, followed by some comments about the uses and limitations of each method.

Interviews

Thirty-five years after it was first presented, Sullivan's *Psychiatric Interview* (1954) still stands as one of the most valuable guides a practitioner can find for the study of interpersonal relationships. The main emphases in Sullivan's definition of the interview are inherently appropriate. Communication is *primarily vocal*. Not verbal, not only vocal, but primarily vocal. The relationship is that of *expert* to *client*. Not friend to friend, not interrogator to witness, but expert to client. The purpose of the interview is to elucidate *characteristic patterns of living*, as discussed previously in this chapter. For his efforts, the client expects to derive some *benefit*. Not the interviewer, but the client. Some readers these days will take issue with Sullivan's more arbitrary declarations, e.g., "it is practically impossible to explore most of the significant areas of personality with a third person present" (Sullivan, 1954, p. 9). Regardless of viewpoint, however, relatively inexperienced interviewers can scarcely fail to profit from Sullivan's sensible suggestions about the inception of the interview, the various stages of reconnaissance, transitions from one topic to another, and ways of bringing interviews to a close. Even experienced interviewers may benefit from rereading Sullivan's comments on the interviewer as participant-observer, the linkage of anxiety with parataxic distortion, and the incapacitating effects of the professional's own extreme emotions should these arise in the course of the interview.

Since Sullivan's time, many volumes have been written about interviews. The most radical change in interviews directed toward understanding interpersonal relationships has been the shift from individual to conjoint groupings, and with that a move beyond "primarily vocal communication" to use of the interview as a setting for direct social interaction. Among the various guides for conducting first interviews, those proposed by Haley (1976) seem particularly straightforward and compatible with the problem-directed focus suggested in this chapter. Following contact and arrangements for meeting, the initial interview proceeds through four stages. In the *social* stage, those attending are allowed to seat themselves as they wish. The interviewer introduces himself or herself, and then speaks to each member to obtain his or her name. As a response is obtained from each person, the situation is immediately defined as one in which all are involved. At this stage it is necessary to observe and legitimate to conjecture, but important to keep conclusions tentative. Prematurely set ideas restrict observation and the prospect of better ideas later on. Haley also enjoins interviewers to keep their guesses to themselves, not only because they might be wrong but also because even accurate comments require responses that clients are not yet ready to provide.

After introductions and any other social amenities that may be appropriate, the interviewer moves to the *problem* stage. Most people who come for help do not know quite what to expect of professionals or what their own parts in the process will be. When the interviewer inquires about their problems, as they see them, they are all clearly getting down to business, and the interviewer is showing that he or she needs to know how each of them perceives the difficulty. A common way to begin is to say something like, "I recall what was said on the telephone, so I have some idea what the problem is, but I asked you all to come in so that I could get everyone's ideas about it." The interviewer then proceeds to get a statement from everyone present about the problem as that person views it. As before, all comments are registered and observations are made throughout, but the interviewer still remains silent about any conjectures that may be forming. The central task in this early period is to encourage people to talk and to listen to the meanings in what they say.

In the next stage of the interview, the *interaction* stage, clients are encouraged to talk to each other. The interviewer removes himself or herself from the center of the conversation and turns the members more and more toward one another. The shift usually occurs naturally, as people disagree about the nature of the problem or wish to qualify one another's remarks. If a change to direct interaction does not occur spontaneously, the interviewer instigates it, if necessary by moving people toward each other physically. When any two people start talking, others can be brought into the conversation: "Do you have any thoughts on that?" "Could you help them out with this one?" Actions as well as words are encouraged to facilitate the exchange and to get people to show as well as to say how they deal with each other.

By this time, the members of the group will have revealed a good deal about themselves and their relationships. They will have presented a set of issues that at least someone present regards as a problem. The task of the interviewer then becomes one of *defining desired changes*. In contract with the clients, a reasonably clear statement is formed of the goals of treatment. Ideally and not uncommonly, one attempts to identify a change that all members present consider desirable and that offers a reasonable chance for improved solution. In more active forms of treatment, directives may be given so that work toward improvement can begin immediately and the involvement of clients maintained between the first interview and the next.

Haley is just as firm as Sullivan was about the inclusion of third parties, but his position is exactly opposite from Sullivan's: "Today it is assumed that to begin therapy by interviewing one person is to begin with a handicap" (Haley, 1976, p. 10). To this writer, it seems most reasonable to base invitations to the first interview on the client's initial definition of the problem. If the problem is perceived as individual, the person with the problem is seen first. If the problem is considered interpersonal, the interviewer can find out who might be most directly involved and invite them in. In either case, moves from individual interviews to larger and smaller groupings may be anticipated as perceptions of problems and functional interdependencies in the maintenance of problems suggest.

The interview is by far the most commonly used procedure in clinical practice, both for treatment and assessment. Among experts concerned with accuracy of measurement, however, the interview is not a favored technique. Anastasi (1976) devotes less than a page in a chapter on "Other assessment techniques" to the "time-honored source of information" provided by interviews. Although she concedes that interviews can serve many purposes in applied psychology, she concludes her brief statement with comments about the need for skill and sensitivity on the part of the interviewer and the dangers of error from failure to obtain needed information or from misinterpretation of data that have been obtained. Nunnaly (1970) uses less than a page to discuss the interview as a method for personality assessment and concludes that it "does not provide a valid general tool for the measurement of personality traits." A somewhat more charitable view is expressed by Cronbach and Gleser (1965). Despite the "preponderantly negative" evidence on the validity of the interview, as they see it, Cronbach and Gleser are willing to admit the method as a "flexible wideband procedure" for "obtaining information on characteristics that formal measurement procedures do not reveal." Like any wideband technique, however, the interview offers its advantage of comprehensiveness only at the price of limited fidelity. Cronbach and Gleser recommend interviews mainly as early screening operations in sequential decision strategies. Firm decisions that affect the lives of clients need to be based on more precise information which is gathered by other means.

Research on the reliability and validity of the interview is not reassuring. For example, Radke-Yarrow and her colleagues (1964) found a median r of only .37 between ratings from a retrospective interview with mothers and baseline data gathered while the children were in nursery school. Haggard, Brekstad, and Skard (1960) found reasonably close correspondence between anamnestic accounts obtained by interviewing mothers and "hard fact" data concerning such infant characteristics as weight and length, but much lower correspondence for various forms of attitudinal ratings, and scarcely any agreement beyond chance when the retrospective accounts concerned topics about which some anxiety or other affect was likely to be experienced. Unfortunately, it is just those topics about which clinicians and their clients are most seriously concerned. When the characteristics to be inferred from interviews are current and reasonably well defined, higher reliabilities appear (Weiss, Hops, & Patterson, 1973; Boals, 1979), but reliability correlations still tend to hover around .70 and rarely exceed .80. Validity correlations are lower still. The interview is a dominant method of the softer social sciences, such as anthropology and sociology. Clinicians are not likely to abandon it just because some psychometric researchers have declared it unreliable. But the merit of the interview as an assessment method needs far better documentation than it has received to date, and its use as the only method for studying interpersonal relationships cannot be justified at all.

Observation

Behaviorally inclined clinicians have tried to avoid the perils of subjectivity and unreliability by basing their descriptions on observation. They enter the settings in which behavior occurs and record the events that take place there. Patterson and his colleagues at the University of Oregon have developed systems for coding parent-child interactions (Patterson, Ray, Shaw, & Cobb, 1969) and marital interactions (Weiss, Hops, & Patterson, 1973) that have been widely used in outcome research on interpersonal behavior. The Marital Interaction Coding System (MICS) allows observers to classify interactive behavior as it occurs into any of 29 categories (e.g., agree, approve, criticize, excuse, interrupt, command, laugh), and then to combine occurrences of discrete codes into six larger aggregates, namely Problem Solving, Problem Description, Negative Verbal Behavior, Positive Verbal Behavior, and Negative and Positive Nonverbal Behavior. Trained observers maintain acceptably high levels of agreement in use of the categories, and the aggregate indices are clearly sensitive to planned intervention. Thus, direct attempts to teach married couples to replace criticisms, complaints, and other aversive controls with more positive influences are reflected by changes in the corresponding codes.

So far, however, the coding systems have been used most successfully to record relatively brief segments of behavior deliberately elicited by the investigator. Direct observation of clinically important interactions in natural settings is exceedingly difficult to do. For one thing, the interactions that matter may occur very infrequently. If all interbehavior is recorded over a long enough time to include dependably registered "significant" interactions, the record is also likely to contain an overwhelming mass of humdrum, clinically trivial material. Furthermore, unless observers follow their subjects everywhere they go, many of the most interesting interactions are likely to occur "out of range," in bed, on the way to visit relatives, on the golf course, or anywhere else. If observers actually follow the subjects over a wide range of settings, obvious problems of reactivity arise, as well as the problem of "dross" mentioned before. Even if useful information can be obtained by naturalistic observation, the costs are often prohibitive for many practical clinical purposes.

Christensen (1978) has been doing some very interesting work with randomly activated audio recordings through omnidirectional microphones placed at various locations in the home. Ingenious methods of these kinds may eventually provide naturalistic observations of important behavioral occurrences at low enough costs for common clinical use. Until then, naturalistic observation seems more useful for getting information about the environments in which behavior occurs than for systematic recording of the behavior itself.

Records

Behaviorally oriented clinicians of the "broad spectrum" sort (e.g., Lazarus, 1976) frequently ask clients to record their own behavior or that of others they are in a position to observe. Fluctuations in weight, numbers of cigarettes smoked, tantrums, quarrels, and numerous other forms of behavior are thus registered systematically by people involved in or otherwise close to the problems under study. Records of these kinds are obviously not as "objective" as those obtained by outside observers, but they are at the same time free of the reactive effects any observer must introduce, can be focused on significant events over the full range of settings in which the events occur, and can be obtained at relatively low cost.

In the study of interpersonal behavior, interesting material can be obtained by means of *interaction records* (Peterson, 1979a, 1979b). The procedure we have used with married couples contained the following instructions:

Please use this form to describe the most important interaction you two had today. In your own words, from your own viewpoint, tell:
1. *The conditions under which the exchange took place.* Where and when did it happen? How were you both feeling as the interaction began?
2. *How the interaction started.* Who made the first move? What did that person say or do?
3. *What happened then.* Please write a fairly detailed description of the exchange from start to finish. Who did and said what to whom? What were you thinking and feeling as the action went on? What ideas and emotions did your partner seem to have? How did it all come out?

The records people write are frequently revealing. Some are long. Some are short. Some concern very difficult, troubled exchanges. Others relate deeply intimate and satisfying encounters. Here is one from a couple in treatment:

I was trying to convince Donna to wear a pair of slacks which I liked. She said OK to my idea at first, but it evidently bothered her because she refused to wear the clothes I suggested and complained about my trying to dominate her later. I decided to apologize and said she could wear anything she wanted, somewhat for the reason that I knew she was right, but mostly because I wanted to avoid an argument at my parents' house. My apology made no difference to her and she continued arguing. This made me very mad, as I feel the argument should be over when I admit I am wrong. The arguing which followed mostly concerned my dominating her, which was a subject I wanted to avoid. Defending myself, I told her she wanted and liked to argue, just for something to do. Things were then said which we did not mean at all (you're pathetic, I can't stand you, we'll go home today). I even threatened to hit Donna, which scares me even now. The thing lasted about 30 minutes. There was no satisfaction at all and no good came of it.

Here is another record, this time from one of the "happy couples" in our research on the assessment of interpersonal relationships:

Jim rolled over quietly and started loving me. We were both well rested and relaxed. We made love very passionately. Marvelous!

In obtaining records from married couples, we have asked husbands and wives to write independent accounts as soon as possible after each exchange is over. The two accounts naturally differ somewhat, and the discrepancies are interesting in their own right. If the accounts are written soon after interactions have occurred, however, they are usually closely parallel and a single interaction sequence can be described. In analyzing any interaction, we first identify the major acts or moves that each person has made in the course of the exchange. Then an interpersonal meaning, or "message," is inferred for each act. As indicated in the first section of this chapter, each message contains three kinds of meaning, namely a report of the emotion the person is feeling at the time, a report of the way the person construes the situation, and an expectation about the response of the other. The first two acts in the quarrel reported above, for example, can be described as

Act	Message	Affect	Construal	Expectation
Husband asks wife to wear slacks he likes	Dress to please me	Neutral attention	Advice will be helpful	Wife will conform
Wife refuses	You are trying to dominate me, and I will not submit	Resentment	Husband's request is part of a general pattern of domination	Husband will reduce controls

Despite the rather high level of inference required for these interpretations, clinicians agree fairly closely about them (Peterson, 1979a). The kinds of affect, construal, and expectation most commonly reported by couples in treatment for marital problems are widely different from those reported by couples who claim they are "happily married." Sequential interaction patterns also differ in interesting ways. Aggression followed by "fighting back," for example, was more commonly reported by satisfied couples than by disturbed couples. Couples in clinical treatment more frequently reported cycles of aggression followed by angry withdrawal.

Although interaction records have been obtained so far only from married couples, there is no reason they could not be obtained from parents and children, cooperating employees, or any other literate people in various relationships with one another. The instructions in our research called for identification of the "most important" interactions of the day. In clinical use, instructions could be varied to suit each case. For some people, reports of conflict might be most useful. For others, detailed accounts of communicative failures or sexual experiences might be helpful. As self-reports, interaction records are subject to the limitations of all verbal accounts. Interpersonal events and reports of those events are not the same. The reports, however, are interesting in their own right, and in convergence with other kinds of evidence can help identify the recurrent patterns of interaction that make up any relationship.

Analogues

An analogue is a contrived situation that resembles some class of natural situations and is designed to elicit some particular class of behavior of scientific or professional interest. The contrived situation is "analogous" to a natural one, and thus resembles a test. "Tests," however, often elicit responses that are unique to the testing situation and are of interest only as signs of other characteristics. Where else but on the Rorschach can M or C responses be seen? An analogue comes as close to the "real" situation as ethical and practical constraints allow, and the behavior that emerges is examined directly rather than indirectly.

Many situations have been devised to elicit interpersonal behavior. In the most general sense, all the procedures employed by experimental social psychologists can be seen as analogues. From this view, all the "gaming" methods, "Prisoner's Dilemma," "Chicken," and the rest (see Pruitt & Kimmel, 1977) might be seen as potentially useful clinical procedures. The generality of behavior observed in those situations is questionable, however, even from one experiment to another, let alone from the laboratory to wide ranges of naturally occurring situations. For use in professional assessment, an analogue must draw out behavior of genuine significance in the lives of clients. Not many analogues do that.

The most promising procedures appear to be those that represent universal or near universal issues of generally acknowledged importance in close relationships. The "Improvisation" methods used by Raush and his colleagues (1974), for example, set up a situation in which each husband is brought into a mood of distance from his wife. The husband is asked if he has ever known the feeling of not wanting another person next to him, of wishing to be left alone. (Everybody has.) The husband is then told that this is just the way he feels about his wife now. If his wife has ever done anything to make him feel that way (many will acknowledge that such occasions have occurred) he is asked to dwell on the memory for awhile. If he cannot think of any alienating experiences (many newlyweds will deny them) he is encouraged to imagine an incident or quality about his wife that would make him feel distant from her. Meanwhile, the wife is asked to imagine that her husband has become like a stranger to her—cold, distant, and irritable. This has gone on for several days. She has decided it cannot continue. Tonight she must try to bridge the gap between them and draw the two of them together again. The scene begins with the husband staring out the window as the wife enters the room.

Other improvisations are included in the set that Raush et al. employed. Couples begin with some relatively innocuous conflicts about dinner for an anniversary and a choice of television programs. Roles are reversed in a second run through the distance scene. Anyone who has employed the technique with married couples is likely to be impressed by the ease with which most participants can get into the moods of the various situations and find themselves behaving in ways that seem quite spontaneous and authentic. As Raush and his colleagues have shown, the behavior that emerges can be reliably coded and some interesting differences appear between distressed and nondistressed couples. Distressed husbands, for instance, tend to be relatively submissive during the "issue-oriented" anniversary and television scenes, but then turn on their partners and attack in the "relationship-oriented" distance scenes.

Gottman (1979) has employed a procedure in which couples discuss and then resolve a conflict they have actually experienced. In our research at Illinois and Rutgers, we have also had couples enact conflicts that they consider important in their lives. Following an interview in which "the main problems in the family" are discussed, people are asked to recall a recent episode in which the problem occurred. They go over the scene in conversation with the interviewer so that each party will have a fairly clear script in mind, and then enact the episode as authentically as they can. The ensuing interaction is recorded on videotape. In one variation of the procedure, the scene is then replayed before the couple in much the manner of Kagan's Interpersonal Process Recall (Kagan, 1973). The tape can be stopped at any time to allow for questions and comments from anybody present. Kagan encourages relatively free comment and appears to obtain very rich data by doing so. More specific questions about communicative meanings and covert processes, such as "What did you think he meant by that?" "How were you feeling just then?" can be asked as examiners and participants may wish. In our experience, direct enactments of significant problems have proved to be highly volatile situations with severely distressed clients. People who are deeply disturbed about their problems either avoid them and enact trivial scenes or seize the opportunity to show how bad things really are. Sometimes they get into quarrels that are difficult to control. If problem enactments are used with badly distressed clients, it is probably best to introduce them only after a firm professional relationship has been established by other means, such as interviews. When the enactments are set off, the professional in the room had better be prepared to deal therapeutically with the effect.

The analogue procedures just described, of course, are only a few of the many that might be used. The chapter on analogues in any book on behavioral assessment (e.g., Nay, 1977) will suggest a wide range of other possibilities. In general, analogues offer the advantages of a "command performance." Examiners can summon up any kind of interaction for which appropriate stimuli can be devised. The behavior can be recorded and examined in detail after it has happened. Highly reliable appraisals of some characteristics of interpersonal behavior can be made. On the other side, it is important to remember that analogues *are* analogues, and not the "real thing." The behavior that occurs under contrived conditions is subject to all the demand characteristics and other perturbations that affect behavior in any controlled situation. Questions of generalizability are just as pertinent for analogue data—no less and no more—as for data from other sources.

Functional analysis

From the procedures described above, descriptions of recurrent interaction patterns can be derived. Beyond description, the causal conditions governing regularities in interpersonal behavior can be provisionally inferred. When that stage of tentative understanding has been reached, the next and most decisive step in the clinical process can be taken. Influences are exerted to change the causal conditions that maintain disturbing interactions. This is treatment, but it is also a form of assessment. Changes will occur or they will not occur. In general, changes in predicted directions confirm hypotheses about the causes of disorder. Persistence of the problem tends to disconfirm the hypotheses and requires conceptual reformulation. The cyclical process of describing interaction patterns, formulating ideas about the conditions that maintain the patterns, testing the propositions by planned intervention, and describing the interaction patterns that follow, can be regarded as a *functional analysis of interpersonal behavior.*

The term "functional" has several meanings. One meaning is physical. Functional characteristics are distinguished from the structural components of machines or organisms. This is the difference between physiology and anatomy, between the process of carburation and a carburetor, between the way an entity works and the components that make it up. Another meaning is doctrinal. In psychology, Functionalism refers to an emphasis on the goal-directed nature of behavior and to its adaptive quality in reference to goal attainment. Contrast with Structuralism is usually implied. A third meaning is mathematical. A mathematical function expresses the relationship between one set of variables and another. Without pretending that functional analysis in clinical psychology is mathematically precise, without endorsing the doctrines of an extreme Functionalism and thereby rejecting all other viewpoints, and without advocating a disembodied study of process to the negelct of substance, I suggest that the major connotations of all three meanings apply in the present case.

The general logic of functional analysis is well established in psychology. It is the fundamental method of Descriptive Behaviorism as proposed by Skinner (1938, 1953) and pursued by all investigators who follow a behavioral course of investigation. In studying any behavior, one first establishes the rate and the topography of the behavior itself. These are the dependent variables of experimental inquiry. One then alters some influence that affects the rate or form of behavior. The influences are the independent variables of experimental inquiry. Effects on behavior are observed. If effects occur systematically, cause-effect relationships are established. These are the laws of behavioral science. Their synthesis provides a comprehensive picture of the organism as a behaving system. The same logic appears within a different epistemology in the psychology of personal and interpersonal constructs proposed by George Kelly (1955). Through observational and elicitative procedure, social behavior is described. By inference, hypotheses are formed about the covert processes governing social behavior. The hypotheses are then tested by other operations, including the influences of clinical therapy. The general pattern of inquiry in functional analysis is that of experimental psychology. In clinical use, the most commonly applicable design is some form of single-subject investigation in which determinations of cause-effect relations are made by comparing behavior at one time under one set of conditions with behavior at other times under other conditions. In application to human relationships, the "subject" becomes a couple, a family, or some other pair or larger group.

As suggested already, four steps are involved in the functional analysis of interpersonal behavior. First, recurrent patterns of interactions are described by some combination of descriptive methods. Second, the relatively enduring causal conditions that maintain dysfunctional patterns of behavior are provisionally inferred. Third, influences are exerted to change the causal conditions by whatever means the stock of methods for treating relationships may suggest. Fourth, changes in interaction patterns and therefore in the relationship are observed. If no changes occur, the causal inferences were wrong or the influences were ineffective. Different treatments may then be attempted or ideas about maintaining conditions may be revised. If changes occur, and extraneous influences are ruled out, the treatment has been effective and the credibility of the cause-effect formulation has been improved.

The practice of functional analysis in professional psychology is most securely established in the modification of individual behavior by changing external stimulus conditions that influence behavior. Thus, children's tantrums are reduced by cessation of parental reinforcement and use of time-out procedures. Bizarre actions of psychotic patients are changed by satiation of the bizarre activity and simultaneous reinforcement of incompatible, socially acceptable behavior. The many reviews of behavior therapy now available (e.g., Franks & Wilson, 1979) offer literally thousands of examples. Recently, the same principles have been applied to covert activities in cognitive behavior modification (Meichenbaum, 1977). Not only external stimuli but such internal events as subvocal speech and images are shown to play a part in determining behavior. Various clinical procedures are therefore used to change the covert processes, and effects are observed both in reports about the internal activities themselves and in explicit behavior related to the covert processes. The functional analysis of interpersonal behavior has only begun in clinical practice. As was true in the evolution of individual behavior analysis, the first efforts have focused on external stimulus conditions. Weiss, Hops, and Patterson (1973) and Stuart (1976) have modified the reciprocally aversive interactions of husbands and wives, mainly by determining what kinds of interaction both parties see as undesirable, defining desired changes in behavior, contracting for replacement of one class of interactions by another, and helping people learn to treat each other in the more satisfying ways by any of several procedures.

Extension of a functional analytic approach to more complex aspects of interpersonal behavior will not be easy. The conception of interpersonal relationships outlined in the first part of this chapter included such ideas as interpersonal meaning, causal condition, script, agenda, and unawareness. It does not seem likely that complex interpersonal relationships among intelligent, sensitive, mobile adults can be understood unless concepts of these kinds are introduced. This makes the practice of functional analysis in the study and change of interpersonal relationships difficult. Rules for inferring "causal conditions" are indefinite. Principles governing choice of intervention are still primitive. No convincing demonstrations of the method with the most complex and interesting features of interpersonal relationships have yet appeared. For all this, the principle of functional analysis seems inherently sound. Scientific psychology proceeds within two main disciplines, correlation and experiment. Professional psychology involves two main pursuits, assessment and change. In the functional analysis of interpersonal behavior, these pursuits and disciplines stand a chance to be united.

REFERENCES

Anastasi, A. *Psychological testing*, 3rd ed. New York: Macmillan, 1976.

Berne, E. *Games people play*. New York: Grove Press, 1964.

Boals, G. F. *The reliability and utility of three data modes in the assessment of marital relationships.* Unpublished doctoral dissertation, Rutgers State University, 1979.

Bowen, M. Family therapy and family group therapy. In D. H. L. Olson (Ed.), *Treating relationships*. Lake Mills, Iowa: Graphic Publishing Co., 1976.

Carson, R. C. *Interaction concepts of personality.* Chicago: Aldine, 1969.

Christensen, A. Naturalistic observation in families: A system for random audio recordings in the home. Department of Psychology, University of California at Los Angeles, 1978.

Cronbach, L. J. & Gleser, G. C. *Psychological tests and personnel decisions*, 2nd ed. Urbana, Ill.: University of Illinois Press, 1965.

Franks, C. M. & Wilson, G. T. *Annual review of behavior therapy: Theory and practice*, Vol. 7. New York: Brunner/Mazel, 1979.

Gottman, J. M. *Marital interaction: Experimental investigations.* New York: Academic Press, 1979.

Haggard, E. A., Brekstad, A., & Skard, A. G. On the reliability of the anamnestic interview. *Journal of Abnormal and Social Psychology*, 1960, **61**, 311–318.

Haley, J. *Problem-solving therapy: New strategies for effective family therapy.* San Francisco: Jossey-Bass, 1976.

Harris, T. A. *I'm OK—You're OK: A practical guide to transactional analysis.* New York: Harper & Row, 1967.

Kagan, N. Can technology help us toward reliability in influencing human interaction? *Educational Technology*, 1973, **13**, 44–51.

Kelley, H. H. *Attribution in social interaction.* New York: General Learning Press, 1971.

Kelley, H. H., Berscheid, E., Christensen, A., Harvey, J. H., Huston, T. L., Levinger, G., McClintock, E., Peplau, L. A., & Peterson, D. R. *The psychology of close relationships.* Book in preparation, 1981.

Kelly, G. A. *The psychology of personal constructs.* New York: Norton, 1955.

Lazarus, A. A. (Ed.) *Multimodal behavior therapy.* New York: Springer, 1976.

Meichenbaum, D. *Cognitive-behavior modification: An integrative approach.* New York: Plenum Press, 1977.

Minuchin, S. *Families and family therapy.* Cambridge, Mass.: Harvard University Press, 1974.

Nay, W. R. Analogue measures. In A. R. Ciminero, K. S. Calhoun, & H. E. Adams (Eds.), *Handbook of behavioral assessment.* New York: Wiley, 1977.

Nunnaly, J. C., Jr. *Introduction to psychological measurement.* New York: McGraw-Hill, 1970.

Patterson, G. R., Ray, R. S., Shaw, D. A., & Cobb, J. A. *Manual for coding of family interactions.* Eugene, Oregon: Oregon Research Institute, 1969.

Peterson, D. R. *The clinical study of social behavior.* New York: Appleton-Century-Crofts, 1968.

Peterson, D. R. A functional approach to the study of person-person interactions. In D. Magnusson & N. S. Endler (Eds.), *Personality at the crossroads: Current issues in interactional psychology.* Hillsdale, N.J.: Erlbaum, 1977.

Peterson, D. R. Assessing interpersonal relationships by means of interaction records. *Behavioral Assessment,* 1979, **1**, 221–236. (a)

Peterson, D. R. Assessing interpersonal relationships in natural settings. *New Directions for Methodology of Behavioral Science,* 1979, **2**, 33–54. (b)

Pruitt, D. G. & Kimmel, M. J. Twenty years of experimental gaming: Critique, synthesis, and suggestions for the future. *Annual Review of Psychology,* 1977, **28**, 363–392.

Radke-Yarrow, M., Campbell, J., & Burton, R. V. Reliability of maternal retrospection: A preliminary report. *Family Process,* 1964, **3**, 207–218.

Raush, H. L., Barry, W. A., Hertel, R. K. & Swain, W. A. *Communication, conflict, and marriage.* San Francisco: Jossey-Bass, 1974.

Schutz, W. C. *FIRO: A three-dimensional theory of interpersonal behavior.* New York: Holt, Rinehart & Winston, 1958.

Skinner, B. F. *The behavior of organisms.* New York: Appleton-Century, 1938.

Skinner, B. F. *Science and human behavior.* New York: Free Press, 1953.

Stuart, R. B. An operant interpersonal program for couples. In D. H. L. Olson (Ed.), *Treating relationships.* Lake Mills, Iowa: Graphic Publishing Co., 1976.

Sullivan, H. S. *The psychiatric interview.* New York: Norton, 1954.

Swensen, C. H., Jr. *Introduction to interpersonal relations.* Glenview, Ill.: Scott Foresman, 1973.

Watzlawick, P. *Change: Principles of problem formation and problem resolution.* New York: Norton, 1974.

Watzlawick, P. *The language of change.* New York: Basic Books, 1978.

Weiss, R. L., Hops, H., & Patterson, G. R. A framework for conceptualizing marital conflict: a technology for altering it, some data for evaluating it. In L. A. Hamerlynck, L. C. Handy, & E. J. Mash (Eds.), *Behavior change: Methodology, concepts, and practice.* Champaign, Ill.: Research Press, 1973.

Chapter 9

Symptoms and Interpersonal Problems: The Prototype as an Integrating Concept*

Leonard M. Horowitz, Rita de Sales French, Jeffrey S. Lapid, and David A. Weckler

Complaints that bring people to psychotherapy fall into conceptually different classes. One class consists of symptoms, which are often adjectives expressed in noun form, such as depression, loneliness, suspiciousness, anxiety, and tension. A second class consists of self-defeating thoughts, such as "Something is wrong with me"; "I am a failure"; and "I am a cold person." A third class consists of specific behavioral disabilities, typically interpersonal ones, such as "I can't seem to make friends" and "I find it hard to say 'no' to my friends."

These and other kinds of complaints frequently occur in intake interviews, but we do not know how they are related to each other. If a person complains of depression, for example, what are the person's most distressing thoughts or the person's major interpersonal problems? If a person thinks "I am passive" or "I am ungiving," what is the person's most probable symptom or most probably interpersonal difficulty?

In our work, we have conceptualized the relationship between symptoms, self-defeating thoughts, and interpersonal problems in the following general way. We regard a symptom like depression as an abstract conceptual category. Ingredients of the category would include many features—feelings, thoughts, and behaviors—that summarize the meaning of that symptom. These features are themselves abstractions composed of more specific features. Thus, a statement like "I am depressed" summarizes ingredients that can be expanded into increasingly specific feelings, thoughts, and behaviors.

When a person reports being depressed, an interviewer therefore asks questions to determine which particular ingredients characterize that person's situation. The inter-

*The research reported in this article was supported in part by funds from the Boys Town Center for the Study of Youth Development at Stanford University. The opinions expressed and the policies advocated herein do not necessarily reflect those of Boys Town.

We would like to express our gratitude to Jean Amrhein, Muriel Gani, Joseph Gerber, David Grandin, Jeffrey Hoffman, Betsy Lamson, David Post, and Kathryn Tucker for their help in the collection and analysis of the data. We are also grateful to Dr. Perrin L. French for facilitating the work with patients at the VA Hospital.

viewer can only understand the person's depression by probing further into its meaning since the meaning of depression for one person is different from the meaning for another person. If an interviewer learned through questioning that the person was feeling inferior, closed, and lonely, the interviewer might investigate further and learn that the person was finding it hard to make friends, relax on a date, and say 'no' to other people. Successive questioning would eventually lead the person to describe specific thoughts and interpersonal problems which could then be treated by the interventions of psychotherapy. These thoughts and interpersonal problems are thus critical in explaining the more abstract symptom.

This chapter describes our progress in exploring the relationship between a symptom and interpersonal problems. A symptom is viewed as a prototype, an organized collection of features that conveys the "average meaning" of the concept in an idealized form. By appropriate questioning, an interviewer traces a pathway into the prototype, articulating the meaning of the symptom for a particular person. Each relevant feature is investigated further, and the symptom is analyzed into sharper components of meaning. In this chapter we shall trace depression through components of its meaning to particular interpersonal problems. These interpersonal problems will then be examined further to clarify their meaning and to identify their implications for therapy.

There are methodological reasons for wanting to distinguish among the different classes of complaints and to clarify their relationship to each other. For one thing, investigators studying the effectiveness of psychotherapy have devised procedures to generate individualized lists of problems for evaluating the outcome of each patient's treatment (Garwick & Lampman, 1972; Kiresuk & Sherman, 1968; Klonoff & Cox, 1975; Malan, 1973). A study of the problem lists themselves, however, has shown low interobserver reliability (Bloch et al., 1977). Expert clinicians who viewed the same intake interviews did not agree well about the patients' major problems. One reason for the lack of interobserver agreement was that different observers described the problems at different levels of abstraction. That is, three observers viewing the same interview disagreed as to whether a patient's major problem was "depression," "low self-esteem," or "an inability to express anger." These forms of a problem are not incompatible with each other—they may simply involve different levels of abstraction in stating the problem—and observers would probably show more agreement if the form of the problem were kept constant.

Furthermore, studies of psychotherapy outcome (e.g., Sloane et al., 1975; Frank et al., 1978) largely focus on changes in *symptoms* that follow psychotherapy; but the interventions of psychotherapy usually focus on *interpersonal problems*. Thus, there is a general disparity between the content of a treatment and the evaluation of that treatment. If a reduction in symptoms does not immediately follow a resolution of interpersonal problems, then an assessment through a symptom checklist might fail to capture changes that did in fact occur during the treatment. This is another reason for wanting to relate the different levels of possible change.

THE PROTOTYPE AS AN EXPLANATORY CONCEPT

To begin, let us consider an abstract kind of complaint like the symptom "depression." Because of its abstractness, the concept is not well defined; its meaning varies somewhat from person to person, and people seem to apply different standards when they judge depression in themselves and in others. Therefore, when people say "I feel depressed," their intended meanings are not precise. Three people who begin psychotherapy with a complaint of depression may have quite distinct problems in mind; one may be experiencing deep feelings of inferiority and inadequacy; a second may be experiencing poor inner controls (overeating, oversleeping, excessive drinking); a third may be experiencing existential feelings of separateness and alienation.

Because of this diversity in meaning, some method is needed that not only describes the "average" meaning of depression but also allows us to describe variability in people's usage. We want to be able to identify features that apply to a given person and then investigate those features further.

For this reason, we have adopted the concept of a prototype to describe depression. We believe that depression should not be conceptualized in terms of a traditional trait or type, but rather in terms of a more modern conception which describes a theoretical ideal or standard against which real people can be evaluated. The following section describes the concept and reports an empirical method for portraying it.

The Concept of a Prototype

Recent research in cognitive psychology (Cantor & Mischel, 1979a; Cantor, Smith, French, & Mezzich, 1980; Rosch, Mervis, Gray, Johnson, & Boyer-Braem, 1976) has focused on the prototype as a way of defining a concept or category. A prototype is a theoretical notion, consisting of the most common features or properties of members of a given category. All of these properties characterize at least *some* members, but in actual practice, no one property is either necessary or sufficient for membership in the category.

At one time, a category was typically defined in terms of a discrete set of features that were individually necessary and jointly sufficient for membership in that category. The category "girls," for example, was defined by a set of critical features like: +animate, +human, +young, −male. Each feature was considered necessary, and the features were collectively sufficient for classifying any object as a member of the category or not.

In more recent years, however, psychologists have come to view certain important categories in more probabilistic terms. Members of the category "birds," for example, share many properties with each other. Some birds are all alike in being small; others are alike in being colorful; still others are alike in producing sweet songs. We could list all the features that people cite most often when they describe birds, and the composite of the most frequent features would define a kind of theoretical ideal—the prototype. No actual bird would have all of these features, and very few features would apply to all birds. In practice, however, some birds have more of the specified features than others, and a bird with a large number of these features (or the more important ones) would generally be a good example of that category, while a bird with fewer (or less important) features would be a poorer example. Thus, a sparrow (which has *many* features) is a good, or prototypic, example while a penguin (which has fewer features) is a poorer, or less prototypic, example; an owl, (with an intermediate number of features) is an intermediate example (Rosch et al., 1976). Concepts from the literature of personality and psychopathology have also been subjected to this kind of analysis (Cantor & Mischel, 1979a, 1979b; Cantor, Smith, French, & Mezzich, 1980). In the work described below, we adapted procedures of these studies to examine the prototype of a "depressed person."

DEPRESSION AS A PROTOTYPE

Thirty-five introductory psychology students at Stanford University were selected on the basis of their scores on the Beck Depression Inventory (Beck & Beamesderfer, 1974); 12

had obtained high scores (9 or above), 11 had obtained the moderate score of 3, and 12 had obtained the low score of 0. First, these subjects were asked to think of the best example they could of a person that they knew who was depressed; they were also asked to state the approximate age and sex of the person they were describing. They were then asked to describe the person—to write down the person's most usual feelings, thoughts, and behaviors. The writers were encouraged to be as specific as they wished and to feel free to include descriptive statements, even if the statements could not be easily labeled as a feeling, thought, or behavior. They spent about half an hour describing the person's feelings, thoughts, and behaviors.

It is interesting to note, parenthetically, that 11 of the 12 depressed subjects described depressed people who were of the same sex and age as themselves, while subjects of the other two groups were about equally divided in this respect (8 of 11 for the moderate subjects and 5 of 12 for the nondepressed subjects). Thus, the depressed subjects described someone very much like themselves (perhaps themselves) more often than the nondepressed subjects.

Each subject's description was typed and then submitted to a panel of three judges. Each judge independently tabulated every feature, and the judges met to discuss the features they had identified. The group's consensus was then recorded to obtain separately for each group a final listing and frequency count of features for subjects in that group.

The three groups of subjects did not differ in particular features that they contributed, nor in the overall number of features. The mean number of features mentioned by depressed, medium, and nondepressed subjects was 33.7, 29.0, and 25.6, respectively; $F(2,32) = 2.38, p > .10$. Since the groups did not differ significantly, we combined features from all 35 subjects to derive a more stable description. Features that had been supplied by 17 percent or more of the subjects (i.e., six or more subjects) formed the final prototype. There were 41 features that met this criterion. The most common features (and their relative frequencies) were: "feels inferior, worthless, inadequate" (.60); "has a pessimistic attitude, expects the worst" (.49); and "avoids social contact, isolates self from others" (.66). Overall, there were 17 feelings, 11 thoughts, and 13 behaviors.

We checked whether the depressed, medium, and nondepressed subjects differed in the number of final prototypic features that they had mentioned in their original descriptions. These means for the three groups were significantly different—12.9, 10.7, and 9.8, respectively; $F(2, 80) = 4.00, p < .05$. The mean number of prototypic features was also computed separately for feelings, thoughts, and behaviors: for feelings, 5.3, 4.4, and 3.7; for thoughts, 4.0, 3.1, and 2.8; for behaviors 3.2, 3.1, and 3.0. It is interesting that the groups did not differ in the number of prototypic *behaviors* (which are public and observable), but they did differ with respect to the more private feelings and thoughts.

Finally, in order to determine the cognitive organization of these 41 features, we performed a hierarchical clustering procedure (Johnson, 1967). In this procedure, 50 subjects were each given a stack of 41 cards that contained the features, one to a card. The subjects were asked to sort the cards into categories, showing which features seemed to go together. We then computed a matrix showing how often each feature was categorized together with each other feature.

This matrix of proportions was then subjected to a hierarchical clustering procedure (Johnson, 1967; Everitt, 1974). The method identified major clusters within the set of features. The resulting clusters are shown in Figure 9.1. Features that are enclosed in the innermost rectangles were the most tightly clustered. As the rectangles become larger, the denoted cluster is weaker. The figure also shows the criterion for each cluster, i.e., the proportion of subjects who placed the features in a common category.

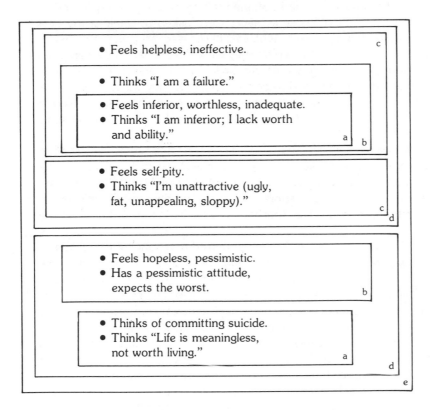

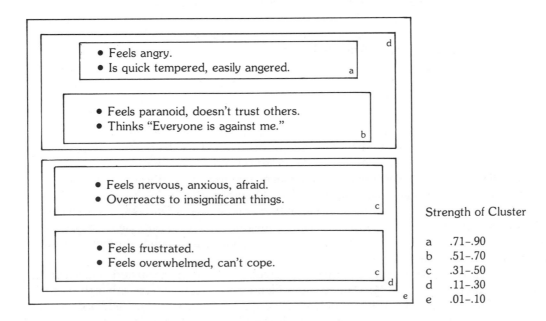

Strength of Cluster	
a	.71–.90
b	.51–.70
c	.31–.50
d	.11–.30
e	.01–.10

Fig. 9.1. Prototype of a depressed person.

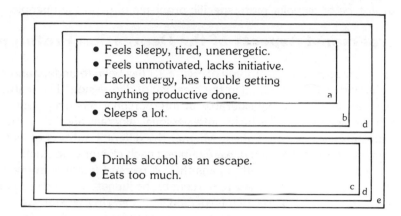

- Feels sleepy, tired, unenergetic.
- Feels unmotivated, lacks initiative.
- Lacks energy, has trouble getting anything productive done. a
- Sleeps a lot. b

d

- Drinks alcohol as an escape.
- Eats too much. c

d

e

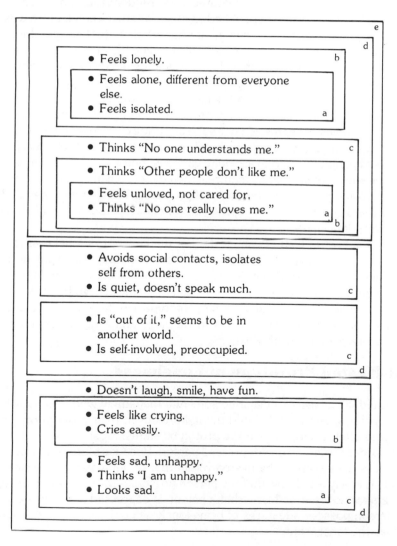

e

d

- Feels lonely. b
- Feels alone, different from everyone else.
- Feels isolated. a

- Thinks "No one understands me." c
- Thinks "Other people don't like me."
- Feels unloved, not cared for.
- Thinks "No one really loves me." a

b

- Avoids social contacts, isolates self from others.
- Is quiet, doesn't speak much. c

- Is "out of it," seems to be in another world.
- Is self-involved, preoccupied. c

d

- Doesn't laugh, smile, have fun.
- Feels like crying.
- Cries easily. b

- Feels sad, unhappy.
- Thinks "I am unhappy."
- Looks sad. a

c

d

Figure 9.1, thus, describes the overall meaning of depression. The next step is to use this prototype to pinpoint more specific problems of depressed people.

Interpersonal Aspects of the Depression Prototype

One goal in studying the prototype of Figure 9.1 has been to understand how interpersonal problems may be embedded in the meaning of depression. The features of the figure, however, seem to vary considerably in interpersonal meaning. One feature, "Thinks 'Everyone is against me,' " is highly interpersonal, whereas another feature, "Feels sleepy, tired, unenergetic," is not. To test whether the different subsets of features vary significantly in interpersonal meaning, we examined each cluster of strength d (see Figure 9.1). This degree of cluster strength means that all pairs of features in the cluster had been classified together by more than 10 percent of the judges. There were nine such clusters.

To determine the degree of interpersonal meaning in a cluster, we obtained ratings of the different features. The 41 features were randomized and presented to students at Stanford University who were asked to judge whether each feature was interpersonal or not. Ratings were made on a five-point scale from "1" (definitely not interpersonal) to "5" (definitely interpersonal). The means of the nine clusters varied from 1.63 to 4.05. An analysis of variance showed that the nine clusters did differ significantly; $F (8, 32) = 9.38$, $p < .001$. The cluster that received the highest mean rating was the one involving loneliness, and the one that received the lowest mean rating was the one involving sleepiness. Thus, the concept of depression is not uniform in interpersonal meaning.

The meaning of depression has such disparate elements that we would not necessarily expect two depressed people to be alike with respect to their interpersonal problems; depressed people as a group are quite varied. If, however, depressed people were selected for some subset of prototypic features, then their problems should be more alike, perhaps even exposing particular interpersonal problems. We therefore decided to focus on the cluster that had received the highest ratings of interpersonal meaning, namely the cluster concerning loneliness.

This subset of features suggests that the concept of loneliness is nested within the prototype of depression. As a more delineated concept, it might be one route toward articulating interpersonal problems subsumed under depression. In order to examine the concept of loneliness more closely, we used the same procedure to derive the prototype of a "lonely person," expecting a similar prototype with fewer features and a sharper meaning. We also expected its features to be more uniformly interpersonal and to include explicit interpersonal problems.

The Nested Prototype of Loneliness

We asked 40 subjects to describe someone they knew who was their best example of a lonely person, and we tabulated the features from their descriptions. Eighteen features occurred often enough to achieve prototype status. Most of these features also occurred in the larger prototype of a depressed person. Because of this embedding, the concept of loneliness does seem to be nested within that of depression. Therefore, to know that a person is lonely is to know that the person possesses major features of depression, but the converse is not true: to know that a person is depressed does not necessarily imply that the person possesses features of being lonely since there are other routes to depression besides the lonely route.

Features of the lonely prototype were subjected to a hierarchical clustering scheme that yielded the results shown in Figure 9.2. There were four clusters with strength d, and we computed the mean interpersonal ratings of these clusters. The mean ratings ranged from 2.67 to 3.97. The clusters differed significantly, but not as markedly as those of depression; $F (3, 14) = 7.27, p < .01$.

Also, the mean interpersonal rating across all features was significantly higher for the lonely prototype than it was for the depressed prototype; $t (57) = 2.28, p < .05$. In general, the lonely prototype is more interpersonal in meaning than the depressed prototype.

Finally, the lonely prototype contained two prototypic thoughts that explicitly described an interpersonal problem. These two thoughts were: "I want a friend" and "I don't know how to make friends." They clearly express a problem (i.e., a frustrated interpersonal goal and a wish to achieve it). Although the depressed prototype contained features related to this problem, the problem was not as clearly expressed as it was in the lonely prototype. The clarity of the problem suggests that lonely people experience interpersonal problems related to the prototypic thought, "I don't know how to make friends." We wanted to identify these characteristic interpersonal problems, so we compared lonely and nonlonely people. Our results did show a systematic difference between the two groups, but before we report that difference, we need to discuss interpersonal problems in a broader context. Therefore, in the following section we shall discuss the domain of interpersonal problems and then return to the lonely person's problems.

THE NATURE OF INTERPERSONAL PROBLEMS

Interpersonal problems are often stated in a form that begins "I can't (do something)," expressing the frustrated goal. Some examples are: "I can't say 'no' to my friends" and "I can't express affection to my wife." Norms showing the range or frequency of such problems do not exist and we wanted to examine their occurrence in a general psychiatric population.

In an intensive study of a single case (Horowitz et al., 1978, Observation 3), we examined all the interpersonal problems that were mentioned during the first 100 hours of treatment of a woman who suffered from sexual frigidity. All complaints that began with a synonym of "I can't" were identified and systematized. Very few of these complaints mentioned the sexual frigidity directly, but the majority of them, like the sexual problem, reflected difficulties with intimacy—difficulties in trusting, believing, praising, helping, comforting, and getting close to other people. Like the symptom, the interpersonal problems could be organized around problems with closeness.

In another study, we examined 28 intake interviews of patients who were about to begin psychotherapy (Horowitz, 1979), and we systematically identified all statements that began with some variation of the phrase "I can't." The resulting problem statements were primarily statements about interpersonal problems. Problems that were not interpersonal (like "I can't fall asleep at night") were in the minority.

The problematic behaviors themselves (e.g., saying "no" to other people) were then studied semantically and scaled. A multidimensional scaling showed that these problematic interpersonal behaviors varied along three dimensions, any of which (alone or in combination with others) could be the cause of the problem. The three dimensions resembled dimensions like friendliness and power that have been postulated theoretically (e.g., Ben-

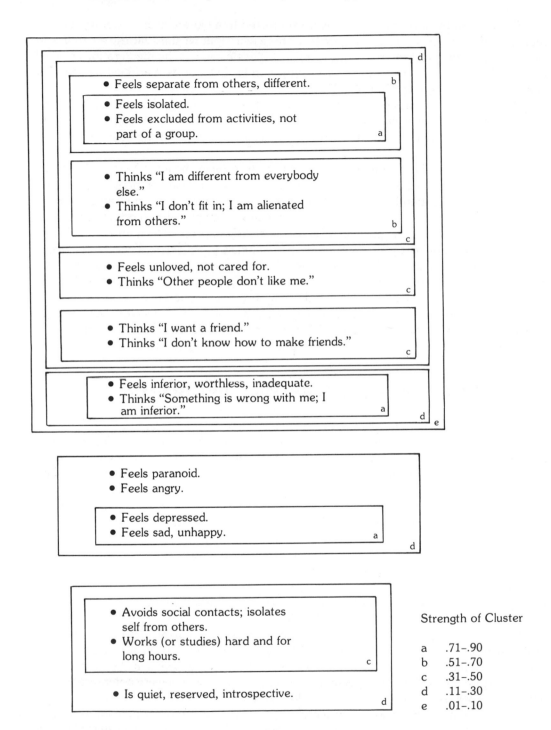

Fig. 9.2. Prototype of a lonely person.

jamin, 1974, 1977; Leary, 1957). They also resembled dimensions derived empirically in nonclinical contexts (Fillenbaum & Rapoport, 1971; Joncas, 1977; Maccoby & Masters, 1970; Marwell & Hage, 1970; Osgood, 1970; Rosenberg & Sedlak, 1972; White, 1978; Wish, Deutsch, & Kaplan, 1976).

The dimensions were labeled (1) the nature of the subject's involvement with the other person (hostile or friendly), (2) the subject's intention to influence, change, or control the other person, and (3) the degree of psychological involvement between the subject and the other person. "Being friendly and sociable," for example, which was derived from the problem "I find it hard to be friendly and sociable," connotes friendliness (Dimension 1) and a relaxation of control (Dimension 2). "Reading the other person's point of view" connotes a subjective involvement with the other person (Dimension 3).

In addition to the multidimensional scaling, we also performed a hierarchical clustering scheme. This technique organized the problematic behaviors into thematic clusters that occupied different regions of the three-dimensional space. Examples of the major clusters are listed in Figure 9.3. Problems of intimacy and aggression were the most numerous; they comprised about two-thirds of all the problems in the original interviews. In general, problems of intimacy connoted friendliness, a relaxation of control, and some subjective involvement with the other person. Problems of aggression, on the other hand, were generally unfriendly and connoted less subjective involvement with and more control over the other person. The arrangements of the different clusters in the three-dimensional space is reported in detail by Horowitz (1979).

These procedures, thus, characterized the semantic meaning of problematic interpersonal behaviors. Two behaviors which have similar coordinates would have similar meanings. They could be quite different behaviorally, of course, even if they were semantically similar. For example, "expressing affection" and "revealing personal things," which are in the same cluster, both reflect friendliness, a moderate involvement with the other person, and a relaxation of control; hence, they are similar in meaning. A question arises, though, as to whether their similar meaning would cause them to co-occur as problems. Would a person who had difficulty expressing affection have difficulty revealing personal things? On the one hand, semantically similar problems may be *behaviorally* specific: A difficulty in executing one behavior may not necessarily imply a difficulty in executing the other. On the other hand, if problems arise from underlying dimensions of interpersonal meaning (like a relaxation of control), then two behaviors with a similar meaning would co-vary as problems.

To compare these alternative hypotheses, we administered a deck of interpersonal problems to 100 students at Stanford University (Horowitz, French, Gani, & Lapid, 1980). The students sorted the cards by the Q-sort method into nine categories, from Category 1 ("least familiar as a problem of mine") to Category 9 ("most familiar as a problem of mine"). The category number (1–9) served as a rating that described how familiar the problem was for that subject. The value of r was computed between the category assignment of each pair of problems. We hypothesized that if two problems were in the same cluster (hence, similar in meaning), they would correlate more highly than problems in different clusters.

The results supported this hypothesis. Although the mean r across the pairs of all problems in the deck was 0.00, the mean r between pairs within a given cluster was always positive. Therefore, if a person reports one problem of socializing (e.g., relaxing on a date), the probability is higher that the person will also report a problem participating in groups, enjoying parties, and making friends. These results suggest that a person may experience a behavior as difficult because of its meaning—criticizing other people and

I. BE INTIMATE: "It's hard for me to . . .

- commit myself to another person.
- trust other people.
- tell personal things to other people.
- love another person.

II. BE AGGRESSIVE. "It's hard for me to . . .

- tell another person that I have a different opinion.
- say 'no' to other people.
- make demands of other people.
- criticize other people.

III. NOT BE AGGRESSIVE. "I . . .

- get annoyed by other people too easily.
- talk back to other people too much.
- criticize other people too much.
- put too much pressure on other people.

IV. BE SOCIABLE. "It's hard for me to . . .

- have fun at parties.
- telephone other people and arrange to get together with them.
- join in on groups.
- make friends in a simple, natural way.

V. BE INDEPENDENT. "It's hard for me to . . .

- end a relationship when I want to.
- 'make it' without other people.
- do as I please without feeling guilty toward other people.
- go out to do my work and leave the other person at home alone.

VI. NOT BE COMPLIANT. "I . . .

- let myself be persuaded by other people too easily.
- find myself joking and clowning around too much to get other people to like me.
- care too much about other people's reactions.
- always act like a helpless, little child in front of others.

Fig. 9.3. Examples of problem statements in the form "It's hard for me to . . . ."

making demands of other people are both perceived as unkind—and the meaning, rather than the behavior per se, creates the problem.

INTERPERSONAL PROBLEMS OF PEOPLE WHO ARE LONELY

The prototype of loneliness, which is nested within the prototype of depression, suggested a particular class of interpersonal problems. The prototypic thought, "I don't know how to make friends," corresponds to one of the more common interpersonal problems observed in our study of interpersonal problems, namely, the problem "I find it hard to make friends in a simple, natural way." That particular problem was part of a cluster of problems in socializing—making friends, having fun at parties, and relaxing on a date. These problems reflected a difficulty in being friendly, uncontrolling of the other person, and pscyhologically uninvolved. It was hypothesized that people who report feeling lonely would more often report problems from this cluster.

To test this hypothesis, we asked lonely people and nonlonely people about their major interpersonal problems (Horowitz & French, 1979). We administered the UCLA Loneliness Scale (Russell, Peplau, & Ferguson, 1978) to undergraduate students at Stanford University and identified individuals at each extreme. We then administered a deck of cards describing interpersonal problems. Each subject arranged the cards by the Q-sort technique into nine categories, from Category 1 ("least familiar as a problem of mine") to Category 9 ("most familiar as a problem of mine"). The Q-sort technique required the subjects to place a prescribed number of problems into each category.

We then determined which problems the subjects most often placed among their top problems. As hypothesized, the most common type of problem for the lonely subjects were those describing difficulties in socializing. This category contained 13 different problems, which are shown in Table 9.1. We recorded the mean number of times that each of these problems was placed in Cateogry 9 by lonely and notlonely subjects. The results in Table 9.1 showed that lonely people suffered from problems of this type significantly more often.

We also recorded the number of the category into which each problem of socializing was placed and averaged the category placements. As shown in Table 9.1, lonely subjects, on the average, placed every problem of socializing into a higher category. Thus, lonely people can be characterized by a greater prominence of problems of socializing.

The problem that lonely people most frequently placed in the top category was "I find it hard to make friends in a simple, natural way." Apparently this problem occurs frequently enough for lonely people that it appeared as a feature of the lonely prototype. All the other problems of socializing also differentiated between lonely and nonlonely people, but apparently they were not salient enough to have achieved prototype status.

In this work we have studied loneliness because of its position within the prototype of depression. "Depression" is a variegated concept. As an interviewer focuses on specific features, the concept becomes more precise. The most interpersonal features of depression concerned loneliness, and that is why we examined the subsidiary prototype of a lonely person. As expected, that prototype was sharper in meaning than the one for depression. Furthermore, features of the lonely prototype suggested interpersonal problems over socializing, and the data showed that problems of socializing were consistently more probable for lonely people.

TABLE 9.1. PROBLEMS OF INHIBITED SOCIABILITY.

Problem: I find it hard to . . .	Probability of Being Among Top 5 Problems		Mean Category Placement	
	Lonely	Not Lonely	Lonely	Not Lonely
make friends in a simple, natural way.	.28	.00	6.16	2.84
introduce myself to O(s) at parties.	.24	.18	6.36	5.84
make phone calls to O to initiate social activity.	.20	.02	6.12	4.76
participate in groups.	.16	.04	5.12	4.60
get pleasure out of a party.	.16	.02	5.64	4.64
get into the swing of a party.	.12	.07	6.00	4.89
relax on a date and enjoy myself.	.12	.00	5.84	3.56
be friendly and sociable with O.	.08	.00	5.36	3.78
participate in playing games with O.	.04	.02	5.04	4.49
get buddy-buddy with O.	.04	.00	5.64	4.93
entertain O at my home.	.00	.04	4.84	4.56
get along with O.	.00	.02	6.08	5.04
extend myself to accept O's friendship.	.00	.00	4.48	3.33

TWO OTHER PATHWAYS TO DEPRESSION: ILLUSTRATIVE CASES

Because depression is a variegated concept, two individuals who are depressed might differ substantially in their interpersonal problems. We have not yet applied our method to clusters other than loneliness, but we have examined individual cases that illustrate some of these other pathways to depression. The following case descriptions illustrate two other possible pathways. One, Mr. A, suffered low self-esteem and a tendency to avoid social contact. When Mr. A's reasons for avoiding social contact were investigated, the interviewer learned about severe fears of intimacy. The other patient, Mr. B, felt frustrated, angry, and anxious over his own anger. When his frustration and anger were investigated, the interviewer learned about extreme difficulties with aggression.

The patients were participants in a study of 12 male inpatients at the VA Hospital who were receiving individual psychotherapy and were being discussed in depth at a weekly case conference. Before the therapy began, the patients were shown an inventory of interpersonal problems (see Horowitz, French, Gani, & Lapid, 1980) and asked to indicate the problems that they recognized as similar to their own. They were then asked to designate the ten problems that they regarded as the most severe.

Mr. A—Problems of Intimacy

Mr. A's top ten problems included difficulties with loving another person, trusting other people, telling personal things, accepting love when it was offered, and performing sexually. These problems reflected difficulties in being friendly, subjectively involved with another person, and uncontrolling.

Mr. A was a quiet, unmarried, 38-year-old man who smoked and drank heavily; he sought treatment to overcome severe depression and alcoholism. He noted that whenever he visited his parents' home, he would get embroiled in family squabbles that would leave him feeling depressed. He felt particularly low in self-esteem and regarded himself as a failure. He felt helpless, ineffective, inadequate, and inferior. Our formulation of the case will relate these prototypic features of depression to Mr. A's interpersonal problems over intimacy.

Mr. A's mother was a passive, quietly angry, and quietly complaining woman who felt chronically dissatisfied with her life. She was continually exerting subtle pressure on her son to share her dissatisfaction and experience her discontent. He felt that he should help her, but she would generally rebuff any constructive suggestions he might make. She subtly encouraged a blending of moods and thoughts, expecting him to understand her needs and wishes intuitively. As one example of such expectations, she was known to telephone people and, without identifying herself, begin talking as though they knew by magic who was calling.

Mr. A was very sensitive and responsive to his mother's moods and wishes. In a similar way, he also took on other people's worries, troubles, and miseries, and generally felt that he ought to help them. If he was unable to help (as was often the case), he felt ineffective, helpless, and guilty. On the ward, for example, patients would sometimes complain of depression, and Mr. A would then become depressed. Many of his problems could be organized around an inability to "separate" from other people.

Intimacy was apparently a problem because Mr. A was affected too strongly by other people's needs; he too readily participated in other people's moods and problems. Staff members had observed this tendency; when they rated him on Benjamin's (1974) SASB, they asssigned the highest ratings to the following behaviors: empathizes with staff members' views, actively listens in a nonjudgmental and friendly way, looks after their interests, takes steps to protect them, and considers their side of things. In a sense, Mr. A was *too* skillful with intimacy, and his difficulties had to do with his inability to disengage himself from other people. The therapy was designed to help him separate his own needs and wishes from those of other people and to judge more realistically when he could and should be expected to help.

Mr. B—Problems of Aggression

Mr. B was a 30-year-old, unmarried man who complained of feeling nervous, shaky, and depressed. He had been characterized at different times as manic-depressive, paranoid schizophrenic, and schizoaffective schizophrenic. When he was functioning well, he was regarded as convivial, intelligent, and witty. The staff's ratings on Benjamin's (1974) SASB reflected his congenial nature. Items with the highest ratings were: he invites others to be with him, warmly welcomes others, and lets others know where he is so they can maintain friendly contact. His largest group of interpersonal problems were problems of aggression— difficulties confronting other people, telling people about his anger, and fighting. These problems left him feeling silently angry, frustrated, and helpless. Furthermore, as described below, anger had a distressing meaning for him and aroused anxiety. Thus, the important features of depression for Mr. B were anger, frustration, and helplessness—a different route to depression from Mr. A's. The case formulation will clarify the source of these problems and explain the role of anger and anxiety in his depression.

Mr. B described his mother as a physically strong woman who dominated the family, using brute force on him in battles over haircuts, household chores, and the like. His mother set rules about eating, dressing, and washing, and she enforced these rules in a way that left him feeling small. He developed an impression early in life that rules could diminish him out of existence and as an adult, felt particularly demeaned by the hospital confinement and its rules. In contrast, driving his car alone at very high speeds gave him a pleasurable feeling of freedom, power, and control.

Mr. B could not comfortably rebel against rules, however, because his aggression signified danger. His mother openly regarded him as a troublemaker and led him over the years to believe that his actions had repeatedly caused unhappy consequences. For example, when his older sister, as an unmarried teenager, became pregnant, Mr. B came to believe that he was in some way responsible. Also, during his teenage years, his mother died of cancer, and he believed that he had caused her illness and death. He had also come to believe he had caused the death of other family members.

Because of these "omnipotent" ideas concerning his own mismanaged power, he drastically curbed his aggression and hostility. His own hostility made him anxious. Once, working as a volunteer with retarded children, he found himself unable to set limits on the children, experiencing that use of power as extremely unkind. He finally resolved the conflict by quitting the job.

It is not surprising that Mr. B's list of problems would express his wish to be more aggressive and controlling—to talk back, to tell people when he was angry, and say "no" to people. The goal of his treatment, quite different from Mr. A's, was to help him more realistically assess the effects of his firmness, nonpassivity, and appropriate aggression.

DIFFERENT MEANINGS OF "I CAN'T" IN INTERPERSONAL PROBLEMS

An important part of treating a symptom like depression, then, is to investigate the symptom until specific interpersonal problems are identified. Specific problems in the form "I can't (do something interpersonal)" are then the focus of therapeutic interventions. Phrases like "I can't" and "I find it hard to," however, are themselves ambiguous. When Mr. A reports that he can't trust people, when Mr. B reports that he can't fight, and when lonely people report that they can't make friends, the meaning of "can't" varies considerably from case to case.

At times "I can't" refers to a lack of competence, meaning "I don't know how to." The lonely person's "I can't make friends" may have this kind of meaning, suggesting that the person needs help in gaining a particular skill. At other times, the phrase refers to an inhibition against executing some desired behavior; the person has the necessary skill but restrains him or herself from executing the behavior. In that case, "I can't" means "I can't bring myself to." This is probably the meaning Mr. B intended when he expressed difficulties with aggression. His fantasies may reveal a higly developed competence for aggression, but his overt behavior, at least in some situations, would show the self-imposed restraint. At still other times, "I can't" may mean that performance anxiety (rather than a conflicting motive) interferes with the person's performance, masking a competence that otherwise exists.

We need therefore to understand the intended meaning of the problem statement if we are to formulate appropriate treatment strategies. If the person's problem implies a lack of competence, then the treatment should help the person acquire relevant skills. If the problem reflects a conflict and a self-imposed inhibition, then the treatment should clarify the conflict, reduce whatever conditions had caused the inhibition (e.g., guilt), and help the person choose freely among response options. If the problem reflects the interfering effects of anxiety, then the treatment should desensitize the person to anxiety.

To start with the simplest case, we wanted to develop a procedure that would show whether a particular problem reflects a lack of competence. If so, then remedial skill training would be appropriate; if not, then some other treatment would be needed. An assessment procedure was therefore needed that would show whether a deficit exists in the person's competence.

To distinguish between a lack of competence (I don't know how to) and an inhibition (I can't bring myself to), we decided to investigate the lonely person's difficulty with socializing. Does that difficulty reflect a lack of competence or an inhibition? The lonely person's top-rated problem, "I find it hard to make friends in a simple, natural way," corresponds to the prototypic thought, "I don't know how to make friends" and implies a lack of know-how, a lack of competence. Problems of socializing in general may reflect a lack of competence. If so, when the lonely person's competence is assessed—even for benign social situations—the person's performance should be poorer.

Assessing Competence

We therefore wanted to compare lonely and nonlonely people on a simple test of interpersonal competence. Many interpersonal tasks, however, might arouse anxiety in lonely people, and a performance decrement could arise not from lack of competence, but from the interfering effects of anxiety. Therefore, we searched for a test of competence that was relatively impersonal and nonthreatening, a task that the subject could approach in a relatively leisurely and nondefensive way, one that would test the limits of the subject's competence rather than assess the net performance observed under anxiety and interpersonal stress.

The task we selected was adapted from a task developed by Platt and Spivack (1975). This task requires the subject to consider hypothetical situations that posed different kinds of problems and to generate possible solutions. The subject was free to think about each situation and, in a leisurely way, to write a possible solution. The task was scored for the number and quality of methods, or "means," that the subject generated. Each situation was described in impersonal terms, about some fictitious character (in order further to divert the subjects' attention from themselves and possibly reduce stress). The task was therefore benign in that the subjects (a) were under no time pressure, (b) focused their attention on a fictitious character, and (c) were not required to enact the behavior itself.

The subjects were presented with a set of 11 situations. Each situation described the problem and a successful outcome in which some fictitious person successfully fulfilled his or her needs. The subjects were asked to supply the means by which the successful end was achieved, telling how the person managed to solve the problem. Here is one example:

C. had just moved in that day and didn't know anyone. C. wanted to have friends in the neighborhood. The story ends with C. having many good friends and feeling at home in the neighborhood. You begin the story with C. in his (her) room immediately after arriving in the neighborhood.

Most of the situations were interpersonal and involved different themes, particularly ones concerned with socializing—making friends in a new neighborhood, getting to know a new roommate, meeting new people at a party, meeting someone of the opposite sex, participating in a neighborhood meeting. One situation, however, was different from the others in that it was not interpersonal; it concerned a person who lost and later recovered a watch. A separate group of judges read the situations and rated them along various dimensions—how interpersonal they seemed, what skills they called for—and the judges' ratings corroborated our judgment that this situation was different from the others. Lonely people were expected to perform more poorly on the interpersonal situations that called for skills at socializing, but not on this control item.

The UCLA Loneliness Scale was administered to a large class in introductory psychology at the beginning of the term. Subjects were selected from this pool to have high, medium, or low scores of loneliness, corresponding to the top, middle, and bottom fifths of the distribution. There were 39 subjects in all—15 nonlonely subjects (7 males, 8 females) who had scores below 30; 10 medium subjects (7 males, 3 females) who had scores between 40 and 45; and 14 lonely subjects (9 males, 5 females) who had scores above 55. The subjects were contacted by telephone several weeks after they completed the Loneliness Scale, and they were tested in groups of fours. Each situation was presented at the top of a separate page, and the subjects wrote their responses on that page. Situations for male subjects were written about a male person, those for female subjects, about a female person. The entire procedure took about half an hour.

Three naive judges rated each response independently and blindly. To check that the three groups of subjects were comparable in verbal productivity, the judges first counted the total number of words in each response. The three groups of subjects did not differ; F

$(2, 36) < 1$. The judges also examined other characteristics of the subjects' verbal style, such as the frequency with which positive and negative affect were expressed and the frequency with which personal names were used. The three groups of subjects did not differ significantly in any of these respects.

Then the judges counted the number of methods (or "means") that the subjects generated as a way of solving the problem. The scoring procedures of Platt and Spivack (1975) were adapted in order to identify and score the number of methods that the subjects generated. Corresponding scores of the three judges were then averaged to yield a single stable index of each subject's performance.

First we examined the subjects' performance on the control item (methods of recovering a lost watch). The three groups did not differ signficantly on this task in any way. For the total number of methods produced, $F(2, 36) = .07, p > .93$. This F was smaller than the corresponding F for any other item.

Having established the comparability of the groups on the control item, we then examined the number of methods produced. In each of these situations, the lonely subjects produced fewer methods for solving the problem. The three groups differed significantly; $F(2, 36) = 4.28, p < .02$. The mean numbers of methods per item were 2.17, 2.95, and 2.74, respectively, for lonely, medium, and nonlonely subjects.

In addition, the judges rated the overall quality of each response as a way of solving the problem. These global ratings ranged from 1 ("poor") to 5 ("excellent"), and the three groups differed significantly in this respect as well; $F(2, 36) = 4.85, p < .01$. The mean ratings for the three groups were: 1.73, 2.24, and 2.07. Thus, lonely subjects produced fewer methods of solving the problems, and their responses in general were judged to be of poorer overall quality. Subjects of the lonely group also used more fantasy in their responses, $F(2, 36) = 3.52, p < .05$, and they more often failed to generate any method at all, $F(2, 36) = 3.32, p < .05$.

These results show that people who complain of feeling lonely (hence experience difficulties in socializing) think of fewer ways of handling hypothetical social situations. They performed as well as nonlonely people on the impersonal situation, but not on the interpersonal situations. In this sense, a lonely person who reports a difficulty in making friends reveals less competence than a nonlonely person.

Adjectives other than lonely, however, may reflect other kinds of impairment. The complaint "I am timid," for example, suggests a difficulty with aggression that does not necessarily imply a lack of competence. People who describe themselves as timid may only have difficulty in exercising the competence that they possess. In that case, we would not expect them to perform poorly on a benign test of hypothetical situations.

One natural next step, then, would be to study other self-descriptive adjectives, like "timid," in the way that we have studied the word "lonely." But which adjectives should be studied? Norms do not exist to help us identify the most common self-descriptive adjectives that occur in psychiatric interviews. We therefore needed to collect norms and identify groups of adjectives that might correspond to particular groups of interpersonal problems.

We had a second theoretical reason for wanting to study interpersonal adjectives that occur in presenting complaints. In our view, a statement like "I am lonely" subsumes observations about the self that include interpersonal problems. If interpersonal problems do contribute significantly to the meaning of adjectives, then the semantic organization of interpersonal adjectives should be similar to that of interpersonal behaviors. That is, we would expect adjective complaints to vary along dimensions similar to those of interpersonal behaviors and to fall into similar clusters. The two domains should reveal a basic similarity. The following study tested this hypothesis.

THE STRUCTURE OF COMPLAINTS IN ADJECTIVE FORM

Horowitz and Post (1980) studied the self-descriptive adjectives that occurred in interviews of people who were about to undergo psychotherapy. The adjectives of interest were those describing *interpersonal* problems, so some procedure was needed to determine which adjectives had an interpersonal meaning. The words were therefore presented in a booklet to 36 judges who judged each word as being interpersonal in meaning or not. The proportion of judges who classified a word as interpersonal served as an index of its interpersonal meaning.

Adjectives as a group were judged to be less interpersonal in meaning than the problem behaviors of the earlier study. In the study of problem behaviors (Horowitz, 1979), two-thirds of the items were unanimously judged interpersonal by a panel of judges; in contrast, less than 10 percent of the adjectives met this criterion. Adjectives are often used to ascribe stable qualities to the self, whereas verbs more often characterize interactions between people. As a person comes to view a personal problem in the adjectival form, the complaint takes on an internal rather than an interpersonal meaning and imputes undesirable qualities to the self.

An adjective in our study was regarded as interpersonal if the proportion of judges who rated it as interpersonal exceeded .50; 131 words met this criterion. Naive subjects sorted the words into semantic categories, and a matrix was formed that showed, for each pair, what proportion of the people placed the two words in the same category. A hierarchical clustering procedure (Johnson, 1967) and a multidimensional scaling procedure (Shepard, 1974) were then performed on this matrix.

The multidimensional scaling procedure yielded three major dimensions that were similar to those of the earlier study. The first dimension described the degree of the subject's psychological involvement with the other person. The second dimension reflected a sense of efficacy and corresponded to the control dimension of the earlier study. The third dimension expressed the degree of hostility conveyed by the adjectives and corresponded to the hostile-friendly dimension of the earlier study.

The hierarchical clustering procedure yielded six separate clusters similar to those of the earlier study The largest contained 51 words, some of which are shown in Table 9.2. These words describe the way people feel if they have difficulties in getting close to other people; they correspond to the largest cluster of the earlier study (difficulties in trusting, opening up to, and being affectionate with other people). The second largest cluster contained 29 words and corresponds to the other largest cluster of the earlier study (difficulties in defending oneself assertively and aggressively).

A third small cluster described a person who feels overly aggressive and manipulating, corresponding to one of the clusters of the earlier study; the mean coordinates of the adjectives were quite close to those of the earlier problem behaviors.

Finally, two other clusters are worth noting. One contained 15 adjectives like "lonely" and corresponded to problems in socializing with other people. The other contained 21 words like "passive," "self-conscious" and "not free," which reflected an inability to behave independently of other people's reactions and wishes.

The words in this last cluster contrast in an interesting way with those in the lonely cluster. A difficulty in behaving independently would seem to reflect not so much a lack of

TABLE 9.2. REPRESENTATIVE WORDS IN THE ADJECTIVE CLUSTERS.

N of Words in Cluster	Representative Words	Hostile (−) to Not Hostile (+)	Ineffective (−) to Effective (+)	Uninvolved (−) to Involved (+)
51	severe, ungiving, mistrustful, angry, resentful, irritable	−.85	.10	.18
29	vulnerable, needy, inferior, unmanly, ineffective, victimized	.73	−.39	.12
6	aggressive, competitive, manipulative, calculating, responsible, stimulated	−.74	1.10	−.24
15	isolated, lonely, withdrawn, shy, emotionally uninvolved, timid	.71	.08	−.33
21	pressured, cautious, guilty, insecure, defensive, passive	.51	.21	−.07
9	immature, irresponsible, stupid, childish, clownish, unpredictable	−.15	−.63	−.56

competence as a self-imposed restraint (inhibition). Under relaxed conditions, a person who feels passive would know how to act, but that person's social competence might be masked in everyday social situations. People who regard themselves in these ways should show no lack of competence on a benign pencil-and-paper test involving hypothetical interpersonal situations.

This kind of analysis also exposes possible semantic confusions. The lonely and passive clusters were spatially close in the adjective space (both connoted nonhostility and relatively little involvement with the other person), but the corresponding behavioral clusters were not close together. If two clusters of adjectives are close together in the adjective space, yet the corresponding problem behaviors are far apart, the adjectives from the two clusters (e.g., "withdrawn" and "passive") might seem semantically similar, while their behavioral origins would be quite different. Indeed, a passive person might be incorrectly viewed as withdrawn and wrongly judged to be suffering from problems of socializing. These sources of misunderstanding need to be studied further.

FUTURE RESEARCH

This chapter has described our progress in exploring the relationship between symptoms and interpersonal problems. We have portrayed a symptom like depression as a prototypic set of features that conveys the "average meaning" of the concept. By appropriate questioning, an interviewer traces a pathway into the prototype and articulates the meaning of the symptoms for a particular person. Each relevant feature is investigated further, and progressively refined prototypes contain sharper features that are more uniform in meaning.

We have traced depression through loneliness to interpersonal problems with socializing. Problems involving socializing have implied a deficit in social skills that seems to call for remedial training. On the other hand, alternative pathways through the prototype may lead to other kinds of problems that call for other kinds of interventions (guilt reduction, desensitization, etc.).

In future research we hope to apply the concept of a prototype in several ways. First, prototypes vary in their precision of meaning, and judgments about a more precise concept should be more reliable. Since depression, with its many disparate features, is imprecise, ratings of depression should be less reliable. On the other hand, the concept of loneliness (which contains fewer prototypic features) is more precise, so ratings of loneliness should be more reliable.

Second, as observers become trained in the use of a concept, the prototype should reflect an increased sophistication. The prototype of "an aggresssive child," for example, might be compared among groups varying in expertise—novices, trainees, and professionals. Three such groups would undoubtedly have many features in common, but with increasing degrees of expertise, the subtler features should become more prevalent.

Third, the meaning of a concept varies among users, and a user whose meaning better approximates the prototype would seem to apply the concept in the more standardized way. For this reason, some judges use depression in a more conventional way than others, and for them, judgments of depression should show higher reliability.

Finally, a prototype with a varied set of features could be misleading, and the process by which one is misled needs to be explored. A prototype is more than a list of features; it is an *organized* list. We have tried to capture the organization through a clustering procedure. When the description of a person includes enough prototypic features, the full prototype is activated. Once activated, the prototype suggests other features that were not included in the original description and the person is judged to possess those features as well. (Sometimes the inference is accurate, and sometimes it leads us astray.) Our depressed patient, Mr. A, for example, suffered a fear of intimacy and avoided social contacts as a way of minimizing interpersonal entrapments. If features like his social isolation activated the lonely prototype, an observer might incorrectly infer a deficit in social skills. Processes of this kind need to be studied further.

REFERENCES

Beck, A. T. & Beamesderfer, A. Assessment of depression: The depression inventory. In P. Pichot (Ed.), Psychological measurements in psychopharmacology. *Modern Problems of Pharmacopsychiatry*, 1974, **7**, 151–169.

Benjamin, L. S. Structural analysis of social behavior. *Psychological Review*, 1974, **81**, 392–425.

Benjamin, L. S. Structural analysis of a family in therapy. *Journal of Consulting and Clinical Pscyhology*, 1977, **45**, 391–406.

Bloch, S., Bond, G., Qualls, B., Yalom, I., & Zimmerman, E. The evaluation of outcome in psychotherapy by independent judges: A new approach. *British Journal of Psychiatry*, 1977, **131**, 410–414.

Cantor, N. & Mischel, W. Prototypicality and personality: Effects on free recall and personality impressions. *Journal of Research in Personality*, 1979, **13**, 187–205. (a)

Cantor, N. & Mischel, W. Prototypes in person perception. In L. Berkowitz (Ed.), *Advances in experimental social psychology*, Vol. 12. New York: Academic Press, 1979. (b)

Cantor, N., Smith, E., French, R. de S., & Mezzich, J. Psychiatric diagnosis as prototype categorization. *Journal of Abnormal Psychology*, 1980, **89**, 181–193.

Everitt, B. *Cluster analysis.* New York: Wiley, 1974.

Fillenbaum, S. & Rapoport, A. Verbs of judging. In *Structures in subjective lexicon.* New York: Academic Press, 1971.

Frank, J. D., Hoehn-Saric, R., Imber, S. D., Liberman, B. L., & Stone, A. R. *Effective ingredients of successful psychotherapy.* New York: Brunner/Mazel, 1978.

Garwick, G. & Lampman, S. Typical problems bringing patients to a community mental health center. *Community Mental Health Journal*, 1972, **8**, 271–280.

Horowitz, L. On the cognitive structure of interpersonal problems treated in psychotherapy. *Journal of Consulting and Clinical Psychology*, 1979, **47**, 5–15.

Horowitz, L. M. & French, R. de S. Interpersonal problems of people who describe themselves as lonely. *Journal of Consulting and Clinical Psychology*, 1979, **47**, 762–764.

Horowitz, L. M., French, R. de S., Gani, M., & Lapid, J. S. The co-occurrence of semantically similar interpersonal problems. *Journal of Consulting and Clinical Psychology*, 1980, **48**, 413–415.

Horowitz, L. M. & Post, D. Interpersonal meaning of adjectives appearing in psychiatric complaints. *Journal of Consulting and Clinical Psychology*, 1980, **48**, 409–411.

Horowitz, L., Sampson, H., Siegelman, E. Y., Weiss, J., & Goodfriend, S. Cohesive and dispersal behaviors: Two classes of concomitant change in psychotherapy. *Journal of Consulting Clinical Psychology*, 1978, **46**, 556–564.

Johnson, S. C. Hierarchical clustering schemes. *Psychometrika*, 1967, **32**, 241–254.

Joncas, E. Action expectation in social situation. Unpublished doctoral dissertation, Yale University. Cited in Abelson, R. D., & Schank, R. C. *Scripts, plans, goals, and understanding: An inquiry into human knowledge structures.* Hillsdale, N.J.: Erlbaum, 1977.

Kiresuk, T. J. & Sherman, R. E. Goal attainment scaling: A general method for evaluating comprehensive community mental health programs. *Community Mental Health Journal*, 1968, **4**, 443–453.

Klonoff, H. & Cox, B. A problem-oriented system approach to analysis of treatment outcome. *American Journal of Psychiatry*, 1975, **132**, 836–841.

Leary, T. F. *Interpersonal diagnosis of personality.* New York: Ronald Press, 1957.

Maccoby, E. & Masters, J. C. Attachment and dependency. In P. Mussen (Ed.), *Carmichael's manual of child psychology.* New York: Wiley, 1970.

Malan, D. H. The outcome problem in psychotherapy research: An historical review. *Archives of General Psychiatry*, 1973, **29**, 719–729.

Marwell, G. & Hage, J. The organization of role-relationships: A systematic description. *American Sociological Review*, 1970, **35**, 884–900.

Osgood, C. E. Interpersonal verbs and interpersonal behavior. In J. L. Cowan (Ed.), *Studies in thought and language.* Tucson, Arizona: University of Arizona Press, 1970.

Platt, J. J. & Spivack, G. *Manual for the mean-ends problem-solving procedure (MEMPS): A measure of interpersonal cognitive problem-solving skill.* Philadelphia: Hahnemann Medical College and Hospital, 1975.

Rosch, E., Mervis, C. B., Gray, W. D., Johnson, D. M., & Boyer-Braem, P. Basic objects in natural categories. *Cognitive Psychology*, 1976, **8**, 382–439.

Rosenberg, S. & Sedlak, A. Structural representations of implicit personality theory. In L. Berkowitz (Ed.), *Advances in experimental social psychology*, Vol. 6. New York: Academic Press, 1972.

Russell, D., Peplau, L. A., & Ferguson, M. L. Developing a measure of loneliness. *Journal of Personality Assessment*, 1978, **42**, 290–294.

Shepard, R. N. Representation of structure in similarity data: Problems and prospects. *Psychometrika*, 1974, **39**, 373–421.

Sloane, R. B, Staples, F. R., Cristol, A. H., Yorkston, N. J., & Whipple, K. *Psychotherapy versus behavior therapy.* Cambridge, Mass.: Harvard University Press, 1975.

White, G. Conceptual universals in personality description. Unpublished manuscript. Department of Anthropology, University of California, San Diego, 1978.

Wish, M., Deutsch, M., & Kaplan, S. J. Perceived dimensions of interpersonal relations. *Journal of Personality and Social Psychology*, 1976, **33**, 409–420.

Chapter 10
Use of Structural Analysis of Social Behavior (SASB) to Guide Intervention in Psychotherapy*
Lorna Smith Benjamin

"In most branches of medicine the value of diagnosis is never questioned. Its importance is self-evident because treatment and prognosis are largely determined by it . . . where mental illness is concerned the situation is rather different . . . the fundamental reason why the importance of diagnoses is not self-evident in psychiatry [is] . . . because the therapeutic and prognostic implications of psychiatric diagnosis are relatively weak, and the diagnosis themselves relatively unreliable" (Kendell, 1975, pp. 1–2). Psychiatry's most recent response to such criticisms of its nosology is the creation of the DSM-III (American Psychiatric Association, 1980) which moves in the direction of objectivity by defining mental disorders in more purely descriptive, operationally defined terms. Because of its descriptive approach, DSM-III is generally atheoretical with regard to etiology: "making a DSM-III diagnosis represents an initial step in a comprehensive evaluation leading to the formulation of a treatment plan. Additional information about the individual being evaluated beyond that required to make a DSM-III diagnosis will invariably be necessary. . . . For instance, the clinician considering a psychodynamically oriented treatment will pay particular attention to . . . interaction, fantasy, attitudes, expectations about interpersonal relationships . . . early developmental experiences and conflicts that underlie the current disturbance . . . unconscious conflicts and defensive style" (American Psychiatric Association, 1980, pp. 6–7).

By emphasizing description, the DSM-III has improved the reliability of psychiatric diagnosis but has not yet provided a system which explicitly accommodates and organizes information relating to etiology or to treatment—two of the major purposes of diagnosis. Further, the DSM-III includes social behaviors only informally.

*I would like to thank R. Dallas Jones and Dee Jones for their invaluable assistance in this and many other SASB projects. Thanks are also given to Angelica Johnson and Al Cheung for their helpful comments on an earlier draft of this chapter. Analyses in this paper were supported by a grant to L. S. Benjamin from the National Institute of Mental Health, #1, RO MH33604-01.

Over 20 years ago, Leary and co-workers (Leary, 1957) noted that "much of the conceptualization in psychology and the nomenclature of psychiatry has been noninterpersonal. Terms such as *depressed, impulsive,* and *inhibited,* for example, refer to characteristics that possess maximum meaning when their interpersonal purpose is added" (p. 5). In this same vein, Leary (1957) observed that "most of the popular diagnostic labels have vague, undefined, but fairly effective functional power. They have interpersonal correlates. . . . [T]o be inflexibly distrustful and withdrawn is invariably maladjustive. Many psychiatrists would call it schizoid. Thus we see the possibilities of redefining the classical language of administrative psychiatry in interpersonal terms. This preserves the usefulness of the older terminology while sharpening its denotative power" (p. 57). Leary then went on, in one of the classic monographs of psychology, to propose an interpersonal nosology and to relate it to some psychiatric categories. Many others (see a review by McLemore & Benjamin, 1979) have also emphasized social implications of psychiatric labels. Until recently these efforts have been largely ignored by both psychology and psychiatry.

The purpose of the present chapter is to demonstrate with a single case how to apply an operationally defined, reliable (and refutable) method for systematically describing social and intrapsychic behavior in a manner which has both etiological and treatment implications. The method is called Structural Analysis of Social Behavioir (SASB) and it is presently being used in a research study funded by NIMH to determine whether SASB descriptions of social behavior in patients can be usefully integrated into the DSM-III nomenclature. An alternative goal of the project would be to determine whether the SASB descriptions can serve as the basis of a formal interpersonal nosology.

THE CASE HISTORY

The patient was a 34-year-old male, without formal psychiatric history until about a year ago when he made an unusual and very painful suicide attempt following an extreme disappointment in a relationship with a girlfriend. After discharge from the hospital, he broke probation associated with writing bad checks and was jailed. Just prior to his release, he escaped from the minimum security prison, sought out his wife (from whom he'd never been divorced), and took an overdose.

THE DSM-III DIAGNOSIS

Various diagnoses entered on the patient's chart were primary affective disorder, unipolar affective disorder, mixed features with character disturbance. The Interpersonal Diagnostic Research Study uses the official NIMH Diagnostic Interview Schedule (DIS) to identify symptoms. Two trained interviewers attended a DIS interview conducted by one of them and then independently interacted with a computer programmed by Harold Erdman (under the direction of Drs. John Greist, Marjorie Klein, and James Jefferson) to follow the official DSM-III decision tree. A patient is accepted for the study only if the two trained DIS interviewers independently obtain the same diagnosis using computer algorithm.

Selected excerpts from the hard copy of the computer-interviewer interaction are included to illustrate how the DSM-III diagnosis was made in this case. Interviewer answers appear in parentheses:

Does any of the following apply to your patient: 1) delusions, hallucinations, incoherence, derailment, poverty of thought, markedly illogical thinking, behavior that is bizarre, grossly disorganized, or catatonic. 2) depressed, irritable or expansive mood. 3) irrational anxiety or avoidance behavior. 4) antisocial, aggressive, violent, defiant, oppositional or negativist behavior. 5) physical complaints or irrational anxiety about physical illness. 6) don't know. 7) none of the above. (Answer: 2)
. . . Because of your patient's depressed or expansive or irritable mood, the program will check for affective disorders. Criteria for manic disorder follow.
Has your patient had one or more distinct periods with the mood described by any of the following: 1) elevated. 2) expansive. 3) irritable. 4) don't know. 5) none of the above. (Answer: 5)
Criteria for major depressive disorder follow.
Does your patient have a dysphoric mood or loss of interest or pleasure in all or almost all usual activities and pastimes, characterized by symptoms of depression, sadness, hopelessness, irritability, worry, etc. (Yes)
Does your patient have any of the following symptoms: 1) poor appetite or weight loss or increased appetite or weight gain. 2) sleep difficulty or sleeping too much. 3) loss of energy, fatigability or tiredness. 4) psychomotor agitation or retardation. 5) loss of interest or pleasure in usual activities, or decrease in sexual drive. 6) feelings of self-reproach or excessive or inappropriate guilt. 7) complaints or evidence of diminished ability to think or concentrate, such as slow thinking. 8) recurrent thoughts of death or suicide or any suicidal behavior. 9) none of the above. (Answer: 1,2,3,4,5,6,7,8)
Did your patient's depressive symptoms last two weeks or longer? (Yes)
Can you rule out a simple bereavement following a loss of a loved one as being responsible for your patient's symptoms? (Yes)
Diagnosis made: Major Depression

On interview and on the ward, the patient did not show any of the behaviors often seen in a person who is sent to the hospital from the prison system. He was affable, cooperative, and friendly. In fact, the guards spontaneously offered, "He doesn't seem like a prisoner; he seems like one of us."

Because of the "mixed" diagnosis suggested at some points in the patient's chart, the diagnostic program was rerun deliberately choosing the "antisocial" branch even though neither of the DIS interviewers felt that the antisocial branching question applied to this affable, compliant man. The antisocial branch of the program noted the presence of some "psychopathic" symptoms which seemed related to the episode of forging a check (a felony), and writing others with insufficient funds; "running away" for a month after breaking parole also was noted. The diagnosis made from this program branch was: conduct disorder, socialized, nonaggressive.

In conclusion, the primary DSM-III diagnosis was Major Depression, with a possible secondary diagnosis: conduct disorder, socialized, nonaggressive.

THE SASB INTERVIEW STYLE

1. Description

The starting point for an SASB interpersonal diagnosis is traditional: identify the chief complaint and the reason for hospitalization now. Symptoms (such as complaints about irritability, sleeplessness, loss of appetite, statements of how bad one is, and so on), however, are not allowed focus. Rather, there is an attempt to understand the phenomenology, the experience, the meaning of the symptoms. The assumption is that the patient's presentation has been very much affected by past learning (developmental history) and the current social network (family and work or school). Symptoms are presumed to have a purpose and the task is to understand how, from the patient's point of view, the symptoms are adaptive. This phenomenological diagnosis of symptoms within the social network is described by and related to the intrapsychic state by use of the SASB model.

In order to get "underneath" the symptoms and into the patient's phenomenology, the interviewer needs to use a style quite unsuited to making a DSM-III diagnosis. Rather than controlling the flow of the interview by asking questions that focus on symptoms, the interviewer needs to assume a much more reactive interpersonal posture and flow quite freely with the patient and his or her stream of consciousness. The interviewer talks with rather than at the patient and frequently uses "soft" interviewing skills described, for example, in texts appropriate to counseling and guidance (e.g., Brammer, 1973). The interviewer paraphrases often and takes care to be nonjudgmental of the patient; he or she also uses fantasy, metaphor, and intuition to facilitate communication. Generalities are avoided and specific examples are encouraged. The interviewee is frequently asked to specify feelings and expectations.

Despite this reactive posture, a great amount of interviewer attention is given to tracing the meaning and flow of the conversation. "Listening with a third ear" (Reik, 1948) is in order. Each relationship with each person in the social milieu is discussed and silently coded by the interviewer in terms of the SASB model. An interpersonal assessment is complete when each important member of the family, community, and the school or work situation has been considered as well as the patient's feelings about him or herself.

After developing an understanding of the symptomatology, how it has grown out of the patient's experience and is therefore reasonable and logical from his or her point of view, the interviewer is then ready to consider treatment implications. There is an effort to support strengths and develop potential alternative responses to meet the same needs more constructively.

2. Example

To illustrate the interviewer style, the first seven exchanges between the interviewer and this patient are shown:

Interviewer: I heard a brief description of what's been happening to you and the story kind of makes me sad and I wonder how you feel about it. (*Authentic self-disclosure along with an exploratory statement.*)
Patient: Well I feel pretty passive I guess.
Interviewer: Passive? (*Paraphrase.*)
Patient: Ya.
Interviewer: Can you say more about that? (*Attempting to explore at a deeper level the self-description.*)
Patient: Well I guess I just have a, a don't care attitude about it now.
Interviewer: Um, hm. You say now. Was there a time when you didn't feel that way? (*Interviewer focuses on strength and tries to develop a time frame.*)
Patient: Well there must have been somewhere down the line when I cared, but it's been probably in the last maybe year or two I've just, well, I guess I just feel there's nothing left to try for, or I've just basically given up I guess.
Interviewer: Um, hm. What did you used to try for? (*Again, focusing on strength and avoiding reinforcing symptomatology.*)
Patient: Well I used to try to enjoy life, try to be productive I guess would be the word, get the most out of life. Apparently I was doing it the wrong way.

These opening exchanges show how dedicated the patient was to making self-derogatory remarks. It was followed by several exchanges in which the interviewer insisted on concrete examples which, in reality, did not support the thesis that the patient was a totally bad and hopeless person. Gradually the number of self-derogatory remarks decreased and self-disclosing ones began to come in, until on the 23rd exchange:

Interviewer: Well I hear that you're very self-critical about this. But I wonder what your reaction was to their fighting? Did it make you feel angry, afraid, or numb, or what? (*Interviewer acknowledges the self-oppression, but pushes for specific interpersonal data as well as expression of feeling*.)
Patient: Well it made me feel a little angry and also probably made me a little afraid because I didn't exactly know how to handle it. And I don't know, I just never had anybody to talk to. I think that had a lot to do with it. If I had something bothering me I just couldn't talk to anybody.

In the next section, there will be a description of the SASB model. Once the language for SASB has been established, the phenomenology of the patient's most recent suicide attempt will be described as it evolved in the later segments of this interpersonal interview.

THE SASB MODEL

The relation of the SASB model to the previous interpersonal models such as Leary's Interpersonal Circle (Leary, 1957), and Schaefer's circumplex model of parent behavior (Schaefer, 1965), along with several others, was presented in Benjamin (1974). SASB also has much in common with the interpersonal problems approach discussed by Leonard Horowitz and his coworkers in Chapter 9 of this volume. Since 1968, five different versions of questionnaire items describing the points of the SASB model have evolved, each improving on the preceding in terms of validity as measured by circumplex analysis, factor analysis, an autocorrelation procedure, and a dimensional ratings procedure. An early report on validity and reliability appeared in the 1974 paper and an update on the much improved 1980 version will be completed shortly.

The SASB model, presented in Figure 10.1 is divided into three parts: The first group of behaviors (appearing at the top) involve focus on another person and transitive action. The second group of behaviors (appearing in the middle) are behaviors that involve focus on the self and an intransitive state. The top two groups, focus on other and focus on self, are interpersonal in nature and describe complementary behaviors. The third group appears at the bottom of the figure and respresents intrapsychic behaviors resulting when focus on other is turned inward on the self (introjection). The principles of complementarity and introjection will be illustrated shortly.

Each of the three surfaces or planes of the model is built on two axes. The horizontal axis runs from disaffiliation on the left to affiliation on the right; the vertical axis runs from maximal interdependence at the bottom to maximal independence at the top. These axes define four quadrants on each surface; the total result is eight interpersonal quadrants and four intrapsychic quadrants which are discussed elsewhere (Benjamin, 1979a) and would be useful to those who would prefer to work with a version of the SASB model which is less complex than Figure 10.1.

In the full model shown in Figure 10.1, each of the points located within the quadrants is made up of mathematically defined proportions of the behaviors described by the axes. For example, Chart Point 113, confirm as OK as is appears in the first (upper, right-hand)

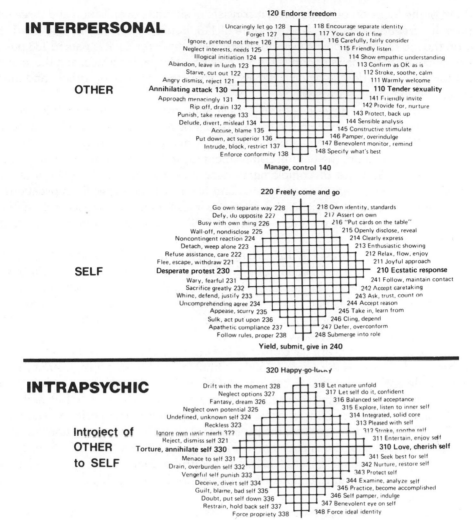

INTERPERSONAL

OTHER

SELF

INTRAPSYCHIC

Introject of
OTHER
to SELF

Fig. 10.1. Model for Structural Analysis of Social Behavior. The top plane describes focus on other or transitive action; the middle plane describes focus on self or intransitive state; the third plane describes focus on other introjected upon the self. Each surface is built upon an affiliative axis on the horizontal and an interdependence axis on the vertical. Points between the poles are made up of proportionate amounts of elements described by the poles. The model describes 54 pairs of opposites (e.g., 123, abandon versus 143, protect, back up on the first surface). Thirty-six complementary pairs are found at comparable places on the first two surfaces (e.g., 143, protect, back up is matched or complemented by 243, ask, trust, count on). Thirty-six introjections are detailed by considering what happens if points on the focus on other surface are turned inward (e.g., 143, protect, back up turned inward yields 343, protect self). Antitheses are found via the complement of the opposite (e.g., the antithesis of 223, detach, weep alone is 143, protect, back up). (From "Structural Analysis of Differentiation Failure" by Lorna Smith Benjamin, *Psychiatry*, 1979. Copyright 1979 by the William Alanson White Psychiatric Foundation. Reprinted by permission.)

quadrant of the focus-on-other surface; it consists of six units of affiliation and three units of endorsing freedom (+6, +3). The opposite of 113, confirm as OK as is, is located 180° away on the model, has opposite signs for its coordinates (−6, −3); it is named 133 punish, take revenge. Eighteen pairs of opposites are described by each surface, and these offer a means for describing double-binding behavior (when the focus is on other) and ambivalence (when the focus is on self).

The second surface describes focus on self and represents behaviors that are complementary to those described on the first surface. For example, the complement to 113, confirm as OK as is, is 213 enthusiastic showing. If one person is focusing on the other with friendly confirmation, the natural complement is for the other to unveil him or herself comfortably. The 37 pairs of complements described by the first two surfaces allow definition of complementarity in relationship and have clear and specific implications for the relevance of the patient's significant others to interpersonal diagnosis and treatment (see Benjamin, 1977; McLemore & Benjamin, 1979). Complementarity is important in understanding etiology.

The third surface represents the turning inward of behaviors described by the first surface. For example, the introjection of point 113, confirm as OK as is, is 313, pleased with self. One implication of the intrapsychic surface is that if a given individual exhibits behaviors described by this part of the model, it is possible to infer what treatment has been received at the hands of significant early and/or current figures. Introjection is also important in understanding etiology.

Treatment implications are developed by the principle of antithesis. For interpersonal behaviors, the antithesis is the opposite of the complement. For example, the antithesis of 233, whine, defend, justify, is 113, confirm as OK as is. If the whiny, defensive patient chooses a genuinely confirming spouse, the defensiveness can give way to free and enthusiastic disclosure. Of course, mere assumption of the antithetical position usually does not suffice. Clinical wisdom suggests the process is slow and other transactions (probably involving combinations of dominance and warmth) are necessary. The SASB model provides a descriptive language for studying what has to be done before natural identifications, complements, and introjections of behaviors from current benevolent significant others can occur.

The rules for generating the code numbers useful in locating the points on Figure 10.1 are: The 100s digit describes the surface: 100s = focus on other surface, 200s = focus on self surface, and 300s = introject surface. The 10s digit represents the Cartesian quadrant defined by geometric convention. The 1s digit represents the subdivisions of the quadrant and it ranges from 0 to 8, for a total of nine subdivisions.

These subdivisions of quadrants describe sets of behaviors having similar topics, and they are named tracks. In other words, every chart point ending in the same units number belongs to the same track, and the topics covered by the tracks are as follows: 0 = primitive basics; 1 = approach-avoidance; 2 = need fulfillment, contact, nurturance; 3 = attachment; 4 = logic and communication; 5 = attention to self-development; 6 = balance in relationship; 7 = intimacy-distance; 8 = identity. The items belonging to each track can be identified in Figure 10.1 by their common units numbers.

To classify an interpersonal event, a rater locates the quadrant by making a sequence of three decisions about focus, affiliation, and interdependence. Following the identification of the quadrant, the rater names the specific chart point by identifying the topic (track) and checking with a detailed description of the chart point offered by items on the associated questionnaires. (For examples of coding, see Benjamin, 1979b.)

USING THE SASB MODEL TO UNDERSTAND THE PHENOMENOLOGY OF SUICIDE ATTEMPT FOR THE PATIENT

Introject theory would require that the patient perceive important others in his environment as attacking, rejecting, destructive, and that he, for one reason or another, would have turned his destructiveness on himself in a process described best by the German word for suicide, "self-murder." In the interview, however, the patient maintained that neither his wife nor his mother nor his father nor his grandfather nor anyone else abused him. He acknowledged rejection from them, but never hostile power or overt attack. If the introject theory applies to this suicide attempt, the attack from others has to be inferred, and presumed to be unconscious.

The Meaning of the Suicide Attempt in Relation to His Father

During the interview, there was an exchange about possible abuse from the father:

Patient: I think I was following orders when I was five years old.
Interviewer: Whose orders? (*Seeking specific definition of the interpersonal milieu.*)
Patient: My father's.
Interviewer: Can you say more about that? (*Encourage detail concerning a likely key figure.*)
Patient: Well it's simple. If I didn't follow orders I'd be over his knee.
Interviewer: And then what? (*Seeking extensive detail on an important social interaction.*)
Patient: Well I'd get spanked.
Interviewer: With what? (*Seeking more specific detail.*)
Patient: With his blackjack.
Interviewer: His blackjack? (*Selectively emphasizing a major issue defined by introject theory.*)
Patient: Ya, it was a blackjack. It was the small end of his blackjack. So I learned to jump and take orders at a very early age.
Interviewer: How often did it happen that he would hit you with a blackjack? (*Establishing a time frame.*)
Patient: Once a week probably.
Interviewer: Once a week? (*Paraphrasing in a tone communicating understanding.*)
Patient: Oh ya.
Interviewer: Why are you laughing? (*Picking up affect around a major event hypothesized by introjection theory to relate to the suicide presentation.*)
Patient: Because it sounds so cruel, and to me it seemed so normal.
Interviewer: It does sound cruel. (*Trying to reinforce an insight.*)
Patient: To me it was just, it was just something that had to be done.
Interviewer: You were used to it? (*Patient is backing off the insight. Paraphrase is slanted to reemphasize it.*)
Patient: I guess so, ya, but he had strict orders and you had to, you had to stick to them.
Interviewer: So you were used to being knocked around and beaten up? (*Trying to consolidate his understanding of this interaction.*)
Patient: Oh, ya, oh, ya.
Interviewer: That's just a normal thing in relation to your father. (*Acknowledging the patient's view that the beatings were normal because the insight about cruelty is too discrepant. The interviewer shouldn't go too far "ahead" of where the patient "is."*)
Patient: I'm not saying I like it, but I was used to it.

In short, in the context of discipline, the patient describes severe abuse yet he does not really acknowledge attack from his father. In interview, more conscious phenomenology of the suicide attempt in relation to the father emerged.

Interviewer: What is he (*the father*) thinking about you right now? (*Using fantasy to assess interpersonal expectations in relation to key figures.*)

Patient: I have no idea. I'm sure he's thinking something like, what a fool. I would imagine that's what he's thinking.

Interviewer: What a fool for what? (*Elicit detail for 136, Put down, act superior.*)

Patient: What a fool for trying such a dumb stunt. That's exactly what he would say.

Interviewer: Which thing, you mean the—

Patient: Overdose.

Interviewer: Not a lot of sympathy here, huh? (*114, Show empathic understanding is nearly opposite 136, Put down, act superior.*)

Patient: No I don't think so.

Interviewer: What if you had succeeded, what would he have said? (*Eliciting detail of the fantasy.*)

Patient: Well he probably would have said, well I guess he really did it this time. I don't know what he would say.

Interviewer: You seem a little bit amused. (*Picking up on affect suggesting the suicidal behaviors have their positive value.*)

Patient: I am because I just wonder. I've often thought about that. I wonder if he would think about, if it would shock him or how he would take it. I suppose it would shock him, I would think. I can't say for sure.

Interviewer: If he was shocked what would he feel? (*Encouraging more specificity.*)

Patient: He'd probably go on the same guilt trip that I'm on now. He would say, well why didn't I give him a little more of my time or, and why didn't I do more things with him.

Inteviewer: He might feel a little remorseful? (*Consolidating the finding that the suicidal act may have been 133, Punish, take revenge.*)

Patient: Yes I would say so.

Interviewer: Bring him to his senses a bit maybe? (*Emphasizing the desire to communicate with the father.*)

Patient: Well I hope he'd think that way.

Interviewer: Thinking about that makes you feel good? (*Clarifying positive aspects of suicide act.*)

Patient: No, cause I don't like to hurt people.

Interviewer: But it would hurt him? (*Patient is backing off his angry feelings; interviewer is trying to bring him back.*)

Patient: I think it probably would.

Interviewer: In a funny kind of way you might get back at him that way? (*Pressing for more explicit acknowledgment of the view he showed earlier.*)

Patient: I really wouldn't want to get back at him.

Interviewer: You wouldn't? (*Acknowledging the patient's wish to back off of this view.*)

Patient: No, I really wouldn't.

Interviewer: Why not? (*Exploring why this idea of retaliatory anger at his father is ego-alien.*)

Patient: Oh he's my father. Anybody else I might have a little bit of vengeance or wanting to get back, but he's my father and he raised me the way he thought was best and I can't knock him for it.

In other words, for a brief time, the anger toward the father emerged into consciousness and the patient's view of the suicide as revengeful (punish, take revenge, 133) and blaming (accuse, blame, 135) were fantasied as drawing out in the father the expected complements (whine, defend, justify, 233, and appease, scurry, 235) along with at least one of the expected introjections (guilt, blame, bad self, 355). When the interviewer persisted, however, in making the revenge wishes clear, the patient backed off of it and denied it again under the logic that what the father did or didn't do was with the best of intentions.

The Meaning of the Suicide Attempt in Relation to His Wife

About one-third of the way through the interview, the patient was describing the moment when he escaped from prison for the purpose of telling his wife about how he felt about the marriage and family and his own life before killing himself. He said:

Patient: I told her how I basically was feeling, that I just didn't, I really didn't care anymore. She could do what she wanted.
Interviewer: Meaning what? (*Interviewer suspects this comment is "loaded."*)
Patient: Well, she really wanted to go through the divorce and I'd leave her alone.
Interviewer: Meanwhile you were planning to kill yourself. Right? (*Interviewer guesses.*)
Patient: Right, I was making her happy. I guess I was telling her what she wanted to hear or what I thought she wanted to hear.
Interviewer: You thought she wanted to hear that she'd be free of you? (*Restatement of patient's words in this context in an interpretation of the suicide as a "gift" to the wife.*)
Patient: Right.

Classifying the patient's relationship with the wife in terms of the SASB model, it is clear he was most concerned about her angry dismissal and rejection of him. Severe rejection is plotted as SASB point 121 and is adjacent to murderous attack, 130. Severe rejection calls for the complementary behaviors; flee, escape, withdraw (221). Instead of giving the complement to the angry, nearly murderous rejection, he appears to have introjected them to show behaviors described as reject, dismiss self (321). At the same time, through the suicidal gesture, the patient gave his wife a near opposite of what she gave him, namely 142, provide for, nurture (I was making her happy). Simultaneously he showed submission (telling her what I thought she wanted to hear) described by SASB point 248, (feels, becomes what he thinks the other person wants). This fusion or confusion of submission and "love" is fairly common in normative samples (especially of females). The unusual dynamic here is that the "loving" submission involves following the presumed directive to "drop dead" (a complementary fusion of attack and control). The discovery that a suicidal gesture is in a peculiar way an act of "love" is not uncommon when exploring patient phenomenology using the SASB model.

The Meaning of the Suicide in Relation to His Children

Looking at his understanding of his own suicide from the point of view of his children, he comments:

Interviewer: Well what do you think your kids would feel if you succeeded in killing yourself? (*Again using fantasy to assess interpersonal expectations in relation to key figures.*)
Patient: Oh I think they'd feel bad, but I think they'd forget it. . . . I don't know, I've tossed that around. Boy I've tossed that around and that's the conclusion that I came to. That they would, that they would forget about it in time. I figure in the long run, it wouldn't hurt them as much as me being around.
Interviewer: Um, hm. Well you don't think much of yourself do you? (*A "reflection" which is really an interpretation.*)
Patient: No, not very much at all.

SASB classification of this communication would be that while in reality he was abandoning the children (abandon, leave in lurch, 123), he perceived quite the opposite, namely that he was protecting them (143, protect, back up). His notion of protecting the children by removing himself from them, of course, depends heavily on his understanding of himself as a bad, destructive person (321, reject, dismiss self). He also referred later on in the context of discussing the suicide in relation to his children as "the ultimate sacrifice." Here again from the patient's point of view, given his assumption of being an extremely bad person (321), removing himself from his children's world was an act of "love."

Summary of the Phenomenology of the Suicide Attempt

The interview method, then, has shown that from the patient's vantage point, taking an overdose was an act of kindness and love for his wife and children, and, though fleetingly admitted, an act of revenge toward his father. Many of the classifications of these views on the SASB model were on Track 3, the attachment track. Frequently, the SASB classifications of the phenomenology of the suicide attempt involved simultaneous opposites: while "protecting" the children (143) he abandoned them (123); while taking revenge on the father (133), he said the father meant well and did the best he could (113); he was giving his wife what she wanted (240) while going his own separate way (228).

This analysis would suggest a formulation of this patient's conflict in terms of attachment (Track 3) and separation problems with a strong tendency to contradiction. The patient clearly states that there was a disruption of an attachment with an important woman before each suicide attempt. In the first incident involving the unusual and extremely painful attempt, his girlfriend had left him. The current suicide attempt followed the wife's active initiation of divorce proceedings. His explanation of the buildup to the attempt was:

Interviewer: So she wants divorce. She wants to be free of you. Is that right? (*Paraphrase.*)
Patient: The way I take it, yes.
Interviewer: Well you qualify like maybe that isn't right. (*Picking up on ambivalence.*)
Patient: Well I, a long time ago tried to, quit trying to second guess.
Interviewer: Ya. Isn't she straight, doesn't she give straight answers? (*Paraphrase.*)
Patient: Ah, she's a typical woman. I shouldn't say that, she's unpredicting.
Interviewer: Unpredictable? (*Reflection.*)
Patient: Unpredictable. I just quit trying to second guess her.
Interviewer: What's one thing she switched on you that bugged you? (*Looking for specifics in a key relationship.*)
Patient: Well, when I was in jail I got a short letter from her at Christmas time and she said I'm really busy this season. All, how did she put it? First she put something like this is the first Christmas in years I've really felt good. I really have the Christmas spirit which makes me feel like, wow, I'm not here. This is my first Christmas away and she's feeling good. And then she wrote I'll write you right after Christmas, and she never wrote again. I thought, wow.
Interviewer: Hm. That must have hurt. (*Empathic pressing for deeper feeling.*)
Patient: Well, Christmas is a bad time . . . and I just kinda quit the whole scene and I just kinda forgot it and as the months went by I just seemed to care less and less about, about everything.

RELATING THE PHENOMENOLOGY OF THE SUICIDE ATTEMPT TO THE INTREX RATINGS OF HIMSELF AND HIS FAMILY MEMBERS

The Patient's Self-concept

Following the interview, the patient was given the questionnaires associated with the SASB model and the data were analyzed by an interpretive computer program which yields a narrative text called the INTREX report. The INTREX report divides the model into clusters (see Benjamin, 1980), which is midway in complexity between the simple quadrant version and the full model in Figure 10.1. Direct quotations from the INTREX report summarize the patient's response to the questionnaire measuring his self-description in terms of the introject surface of the SASB model:

Self-indicting and oppressing. The person rated is described as self-oppressing. Internally directed accusations of inadequacy are likely, along with guilt and shame. Uncertainty and guilt may blend into fooling the self by doing what is known to be not good for the self. Vicious self-punishment may be present and the possibility of self-destructive behavior probably should be discussed with a therapist.

Self-rejecting and destroying. The person rated is described as very hurtful of self. This may include ignoring illness and injuries, overburdening and depleting the self; rejecting and depriving the self; generally being one's own worst enemy. In its harshest form, this may include torture and annihilation of the self. The possibility of self-destructive behavior should be discussed with a health professional.

Several days later, the patient rated the items on the introject surface again, using two different mental sets—once for how he felt when he was at his very best, and again for how he felt when he was at his very worst. All three ratings: the "average," the best, and the worst, yielded the same two clusters for the introject: self-indicting and oppressing, and self-rejecting and destroying. The only difference was that the internal consistency (defined in Benjamin, 1974) was less when he was at his best (.820), than when he was at his worst (.989). In other words, when he was at his best, his highly consistent orientation around self-destruction and self-oppression broke up slightly. The patient's dedication to putting himself down was demonstrated by the excerpts from the beginning of the interview.

The Patient's Relationship with His Wife

His perception of the wife as unpredictable was reflected at several places in the INTREX report. For example, when the patient rated his wife at her best, the program described the wife as:

Affirming and understanding—the person rated is described as appreciating, understanding, affirming and showing empathy for the other person. Additional behaviors that may be present include fairly treating the other person and actively listening even if there is disagreement.

Helping and protecting. The person rated is described as actively helping the other person through protection, support, constructive advice and possibly teaching. Such active helpgiving may, if pushed to extremes, take on the characteristics of pampering and perhaps overindulgence.

The consistency report read: "The ratings for this group of behaviors were not particularly consistent. This implies a fair amount of instability/variability in behavior. Such variability can be manifested by quick changes from moment to moment in a given situation, and/or by noticeable shifts in mood (movement from one cluster of items to another)."

The focus on other parts of the patient's ratings of his wife at her worst are shown in Figure 10.2. In stark contrast with the ratings of his wife at her best, when rating his wife at her worst, the two emergent clusters were freeing and forgetting plus ignoring and neglecting. The text for these clusters can be read in the Figure. Note that his ratings of his wife at her best showed her to be unpredictable, but when at her worst, there was consistent contradiction. The INTREX consistency report for ratings of his wife at her worst read: "The ratings for this group of behaviors show a strong 'reverse' internal consistency. There was a tendency to endorse (and/or avoid endorsing) blocks of items having opposite meanings. This kind of interpersonal posture is sometimes called 'double-binding' in that if one kind of interpersonal message is given, it is likely that it would be associated with a strong consistent statement of an opposite message."

In sum, the ratings of his wife at her best showed her to be somewhat supportive, although unstable in that posture, and to be mostly rejecting and independent at her worst. The rejection was contradicted by a strong tendency to endorse items of opposite meaning. Inspection of Figure 10.2 suggests contradiction came between friendly influence versus neglect plus some hostile control versus friendly emancipation.

The Patient's Relationship with His Mother

Consistent with the traditional clinical wisdom which suggests that people tend to pick partners who either recapitulate or complement their own early experience, this man's description of his mother when rating the interpersonal history showed important similarities to his description of his wife. The INTREX report describing his mother's behavior when focusing on him included the clusters freeing and forgetting, helping and protecting, and watching and managing. A consistency report of contradiction and double-bind was obtained from the ratings of the mother just as from the ratings of the wife at her worst.

Interviewer style is different when giving patients their INTREX reports. It is concerned with checking accuracy, and if accuracy is confirmed, with interpretation and teaching. In the session during which the patient was shown his INTREX report, he was read the clusters describing the mother's focusing on other behavior and then the interviewer asked:

Interviewer: Does that sound like your mother when you were little? (*Checking for accuracy*.)
Patient: As much as my mother as I can remember when I was little.
Interviewer: Do you have trouble remembering? (*Checking*.)
Patient: Yes I do.
Interviewer: Okay. She showed the same reverse tendency (as your wife) and when it involves focusing on you, we call it double-binding. If one message is given it's likely to be associated with an opposite message. And the main oppositions we're seeing here are the independence or letting you do your own thing by forgetting about you, alternating with being very controlling and watchful. (*Teaching*.)

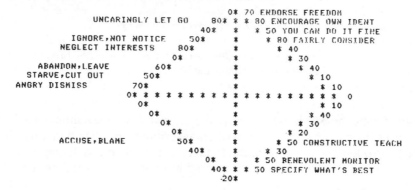

```
SUBJECT NUMBER 006.  MALE.  MAY, 1980.
RATING NUMBER  14  WAS OF YOUR PERCEPTION
MY SIGNIFICANT OTHER AT HIS/HER WORST (HE OR SHE IS RATED)

BEHAVIORS SHOWN INVOLVE FOCUSING ON ANOTHER PERSON. THERE IS ACTIVE
INITIATION, ACTION, OR PARENTLIKE BEHAVIOR
THIS IS THE FIRST OF TWO PARTS FOR THIS RATING

                                        0* 70 ENDORSE FREEDOM
              UNCARINGLY LET GO       80* * * 80 ENCOURAGE OWN IDENT
                               40*      *    * 50 YOU CAN DO IT FINE
         IGNORE,NOT NOTICE    50*       *      * 80 FAIRLY CONSIDER
         NEGLECT INTERESTS  80*         *      * 40
                          0*            *      * 30
       ABANDON,LEAVE     60*            *     * 40
      STARVE,CUT OUT    50*             *     * 10
    ANGRY DISMISS      70*              *      * 10
                     0* * * * * * * * * * * * * * * * * * * * 0
                      0*                *        * 10
                       0*               *       * 40
                        0*              *      * 30
                         0*             *     * 20
        ACCUSE,BLAME    50*             *      * 50 CONSTRUCTIVE TEACH
                       40*              *    * 30
                      0*    *       * 50 BENEVOLENT MONITOR
                     40* * * 50 SPECIFY WHAT'S BEST
                      -20*

IN THE STATEMENTS WHICH FOLLOW, READ IN 'HE OR SHE' AS SUBJECT AND 'ME'
AS OBJECT OF THE DESCRIPTION.  FOR EXAMPLE, IF THE REPORT SAYS: 'IG-
NORES THE OTHER PERSON, NEGLECTS HIS/HER INTERESTS', READ 'HE/SHE IG-
NORES ME, NEGLECTS MY INTERESTS.  THE LISTED IMPORTANT PERSON IS BEING
DESCRIBED AND RATINGS CAME FROM THE 'HE/SHE' FORM OF THE QUESTIONNAIRE.


**************************************************************************
                          CLUSTER ANALYSIS

   FREEING AND FORGETTING.  THE PERSON RATED IS DESCRIBED AS EMANCIPATING
   OR FREEING THE OTHER PERSON BY EXPRESSING CONFIDENCE IN THIS PERSON AND
   BY ENCOURAGING THIS PERSON'S INDEPENDENT IDENTITY.  HOWEVER, THIS
   EMANCIPATION MAY AT TIMES BORDER ON LACK OF CARING OR FORGETFULNESS.


   IGNORING AND NEGLECTING.  THE PERSON RATED IS DESCRIBED AS BASICALLY
   IGNORING AND/OR NEGLECTING THE OTHER PERSON'S NEEDS AND INTERESTS.  SUCH
   INATTENTION MAY RESULT IN OR BE CAUSED BY UNUSUAL IDEAS AND PERCEPTIONS.
   HOW THE PERSON RATED TREATS THE OTHER MAY SEEM TO HAVE NO RHYME OR
   REASON.  THE PERSON RATED MAY ABANDON THE OTHER AT CRITICALLY IMPORTANT
   TIMES.


**************************************************************************
   BRIEF TECHNICAL REMARKS
      THE RATINGS FOR THIS GROUP OF BEHAVIORS SHOW A STRONG 'REVERSE' INTERNAL
      CONSISTENCY.  THERE WAS A TENDENCY TO ENDORSE (AND/OR TO AVOID ENDORS-
      ING) BLOCKS OF ITEMS HAVING OPPOSITE MEANINGS.  THIS KIND OF INTERPER-
      SONAL POSTURE IS SOMETIMES CALLED 'DOUBLE-BINDING' IN THAT IF ONE KIND
      OF INTERPERSONAL MESSAGE IS GIVEN, IT IS LIKELY THAT IT WILL BE ASSOCI-
      ATED WITH A STRONG CONSISTENT STATEMENT OF AN OPPOSITE MESSAGE.
```

Fig. 10.2. The INTREX analysis of the patient rating his wife at her worst. The figure shows his perception of rejection contradicted by a tendency toward benevolent control. There is a discussion of the "double-bind" in the text.

Patient: Sounds right.

Interviewer: That sounds right? Can you think of an example that might illustrate that? (*Probing for specifics to illustrate the trend and consolidate his learning.*)

Patient: Oh, if I wanted to go down to a friend's house to stay during the summer, she might say be back by 10:00 o'clock. But then I'd call her up about 7:00 o'clock to ask to stay and she'd say, stay on there overnight.

Interviewer: So she had tight control about getting home at first and then later didn't even care. (*Highlighting the sides of the conflict.*)

Patient: Then she probably would say, ask your father first.
Interviewer: I see. So it was hard to know whether she cared or not. (*Making the implicit explicit.*)
Patient: Right.
Interviewer: Okay. Do you feel close to her? (*Exploring feelings.*)
Patient: No. I probably was closer to her than my father, but I wasn't very what you'd call close to her. We didn't talk to her at all.
Interviewer: How come you didn't talk to her? (*Exploring further.*)
Patient: I don't know. I guess we were just never that close. I don't have a good answer for that.
Interviewer: Okay. Maybe she's not available. (*Interpretation in terms of 226, Busy with own thing.*)
Patient: Oh she was always busy doing something and I guess maybe I just didn't want to bother her. I'd just forget about it and go do something else.

As predicted by the SASB theory, the patient showed complementarity to the mother both in terms of the clusters he endorsed when describing himself in relation to her when he was age five to ten and in terms of the tendency toward contradiction. Focus on self clusters obtained from his description of himself in relation to his mother are shown in Figure 10.3

The complementarity between the patient as shown in Figure 10.3 and his perception of his mother was described by the following INTREX program segment:

There was a search for complementarity in the following ratings.
My mother when I was age 5–10 (she is rated).
As I saw myself in relation to my mother when I was age 5–10 (I am rated).
The complementary clusters listed here, if any, will be of the form He/she focuses on me and I focus on myself.
His/her Freeing and Forgetting reinforces Asserting and Separating in me and vice versa.
His/her Helping and Protecting reinforces Trusting and Relying in me and vice versa.
His/her Watching and Managing reinforces Deferring and Submitting in me and vice versa.
The complementary clusters listed here, if any, will be of the form I focus on him/her and he/she focuses on him/herself.
My Freeing and Forgetting reinforces Asserting and Separating in him/her and vice versa.
My Affirming and Understanding reinforces Disclosing and Expressing in him/her and vice versa.

The INTREX consistency report for Figure 10.3 was: "The ratings for this group of behaviors showed a strong 'reverse' internal consistency. There was a tendency to endorse (and/or to avoid endorsing) blocks of items having opposite meanings. In this case where the focus is upon the self, such a tendency to endorse contradictory blocks reflects ambivalence. There is reaction in opposite ways on at least one well-defined interpersonal theme."

In sum, there was complementarity in terms of the interpersonal orientations described by the clusters and also in terms of the tendency to opposition. The wife and the mother were identified by the INTREX program as showing a highly uniform tendency to give opposite messages when focusing on other, and this was given the label double-binding. When focusing on self in relation to his mother, the patient also had a very high coefficient of contradiction, and when this occurs on the focus on self surface, it is named ambivalence. The patient's ambivalence about his mother may have contributed to his perception (or selection) of his wife as "double-binding." It should be noted that the consistency report of the wife's description of herself at her worst suggested "extreme unpredictability . . . chaotic" behavior.

```
SUBJECT NUMBER 006.  MALE.  MAY, 1980.
RATING NUMBER   5  WAS OF YOUR PERCEPTION
AS I SAW MYSELF IN RELATION TO MY MOTHER WHEN I WAS AGE 5-10 (I AM RATED)

BEHAVIORS SHOWN INVOLVE FOCUSING UPON THE SELF.  THERE IS REACTION, BEING IN
A STATE OR CHILDLIKE BEHAVIOR.
THIS IS THE LAST OF TWO PARTS FOR THIS RATING
                                     0* 10
              GO OWN SEPARATE WAY  60* * * 60 HAVE OWN IDENTITY
            DEFY,DO OPPOSITE     80*   *    * 50 ASSERT ON OWN
           AVOID BY BEING BUSY  40*        * 10
         WALL-OFF,NONDISCLOSE 40*      *      * 0
                         0*            *      * 20
      GRIEVE,WEEP ALONE    50*         *      * 10
                   0*                  *        * 40 RELAX,FLOW,ENJOY
               0*                      *        * 0
           0* * * * * * * * * * * * * * * * * * * * 0
               0*                      *        * 20
                0*                     *        * 20
                 0*                    *      * 60 ASK,TRUST,COUNT ON
                  0*                   *      * 50 ACCEPT REASON
                   10*                 *      * 40 TAKE IN,LEARN
      SULK,ACT PUT UPON   40*          *    * 30 CLING,DEPEND
      APATHETIC COMPLIANCE 70*         *  * 20
        FOLLOW RULES,PROPER  70* * * 40 SUBMERGE INTO ROLE
          YIELD,SUBMIT,GIVE IN 50*
```

IN THE STATEMENTS WHICH FOLLOW, THINK OF 'I' AS THE SUBJECT AND THE
LISTED IMPORTANT PERSON AS THE OBJECT OF THE DESCRIPTIONS. FOR EXAMPLE,
IF THE REPORT SAYS: 'IGNORES THE OTHER PERSON, NEGLECTS HIS/HER INTER-
ESTS', READ: 'I IGNORE HIM/HER, NEGLECT HIS/HER INTERESTS'. YOU ARE
DESCRIBING YOURSELF AND THE SOURCE IS THE 'I' FORM OF THE QUESTIONNAIRE.


```
*********************************************************************************
                            CLUSTER ANALYSIS
```

ASSERTING AND SEPARATING. THE PERSON RATED IS DESCRIBED AS BEHAVING
INDEPENDENTLY BY ASSERTING, ACTING ACCORDING TO INTERNAL STANDARDS AND
FREELY COMING AND GOING WITHOUT WORRYING OVER WHAT IS SAID ABOUT IT.
THIS STRONG AUTONOMY MAY TAKE THE FORM OF 'GOING ONE'S OWN SEPARATE
WAY', AND IN SOME CASES MAY ALSO BE ACCOMPANIED BY DEFIANCE OR
OPPOSITIONALISM.

TRUSTING AND RELYING. THE PERSON RATED IS DESCRIBED AS TRUSTINGLY
EXPECTING AND ACCEPTING IDEAS, PERSONAL ADVICE AND KINDNESS. THERE IS A
WILLINGNESS TO TAKE IN AND LEARN FROM THE OTHER PERSON. IN ITS MOST
PASSIVE OR SUBMISSIVE FORM, THIS TRUST MAY TAKE THE FORM OF
OVERDEPENDENCE AND CLINGING.

DEFERRING AND SUBMITTING. THE PERSON RATED IS DESCRIBED AS YIELDING,
SUBMITTING AND GIVING IN. FRIENDLY FORMS OF THIS INTERACTIONAL STYLE
MAY ENTAIL OVERCONFORMING AND DEFERRING, WHILE LESS FRIENDLY FORMS MAY
INVOLVE EXAGGERATED ADHERENCE TO RULES, AND 'BEING PROPER'. THE MOST
DISAFFILIATIVE FORM WOULD BE TO GIVE UP ALL SPARK, TO BE SPIRELESS.

WALLING OFF AND AVOIDING. THE PERSON RATED IS DESCRIBED AS WALLING OFF
AND AVOIDING THE OTHER PERSON, NOT HEARING OR REACTING AND/OR BY DOING
SOLITARY ACTIVITIES. BEHAVIOR THAT SEEMS UNRELATED OR IRRELEVANT TO
WHAT IS GOING ON IS LIKELY; THE PERSON IS OFTEN 'ON OWN TRIP'.
DETACHMENT, REFUSING TO ASK FOR ANYTHING, AND SOLITARY WEEPING MAY BE
OTHER TYPES OF DISTANCING BEHAVIORS.

```
*********************************************************************************
BRIEF TECHNICAL REMARKS
```
THE RATINGS FOR THIS GROUP OF BEHAVIOR SHOWED A STRONG 'REVERSE'
INTERNAL CONSISTENCY. THERE WAS A TENDENCY TO ENDORSE (AND/OR TO AVOID
ENDORSING) BLOCKS OF ITEMS HAVING OPPOSITE MEANINGS. IN THIS CASE WHERE
THE FOCUS IS UPON THE SELF, SUCH A TENDENCY TO ENDORSE CONTRADICTORY
BLOCKS REFLECTS AMBIVALENCE. THERE IS REACTION IN OPPOSITE WAYS ON AT
LEAST ONE WELL-DEFINED INTERPERSONAL THEME.

Fig. 10.3. The INTREX analysis of the patient rating himself in relation to his mother when he was age 5–10. His defiance alternating with his deference and his withdrawal alternating with trust explained the "ambivalence" label given to this rating.

The Patient's Relationship with His Father

Ambivalence also appeared in the patient's rating of himself in relation to his father. For the patient's self-description here, several opposing clusters emerged: asserting and separating versus deferring and submitting; trusting and relying versus walling off and avoiding. Sulking and appeasing was the remaining cluster and the INTREX program reported "a strong 'reverse' internal consistency." The father was described by the clusters affirming and understanding, watching and managing, and ignoring and neglecting. The consistency report for the father's focus on other behavior read: "The ratings of this group of behavior showed essentially no consistency. There probably is extreme unpredictability with frequent changes from momemt to moment. In general it can probably be said that this group of behaviors is not stable or 'together.' In many cases the word 'chaotic' would be appropriate."

When going over the INTREX report with the patient, the interviewer noted that no abuse was endorsed on the questionnaire and yet it had been discussed during the interview:

Interviewer: What surprised me about this (report), after I talked to you, was that you didn't rate your father as more harsh, more attacking. (*Self disclosing and checking.*)
Patient: You know, I never considered him harsh or attacking. I put it down the way it happened.
Interviewer: That's the way you felt it was. What I felt was harsh, you saw as discipline and therefore okay. (*Self disclosing and checking.*)
Patient: Right . . . well I wouldn't consider him harsh.
Interviewer: You wouldn't consider him harsh? That's just normal discipline? (*Checking.*)
Patient: That's right . . . they were really doing it for my own good anyway.
Interviewer: Oh, I see, their intentions were good? (*Checking.*)
Patient.: Right.
Interviewer: I see. Ya, okay. Well people see things differently depending on what they think the purpose is. What do you think your parents' intentions were? (*Affirming and checking.*)
Patient: Just to raise me to the best of their ability.

Summary of the Interview Data and Self-Ratings in Relation to the Suicide Attempt

In summary, the patient's self-ratings on the INTREX reports showed that he experienced his wife and his mother as consistently giving opposing messages, particularly in the interpersonal regions of rejection and nuturance (ignoring and neglecting versus helping and protecting). Both partners were described as very controlling (watching and managing) and also as the opposite (freeing and forgetting), but no overtly attacking behaviors from mother, father, or wife were reported by the patient to account for the very oppressive introject measured on the INTREX report.

During interview, it was learned that the severe and frequent beatings from the father at the mother's request were not experienced as attack, but rather as "justified" punishment. On interview, the suicide attempt itself was interpreted as an effort to please the wife and protect the children while at the same time abandoning them (and himself) and punishing himself. The suicide attempt was, in the coding language of SASB methodology, a *multiple communication* meaning several points of the model were needed to code it (Estroff and Benjamin). (Self) abuse was done according to family tradition—namely with the "best" of intentions.

TREATMENT PLANS BASED ON THE SASB MODEL

Both the self descriptions on the INTREX questionnaires and codings of the phenomenology of the suicide attempt involve multiple communication about the issue of attachment and, because no direct perception of attack from significant others could be measured, the suicide attempt is hypothesized to be more of a communication of conflict about attachment with emphasis being on the self-punishment part of the attachment track (133 punish, take revenge introjected to become 333, vengeful self-punish). Consequently, the suicide attempt is not viewed as a pure case of self-murder. This is not to say the attempt was not serious, nor that it could not reoccur. Rather, the treatment implications are that the suicidal behavior has much to do with the introjections of punishment from and a wish to revenge the father; in relation to the wife and mother, the suicidal behavior had to do with a complementary withdrawal as well as the introjection of their rejection. Therefore, family therapy including these members and addressing these issues would be the treatment of choice.

The dynamic SASB formulation would be that this man specializes in self-critical and self-abusive behaviors. They become acute when there is a major conflict with an attachment object. In general, his recent life history involves escalating the level of punishment inflicted upon him. Lack of space precludes an examination of this issue, but it is reasonable to hypothesize that the legal system in this case was unreasonably harsh (associated with the behavior of one particular probation officer) and also that the patient developed a sense of timing and "footwork" which assured that he would come up with the least desirable outcome at any given choice point. This formulation suggests that returning him to a higher security prison because of his recent escape would only play further into the self-punitive pathology.[1]

A knowledge of treatment implications of SASB allows the interviewer to set up a treatment plan even on initial interview. In the following passage, the interviewer does that, using the contradictory language of the patient and metaphors with multiple meaning. Talking with patients at their own level of complexity usually is appreciated by them and seems to have a greater impact.

Patient: I think so and I'm real wishy washy. I one day feel like I don't want to kill myself and the next day I think ya, I do.
Interviewer: Well, I'm sure that you believe some people would be pleased, your ex-wife. And it would get back at your father. (*Interpretation.*)
Patient: I don't want to get back at my father.
Interviewer: Well, it would. You've given these other people a lot of power, I would say, while you're taking control. (*Interpretation with contradiction.*)
Patient: I don't want to take control either.
Interviewer: Well, that's what killing yourself is to do, it's predictable. You "make sure you're not hurt." Kill several birds with one stone too you see. (*Interpretation with contradiction and metaphor.*)
Patient: Oh I would, definitely.

During this treatment section of the interview, the interviewer talked in paradox matching the patient's contradictions, but reversing the thrust of the implications. While the patient was gaining control through losing control (suicide), the interviewer tried to make it ego-alien to show that as he gained it in this way, he gave it away. At a point like this in an SASB interview, if the interviewer stops to ask, "Am I making sense or does this sound crazy?" patients usually will say, "I follow you, I know what you mean."

In addition, the interviewer deliberately invoked guilt in order to attempt to inhibit the suicidal tendencies. Recognizing that the patient's reasoning was that he would "protect" the children if he suicided, the interviewer used the patient's predilection toward guilt to lead to the opposite conclusion—namely that he should not suicide.

Interviewer: Well what do you think your kids would feel if you succeeded in killing yourself? (*Exploring through fantasy.*)
Patient: Oh, I think they'd feel bad, but I think they'd forget it.
Interviewer: Very unlikely. (*Teaching and invoking guilt.*)
Patient: That's really hard to tell.
Interviewer: Well, children who have parents who suicide take it hard. (*Invoking guilt.*)
Patient: Probably knew what the parents went through.
Interviewer: They'd understand? (*Checking.*)
Patient: I would think so. Right.
Interviewer: Ya? They're unlikely to do that too. (*Invoking guilt.*)

The interviewer invoked guilt with a constructive thrust rather than simply maintaining the antithetical position of friendly listening 115, and empathic understanding, 114, because interviewer provision of positive antithesis rarely works alone. Dr. Glen Shaurette, Chief of Psychiatry, VA Hospital, the University of South Carolina at Columbia, believes that rather than starting with the antithesis, the inpatient milieu should complement the patient's present interpersonal posture and then move in a counterclockwise direction toward the desired antithesis. Further discussion of this Shaurette principle appears in Benjamin (1980).

In the following passage, the interviewer highlights the needed antithesis and shows understanding of the patient's "resistance" to constructive change:

Interviewer: Well let's just talk one little bit more about those two parts of you that we mentioned before. The part that doesn't want to be hurt and kicked around and the part which thinks you might put it back together. (*Paraphrases internal conflict.*)
Patient: Okay.
Interviewer: If we were to give that part which might put it back together another chance, what could we do? (*Emphasis on constructive side.*)
Patient: Well I'd have to extend myself, I'd have to trust myself and boy you are really probing. I am apprehensive about trying to trust.
Interviewer: You need to find somebody that would be predictable and kind except you get along with ornery folks. (*Antithesis is specified.*)
Patient: I do. Must be my . . .
Interviewer: It's what you've learned. (*Teaching.*)
Patient: If I extend myself I'm going to get hurt, that's just the way I look at it. I don't want that at all.

In this passage, the interviewer is describing the need for antithetical experiences (you need somebody that would be predictable and kind) and elsewhere, starts to provide it by being friendly and directive:

Interviewer: I see the going to jail and all that stuff as your fight with your father and would suggest that you begin to fight with him up front. We could help you with that. That would be a way out. And work that thing through so you stop being the sacrificial lamb, if you know what I mean. And you'd do yourself a favor and your kids a favor, the kids a big favor, a real favor, if you would try to get it back. (*Trying to provide alternative constructive responses and beliefs.*)
Patient: I'd do anything for my kids.

THE PATIENT'S REACTION TO THE SASB INTERVIEW

The impact of the SASB interview was measured informally by inspection of the notes in the patient's chart. These came from his nurses, a medical student, and a resident. Prior to the conference, all entries had to do with symptoms, mostly documenting the patient's dedication to harming himself and his agreement to daily suicide contracts.

The first entry following the SASB interview was "patient retreated into room after conference with Dr. B. He curled up in a ball on his bed and felt quite confused over what had happened. In reflecting the conference, he expressed surprise at Dr. B.'s perceptiveness, admitting that she was right most of the time. He wanted to know what Dr. B.'s thoughts on his survival chances were and what would happen with him now. For the time being this R.N. handed him the tape from the recorded session for him to keep and reflect on. He is putting his fate in the professionals' hands. Recommend short passses with (prison) guards, engage in plenty of activities."

The medical student entered: "Recurrent theme developed by Dr. B. during staffing today was his desire to see something new happen in his life and his fear of being hurt. Patient states that one thing he could possibly see living for is to try and make things better with his children. The fear of being hurt if he reached out, however, is paralyzing. Feeding this is his huge feeling of guilt which makes him convinced he will fail because of his worthlessness if he does try to make contact with people."

In the following days, staffing notes continued to make some references to the conference and to the listening of tapes which the patient regarded as very important ("the tape is my deep, dark secret. My family can't understand me until they understand themselves. I've always been a screwball, but underneath I'm serious and cautious"). A nursing note ten days later said: "Right now I'm living just for my kids. I don't think enough of myself to do it for me." Two days after that: "Right now my kids are my only reason I can see for going on and only 1% of me wants to go on for them. Has been talking with children by telephone, low self-esteem." Two days later: "Wife told him she'd rather buy children's shoes than spend money going to the family conference. (The wife rejects him using his caring about the children, the one area of strength he has remaining). Patient responds self punitively: 'Maybe if you give me those electric shocks it would help, antidepressants aren't working.'" It seemed the impact of the interview faded with time and destructive input from the wife. The SASB approach, like any other, requires consistent followup to implement the principles. There is no such thing as one trial "relearning."

COMPARISON OF THE DSM-III AND THE SASB DIAGNOSES

The DSM-III diagnosis had the treatment implication of an antidepressant and the patient was given Imipramine. Though neither approach provided a "cure," compared to the DSM-III, the SASB interview plus the INTREX ratings provided much greater understanding of the phenomenology of the suicidal act, of its social etiology, of how to interact with the patient to "connect" and inspire the will to change, and suggested what types of social relearning probably would be helpful. To summarize briefly: the patient has a highly consistent destructive objective; the suicide was interpreted by him as an effort to give his wife "what she wanted"—240 (while controlling the separation himself—140); to "protect" his children—143 (while abandoning them—123); to take revenge on his father—133 (while showing empathic understanding of his position—113 + 114); and to protect

himself—343 (while being extremely reckless—323). These themes occur on the attachment track of the SASB model. The INTREX ratings showed perception of double-binds
coming from the wife and the mother, the major contradictions occurring in the regions
ignoring and neglecting versus helping and protecting. These observations about conflict
involving attachment; the absence of perception of overt attack from loved ones, led to
the interpretation of the suicide· as a communication rather than as a "pure" case of
self-murder. The treatment implications involve first the fact that the patient felt understood; for the first time he showed a little will to fight to get better in that he developed an
interest in taking care of his children and that he began to think about expressing anger
directly toward his father (i.e., developed an alternative set of responses to the suicidal
ones). A family conference was proposed as an initial step toward making room for him to
function in a constructive fashion as a father and to begin to relate to his own father in a
less intropunitive fashion.

At this early point in the research study, it is difficult to predict how a formal category
for patients like this would look. Probably it would include SASB descriptors about self-
concept, perception of significant others, and contrast of patient perception with observer
descriptions. In this case, for example, the wife's ratings of the patient were available but
space limitations preclude an examination of some interesting discrepancies in their
views. For example, the wife described herself as belittling and blaming the patient when
she was at her worst, but Figure 10.2 suggests that he did not perceive her that way. His
near total blockage of perception of others as exerting hostile control (which is the
theoretical root of his own self-oppression) may be a key factor in his self-punitive activities. The old clinical truism for this phenomenon is "anger inward rather than anger
outward." Such blockage measured by discrepancy in self and observer ratings may turn
out to be characteristic of patients in this category. Then too, the extreme submissiveness
shown in Figure 10.3 may be characteristic of depressed patients (see also Essex, Klein,
Jones, & Benjamin, submitted for publication).

GENERAL DISCUSSION OF THE TREATMENT IMPLICATIONS OF SASB

The preceding has demonstrated uses of SASB and the associated INTREX questionnaires in the analysis of an initial encounter with an inpatient participating in the Interpersonal Diagnosis Study. Use of these methods in other contexts seems unlimited. In
ordinary outpatient therapy, for example, the SASB therapist would continually code
patient statements according to the model. Such constant coding has many implications.
The first is that it directs inquiry so that the time is not wasted on vague generalities. For
example, "I feel upset today" is followed by inquiry until something specific and interpersonal can be identified and coded. Of all of the outcome studies of psychotherapy, one
stable finding is that the more specific therapies are, the more effective they are (Garfield
& Bergin, 1978).

Coding patient statements in terms of the SASB model also has direct implications
about others in the social milieu, including transference reactions. The therapist should be
continually aware of the patient's interpersonal posture toward him or her independently
of the content of what is being said. Through the principle of complementarity, the
therapist can infer how he or she is being perceived. An example is if a patient is seeming
to be defensive or whiny, the therapist might say something like, "Are you feeling challenged or criticized by me right now?" The patient might respond with; "Yes, I guess so,
when you said . . ." and go into the detail. If discussed in this friendly, nonadversarial way,
a developing resistance can be aborted.

Generally speaking, SASB codings can facilitate the use of the tried and true rules of "dynamic" therapy: constantly interrelate the past, the present, and the transference. Sharpened therapist perception and communication about the connections among these three is likely to be constructive. If space permitted, there might be a cataloging of examples of improved understanding, communication, and relearning using each of the features of the SASB model.

The therapist-reader is invited to try the following exercise in his or her next couple's therapy session: every time there appears to be a misunderstanding or disagreement, code each person's point of view. Then reflect for both, the differences in view. Explore their reactions to the new perceptions. When coding, remember to address the separate issues of: (1) *Focus. Example*: he was focusing on himself rather than on her when he went back to work after their fight that night, so he was showing 221, flee, escape, withdraw, and not 121, angry dismiss, reject. (2) *Affiliation. Example*: she was feeling friendly when she asked why he was late; it was 141, friendly invite, rather than 131, approach menacingly. (3) *Interdependence. Example*: He thinks that just listening to her without actually trying to do something to fix it (which would be 115, friendly listen) is "weak" and submissive (which would be 240, yield, submit, give in). (4) *Complementarity. Example*: if she appeases, scurries, and cringes so much (235, appease, scurry; 233, whine, defend, justify), she just draws out more put downs (136, put down, act superior) and punishment (133, punish, take revenge) from him. (5) *Opposition. Example*: his father was pushed around by his mother (136, put down, act superior; 137, intrude, block, restrict), and he thinks the opposite of that is to give in (237, apathetic compliance). He believes if you are not one up, you must be one down. Separation of the ideas of complements and opposites can be very helpful. Asserting (216, put cards on the table) does not need to involve attack or put down (136). (6) *Antithesis. Example*: she was a neglected child (126, ignore, pretend not there; 125, neglect interests, needs; 123, abandon, leave in lurch), leading her to be a "loner" as a child (wall off, nondisclose, 226; busy with own thing, 225; detach, weep alone, 223) and so she "overmothers" (146, pamper, overindulge; 147, benevolent monitor, remind; 148, specify what's best) to be sure that her children don't suffer what she suffered. (7) *Introjection. Example*: both his parents were extremely controlling (140, manage, control) so it's difficult for him to let himself go (320, happy-go-lucky; 138, let nature unfold; 317, let self do it, confident).

The INTREX reports of the self-descriptions, of course, facilitate such SASB formulations. A very recent discovery is that psychotics can and will rate hallucinations as a relationship, and the INTREX program will show how the hallucination derives from the social environment. "Craziness" usually "makes sense" when interpreted within the SASB framework. More information about INTREX can be obtained in Benjamin (1980).

Therapists who elect to use SASB to guide thier interventions in psychotherapy are unlikely to become bored or burned out. The challenge of classifying and thinking of principles of opposites, complements, antithesis, and introjection as they relate to the past, present, and transference can keep one alert even through a day of seeing many patients "back to back."

NOTE

1. One judge was sympathetic to this analysis but the other was not. Suddenly, one Friday afternoon, much to the surprise of the patient and staff, the patient was transferred back to jail, and one of his nurses wrote: "At that time all previous treatment efforts and minor accomplishments evaporated in front of my eyes."

REFERENCES

American Psychiatric Association. *Diagnostic and statistical manual of mental disorders*, 3rd ed. Robert L. Spitzer, Chairperson, Task Force on Nomenclature and Statistics, Washington, 1980.

Benjamin, L. S. Structural analysis of social behavior. *Psychological Review*, 1974, **81**, 392–425.

Benjamin, L. S. Structural analysis of a family in therapy. *Journal of Consulting and Clinical Psychology*, 1977, **45**, 391–406.

Benjamin, L. S. Structural analysis of differentiation failure. *Psychiatry*, 1979, **42**, 1–23. (a)

Benjamin, L. S. Use of structural analysis of social behavior (SASB) and Markov chains to study dyadic interactions. *Journal of Abnormal Psychology*, 1979, **88**, 303–319. (b)

Benjamin, L. S. *INTREX users manual*. Madison, Wisc.: INTREX Interpersonal Institute, 1980.

Brammer, L. M. *The helping relationship: Process and skills*. Englewood Cliffs, N.J.: Prentice-Hall, 1973.

Essex, M. J., Klein, M. H., Jones, R. D., & Benjamin, L. S. Social and psychological strains and resources affecting depression in older women. Submitted for publication.

Estroff, S. & Benjamin, L. S. Manual for using SASB to code videotape and typescripts. Unpublished manuscript.

Garfield, S. & Bergin, A. E. *Handbook of psychotherapy and behavior change: An empirical analysis*. New York: Wiley, 1978.

Kendell, R. E. *The role of diagnosis in psychiatry*. Oxford: Blackwell Scientific Publications, 1975.

Leary, T. *Interpersonal diagnosis of personality*. New York: Ronald Press, 1957.

McLemore, C. W. & Benjamin, L. S. Whatever happened to interpersonal diagnosis? *American Psychologist*, 1979, **34**, 17–34.

Reik, T. *Listening with the third ear*. New York: Grove Press, 1948.

Schaefer, E. S. A configurational analysis of children's reports of parent behavior. *Journal of Consulting Psychology*, 1965, **29**, 552–557.

Part III:
Interpersonal Process Models for Psychotherapy

Part III

Chapter 11
Interactional Psychotherapy: Using the Relationship
Sheldon Cashdan

The notion that the personal interaction between therapist and client constitutes an important aspect of the psychotherapy process is nothing new. The extent and the manner in which the interaction figures into the change process is another matter. Behavior therapists, for example, view the therapist-client relationship as facilitative rather than substantive. The relationship, as they see it, is significant only if it increases the probability that the client will follow instructions or attend to appropriate reinforcers. Even psycho-analytically oriented therapists treat the relationship as facilitative, its major function being to promote insight. Manifestations of the relationship are consequently construed in transferential or countertransferential terms, not as legitimate expressions of a contemporary exchange between two human beings with significance in its own right.

The therapist-client relationship can, in contrast, be viewed as the *primary* arena for meaningful psychotherapeutic change. This is the position I take in my own work with clients and the one to which most of the contributors to this volume subscribe. It is a position that derives from a more pervasive interactional perspective in which human relationships and the interactions that comprise them form the motivating force behind most if not all human behavior. This philosophy is succintly expressed by Lennard, who writes:

Human beings are characterized by the striving for and dependence upon interactions with other human beings. Such interaction is an end in itself, and interaction deprivation leads to anguish, loneliness and depression. Interaction defines and affirms the humanness of the self. [Lennard & Bernstein, 1969, p. 48.]

An increasing number of social scientists including Blumer (1969), Carson (1969), and Guntrip (1973) concur with Lennard in the belief that human interaction is in itself motivating. A logical extension of this belief is that meaningful change may not be so much an intrapsychic event as an interpersonal one.

Merely to assert, however, that therapeutic change is interpersonal, or relational, leaves much unsaid. What precisely is it about the therapist-client relationship that produces change? Upon what types of interactional events need one focus? How do changes that occur in the therapy room generalize to changes outside of it? These are some questions I tried to answer in my book *Interactional Psychotherapy* (Cashdan, 1973). Focusing exclusively on the relationship between therapist and client, I outlined the basic ingredients of a relational treatment process in which the here and now interactions between therapist and client took center stage. The result was a description of the various devices an interactional therapist relies upon to produce change. This change in large part centered in the concept of a "strategy."

STRATEGIES AND PSYCHOPATHOLOGY

Every system of psychotherapy, ranging from systematic desensitization to Gestalt therapy, zeroes in on a specific class of behavior that it purports to change. In some systems, the target behaviors are "habits," in some "repressed feelings," and in still others, "irrational assumptions." In interactional psychotherapy, target behaviors take the form of "strategies." Broadly defined as ingrained patterns or maneuvers by which people structure their interpersonal relationships, "strategies" constitute the pathology of interpersonal relationships.

The concept of a strategy emerges from the assumption that human relationships are built upon implicit contractual agreements and that the interactions comprising these agreements have reward-cost tags attached to them. The idea that interpersonal behavior could be expressed through social economics was first proposed by Homans in his work, *The Human Group* (1950), and later expanded upon by Gouldner in an article entitled "The Norm of Reciprocity" (1961). More recently, in his book *Interaction Concepts of Personality* (1969), Robert Carson showed how a theory of personality could be based solely on interpersonal constructs. Integrating the interpersonal formulations of Leary, the interpersonal psychiatry of Sullivan, and the social psychology of Thibaut and Kelly, he demonstrated how one could explain much of human motives on the basis of implicit contractual agreements. Strategies represent the behavioral expression of these agreements. As might be expected, there are adaptive strategies and maladaptive strategies.

Adaptive strategies are behavioral patterns in which the meaning of social actions are agreed upon by the participants. Such patterns typically are described by terms such as "above board," "two way," and "up front," and more often than not tend to be found in meaningful friendships, fulfilling marriages, and productive work relationships. At their core lies a mutual understanding, an implicit quid pro quo, that leads the participants to assume with some degree of confidence that what they get from the relationship will be more or less equivalent to what they put in.

Maladaptive strategies, in contrast, are exploitative. The result of lopsided contracts, they primarily benefit only one of the parties. Like adaptive strategies, maladaptive strategies are devices by which people bind one another in sustained relationships. But unlike their adaptive counterparts, they are rooted in inequitable exchanges.

The subtlety of maladaptive exchanges often leads to their persisting over long periods of time. Ultimately, however, the person who is the target of the strategy comes to realize what has been going on and responds either with rage or withdrawal. This in turn produces anxiety, depression, and sometimes physical symptomatology in the perpetrator who, sensing the failure of the strategy, begins to decompensate relationally.

Of the various maladaptive strategies, four in particular stand out. They are the dependency, martyr, sexuality and power strategies. Presented below in capsule form, each represents a stylistic mode of structuring close relationships. Each is made up of a set of unique communications and metacommunications. Each in its own way constitutes a form of interpersonal pathology.

STRATEGIES AND HUMAN COMMUNICATION

Among the four strategies, dependency strategies are perhaps the most prevalent. Along with martyr strategies, they are commonly seen in clinical depression. Dependency strategies, however, are not restricted to depression; they play a part in most disturbances where psychological invalidism is evident. The hallmark of a dependency strategy, accordingly, is the use of helplessness as a means of forming and maintaining personal relationships.

Persons who employ dependency strategies spend an inordinate amount of their time asking for directions, soliciting opinions, and maneuvering people into a position where they will make decisions for them. Communications in relationships where a dependency strategy is operating typically take the form of:

- What do you think about—?
- Can you help—?
- Should I—?
- I fall apart when—.

The tone of the relationship is one of ineptitude with an implicit threat of imminent collapse should help or advice not be forthcoming. Underlying the use of most dependency strategies is the metacommunicative "I can't live without you," a threat that in some cases is expressed through suicide attempts.

The martyr strategy, in contrast, is founded on duty and sacrifice. Basing their relationship with others on ingratiation, martyr strategists tend to be obsessed with doing things for others. I recall a woman in family therapy who drove her family to distraction by constantly reminding them to wear their scarves, take their vitamins, and to take along their boots whenever the weather looked threatening. One specific ritual entailed checking out the safety latches on the car doors—one by one in sequence—every time the family went on a trip, even if it was just to a neighborhood movie. When I asked her in one session why she felt compelled to do such things in the face of her family's obvious annoyance, she replied in a rather pathetic tone of voice, "What use would they have for me otherwise?"

Martyr strategies sometimes crop up in therapy in offers of clients to be therapeutic guinea pigs ("You can try new techniques on me if you like"). It also can be seen in group therapy in the case of the member who makes sure that the chairs are all set up or that the coffee is brewing. As in the case of other strategies, the martyr strategy contains a metacommunication which accompanies the more overt communication. In the case of the martyr strategy, it takes the form "You owe me," and no matter how self-sacrificing or ingratiating the martyr strategist appears to be, he ultimately expects his due.

Sexuality strategies rely on eroticism as the basis for relationship formation. The primary mode of interaction is seductiveness with the eventual goal of sexual entanglement. People who rely on sexual strategies as their modus operandi communicate their intentions through suggestive posturing, double entendres, and other forms of interpersonal erotica. In therapy this may take the form of tight-fitting clothing (by both males and females), the use of double entendres, and detailed accounts of sexual escapades. Very often such tales seem designed to titillate rather than inform, and function to turn the therapy session into a verbal massage parlor.

The use of a sexual strategy was evident in the case of one client who spent a great many of our early sessions describing his sexual escapades, some of which involved the seduction of two of his wife's best friends. The particular dynamics of these seductions—i.e., his vengeful feelings toward his wife—was not as revealing as the fact that each and every episode had to be recounted in minute detail. It was not until he was confronted with what he was doing—i.e., attempting vicariously to ally himself with me along sexual lines—that the strategic nature of his story telling was exposed. Then and only then could we discuss the possibility of his structuring his relationships along other than sexual lines.

The thing that sets sexuality strategies apart from sexuality per se is the use of eroticism as an exclusive and manipulative mode of social exchange. Sexuality for the sexual strategist is not just another realm of social experience, situated alongside other realms. It is the primary realm. Thus, the sexual strategist uses sex to buy love, patch up arguments, relieve boredom, and get ahead in the work world. The epitome of a sexuality strategy was expressed in the words of one client who had spent the past six years stumbling in and out of disastrous affairs. When I asked her why sexuality played such a dominant role in all her relationships—to the virtual exclusion of other forms of relating—she confessed sadly, "The only thing I know how to do well is fuck."

The three strategies already mentioned—dependency, martyr, and sexuality—all involve elements of control. Most of the time though, the control elements seem to be downplayed, or at least disguised. This is less the case with power strategies where issues of dominance and submission become central.

Power strategies are essentially interpersonal control maneuvers that are based on fear and intimidation. Persons who employ such strategies seem unable to share responsibility or to take suggestions. Instead, they are experts at telling people when and how to do things. Communications associated with power strategies accordingly take the form of "Do what I say!" or "You must—," followed by the implicit "or else." The "or else," which is hardly ever spelled out, typically has less to do with physical harm than with predictions that the person at whom the strategy is directed will fall apart or deteriorate.

Power strategies are often seen in despotic work relationships, although I have seen it operate countless times in dysfunctional marriages. In such cases, the power strategist, usually the husband, controls the wife with the implicit threat that she would go to pieces if he weren't around. The metacommunicative threat behind the strategy usually becomes explicit at the time the wife has had just about all she can take and decides to leave. It is at this point that we hear the husband say something to the effect of, "Go ahead. See if you can make it on your own. You'll be back on your hands and knees before the week is out." It is clear in such instances that the implicit threat—the metacommunication—has to do with predictions of personal collapse.

The four strategies described above in summary fashion are schematically depicted in Table 11.1, along with the communicative and metacommunicative patterns associated with each. I suspect that more maladaptive strategies exist and that the four already described do not exhaust all the possibilities. They do, however, highlight some of the more common ways in which human beings manipulate one another and some of the more common patterns one comes across in psychotherapy.

INTERACTIONAL PSYCHOTHERAPY: THE PROCESS

Interactional psychotherapy is a systematic way in which maladaptive strategies are dealt with in the context of the therapist-client relationship. The therapy process, made up of five relatively distinct phases, or stages, constitutes the way in which strategies are challenged, negated and ultimately replaced. The five stages, listed below, are indexed by

TABLE 11.1. MALADAPTIVE STRATEGIES.

Strategy	Modality	Communications	Metacommunication
Dependency	Helplessness	"What do you think?" "What should I do?" "Can you help?"	I can't survive without you
Martyr	Ingratiation	"I try so hard." "How can I help?" "I work my fingers to the bone."	You owe me
Sexuality	Eroticism	Double entendres Flirtatiousness Suggestive dress	I ___, therefore I am*
Power	Control	"Do what I say." "Obey, . . . or else." "You must. . . ."	You can't survive without me
?	?	?	?

*With apologies to Descartes

a series of therapeutic techniques that are unique to that stage and a corresponding shift in the client's behavior:

Stage One: Hooking
Stage Two: Maladaptive Strategies
Stage Three: Stripping
Stage Four: Adaptive Strategies
Stage Five: Unhooking (Termination)

The goal of treatment is to guide the client through each of the stages, thereby providing him with a set of sequential learning experiences which culminate in the replacement of maladaptive strategies with more adaptive ways of relating. A brief synopsis of the process follows.

Stage One: Hooking

Interactional psychotherapy begins with the therapist establishing the conditions that enable him to be viewed as a "significant other." When clients first visit a therapist they tend to cast him in the role of expert, as someone who through some magical process will give the client answers he or she is missing. This is obviously nonsense. If therapy is to meet with some measure of success, it cannot be based on some mystical notion about an omnipotent therapist who wields a psychological wand.

The techniques employed in the first, or "hooking," phase of treatment, are accordingly designed to counter magical perceptions and to "humanize" the therapist. One of these techniques, "emotional coupling," simply entails tapping into the emotional component of a client's statements; the other involves offering relatively innocuous advice so as to make the client's life a bit more manageable. Both can be seen operating in the case of a gay woman who sought me out for help with a depression that developed over a broken love affair with an older woman.

The client, named Beth, seemed anxious from the very first moment I saw her. It turned out that this had less to do with the broken love affair than with an upcoming meeting with her mother whom she had not seen for many years. While eagerly looking forward to the reunion, the client also was "concerned." She could not quite put her finger on what her concern was all about; it just bothered her.

Emotional coupling merely entailed making statements to Beth to the effect that she seemed apprehensive or anxious. Extracting the more emotionally tinged "I am frightened" from the somewhat intellectualized "I have concerns" functioned to establish me in Beth's eyes as someone who could feel for her as well as someone who could analyze her problems.

But what was Beth frightened of? Brief exploration revealed that her anxiety centered on where she and her mother had arranged to meet—the mother's motel room in Washington, D.C. It was not difficult to surmise, knowing some of the details of the client's life, that her "concerns" probably had to do with unrecognized fears that something sexual might take place in the mother's room. Since it was much too early in therapy even to broach the subject of mother-daughter sexuality, I simply advised Beth to meet her mother at the Lincoln Memorial. I furthermore suggested that she and her mother spend the day taking in the Washington Monument or strolling around the reflecting pool. Beth returned for her next session ecstatic about the beautiful time she had spent with her mother. She thanked me profusely for my help.

The reasons for taking the time to engage the client in the hooking process is twofold. One, mentioned earlier, is to establish the therapist as a "significant other." Unless the therapist is regarded as someone who potentially holds strategic value for the client, the strategy will not emerge. The second reason has to do with confrontations which take place somewhat later in the therapy that conceivably might precipitate premature termination. Hooking sets the groundwork for personal relatedness so as to prevent the client from bolting when the going gets rough.

Stage Two: Maladaptive Strategies

The second stage of treatment sees the client's maladaptive patterns of relating start to emerge. This occurs spontaneously as a normal consequence of the client's changing perception that the therapist is not just a distant figure but someone who potentially is capable of gratifying relational needs. Yalom comments on this phenomenon as it occurs in group therapy. He writes:

given enough time, every patient will begin to be himself, to interact with group members as he interacts with others in his social sphere, to create in the group the same interpersonal universe which he has always inhabited. In other words, *patients will begin to display their maladaptive interpersonal behavior in the group; no need for them to describe their pathology—they will sooner or later act it out before the group's eyes.* [Yalom, 1975, p. 29, emphasis added.]

Yalom's description of what happens in groups merely mirrors what happens in individual therapy. The main difference is that the therapist is the target of the maladaptive interpersonal behavior (the strategy) since he is the only other person in the room.

The critical development in stage two is the full blown emergence of the strategy in the therapist-client relationship. Just talking about the strategy does not suffice. It must be behaviorally expressed in the relationship if one hopes to eliminate it and replace it with something new. The goal of stage two therefore is to transform vague, nebulous expressions of the strategy into clear, concrete statements so that it can be dealt with as directly as possible.

How does the therapist accomplish this? By drawing the client through various levels of communicative involvement until the strategy becomes part of the ongoing therapy relationship. Beginning with the most remote level and moving to the most immediate one, they are:

Level 1: Communications regarding *early relationships* (parents, childhood friends, etc.);

Level 2: Communications regarding *current relationships* (spouse, employer, lover, etc.); and

Level 3: Communications regarding *therapy relationship* (therapist-client, or group members if in group therapy)

Thus, whenever discussion gets mired in the past (Level 1), the therapist endeavors to bring it to the present level (Level 2). Whenever it gets mired in the present (Level 2), the therapist directs it into the room (Level 3). Since clients rarely bring the strategy into the room on their own, at least in the early stages of treatment, it is the therapist's job to transform it from a there and then event into one in the here and now. Unless the strategy is experienced by both client and therapist in this way, it will be practically impossible to deal with it therapeutically.

Techniques that the therapist can use to accomplish this transformation fall under the rubric of *direct confrontation* and *dare ploys*. In the first, the therapist takes statements which allegedly are intrapersonal (monadic) and turns them into interpersonal (dyadic) ones. Thus, the client's remarks, "I sometimes have an overwhelming urge to cry," or "I often get angry," need to be rephrased by the therapist as "*I* sometimes make *you* feel like crying," or "*I* make *you* angry." In the second, the therapist takes conditional statements of the sort, "What if . . . ?" or "I wonder if . . . ?" and literally dares the client to restate them in terms of the requests or demands they actually represent.

In the case of the dependency strategy, for example, the therapist might respond, "Why don't you ask and find out" to the client's conditional, "What would you do if I asked you to tell me whether to get a divorce?" The same holds true for other strategies. Thus, during one session, one client who had a tendency to get herself sexually entangled with men very early in her relationships, asked me, "I wonder how you'd react if I asked you up to my apartment?" I responded, "I think you're saying you'd like to ask me" (Cashdan, 1973, p. 78). Whatever strategy is employed, the goal is to elicit as direct an expression of it as possible so as to be able to deal with it in stage three.

Stage Three: Stripping

Stage three is the phase in treatment in which the client's strategy is confronted, challenged, and ultimately refuted. It is perhaps the pivotal stage in the therapy process for it is the one in which the strategy is negated and ultimately rendered ineffective. Stage three sees the client divested or "stripped" of his maladaptive ways of relating.

The procedures used to bring this about can be seen in a series of interactions in which the strategy is refuted while the relationship is simultaneously affirmed. Referred to as "refutation-affirmation" techniques, they require that the therapist tell the client of his unwillingness to respond to him in strategic ways while at the same time expressing a continuing commitment to the client and the client's welfare. At a deeper level, it is the therapist's way of saying "I care for you but I don't care for what you do to me."

Using dependency strategies again as an example, the therapist communicates to the client that he is not going to answer every question or solve every problem. Nor will he be continually "on call." Over and over, the therapist needs to drive home the point that the relationship with the client involves more than just being a caretaker. Once, when faced with a mounting barrage of "problems," I told a client, "I have the feeling you'd make up some problem to bring to me if one didn't actually exist." At first the client seemed hurt, but then admitted that he didn't think I would want to see him if he didn't have a problem that day. The fact that some human beings can conceive of a relationship only in terms of problems and their solution points up the sterile quality of interactions in which dependency strategies have gained the upper hand.

It would be nice to be able to report that once stage three is underway, things progress smoothly. Unfortunately, just the opposite seems to be the case. People do not relinquish their strategies without a fight, which is understandable given that strategies represent a persons's interpersonal modus vivendi. It is precisely because the strategy is so much a part of one's being that rejection of the strategy becomes experienced as a rejection of the self. The typical result is extreme anger or depression, and is almost always accompanied by an impulse to flee.

It is at this point that the benefits of the earlier hooking procedures are realized. If hooking was carried out successfully, the chances are good that the client will remain in treatment in the face of what seems to him like rejection and withdrawal. This, coupled with the therapist's faith in the client, expressed interpersonally through affirming communications, helps the client see matters through to their conclusion. It is the living through of this admittedly trying situation by both therapist and client—with the accompanying recognition that the relationship has survived—that leads to the kind of learning that makes up the fourth stage of interactional therapy.

Stage Four: Adaptive Strategies

The fourth stage of treatment is the stage in which the client, bereft of his time-honored way of relating to people, begins to make his first fledgling attempts to relate in more meaningful ways. The difficult exchanges that took place in stage three, the threats to leave, the anger over perceived rejection, are now largely things of the past. (In some instances, clients occasionally will fall back on a secondary strategy, exhibiting dependency when sexuality fails, for example. When this occurs, it is necessary to backtrack a bit and repeat the procedures in stage two with specific reference to the new strategic behaviors.) The client and therapist now enter a phase in therapy in which the major consideration becomes filling the void that has been created by the elimination of strategic ploys.

It is in stage four that clients first begin to voice some very basic doubts about themselves as well as about things that hurt them deeply. Though clients may have revealed things about themselves earlier in therapy—e.g., symptomatic concerns, taboo thoughts, angry feelings, and so on—the self-revelations in stage four seem to center on deeper concerns. Yalom (1975) indicates that these concerns revolve about two major themes: worthlessness and sexuality. Clients either reveal doubts about their basic worth and/or about their feelings about themselves as sexual beings.

While I certainly agree that Yalom has hit upon two issues of critical importance, I would add one more: fear of abandonment. I have repeatedly found that many people bear secret anxieties about intimacy and abandonment, almost as if getting close to another human being and letting oneself truly be known will inevitably lead to rejection and aloneness. Whether we are speaking about worthlessness, sexual identity, or abandonment, revelations about these three areas constitute the significant events of stage four.

In this stage, the therapist continues to respond in the supportive, affirming manner that marked his earlier behavior. What is most critical at this point in the therapy, however, is not so much the social bolstering and encouragement the therapist provides but "transactional feedback." This entails offering the client an interpersonal mirror for the ways his strategy affects other human beings—in this instance, the therapist. Thus, the sexual strategist is shown how his behavior places constraints on a relationship where sexuality dominates. Power strategists are shown how their tone of voice and imperious pronouncements frighten and intimidate others. Similar considerations could be spelled out for the other strategies as well. It is precisely because the therapist has become a "significant other" that his feedback is regarded as meaningful by the client and is openly accepted.

At another level, though, the client receives much more than just "information." He learns for the first time what it is like to have a best friend, to be loved in the broad relational sense of the word. He learns what it is like to be in a relationship where one feels confident enough to be trusting, rather than in a relationship which is always hanging under the Damoclean sword of imminent rejection and certain abandonment. It is this perhaps more than anything else that constitutes the powerful learning experience around which interactional therapy is built. And it is at this point that the therapy begins to draw to a close.

Stage Five: Unhooking (Termination)

The "self-revelation–transactional feedback" process is a finite one. There is, after all, just so much one human being can reveal and a limit to how much feedback can be provided. From a reward-cost perspective, both theapist and client are getting less than they are putting into the relationship—the therapist in terms of usefulness, and the client in terms of time and money. When both parties begin to apprehend this, it marks the beginning of a letting-go process which signals the treatment's termination.

The significant occurrence in stage 5 is the turning outward of therapy. The interior stages of the process, stages 2, 3, and 4, saw the focus of treatment placed entirely on the one-to-one interaction that was taking place in the therapy room. If the client is to benefit from what he has learned about relationships, he will have to develop relationships with persons who can give him more than the therapist possibly can, given the realities of professional involvement. As just one difference, there is the on-call nature of extended relationships which the therapist cannot provide if he wants to remain a therapist. The client's growing recognition of this indicates that the therapy is nearing completion. When it is fully acknowledged, and the experience of separation and loss is openly discussed, the therapy comes to a close.

Assuming that all has gone well—that is, that the stages have been faithfully negotiated—the client will possess some of the rudimentary interpersonal tools he or she needs to form meaningful, lasting relationships. This, coupled with the experience of having survived a relationship without having to rely exclusively on one's trusted weapon—the maladaptive strategy—places the client in a vastly improved position with regard to future involvements. To the degree that people continue to grow in their interpersonal relationships, the last stage of interactional psychotherapy represents the first stage of a significant interpersonal growth process.

What I have tried to do in the preceding pages is to describe in a somewhat idealized fashion how a therapist uses himself in the therapy process to promote change. The emotional nuances of the process as well as differences among therapists and clients were glossed over in favor of emphasizing the more systematic aspects of the process. The focus consequently was on ways of eliciting the strategy in the therapy relationship and on ways of dealing with it as directly as possible so as to provide the client with a novel and educative experience. This more than anything else constitutes the basic ingredients of any therapy with an interactional emphasis.

But what takes place in psychotherapy is only a small part of the overall picture. The drama of therapist and client takes place not in a vacuum but in the larger context of social interaction. The question therefore arises, why strategies? Why do people resort to these maneuvers in the first place? What function do they play in the lives of human beings? The answer has to do with something called the "self."

STRATEGIES AND THE SELF: TOWARD A THEORY OF RELATIONSHIPS

What exactly is the self? Authors ranging from Jung to Maslow to Laing have addressed themselves to this question. None, however, has articulated a clinically useful definition of what the self truly is. The field of psychiatry is singularly lacking in theoretical perspectives in which the self plays a central and substantive role.

Perhaps one exception is object relations theory as depicted in the work of Guntrip (1973), Fairbairns (1954), and Winnicott (1965). Through a focus on the way in which people internalize their relationships, specifically their early ones, object relations theorists have tried to show how different sorts of interactions are transformed into a sense of being, in other words, a sense of self. The particulars of this transformation, including the ways in which bad parts of the self (infantile libidinal and antilibidinal components) are split off from the good parts, form the foundation for a theory of psychic functioning in which the mother-child interaction plays a prominent role. The significance of object relations is that it substitutes the notion of "person-ego" (Guntrip, 1973, ch. 5) for the traditional psychoanalytic "system-ego," arguing that *person seeking* rather than *tension reduction* is the major motive behind human behavior.

The major problem with object relations theory is its heavy emphasis on the mother-child relationship as the prototype for understanding the makeup of the self. Contemporary relationships, strictly speaking, are not seen as significant in their own right, only to the extent that they augment or rectify the consequences of good or bad mothering. This perspective is carried over into therapy where what goes on between therapist and client is construed almost entirely in terms of transference and countertransference. As such, object relations remains historical and deterministic, and fails to realize its potential as a contemporary, relational theory of self.

The only position which truly adopts an interpersonal perspective on the self comes not out of psychiatry or psychology but out of sociology. Termed "Symbolic Interactionism," it was founded by George Herbert Mead, who developed a theory of human behavior in the early 1900s that took into account the thoroughly social nature of human beings. His theorizing, currently expressed in the writings of Blumer (1969), Cottrell (1969), and others, focuses on the way human beings symbolically internalize one another and how this mediates their ongoing interactions with the significant people in their world. Within this formulation, the self plays a critical role.

For symbolic interactionists, the self is a dynamic process that encompasses two distinct but intertwined elements. One of these, the part of the organism Mead chose to call the "I," is the part that is spontaneous and responsive, the part which reacts to changes in the environment in an immediate fashion. The other component, referred to as the "Me," is the part that molds, controls, and inhibits the initial inclinations of the "I." The "I" and "Me" represent, respectively, the reactive and reflective components of the human psyche. Both act in concert to produce the dynamic inner process that is phenomenologically experienced as the self.

The important thing to bear in mind is that the self is thoroughly and irreducibly interpersonal. It is the organism's way of inwardly constructing probable action sequences and then internally responding to them from the perspective of others. By internally playing out the "responses of others" to one's incipient acts, human beings become objects to themselves, responding to themselves as others might. At its very core, self-knowledge is other-knowledge. In the words of Cottrell, "We literally do not 'know what we are doing' nor even what or who we are except in terms of the responses of others that give meaning to our acts and define us to ourselves" (1969, p. 547).

The question arises as to how the "responses of others" are evoked. How does one internally incorporate the ongoing reactions of others so as to produce the inner transactions that are the self? The answer is, through conversation. The ways that other human beings are incorporated into oneself (one's self) occurs largely through the psycholinguistic transformation of outer "face-to-face" conversation into "inner" conversation. The "self" in symbolic interactionism is basically an "inner forum" that dictates how people feel about themselves as well as how they are apt to behave.

But clients do not seek psychotherapists out for problems with their "inner forums" or because their "I" and "Me" don't see eye to eye. They come to therapy because their marriages are failing, because they can't seem to find fulfillment in their work, and because their sex lives are less than satisfactory. What has this to do with psycholinguistic transformations and the self? The answer becomes clear once we examine the self's *content* more closely.

If one looks closely at the kinds of figures or voices that make up the "Me," it becomes apparent that they are more than a generalized amalgam of past and present voices. Despite Mead's use of the term "generalized other" to depict the broad societal constraints embedded in the "Me," people's inner voices tend to group into fairly discrete clusters. Thus, some voices affect how you feel about yourself as a man or woman, others affect your feelings about yourself as a husband or wife, and still others affect how you feel about yourself as a doctor, teacher, nurse, or homemaker. Each of these represents different parts of yourself (your self), suggesting that the self is not a single "I-Me" configuration, but is actually a series of "I-Me's."

Cottrell (1969) refers to these as "self-other systems." I prefer simply to call them identities and to talk about sexual identity, work identity, affiliative identity, etc., each internalized as a specific experiential feeling state. Thus, sexual identity can be experienced through feelings about oneself as a male, female, heterosexual, bisexual, or homosexual, while affiliative identity may be experienced through feelings about oneself as a husband, wife, divorcee, or single person. Identities, in short, exist within people as "relational enclaves" and are constantly being carved out of their interactions with significant others. In the words of the symbolic interactionists, "We are our others."

Integrating all this with what was said earlier, we can perhaps gain some appreciation for the function that strategies fulfill in human relationships. Strategies, very briefly, are meant to protect the self. To the extent that they are "self-protective," strategies are nothing less than the guardians of personal identity. Once one accepts this, it becomes apparent why people cling to their strategies so tenaciously and resist any efforts, therapeutic or otherwise, to do away with them. The sexual, martyr, dependency, and power strategies all in their own way bind people in relationships so as to maintain some semblance of psychic (self) integrity while keeping those same people at arm's length to defend against shaky identities.

Persons who seek psychotherapeutic help are persons who experience pervasive and chronic difficulties in one or more of their identities. The strategies they employ to deal with their difficulties only compound their problems and produce the kinds of reactions we call neurosis and psychosis.

However one chooses to address the issue of identity, by directly engaging the inner voices or by precipitating a "strategic identity crisis" in the confines of the therapy room, it is through the therapist-client relationship that the identity issue is ultimately resolved. It is perhaps appropriate to end with a quote from Guntrip, who writes: "the identity problem is the biggest single issue that can be raised about human existence. It has always been the secret critical issue; only in our time have we become explicitly conscious of it" (1973, p. 119). Interactional psychotherapy is a modest attempt to bring this consciousness into the therapy room.

REFERENCES

Blumer, H. *Symbolic interactionism.* Englewood Cliffs, N.J.: Prentice-Hall, 1969.

Carson, R. C. *Interaction concepts of personality.* Chicago: Aldine, 1969.

Cashdan, S. *Interactional psychotherapy: Stages and strategies in behavioral change.* New York: Grune & Stratton, 1973.

Cottrell, L. S. Interpersonal interaction and the development of the self. In D. A. Goslin (Ed.), *Handbook of socialization theory and research.* Chicago: Rand, McNally, 1969.

Fairbairns, W. R. D. *An object relations theory of personality.* New York: Basic Books, 1954.

Gouldner, A. W. The norm of reciprocity: A preliminary statement. *American Sociological Review,* 1960, **25,** 161–178.

Guntrip, H. *Psychoanalytic theory, therapy, and the self.* New York: Basic Books, 1973.

Homans, G. C. *The human group.* New York: Harcourt, Brace, Jovanovich, 1950.

Lennard, H. L. & Bernstein, A. *Patterns in human interaction.* San Francisco: Jossey-Bass, 1969.

Winnicott, D. W. *The maturational process and the facilitating environment.* New York: International Universities Press, 1965.

Yalom, I. D. *The theory and practice of group psychotherapy.* New York: Basic Books, 1975.

Chapter 12
Relational Psychotherapy:
The Clinical Facilitation
of Intimacy*
Clinton W. McLemore and Phyllis P. Hart

We are going to describe an approach to psychotherapy that revolves around what we call "The Disclosure." Like the other therapies described in this *Handbook*, ours is vitally concerned with the patient's interpersonal relationships. The nature of these relationships is, we believe, both indicative *and* determinative of a person's psychological well-being. Intimate relationships reflecting a balance between dependence and independence are taken to be more wholesome than nonintimate relationships, which usually involve either symbiosis (excessive dependence), detachment (excessive independence), inordinate ambivalence (behavioral vacillation), or confusion (jumbled communication). Emotional closeness between persons is typically benevolent, although certain people seem to achieve an approximation to intimacy through mutual aggression—hostile contact, for example patterned domestic war, is often preferred to no contact by people who know only this way of interacting.

It has been many years since Harry Stack Sullivan (1940; posthumous publications, 1954, 1956, 1962, 1964; see especially 1953, p. 246) made intimacy a well-known and respected clinical concept. Through the years, intimacy has become a shibboleth. Nearly everyone wants more of it but few people can tell you exactly what it is.[1] Like many important constructs in psychology, intimacy is probably impossible to define rigorously. This is because it is closely tied up with mental events. What is primary (mental or first order) data for one person can never be primary data for another. An individual's states of consciousness are, ultimately, only his or her own. Terms like love, anxiety, and despair— and intimacy—are by nature incapable of being fully operationalized. To reduce them to objectives is to lose much of their essence. For better or worse, no string of predicates and no set of factor analyses can entirely portray experiential states.[2] At the same time, people often present themselves for therapy in the hope of altering these states. They want to *feel* better. Thus, we are sometimes forced to use terms that have more intuitive than scientific appeal. There is, correspondingly, probably no better word than intimacy to depict that quality of interpersonal relationships that is most conducive to happiness, fulfillment, and meaning in human life.

*The authors express their appreciation to Dr. Hendrika Vande Kemp for her helpful comments during the writing of this chapter and to Mrs. B. J. Jacklitch for her very competent secretarial assistance.

Having alluded to objectivity versus subjectivity—knowledge is by nature subjective and, indirectly, to the difference between mental and physical events (and by implication to the mind-body problem), a review of the distinction between a scientific and a philosophic question may help lay the foundation for our clinical discussion. Questions of ethics and metaphysics *cannot* be answered in the laboratory, at least not without begging these questions (see, for example, the comments on pp. xiii, xiv of Bertrand Russell's *History of Western Philosophy*, 1945). "Should I tell my mother off?" is as much a philosophic question as a scientific one unless, of course, one is simply asking what the *effects* of doing this will be. What is good? What is of ultimate value? What is the ideal for human contact and for human thoughts, feelings, and actions, or is there no ideal? To what extent should people be allowed to decide these things for themselves? What is the nature of the human person? Are we, after all, just a conglomeration of physical processes or are we something more and, if so, what? These sorts of questions relate directly to our notions of mental health and, as a corollary, to the practice of psychotherapy (see Halleck, 1971; London, 1964). For this and other reasons, therapy will never be a purely scientific enterprise. It is, at best, an art that is informed by science.

Since a fair amount of what we call psychotherapy, then, seems to boil down to applied clinical *philosophy*, it is a good idea for the advocates of any clinical approach to highlight the scientific *and* philosophical assumptions upon which their approach is based. Consequently, we will begin our discussion by presenting some of our theoretical premises. We have already noted a few of them, but we want to list several more. Then, we will survey a number of theoretical roots which inform our methods. Space limitations prohibit an exhaustive literature review, but we can at least point to some major sources of influence. We will then describe several important social assessment advances made in recent years, most of which are described in other chapters of this book. After our discussion of assessment, we will outline the typical course of relational psychotherapy. What can the clinician expect as therapy progresses? In attempting to augment the intimacy of a client's interpersonal relationships, are there predictable stages through which therapy, and the therapist-client relationship, tend to move? We will also consider The Disclosure procedure per se. What is it? What are its risks and benefits? How should the client be prepared for it? How should significant others be prepared? What is required of the therapist in relational therapy and, in particular, *during* The Disclosure? To give concrete meaning to our discussion, we will present several case summaries. Finally, we will consider the empirical implications of intimacy training. What research studies need to be done? What would their results tell us? How does all this affect the clinical education of therapists?

In order to provide a preliminary glimpse of what we mean by The Disclosure in relational therapy, let us briefly describe it now. The Disclosure involves bringing into the consulting room, at the same time, the client and one or more significant others. *Which* others depends on the particular difficulties of the client. In some traditional marital and family therapies, of course, two or more persons meet simultaneously with the therapist, as is the case with group therapy. Our method differs from these in at least two ways. First, in most forms of marital, family, and group therapy, most if not all persons involved in treatment are conceptualized by the therapist as clients or patients. The group, or the "system," is under care. In our approach, there is a single identified client. Significant others may benefit from disclosure meetings, but the principal intent of these meetings is to help the primary client. Second, the other therapies to which we have referred usually involve many sessions, over a period of months (or years), with all persons attending the sessions. The Disclosure in relational therapy ordinarily occurs during a single two-hour convocation. Additional disclosure sessions may be scheduled later, but these are not routine. We will outline what specifically happens in The Disclosure later in the chapter.

THEORETICAL ASSUMPTIONS

As anyone who has completed a good course in logic can tell you, primary (major) premises are not demonstrable, that is, you cannot "prove" the validity of basic assumptions. This makes it especially important for psychological theorists to be explicit about those foundational beliefs that condition their clinical formulations and procedures. To this end, we will cite some of our major theses. Some of these are more philosophical than psychological but, as we have argued above, the line between the two is often fuzzy.

1. *People are by nature relational.* To be human is to be affiliative—to maintain interpersonal relationships and to give and recieve intimate social communications. This is an ontological assumption about the nature of people. It is buttressed (but not proved) by much formal and informal observation, and it has been a fundamental building block of interpersonal traditions in clinical psychology and psychiatry since their inception.

2. *Intimacy is a pivotal criterion of psychological integrity.* The ability to achieve and maintain emotional closeness with others is a uniquely important index of "mental health." Note that, on the basis of our first thesis, we assume that persons who *can* achieve and maintain intimacy *will* do so. Note also that, while sociability is no doubt positively correlated with the intimacy of a person's relationships, a large number of superficial social involvements is not to be taken for intimacy (although it may reflect a very functional social skill).

3. *States of consciousness are intrinsically important.* People consult therapists for problems of behavior and/or problems of consciousness. Anxieties, depressions, and other dysphorias are representative of the latter, while elevator phobias, unassertiveness, and social ineptitude are representative of the former. Behavioral problems, however, have their cognitive-emotional concomitants (e.g., feelings of distress), which is why people with behavioral difficulties present themselves for treatment in the first place. The importance of mental states and processes militates against a radical *clinical* behaviorism, although behavioral science must rely on *methodological* behaviorism in the conduct of research (re: operationalism).

4. *Mind and behavior are in reciprocal regulation.* Mental events (thoughts, feelings, attitudes, etc.) and behavioral events (actions) influence each other, although it is probably more accurate to say that mental events and one's *perceptions* of behavioral events (and their consequences) do the influencing. The therapist can presumably enter this circular feedback system at any point with good effect. Patients can act their way into new thoughts and feelings, or they can think/feel their way into new forms of behaviors.

5. *Avoidance is central to psychological dysfunction.* Many therapists have said this. Consider, for example, Fritz Perls' well-known comment that "the essence of neurosis is avoidance" (see also Perls, Hefferline, & Goodman, 1951, p. 142: "the therapist keeps leading the patient back to that which he wishes to avoid"). Avoidance of whatever triggers off unpleasant emotions may not be the origin of all psychological problems but it certainly seems to perpetuate a large number of them. Wachtel (1977) has published a landmark analysis of how avoidance and its extinction relate to psychopathology and psychotherapy.

6. *Introjects often mobilize avoidance.* Among main contributions of Ellis' (1962) rational-emotive therapy and other cognitively oriented treatments (e.g., Beck, 1973, 1976)

is the clear recognition that internalized conversations can markedly affect emotions *and* behaviors. Exactly *what* a particular patient avoids is largely conditioned by the content of introjected dialogues, which often seem to the patient to be mere "self-talk." Bringing into the client's awareness how such internal conversation relates to experiences with signifi- cant others is an important goal during the early phases of relational therapy. Sometimes introjects (re: personifications in Sullivan's theory) are heavily infused with fantasy mate- rial, such that the introject (mental representation) of another person may differ substan- tially from what the person actually is. Correcting such distortions is a key part of treat- ment. Parenthetically, as a recent movie indicated, "death ends a life but it does not end a relationship."

7. *Interpersonal realities are not entirely arbitrary.* Theorists like the gifted Paul Watzlawick of the Mental Research Institute in Palo Alto have pointed out the large extent to which our experiences are determined by how we "frame" them. In *How Real is Real?* (Watzlawick, 1976), he writes, "there is no absolute reality but only subjective and often contradictory conceptions of reality" (p. 140). While, from a philosophic point of view, this statement cannot easily be refuted—but is the statement itself "only a subjective and . . . contradictory conception of reality"?—and while it is a healthy antidote to "hardening of the categories," it does seem to us that clients' perceptual interpretations of interpersonal transactions *do* vary along a continuum of objective accuracy. Coherence theories of truth always fare better than correspondence theories. Nevertheless, we want to stand in the middle ground between absolutism and relativism.

8. *Communication is not a panacea.* Because it is impossible to be emotionally close to someone whom you do not know, communication is the ocean that keeps intimacy afloat. Without communication, the good ship intimacy runs aground. Sullivan, of course, stressed this in his teaching. At the same time, accurate communication does not by itself guarantee intimacy. To elaborate our analogy, when malevolence or incompatible desires make the waters rough, intimacy can be swallowed up in the storm. Under certain adverse conditions, clear communication only exacerbates interpersonal trouble, for example, by bringing opposite vested interests into sharp relief (good negotiators know this). Effective therapy in such cases must alter something more basic than communicative skill. It must reach feelings and motivations. It must, for instance, make its way through the smoke screen of anger to the more basic level of hurt and pain.

9. *Face-to-face self-disclosures by the client to significant others can have powerful therapeutic effects.* Communicating one's private thoughts and feelings to those people who are most important in one's life can accomplish a number of things all at once. First, it undercuts avoidance and thereby facilitates the extinction of fear and defensive manuev- ers. People will sometimes go to great lengths in order *not* to experience the uneasiness or embarrassment that might attend self-disclosure, especially to significant others such as parents. Since one can only verbalize what one "knows," repression affords a certain amount of protection against frightening self-disclosures. Relatedly, patients' fears that self-disclosures will lead to violent reactions in others, and sometimes in themselves, are typically inordinate and often strikingly irrational. Second, characteristically, a patient's closely guarded thoughts and feelings relate directly to those persons who have been introjected. When the patient takes the seemingly ultimate risk of telling *these* people of his or her private ideas, feelings, wishes, and fantasies, their unrealistic nature often becomes apparent. This facilitates correction of the introjected content. Third, face-to- face disclosure to a significant other gives the patient expressive practice. Like the therapy relationship itself, only more so, it serves as an important forum for risk taking. Fourth, such self-disclosure, if done under proper therapeutic guidance, can immeasurably deep-

en intimacy between the particular persons involved. It tends strongly to open channels of benevolent communication, to establish precedents for self-disclosure, and to disrupt ingrained patterns of scripted avoidance and interpersonal ritual (which inhibit intimacy). This seems to be the case even when the basic content of the disclosed information is significantly negative.

Naturally we hold more than these nine assumptions. Like many other therapists, for example, we believe that the processing of deep feelings is at the heart of effective psychotherapy. Nevertheless, this list of assumptions will at least orient the reader to what may be distinctive about our methods.

THEORETICAL ROOTS

It is difficult within the compass of a few pages to summarize all of the prior work that even directly influenced the development of one's psychotherapeutic methods. This is especially true when the approach under consideration reflects, as ours does, contributions from several different clinical and research traditions. We will briefly describe the general nature of relational psychotherapy and then trace its principal origins.

Relational therapy is quintessentially an interpersonally focused treatment. Our concern, from start to finish, is on the nature of the patient's social relationships. These relationships, however, may be intrapsychic as well as tangible—they can be "in the head." Psychotherapy, in our view, largely consists of intimacy training. It teaches the client how to attain and perpetuate emotional closeness with others. This is done by helping him or her extinguish crippling anxiety and the avoidance behaviors that both reflect and sustain it. As anxiety diminishes, and tolerance for unpleasant emotions such as embarrassment grows, the person is less likely to perform reflexive behaviors that ward off troubling feelings at the expense of sacrificing interpersonal closeness. The therapeutic relationship serves as: (1) a way to analyze the client's everyday interpersonal experiences, with a view toward discovering impediments to intimacy; (2) a means to practice relating openly and intimately to another human being, who responds benevolently and sensibly; (3) a forum for the expression of deep feelings, which is primarily what most people resist sharing; (4) a support for continued interpersonal risk taking, within and beyond the therapeutic hour; (5) a catalyst for such risk taking; and, (6) an opportunity for the client to learn which risks are most likely to facilitate intimacy (e.g., there is a difference between "owning" one's feelings and acting them out, even though both are often called "expressing one's emotions"). These six benefits are neither exhaustive nor mutually exclusive, but they represent some of the more salient ones associated with relational psychotherapy.

Nearly every interpersonal therapy owes its greatest debt to the neo-Freudians, in particular to Harry Stack Sullivan. What we are calling relational psychotherapy is no exception. Long before terms like "meaningful relationship" became fashionable, Sullivan realized how critically important *intimacy* is to human health and happiness. Indeed, he saw that what it means to be human is very tied up with the ability to be emotionally close (see Sullivan, 1953, p. 261). This, in turn, is heavily dependent on one's capacity to communicate clearly. "Security operations," while designed to preserve one's sense of well-being, have the untoward side effects of restricting awareness, limiting open communication, and thus hindering intimacy. Sullivan's comment to the effect that it takes people to make people sick and it takes people to make people better reflects his view of therapy. The therapist is a *person*, expert in the ways of human relationships, with whom the client attempts to engage. His or her own personality, enriched by clinical training, is the therapist's most important tool. During the therapeutic interview, the clinician attends carefully to: (1) what makes the patient uncomfortable and, by implication, what the patient tries to avoid (often with great subtlety); (2) the patient's specific forms of anxiety avoidance (security operations, self dynamisms, etc.); (3) what the clinician him or herself experiences when interacting with the patient; (4) the nature of the patient's outside interpersonal relationships, especially those with significant others, present and past; and (5) what the patient seems to be trying to do, to and with the clinician—i.e., how the patient attempts to structure *their* relationship. The interpersonal behaviors of the client in the therapy situation are taken as at least somewhat indicative of what the client does in certain other situations. While Sullivan may have overstressed the benefits of insight and the role of clear communication, his clinical sensitivity was unexcelled. His ideas and methods represented a radical and fundamentally important departure from both traditional psychiatry and orthodox psychoanalysis. The relationship between doctor and patient was no longer an aside, a secondary or tertiary contribution to diagnosis and treatment. With Sullivan, the relationship and the corrective experiences that informed it *became* the treatment, a theme reflected in such recent approaches to treatment as Patterson's (1974). This is why Sullivan stressed that the patient is continually evaluating the kind of human being the doctor is, e.g., how the doctor reacts to irritations, even how he or she holds a coffee cup. The client wants to know, in the most basic sense, *who* is doing the treatment. Readers interested in the impact and history of Sullivan's interpersonal theory of psychiatry may consult, in addition to his books, Chapman (1976, 1978), Chrzanowski (1977), Kvarnes and Parloff (1976), Mullahy (1948, 1970), Thompson (1950), and Witenberg (1973).

Other neo-Freudians also made important contributions to the development of interpersonal therapies, ours included. Next to Sullivan, Karen Horney (1937, 1939, 1942, 1945, 1950) has probably been most influential. Like Sullivan, she did not find libido formulations very enlightening. As a consequence, she began to look at culture, especially as it is expressed through such primary transmission agents as the family and the school. It became her conviction that neurosis is, in essence, learned. Although her writings do not give us the details of *how* this learning takes place, nor do they tell us very much about the actual operations of therapy, they do provide illuminating discussions of how neurotic needs disrupt relationships. Her comments on competitiveness, for example, are strikingly accurate (Horney, 1936). Horney's list of dysfunctional needs and her suggestion that there are three basic interpersonal orientations—toward, against, and away from people—are among her most helpful contributions. A recent biography (Rubins, 1978) appropriately calls her a gentle rebel of psychiatry.

Erich Fromm (1941, 1947, 1955) and Erik Erikson (1950, 1968) have also had their impact on interpersonal theories, although neither can properly be called an interpersonal theorist. Fromm is really more of a societal analyst and Erikson is still, in actuality, a psychoanalyst. Nevertheless, Fromm said some important things about how society shapes character (which in turn conditions interpersonal behavior). People with "marketing orientations," for example, are not likely to be very good at intimacy. Erikson highlighted some crucially significant interpersonal issues and related them to development over the life span—to trust or not to trust, to assert or not to assert, and so on. Of most interest to us is Erikson's suggestion that persons in early adulthood face the psychosocial crisis called "intimacy versus isolation."

Turning for a moment or two to empirical lines of influence, Timothy Leary (1957; Leary & Coffey, 1955) took the ideas of the neo-Freudians and others and tried to operationalize them. Specifically, he constructed a circumplex model of social behavior built around two orthogonal axes, dominance-submission and love-hate, and he developed ways to map a person's interpersonal style onto the model. The Interpersonal Check List, which we will discuss later in this chapter, is an example of such a mapping device (LaForge & Suczek, 1955). Following Sullivan, Leary reasoned that mental health is positively correlated with the flexibility of a person's interpersonal behaviors, which tend to be reflexive instead of planned. Leary's work has stood up well to independent scrutiny (see, for example, Lorr, Bishop, & McNair, 1965; Lorr & McNair, 1963, 1965); his brilliant *Interpersonal Diagnosis of Personality* (1957) is still a widely read classic. The research it describes represented the first large-scale attempt to apply scientific rigor to the study of interpersonal relationships.

Several other researchers (e.g., Becker & Krug, 1964; Schaefer, 1965) also put forward models of interpersonal behavior (see Benjamin, 1974, for a brief historical review of these developments). By far the most scientifically rigorous and clinically astute model published to date is Lorna Benjamin's (1974, 1977, 1979) "Structural Analysis of Social Behavior." It is constructed around three axes: affiliation (love-hate), interdependence (high-low, with both dominance and submission representing high interdependence), and focus (self versus other). Since the clinical use of the Benjamin model is described elsewhere in this *Handbook*, we will not present an extended decription of it here. The reader may consult McLemore and Benjamin (1979) for a discussion of how this model, and others like it, relate to traditional psychiatric diagnosis.

Another highly influential publication was Robert Carson's (1969) *Interaction Concepts of Personality*, in which Carson demonstrated the clinical and empirical utility of systematic social behavioral concepts. Using a four-quadrant version of the Leary circle, he applied interpersonal concepts to such traditional areas of social psychology as bargaining and negotiation, and to such clinical activities as verbal psychotherapy. Carson's book remains the best, rigorous, yet readable, survey of the interpersonal point of view.

Still another empirical tradition that informs our clinical approach is the research on self-disclosure (Jourard, 1971). We are not entirely comfortable with the methodologies undergirding much of this work, and we debate the ways self-disclosure is sometimes defined by investigators. It seems to us, for example, that the most important self-disclosures have to do with a person's *immediate* affective-cognitive responses, or with closely held emotional secrets, not with "factual" data, however embarrassing (e.g., a man's "income" last year or a woman's "sexual history"). Nonethelesss, the self-disclosure literature has drawn attention to a very important kind of interpersonal behavior, one that is directly related to intimacy (see Hillix, Harari, & Mohr, 1979).

Transactional analysis, to the extent that it has catalogued scripts and games, has provided interpersonally oriented therapists with valuable understandings of the highly programmed ways that people prevent or destroy intimacy. Eric Berne's (1964) *Games People Play* is still worth reading, as are his other books (e.g., Berne, 1961, 1963). Although we do not find transactional analysis techniques completely satisfying—they seem at times either too superficial, too cognitive, or both—it is our opinion that careful study of the patterned social disruptions elucidated by transactional analysts is indispensable for the interpersonal therapist.

In our development of the procedure we call The Disclosure, we have also been influenced by Gestalt therapy (Perls, 1947, 1969; Perls, Hefferline, & Goodman, 1951). We especially appreciate the Gestalt emphasis on owning feelings and on how repressed or retroflected emotions often express themselves somatically. This last observation, of course, is closely related to the watershed insights of Wilhelm Reich (1949). The Gestalt emphasis on emotional expression has been continued, perhaps with good effect, in such nontraditional treatments as Primal Therapy (Janov, 1970; Janov's *Primal Scream*, while it includes some ambitious clinical claims, is also worth reading). We also value the use of dialogues in Gestalt therapy. Gestalt practitioners commonly have their patients engage in conversations with important others. These others, however, are present only in fantasy. Among the benefits of such conversation is the laying bare of introjected irrationalities, the same sorts of irrationalities that rational-emotive therapists try to combat.

Finally, we have already mentioned Paul Wachtel's (1977) work. His *Psychoanalysis and Behavior Therapy* is an incredibly cogent discussion of therapeutic method. He has successfully shown, and with considerable flair and documentation, what many of us have always believed: the intelligent clinician need not choose between the two schools. Finding one's way in clinical practice is not an election in which the various therapies are rival candidates. Quality clinical service demands that the practitioner find and use the particular procedure (from whatever school) that will best help this particular client, with this particular problem, in this particular setting, under these particular circumstances. Understanding (insight) *and* action (behavioral prescriptions such as Sullivan's "homework") have value.

There have been other academic and applied contributions to the development of relational therapy and the disclosure procedure. Our theological beliefs (Judaeo-Christian) have, no doubt, encouraged our individual valuations of intimacy and self-revelation, and our view of the human person as fundamentally relational. We do not, however, have space to go into all that here.

WHAT'S NEW IN RELATIONAL PSYCHOTHERAPY?

It seems that nearly every therapist has a new brand of therapy to sell under a new label (sometimes only the label is new). We must ask if we are saying anything innovative.

Much of what we do with clients is traditional. Many therapists (notably Sullivanians) cultivate intimacy, and many therapists draw from the clinical and empirical sources we have outlined above. We do believe, however, that we have extended some of these prior contributions, especially with our disclosure-confirmation procedure.

On the basis of over 50 cases, spread over nearly a decade, it is our conviction that when the patient and significant others are properly prepared for it, and when the interview is well conducted, The Disclosure can be richly therapeutic. If, as Confucius suggested, one picture is worth a thousand words, perhaps one face-to-face disclosure session is worth many sessions of talking *about* disclosure. Even Gestalt (fantasy) dialogues are often a quantum leap up from the patient telling the therapist what he or she would *like* to tell so and so. The Disclosure is a quantum leap up from this. The focal point of relational therapy is to get the patient, at the appropriate time and in an appropriate manner, to inform his or her significant other(s) of what the patient thinks and feels about some private "something." This is done with the therapist present to ensure clear communication, to encourage benevolence, and to prevent the patient from getting stuck or diverted. If the significant other(s) is no longer alive or is unavailable, fantasy work is, of course, the method of choice. Until intimacy is established with one's significant other(s), at least mentally, intimacy in other relationships will be hindered by unresolved introjected material.

Encounter groups, of course, have been geared toward the cultivation of interpersonal closeness, but like Gestalt therapy, they fail to bring the client face to face with actual significant others and, therefore, with the strong feelings that attend disclosing to them. Many Sullivanian therapists, despite Sullivan's early emphasis on milieu treatment, also underemphasize the need to bring patients face to face with the objects of their introjects or personifications, even though Sullivan seemed to believe that any two people could "collaborate together in real intimacy" if the motivation was present (Sullivan, 1956, p. 104). Even very disturbed clients can profit substantially from such confrontation. O. Hobart Mowrer (1964) has urged people to tell their secrets, but to our knowledge he makes no routine systematic effort, after working with the client to facilitate intimacy skills, to get significant others together in the consulting office. Like the encounter tradition, Mowrer's methods rely heavily on groups.

Family therapists have, for years, encouraged clinicians to bring significant others into the treatment office. Their emphasis most typically seems to be either on diagnosis or on change in the family system (see Harper, 1975, p. 1). Our emphasis, by contrast, is simply on self-disclosure, by the client, for the client. In relational therapy, we ordinarily make no attempt to involve significant others in ongoing therapy. Although Framo primarily treats couples, of all the family therapists his work seems most similar to ours. We especially like the subtitle of his insightful 1976 paper, "You Can and Should Go Home Again."

Many people carry around strong feelings having to do with others such as parents. These feelings are closely associated with introjects (personifications). Rarely will a client spontaneously reveal these deep feelings to the very people the feelings concern. In fact, people often go to great lengths to avoid such disclosures, as mentioned above. Talking to a therapist *about* significant others, but never facing them and the feelings that come with this, sometimes just perpetuates the avoidance. Getting clients and significant others together simply to "observe their interactions" may be similarly inefficacious. For the session to be most conducive to the development of intimacy in the client's life, the client must be ready and willing to carry out a *planned agenda*. This agenda is for him or her to walk through what feels like the Valley of the Shadow—to tell the other(s) that which is hardest to tell (whatever it is). The most difficult material is almost always central to the pathology. "I'm afraid of you, Dad." "I always felt you loved my sister more." "I'm a homosexual." These are the sorts of things that must be said. It is the therapist's job to find out, with the client, what these things are in each case.

CLINICAL ASSESSMENT

We have said that the focal point of relational psychotherapy is intimate disclosure to significant others. This assertion needs qualification. First, the often used phrase "here and now" should not be said as if it were hyphenated, i.e., what is "now" (present in the patient's psyche) may not be "here" (present in the patient's immediate environment). One's most significant interactions may have occurred long ago, with persons no longer living or at least no longer accessible (e.g., senility). In such instances, the therapist must be content to work directly with the patient's introjects, both through fantasy methods and through careful scrutiny of the therapeutic relationship (re: transference, in psychoanalytic terms, and parataxic distortions in interpersonal psychiatry terms). Second, although the focal point—the therapeutic crisis—may be one or more disclosure meetings with significant others, it is useful to remind ourselves that such meetings (and most of the rest of therapy) stand in the service of facilitating *intimacy*. The Disclosure is essentially a tool, a "technique," intended to assist in this more general effort. Third, work with significant others from the past is intended primarily to alter the nature of the client's relationships in the present. Many times, as we have noted, significant others "then" continue to be significant others "now," but introjected material is only addressed insofar as it creates present intrapsychic distress. Since maladaptive social behavior (often fueled by introjects) leads to aversive consequences, our interest in intrapsychic content usually takes on a behavioral slant. Finally, since the ultimate concern of therapy is with the client's ongoing relationships, it is important for the therapist to have accurate information about exactly *how* the client relates to *whom*. Wachtel (1977, p. 70) points to the need for systematic analysis of the patient's interpersonal behaviors.

In *The Psychiatric Interview*, Sullivan (1954) stressed the importance of keen observations during the treatment hour, including the need for the therapist to attend carefully to what the patient says, and how he or she says it. He also highlighted the importance of taking a careful interpersonal history. We agree. It should be noted, however, that history taking need not be an excessively formal affair. As Sullivan suggested, it can be done smoothly and often unobtrusively. In recent years, several new methods have been put into the hands of the clinician. Collectively they hold great promise, particularly in our efforts to get *beyond* the therapeutic transaction to understand the patient in his or her ordinary interpersonal environment or network. Mental health may consist largely of the ability to keep from becoming enmeshed in various forms of interpersonal chess, with its moves, countermoves, gambits, and strategies. As a treatment specialist, one wants to know how much of which kinds of chess the patient plays, and with whom. These assessment methods go a long way toward telling us.

We are currently in the process of putting together a standard interpersonal assessment battery. Taking a good history is, as we said, a crucial part of any such battery, as is a careful charting of the therapist's impressions of the patient's intimacy-avoidance patterns. Impressionistic notes, of course, go into the client's clinical file. Over the years we have used a variety of aids to the gathering of anamnestic data, such as biographical information forms and Sullivanian style chronology sheets that allow the patient to list ages along the left margin and corresponding events (people, places, etc.) to the right of these. The more systematic indices of relationships we have used, or are exploring, are these:

1. *Structural Analysis of Social Behavior (SASB)*. We have already mentioned Benjamin's (1974) model of social behavior. In our judgment, the SASB has a great deal of clinical potential, owing to the logic of its construction, the empirical evidence supporting this logic, the flexibility and precision of the model, and our own experience in using it with clients and in research. Since another chapter in this book treats the SASB in detail, our comments will be brief. When the questionnaires from an SASB interpersonal history are computer analyzed, the results include "maps" (diagrams) of and interpretive narrative for a fair number of clinically significant relationships (e.g., patient's relationship to mother and to father as a child; mother and father's relationship to each other; patient's relationship to a significant other such as a spouse).

2. *Interpersonal Check List (ICL)*. The ten-minute checklist (LaForge & Suczek, 1955) used to map self and other ratings onto the Leary circle (see above) is easy to use and often clinically revealing. An advantage of this checklist is its ease of administration, which makes it relatively easy to get ratings of the client by others. On the other hand, the checklist may not pick up the nuances of relationships grounded in the giving and taking of autonomy (see McLemore & Benjamin, 1979, p. 22, for details).

3. *Impact Message Inventory (IMI)*. Kiesler and his colleagues (Kiesler, Anchin, Per-

kins, Chirico, Kyle, & Federman, 1975, 1976; Perkins, Kiesler, Anchin, Chirico, Kyle, & Federman, 1979) have developed a 90-item, self-report inventory keyed to a conceptual framework (Kiesler, 1973, 1979; Kiesler, Bernstein, & Anchin, 1976) similar to Leary's (1957) and Lorr and McNair's (1963). The IMI indexes the affective, behavioral, and cognitive reactions of one individual to another with whom he or she has just interacted. Results include scores on fifteen subscales, each empirically anchored to one of the interpersonal catagories used by Lorr and McNair in their Interpersonal Behavior Inventory. The IMI allows the psychotherapist and/or researcher to obtain systematic, clinically useful information about the patient's "social stimulus value" based on *specific interpersonal behavior samples*. For example, the IMI may be completed (in response to the patient) by the therapist, a clinical assistant, or significant others.

4. *Inventory of Interpersonal Problems (IIP)*. Leonard Horowitz (1979) has done what many of us have thought about doing for years and, in the process, has filled a critical gap in the assessment of interpersonal behavior. He has developed an efficient way for patients to indicate what they perceive to be their principal interpersonal difficulties. They simply read through a list of potential problems and select the ones that apply.

5. *Fundamental Interpersonal Relationship Orientation (FIRO-B)*. Like the Leary checklist, the FIRO-B (Schutz, 1960) can be administered in about ten minutes. It gives a number of scores, including expressed and wanted affection, control, and inclusion. How these scores relate to those of other interpersonal measures, such as the SASB and the ICL, is still uncertain. Stated differently, we are not yet entirely clear about what the FIRO-B indexes.

6. *Self-Monitoring of Expressive Behavior (SMEB) Scale*. For his doctoral dissertation at Stanford, Mark Snyder (1974) constructed and validated a scale that seems to measure the extent to which persons control their social expressions in response to environmental circumstance. Such expressive control is probably closely related to what a lot of people refer to as social skill. Surely a certain amount of self-modulation is desirable (none would be autistic), but beyond some unknown point expressive self-control is probably dysfunctional (it my help sell used cars, but it prevents intimacy). Even in view of these ambiguities, the SMEB scale seems worth further exploration. See Briggs, Cheek, and Buss (1980) for a recent critique.

7. *Interpersonal Inkblots (IIB)*. To mention inkblots to some psychologists it to wave a cape before bulls. Nevertheless, it is difficult to discount totally a technique that has received so much clinical attention over the span of so many years. The Rorschach has intrigued practitioners with its alleged potential to reveal "deep character structure," and most of us have had the experience of obtaining floridly bizarre inkblot protocols from persons who seem pretty normal on interview (and on the MMPI!). What such apparent discrepancies mean, of course, is a moot issue. Despite such controversy, it seems worthwhile to attempt to measure the patient's preconscious or unconscious interpersonal percepts. Leary (1957) attempted such measurement with a modified form of the TAT. To this end, we have begun to experiment with 20 blots that strongly "pull" perceptions of people, and we have developed a standardized mode of administration and scoring.[3] Given the attention Rorschachers pay to M (human movement) responses, our assessment device may be worth continued exploration. Our observations to date support such a conclusion. Skeptical readers may do well to recall Paul Meehl's (1972) comment about *his* skepticism toward any psychologist who could not get excited about both factor analysis and psychoanalysis.

STAGES OF RELATIONAL PSYCHOTHERAPY

Successful relational therapy seems, more or less, to follow a pattern. Before outlining this pattern, we would like to comment on the "foci" of therapy. The patient typically comes in demoralized (Frank, 1961) and preoccupied with his or her troubles. The therapist, by listening carefully, can usually determine something of the nature of the patient's internal conversations (introjective communications) and interpersonal relationships. As the therapist begins to reflect these determinations back to the client, the latter begins to focus more and more on his or her relationships and, eventually, on how these relate to prior relationships (via introjected content). This comprises the bulk of therapy and takes the most time. It is during this stage of therapy that disclosure sessions, if any, occur. Finally, the client begins to examine the quality of his or her relationship with the therapist.

Such scrutiny requires courage and a sense of confidence in the solidity of the therapeutic alliance. Although the relational therapist desires and encourages the patient's focus on the therapy relationship at the proper time, extended analysis of the transference does not consitute the core of the treatment.[4] This is because the therapist's behaviors are only a small sample of all possible interpersonal behaviors, which may or may not resemble the behaviors of, say, parents. It is well established that even passive therapists "shape" their clients' behaviors. We believe it is unrealistic to assume that the patient's "dispositions" are so strong as to be unaffected by "situations" (see Mischel, 1973). It is also because our focus in relational therapy is pragmatic. We want to improve the patient's interpersonal relationships as quickly as possible. Long-term transference work seems to us both inefficient and, for most people, an unnecessary luxury. Let us now outline the stages of relational therapy as we conceptualize them.

Stage I. Inquiry

During the first few sessions, the therapist gathers information about the client and his or her presenting problems (see Sullivan, 1954). The client, at the same time, evaluates the therapist on dimensions like trustworthiness, stability, competence, and similarity of basic values. Through these first sessions, the therapist usually asks a lot of questions. We should point out that asking questions in such a way as to open up rather than shut down a client is among the most difficult clinical skills to master (see Bugental, 1966). The assessment battery is usually given in Stage I.

Stage II. Stabilization

For therapy to succeed, therapist and client must "hit their stride" together. They have to establish a rhythm into which both can settle for the purpose of joint exploration of the client's life, and in particular the client's feelings. For most clients, triadic reflection (Truax & Carkhuff, 1967) by the therapist works well. It is usually important for the patient to take the lead in this stage as early as possible. Emotional immersion (see Bugental, 1966) is primary. The therapist only rarely asks questions.

Stage III. Assimilation

By the time the treatment relationship has stabilized, the client is beginning to pay more attention to mental representations of significant others. The existence of powerful introjects, or personifications, is becoming apparent (see Schafer, 1968). At this juncture in therapy, the client is taught to free associate, using Sullivan's (1954) almost offhand question, "What comes to mind when you think of . . . ?" The client may also be encouraged to talk aloud to significant others, in the mode of Gestalt dialogues (Perls, 1969). When this is done, as with free association, the therapist introduces the idea as smoothly as possible, without fanfare. Decades ago, Perls (1947) pointed to the importance of assimilating introjects. Borrowing from certain psychoanalytic formulations, he noted the "undigested" quality of introjected psychic content. The people who have come to populate our psyches as personifications are more often than not almost separate or dissociated parts of us. They remain, as it were, undisturbed, though they may greatly disturb us. Introjects are very nearly ego-alien without our recognizing them as such. Good psychotherapy brings the person face to face with his or her mental inhabitants. It helps the person accept those aspects of an introject that he or she deems desirable and reject the rest. Coming to terms with one's introjects provokes much anxiety. Living through this anxiety is at the crux of the therapeutic process.

Stage IV. Confrontation

Once the patient has encountered his or her introjects in the consulting room, which often takes many sessions of hard and upsetting work, it is usually helpful to extend the encounter(s) to ongoing relationships. If the client's parents are still living, we sometimes suggest that they be brought in. In some cases, the significant other may be a girlfriend or a boyfriend. Occasionally it is a teacher, a sibling, an employer, or a spouse, which brings up the issue of marital therapy.

It seems well established that when there is marital trouble, both spouses should be treated (Bergin & Lambert, 1978). At the same time, a lot of what gets passed off as marriage therapy consists of little more than people rehearsing in front of the therapist for a fee the same destructive script they play out for free at home without a professional audience. Allowing this to go on for long is probably damaging, insofar as the presence of the therapist seems only to exacerbate the drive for self-justification. Because so much marital work involves, in our experience, the breaking of a symbiosis—each spouse needs to take responsibility for his or her own happiness—it seems advisable for each of the two to have an individual therapist (in addition to conjoint sessions).

We use The Disclosure in the confrontation stage of therapy. Aside from whether or not significant others are brought in, it is also the time for patient and therapist to examine *their* relationship carefully. How close are they? What has each done that has helped or hindered intimacy? What can each do to help now? This is the time for concentrated scrutiny of the transference and, after this, for the therapist to reveal a little more about his or her life. It is the time to make the client a peer, as much as possible—to make sure he or she is *not* one down (see Haley, 1963).

Stage V. Transition

Bearing in mind Sullivan's (1954) wise advice that a therapist stick to the business of being an expert, it is our desire that clients continue their relationship with us after they stop coming for regular sessions. It seems best for patients to regard us as experts whom they may consult at any point in their lives. They are told that they can come and go in therapy as they please, which tends to get rid of the notion that at some undefined point we will give them a graduation certificate or an imprimatur of mental health. Consequently, we do not speak of termination but of discontinuance of regular visits. The idea is for the client gradually to taper off, to reduce the freqeuncy of sessions over time. If we have not heard from a client in six months, we ordinarily make a follow-up phone call to find out how things are going. We also intend to accomplish during the transition stage a careful analysis of the degree to which the patient's original goals have been reached.

THE DISCLOSURE

We will now discuss the method of bringing the client's significant others into the consulting room which, if it is to happen, ordinarily takes place during the confrontation stage of therapy. Let us note, in passing, that what we have described as the pattern of treatment is not invariant. Sometimes, for example, disclosure meetings are conducted long before the assimilation stage is completed. The nature of disclosure sessions is probably best communicated through brief case histories and, to this end, we present some below. At this point we want to discuss some of the clinical details that the relational therapist must attend to in using the disclosure procedure.

It usually takes a couple of hours to do a disclosure, since the client may need quite a bit of time to get everything said, and it is important to allow time for "processing." Because of the intensity that often attends such work, most clients and their significant others do not tolerate longer sessions very well. The client will almost always be ambivalent and approach the meeting with a certain dread, mixed with anticipation, but it is imperative that he or she *want* to do it. This implies that the client should perceive the session as his or her choice and responsibility. Along with this, the client should have a clear idea of the sorts of things he or she intends to say in the meeting (the actual content of the session, for example how far the client will go, is always determined in the moment, but the "ideal" should be explicit to client and therapist). The therapist, in preparation, encourages the client to verbalize the disclosures as early in the meeting as possible, within the limits of anxiety tolerance. Clients are further coached in how to say what is to be said. Statements need to be direct but nonaccusatory. Significant others should be told, in preparation, that the meeting is intended to gain further understanding of the *client* in order to facilitate therapy, and to give the client a chance to share some personal information. These things are customarily communicated by the client.

During the meeting the therapist makes every effort to ensure that no one is devastated or, to use Whitaker's (1976) phrase, that everyone's dignity be preserved. At the start of the session, the therapist gives a short introduction to the process and, as prearranged, turns the floor over to the patient. In this introduction, which is positive and affirming, their value to the healing task is indicated to the significant others, as is the intrinsic value of simple self-disclosure, which the client will now do. We have found that this communication of value to the visitor(s), in a warm and friendly way, noticeably decreases their anxiety over what is to come.

The success of the disclosure session obviously hinges to some extent on the benevolence and openness of the significant others. Bacon knew what he was talking about when he said that "knowledge is power." Others *can* abuse the patient's self-disclosures, his or her vulnerability. This, together with the possibility that the client will panic over feeling exposed, are the major risks. We have found that if the therapist takes the trouble to preserve participants' dignity, people rarely victimize the client. In instances when the material to be communicated is likely to have high threat value for the visitor(s), it is a good idea to include a second therapist in the session. This therapist can be an ally to the client's significant other(s) during awkward moments. Returning to the issue of power,

The Disclosure allows the patient to give up one kind of power for another. He or she must surrender the power that seems to come from secrecy, avoidance, and careful image management. Such power is, of course, largely illusory. While it may ward off embarrassment or censure, it prevents real intimacy. Karen Horney long ago pointed out how people who present an idealized self to others do not—indeed cannot—feel loved, since such love as others bestow must be discounted—it is, alas, not love of the real person but of a facade. The power that the patient stands to gain is the inner strength that comes from the abolition of fear. By actively telling others what the client most dreads they might find out, the sting of exposure is reduced if not removed. The Disclosure, as it were, is one grand exercise in desensitization.

What are the contraindications to The Disclosure? This is difficult to answer, since we are not sure that we know of any. If the patient or the significant others are psychotic or borderline psychotic, perhaps the method would be harmful, but we have seen positive effects even in such cases. The crucial considerations seem to be the adequate preparation of the client for the meeting, not using the procedure prematurely in treatment, and the skill of the therapist. What, then, is required of the therapist? We will discuss this with a view toward the entire process of therapy.

The therapist needs to be capable of the behaviors represented in the Rogerian triad (Truax & Carkhuff, 1967): nonpossessive warmth, accurate empathy, and authenticity or genuineness. Interpersonal flexibility, the ability to behave in a wide variety of ways, is also important (see Carson, 1969). A certain comfort with strong emotion (Janov, 1970) and skill at facilitating the experiencing of emotion in clients (Perls, 1969) seem conducive to effective therapy, but we take caution from the finding that "intense" therapists can do damage (Bergin & Lambert, 1978). Related to this skill seems to be a certain clinical subtlety, the talent to rachet up, step by step, the *client's* emotional involvements (see Wachtel's comments on treating obsessives, 1977, pp. 258, 259). We are also of the opinion that therapists need the kind of general clinical savvy that comes only through a good psychiatric-psychological education. This includes a knowledge of psychodynamics and a solid sense of diagnosis and prognosis, and it probably reflects itself partly in the therapist's interpretive acumen. Familiarity with behavioral methods (Goldfried & Davison, 1976), and the pragmatic realism that prompts one to use them appropriately, is also important, as is the courage to speak candidly but tactfully to clients when necessary. And, the therapist must be able to self-disclose *to* the client at the right moments, but in a way that keeps the focus of therapeutic concern on the client (disclosures must be succinct). Finally, as has been said by many other therapists, it is important to offer realistic hope to the patient, to generate a sense of confidence in therapy, in the therapist, and most of all, in the client. Perusal of this long but incomplete list of therapist qualifications reveals why we believe it is unwise and naively provincial to embrace a single school of treatment for all patients.

ILLUSTRATIVE CASES

Case reports of all sorts abound. We will use our limited case study space to demonstrate what we believe to be unique to our therapeutic approach. What follows are examples of the clinical use of The Disclosure.

1. After several months of therapy, John, a professional man in his twenties, met with his father, his therapist, and a clergyman. The client's presenting problem was an inability to make his peace with an occupational crisis. It became increasingly evident that what he

had trouble accepting was "failure," which in turn related to his father, whom he viewed as demanding and never satisfied. Through the medium of Gestalt dialogues, he began to stand up to his introjected father. When they would talk by phone, however, the paternal introject (with its demands) was revitalized. During The Disclosure, the client told his father, in an impressively loving way, of feeling that he was "a failure, never enough," etc. The father, who was a very successful member of the same highly verbal profession as his son, seemed to feel deep concern if not agony. When he became defensive, the clergyman, who was closer in age than the therapist to the father[5] and very skilled psychologically, assuaged the latter's anxieties, and the process continued. The session represented a significant breakthrough, both for John and for their father-son relationship.

2. Paul, a man in his early forties, brought in his mother. He told her of feeling displaced by his younger sister as a child, and of his memories of his mother beating him with a belt. As they talked, he recalled that they had had a rift over an ideological issue, at which point he had "pushed her away." They then continued to share memories of his childhood, of his "sitting on the kitchen sink swinging [his] feet," etc. He abruptly stopped talking and, with moist eyes, said, "I don't think you ever did beat me with a belt. I must have filled that in because of my other feelings." The session ended years of distance between them. They left embracing, their first authentic closeness in years.

3. Shelly, a woman in her twenties, came for therapy because of a longstanding melodramatic fantasy life which she sensed was "not healthy." In the course of therapy, she indicated a desire to get closer to her father, who, like her, was emotionally reserved and socially hesitant. During The Disclosure, she told her parents of her fantasies, which were radically different from her actual life. Her ongoing fantasy life, which extended back for many years, reflected continuity of plot and complete character development, and it included scenes of romantic suicides, motorcycle gang involvements, sexual acting out, and "Patty Hearst episodes." Telling these things to her parents was difficult and embarrassing, especially because she had given them no prior information about her fantasies. Under the gentle reassurance of the therapist, all three left feeling very good about the meeting, which brought them noticeably closer.

4. Robin, a woman in her forties, was raised in a cold, harsh family atmosphere in which work and thrift were dominant values. She was urged to bring her parents in but elected not to, stating that they would resist. She also indicated that she did not feel ready for such an emotionally taxing encounter. Because the client's mother was dying of metastasized cancer, the therapist suggested that she do what she could to open lines of communication with her. In steps, the client began to write letters, then to phone, and then to make regular visits to see her mother. She is still in the process of getting closer to both parents, and the results so far are very encouraging. We hope to see her and her parents in the office soon.

5. Randy, a man in his thirties, came to therapy for a number of reasons, including an unsuccessful relationship with a woman he had hoped to marry. When the therapist suggested that he bring her in if she were willing, the client turned white and said with dread in his voice, "I don't think I'm ready for that!" The therapist did not press the issue, but did remark matter of factly on the client's discomfort in the face of confronting the woman. We cite this case to show that the significant other is not always a parent. This and the last case also demonstrate that clients are not routinely eager to undertake The Disclosure. In any event, it is the therapist's job to bring the client to the brink of this decision. Even an unwilling client may profit from realizing the "terror" summoned up by the possibility of self-disclosure to certain others.

6. Helen's session with her parents was unexpected, since they lived 3,000 miles away. She had been separated from her husband, but when a rift occurred between her and her best friend, she panicked and went home to him. He too panicked, fearing that he was going to be burdened with a suicidal wife while he was emotionally preparing for a divorce. He called her parents for help. Their immediate flight to the West Coast in itself communicated more concern to Helen than she believed they had for her, but Helen still felt that she would not know what to say to them when they arrived. By the time the three came in, they had already discussed how Helen's mother had always intervened between the children and their father which, she explained, was "to protect everyone from each other." During the session, with the help of two parents who were also willing to be very vulnerable, Helen was able to reveal her feeling that her mother was never real and genuine with her. The mother, in turn, said she had always feared that Helen was too fragile for honest, open communication. The lasting effect of the session was that all three felt they "were a family again" and that Helen felt she now had strong emotional support from formerly alienated parents.

EMPIRICAL CONSIDERATIONS

Since this is a handbook of interpersonal therapies and not a research manual, we will mention here only general directions for empirical investigation. Those lines of research that promise to yield concrete clinical applications are highlighted.

1. We have mentioned that no single approach to treatment is likely to be optimal for all clients. People are just too complex and multifaceted for one mode of psychotherapy to be ubiquitously ideal. Relational therapy, as we have shown, is designed to increase *intimacy*. As part of the treatment process, we work toward the assimilation of introjects, the extinction of fear, and the clear representation of feelings in both the patient's consciousness and communicative behaviors. The principal empirical question to be answered has to do with the effective range of intimacy training. How broad-spectrumed is our treatment? How helpful is it for particular categories of problems? For what clients, with what difficulties, is relational therapy the treatment of choice? Are the benefits of relational therapy more, or less, permanent than those of other treatments?

2. A related question has to do with the adequacy of the various social behavior models (e.g., Benjamin, 1974) for understanding and predicting human affairs. This question relates directly to psychodiagnosis and, by implication, to prognosis and the specification of treatments, since a robust diagnostic system generates both prognostications and prescriptions. Leary (1957) and McLemore and Benjamin (1979) have attempted to demonstrate the value of interpersonal diagnosis, and preliminary results (e.g., Cerling, 1979) are encouraging. Lorna Benjamin is currently administering a large funded research project intended to explore in detail the value of social diagnosis.

3. There is currently a welcomed shift in psychotherapy research away from simple outcome studies toward the careful study of process. What exactly goes on *in* therapy that facilitates client improvement? On the assumption that intimacy training is as helpful as we think it is, what are its "active ingredients" (and in what "proportions," i.e., how should they be weighted)? What therapist behaviors most promote healthy interpersonal closeness in the patient's life?

4. Following Leary (1957), we have said that a great deal of social behavior is reflexive, that is, automatic rather than planned. This is not to deny the operation of general

plans and strategies (see Carson, 1969) but simply to argue that moment-to-moment interpersonal responses are not under all that much cognitive control. Quite aside from "techniques," are certain *therapists* more effective with certain clients in augmenting intimacy? If so, can we learn to match the right therapist with the right patient?

5. Is it possible to formalize intimacy training? Can we devise self-contained training modules that would require little or no direct clinician time? How far would such modules go in accomplishing what our relational therapy seems to accomplish? A variety of relevant programs already exist, and the Marriage Encounter movement—which many people claim is of significant value—is an example of what can be done without formal therapy. How about lay therapists?

6. How can we best train relational therapists? Given the obvious similarities between relational psychotherapy and traditional Sullivanian approaches, teachers at such highly respected training centers as the William Alanson White Institute may have the most to offer in answering this question. We are, however, relatively certain that the intimacy skills of a patient in therapy will rarely advance beyond the level of the therapist's intimacy skills. The effective conduct of relational therapy cannot, we are sure, be taught in any other way than through *intimate interpersonal experience* itself, supplemented by appropriate clinical instruction.

SUMMARY

We have described an approach to psychotherapy that centers around the cultivation of intimacy in the patient's life. Often catalytic to such cultivation is the bringing together, under the therapist's guidance, of the client and one or more significant others, for purposes of The Disclosure. The procedure entails the client simply sharing with these others one or more bits of personal, previously undisclosed information. Early in this chapter we enumerated a number of theoretical assumptions upon which our methods are based. The theoretical roots of relational psychotherapy include the work of the neo-Freudians—most notably Harry Stack Sullivan, the contributions of other schools such as Gestalt therapy and transactional analysis, the writings of such pioneers of the interpersonal point of view as Robert Carson and Timothy Leary, the literature on self-disclosure, and the recent theoretical statements of Paul Wachtel. We have also considered, in separate sections, the need for an interpersonal assessment battery and the stages through which relational therapy seems ordinarily to progress. To flesh out our theoretical description of The Disclosure, we cited several short case histories. We ended the chapter with some suggestions for empirical research.

There is more we would like to say but the space limitations of a single chapter prevent further exposition at this time. We will have to be content with an outline of the essence of what we believe to be a method of psychotherapy that is both clinically and empirically informed.

NOTES

1. In *Clinical Studies in Psychiatry*, Sullivan (1956, p. 251) notes that "Americans [are] among the world's most insecure people so far as close approaches to intimacy are concerned."

2. It is worth noting that all the physiological research in the world will never, indeed could never, impart the *experience* of the subject(s) to the researcher(s).

3. Interested readers are invited to correspond with Clinton McLemore about these.

4. Jack Boghosian, one of our doctoral students, has written an excellent paper on transference from an interpersonal point of view, entitled "Transference and Interactionalism: A Convergence of Psychoanalytic and Interpersonal Perspectives." Copies are available.

5. As much as possible, when two therapists are involved in disclosure sessions, they should be similar to the client and significant other in their respective ages.

REFERENCES

Beck, A. T. *The diagnosis and management of depression*. Philadelphia: University of Pennsylvania Press, 1973.

Beck, A. T. *Cognitive therapy and the emotional disorders*. New York: International Universitities Press, 1976.

Becker, W. C. & Krug, R. S. A circumplex model for social behavior in children. *Child Development*, 1964, **34**, 371–396.

Benjamin, L. S. Structural analysis of social behavior. *Psychological Review*, 1974, **81**, 392–425.

Benjamin, L. S. Use of structural analysis of social behavior (SASB) and Markov chains to study dyadic interactions. *Journal of Abnormal Psychology*, 1979, **88**, 303–319.

Bergin, A. E. & Lambert, M. J. The evaluation of therapeutic outcomes. In S. L. Garfield & A. E. Bergin (Eds.), *Handbook of psychotherapy and behavior change: An empirical analysis*, 2nd ed. New York: Wiley, 1978.

Berne, E. *Transactional analysis in psychotherapy: A systematic individual and social psychiatry*. New York: Grove Press, 1961.

Berne, E. *The structure and dynamics of organizations and groups*. Philadelphia: Lippincott, 1963.

Berne, E. *Games people play: The psychology of human relationships*. New York: Grove Press, 1964.

Briggs, S. R., Cheek, J. M., & Buss, A. H. An analysis of the Self-Monitoring Scale. *Journal of Personality and Social Psychology*, 1980, **38**, 679–686.

Bugental, J. F. T. *Psychological interviewing*, rev. ed. Westwood, Calif.: Psychological Service Associates, 1966.

Carson, R. C. *Interaction concepts of personality*. Chicago: Aldine, 1969.

Cerling, D. C. Interpersonal dimensions of psychopathology. Unpublished doctoral dissertation, Fuller Theological Seminary, Graduate School of Psychology, 1979.

Chapman, A. H. *Textbook of clinical psychiatry: An interpersonal approach*, 2nd ed. Philadephia: Lippincott, 1976.

Chapman, A. H. *The treatment techniques of Harry Stack Sullivan*. New York: Brunner/Mazel, 1978.

Chrzanowski, G. *Interpersonal approach to psychoanalysis: Contemporary view of Harry Stack Sullivan*. New York: Gardner Press, 1977.

Ellis, A. *Reason and emotion in psychotherapy*. New York: Lyle Stuart, 1962.

Erikson, E. H. *Childhood and society*. New York: Norton, 1950.

Erikson, E. H. *Identity: Youth and crisis*. New York: Norton, 1968.

Framo, J. L. Family of origin as a therapeutic resource for adults in marital and family therapy: You can and should go home again. *Family Process*, 1976, **15**, 193–210.

Frank, J. D. *Persuasion and healing: A comparative study of psychotherapy*. Baltimore: Johns Hopkins University Press, 1961.

Fromm, E. *Escape from freedom*. New York: Farrar & Rinehart, 1941.

Fromm, E. *Man for himself*. Rinehart, 1947.

Fromm, E. *The sane society*. New York: Rinehart, 1955.

Goldfried, M. R. & Davison, G. C. *Clinical behavior therapy*. New York: Holt, Rinehart & Winston, 1976.

Haley, J. *Strategies of psychotherapy*. New York: Grune & Stratton, 1963.

Halleck, S. L. *The politics of therapy*. New York: Science House, 1971.

Harper, R. A. *The new psychotherapies*. Englewood Cliffs, N.J.: Prentice-Hall, 1975.

Hillix, W. A., Harari, H., & Mohr, D. A. Secrets. *Psychology Today*, 1979, **13** (4), 71–76.

Horney, K. Culture and neurosis. *American Sociological Review*, 1936, **1**, 221–230.

Horney, K. *The neurotic personality of our time*. New York: Norton, 1937.

Horney, K. *New ways in psychoanalysis*. New York: Norton, 1939.

Horney, K. *Self analysis*. New York: Norton, 1942.

Horney, K. *Our inner conflicts*. New York: Norton, 1945.

Horney, K. *Neurosis and human growth*. New York: Norton, 1950.

Horowitz, L. M. On the cognitive structure of interpersonal problems treated in psychotherapy. *Journal of Consulting and Clinical Psychology*, 1979, **47**, 5–15.

Janov, A. *The primal scream*. New York: Dell, 1970.

Jourard, S. M. *Self-disclosure: An experimental analysis of the transparent self*. New York: Wiley-Interscience, 1971.

Kiesler, D. J. *A communications approach to modification of the "obsessive personality:" An initial formulation*. Unpublished manuscript, Emory University, Atlanta, Georgia, 1973.

Kiesler, D. J. An interpersonal communication analysis of relationship in psychotherapy. *Psychiatry*, 1979, **42**, 299–311.

Kiesler, D. J., Anchin, J. C., Perkins, M. J., Chirico, B. M., Kyle, E. M., & Federman, E. J. *The Impact Message Inventory*. Richmond: Virginia Commonwealth University, 1975; 1976.

Kiesler, D. J., Bernstein, A. J., & Anchin, J. C. *Interpersonal communication, relationship and the behavior therapies*. Richmond: Virginia Commonwealth University, 1976.

Kvarnes, R. G. & Parloff, G. (Eds.) *A Harry Stack Sullivan case seminar: Treatment of a young male schizophrenic*. New York: Norton, 1976.

LaForge, R. & Suczek, R. The interpersonal dimension of personality: III. An interpersonal check list. *Journal of Personality*, 1955, **24**, 94–112.

Leary, T. *Interpersonal diagnosis of personality: A functional theory and methodology for personality evaluation*. New York: Ronald Press, 1957.

Leary, T. & Coffey, H. S. Interpersonal diagnosis: Some problems of methodology and validation. *Journal of Abnormal and Social Psychology*, 1955, **50**, 110–124.

London, P. *The modes and morals of psychotherapy*. New York: Holt, Rinehart & Winston, 1964.

Lorr, M., Bishop, P. F., & McNair, D. M. Interpersonal types among psychiatric patients. *Journal of Abnormal and Social Psychology*, 1965, **70**, 468–472.

Lorr, M. & McNair, D. M. An interpersonal behavior circle. *Journal of Abnormal and Social Psycholgy*, 1963, **67**, 68–75.

Lorr, M. & McNair, D. M. Expansion of the interpersonal behavior circle. *Journal of Personality and Social Psychology*, 1965, **2**, 823–830.

McLemore, C. W. & Benjamin, L. S. Whatever happened to interpersonal diagnosis?: A psychosocial alternative to DSM-III. *American Psychologist*, 1979, **34**, 17–34.

Meehl, P. E. Second-order relevance. *American Psychologist*, 1972, **27**, 932–940.

Mischel, W. Toward a cognitive social learning reconceptualization of personality. *Psychological Review*, 1973, **80**, 252–283.

Mowrer, O. H. *The new group therapy*. Princeton, N.J.: D. Van Nostrand, 1964.

Mullahy, P. *Oedipus: Myth and complex*. New York: Grove Press, 1948.

Mullahy, P. *Psychoanalysis and interpersonal psychiatry*. New York: Science House, 1970.

Patterson, C. H. *Relationship counseling and psychotherapy*. New York: Harper & Row, 1974.

Perkins, M. J., Kiesler, D. J., Anchin, J. C., Chirico, B. M., Kyle, E. M., & Federman, E. J. The Impact Message Inventory: A new measure of relationship in counseling/psychotherapy and other dyads. *Journal of Counseling Psychology*, 1979, **26**, 363–367.

Perls, F. S. *Ego, hunger and aggression: The beginning of Gestalt therapy*. New York: Random House, 1947.

Perls, F. S. *Gestalt therapy verbatim*. Lafayette, Calif.: Real People Press, 1969.

Perls, F. S., Hefferline, R. F., & Goodman, R. *Gestalt therapy: Excitement and growth in the human personality.* New York: Julian Press, 1951.

Reich, W. *Character-analysis.* New York: Farrar, Straus & Giroux, 1949.

Rubins, J. L. *Karen Horney: Gentle rebel of psychoanalysis.* New York: Dial Press, 1978.

Russell, B. *A history of western philosophy.* New York: Simon & Schuster, 1945.

Schaefer, E. S. A configurational analysis of children's reports of parent behavior. *Journal of Consulting Psychology,* 1965, **29**, 552–557.

Schafer, R. *Aspects of internalization.* New York: International Universities Press, 1968.

Schutz, W. C. *FIRO: A three-dimensional theory of interpersonal behavior.* New York: Holt, Rinehart & Winston, 1960.

Snyder, M. Self-monitoring of expressive behavior. *Journal of Personality and Social Psychology,* 1974, **30**, 526–537.

Sullivan, H. S. *Conceptions of modern psychiatry.* New York: Norton, 1940.

Sullivan, H. S. *The interpersonal theory of psychiatry.* New York: Norton, 1953.

Sullivan, H. S. *The psychiatric interview.* New York: Norton, 1954.

Sullivan, H. S. *Clinical studies in psychiatry.* New York: Norton, 1956.

Sullivan, H. S. *Schizophrenia as a human process.* New York: Norton, 1962.

Sullivan. H. S. *The fusion of psychiatry and social science.* New York: Norton, 1964.

Thompson, C. *Psychoanalysis: Evolution and development.* New York: Hermitage House, 1950.

Truax, C. B. & Carkhuff, R. R. *Toward effective counseling and psychotherapy: Training and practice.* Chicago: Aldine, 1967.

Wachtel, P. L. *Psychoanalysis and behavior therapy: Toward an integration.* New York: Basic Books, 1977.

Watzlawick, P. *How real is real?: Confusion, disinformation, communication.* New York: Random House, 1976.

Whitaker, C. A family is a four-dimensional relationship. In P. J. Guerin (Ed.), *Family therapy: Theory and practice.* New York: Gardner Press, 1976.

Witenberg, E. G. (Ed.) *Interpersonal explorations in psychoanalysis: New directions in theory and practice.* New York: Basic Books, 1973.

Chapter 13
A Brief, Strategic Interactional Approach to Psychotherapy
James C. Coyne and Lynn Segal

One of Harry Stack Sullivan's radical notions was that personality is most profitably viewed as the pattern of recurring situations that characterize a person's life, rather than as a collection of hypothetical entities interacting under the skin. This conceptualization seems to prescribe that the interpersonal field replace the isolated individual as the focus of study and treatment, but Sullivan himself never developed its full implications. He was probably more immersed in the Freudian tradition than is generally recognized, and in his time the technology of therapy was considerably less developed than it is today. "Sullivan had few potent options to consider in formulating the view that the therapist should essentially stick to uncovering and leave the rest to the patient" (Wachtel, 1977, p. 68).

Sullivan held to an essentially Freudian model of therapy, and believed in the virtue of minimal intervention. Yet, we who are free of the constraints he faced can take his emphasis on process and context as the point of departure for a very different interpersonal psychotherapy. Pursuing Sullivan's focus on evolving patterns of relationships rather than the patient's putative inner life, we can intervene directly to modify the contexts, complex feedback processes, and characteristic responses of others that maintain the patient's predicament.

Consistent with this, the Mental Research Institute group (Watzlawick, Weakland, & Fisch, 1974; Weakland, Fisch, Watzlawick, & Bodin, 1974) has developed a brief strategic approach to therapy, one that conceptualizes clinical problems as aspects of ongoing interpersonal systems. It is assumed in this approach that the client's distress and symptoms arise from the mismanagement of life transitions such as marriage or divorce or from the mishandling of everyday life difficulties. Severe symptomatology may merely reflect the exacerbation of initial difficulties by the repetition of reasonable but inappropriate problem-solving efforts of patients and those around them.

In the MRI approach, therapeutic interventions typically focus on the attempted solutions of patients and their significant others—what is being done to deal with their difficulties—rather than the difficulties themselves. The interventions involve deliberate attempts to prevent the occurrence of problem-maintaining behavior, typically by reframing or redefining problems so that the existing beliefs and values of involved persons can lead to very different behavior. The intent is to get them to act in relevant new ways through the use of homework, direct and indirect suggestion, and paradox. Therapeutic goals are typically small but definite changes in behavior that are intended to instigate change of a more generalized nature.

Although our ideas grew out of work with families, the basic theory and therapeutic techniques can be applied in any interpersonal context. It is our assumption that therapists are rarely in a position to disregard the relation of the clients to other people. Invariably, others are involved in clients' presenting problems as objects, helpers, opponents, or observers and commentators. Brief strategic therapy has been used with couples, families, friendships, work relationships, client-professional problems, and larger organizations. Working with single adults, brief therapists capitalize in novel ways on their salience in clients' interpersonal fields.

Watzlawick and Coyne (1980) have recently presented a case that takes to an extreme the MRI approach's emphasis on the interpersonal context of clinical problems. The identified patient, a 58-year-old man who was suffering from depression secondary to two strokes, attended none of the five sessions! Rather, his immediate family met in an attempt to modify their efforts to be helpful that had previously only seemed to make matters worse. The complete absence of the "patient" makes the case somewhat atypical, but it highlights the assumption that an interactional system approach does not require that all members of the system attend therapy sessions; appropriate changes in a subsystem (i.e., one or more significant persons) can bring about major changes in the entire system. It may be useful to describe this case further in order to illustrate other characteristic features of brief strategic therapy.

THERAPY IN THE ABSENCE OF THE PATIENT: A CLINICAL EXAMPLE

The identified patient had suffered his second stroke 12 months prior to therapy. After physical and speech therapies, he showed only a few residual deficits, but his neurologist called for a family interview when it appeared that a deepening depression had halted his recovery and even reversed earlier gains. The man was now spending up to 14 hours a day in bed, watching television, and seldom left the house except when pressured by his wife to walk around the block. In the interview, the entire family conceded that they seemed to aggravate his problems, despite the best of intentions. All agreed that therapy would be helpful, but the man indicated that he himself would not participate. With his permission, the remaining family members were referred for five sessions of therapy at the MRI Brief Therapy Project.

The first session of therapy was attended by the patient's wife and two sons. Responses to questions concerning the family's characteristic problem-solving efforts suggested a recurring interactional pattern. The man's wife and sons would encourage him to pull himself together, try harder, and to see his situation more optimistically. He in turn would respond with increased helplessness and displays of deficiency, to which the family responded with more optimism and encouragement. The family, and particularly the wife, had become increasingly demoralized by the failure of their best efforts. In desperation they sometimes resorted to coercion and harsh verbal attacks, and found themselves inadvertently stifling any signs from the patient of initiative and self-responsibility. They admitted setting the times he arose from and retired to bed, taking charge of his basic self-care and personal hygiene, and even impatiently finishing his sentences and answering for him.

While the interactional pattern was remarkably consistent, there were notable occasions when it broke down, and even when the man was "his old self" again. For instance, at one point, the wife mistakenly ingested sleeping medication instead of a tranquilizer.

The man found her lying half-conscious in their living room. He took a number of appropriate steps including summoning help, informing one of the sons by telephone, and attending to her needs until it was clear that she was out of danger. When the crisis passed, he sank back into his usual state of apathy and depression.

In raising the question of goals, the therapist was careful not to give the family any false hope about a sudden or dramatic change. Rather, he suggested that they focus on some small but noticeable change in his everyday activities, something that would indicate that he was resuming normal activities. It was stressed that the targeted change should be of a nature such that if it were to occur, it would indicate that there had been a significant change in the patient's general attitude. This particular framing of goals was chosen because the family had repeatedly spoken of the man's problem as being attitudinal in nature. Before becoming more specific, the therapist reviewed the family's efforts to help the patient. Even while praising the family's dedication, competency, and efficiency in attending to him, he noted how their "common-sensical" strategy had failed. The therapist recalled that the instances in which the patient had at least temporarily showed improvement were typically ones in which there was breakdown of the family's helpfulness or competency. He suggested that perhaps the family could deliberately stage such incidents. He then pessimistically mused, however, that the family was so exceptionally reasonable and motivated to be helpful that it would be too much to expect that they could behave so counterintuitively. They in turn repeatedly protested that they would and that they were committed to doing anything the therapist requested.

The therapist and the family collaborated in developing plans for situations in which the family members' usual competence could be suspended. For instance, it was decided that the wife should prepare an elaborate breakfast, but then fall asleep in the living room without calling her husband. She was then to apologize and indicate that she was overwhelmed. She was also to become less efficient in cleaning up the kitchen and attending to the patient's needs. She was to serve him pork roast, a meat he detested. She was then to apologize, explaining that she was having trouble making decisions about meals and that the meat seemed like a good choice because she served it so seldomly. The man responded to her efforts by beginning to get up in the morning without assistance, helping her with chores, and generally being more attentive to her. She reported that he was showing the most affection toward her that he had demonstrated since his second stroke.

At times, however, the woman showed signs of slipping into coercive strategies aimed at motivating the husband. She was particularly vulnerable to what she saw as displays of stubbornness by her husband. The therapist reframed this as the form in which pride is expressed when someone is depressed. He agreed with her that the patient was proud and stubborn, and suggested ways in which she could be helpful if she "encouraged him by discouraging him." For instance, rather than arguing with the patient when he attempted to go to bed early, she was urged to sympathize with him and offer to help him get to bed even earlier.

The man progressed well in the five weeks of therapy and took a number of initiatives. He began attending church again and having brunch at a restaurant afterward. He also reorganized his shop and began working in it, took his wife on a brief vacation, and bought a small boat with his sons. The course of this case illustrates a number of features of brief therapy that we will consider at greater length.

The Persistence of Clinical Problems

Traditional intrapsychic approaches to therapy have often made the assumption that if a person persists in a self-defeating pattern of behavior, then he or she must have an unconscious need to achieve these particular results. Family therapists have shifted the blame to other family members, hissing at them as villains and implicating the satisfaction of their unconscious needs in the persistence of the patient's problems. In contrast, brief strategic therapy does not make the assumption that someone must gain from disturbed behavior. It does assume, however, that even reasonable and well-motivated people can create unsatisfactory situations such that the very actions that seem necessary to remedy them actually *maintain* them. That is, people can create contexts where behavior that would usually be reasonable and adaptive leads to adverse outcomes. The failure of their efforts only convinces them that more of the same behavior is required and, further, that to deviate from this would make matters worse.

In conceptualizing the problems presented by their clients, brief strategic therapists are guided by the postulate that, from the framework of the persons involved, actions that serve to perpetuate the problems are meaningful problem-solving efforts and perhaps even the best that can be expected, given the circumstances. Operating with such a "principle of charity," one should always look very closely at apparently irrational behavior to see whether there is not some pattern there after all, and one can expect to find clues to this pattern in the interpersonal context.

Although there are many ways in which people take self-defeating actions to solve problems, five basic metapatterns of attempted solutions have been repeatedly observed in our clinical work (Fisch, Weakland, Watzlawick, Segal, Hoebel, & Deardoff, 1975).

1. Attempts to be spontaneous deliberately

This pattern is found in cases involving sleep disorders, sexual difficulties, substance abuse, and blocks to creative endeavors. It also occurs in a wide range of situations in which people attempt to force a particular emotional reaction in themselves when their appraisal of their circumstances is contrary to it. Despite folk wisdom that if one does not succeed at first, one should try again and harder, many desired results simply do not yield to such efforts. One cannot "will" an erection. Other desired results are exceedingly difficult or impossible to achieve except as byproducts of activities undertaken for other ends. One cannot force oneself to have a pleasurable experience socializing at a party unless at some point socializing becomes an end in itself.

It is assumed that most people will occasionally have difficulty with bodily functioning or performance, and feelings wax and wane. If such difficulties were seen as normal life difficulties which self-correct with time, all would be well. But once a person sets about deliberate correction, he risks getting caught in the paradoxical predicament of attempting to force spontaneous behavior. The patient-to-be may try to force himself to sleep, be potent, or cheer himself up and feel happy. When such methods as will power, reasoning, or positive thinking fail to bring about the desired response, more of the same is tried, setting the stage for a full-fledged problem. With each failure, the person becomes more convinced of the severity of the problem and the need to try harder.

2. Attempts to have others behave in a desired fashion even while requiring that they do so spontaneously

A woman who sought therapy after her son was apprehended for delinquent activities expressed her problem in this fashion: "I want Bobby to do things, but I want *him* to want to. He shouldn't follow orders blindly and not want to. I realize I am making a mistake, but I cannot pinpoint what I am doing wrong. I won't dictate to him, I want him to learn things on his own. Yet a boy his age can't be left on his own." Jean-Paul Sartre has discussed at length the basic human dilemma of wishing that others do as we desire while requiring that they act freely and spontaneously. Advice often has to be made between getting a specific response from others and getting a spontaneous response, particularly in matters of affection or authority. People, however, sometimes attempt to obtain both with unfortunate consequences. They then cannot clearly articulate their wants because it would interfere with the spontaneity of the other's responses. At that same time, they seek specific responses and become frustrated when they are not forthcoming. As such a situation develops, communication of needs must become muddled in order to protect spontaneity, and obtaining desired responses can become paradoxically undesirable because it indicates that spontaneity has been lost.

3. Seeking a non-risk method where some risk is inevitable

This self-defeating way of solving problems is frequently found in the areas of work and dating. It often arises when a person feels that further failures would be intolerable and that the next effort therefore has to be perfect. For instance, the shy single male may try to avoid the risks of rejection when attempting to make new female friends. He becomes so concerned with finding the perfect opening gambit that he never begins a conversation with someone of the opposite sex. Similarly, the salesman or the job seeker can both run into variations of this pattern in trying to make a perfect first impression. They plan out every move or statement in a way that does not allow for any variation in the response of others. Alternatively, they become so sensitive to the nuances of the other's response that it becomes uncomfortable for both. In either case they alienate the other person and convince themselves that they did not plan carefully enough or that they were not interpersonally sensitive enough, so that they redouble their efforts.

4. Attempting to reach accord through argument

There is a Monty Python sketch in which a man goes to a clinic where people pay to be in an argument. The experience, however, with which he is provided is not what he has expected. He becomes embroiled in disputes as to what the fees are, whether the argument has started, whether it has ended, and whether it is even an argument rather than a series of contradictions. Absurd as the sketch may be, it illustrates a common result when people attempt to resolve differences through argumentation: namely, they may find themselves fruitlessly exploring their lack of consensus concerning ground rules and relevant information. It is also common in such situations that one or all parties involved will shift their attention from content issues to how they might impress, win, or dominate. As many arguing spouses or parents and adolescents have discovered, winning an argument can become more important than resolving the issues involved. Furthermore, arguing parties can become co-opted so that reasonable or reconciliatory action come to represent defeat. In our clinical work, we have frequently found that adolescents will persist in delinquent activities when the only conceivable benefit is that they can thereby refute their parents' claims of authority and control. The parents in turn feel pushed to reestablish order with the enforcement of increasingly unreasonable rules, giving further impetus to the adolescents' delinquent activities. Coyne and Fabricatore (1979) have described the same pattern of escalation between prisoners and guards in a community corrections center.

The human potential movement stressed full discussion and sharing of one's feelings as a panacea for all human problems, and it paid little attention to the instances when this is an unproductive and even destructive approach. We can never say just one thing, and the ineffectiveness with which we communicate can amplify normal fluctuations in the closeness and comfort that accompany all relationships. When relationships are in transition, it is possible that the tensions arising from attempts to reach accord through argument can become more problematic than the differences that are to be resolved. This is particularly true when there has been a breach of trust in a relationship that nonetheless offers considerable satisfaction to its participants. Rounds of accusations and defense take up time and create more ill feelings while they block the occurrence of more positive interactions.

5. Attracting attention by attempting to be left alone

Many problems, from marital discord to depression and even paranoid behavior, can be maintained by this attempted solution. A person can become inducted into this approach when he or she defines some behavior by others as insidious, as indicating their lack of esteem or respect. The person then attempts to solve the problem by emotional or physical withdrawal, by hesitant inquiries or even counterattacks. While these efforts may succeed, they may also increase the other's undesired behavior. Coyne (1976a, 1976b) has described the accumulation of negative interactions by depressed persons. Depressed persons believe that others are handling them gingerly and not really expressing their true feelings, and so they withdraw or alternatively express their sense of rejection. In either case, their obvious distress and hypersensitivity increase the problematic behavior of others, further validating the depressed person's negative perception.

In summary, the vicious cycle of interaction between the problem and attempted solution is a self-perpetuating system. Segal (1980) has compared the patient with a persisting problem to a man caught in quicksand. The more he struggles, the more he sinks. The more he sinks, the more he struggles. These attempted solutions perpetuate and even aggravate problems in a way that traditional therapists interpret as signs of deep underlying problems of an intrapsychic nature. From the brief strategic therapy viewpoint, a preoccupation with occult inner entities and hidden causes distracts traditional therapists from observing the interpersonal contexts in which the patient's behavior is perpetuated. The brief strategic therapist finds no usefulness in seeking causes removed from this context and assumes that, for the purposes of intervention, the interpersonal context is sufficient as its own explanation. The theory and practice of brief therapy rests on two major assumptions: "regardless of their basic origins and etiology—if, indeed that can ever be reliably determined—the kinds of problems people bring to psychotherapies *persist* only if they are maintained by the ongoing current behavior of the patient and others with whom he interacts. Correspondingly, if the problem-maintaining behavior is appropriately changed or eliminated, the problem will be resolved or vanish, irrespective of its nature, origin, or duration" (Weakland et al., 1974, p. 144).

THE CONDUCT OF BRIEF STRATEGIC THERAPY

Pretreatment Considerations

In conventional psychotherapy, it is assumed that the person for whom an appointment is made will become the identified patient or client, and ipso facto the focus of treatment. In brief therapy, however, we do not assume that asking to be seen means that a person is either committed to change or the most appropriate point of intervention in an interpersonal system. Many people seek therapy not because of their distress with their problems but because they are under pressure from someone else who is more distressed or more motivated. Thus, an alcoholic may seek therapy because of the threat of divorce, or an adolescent because his parents insist.

It is assumed in brief therapy that treatment will be most effective if the therapist works with those members of an interpersonal system who are most committed to change. Therefore, in the earliest contact with a case, whether it is a phone conversation or an initial session, it is important to assess who is most bothered by the problem since this person is likely to offer the best leverage for change. This person will not necessarily be the one who would be designated as the identified patient in conventional therapy. Ideally, the person selected will communicate the following: (1) I have a problem; (2) I have tried to solve it and have been unsuccessful; and (3) I am asking for your help.

If the person calling for an appointment or coming to the first session fails to meet these criteria, there are a number of strategies available either to increase motivation or to identify a more appropriate point of intervention in the system (Fisch et al., 1975). Working with an adolescent who does not believe he has a problem that requires therapy, for instance, the therapist can echo his reservations while pointing out that he does have a problem, i.e., that others are applying pressure to him. The client might then commit himself to treatment with the focus of seeing how he might deal more effectively with those he finds coercive. This commitment, however, leaves the therapist free also to explore ways of making changes in the original presenting problem.

Other strategies are available but for our present purposes we merely wish to emphasize the pitfalls attending the assumption that every person who requests therapy is ready to work on the stated problem. Failure to identify an appropriate contact person in a system can lead to a situation in which the therapist will find it difficult to gather information, to get the person to accept new ideas, or to take an alternative tack in dealing with the problem. Such an illusion of treatment can persist until the person runs out of time or money or until the therapist makes a referral to another therapist.

Obtaining a Problem Description

Throughout brief strategic therapy, the therapist's principal activity is the gathering of clear and concrete information about the ongoing interactions that characterize a problem. This information is used first in grasping the problem, next in making interventions, and finally in checking their outcomes. We seek sufficient information for the therapist to visualize a motion picture of any situation under discussion. Although we expect a therapist to be intuitive and empathic, such a "film" should be based on detailed information, not guesswork. Minimally, any inference or interpretation by the therapist should be explicitly checked against the reports of the patients.

Treatment begins by simply asking the patient or patients, "What is the problem that brings you here?" In the ensuing questioning, the therapist seeks an explicit statement as to: (1) the particular problem that has led the clients to seek treatment; (2) how the problem is expressed in their daily lives, i.e., what it prevents them from doing or makes them do unwillingly; (3) why therapy is sought *now* rather than earlier or later; and (4) how this particular agency or therapist was chosen. In an exceptional case, the immediate answer would be, "My husband and I have generally not been getting along, and the situation became aggravated when his parents announced that they would spend their vacation with us. The children are sensitive to our constant bickering and are becoming less obedient. I could not endure the added strain of my husband's parents living with us unless we reduced these other tensions. My physician recommended you because other patients of his had spoken highly of you."

More likely, clients initially make one of a number of unsatisfactory responses. Some offer answers that are too vague or general to provide a picture of the ongoing problem, such as "we don't communicate" or "I have been depressed." In such cases, more focused questioning is necessary, such as asking for a specific incident or asking exactly how this problem most interferes with their daily lives. Other clients provide an endless list of complaints and it becomes necessary to ask, "What is the most important of these?" or "Can you select the one difficulty the resolution of which would give you a needed boost in coping with your other problems?" Still other clients simply respond, "I don't know what my problem is," and require assistance in reconstructing how they decided to enter treatment, how they are distressed, and how this is evident in their daily lives. However a problem statement is derived, it is important that one be obtained. Brief strategic therapy is a structured, problem-oriented approach, and its brevity requires the focus of a clear problem statement.

Describing Attempted Solutions

Answers to the question, "How have you been attempting to handle or resolve this problem?" generally come more easily than the initial problem description. The emphasis is again on obtaining behaviorally relevant descriptions of specific interactions. Clients frequently focus on affective reactions and thoughts instead of observable behavior, and it then becomes necessary to restate the question as, "What do you *do* leading up to those thoughts or feelings, and then how do you deal with them?" At other times, clients will give helpless answers of the form "nothing" and it is then useful to inquire specifically how they go about doing nothing. For instance, a depressed and withdrawn man may be sitting at home listening to music that reminds him of a former girlfriend and ruminating how no one else could ever be as wonderful. With other clients who give a helpless response, the therapist persists with "I can see that this problem is getting the best of you or you would not be here to see me. But everyone tries as best they can to deal with problems, and I wonder what you have been trying, even though it has not worked as well as you would have liked."

Although people typically try a variety of problem-solving strategies, there is usually a basic rule or logic that can summarize their efforts. This is not to say that the client is explicitly following any rule; rather, the term is a metaphor pointing to the possibility of a general pattern or common denominator. Usually, the therapist looks for commonalities in what the clients are trying to accomplish—the objective—and how they go about doing this (Segal, 1980).

For instance, a woman who wishes to meet someone new for a possible relationship may go to parties but always with the security of a large group of friends; she may go to cafes but always brings a newspaper in which she can be engrossed; and she may take a crafts class but acts so task-oriented that others accept that she does not want to be disturbed. In each case, the woman takes an important initiative but is too thorough in attempts not to appear obvious.

The therapist should be careful not to neglect the role of the response of others, even when the presenting problem does not appear to be interpersonal in nature. For instance, a woman complained about not being able to finish her dissertation. Initial discussions of what she did about this problem centered on her own efforts to write. Yet, in passing she mentioned that her boyfriend tried to be supportive, but that she was not fully appreciative of this. When the couple was then interviewed together, it became clear that the boyfriend became hostile and verbally abusive when his statements of encouragement and support failed to make a difference. The issue had become so intense that she was now avoiding even trying to work on the dissertation and she was questioning whether they should stay together. He was taking the position that she should finish the dissertation as soon as possible or abandon it in order to avoid further threat to the relationship, thereby increasing the pressure on her. Cases such as this one highlight the need to inquire how others react to what the client is doing to solve the presenting problem.

Eliciting a Goal Statement

The goal of therapy is formulated from the client's answers to direct questioning of the form, "At a minimum, what would you hope to happen as a result of coming here?" What is sought is a behavioral description of the interaction that could signify that the problem had been resolved. The client's initial goal statement is likely to be too vague or general, such as "to communicate better" or "to be less depressed." It is important to pursue questioning of the form, "Can you describe a situation that, were it to occur, you would know that positive change had been achieved?"

A number of considerations influence the therapist's reformulation of the client's initial goal statement. First, it is preferred that the goal be stated in terms of the occurrence of a positive event rather than the mere absence of negative conditions. For instance, in one case, parents complained that they had been unsuccessful in controlling the behavior of their two adolescent sons, and it was clear that the parents tended to provoke rebellious behavior by their constant inquiries, warnings, and intrusiveness. They initially indicated that their goal was for the boys not to act rebelliously. For the purposes of treatment, however, the goal was rephrased as the parents comfortably going out for an evening without having to maintain a monitoring of the boys by telephone. This positive move was inconsistent with the interpersonal pattern that had characterized the problem situation.

A second consideration in accepting the client's goal is that it should involve a change that is small but strategic. Even under optimal conditions, it is difficult to take a different tack in solving a problem that has resisted all previous efforts. The client is likely to be demoralized and skeptical about the usefulness of renewing efforts. The client might, however, be encouraged to make a small change, precisely because of its significance in comparison to the total problem. If the step can be induced in a way that leads to change in even a trivial aspect of the all-embracing problem, it may become apparent that the problem is not as monolithic as it first appeared (Watzlawick, 1978, p. 72). It is frequently the case in depression, for instance, that people are able to validate feelings of ineptitude, worthlessness, and rejection in the performance of everyday activities. Whereas the depressed person may be resistant to suggestions of any major new effort, he or she may be open to small concrete changes in daily routine that may potentially be a break in a seemingly endless string of failures and frustrations.

The third consideration has been termed the principle of the unresolved remnant (Watzlawick, 1978, p. 73). In essence, the rule is that the therapist should never suggest the possibility of totally resolving a problem, but only its improvement. The goal is thus for the depressed person to interact with others *somewhat* more comfortably or sleep a *little* longer, even though continuing to experience noticeable discomfort. The strategy has a twofold effect. It rejects an all-or-nothing conception of change, thereby freeing clients from the burden of having to be totally successful or an utter failure. It also sets the stage for the clients to achieve more than the therapist's apparent expectations and to do so with a sense of self-initiative.

Strategic Planning

The brief therapist is committed to helping the client achieve a goal while recognizing the necessity of blocking, frustrating, or redirecting existing problem-solving efforts. The basic solution abstracted from the client's description of coping efforts alerts the therapist to what must be avoided. The intent is to influence the client to take a new tack that is not a variation of the basic solution so that the behaviors perpetuating the problem are abandoned.

Thus, a person who is anxious when speaking in public reports trying all of the following: practicing in front of a mirror, making extensive notes and outlines, doing breathing exercises, and taking tranquilizers. These solutions differ but share the common feature of being attempts to reduce anxiety. The brief therapist should be careful not to suggest variations on this theme, but rather than merely avoiding it, he or she would do best to suggest any of a number of strategies that represent its *opposite*. The client could be encouraged to (1) announce to the audience that he is nervous; (2) make a mistake on purpose; (3) act as if he forgot what he was saying and ask the audience for help; or (4) drop his notecards in the middle of his talk. Each of these represents a 180-degree shift from previously attempted solutions (Segal, in press).

Brief strategic therapy emphasizes interventions in the form of comments, suggestions, prescriptions, and asides which run counter to the strategies clients consider logical. Obviously, getting them to carry out counterintuitive assignments is not easy since such advice would only seem to make matters worse from their perspective. It becomes important, then, to change their views of their situations so that new solutions can become easier and so that existing solutions that are perpetuating the problem become more difficult. The general approach is termed "reframing," by which we mean "to change the conceptual and/or emotional setting or viewpoint in relation to which a situation is experienced and to place it in another frame which fits the 'facts' of the same concrete situation equally well or even better, and thereby changes its entire meaning. . . . What turns out to be changed as a result of reframing is the meaning attributed to the situation, and therefore its consequences, but not its concrete facts" (Watzlawick et al., 1974, p. 95).

Any of the following framings might be suitable for the speech-anxious client who is asked to make a deliberate mistake: (1) it is a method of *in vivo* desensitization; (2) exaggeration of a problem is a way of learning how one does it, and is therefore the first step in learning how not to do it; (3) it is likely to produce some insights that would take much longer with conventional verbal therapy. Some clients become intrigued with the question, "Do you know how to give a really bad presentation or only how to give an amateurishly bad one?" In still other cases, we might use an intervention called "the devil's pact." The client must agree to follow the therapist's assignment without knowing what it is or discussing it once it has been presented. The client is then requested to recontact the therapist only when the assignment has been completed.

The particular reframing that is chosen with a given case will reflect the client's values, beliefs, and attitudes. Starting with the client's opening statements in the first contact, the therapist attempts to grasp the concepts organizing the client's coping efforts. Reframing typically involves an active acknowledgment of them and the addition of a new twist or new direction that makes alternative behaviors more likely. There are many ways of motivating clients to behave differently. Angry and frustrated parents can be given assignments framed in a way that allows them to vent their feelings harmlessly and therapeutically, while parents stressing their caretaking role can be given suggestions in a way that calls upon them to be helpful and sacrificing. The curious and insight-oriented can be motivated to try out new ideas, to see what they can learn from new experiences, while resistive clients can be encouraged to change.

Reframing is most likely to prove successful when it requires the smallest possible shift in concepts and behavior. Milton Erickson convinced a patient who would not talk to anyone to attempt to do so in a public library. While a small change, it shifted the meaning of the man's behavior. To be quiet in a library is appropriate. With the pressure to maintain a conversation reduced, the man was able to interact with others, leading up to the initiation of a relationship.

Interventions—General Themes

Brief therapy requires that the therapist adapt to the particular style, language, and behavior of a client, and any interventions are likely to capitalize on idiosyncratic features of a client's situation. There are, however, some recurring themes or positions that characterize the brief therapist's activity, and it would be useful to note them briefly.

Taking a one-down position

Brief therapists use a number of tactics to diminish their implied distance from the client, conveying that therapists are modest people with frailties and insecurities. It is assumed that clients are more likely to accept mere ideas, try out assignments, and give more complete information if the ambience of treatment is kept low key. When collecting information, an explicit one-down position is used for clarification purposes. We are likely to say, "Would you please go over that again? Sometimes I have to hear things five times before I can get a handle on them. Please bear with me." In the later stages of treatment, when new ideas or directives are presented, they are framed as "not very important" or "just an experiment from which something might be learned." Alternatively, the therapist might propose a homework assignment and then reject it as reflecting an inappropriate "therapeutic optimism" only to have it predictably defended by the client.

Going slow

Treatment generally proceeds most quickly when the client is not under undue pressure to solve the problem immediately or facing some real or imagined deadlines. In a wide range of situations, people perform best when their sense of being evaluated is reduced (Lavelle, Metalsky, & Coyne, 1979). Consequently, a number of therapeutic maneuvers are designed to convey a message of "Go slow." In many instances, clients are admonished not to change too quickly. Clients are frequently asked to think about an assignment for a week prior to carrying it out. The effectiveness of this is enhanced if there is a constant reminder of the delay. A depressed man having difficulty taking any initiative whatsoever spoke of wanting to build a rock garden. The therapist suggested that it was premature because his depression had clearly sapped his energy. The man might, however, note the appropriateness of rocks he encountered in the next week, but should under no circumstances collect any. His attention to rocks was further developed with a monologue by the therapist describing the shape and location of various rocks. Similarly, a social isolate might be urged to begin attending parties but to avoid meeting anyone new. These ventures might be framed metaphorically as beachheads in her assault on loneliness, in which case it is important not to advance too far until her forces are properly assembled. In the interim, she should be prepared to fend off others as best she can.

When clients return, happily explaining that they are nonetheless making progress, the brief therapist is likely to acknowledge this but also to warn them to slow down. It can be further suggested that the progress they have made precludes much more for at least a week or so. In doing so, the therapist puts clients at ease, helping them avoid a sense that they must follow up on initial gains or be considered failures, and allowing them to take credit for whatever positive change does occur in the coming week.

Pessimism

Traditional conceptions of thoughts and attitudes as mental elements ignore the extent to which they can be usefully considered social phenomena through and through. Traditional therapists are therefore unprepared for the extent to which clients' irrational hopelessness is maintained by the equally irrational optimism and false reassurance of those around them (Coyne, 1976a). Mabel Cohen et al. (1954) have noted how therapists typically meet their clients' pessimism with seductive promises that are too great to be fulfilled, followed by rejection when the clients fail to respond favorably. In contrast, brief strategic therapists actively avoid optimism and false reassurance, offering instead a calculated pessimism. When clients inquire, "Doctor, can you help me with my problem?", the brief therapist's response is likely to take the form of, "I have helped some people, but there are others with whom I could not do anything. But even if I could tell you that I have been successful in every single case, you would still have the right to think, 'Yes, but I'll be his first failure' " (Fisch et al., 1975). Beginning brief therapists are generally surprised how quickly clients abandon a pessimistic position when a therapist counters them with more pessimism.

Dangers of improvement

Most personal change involves a balance of positive and negative elements and it makes good sense to caution clients that there are drawbacks and even dangers to improvement. The necessity of change can then be seen as less urgent, the clients are less pressured, and they are more realistically prepared for the negative side of progress. There are, however, additional strategic advantages for the therapist warning of the dangers of improvement (Segal, 1980). Some clients request help, but put the onus of change on the therapist. In arguing for the dangers of improvement, the therapist puts the burden back on such clients to demonstrate their willingness to make an effort.

In other cases, the therapist's "dangers of improvement" position can be used to disrupt destructive patterns of nagging and resistance. A husband might be urging his wife to quit smoking in a manner that makes her feel guilty but nonetheless makes it more difficult for her to quit. If the therapist suggests that he is nagging her precisely because he is aware of its boomerang effect (even if "unconsciously"), the wife's wish to avoid being badgered no longer must lead to more smoking. As Fisch et al. (1974) note, "It is one thing to be nagged, it is entirely another to be subtly snookered" (p. 35).

Symptom prescription

A broad class of problems are maintained by efforts to stave off their occurrence. This class includes problems associated with the be-spontaneous paradox such as sleep disturbance, sexual difficulties, and writer's block. Athletes trying hard to avoid a characteristic mistake and couples trying to avoid yet another argument also fall into this pattern. Their preoccupation with the need to avoid the usual negative outcome distracts them from the task at hand and makes failure more likely. This in turn leads to the conclusion that they did not try hard enough, when what is needed is for them to free themselves from the self-defeating demands they are making on themselves. Admonitions that they relax or not try so hard seldom have the desired effect, and it becomes necessary to suggest instead that they actively bring on the undesired outcome. There are many rationales that can justify such a tack. Ascher and Efran (1978) have described symptom prescription with persons suffering from insomnia with the rationale that staying awake would allow the clients to collect instances of thoughts that would keep them from sleeping, data that are vital to any treatment planning. A controlled comparison revealed this approach to be superior to relaxation techniques. Brief therapists use similar rationales, but are likely to embellish them with the added suggestion that the longer that clients stay awake on a given night, the more thoughts they will collect, and therefore the better the data base.

Depending on the context of the problem-maintaining efforts, a variety of other rationales can be invoked for symptom prescription: (1) "If the problem is truly inevitable, making it occur deliberately will at least make it predictable"; (2) "If you must do it, do it with a bit more of a flourish"; (3) "If the problem has never occurred more than three times in a week, you might try having it occur five times by Tuesday so that it might be less likely to happen again on Wednesday."

In one case, a man regularly took to lying on his couch for hours at a time, ruminating on the hopelessness of his financial situation, which was actually not that bad. It was pointed out to him that he and his wife were greatly relieved when such a spell ended, and that when it did, they typically were then more communicative, appreciative, and affectionate. Other couples might first require a destructive argument in order to "make up" in such a fashion. The couple was told that they clearly had this option, and could use it if either partner felt their situation was an emergency, or that therapy was progressing too slowly. Until they discovered the third alternative, however, they should probably stick with the husband's rumination attacks. The couple agreed that two or three nights a week with greater closeness would be desirable, and so it was suggested that the man surprise his wife with rumination attacks of approximately that frequency. The therapist offered that this was a sacrifice and that a good argument might be easier, but the couple rejected the latter option. They subsequently reported that they were trying hard, but it was impossible to prolong a rumination attack. They were enjoying their time together much more, and their sex life had been revitalized. They confessed, however, that they were puzzled by what the therapist meant by the "third alternative."

CONCLUDING REMARKS

In this last example, the therapist suggested to the couple that the husband should have attacks of depressive ruminations or alternatively, they could argue in what could prove to be a destructive fashion. In the larger context of the goals of therapy, neither would be seen as desirable outcomes. The therapist was not seeking more ruminations or more arguments as a goal, but was arranging a situation so that the couple would take more responsibility for their behavior and would initiate change. They were being tricked out of their problem.

Clients frequently accept such absurd behavior prescriptions happily and with big smiles, as if they somehow had caught on to the essentially humorous nature of this dead serious play. Some will say, "You're using reverse psychology on us, and you really do not want us to have the problem." In such cases, the therapist merely agrees, since their "awareness" is irrelevant as long as the directive is given and followed (Haley, 1976, p. 204).

The use of paradox and symptom prescription offends therapists who believe that whether clients achieve change is less important than whether they have an open and honest human experience with a therapist who is sharing understanding with them. Haley (1976, p. 208) has countered that such therapists ignore that the therapeutic context is a *paid* relationship, not an honest human experience, and there is something inhuman about a therapist receiving money merely to be human with clients. Such arguments, however, are not likely to prove persuasive for all. Some therapists are simply too honest to play the games described in this chapter. They prefer instead to play the game of not seeing that they are playing games (Laing, 1970).

An entirely different set of concerns arises around the issue of contracting with a set of persons to change the behavior of someone else. We do not minimize the issue, but invoke the counterargument that most clinically relevant behaviors occur in the context of significant relationships, and changes in these behaviors are associated with change in the relationships. We assume that clients and those around them are unavoidably influencing each other, and that the therapist is faced with the responsibility of deciding how this is to be taken into account in the most humane, ethical, and effective manner. We no longer have the luxury of construing our ethical responsibilities in myopically unecological terms.

REFERENCES

Ascher, L. M. & Efran, J. S. Use of paradoxical intention in a behavioral program for sleep onset insomnia. *Journal of Consulting and Clinical Psychology*, 1978, **46**, 547–550.

Cohen, M. B., Baker, G., Cohen, R. A., Fromm-Reichmann, F., & Weigert, E. A. An intensive study of twelve cases of manic depressive psychoses. *Psychiatry*, 1954, **17**, 103–37.

Coyne, J. C. Depression and the response of others. *Journal of Abnormal Psychology*, 1976, **85**, 186–193. (a)

Coyne, J. C. Toward an interactional description of depression. *Psychiatry*, 1976, **39**, 28–40. (b)

Coyne, J. C. & Fabricatore, J. Group psychotherapy in a corrections facility: A case study of individual and institutional change. *Professional Psychology*, 1979, **10**, 8–14.

Fisch, R., Weakland, J., Watzlawick, P., Segal, L., Hoebel, F., & Deardoff, M. *Learning brief therapy: An introductory training manual*. Palo Alto, Calif.: Mental Research Institute, 1975. (No longer available)

Haley, J. *Problem-solving therapy*. New York: Jossey-Bass, 1976.

Laing, R. D. *Knots*. New York: Pantheon, 1970.

Lavelle, T. L., Metalsky, G., & Coyne, J. C. Learned helplessness, test anxiety, and acknowledgment of contingencies. *Journal of Abnormal Psychology*, 1979, **88**, 381–387.

Segal, L. Focused problem resolution. In E. Tolson & W. J. Reid (Eds.), *Models of family therapy*. New York: Columbia University Press, 1980.

Segal, L. Brief Therapy: Focused problem resolution. In R. J. Corsini (Ed.), *Innovative psychotherapies*. New York: John Wiley & Sons, in press.

Wachtel, P. L. *Psychoanalysis and behavior therapy*. New York: Basic Books, 1977.

Watzlawick, P. *The language of change*. New York: Basic Books, 1978.

Watzlawick, P. & Coyne, J. C. Depression following stroke: Brief, problem-focused family treatment. *Family Process*, 1980, **19**, 13–18.

Watzlawick, P., Weakland, J., & Fisch, R. *Change: Principles of problem formation and problem resolution*. New York: Norton, 1974.

Weakland, J., Fisch, R., Watzlawick, P., & Bodin, A. Brief therapy: Focused problem resolution. *Family Process*, 1974, **13**, 141–168.

Chapter 14

Being Asocial in Social Places: Giving the Client a New Experience

David M. Young and Ernst G. Beier

INTRODUCTION

The purpose of this chapter is to acquaint the reader with the idea that effective therapeutic communication is, by definition "asocial." That is, the potential for change is created when a therapist does not provide a client with the type of response that the client is covertly trying to evoke. The nature of the engagement and disengagement processes in therapy are discussed. Methods of learning to respond asocially in therapy and the basic modes of asocial response are presented and illustrated with case material.

ON SOCIAL ENGAGEMENT

A major tenet of the communications approach to psychotherapy described by Beier (1966; Beier & Valens, 1975) is that a client's characteristic behavior or style of communicating, whether it produces conventional reward or punishment, is strengthened whenever he or she receives an expected or social response from the interpersonal environment. Social responses are not defined in the traditional sense as nice, friendly, or gregarious; rather they are behaviors that are predictable. If a client behaves in a manner that is often caustic and critical, the expected outcome or socially engaged response might include frequent arguments with others and special negative attention. Conversely, if an individual frequently engages others with a pattern of behavior that is instantly agreeable, replete with head nods and smiles, the predictable or social response created by this type of emotional climate might include social situations in which many special favors or requests are made. The idea of typical or stylistic patterns of emotion "pulling" (Kiesler, 1978) is based on the assumption that individuals are motivated to achieve predictability and control in their social interactions, whether or not the resulting responses are painful.

One has only to observe infant-parent interaction for a short time to conclude that children learn early in life to make things happen with idiosyncratic social styles. If life could not be *made* predictable by the young child, what chance of physical or psychological survival would there be? Consider the child whose mother is "turned on" to the child whenever it is bouncing with joy, but indifferent to the child when it is sad. The child learns very quickly which of his or her behaviors elicit the predicted response from mother, and the child also learns that the mother can be punished by withholding a happy, bouncing response.

Another mother might respond positively to a child's wide variety of moods and actions but negatively to sexual self-touching, and again the boy learns how he can socially engage mother—negatively or positively. Parents are constantly scanned and the child learns what works with each. We are assuming that training in styles of social engagement occurs without awareness, on the part of parent or child.

THE CLIENT'S DESIRED DILEMMA

It is not suggested that the display of established patterns of social engagement is manipulative or pathological. All people engage in a variety of stylistic behaviors and most exhibit flexibility in being able to communicate in a manner congruent with the social responses or interpersonal goal they seek. Individuals suffer psychological pain because they are in a state of communication deficit; they obtain responses to their communication which they have not "willingly" elicited and for which they cannot account. They feel that they are victims. They totally deny the fact that they have—probably repeatedly—evoked the aversive responses. Within this framework of the neurotic paradox, (e.g., Mowrer, 1948), the patient or client painted her or himself into a corner. The client is suffering as he or she feels like the recipient of unsatisfactory responses from the social world; yet, the client has helped to evoke these responses because, while aversive, they are also meaningful; they help to create a predictable world. Many theorists imply that the client's problem stems from a lack of knowledge or from a lack of social skill or a simple inability to cope with stress. We argue that the client's problem messages actually provide the client with both satisfaction and disappointment. When the client sends problem messages, it appears that he or she is unable to learn from experience. Actually, these messages are the result of two mutually exclusive motivations, and the message represents a compromise between these motives. The most general labels for these motivations are: (1) the individual's sense of integrity, and (2) the social pressures he or she is under. The resulting compromise between these two pressures represents the client's way of "having his cake and eating it too." He or she can engage another person, evoke some response which is important to make the world predictable and which is at least partially "wanted," but he or she can also complain about the pain which the responses cause.

Some examples of the power of covert social engagement are in order. Take the case of a depressed client who complains about her spouse's anger. The "downtrodden" wife subtly encourages her husband's attacks, yet she can always deny that she desired an "unhappy" result such as a divorce. With her pain, the wife is able to think of herself as free from the responsibility for her subtle maltreatment of her husband. Her pain permits the denial of both the manipulation of the relationship with the husband and the fact that she—on some level of awareness—wants the divorce. We are not suggesting that the wife in this case, or clients in general, are consciously deciding on how to create covertly an emotional climate in others to yield a "desired" behavior. The conscious use of covert manipulation is the trade secret of a conman, even though we all use it occasionally. The client, on the other hand, is indeed unaware of certain of his or her motivations and of the compromise he or she is achieving to obtain at least partial gratification from their expression.

Another clinical example of how an adaptive compromise (Mahl, 1971) operates via the client's symptoms is offered. A young man at the student counseling center loudly proclaimed his dismay that "Nobody will go out with me!" Further inquiry revealed that he was collecting these rejections (injustices) in response to requests that sounded more like harassments than social invitations. This type of social engagement surely creates a predictable emotional climate, namely rejection; yet why did the client set up the situation to find this particular result? The therapist in this case learned that the client had a lot of pressure on him to "make friends," and to "find a girl," and had been repeatedly told that "loners" are odd and dangerous. The client's invitation to others to go out with him represented the social pressure instruction. He could then say: "I'm trying, right?" His gruffness and his harassing comments, on the other hand, represented his motivation to maintain his integrity—he is his own man, beholden to none. He remained "strong" and lonely, but he received rejections which proved to him that others were wrong, even though he did what they told him to do. He also combined personal strength with obedience to others in his particular style and with this message could predict the outcome which left him with at least partial satisfaction.

From this description of the client's compromise, it follows that therapeutic communications are messages which are effective because they interrupt the client's communications. They consequently help to extinguish the expected pattern of social interaction which is prompted by the client's style of behavior. That is, therapy may be seen as taking place when the therapist interrupts, in an "asocial" or disengaged way, in response to the client's typical interaction styles. When the customary, preferred, or expected response is withheld in the therapy session, the client experiences a sense of "beneficial uncertainty" (Beier, 1966). The client's reaction is one of uncertainty because preferred styles of communicating no longer produce the familiar responses that have been a mainstay of the client's psychological diet. This uncertainty is labeled beneficial because the asocial behavior is originating from a caring person in the safe, confidential environment of the consulting room and not in the "real" world where the interpersonal stakes are high. Thus, the client is receiving a new experience in response to old patterns of engagement attempts.

In the therapy setting, where a client's typical attempts of engagement do not result in the expected response, the client is obliged to discover new behavior styles. As this model is based on extinction procedures, it is expected that extinction attempts will first cause an increase of the old behavior pattern. Eventually the client will experiment with new social engagement styles, and it should be noted that it is essential that the therapist continues his extinction procedure throughout by disengaging with asocial responses. Where the therapist approves or rewards certain of the client's responses, he or she would be "engaged" and remain the author of the change. Through asocial, disengaged responses, the therapist shifts to the client the responsibility for his/her conduct. A case illustration follows in which an anorexic client whose engagement style of dependence and symptomatic complaints has shifted to one in which the client is seeking support for her accomplishments:

Client: I'm feeling pretty good today. I had a good week! (*smiling*)
Therapist: Tell me more about that.
(*Disengaged response. This response, as most other reflective respones, is "disengaged" in the sense that the therapist does not really respond in the required mood evoked by the client. With such a response, the therapist also shifts responsibility to the client. He says to the client between the lines, "You go ahead and elaborate.")*
Client: Well, I actually straightened out that problem at work with my boss. I just opened up to her

and honestly told her about my problem with working weekends and she, uh—said "Okay" that I didn't have to. (*In the voice there was much enthusiasm with a bid for therapist to join in her joy.*)
Therapist: Um hum. (*A delay response, but disengaged as the client was pulling for much more involvement and approval.*)
Client: (pause) Oh, . . . I also really talked with Frank (*husband*) about needing, you know, to have more communication with him and less bossing and fighting. He really listened . . . for the first time, really! (*While changing the structure of the content, the client's attempt at engagement continues in the same mode. The bid here is still for the therapist to approve of the client's growth.*)
Therapist: You'd like me to know about all your progress and that you're feeling good. (*Another reflective response, disengaged as it does not reward the client's achievement by responding with personal approval. Reflective statements have come into use in so many therapies because they are asocial in nature—beyond reward and punishment.*)
Client: (awkward pause) Oh, and guess what? I only threw up about twice this week! (*The client plays her ace by presenting improvement with her most important or scariest symptom. Who could be so cold-hearted as not to rejoice with a person who has stopped starving herself to death? Or, in this covert way, says "thanks!"*)
Therapist: Um hum. (*An effective asocial listening response, but not entirely sufficient. A longer statement, perhaps reflecting the increase in the demand for approval and the hidden "thanks" would have been closer to a "maximum response." A maximum response includes the major themes and "catches the client in the act" of acting out on these themes.*)
Client: (All nonverbal. Looks downward, maintains a sad facial expression and a slumping posture. Silent. The client is covertly switching engagement styles back to her previous mode of suffering. At the same time she is showing her anger at the therapist for not rewarding her for her reports of an "almost" symptom-free week.*)
Therapist: You look pretty sad now. I think you're disappointed in me, that I didn't show approval and look pleased when you talked about having a good week, about not throwing up. (*The therapist is disengaged and reflects on this major theme while they are "acted out." An excellent response. We must, however, warn that the purpose of this response is not to provide insight. In communication theory, disengagement is useful because it suggests new choices to the client.*)
Client: Who cares! I'm thinking of killing myself right now. (*With anger*) Can I leave? (*The client makes a last attempt to engage the therapist into caring with the double threat of walking out and suicide.*)
Therapist: (*In an exaggerated manner with a friendly smile*) Boy, am I a jerk for not being pleased with you. You came in here all smiles and now look what I've done! (*Therapist disengages with a paradigmatic response that exaggerates the client's resistance.*)
Client: (Laughs) I suppose I am angry with you. I thought you would be pleased. Sometimes I don't think you care for me and . . . (*the client was able to drop her manipulative styles and explore hidden feelings because of the uncertainty that was provided in a caring way*).

In the above example, when the anorexic client's "Please pat me on the back" engagement attempt failed to evoke the preferred response, she escalated to a preferred threatening posture, complete with termination threats and talk of suicide. If the therapist had not responded with his asocial response, the client would have maintained her particular counterproductive method of winning favors. It was especially important for the therapist to disengage from the client's escalation toward suicide as otherwise, the client would have reexperienced in therapy the success of her most dangerous skills: "If I can't win approval with my conventional accomplishments, presenting my symptoms can generally evoke the social caring I want."

An example from one of our laboratory studies can help illustrate how behavior change may result from an unexpected or asocial response (Young, Beier, Beier, & Barton, 1975). Male college students were asked to "help test equipment for a new aggression game involving the use of padded clubs designed electronically to record impact." In pretesting, the sample was divided into two groups: those favoring a social role for women that was equal to that of men (liberals), and those who preferred women to stay at home and take care of the home or children (traditionals). Each student in the study had two game bouts with a female confederate. In the first bout, the female opponent maintained a defend-only posture. In the second match, the confederate switched to a strong offense. The liberal group of students played the game with vigor during both bouts. The traditionals, on the other hand, played quite gently during the defend-only condition but equalled their liberal counterparts when confronted with the unexpected and presumably undesired change in their opponents' behavior. Even though our sample of traditionals seemed to prefer a delicate exchange, they did modify their behavior when confronted with an unexpected or asocial response.

In the therapy setting, when a client's communications do not result in the "expected" or social response from the therapist, a similar shift may occur. A client displays sadness or cries and the therapist does not respond as family members or close friends would respond. The therapist simply does not offer a sense of closure which the expected or social response does. Instead, the therapist has a repertoire of asocial responses available to him. The therapist may ask, "What are the words that go with these tears?" gently reminding the client that he or she is here to work, or the many common listening responses such as, "Go on, tell me more," or "um hum" also serve asocial disengagement and tend not to reinforce the client's communication pattern in that they do not provide the expected emotional response necessary for closure. The therapist might also choose to disengage by interpreting the communication process (metacommunication) or by exaggerating the client's resistance. In any event, the client is getting a new experience; the lack of closure almost forces him or her into new explorations. When the therapist is able to disengage and deny closure, the client is provided with an experience of beneficial uncertainty.

In a sense, communication theory is close to a general theory of psychotherapy. In many varieties of psychotherapy, the old patterns of client communication are not met with familiar rewards or responses from the therapist. The process may be seen as operating in psychoanalysis when the analyst does not relate to the social meaning of a statement, but to the underlying dynamic meaning. In Rogerian work we have reflections which surely are asocial. In Gestalt-transactional work, we have the analysis of the impact of a statement with an analysis of the social consequences. In behavior theory, therapists try not to enter the social arena at all but present a reward which is more symbolic than real.

MAKING UNCERTAINTY BENEFICIAL

In presenting a communication approach to the therapeutic process, we have attempted to answer the question of how behavior is changed by asocial communication. But should we knowingly aim for uncertainty during psychotherapy? The task of the therapist is often seen as helping a client to cope better. The client is often seen as indecisive and uncertain in the first place. When we give such high value to the arousal of uncertainty, we need to explain this further. In the psychotherapeutic process, the somewhat unsettling experience of uncertainty is introduced along with positive values: love, hope, and safety. The therapist must care. He must induce a sense of hope and the therapeutic hour must reduce the threat of anticipated consequences in order to produce "beneficial" uncertainty. The lack of closure produced by the elimination of social responses brings about challenge and uncertainty. The positive values attached to uncertainty permit the client to become a creative artist. The client starts asking, "Must I really?" "Must I really produce my preferred closure pattern?" "Are they really necessary?" "Can I accept responsibility for my harmful and counterproductive communications and change them?" The experience of uncertainty permits this type of questioning, provided that there is some sense of love, hope, and freedom from threat.

There is a further characteristic of asocial communication which especially helps to provide the client with a sense of freedom; it is the artificial nature of the setting. The consulting room is a sanctuary. It is unique in that most interactive consequences are explicit; the client is in control of coming to visit and paying for it. The therapist must keep all information confidential and there are no social consequences. The hour is in this sense playful and gamelike, a condition which enhances creativity. Discussion of taboo topics, role playing, role reversals, memories of childhood, the sole caring attention of another person, all make this hour unreal. These unusual experiences are valuable because new ways of coping can be examined in the safety of the hour. The sting of confronting real problems is diluted with unreality and maximizes the hope for change. When critics speak about the manipulative nature of communication therapy, they do not seem to understand that in psychotherapy the therapist cannot play the social role of a friend and that it is the unique asocial nature of the setting which enhances the business of change. The therapist who disengages from the client's social expectation with asocial responses is arousing uncertainty. In a sense the therapist is "confronting" the client, presenting a challenge in order to make change possible, and it is the therapist's task to formulate communications which are perceived as challenge rather than as threat. Challenge arouses hope; threat creates injurious uncertainty and causes withdrawal and fear.

LEARNING TO BE ASOCIAL

It is ironic that some of the frequently offered reasons for wanting to become a psychotherapist may serve as obstacles to effective treatment. Wanting to comfort people in distress, being sensitive to the needs of others, being likable, and even caring certainly have a place in therapy, but they can be counterproductive. Such needs can be used all too easily for social engagements (clients have great skill with the conventional needs and therapists should be aware of their own needs, particularly the ones which make them vulnerable). The client scans the therapist's subtle and often nonverbal cues and then uses the information for purposes of his own resistance to play out a social role with the therapist. Therapists who want to be liked are easy targets; their very desire can become their Waterloo. We do not claim that all is lost when the therapist gets engaged. As we have grow up in Western culture and are tuned into many of the cues of others, such engagements are hard to avoid. We overlearn to respond with hurt to unfair criticism, with horror to violence, and with a degree of acceptance when our praise is sung. To short-circuit these overlearned and largely unconscious reactions is a tall order. To become aware enough to disengage from a client's engagement style, the therapist must first of all know and then use his or her own "natural" reactions as a diagnostic instrument. The therapist should ask him or herself the phenomenological questions: "how does the client make me feel?" and "what procedures is the client using to make me feel this way?" To answer these questions, the therapist must be able to understand the emotional climate evoked in him or her and to observe the subtle methods the client is using to do so. The therapist is not only scanning the client's feeling and behavior, but his or her own as well.

The therapist undoubtedly will get engaged often enough with this client, but his or her art is to disengage, reading him or herself as the diagnostic instrument. The effective therapist of this model becomes a very sensitive individual with the flexibility to alter or control his or her own natural response biases. The therapist should not have the goal of remaining "emotionally cool." The client has years of practice and the skill to engage others; his or her psychological survival seems to depend on it. It is not an error for the therapist to become engaged. It *is* an error to stay engaged.

It is easier for new students of this model first to practice disengagement via asocial responding outside the therapy setting. Many budding therapists feel more at ease in this manner. They learn to observe their own preferred behavior and then to vary it. The fellow with a serious demeanor will see what happens to him when he smiles at others in an elevator; another alters an idiosyncratic nonverbal habit, such as a pointing of a finger; a woman who typically lets her friend suggest where to go is now taking the initiative. And all learn to observe in this manner the impact of their own asocial responses. They simply respond in a way that is not expected of them. The essential training of communication analytic psychotherapists involves a deep understanding of their own impact on others. This can be learned as a role-playing interaction and through supervision of audio and videotaped sessions. The use of role playing is a particularly helpful technique. Although the content of the hour may be fabricated, subtle cues are always sent in the attempt to engage the other person on a covert level, and these can be analyzed for style.

The need for ongoing supervision or consultation should be stressed. All therapists, novice or advanced, become enmeshed in their client's subtle demands. Therapists would do well to remember that the client is always more skillful than the therapist in unconsciously scanning the therapist for avenues of covert manipulation. This is how the client maintains his or her problem. Spending even one hour a month with a colleague in case review can assist even the most experienced therapist in exiting from subtle engagement patterns. (For a detailed discussion of training and supervision in this model, see Beier & Young, 1980.)

BASIC MODES OF ASOCIAL RESPONSE

In this section we attempt to present a few of the basic kinds of disengagement techniques that are available to the therapist. The variety of techniques will be illustrated with actual case examples. Of course, this listing only provides a bare bones outline of the many maneuvers available. We are not claiming that these techniques are exclusive to the realm of our model. We expect that most therapists utilize these tools to some extent regardless of the theoretical model they have adopted, yet we believe the efficacy of these tools is based on their asocial qualities within the interaction rather than on other theoretical considerations.

Delay Responses

These simple tools are basic to most therapists' repertoires. Often called "minimal encouragers" or "listening responses," comments such as "Go on"; "please continue"; "um hum"; "tell me more" often prove to be of greater value than simply keeping the interaction going on or eliciting more information from the client. It is actually a mini-disengagement response. The therapist is about to be "engaged" by the client's demands, and the response provides the therapist with some time while not succumbing to engagement. It also permits the therapist to get a clearer picture of the procedures the client uses to engage the therapist and perhaps of the client's motivation to constrict the therapist's emotional climate. Consider the following example:

Client: Doctor, I can't take it with my wife any longer. She is really neglecting the kids, refuses me sex, and can't hang on to money at all. I've no alternative but divorce, right?
Therapist: (*Pause*) Go on.

With such a simple yet effective phrase, the therapist is able to avoid the trap of the client's polarizing engagement attempt and to buy time to reflect on several unanswered questions. Why is the client seeing a therapist and not an attorney if he wants a divorce? If the wife is such an "evil creature," why must the client immediately work so hard at proving this and gaining the therapist as an ally? With the help of the time gained through this and similar disengagement techniques, the therapist was eventually able to answer these questions. The client needed a therapist instead of a lawyer because he set the stage and collected injustices from his wife; he wanted to get out but could not see himself taking responsibility for his wish to withdraw from the marriage. These cross-motivations translated into such actions as demanding sex when his wife was busy, keeping financial information hidden from her, and then complaining about her financial incompetence and attempting to engage the therapist to support his victim posture.

We should note here that we should not assume that any particular response *must* have an asocial impact. A response may be most likely to have an impact, but it may not be perceived that way by the client. A response that produces uncertainty in one client can be perceived as a reward by another. The continuous use of delay with a long-winded client who is boring the therapist to tears may make things comfortable for the therapist who unconsciously wishes to rid himself of the dullness. In this case, however, the wish for distance does not mean disengagement. In fact it would rather serve to reinforce the client's view of the world that nobody pays attention to him. Whenever a therapist's routine responses become too stylized with a particular client or when a therapist becomes too "comfortable," it is time to look again at the client's mode of subtle manipulation.

Reflection of Content and Feeling

In addition to providing important feedback to the client and keeping the responsibility "ball" in the client's court, these reflections are universally recognized tools which also help the therapist maintain an asocial posture. By paraphrasing content or bringing feelings into the open, the therapist is able to provide the message of caring and understanding which is so essential for change. Consider the following example in which reflecting maintains client responsibility and prevents the therapist from acting in a socially engaged manner:

Client: It was a disaster of a date. Everything went wrong. My hair was still in curlers and I kept him waiting. When we finally got out, I had too many drinks on an empty stomach and became obnoxious in addition to getting sick. He took me home early and I didn't get to the party. I just felt terrible.
Therapist: You're pretty upset about the lousy time you had.

The therapist delayed with this reflection. The client's opening was eventually interpreted as saying, "I'm really screwing up my social life and what are you going to do about it?" In addition, the client was even covertly asking the therapist to "chew her out" for making a mess of things once again. With the use of delay and reflection, the therapist was able to throw the ball back to the client, telling her that he was expecting to hear more about the underlying feelings.

Labeling Style of the Interaction

Talking with the client about his or her communication style or using "metacommunication" (Haley, 1969) provides the therapist with another means of disengagement and with a valuable teaching technique. When the therapist analyzes communication style and implies that the covert message is intended, the therapist is teaching the client that he or she is choosing to experience his or her problems, and is not a victim of them. By making unconscious communication explicit (as it occurs), the therapist gives the client the experience of having control over these subtle manipulations. In this manner the therapist arouses uncertainty. By verbalizing the impact of discordant messages and their discordant motivation, the therapist alerts clients to the existential fact that they are helping to create their problems. In many cases the covert elements of a client's discordant messages are sent through nonverbal channels. This necessitates making explicit the part of the client's compromise which is active and present, yet hidden from awareness. Because nonverbal cues travel in a variety of channels such as gestures, paralinguistic cues, facial expression, etc., the interpersonal impact of these hidden cues seems ambiguous and often escapes notice of both the sender and receiver (Harper, Wiens, & Matarazzo, 1978).

Nonverbal information makes unconscious information visible and even measurable. Consider the following portion of a session in which a client who hates being alone is given the opportunity to view how his subtle behavior produced "unwanted" impact:

Client: (After a long pause with eyes downcast, a sad facial expression, and slumped posture) People always make fun of me. I guess I'm just the type of guy who really was meant to be a loner, damn it. *(deep sigh)*
Therapist: Could you do that again for me?
Client: What?
Therapist: The sigh, only a bit deeper.
Client: Why? *(pause)* Okay, but I don't see what . . . okay *(client sighs again and smiles)*.
Therapist: Well, that time you smiled, but mostly when you sigh and look so sad I get the feeling that I better leave you alone in your misery, that I should walk on eggshells and not get too chummy or I might hurt you even more.
Client: (A bit of anger in his voice) Well, excuse me! I was only trying to tell you how I felt.
Therapist: I know you felt miserable, but I also got the message that you wanted to keep me at a distance, that I had no way to reach you.
Client: (Slowly) I feel like a loner, I feel that even you don't care about me—making fun of me.
Therapist: I wonder if other folks need to pass this test, too?

In this example, the therapist asked for the repetition because he wanted the client to experience the impact of his discordant message. The verbal component was that the client hated to be a loner; the nonverbal component was that he could not be reached by anyone, it was his procedure to create distance. The therapist tried to make explicit the consequences of the "hidden" nonverbal communication and the motivation it represented.

In reviewing the above interaction, it may appear that the therapist was hoping the client might achieve insight into the nature of his dilemma. Actually, we believe that it is the therapist who needs insight, rather than the client. What is important is that the therapist alerts the clients to their typical pattern as they are experienced. It is uncertainty rather than insight which needs to be evoked by the therapist's asocial response. Often while a therapist offers an asocial response, he will also provide insight to clients. That is, however, incidental: providing the client with insight explanations—even accurate explanations about the etiology, maintenance, or steps necessary to "cure" a problem—is not sufficient to effect behavior change. Therapeutic insight for a patient can actually be counterproductive as such communications do not shift the responsibility for the client's conduct to the client. Only when the client's discordant behavior is interrupted and the client experiences the resultant uncertainty will new behaviors be attempted by clients themselves. Offering insight, however, can provide comfort for the therapist.

Paradigmatic Response

One of the potent tools of the therapist using the communications analytic technique is the paradigmatic response (Nelson, 1962; Beier, 1966). This asocial message is transmitted by the therapist as a paradoxical exaggeration of the client's resistance (Watzlawick, Beavin, & Jackson, 1967; Watzlawick, Weakland, & Fisch, 1974; Haley, 1976). With this technique, the therapist produces the experience of beneficial uncertainty for the client by flowing with the resistance. The response is counterpersuasive in that by exaggerating the client's "ploy," the client's manipulative attempt falls flat.

A client whose short-term contract at a university counseling center has two weeks remaining initiates the following sequence after some very intense, soul-searching hours:

Client: Well, you know we only have two weeks left in the semester and I, uh, well, just don't see the point in continuing. I'm sure it's just a waste of your time now—since I'll be leaving soon. Maybe we should just stop now.
Therapist: (*With exaggeration and a smile*) Thank goodness you said something. All I think about is how I could spend my extra hour on Thursday if only you weren't around.
Client: (*Laughs*) I guess I didn't mean it quite that way. I guess I felt sort of sad about stopping and did not want to prolong the agony.

Here the therapist flowed to extremes with the client's covert ploy for special assurance that he was liked and would be missed. The client's subtle style of involving others by putting himself and others down is made explicit by the paradigmatic response. Such a response can be very effective and can come close to one-trial learning. It is a maxi-response.

In view of the above example, the risks involved with the use of paradigmatic responses should be explored. Primarily, danger occurs when the client fails to read the emotional climate of the setting for the exchange as sufficiently beneficial. Therapeutic intent must be clear to the client. The uncertainty produced by such abrupt confrontation cannot be metabolized by the client without the perception of caring. Pain and regression will be the end result of the paradigmatic exchange if the client does not readily see that the therapist is using a posture, a paradigm only for the sake of beneficial impact. It is especially important for the therapist using paradigmatic responses to know and modulate his or her own subtle output. In the event that a paradigmatic response is read as "genuine," that is, as offensive, it is essential that the therapist deal immediately with the client's image of the therapist's intent. In the above exchange, if the therapist coldly stated, "I see your point, let's quit," the impact would have produced a great deal of uncertainty for the client, but it would have been extremely painful—too painful for learning to occur. It is advisable, especially for the therapist just learning the paradigmatic technique, to assess the emotional climate carefully and have a fall-back position available:

Client: (Misunderstands the therapist's paradigm) So, you don't like me at all!
Therapist: I know you are angry that we have such an artificial deadline for our seeing each other. *(The therapist brings the discussion back into focus.)*

CONCLUDING COMMENTS

It is hoped that communications analytic psychotherapy is more than just another model of doing therapy. From a molar perspective, the practice of providing clients with new experiences through asocial responses can be viewed as an attempt to get the most general common principle which affects behavior change. Ambitiously and perhaps arrogantly we propose that uncertainty aroused through the asocial response is the principle of therapeutic gain underlying a variety of treatment approaches.

Consider the statement made by a client: "I just can't stand the thought of visiting my parents any longer." Outside the therapy setting, the client would receive a constricted number of social responses. An argument might be evoked from a relative—"How can you say that after all they have done for you?" A peer might respond with a predictable, "I know, I dread every Christmas!" In the asocial but safe environment of the therapeutic approach, the client will always go through an experience of uncertainty which demands new choices. A Rogerian might respond with, "I really see you struggling with your feelings." An analytic response might be, "You are really afraid of being confronted with your love for your mother." A therapist using a paradigmatic response might say, "Why not forget such an unpleasant encounter?" All of these seemingly different responses to the statement are impacting the client in similar ways. First, clients are getting the experience of having to be responsible for their feelings, their problems, and their conduct. Second, each of these responses is unexpected and arouses uncertainty in the client. The paradigmatic, the analytic, and the Rogerian replies are asocial; they differ from conventional communications. Communication is, after all, the common vehicle underlying all interactions and the therapeutic goal of helping the client to make new choices is most likely the common principle underlying therapeutic services.

REFERENCES

Beier, E. G. *The silent language of psychotherapy: Social reinforcement of unconscious processes.* Chicago: Aldine, 1966.

Beier, E. G. & Valens, E. G. *People-reading.* New York: Stein & Day, 1975.

Beier, E. G. & Young, D. M. Supervision in communications analytic therapy. In A. K. Hess (Ed.), *Psychotherapy supervision.* New York: Wiley, 1980.

Haley, J. *The power tactics of Jesus Christ and other essays.* New York: Grossman, 1969.

Haley, J. *Problem-solving therapy: New strategies for effective family therapy.* San Francisco: Jossey-Bass, 1976.

Harper, R. G., Weins, A. N., & Matarazzo, J. D. *Nonverbal communication: The state of the art.* New York: Wiley, 1978.

Kiesler, D. J. A communication analysis of relationship in psychotherapy. Paper presented at the University of Minnesota Conference on Psychotherapy and Behavioral Intervention, Minneapolis, Minnesota, April, 1978.

Mahl, G. F. *Psychological conflict and defense*. New York: Harcourt, Brace, Jovanovich, 1971.

Mowrer, O. H. Learning theory and the neurotic paradox. *American Journal of Orthopsychiatry*, 1948, **18**, 571–610.

Nelson, M. C. *Paradigmatic approaches to psychoanalysis: Four papers*. New York: Department of Psychology, Stuyvesant Polyclinic, 1962.

Watzlawick, P., Beavin, J. H., & Jackson, D. *Pragmatics of human communication: A study of interactional patterns, pathologies, and paradoxes*. New York: Norton, 1967.

Watzlawick, P., Weakland, J. H., & Fisch, R. *Change: Principles of problem formation and problem resolution*. New York: Norton, 1974.

Young, D. M., Beier, E. G., Beier, P., & Barton, C. Is chivalry dead? *Journal of Communication*, 1975, **25**, 57–64.

Chapter 15
Confronting the Client-Therapist Relationship in Psychotherapy
Donald J. Kiesler

A procession of clients enters the office of the psychotherapist in individual practice: women and men, young and old, brilliant and not so brilliant, different physiques of varying attractiveness. Symptoms range from phobias, anxieties, depression, and psychosomatic disease to amnesia, delusions, hallucinations, and depersonalization. Interpersonal styles range from the shy, withdrawn, and inhibited to the dominant, sarcastic, combative, and exhibitionistic. Indeed, clients present a potpourri of human experience as they reveal their troubles and concerns in the therapist's office.

By listening carefully to these clients, by struggling to understand their private worlds, the therapist is propelled along many different journeys through his own phenomenal world, encountering myriad intensities and varieties of his own private experience as he goes. He stumbles upon feelings toward his clients, including intimacy, sexual attraction, admiration, and respect, as well as frustration, irritation, competitiveness, anxiety, and depression. He notices "pulls" to respond toward a particular client ranging from giving advice and answers, taking responsibility for solving the client's problems, offering dazzling pearls of wisdom, to being cautious about what he says and how he says it, to wanting to interrupt and "talk down" the client, to wanting to prove to the client how stupid he is in certain areas of his life. Further, he detects rapid-fire self-statements attributing hidden and sometimes sinister motives and intents to his clients such as: "He doesn't really want to get better"; "Damn, she loves to be the center of attention"; "The last thing this guy will ever do is see something, *anything*, about himself clearly"; "God, she actually doesn't have any good reason to continue living," and the like. Finally, at various moments he is caught up, both during and between sessions, with fantasies, reveries, and dreams about a particular client that play out in living color and in condensed form a given pattern of interpersonal engagement.

So it goes, and so it must go! In his psychotherapeutic work, the therapist is a captive to varying degrees on "four-wheeler" rides over the dunes and beaches of his own private terrain of inner experiences. My opinion, and my theoretical statement (Kiesler, 1973, 1979, Chapter 1 of this volume; Kiesler, Bernstein, & Anchin, 1976; Perkins et al., 1979), is that the therapist cannot *not* take these "rides" in his sessions with his clients, that his clients are unknowing experts in kidnapping the feelings and behaviors of others whom they encounter. Moreover, if a therapist does not sharply identify and clarify the route and terrain of his captive voyage with a particular client, he cannot help the client confront his central interpersonal problems. In turn, the client cannot discover and experience the freedom of options in his transactions with important persons in his life. Instead, the client will continue to "overprogram" his interpersonal transactions including those with his therapist, and will continue to be trapped, and to trap others, into rigid, incongruous, and self-defeating encounters.

In this chapter, I will share my thinking and clinical experience regarding strategies and principles which govern effective use by the therapist of his inner engagements, pulls, or impacts in his sessions with clients. Since my theoretical position is available elsewhere, I restrict my focus in what follows primarily to clinical applications and examples in an attempt to provide the live, concrete meaning of what are often esoteric conceptual statements (see Chapter 1 for a general framework for this discussion). The principles I develop below are offered as tentative, first attempts to impose some structure on an often bewildering array of therapeutic events. Up front I am aware that my presentation cannot lead easily to systematic operationalizations or direct empirical test since I will not directly address the ultimately crucial issues of how these general principles might be applied systematically and precisely to a particular client or to a homogeneous group of clients. Addressing this issue, however, remains an important future task for interpersonal theorists.

Throughout what follows, the central topic encompasses what I have called the therapist's "impact messages," or what the psychoanalytic literature refers to as therapist "countertransference." What follows, then, can also be described as my interpersonal-communication or transactional model for use of therapist countertransference in individual psychotherapy.

My first task will be to define therapist impact messages more carefully and to provide a brief rationale for their use in interpersonal psychotherapy. I will then offer some general strategic principles, with clinical examples, which can guide the therapist toward effective use of impact messages in his sessions with his clients.

IMPACT MESSAGES

Impact messages refer to all the internal events a therapist experiences and all the overt behaviors he enacts in his sessions with a client which have the therapist's relationship to the client as their referent or target. They include those therapist emotions, action tendencies, cognitive attributions, and fantasies that represent the therapist's engagements or "pulls" in his transactions with a given client. Their occurrence represents repetitive instances during therapy sessions where the therapist linguistically or nonverbally expresses feelings toward the client, or directs feelings, behaviors, or "commands" to the client.

Several classes of therapist impact messages can be distinguished:

1. *Direct feelings.* When the therapist is with the client, the client arouses distinctive feelings, pulls specific emotions from him (e.g., bored, angry, suspicious, competitive, cautious, etc.).
2. *Action tendencies.* The therapist also experiences definite urges or pulls to do or not to do something when with his client (e.g., I should avoid interrupting him; I should leave him alone; I should defend myself; I have to be gentle with this client; I have to find some answers soon, etc.).

3. *Cognitive attributions.* When with the client, various thoughts run through the therapist's head about what he thinks the client is trying to do to him, or what he thinks the client wants him to do—statements the therapist makes to himself about how the client feels toward him, thinks of him (e.g., this client wants me to put him on a pedestal; he thinks I can't be trusted; he would rather be left alone; he is determined to be in control with me, he wants to be the center of attention, etc.).

4. *Fantasies.* When interacting with his client the therapist often experiences more or less vivid images of himself and the client interacting in concrete contexts (e.g., an image of the client and therapist on separate rafts floating out to sea; the therapist holding the client in his lap in a rocking chair; the client and therapist playing poker together, each wearing dark glasses; the client and therapist making love on a white sand beach, etc.). These images can also occur between sessions as day fantasies or night dreams with distinctive themes and overtones.

These classes of impacts all occur internally, covertly in the therapist's experience. From the first session with a given client, however, they lead to constricted overt responding by the therapist. For example, we may observe the therapist increasing his activity by asking more questions, giving more advice, or by more frequent interruptions. Or he may decrease his activity, sitting much longer in silence, feeling cautious about any intervention, and choosing his words carefully. We may notice more frequent light banter with a client, with frequent laughter and spontaneous comments. The therapist may feel increasingly threatened, feeling more and more inadequate with a given client. He may find he feels little or no emotional response to a client. He may become angrily sympathetic about the client's mistreatment by a spouse or family member. He may become increasingly depressed or anxious with a particular client.

The transactional perspective presented above in Chapter 1 emphasizes that the therapist is pushed, shaped, enticed, pulled, overprogrammed, engaged to give a "complementary" response to a given client which, over time, is registered more or less clearly by the therapist as a pattern of emotional, behavioral, cognitive, and imaginal internal engagement. This distinctive pattern, the particular complex of internal engagement, with a given client or person is the impact message.

A first characteristic of the impact message or complementary response is that it is multidimensional; it includes a complex or mixture of positive and negative feelings and engagements. Any overall impact from a given client or person has both positive and negative affective features, has *polarity*. In other words, the very strengths clients present, since they are extreme and rigid, tend also to include their weakness. For example, use of caution, reason, and introspection represents in some situations a valid approach to successful living, is admirable, and impacts others positively. On the other hand, rigid and extreme use of these same behaviors in close interpersonal encounters often leads to miserable failure and pushes others away.

A second feature of the impact complex is the multiplicity of the covert behavior classes detailed above. That is, not only are therapist feelings involved, but also other covert responses including fantasies and cognitive attributions as well as action tendencies. Of necessity, these covert events are reflected simultaneously in the overt verbal and nonverbal actions of the therapist.

In sum, the impact message is the consequence for other persons of the client's distinctive interpersonal style by which he repetitively engages other significant persons in his life. The client's problems in living are manifested in disordered transactions through duplicitous, self-defeating messages to others, through the recurrent ambiguous pattern and negative consequences of his evoking messages. This rigid and extreme style of self-presentation reflects a constricted and incomplete experience of self. The client's evoking pattern pushes others, including the therapist, into rigid, complementary roles in order to ensure that only confirmatory feedback of the client's identity can be obtained. This command of others eventually elicits from them, and from the therapist, ambiguous and/or negative consequences which are baffling to the client since he doesn't clearly perceive his specific responsibility for these consequences.

It follows, then, that the basic task of the interpersonal communication therapist is to disrupt the rigid transactional pattern which the client imposes on the therapy sessions. The therapist does this by continually giving intervention priority to the client's relational messages—by identifying the client's distinctive interpersonal style through the therapist's labeling of his own impact engagements, by disengaging from these pulls or constrictions, by terminating the complementary response, and by various other maneuvers designed to offer what Beier (1966) calls the "asocial" response.

THE MEANING FRAMES

Before more specifically elaborating how the therapist confronts relationship issues with his clients, it is necessary to provide a more precise, working terminology. Figures 15.1, 15.2, and 15.3 outline a model of what I refer to as "meaning frames" (Kiesler, 1973; Kiesler, Bernstein, & Anchin, 1976), which represent the dyadic referential options the therapist has in responding to the explicit or implicit meanings of clients' statements. As I use these terms in the therapy context, E (encoder or sender of the message) is the client, D (decoder or receiver of the message) is the therapist.

Any client statement or nonverbal behavior has both content and relationship meaning, any comment has both report and command, representational and presentational levels of meaning. Further, the relationship (command, presentational) level includes two separate components: (1) The encoder-to-encoder (client-to-client) aspect defines the encoder-client himself, expresses feelings about, evaluations of, and attitudes toward himself. In Figures 15.1 through 15.3, this aspect is designated EE. (2) The encoder-to-decoder (client-to-therapist) component expresses the encoder-client's feelings about, evaluations of, and attitudes toward the decoder-therapist. In Figures 15.1 through 15.3, this aspect is referred to as ED, or the evoking message by which the encoder-client imposes or commands behavior from the therapist decoder. Both relationship aspects, EE and ED, are communicated not only by the statements the client makes, but especially by the distinctive pattern of nonverbal behavior that accompanies his words.

As a participant in the dyad, the therapist-decoder records two corresponding aspects of relationship messages. (3) The decoder-to-encoder (therapist-to-client) meanings are the emotional, cognitive, behavioral, and imaginal internal responses designated in the figures as DE, or the impact message. These DE meanings represent the complementary response to the client's ED-evoking messages, to the client's rigid and extreme self-presentations. (4) The decoder-to-decoder (therapist-to-therapist) meanings are the therapist's own feelings about, evaluations of, and attitudes toward himself, meanings relevant to his own self-definition. These are designated as DD meanings in the figures.

Following any utterance or action by the client in their sessions, the therapist has the following options: (a) to respond directly to the manifest content of what the client has just said, (b) to respond to one of the four relationships aspects (EE, ED, DE, DD)[1], (c) to

ENCODER'S LINGUISTIC MESSAGE

DECODER SCANS REPERTOIRE
OF MEANINGS ELICITED
BY ENCODER'S MESSAGE
↓

MEANING FRAMES

C

Lexical or Manifest Content
Denotative Meaning

EE

Encoder-Encoder Meanings
Encoder Self-Definitions
Self-Evaluations

DD

Decoder-Decoder Meanings
Decoder's Self-Definitions
Self-Evaluations

ED

Encoder-Decoder Meanings
Encoder's Feelings toward Decoder
Encoder's Relationship to Decoder
"Evoking" Message

DE

Decoder-Encoder Meanings
Decoder's Feelings toward Encoder
Decoder's Relationship to Encoder
"Impact" Message

T

Transitional Meanings
Change of Topic
Unrelated to Encoder's Message

↓

DECODER PICKS A MEANING
FROM AMONG THE FRAMES
SENDS MESSAGE BACK

Fig. 15.1. Kiesler's model of content (denotative) and relationship (connotative) meanings implicit in a particular encoder response. In the therapy context, "encoder" is the client, "decoder" is the therapist. The EE, ED, DE, and DD frames register connotative-relationship messages which are sent by the encoder primarily on nonverbal or nonlinguistic channels. C meanings, in contrast, derive almost exclusively from the linguistic channel.

CLIENT'S LINGUISTIC MESSAGE

"What good is talking
going to do?"

↓

THERAPIST SCANS REPERTOIRE
OF MEANING RESPONSES ELICITED
BY CLIENT'S MESSAGE

↓

MEANING FRAMES

C

"We're so close to our feelings, sometimes the
more we think about them the more confused we
get. Someone who is more objective and trained
to listen can be quite helpful."

EE

"You feel *you* should be
able to lick this
problem by yourself somehow."

DD

"I wondered that myself when
I first started seeing clients."

ED

"You're doubtful that *I'll*
be able to help you."

DE

"I felt a tug—like you want
me to take responsibility for
giving you the answers."

T

"We'll get back to that later. But
first I would like to know . . ."

↓

THERAPIST PICKS A
RESPONSE FROM AMONG THE FRAMES.
SENDS MESSAGE BACK

ED   "You're doubtful
that I'll be able
to help you."

Fig. 15.2. An example of Figure 15.1 applied in the psychotherapy situation. In this figure
Ė = client-encoder; D = therapist-decoder.

CLIENT'S LINGUISTIC MESSAGE

"This guy I went to town with
the other day told me I was
no good to nobody . . . I
just want to run away and die."

↓

THERAPIST SCANS REPERTOIRE
OF MEANING RESPONSES ELICITED
BY CLIENT'S MESSAGE

↓

MEANING FRAMES

C
"Where would you go?"

EE
"Here's somebody who meant something
to you. If *he* feels I'm no good to him,
then that just proves I'm no good to
anyone."

DD
"There was a time when I felt
that way about myself."

ED
"Perhaps part of that applies to me . . .
Do I think you're worth anything?"

DE
"I would be quite sad if you
killed yourself."

T
"Perhaps we should look more closely
at what happened with your friend on the
way to town."

↓

THERAPIST PICKS A
RESPONSE FROM AMONG THE FRAMES.
SENDS MESSAGE BACK

DE   "I would be quite
sad if you killed
yourself."

Fig. 15.3. An example of Figure 15.1 applied in the psychotherapy situation. In this figure
E = client encoder; D = therapist decoder.

change topics, or (d) not to respond verbally at all. Which meaning frame the therapist targets in his response depends on his best guess at the moment as to which is the more salient meaning in the client's experience, as well as on what is most "figure" for the therapist at the moment. The therapist's choices are influenced by the total pattern of the client's previous communications, by the therapist's conceptualizations of the central issues permeating the client's problems, and particularly by the degree of congruence evident at that moment between the client's verbal and nonverbal messages.

Whenever the therapist addresses either the ED-evoking or DE-impact frames, he directly addresses the relationship between himself and his client. I define relationship as the momentary and cumulative result of the reciprocal messages, primarily nonverbal, exchanged between two interactants—the continually evolving reciprocal effects of messages sent to and received by two interactants in the ED-evoking and DE-impact meaning frames. The therapeutic relationship, therefore, is the momentary and cumulative reciprocal emotional and other engagements occurring between client and therapist—the continually evolving reciprocal effects of messages sent to and received by client and therapist in the ED-evoking and DE-impact meaning frames.[2]

The remainder of this chapter will focus on maneuvers by which the therapist confronts the client-therapist relationship as articulated in my interpersonal communication theory. It will be helpful to the reader to keep in mind the distinct meaning frames depicted in the figures, as well as EO and OE possibilities. I will first briefly describe my process model and some general statements about using impact messages in therapy. I will then articulate eight principles or rules that can guide a therapist in confronting the ED-DE relationship in therapy via the process of metacommunication.

A GENERAL PROCESS MODEL FOR THERAPEUTIC USE OF IMPACT MESSAGES

Ideally, therapist DE-impact responses are experienced sequentially in two basic stages: the "engaged" or "hooked" phase, and the "disengaged" or "squirmed loose" phase.

The Engaged or Hooked Phase

From the moment the client first enters the therapist's office, the therapy dyad is off and running. Already the therapist is being pushed into a constricted, narrow range of responding to the client. Through his statements and nonverbal behaviors, the client's ED-evoking messages are shaping the therapist to respond to him from a restricted aspect of the therapist's own internal experience and behavior repertoire. That is, the therapist is pulled to provide the complementary response. The therapist cannot *not* be hooked or sucked in by the client, because the client is more adept, more expert in his distinctive, rigid, and extreme game of interpersonal encounter. As Leary (1957) observed, "the more extreme and rigid the person, the greater his interpersonal 'pull'—the stronger his ability to shape the relationship with others" (p. 126).

The client tells the therapist his rehearsed story about his complaints and problems but, since it has led to neither understanding nor change, his rehearsed story has significant omissions or blind spots, as well as under- and overemphases. Along with the story comes a rehearsed, overpracticed, automatic pattern of nonverbal messages which push other persons, including the therapist, into adoption of complementary roles vis-à-vis the client. Others' adoption of their roles in turn confirms the client's own role definition or identity. Underlying both parties' roles are the interpersonal dimensions of affiliation, control, and inclusion with particular manifestations falling around the periphery of Leary's (1957) Interpersonal Circle, and including stances such as Hostility, Mistrust, Nurturance, Submissiveness, Detachment, Exhibitionism, and the like.

Thus, as Chapter 1 elaborates, the therapist's inner experiences and overt behaviors get shaped, moved, restricted to a particular, complementary pie slice of the Circle with a given client. Impact messages are operationalized (Kiesler et al., 1975, 1976; Perkins et al., 1979) as therapist responses which cluster into several of the 15 categories around the Interpersonal Circle. The roles that the client imposes on the therapist, therefore, are various mixtures of positions falling on the dimensions of affiliation, control, and inclusion.

The position the client pushes the therapist to adopt is one that is least threatening as well as most supportive and reinforcing of the roles central to the client's definition of self. By eliciting the complementary role from the therapist, the client continues to validate his self-definition and hangs on to the self-in-world view that organizes his experience. The therapist's and others' complementary responses thus ensure that the client receives feedback which is congruent with his self-conceptualization and confirmatory of his chosen identity. Unfortunately, the complementary responses from others also includes ambiguous, negative, and nonconfirmatory components. These nonconfirmatory consequences occur less clearly and tend to accumulate over time. As a result, it is much more difficult for the client to pinpoint the hook-up of these aversive consequences to his self-presentational pattern, especially to its rarely attended to nonverbal features. In turn, the client is hard put to perceive any responsibility for producing these aversive consequences.

To summarize, in the "hooked" stage, the client's ED-evoking style pulls a distinct pattern of ED-impact messages from the therapist. The therapist cannot prevent this hooking since the client initially is superior to the therapist in shaping the direction their relationship is to follow.

The Disengaged or Squirmed Loose Phase

As the therapist is hooked, he experiences greater or lesser intensities of the various classes of impact messages: feelings, action tendencies, cognitive attributions, and fantasies. If the therapist continues to be hooked, does not squirm loose, he is in effect unwittingly reinforcing the maladaptive style of the client. Over their sessions the therapist will increasingly experience the cumulative impact of the client's maladaptive evoking style by feeling some combination of negative feelings such as anxiety, frustration, irritation, depression, and so on. If the therapist continues to be unaware of his hooking, his experience of these negative feelings is of necessity countercommunicated to the client, usually through a package of his own amgibuous, negative, and incongruent verbal and nonverbal messages. These occurrences not only compound the transactional stalemate, but with his ambiguous and incongruent communications the therapist finds himself in the embarrassing position of modeling maladaptive communication for the client.

Phenomenologically, the extreme experience of the hooked phase is a bad place for the therapist to be. On the one hand, he perceives his role with his client as an accepting, understanding, and nurturant care giver. On the other hand, he increasingly experiences boredom, dread, anxiety, incompetence, irritation, and other feelings during his client's sessions. These negative feelings obviously can threaten the therapist's self-system, and precipitate negative DD self-statements. To prevent this aversive occurrence, the therapist can initiate his own ED-evoking game with the client through what often becomes a power struggle initiated to protect the therapist's identity. This maladaptive possibility on the therapist's part underscores the necessity of arriving at the second stage in therapy through the "disengagement" process.

Since the therapist cannot *not* be sucked in by the client, he of necessity experiences feelings and other engagements with his client *before* he ever notices or labels them. *The first essential step in the disengagement process then, is that the therapist notice, attend to, and subsequently label the engagements being pulled from him by a given client.* Until the therapist notices what is happening internally to him, he is caught in the client's transactional game. Dollard and Miller (1950) point to the necessity of this first step when they define classic psychoanalytic countertransference as instances when the therapist's emotional responses are neither noticed nor labeled by him.

Accordingly, from the first session the therapist must ask himself these essential questions: What is this client doing to me? What am I feeling when I'm with this client? What do I want to do or not do with this client? The Impact Message Inventory (Kiesler et al., 1975, 1976; Perkins et al., 1979) provides a useful format for this self-exploratory process.

In this identification task, the major cue the therapist employs is the emerging outline of a *repetitive pattern* to his internal responses, the general feeling that whatever is happening is recurrent with this client, that the same feelings and tendencies appear over repeated instances. Other important cues are instances when the therapist notices the therapy task "bogging down," when the client seems to abandon his previous immersion in productive self-disclosure and exploration. Or, if things start to get better for the client, they seem to stop. Or, if homework is suggested or assigned, it isn't done. In various ways the client interrupts his previous baseline of pursuing understanding and change.

Other cues available to the therapist to detect his hooking are instances of incongruity on his own part where he feels himself saying things to his client that he doesn't really mean, or with nonverbal expressions that don't seem to fit. Or the therapist may notice himself way off his own usual baseline in therapy—talking more or less than usual, liking or disliking a client more intensely, feeling particularly brilliant or dull with a given client, and so on. At times the therapist may find himself tending to avoid or to emphasize certain topics regardless of the client's interest. Or the therapist may notice his own anxiety at particular moments with his client.

By whatever means the therapist notices or attends to the distinctive transactional milieu experienced within himself, makes "figure" out of what was previously "ground," he thereby takes the initial, crucial step of disengagement. By identifying what is happening to him, by perceiving his personal consequences as one more instance of how the client engages others, the therapist regains a level of understanding and objectivity that permits alternative interventions designed to help the client see and experience the pattern for himself.

The second disengagement maneuver available to the therapist is to discontinue the complementary response. If he realizes he has been pulled to give answers and advice, he must withhold these responses. If he has been pulled to be entertained, he must cease enjoying the entertainment. If he has been feeling cautious and constricted, he must find a way to be more spontaneous. If he has been protecting the client from more intense emotion, he must help the client face the feared feelings.

A third disengagement option for the therapist is through appropriate technique to help the client interrupt his distinctive ED-evoking style. For example, if the client uses abstractions and qualifications in disclosing his problems and concerns, the therapist can consistently push for concrete elaborations through pinpointing and situational analysis. If the client entertains the therapist with anecdotes and histrionic displays, the therapist can reflect the client's feelings of fragility and vulnerability, and encourage him to attend to and elaborate the feelings being avoided. In other words, by selective use of technique, the therapist can assist the client to tune in on aspects of his experience that he is ignoring, under-, or overemphasizing, which underlie the constricted self-presentation which eventually alienates others in his life. By disengaging, the therapist prevents the client from alienating him. Unlike others with whom the client interacts, the therapist "hangs-in" in a supportive fashion to help the client face tuned out aspects of his experience, which the client is avoiding so as to keep his self-definition from being destroyed, to keep himself from emerging naked and vulnerable in a totally unpredictable world.

The last and most powerful disengagement option in the therapist's arsenal is for the therapist to talk directly to the client about the engagements that are transpiring between them. In transactional language, the therapist "metacommunicates" with the client by referring directly to the ED-evoking or DE-impact relationship messages occurring between them. Since it is far from the norm for persons to talk directly to each other about what is transpiring between them nonverbally, metacommunication is very much an "asocial" response. Especially with individuals who have problems in living, others most frequently take the easiest way out by simply leaving the scene. Even those who do not flee usually stay with the implicit agreement that talking about what we are really doing to each other is forbidden. Generally, metacommunication remains a remote option in everyday affairs because of the threat that it can eventuate in rejection, withdrawal of affection, and isolation, that it can lead to disconfirmation of one's self-presentation or identity.

A major result of these everyday implicit pacts is that relationships with significant others continue to be defined exclusively through nonverbal channels. While analogic, iconic, nonverbal signals are powerful, they often are also imprecise, particularly when they include incongruous messages. An unfortunate result is that nonverbal relationship messages between persons are too often susceptible to misinterpretation. Most frequently, we actually prefer these ambiguous and uncertain nonverbal messages to more precise linguistic encodings which can result in clear, unwanted, and feared answers such as rejection, disapproval, and withholding of love. Metacommunication, then, is a relatively infrequent event especially for persons engulfed in problems of living with others.

The advantages of metacommunication, however, are evident. As Villard and Whipple (1976) emphasize, metacommunication produces several distinctly favorable interpersonal outcomes. (1) It reduces the likelihood of problems resulting from inaccurate communication or from misinterpretations, by moving toward a negotiated validation of the actual relationship messages being sent between two persons. (2) Metacommunication brings ambiguities, difficulties, and uncertainties between two parties to a conscious level of awareness so that the parties have the opportunity to clarify together what is happening between them. This negotiated validation labels the intents of both parties so that possible future areas of confrontation and misunderstanding can be avoided more easily. (3) This explicit definition of relationship makes it less likely that the parties will continue to maneuver covertly, nonverbally, with each other to obtain what they want. Instead, in concrete momentary instances it is more possible to state wants directly. (4) Finally, metacommunication increases tolerance for personal differences in that the parties clarify for each other their basic identities. Even with impasses, discussion and elucidation of basic wants and fears provides a perspective for understanding that it is difficult to arrive at solely by inferences from nonverbal messages.

By metacommunicating with his client, then, the therapist provides a very powerful asocial response. By addressing their relationship directly, the therapist models for the client a powerful and unusual technique for communicating with those persons who are significant in the client's life. Further, metacommunication provides the same advantages for the client's relationship to the therapist that it provides for his relationships outside therapy. Namely, it makes inaccurate communication or misunderstanding less likely between therapist and client. Metacommunication brings the attention and labeling of both therapist and client to the relationship issues that are developing between them, permitting pinpointing of the distinctive patterns these maneuvers have taken, which in turn makes it easier for both parties to notice and label subsequent issues as they emerge. As a result, metacommunication interferes with any continued unintended and predominantly nonverbal maneuvers in the therapy dyad. Finally, it provides for increased mutual tolerance and understanding by therapist and client, making it easier for the uniqueness of each party to be preserved with mutual respect for continuing differences. Unquestionably these are constructive consequences, and their implementation in the therapy process provides a relatively unique and powerful human experience.

The success of metacommunication, however, depends crucially on the commitment of the therapist to open, direct, unambiguous communication to the client about the therapist's inner engagements and pulls, and the skill with which he can provide feedback in a manner that is both confrontative as well as supportive and protective of the client's self-esteem. In his use of impact messages, the therapist must always consider the level of potential threat and disruption to the client's EE meaning frame—that is, to the client's conception of self and the integral role he assumes in dealing with his interpersonal world.

The hard work of therapy involves this metacommunicative task. Most crucially, the therapist must break the vicious circle by not continuing to be hooked or trapped by the client's engagement or pull. The therapist must disengage from his impact responses before they build to an intensity which impels the therapist to countercommunicate aversively or incongruently to the client. Furthermore, metacommunication involves the therapist's (1) telling the client both the positive and negative engagements he experiences with the client—an admittedly risky task for both therapist and client; (2) pursuing the extent to which the client intended to elicit that effect from the therapist; (3) identification of the self-definitional and relationship claim the client is intending to impose on the relationship; (4) pinpointing with the client the exact pattern of verbal and nonverbal behaviors which produced the impact (here videotape feedback is often very helpful); (5) analysis of the client's extratherapy relationships with significant others in terms of the identified evoking style of the client; (6) modeling, rehearsal, and reinforcement of alternative, more successful, and flexible client interpersonal styles to be used with persons in his life; and (7) modeling and reinforcement of the metacommunicative process itself for the client to use with important persons in his life—the client thus learns to talk directly with others who matter about their relationship communication.

Let us turn now to some principles of impact confrontation in individual psychotherapy. As stated earlier, these principles are tentative, and deserve close scrutiny, critique, and subsequent modification. Nevertheless, they represent the state of the art as I percieve it at this time.

EIGHT PRINCIPLES FOR METACOMMUNICATION IN PSYCHOTHERAPY

It is important to restate the major rule that underlies any use of relationship confrontation in psychotherapy—namely, the continuing priority for the therapist's disengagement.

Throughout his sessions the therapist must seek to identify and label the pattern of ED-evoking style of his client, and his own complementary DE-impact responses. His continuing goal is to terminate his complementary response as quickly as possible, and to begin to provide other asocial responses which help to disrupt the client's rigid and extreme self-presentation. Among the asocial options available to the therapist are stopping the complementary response, using technique to alter aspects of the client's ED pattern of communication, and metacommunication. The remainder of this chapter focuses on this last option, by offering eight principles that guide the use of metacommunication with clients.

Principle 1

Whenever the therapist is referentially but implicitly included in a client's statement, the therapist's priority is to explore explicitly with the client the ED implications of that statement. This ED exploration is particularly crucial in early sessions with clients, but remains a metacommunicative priority throughout therapy. If a client states in a first session with a therapist, "I really led my former therapist around by the nose," it behooves the therapist very soon to inquire as to how that statement has implications for their own sessions. If a female client states to her male therapist, "I have trouble relating to *men*," the therapist needs to inquire into the meaning of that statement for their own therapy relationship. Other similar client statements are: "I really have trouble trusting *people*"; "Other *persons* don't understand me"; "I have trouble taking responsibility with *people*," and the like.

The client in each of these instances is using indirect and generalized rather than direct and concrete language to refer to a relationship issue. Class-membership words are used (therapist, men, people), and although the therapist is an obvious member of that class, the direct translation is avoided. Clients much more frequently use this indirect language instead of talking directly and unambiguously (e.g., I'm not sure I can relate to you since you are a man"; "I probably will have trouble trusting you"; "I doubt that you will be able to understand me either").

If the therapist does not respond to and explore with the client the ED implications of this kind of statement, he participates in avoiding direct and clear communication. But more relevant to the moment, he avoids clarification of a possible relationship issue that can continue as an interference with the basic therapy task of honest and complete self-disclosure (e.g., if you are a male therapist, and I have trouble relating to men, how can I feel comfortable about disclosing important things to you?). On the other hand, by addressing the issue directly and explicitly, the therapist demonstrates his empathic expertise and can negotiate explicitly with the client strategies for addressing these issues in their subsequent sessions.

The therapist's inquiry takes the form of: "I wonder how that (your leading your former therapist around by the nose; your having trouble relating to men) relates to me," or "I wonder what that means for our relationship." Or in a later session when the client is obviously irritated or angry, the therapist can inquire, "You're obviously pissed off about something today. I wonder if you're pissed off at me."

Principle 2

In feeding back impact messages to the client, it is essential for the therapist to communicate both the positive and the negative polarity of his affective engagements. The client needs a confrontation, but it must simultaneously communicate support and endorsement of the client's self-esteem. The client needs to be told of the negative effects he produces in others, but if it is to be useful, he must first hear the feedback. He cannot open himself to honest exploration of the validity of the feedback if his world view, his identity, is drastically challenged or dramatically disrupted. None of us can let go of the familiar, least of all the ineffective and self-defeating familiar, until the hope of an alternative is provided. The familiar, even when unsatisfactory, is at least predictable and clearly preferable to the panic of sudden unpredictability. Hence, it is vital for the therapist to judge the resultant impact on the client beforehand, especially the level of disruptive anxiety, of any feedback he provides. This empathic judgment by the therapist presupposes his understanding and respect for the real anxiety and pain involved in the client's growth process.

The therapist incorporates positive-negative polarity in his metacommunications in two ways. The most frequent manner is the situation in which the therapist's linguistic messages carries the negative feedback, while his concomitant nonverbal messages signal positive affiliation and respect; that is, the therapist states the negative while nonverbally displaying the positive.

We all have experienced this verbal-nonverbal mixture at various times in our lives. Person A and person B may give us identical verbal feedback; in the case of A we don't hear it and get furious, while with B we hear it and assimilate it. We may dislike A or perceive A simultaneously communicating ridicule, disrespect, or contempt. On the other hand, we respect and like B, and read B as generally respecting us, caring enough to tell us something that is difficult both for him to say and for us to hear. Because of the positive nonverbal messages that accompany B's feedback, we hear and, it is hoped, learn. In contrast, because of the predominantly negative messages coming from A, we tune him out and counterattack.

Our clients are no different in this respect, except that their self-definitions and ED-presentational styles are more extreme and more rigid. The therapist is naive to expect that his feedback will be heard and integrated regardless of his concurrent nonverbal presentations. Instead, it is vital that through his gaze, posture, distance, paralanguage, etc., the therapist commmunicate a clear positive message of respect and concern for the client, for the client's approach to life, and for his struggle to change. When the client-therapist relationship is strong and predictable, when the therapist shows empathy for the client's tolerance for pain and anxiety, the therapist can effectively confront the client, sometimes with incredible frankness, about the invalidity of some of the client's assumptions, labelings, and overt behaviors with significant others in his life.

A second avenue for effective confrontation is to feed back to the client the positive aspect of his evoking style (targeting his intent in what he is doing with others) combined with the negative (the consequences for others of his evoking style, of which he remains relatively ignorant). In this combination, the therapist labels both the ED intent which incorporates the client's strength and positive self-identification (EE), as well as the negative consequences for others of his overt verbal and nonverbal presentations (DE). For example, a therapist might say, "It frustrates me that every time we get close to exploring something important, you immediately run away from it. The message I get from you is that you're very fragile, and I must be very careful not to upset you further by asking you to keep your focus there (DE). But although it's frustrating to me, I realize also that you're trying to protect yourself from discovering some things about yourself that might be painful (EE), or that might make you feel more vulnerable with me (ED)." The first part of this statement reflects the therapist's exasperation with the client's evoking message, "I'm fragile; treat me with kid gloves," which over time pushes the therapist and others away.

The second part verbalizes the therapist's realization that this protective maneuver makes sense, that it is a form of avoiding pain and anxiety which any of us might use to maintain self-respect and identity. The combined statement, therefore, helps the client both to retain self-esteem as well as to begin to discriminate strengths and weaknesses in his approach to living. It thereby facilitates the important learning that valid self-esteem is built upon honest confrontation of one's weaknesses as well as strengths, that weakness is a component of living for us all.

Gendlin (1967, 1968) presents a parallel position from an existential viewpoint: "The therapist must first and foremost respond to the positive tendency which needs to be carried further from out of the negative pattern. . . . There is always a positive tendency which we can 'read' in the negative behavior. Such reading isn't a Pollyanna invention of ours. It is, rather, that something of importance is always just then being defeated, making for a problem" (Gendlin, 1968, p. 224). Gendlin (1967) refers to this bipolar communication as expressing the "two-sided compound":

The reasons against expressing something must also be included. Whatever in my feelings holds me back from expressing something, that too I can express, and in fact, I can express the two-sided compound, whereas I did not feel I could express just the one feeling. For example, to say just "I think you're very scared that you really are crazy," might scare him all the more because he might feel that *I* think he is. Actually, he often makes very good sense about many things and if I express that, too, "Actually, you make very good sense about a lot of things," the first sentence becomes a safe one. This therapist expression becomes possible for me as I decide to voice also that which at first stopped me from expressing my feeling. Another example: "I don't like it when you do that, and I don't want you to do it anymore. But I think you do it . . . and I like *that*." [P. 397.]

By one or both of these polarity communications, then, the therapist softens the threat value, reduces the anxiety of loss of self-esteem for the client so that the feedback can be received—the necessary first step before further exploration and validation can occur. Effective therapist metacommunication thus communicates both negative and positive engagements from the client, thereby expressing the polarity of the impact complex.

Principle 3

In metacommunication the therapist's attitude and intent are crucial to the effectiveness of the feedback given—leading to its being heard and usefully explored by the client. This principle is directly related to Principle 2 which stated that the therapist must communicate affiliation and respect simultaneously with feedback that has threatening and therefore negative connotations for the client. It further emphasizes that the purpose of feedback is to provide a conceptual-experiential framework that will be helpful to the client in understanding and changing his ineffective and self-defeating interactional patterns. For this goal to be accomplished, it is critical that the client perceive the feedback as offered for his benefit, as given to him by someone concerned enough for his welfare to tell him things that are risky to some extent to the teller himself.

It is important, then, that the therapist's feedback not manifest a "win or lose" flavor, or evolve into a contest of power or put-down of the client. To the extent that this power struggle results, the therapist is pursuing his own ED-evoking game, and is forcing the client into a role that supports the therapist's constricted definition of himself.

In contrast, a facilitative attitude accompanying metacommunication is evidenced by nonverbal messages of positive affiliation; by a tentative presentation of the feedback, by a communicated attitude of participatory exploration wherein both therapist and client pursue the validity/usefulness of what the therapist has said to understanding and changing the client's approach to life. Like any other hypothesis, metacommunicative feedback may be shown to be invalid or in need of modification. Invalidating clarification can be just as useful for understanding and change as the case where the therapist's feedback seems to fit precisely.

Principle 4

For effective metacommunication, it is not sufficient for the therapist merely to disclose his impact responses; additionally he must pinpoint instances of the client's specific actions which elicited his responses. By pinpointing, I refer to giving the client concrete instances, specifying in detail the client's overt pattern of verbal and nonverbal behavior which triggers the therapist's impact. It is for pinpointing purposes that videotape feedback can often be more convincing than verbal feedback alone.

Pinpointing presumes the *repeated occurrence* of an aspect of the client's ED-evoking style—usually in the hooked phase when the therapist automatically provides the complementary response. Having identified and labeled the hooking over time, however, the therapist sensitizes himself to future occurrences and can also rehearse a precise statement to the client of the identified pattern. For example, the therapist might offer the following: "I realize it's important for you to be cautious and rational in what you do or say to others, and I agree that it is important in many situations. Yet it seems in our sessions you sometimes send messages you don't intend as a result of this caution. For example, you often show long, silent pauses with me after I've said something to you, and frequently a quick smile flashes on and off. Several times when you did that I felt you were really disagreeing with what I was saying, or were thinking that my comment was a little stupid. But I found out later that wasn't the case, that actually you were feeling a little stupid about yourself . . . I wonder if others might misread you sometimes in the same way, feeling that you are disapproving of them, which is not your intent at all."

The pinpointed portion of this statement is, "you often show long, silent pauses with me . . . and frequently a quick smile flashes on and off." This is a concrete specification of the client's overt ED communication pattern. If the client uses that pattern repetitively with his spouse, parents, friends, and other significant persons, it is likely that it produces negative engagements in them of a similar form, namely cognitive attributions that "He really thinks what I said is stupid, but he won't tell me that"; "He's looking down his nose at me." Accompanying these attributions are varying intensities of irritation and anger toward the client, and a tendency to pull back from any further disclosing or intimate interaction. The client tends to push away persons with whom he wants to be close by this process, in our case by an unintended, disdainful, and negatively evaluative, nonverbal display. If this is a valid description of what the client does both to the therapist and to others, it seems crucial that the client should know about it and get on with discovering and clarifying what it is that keeps him from communicating more clearly with others.

There are exceptions, however, to Principle 4. In some instances the therapist must metacommunicate as a first exploratory step even when he cannot pinpoint at all what it is that is triggering his impact responses. This condition occurs when the therapist abruptly registers an unusual quality or quantity of engagement with a particular client—that is, a sudden increase in physical attraction, in irritation or anger, or most commonly, a sudden confusion about what is going on. In these instances a sudden shift occurs away from the dyadic baseline of therapeutic disclosure and exploration. Since the task is in the process of being disrupted, it is crucial that the therapist focus attention on whatever it might be that *is* going on, even though he initially has little idea what it might be.

For example, during a particular session it might not at first be at all apparent to the therapist that his client's nonverbal pattern has shifted away from his more typical baseline to the point that the client is more frequently avoiding mutual gaze, shifting posture, averting body orientation, having longer latencies, and inserting harsher overtones to his statements. Gradually, however, the therapist experiences the impacts of these shifts by feeling increasingly attacked, things bogging down, loss of direction, difficulty in understanding, frustration, and confusion mixed with some irritation and anger.

Even though the exact pattern cannot be pinpointed, when the fact of disruption becomes clear to the therapist, it is important for him to metacommunicate anyway in something like the following manner: "Something different is happening with us today. I don't know what it is, but I'm feeling attacked (or defensive, or confused, or frustrated). I want to check this out with you since I'm being distracted by something." The purpose of this kind of metacommunication is to clear the relationship air by at least getting the issue on the table, and to pursue precise pinpointing of what is occurring with the client. This may or may not be accomplished, depending on the client's receptivity and on the therapist's ability to monitor and conceptualize during the remaining moments of their session. Regardless, the issue must be put on the table between therapist and client, so that the therapist can at least begin his disengagement and maintain some level of objectivity with his client.

This exception can be called *Principle 4a: When the therapist's impacts shift to a sharply atypical level in a specific instance with a client to the point that the therapy task of disclosure and exploration becomes markedly disrupted, the therapist's priority is to metacommunicate about his impacts as an initial, mutually exploratory move, even though precise pinpointing is not possible at that moment.*

Principle 5

The earlier in their sessions the therapist detects and labels his impact responses to a client, the easier it is for him to disengage from the corresponding affect and thereby pursue his intervention options including metacommunication with his client. Effective metacommunication seems to require mild to moderate levels of DE affective intensity in the therapist, whereas strong levels of therapist emotion make metacommunication quite difficult and problematical.

This principle directly reflects the effects of strong emotion on humans, which is primarily to disrupt perceptual, cognitive, and motor activity. Even though an intense feeling should be easier to detect and label than a mild or moderate level, the effects of strong emotion ensure that the therapist cannot perform in an efficient, objective, and detached manner to use his feelings as corrective feedback for useful exploration with his client. Instead, the therapist is to some extent at least temporarily lost in his own associative fantasies, thoughts, and action tendencies. Generally, the least disruptive action for the therapist at these points is to stall through the remainder of the session, and to attempt to disengage between sessions by supervisory consultation or by personal analysis of the disruptive events.

Intense levels of feelings are not frequent occurrences for most therapists, but seem to be universal happenings at some times for all therapists. Their occurrences reflect the facts that therapists cannot always be maximally efficient, that patients are more adept at their distractive games than the therapist, and that some patient-therapist match-ups present more problems for a given therapist than do others. Finally, they also represent the therapist's potential for introducing his own hangups into the relationship, with certain clients and/or topics triggering instances of the therapist's own ED-evoking responses when his own self-system (DD) is threatened in the therapy session.

All of this underscores the continuing importance of the therapist's consideration of his own idiosyncratic input into the relationship issues that develop with his clients. This possibility is what makes therapy a continual opportunity for both personal growth and personal threat for the therapist. Psychotherapeutic work continues to be therapy for the therapist to some degree throughout his professional career.

The importance of detecting and labeling therapist impact responses as early as possible in psychotherapy sessions also reflects another basic process. It is highly likely that all human feelings which remain unlabeled or unacted-upon tend to "incubate." Incubation has been empirically established for the emotion of fear, and is probably equally applicable to anger and other emotions. By incubation the intensity of unlabeled or unacted-upon emotion tends to increase with the passage of time, apparently through some form of a cognitive rehearsal process. This phenomenon would lead us to predict that the level of undetected therapist affect should increase with intensity over sessions. In addition, the fact that the client will be enacting repeated instances of his ED-evoking style during their sessions ensures cumulative repetitive elicitings of the therapist's DE-impacts. Both these processes again underscore the conclusion that earlier disengagement, by detecting and labeling, is easier and permits more effective metacommunication.

One final consideration leads to the same conclusion. From a transactional perspective, the earlier in his sessions with a client the therapist detects any level of recurrent impact response, the more likely it is that the client is *not* responding to the idiosyncratic characteristics of the therapist, rather that he is responding to the therapist in a generalized role. The earlier in their encounter this occurs, the more likely it is that the client's actions which trigger the therapist's DE-impacts are parataxic distortions or transferences, the more likely it is that the client is pushing the therapist into a restricted, overprogrammed role to protect and validate his identity. In Singer's (1970) language, the earlier this occurs the more likely it is that the client is responding to the therapist in a "disrespectful" manner, as a generalized other carried over from the past, and the less likely it is that the client is discriminating the unique presentations of the therapist in their sessions. For these reasons, the sooner a therapist can detect and label distinctive DE-impacts from his client, the more confident he is that his own idiosyncratic characteristics are being ignored by the client, and that his impacts reflect instead the more generalized ED-evoking style of the client.

It does not follow from Principle 5 that the therapist can *metacommunicate* more effectively with his client in earlier than in later sessions. Application of Principle 5 needs to be balanced with Principles 2, 3, and 4. In other words, effective metacommunication presumes the perception by the client of some stable positive affiliation from the therapist, the client's perception of a respectful, on-task attitude and intent from the therapist, and the availability of specific pinpointed examples. Since some time is usually necessary to ensure these preconditions, it follows that effective metacommunication is not a highly probable event in early sessions. What Principle 5 does assert, however, is that the earlier the therapist can *detect and label* his DE-engagements, the easier will be his task of disengagement from higher intensities of affect. In earlier sessions this labeling can immediately begin to guide appropriate technique by the therapist to alter the client's ED-evoking style in the sessions themselves.

It is my experience, however, and seems theoretically consistent that in some rarer instances, very early metacommunication with a client can be very effective. With a highly motivated client and with a fortuitous client-therapist matchup, it seems that very early metacommunication can facilitate the establishment of a positive relationship with a client, can structure therapy goals, and can provide hope for and reinforcement of the client's attempts at growth. Consider, for example, the following statements by a therapist at the end of a first session with a client: "I want to give you some feedback regarding what's been happening with me in our session today. First, at times I found it difficult to take your pain and hurt seriously. When you talked about painful things you always smiled at the same time. It was only when I looked at your eyes and ignored your mouth that I felt some of your hurt. I guess I'm already wondering whether sometimes other persons in your life might have trouble taking you seriously. Second, when you talk, it is at times difficult to follow your train of thought. You start off in one direction, shift to another, then another, and all the time I'm wondering where you're going and whether you're going to bring it back to the original topic. Again, I'm already wondering whether other persons might experience the same difficulty in following what you're trying to say. Finally, I noticed also that your language tends to be abstract, that you talk in generalities, don't often give concrete examples. As a result, it's hard for me to visualize what you do or don't do with others, hear what you're saying or they're saying. Maybe it will be important for us to look more carefully at concrete situations so that both of us can know more precisely what it is that is producing problems for you." Some of this feedback was immediately confirmed by the client in that she reported instances of similar statements from acquaintances. The exchange also seemed to solidify further her commitment to therapy and became part of our initial articulation of therapy goals. Very early metacommunication seemed in this instance to facilitate both our positive relationship and subsequent constructive progress.

Principle 6

So long as the client is productively (i.e., with congruent communication) pursuing some aspect of the self-disclosure and exploratory task of psychotherapy, metacommunication assumes less of a therapeutic priority. Throughout periods of productive work by the client, the therapist continues to detect and label DE-impacts, but the engagements remain more in the "ground" of the therapist's attention. He continues to monitor them, but puts these labelings "on hold" for possible future confrontation when and if the client's pursuit of the therapy task bogs down.

This principle highlights the essential point that ED-DE metacommunication is only part of what the interactional therapist does with his clients. It is a crucial part, and its continued exploration is essential to the ultimate effectiveness of other therapist interventions. Nevertheless, the task of psychotherapy includes productive/congruent exploration of *all* the meaning frames (EE, ED, DE, EO, OE, and perhaps DD). The therapy dyad is on task when the therapist and client simultaneously are attending to, focusing on, and exploring the same particular meaning frame. Conversely, the dyad is off task, bogging down, when the therapist is focusing on one meaning frame and the client is experiencing and attending to another. When the task bogs down in therapy, it usually is because the therapist is focusing on some frame other than ED-DE, while the client is immersed in some aspect of their relationship. Hence, the maneuver by the therapist that can get things back on task is to direct his attention and statements to the relationship by metacommunication. This is the interactional parallel to the psychoanalytic dictum: when you encounter a resistance, interpret the transference.

Much productive therapeutic work occurs in the nonrelational meaning frames, and indeed these frames represent the majority of the therapist's intervention time. What Principle 6 asserts is that as long as some aspect of that work is being steadily pursued, metacommunication is not a priority. The task, however, inevitably bogs down at distinct points over the sessions as the ED-evoking style of the client recurrently emerges in greater intensity. In order that growth and change continue, stabilize, and transfer stably to the client's extratherapy environment, it remains essential for the therapist to meta-communicate with the client at these disruptive instances.

Principle 7

The therapist's disclosure to the client of his DE-impacts is only the beginning of the metacommunicative process. As Principle 4 already stated, effective exploration of meta-communication feedback also includes precise pinpointing with the client of his ED style of overt verbal and nonverbal behavior. Additionally, *the most effective exploration and elaboration of ED-DE feedback involves "shuttling" around or between the EE, ED, and DE meaning frames as they are relevant in the therapy sessions, and around or between the EE, EO, and OE meanings frames as they are relevant outside the sessions in the client's relationships to significant others.*

This principle reflects the basic interactional assumption that the client's ED-evoking style as manifested to the therapist is the central component of the client's problems in living manifest in his interactions with other important persons in his life. Further, since the therapist's labelings of his distinctive DE-impacts represent hypotheses similar to any other hypotheses he presents to his client, they need to be validated with the client as would any other conceptualization. In the case of labelings of DE-impacts, the crucial validation involves the generality of occurrence of the pattern with other significant persons in the client's life. The ED-evoking style need not be (and most often is not) evident with all other persons in the client's life, but is evident with those "significant others" who are targets for intimacy and inclusion in the client's life. Hence, it is vital to explore the validity of pinpointed ED-DE in-therapy patterns by exploring their occurrence in EO-OE extratherapy encounters. Shuttling among or between the meaning frames is necessary to establish the validity and generality of the client's maladaptive patterns.

Principle 8

The therapist's differential use and sequencing of metacommunication with a given client depends not only on the level of positive affiliation established for their dyad (Principles 2 and 3), but also on client individual differences as reflected in his particular ED-evoking style on the Interpersonal Circle. As discussed previously, with some clients dyadic affilia-tion is established quickly and earlier DE feedback is possible. Affiliation builds more slowly with other clients so that initial focus on other meaning frames is much more appropriate. Likewise, depending on the particular complaints, problems, and/or ED-evoking style of a given client, for one case more effective and efficient metacommunica-tion may be to express the DE component of the therapist's impact (Your refusal to take a stand frustrates me, makes me feel helpless); while with another client it may be more efficient to express the ED component first (You seem to want to avoid taking a stand at all costs).

As I cautioned at the beginning, the crucial task of interactional theorists is to trans-late these general principles of metacommunication as to how they concretely apply and can be specifically sequenced with particular homogeneous groups of clients and/or client problems, with clients with distinctively homogeneous ED-evoking styles—with clients, for example, such as those traditionally labeled as obsessive or hysteric personalities.

Until that occurs, however, the best that can apparently be said is that the timing of metacommunication and optimal sequencing of shuttling among or between the meaning frames varies as a function of the specific ED-evoking style of a given client.

CONCLUSION

It should be obvious that the eight principles I have presented above are only the beginning of an explicit articulation of an interactional theory of countertransference in psychotherapy, of a formulation regarding DE-impact metacommunication with clients.

As I have repeated, for this formulation to be maximally useful, and for it to be of a form that can lead to precise operationalization and empirical test, these general principles need to be translated systematically for specific homogeneous groups of clients and client evoking styles. This more challenging, exasperating, and clearly more creative task remains to be done. It is hoped that we'll get along with it.

But it is also hoped that it is abundantly clear to the reader that a therapist can be nothing other than a *participant* observer with his clients; that a therapist's humanity enters the room with his client; that therapy with the client is to some degree inevitably therapy for the therapist; that *every* aspect of the therapist's experience—feelings, thoughts, fantasies, action tendencies—is engaged in his therapy encounters, and cannot *not* be impacted. Obviously "participant observation" in therapy has significantly more connotations than does the Heisenberg principle of physics.

It seems time for all of us to talk and write openly about our engagements with clients. It seems time for us to conceptualize more precisely, to formulate more comprehensive models, about these DE-impacts. As Gendlin (1967) urges: "We must develop a vocabulary—a science—about the therapist's personal procedure; we cannot leave them private and unnamed. Without detailed vocabulary about what we do inwardly, we cannot talk to each other or train new therapists" (p. 375). To this I add that we also cannot help our clients to face their basic interpersonal problems effectively and efficiently.

What I have attempted to offer in this chapter are theoretical propositions of the form Gendlin (1967) advocates: "If the patient at the moment does so and so, then I find it helpful to do so and so" (p. 375). The reader will decide to what extent I have accomplished this. In any event, my attempt perhaps will stimulate more precise and operational future statements—which is what H. S. Sullivan, the interpersonal "grandfather," had in mind in the first place.

NOTES

1. To make the referential picture for the client's statements complete, it is necessary to add O to designate persons in the client's life other than the therapist. This adds in turn the EO (encoder-to-other, client-to-other), and OE (other-to-encoder, other-to-client) meaning frames. Many therapists as well as client statements refer to what the client feels about, does, or says to others, and to what others such as spouse and family members feel about, do, or say to the client. I have constructed an initial form of a coding system for therapist statements (Kiesler, 1975) based upon a comprehensive elaboration of these meaning frames.

2. For a detailed description of the verbal and nonverbal client and therapist behaviors which index relationship in psychotherapy, see Kiesler (1979) and Kiesler, Bernstein, and Anchin (1976, ch. 5).

REFERENCES

Beier, E. G. *The silent language of psychotherapy: Social reinforcement of unconscious processes.* Chicago: Aldine, 1966.

Dollard, J. & Miller, N. E. *Personality and psychotherapy: An analysis in terms of learning, thinking and culture.* New York: McGraw-Hill, 1950.

Gendlin, E. T. Therapeutic procedures in dealing with schizophrenics. In C. R. Rogers, E. T. Gendlin, D. J. Kiesler, & C. B. Truax (Eds.), *The therapeutic relationship and its impact: A study of psychotherapy with schizophrenics.* Madison: University of Wisconsin Press, 1967.

Gendlin, E. T. Client-centered: The experiential response. In E. F. Hammer (Ed.), *Use of interpretation in treatment: Technique and art.* New York: Grune & Stratton, 1968.

Kiesler, D. J. *A communications approach to modification of the "obsessive personality": An initial formulation.* Unpublished manuscript. Emory University, 1973.

Kiesler, D. J. *A linguistic coding system for dyadic communication.* Unpublished manuscript. Richmond: Virginia Commonwealth University, 1975.

Kiesler, D. J. An interpersonal communication analysis of relationship in psychotherapy. *Psychiatry,* 1979, **42,** 299–311.

Kiesler, D. J., Anchin, J. C., Perkins, M. J., Chirico, B. M., Kyle, E. M., & Federman, E. J. *The Impact Message Inventory.* Richmond: Virginia Commonwealth University, 1975, 1976.

Kiesler, D. J., Bernstein, A. B., & Anchin, J. C. *Interpersonal communication, relationship and the behavior therapies.* Richmond: Virginia Commonwealth University, 1976.

Leary, T. *Interpersonal diagnosis of personality.* New York: Ronald, 1957.

Perkins, M. J., Kiesler, D. J., Anchin, J. C., Chirico, B. M., Kyle, E. M., & Federman, E. J. The Impact Message Inventory: A new measure of relationship in counseling/psychotherapy and other dyads. *Journal of Counseling Psychology,* 1979, **26,** 363–367.

Singer, E. *Key concepts in psychotherapy.* New York: Basic Books, 1970.

Villard, K. L. & Whipple, L. J. *Beginnings in relational communication.* New York: Wiley, 1976.

Chapter 16

Short-Term Interpersonal Psychotherapy (IPT) for Depression: Description and Efficacy*

Myrna M. Weissman, Gerald L. Klerman, Bruce J. Rounsaville, Eve S. Chevron, and Carlos Neu

Short-term interpersonal psychotherapy (IPT) is a brief (12–16 weeks) psychological treatment which focuses on current social and interpersonal difficulties in ambulatory, nonbipolar, nonpsychotic, depressed patients. The main premise of IPT is that depression, regardless of symptom patterns, severity, biological vulnerability, or personality traits, occurs in an interpersonal context and that clarifying and renegotiating the context associated with the onset of symptoms is important to the person's recovery and might prevent further episodes.

IPT is suitable for use, following a period of training, by experienced psychiatrists, psychologists, or social workers. It is designed to be used alone or in conjunction with pharmacologic agents. IPT has evolved over a period of 12 years from the experience of the New Haven-Boston Collaborative Depression Project. Variants of IPT have been tested by this group in two clinical trials of depressed patients—one of maintenance treatment (Klerman et al., 1974; Weissman et al., 1974) and one of acute treatment (Weissman et al., 1979; DiMascio et al., 1979). A third study testing IPT in a sample of depressed methadone-maintained patients, is in process (Kleber, 1979). IPT has been tested with and without the addition of a tricyclic antidepressant. A further testing of IPT against cognitive therapy and a tricyclic antidepressant is currently under way in a collaborative clinical trial sponsored by the National Institute of Mental Health (Psychotherapy of Depression Collaborative Research Program, 1980).

*This research was supported by Alcohol, Drug Abuse, and Mental Health Administration grants MH 26466 and MH 26467, from the Clinical Research Branch, National Institute of Mental Health, Rockville, Maryland.

The concept, techniques, and strategies of IPT have been specified in a procedural manual, which is still being revised (Klerman et al., 1979). This manual is being developed as a training tool so that further refinement of the procedures and replication of the effifacy studies may be undertaken. A program has recently been completed in New Haven to develop methods for the training of experienced therapists of differing disciplines (Weissman, Chevron, & Rounsaville, 1979).

IPT was designed to fill a gap in the field where, for the purpose of conducting serious replication trials, the only therapies that have been sufficiently specified in procedural manuals are those based on cognitive (Beck, 1976) and behavioral (Lewinsohn, Biglan, & Zeiss, 1976) approaches. In contrast, IPT is based on an interpersonal approach, as will be described.

It is our belief that a variety of treatments may be suitable for depression. The depressed patient's interests are best served by the availability and scientific testing of different psychological as well as pharmacologic treatments that can be used alone or in combination. The ultimate aim of these studies is to determine which are the best treatments for particular subgroups of depressed patients. In this chapter, we briefly describe the conceptual framework and goals of IPT, and summarize the efficacy data available thus far.

DESCRIPTION OF IPT

Theoretical and Empirical Framework

IPT derives from a number of theoretical and empirical sources (Klerman et al., 1979). The most prominent theoretical source is Adolph Meyer (1957) whose psychobiological approach to understanding psychiatric disorders placed great emphasis on the patient's psychosocial and interpersonal experiences. Meyer viewed psychiatric disorder as the patient's attempt to adapt to the psychosocial environment. The individual patient's response to environmental change and stress was viewed as having been determined by prior experience, particularly early developmental experiences in the family, and by the patient's affiliation in various social groups. Meyer, strongly influenced by the Pragmatist School and by the views of Darwin, attempted to apply the concept of role adaptation to understanding psychiatric illness.

Among Meyer's associates, Harry Stack Sullivan (1953a, 1953b) stands out for his theory of interpersonal relationships and for his writings linking clinical psychiatry to the emerging social sciences. Sullivan argued that psychiatry was the scientific study of people and the processes that involve or go on between people, in contrast to the study of only the mind, society, the brain, or the glands. Hence, the unit of study is the interpersonal situation at any given time.

The IPT emphasis on interpersonal and social factors in the understanding and treatment of depressive disorders follows the work of others. An interpersonal approach to the treatment of depression, as distinguished from an exclusively intrapsychic or biological approach, has a long tradition, starting with the writings of Sullivan and Fromm-Reichman. More recently, these ideas have been explicated by Mabel Blake Cohen and her co-workers at the Washington School of Psychiatry, in a comprehensive study of the disrupted interpersonal relations in the childhood experiences of 12 manic depressives (Cohen et al., 1954). Results indicated that the early experiences of these manic depressives were reflected in adult personality structures that were consistently associated with particular kinds of interpersonal problems. Moreover, these interpersonal problems were manifest in the way these patients functioned in psychotherapy.

The interpersonal conceptualization was applied to therapeutic strategies in the writings of Jerome Frank (1973) who stressed mastery of current interpersonal situations as an important social-psychological component in psychotherapy. Among others, Becker (1974) and Chodoff (1970) have also emphasized the social roots of depression and the need to attend to the interpersonal aspects of the disorder.

The empirical bases for understanding and treating depression with IPT are the studies demonstrating the impact of stress and life events associated with the onset of depression; the longitudinal studies which demonstrate the social impairment of depressed women during the acute depressive phase and with symptomatic recovery; the recent studies of Brown and Harris (1978) which demonstrate the role of intimacy and social supports as protections against depression in the face of life stress; the studies of Pearlin (Pearlin & Lieberman, 1977) and Ilfeld (1977) which show the impact of chronic social and interpersonal stress, particularly marital stress, in the onset of depression; and finally, the works of Bowlby (1969, 1977) and, more recently, Henderson (Henderson et al., 1978a, 1978b, 1978c) emphasize the importance of attachment bonds or, alternately, demonstrate that loss of social attachments can be associated with the onset of depression.

A considerable body of research has demonstrated the relationship between stress, defined as recent life events, and the onset of psychiatric illness, particularly depression (Pearlin & Lieberman, 1977; Ilfeld, 1977; Paykel et al., 1969; Weissman & Paykel, 1974; Briscoe & Smith, 1973). The Paykel et al. work (1969) is most relevant to the study of stressful life events and depression. This group studied depressed patients and found that exits of persons from the social field occurred more frequently in depressed patients as compared to normals in the six months prior to the onset of depression. This group also found that marital friction was the most common event reported by depressed patients prior to the onset of depression.

Comparable observations were made by Ilfeld (1977) in a survey of about 3,000 adults in Chicago. Depressive symptoms were closely related to stress and particularly stresses in marriage and, less frequently, in parenting. In a closer look at the data, Pearlin and Lieberman (1977) found that chronic, persisting problems within intact marriages were as likely to produce distress and depressive symptoms as was the total disruption of the marriage by divorce or separation.

The most sophisticated empirical work in defining an aspect of attachment bonding (intimacy—a confiding relationship) and examining its relationship to the development of depression has been completed by Brown and Harris (1978). In a community survey of women living in the Camberwell section of London, this group found that the presence of an intimate, confiding relationship with a man, usually the spouse, was the most important protection against developing a depression in the face of life stress.

The impairments in close interpersonal relations of depressed women have been studied in considerable detail by Weissman and Paykel (1974). In a comparison study of depressed women and their normal neighbors, they found that the depressed woman was considerably more impaired in all aspects of social functioning as a worker, wife, mother, family member, and friend. This impairment was greatest with close family, particularly spouse and children, where considerable hostility, disaffection, and poor communication were evident. With symptomatic recovery, most, but not all, of the impairments diminished. Marital relationships often remained chronically unhappy and explosive. There has been some debate as to whether the marital difficulties associated with depression are the cause or the consequence of the disorder (Briscoe & Smith, 1973). Studying the interactions of depressed patients and normal subjects, Coyne (1976) has demonstrated that depressives elicit characteristic, unhelpful responses from others.

This brief review is meant to illustrate some of the key empirical findings that provide a rationale for understanding depression in an interpersonal context and for developing a treatment strategy for depression based on interpersonal concepts. In general, studies show the importance of close and satisfactory attachments to others in the prevention of depression and, alternately, the role of disruption of attachments in the development of depression. The theoretical basis and empirical studies are discussed more fully in the IPT manual (Klerman et al., 1979).

Goals and Focus of Interpersonal Psychotherapy (IPT) for Depression

We view depression as having three component processes.

- *Symptom formation*, involving the development of depressive affect and vegetative signs and symptoms which may derive from psychobiological and/or psychodynamic mechanisms.
- *Social adjustment and interpersonal relations*, involving interactions in social roles with other persons which derive from learning based on childhood experiences, concurrent social reinforcement, and/or personal mastery and competence.
- *Personality*, involving enduring traits such as the handling of anger, guilt, communication, and overall self-esteem, which constitute the person's unique reactions and patterns of functioning and which may also contribute to predisposition to manifest symptom episodes.

IPT attempts to intervene in the first two processes. Because of the brief nature and low level of psychotherapeutic intensity and the focus on the context of the current depressive episode, we do not claim that IPT will have an impact upon the enduring aspects of personality, although personality functioning is assessed.

The overall goals of IPT are reduction of depressive symptoms resulting in restoration of morale and improved self-esteem, and improvement in the quality of the patient's social adjustment and interpersonal relations. The latter may entail assistance in dealing with the personal and social consequences of the depression, or changes in attitudes, expectations, and behaviors in relation to significant others.

The focus of IPT is on:

1. The patient's immediate "here and now" problems;
2. Concern for the patient's current important social and interpersonal relationships;
3. Engaging the patient in mastering the current situation by clarification and modification of current interpersonal relationships and by changing maladaptive perceptions or unrealistic expectations.

In contrast, relatively little attention is focused on the uncovering of deeply unconscious, conflicted areas, the development of a transference, or personality reconstruction.

In summary, the focus of IPT is on the patient in current life situations with the psychotherapist engaging the patient in an evaluation of himself and his current situation, with the goal of alleviating depressive symptoms and helping the patient develop more effective strategies for dealing with current interpersonal problems.

Thus far, IPT strategies have been specified for dealing with the acute depressive syndrome and four problem areas often associated with the onset of depression—grief, role disputes, role transitions, and interpersonal deficits (Klerman et al., 1979). Because IPT is a short-term treatment, it is usually concentrated on only one or two problem areas. Patients may present with a combination of problems in several areas, or there may be no clear-cut, significant difficulties in any one area. The clinician assesses the patient's needs and what the patient considers contributing factors to the depression. For patients with wide-ranging problems, the therapist may be guided in the choice of focus by the precipitating events of the current depressive episode. It should be noted that the classification of problem areas represents an attempt to conceptualize interpersonal problems according to a system that focuses on potential areas of change in treatment. The problem classifications are not intended to represent in-depth formulations, nor do they attempt to explain the dynamics of the depressive disorder. Instead, this classification system assists the clinician in outlining realistic goals and following appropriate treatment strategies.

Interpersonal Problem Areas

Abnormal Grief Reactions

In diagnosing an abnormal grief reaction, it is frequently clear that the patient's depression began with a significant loss, but in other cases there may be only an indirect relationship between the current depression and a previous loss. In reviewing the patient's interpersonal relationships, it is important to obtain a history of significant relationships with those who are now dead or otherwise absent. This should include the circumstances of the death and the patient's behavioral and emotional reaction to the death.

Evidence of the following factors may suggest a pathological mourning process:

1. Overwhelming multiple losses;
2. Inadequate mourning or failure to reminisce about the deceased;
3. Negative behavioral patterns such as avoidance of visiting the grave site or not participating in activities which were shared prior to the death of the loved one;
4. Physical symptoms similar to those of the lost object shortly after death or at a symbolically relevant date (e.g., anniversary, achieved age at which person died, etc.);
5. Negative social factors such as death in an intensive care unit;
6. Evidence of prolonged symptoms such as guilt or continued sense of loss which at the time of death would have been considered part of the normal grief reaction;
7. History of preserving the environment as it was when the loved one died; and/or
8. Absence of family or other social supports during the bereavement period.

Once the therapist has identified the problem as one of depression associated with grief, the two general goals of treatment are to facilitate the mourning process and to help the patient to reestablish interests and relationships that can substitute for that which is lost. The therapist adopts and utilizes strategies and techniques that help the patient bring into focus memories of the lost person, and the emotions related to the patient's experiences with the lost person.

Because grief reactions are often associated with the lack of a supportive social network, the major psychotherapeutic strategy is to encourage the patient:

1. To think about the loss;
2. To present the sequence and consequences of events prior to, during, and after the death; and

3. To explore associated feelings, with the psychotherapist substituting for the missing social network.

Often the patient expresses fear of bringing up that which "has been buried." The patient may express fears of "cracking up," of not being able to stop crying, or of otherwise losing control. In such instances, the psychotherapist may let the patient know that the fears he or she has expressed are not uncommon and that mourning in psychotherapy rarely leads to decompensation.

It is not unusual for a patient with abnormal grief reactions to be fixated around the death itself, thus avoiding the complexities of the relationship with the deceased. The therapist should lead a thorough factual and affective exploration of the patient's relationship with the deceased both during the period when the deceased was alive and in the present context. The patient may not wish to acknowledge angry or hostile feelings toward the deceased. When the mourning process is blocked by strongly negative feelings toward the deceased, the psychotherapist should encourage the patient to express these feelings. This encouragement should not be via confrontation because this may provoke a shift in the hostility from the deceased to the psychotherapist. If negative feelings emerge too rapidly, the patient may decide not to return to psychotherapy because of the guilt which will have developed. If, however, the psychotherapist reassures the patient that these negative feelings will be followed by positive and comforting feelings as well as a positive attitude toward the deceased, the patient may be much better prepared to explore his or her ambivalence. Following these steps, the patient may formulate a new and healthier way of understanding memories of the deceased. For instance, the patient may no longer regard his father as a villain but instead realize that he was a sick person, and thus be able to accept his behavior and his reaction to it.

As the patient loses his investment in maintaining continued, abnormal grieving, he may be more open to developing new relationships to "fill the empty space" left by the lost loved one. At this point, the therapist may be very active in leading the patient to consider various alternative ways to become more involved with others again (e.g., dating, church functions, organizations, work).

Interpersonal Role Dispute

An interpersonal role dispute is a situation in which the patient and at least one significant other have nonreciprocal expectations about their relationship. This definition would probably include every relationship, at least part of the time, because role disputes are an inevitable part of life. The IPT therapist, however, chooses to focus on interpersonal disputes if in his or her judgment they are important in the genesis and perpetuation of the depression. Typical features which perpetuate role disputes are the patient's demoralized sense that nothing can be done, poor habits of communication, or truly irreconcilable differences. Although role disputes are commonly revealed in the patient's initial complaints, and disputes with a spouse are the most frequent problem area presented, at times recognition of important interpersonal disputes may be difficult. Typically, depressed patients are preoccupied with their hopeless feelings and believe that they alone are responsible for their condition. When there is no clear precipitant to a depressive episode and when the patient does not identify problems in current interpersonal relationships, it is important for the therapist to listen as much for what is omitted as for what is said. Failure to elaborate on a current or recent relationship that seems to be important or the presentation of a relationship in overly idealized terms may offer clues to difficulties which the patient is unwilling to recognize and/or to explore in treatment. To understand the interpersonal impact of the patient's depression, it is important to question the patient carefully about how relationships have changed prior to or after the onset of depressive symptoms. An understanding of how interpersonal problems may have precipitated the depression or how they are involved in preventing recovery may suggest a strategy for therapy.

The general goals for treatment of interpersonal role disputes are to help the patient first identify the dispute, then to guide him or her in making choices about a plan of action, and finally to encourage the patient to modify maladaptive communication patterns if present or to reassess expectations in order to bring about a satisfactory resolution of the interpersonal disputes.

In developing a treatment plan, the therapist first determines the stage of the role dispute.

Negotiation implies that the patient and the significant others are openly aware of differences and are actively attempting, even if unsuccessfully, to bring about change.

Impasse implies that discussion has ceased between the patient and significant others, resulting in the smoldering, low-level resentment that is typical of "cold marriages."

Dissolution implies that the relationship is irretrievably disrupted.

The therapist's tasks and expectations at these three stages differ. For example, intervening in an impasse situation may involve increasing apparent disharmony in order to reopen negotiations, while the task of treating a dispute at the stage of unsatisfactory negotiation may be to calm down the participants in order to facilitate conflict resolution. The treatment of disputes at the stage of dissolution has much in common with the treatment of grief in that the therapist attempts to help the patient put the relationship in perspective and become free to form new attachments.

The IPT therapist's general treatment strategy with interpersonal disputes is to help the patient understand how nonreciprocal expectations relate to the dispute and to help begin to take steps that will bring about resolution of disputes and role negotiations. This movement from exploration to action may take place over the entire course of therapy, with early sessions devoted to exploration and communication analysis, and later sessions to decision analysis. In dealing with particular, circumscribed problems, however, the movement from exploration to decision making may take place in a single session.

In exploring the role dispute, the therapist seeks information on different levels. At a practical level, the following questions are answered. What are the ostensible issues in the dispute? What are the differences in expectations and values between the patient and the significant other? What are the patient's wishes in the relationship? What are the patient's options? What is the likelihood of alternatives coming about? What resources does the patient have at his command to bring about change in the relationship?

In understanding how the disputes are perpetuated, special attention to the interpersonal strategies of the disputants frequently reveals problems in communication patterns. For instance, repetitious, painful disputes are frequently perpetuated when participants are overly afraid of confrontation and expression of negative feelings and prefer to ignore solvable problems by simply waiting for things to "blow over." Review and remediation of communication problems are an important part of the IPT therapy process.

When the patient has developed a sufficiently clear understanding of role disputes, including the part he or she plays in them, the process of decision analysis can fruitfully take place. Here, the therapist's role is not to suggest any particular plan of action but to assist the patient in thorough consideration of the consequences of a number of alternatives.

Role Transitions

Depression associated with role transitions occurs when the patient experiences great difficulty in trying to cope with life changes. Role transition problems are most commonly associated with the kind of change that is often perceived as a loss. The transition may be immediately apparent as in the case of divorce, or it may be more symbolic as in the feeling of a loss of freedom following the birth of a child. In either case, the patient feels unable to cope with the change in role, possibly because the situation is experienced as threatening to the patient's self-esteem and sense of identity. In general, a patient's difficulties in coping with role transitions are associated with the following issues:

1. Loss of familiar social supports;
2. Management of accompanying affect, e.g., anger or fear; and
3. Demands for a new repertoire of social skills.

Individuals differ in their overall vulnerability to stress associated with role transitions. In addition, individuals differ in regard to the particular kinds of changes that are likely to produce stress, depending on the "meaning" of the event to the individual's self-esteem.

In IPT we distinguish two components of role transition problems:

1. The patient's feelings about the actual person or thing that has been lost, e.g., spouse, job, etc.; and
2. The patient's reaction to the concomitant role changes occasioned by the loss.

The former is similar to a grief reaction in that the patient is unable to deal with the loss as such and tends to remain fixated around the lost *object*. It is the second component of the role transition problem, involving the inability to cope with the change itself, that distinguishes this problem from a traditional grief reaction. For example, a patient presenting for treatment following the dissolution of her marriage may report that her marriage had been intolerable for many years and that it was, in fact, she who initiated the divorce proceedings with the expectation that her life would markedly improve if only she could extricate herself from an essentially "impossible relationship." Following the divorce, however, she finds that her married female friends, who had hitherto been an important source of support for the patient, have now begun to withdraw from her because they perceive her as a threat to their own marriages. In addition, the patient is experiencing feelings of inadequacy (in the mother role) vis-à-vis her children because they seem to blame her for "sending Daddy away." Feeling lonely, abandoned, inadequate, and deprived of her usual social supports, she seeks treatment. What distinguishes this patient's problem from a traditional grief reaction is that she is not mourning her husband so much as her former role of "married woman"; her depression is not related to the separation from her husband, as such, but to her difficulty in coping with the transition from the role of wife and mother to the role of single parent.

Ordinarily, patients with role transition problems will spontaneously relate their depression to the recent change in their life situation. They may not be aware, however, of the connection between the psychological significance of the change and their diminished self-esteem. As the therapist explores the patient's perception of the old and the new role requirements, and the feelings associated with each, he or she will be better able to formulate a realistic treatment plan.

The two general goals in the treatment of depression associated with role transitions are:

1. To enable the patient to regard the new role in a more positive, less restricted manner, perhaps as an opportunity for growth; and
2. To restore self-esteem by developing in the patient a sense of mastery vis-à-vis demands of the new role-related attitudes and behaviors.

Abnormal grief and role transition problems have much in common in that both involve a reaction to a life change, frequently associated with a loss of some kind. Thus, the IPT strategies and techniques for dealing with problems associated with giving up old roles are similar to those recommended for grief reactions. The therapeutic tasks are to facilitate the patient's realistic evaluation of what has been lost, to encourage the appropriate release of affect, and finally, to help the patient develop a social support sytem and the repertoire of skills that are called for in the new role.

The therapist will help the patient in a systematic review of the positive and negative aspects of the old role and possible new roles. These patients will frequently feel frightened by the change itself, and as a result will tend to romanticize the positive aspects of what has been lost. For this reason, they need to be encouraged to explore the opportunities offered in the new role. As a rule, patients' resistance to change makes it difficult for them to imagine themselves functioning efficiently in different ways. The therapist must actively support these patients as they gradually disengage from the familiar old roles and begin to venture out into the new, as yet unexplored, ways of feeling and behaving.

Interpersonal Deficits

The last problem type identified in IPT is that of interpersonal deficits, which are chosen as the focus of treatment when a patient presents with a history of social impoverishment involving inadequate or unsustaining interpersonal relationships. Such a patient may never have established lasting or intimate relationships as an adult and probably experienced a number of severely disrupted relationships as a child. In general, patients who present with a history of severe social isolation tend to be more severely disturbed than those presenting with other types of problems. Because the treatment strategies for this problem type are similar to those of the traditional psychodynamic approach, the IPT goals and strategies for interpersonal deficits will not be discussed. It should be noted, however, that the brief treatment of interpersonal deficits is a most difficult task, and therefore goals should be limited to merely identifying these issues, not necessarily to resolving them.

EFFICACY DATA

Two trials out of which IPT has evolved and become increasingly more specified have been completed by the New Haven-Boston Collaborative Depression Project, as will be described.

IPT as Maintenance Treatment

The first study, begun in 1967, was an eight-month maintenance trial of 150 women who were treated for six to eight weeks with a tricyclic antidepressant (amitriptyline) and were recovering from an acute depressive episode. Criteria for entrance into the study of acute treatment were definite depression of at least two weeks' duration and of sufficient intensity to reach a total score of seven or more on the Raskin Depression Scale (range 3–15).

The majority of patients (88 percent) were diagnosed as having a neurotic depression according to the APA DSM-II.

This study tested the efficacy of IPT (administered weekly by experienced psychiatric social workers) in comparison to low contact (brief monthly visits for assessments) with either amitriptyline, placebo, or no pill, using random assignment in a 2 × 3 factorial design. The full design, methodology, and results have been reported elsewhere (Klerman et al., 1974; Weissman et al., 1974). For this discussion, the focus will be on the results of IPT as compared to low contact.

The findings showed that maintenance IPT as compared with low contact had no significant differential impact on prevention of relapse or symptom return. IPT, however, significantly enhanced social and interpersonal functioning for patients who did not relapse. IPT's effects on social functioning, assessed by the Social Adjustment Scale (Weissman & Paykel, 1974), took six to eight months to become statistically apparent. Patients receiving IPT as compared to low contact were significantly less impaired in work performance, with the extended family, and in marriage. The overall mean of the assessed social adjustment items reflected these differences between groups as did the rater's overall evaluation of the patient (Table 16.1). The percent score of improvement on social adjustment was substantially greater in the IPT group (44 percent) in contrast to the low-contact group (28 percent) (Figure 16.1).

There were several problems in the maintenance study. First, the all-women sample of depressed patients was not diagnostically homogeneous. In 1967, the new research diagnostic approaches, which included operationalized diagnostic criteria and systematic methods for collecting information on signs and symptoms to make these diagnoses, were not available (Spitzer, Endicott, & Robins, 1978). The set of diagnostic criteria primarily used for depressed patients was the DSM-II, accompanied by a symptom severity measure.

The psychotherapy was described in terms of conceptual framework, goals, frequency of contact, and criteria for therapists' suitability (Weissman et al., 1974). The IPT techniques and strategies had not, however, been operationalized in a procedural manual. Finally, the maintenance study was not the best design for testing out the efficacy of a

Table 16.1. IPT Effects on Social Adjustment after 8 Months of Maintenance Treatment in Depressed Patients Who Did Not Relapse.

Social Adjustment Means[1]	Low Contact	IPT	F-Value
Work	1.7	1.5	5.3*
Social and Leisure	2.3	2.1	1.6
Extended Family	1.7	1.5	5.2*
Marital	2.3	2.0	2.9+
Parental	1.8	1.7	0.5
Family Unit	1.8	1.7	1.1
OVERALL ADJUSTMENT	2.0	1.8	7.2**
RATER'S GLOBAL ASSESSMENT	3.4	2.9	5.0*

[1]All means are adjusted for initial level. The scale for all roles is 1–5, except for the global evaluation which is 1–7. In all cases, higher score means more impairment.

+p = < .10
*p = < .05
**p = < .01

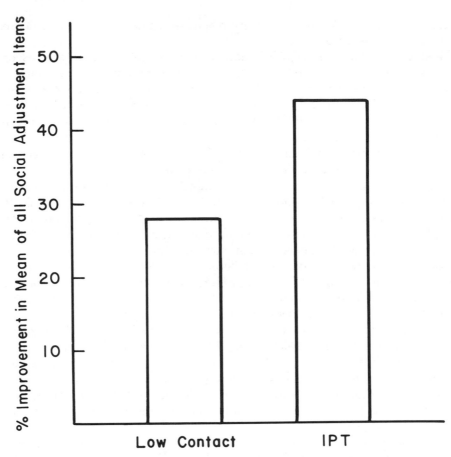

Fig. 16.1. Improvement in social adjustment over 8 months of maintenance treatment.

psychological treatment. Patients who entered into maintenance treatment were all drug responders and the IPT did not begin until the patient had received at least four weeks of drug treatment. Having already established a therapeutic relationship with the psychiatrist who was not administering IPT, the patients were not acutely depressed at the point of randomized assignment to the social worker for IPT treatment.

IPT as Acute Treatment

In 1973, we initiated a 16-week study of the acute treatment of ambulatory depressed patients, including both men and women, using IPT and amitriptyline, each alone and in combination against a nonscheduled psychotherapy treatment. IPT was administered weekly by experienced psychiatrists. There were 81 patients who entered the study and accepted the randomized treatment assignment. On the basis of our experience in the maintenance study, changes were incorporated into this acute treatment study which resulted in a better design for testing psychotherapy in a clinical trial.

By 1973, the SADS-RDC (Spitzer, Endicott, & Robins, 1978; Endicott & Spitzer, 1978) were available for making more precise diagnostic judgments, therefore allowing the inclusion of a more homogeneous sample of depressed patients. Based on the SADS-RDC approach, the inclusion criteria were nonbipolar, nonpsychotic, ambulatory patients who were experiencing an acute primary, major depression of sufficient intensity to reach a score of at least seven on the Raskin Depression Scale.

A procedural manual for IPT was developed (Klerman et al., 1979). Patients were randomized into IPT at the beginning of treatment. The treatment was limited to 16 weeks since this was an acute rather than a maintenance treatment trial. The assessment of outcome was made by a clinical evaluator who was independent of and blind to the treatment the patient was receiving. The patients were followed up one year after treatment had ended to determine any long-term effects of the treatment. The full details of this study have been described elsewhere (Weissman et al., 1979; DiMascio et al., 1979).

The control treatment for IPT was nonscheduled psychotherapy in which patients were assigned a psychiatrist whom they were told to contact whenever they felt a need for treatment. No active treatment was scheduled for these patients but they could call for an appointment if their needs were of sufficient intensity, and a 50-minute session (a maximum of one a month) would be scheduled. Patients requiring further treatment who were still symptomatic after eight weeks (Raskin 9 or over), or whose clinical condition worsened sufficiently to require other treatment, were considered failures of this treatment and were withdrawn from the study. This procedure served as an ethically feasible control for psychotherapy in that it allowed a patient to receive periodic supportive help "on demand" (DiMascio et al., 1980).

For this discussion, the focus will be on IPT as compared to nonscheduled treatment.

Figure 16.2 summarizes the results of the study using lifetime calculations and demonstrates that the probability of symptomatic failure over 16 weeks was significantly lower in IPT as compared to nonscheduled treatment. The results were upheld using other symptom outcome measures, including both self-report and clinical ratings (DiMascio et al., 1979).

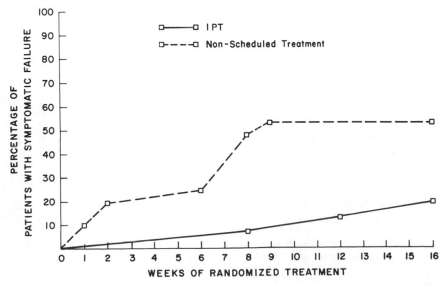

Fig. 16.2.   Life table calculations of the product-limit estimate of symptomatic failure time.

As noted before, differential effects of IPT on the patients' social functioning were not found at the end of four months of maintenance treatment, but took six to eight months to develop. Similarly, in the acute treatment study, which ended at four months, no differential effects of IPT on social functioning were found. At one-year follow-up, however, patients who had received IPT in comparison to those who had not were functioning at a less impaired level in social activities, as parents and in the family unit, and this difference was reflected in the rater's global assessment (Table 16.2).

CONCLUSION

The field of psychotherapy outcome research is rapidly developing. In addition to the use of randomized treatment asssignment and independent and blind clinical assessments of outcome, the clinical trials presented here have incorporated two important methodologic advances: (1) operationalized and defined diagnostic criteria to allow for relatively homogeneous patient groups, and (2) operationalized and defined psychotherapeutic procedures to assure comparability of treatment condition.

Substantively, in two collaborative clinical trials, we have demonstrated the efficacy of maintenance IPT on enhancing social functioning in recovering depressives and the efficacy of IPT on symptom reduction and on social functioning in acute depressives. The effects on social functioning take at least six to eight months to become apparent. The findings are consistent with the general concept of IPT.

As yet, the studies of IPT and of cognitive therapy—therapies developed specifically for depressed patients—are based on relatively small samples. Moreover, the therapeutic trials have been conducted at the centers where the therapies were developed. The results must be replicated elsewhere before definitive conclusions can be drawn. The National Institute of Mental Health, Clinical Research Branch, has initiated a multisite collaborative study of Cognitive-Behavior (CB) therapy, Interpersonal Psychotherapy (IPT) and Pharmacotherapy (Imipramine) as treatment for nonpsychotic, nonbipolar, ambulatory, depressed patients (Psychotherapy for Depression Collaborative Research Program, 1980). This study will be critical in providing answers about the short and long-term

Table 16.2.   IPT Effects on Social Adjustment One Year After Acute Tratment For Depression

Social Adjustment Means[1]	Nonscheduled Treatment	IPT	F-Value
Work	1.5	1.5	.1
Social and Leisure	1.9	1.7	3.6*
Extended Family	1.7	1.6	.6
Marital	1.3	1.4	.09
Parental	1.5	0.9	3.1*
Family Unit	2.1	1.4	9.0**
OVERALL ADJUSTMENT	1.7	1.5	2.6
RATER'S GLOBAL EVALUATIONS	2.9	2.5	3.1+

[1]All means are adjusted for initial level. The scale for all roles is 1–5, except for the global evaluation which is 1–7. In all cases, higher score means more impairment.
+p = < .10
*p = < .05
**p = < .01

differential effects of the various treatments for some types of depressives. The study has other important features. It will include very large samples pooled from three research sites, therapists from each site will receive joint training in the psychotherapy method by the developers of the method, but the therapies will be tested in sites other than those where the methods were originally developed. A one-year follow-up of patients will be included.

Pending the results of this important study, there are now some general guidelines as to the treatment of acutely depressed patients which suggest the value of both tricyclic antidepressants and psychotherapy because of the differential effects that each of these treatments seems to have on both the type and the timing of response.

REFERENCES

Beck, A. T. *Cognitive therapy and the emotional disorders*. New York: International Universities Press, 1976.

Becker, J. *Depression: Theory and research*. New York: Wiley, 1974.

Bowlby, J. *Attachment and loss*. London: Hogarth, 1969.

Bowlby, J. The making and breaking of affectional bonds: II. Some principles of psychotherapy. *British Journal of Psychiatry*, 1977, **130**, 421–431.

Briscoe, C. W. & Smith, J. B. Depression and marital turmoil. *Archives of General Psychiatry*, 1969, **28**, 811–817.

Brown, G. W. & Harris, T. *Social origins of depression: A study of psychiatric disorders in women*. New York: Free Press, 1978.

Chodoff, P. The core problem in depression. In J. Masserman (Ed.), *Science and psychoanalysis*, vol. 17. New York: Grune & Stratton, 1970.

Cohen, M. B., Baker, G., Cohen, R. A., Fromm-Reichman, F., & Weigart, E. V. An intensive study of twelve cases of manic-depressive psychosis. *Psychiatry*, 1954, **17**, 103–137.

Coyne, J. C. Depression and the response of others. *Journal of Abnormal Psychology*, 1976, **85**, 186–193.

DiMascio, A., Klerman, G. L., Weissman, M. M., Prusoff, B. A., Neu, C., & Moore, P. A control group for psychotherapy research in acute depression: One solution to ethical and methodological issues. *Journal of Psychiatric Research*, 1980, **15**, 189–197.

DiMascio, A., Weissman, M. M., Prusoff, B. A., Neu, C., Swilling, M., & Klerman, G. L. Differential symptom reduction by drugs and psychotherapy in acute depression. *Archives of General Psychiatry*, 1979, **36**, 1450–1456.

Endicott, J. & Spitzer, R. L. A diagnostic interview: The schedule for affective disorders and schizophrenia. *Archives of General Psychiatry*, 1978, **35**, 837–844.

Frank, J. D. *Persuasion and healing: A comparative study of psychotherapy*. Baltimore: Johns Hopkins University Press, 1973.

Henderson, S., Byrne, D. G., Duncan-Jones, P., Adcock, S., Scott, R., & Steele, G. P. Social bonds in the epidemiology of neurosis. *British Journal of Psychiatry*, 1978, **132**, 463–466.

Henderson, S., Duncan-Jones, P., Byrne, D. G., Scott, R., & Adcock, S. Social bonds, adversity, and neurosis. Presented at W. P. A. Sect. Comm. on Epidemiology and Community Psychiatry, St. Louis, Missouri, October 18–20, 1978.

Henderson, S., Duncan-Jones, P., McAuley, H., & Ritchie, K. The patient's primary group. *British Journal of Psychiatry*, 1978, **132**, 74–86.

Illfeld, F. W. Current social stressors and symptoms of depression. *American Journal of Psychiatry*, 1977, **134**, 161–166.

Kleber, H. D., Principal Investigator, Weissman, M. M., Co-Investigator: Implications of Psychiatric Diagnosis for Narcotic Dependent Treatment and Psychotherapy of Opiate Individuals. Grant

#RFP 271-77-3410. Psychotherapy of Depression Collaborative Research Program, Revised Research Plan, Clinical Research Branch, NIMH, January, 1980.

Klerman, G. L., DiMascio, A., Weissman, M., Prusoff, B., & Paykel, E. S. Treatment of depression by drugs and psychotherapy. *American Journal of Psychiatry*, 1974, **131**, 186–191.

Klerman, G. L., Rounsaville, B. J., Chevron, E. S., Neu, C., & Weissman, M. *Manual for short-term interpersonal psychotherapy (IPT) of depression.* New Haven-Boston Collaborative Depression Project, Fourth Draft, June, 1979.

Lewinsohn, P. M., Biglan, A., & Zeiss, A. Behavioral treatment of depression. In P. Davidson (Ed.), *The behavioral management of anxiety, depression and pain.* New York: Brunner/Mazel, 1976.

Meyer, A. *Psychobiology: A science of man.* Springfield, Ill.: C. C. Thomas, 1957.

Paykel, E. S., Myers, J. K., Dienelt, M. N., Klerman, G. L., Lindenthal, J. J., & Pepper, M. P. Life events and depression: A controlled study. *Archives of General Psychiatry*, 1969, **21**, 753–760.

Pearlin, L. I. & Lieberman, M. A. Social sources of emotional distress. In R. Simmons (Ed.), *Research in community mental health.* Greenwich, Conn.: JAI Press, 1977.

Psychotherapy of Depression Collaborative Research Program. Clinical Research Branch, National Institute of Mental Health, Rockville, Maryland, 1980.

Spitzer, R. L., Endicott, J., & Robins, E. Research diagnostic criteria: Rationale and reliability. *Archives of General Psychiatry*, 1978, **35**, 773–782.

Sullivan, H. S. *Conceptions of modern psychiatry.* New York: Norton, 1953. (a)

Sullivan, H. S. *The interpersonal theory of psychiatry.* New York: Norton, 1953. (b)

Weissman, M. M., Chevron, E. S., & Rounsaville, B. J. Training Program in Short-Term Interpersonal Psychotherapy. Supplement to U.S. PHS research grant MH 26466, Evaluation of Psychotherapy in Treating Depression, from the Clinical Research Branch, National Institute of Mental Health; Alcohol, Drug Abuse and Mental Health Administration, Rockville, Maryland, 1979.

Weissman, M. M., Klerman, G. L., Paykel, E. S., Prusoff, B., & Hanson, B. Treatment effects on the social adjustment of depressed patients. *Archives of General Psychiatry*, 1974, **30**, 771–778.

Weissman, M. M., & Paykel, E. S. *The depressed woman: A study of social relationships.* Chicago: University of Chicago Press, 1974.

Weissman, M. M., Prusoff, B. A., DiMascio, A., Neu, C., Goklaney, M., & Klerman, G. L. The efficacy of drugs and psychotherapy in the treatment of acute depressive episodes. *American Journal of Psychiatry*, 1979, **136** (4B), 555–558.

Part IV:
Summary and Conclusions

Chapter 17
Interpersonal Approaches to Psychotherapy: Summary and Conclusions
Jack C. Anchin

INTRODUCTION

Previous chapters suggest that if there is one point of convergence across the contributors to this volume, it lies in the assertion that assessing and treating the interpersonal dimension of a patient's current functioning is vital to effecting enduring and generalized clinical change. Beyond this common ground, diversity exists with regard to how interpersonal maladjustment is conceptualized, specific targets and operations comprising one's clinical assessment methodology, and the nature and sequencing of treatment interventions. Clearly, there is no single interpersonal psychotherapy. Rather, interpersonal therapy embraces a variety of distinguishable treatment approaches emanating from the shared view that present-day interpersonal processes are centrally involved in the patient's distress. My goal in this chapter is to project several evolving themes that have emerged from previous chapters, and within this context, to suggest directions for future developments in interpersonal theory, research, and practice.

ECOLOGICAL/RECIPROCAL DETERMINISTIC EMPHASIS

Foremost, an interpersonal perspective on maladjustment is inherently ecological in nature (Chrzanowski, 1977; Chapter 2 above). This means that at the very outset of treatment the interpersonal therapist acknowledges the ongoing, reciprocal interaction between overt and covert processes vis-à-vis social-environmental stimuli in inducing, eliciting, and maintaining abnormality. The reciprocal deterministic conception of causality (Anchin, Chapter 6) formalizes, as it were, the ecological viewpoint, globally classifying events into external-environmental, internal-personal (cognitive-affective), and overt behavioral classes, while positing that "each class may be influenced by variations in any other class over time. *The issue, then, becomes one of specifying the nature of the various relationships over time and determining the stochastic weight accorded any given variable in the functional relationship*" (Hollon & Kendall, 1979, p. 451, emphasis added). This ecological/reciprocal deterministic emphasis is reflected, for example, in Wachtel's (1977a,

1977b; Chapter 3) notion of "interaction cycles," Carson's (Chapter 4) reference to "an unbroken causal loop between social perception, behavioral enactment, and environmental reaction," Peterson's (Chapter 8) guiding conception of interpersonal relationships, and Coyne's (1977, 1979; Chapter 13; Coyne & Lazarus, 1980) transactional perspective, while it operates as a more or less implicit assumption in virtually all other approaches presented in this volume.

Interpersonalists, then, posit a continuous dynamic interplay among four classes of variables—overt behavioral, cognitive, affective, and social-environmental—as operative in human maladjustment. Different theorist-practitioners, however, tend to place particular emphasis upon any one of these classes during the treatment process. Compare, for example, Carson's (Chapter 4) emphasis upon the patient's "errant cognitive system" with Coyne and Segal's (Chapter 13) focus on changing the patient's and/or significant others' actions which represent attempted solutions to problems. Nevertheless, given the interconnection among these four classes of variables, a meaningful change in any one of them is expected to produce changes in the others. An important question, then, in treating a particular interpersonal problem, becomes that of which class of variables is likely to be the most cost-effective point of intervention.

The ecological/reciprocal deterministic emphasis upon behavior, cognition, affect, and social-environmental input also signals two major implications for interpersonal theory, research, and practice. First, it follows that *future theoretical formulations of adaptive and maladaptive interpersonal functioning will need explicitly and systematically to incorporate variables falling within each of these classes.* Consider, for example, that one conceptualizes interactive behavior primarily from the standpoint of interpersonal styles anchored in the Leary Circle or its derivatives. Then, the overarching task guiding theory construction and empirical hypothesis testing becomes that of establishing systematic relationships between characteristic classes of interpersonal-situational input and the distinctive overt interpersonal styles which they characteristically elicit, as well as relationships between these two broad classes of variables and specific cognitive interpretive operations, meanings, and affective experiential factors (see Kiesler, Bernstein, & Anchin, 1976, chs. 3 & 6). Current efforts to establish these kinds of systematic relationships (e.g., Benjamin, in press; Carson, 1979; Duke & Nowicki, Chapter 5; Golding, 1977, 1980; Kiesler, 1977), representing all-important "peripheral" elaborations of "core" interpersonal theories, can only be viewed as positive developments.

A second implication which stems from the ecological/reciprocal deterministic model is that *treatment approaches* (and more specifically, the concepts and operations of which they are comprised) *which highlight variables falling within any one of these particular classes are potentially useful in the overall process of assessing and modifying interpersonal dysfunction.* In the present volume, this capacity to accommodate an array of theoretically diverse concepts and procedures once an interpersonal perspective is adopted can be seen, for example, in Wachtel's (Chapter 3) integration of psychoanalytic and behavioral conceptualizations and interventions (see Wachtel, 1977b); in Cashdan's explanation of interpersonal pathology particularly from the perspective of object relations theory and symbolic interactionism; in the central place accorded the psychoanalytic "introject" concept in the respective approaches presented by Benjamin (Chapter 10), and McLemore and Hart (Chapter 12), as well as the latter's adoption of ideas and techniques from Gestalt therapy; and in the synthesis between an explicitly interpersonal perspective with concepts and techniques emphasized by cognitive-behavioral and social learning approaches to human functioning (e.g., Duke & Nowicki, Chapter 5; Anchin, Chapter 6; Peterson, Chapter 8). These theoretical and technical integrations illustrate the manner in which the interpersonal perspective may serve as a bridge for systematically interrelating different therapeutic approaches, as suggested by Anchin in Chapter 6.

DEVELOPMENT AND EXPANSION
OF SULLIVANIAN THEORY

It is not the function of the pioneer to say the last word but to say the first word. That is the most difficult step. All the pioneer has to begin with is a problem, which has always been there, but hitherto no one has looked at that phenomenon in this particular way. The pioneer suddenly asks a new kind of question. Once the all important start has been made along some new line of investigation, those who come after have only to faithfully follow up every possible line of inquiry it suggests. Some of these will be false trails, others will lead somewhere, but all have to be explored. [Guntrip, 1973, p. 3.]

These comments, made specifically in reference to Freud in the introductory chapter of Guntrip's volume on object relations theory, are equally appropriate when applied to Harry Stack Sullivan's (1940, 1953, 1954, 1956, 1962) interpersonal theory and practice. As discussed in Chapter 1 of this volume, Sullivan was the first to present a systematic theory of interpersonal relationships and psychotherapy, and his work subsequently spawned a number of distinctive lines of interpersonal theory and study. The prophetic nature of Sullivan's theory is suggested by Swensen's (1973) conclusion that "after almost thirty years, Sullivan's theoretical scheme is still able to accommodate most of the facts accumulated in the study of interpersonal relationships between that time" (p. 47). Indeed, this capacity to incorporate the content of most other approaches led Swensen to assert that while the field of interpersonal relations is currently in a preparadigmatic stage of development (see Kuhn, 1970), "when a generally accepted paradigm for the field comes, it will be a direct lineal descendant of Sullivanian theory" (Swensen, 1973, p. 452).

The work of contributors to this volume demonstrates that *Sullivan's formulations continue to serve a critical heuristic function for interpersonally oriented theorists, practitioners, and researchers.* Thus, Kiesler's interpersonal communication theory of psychotherapy (Kiesler, 1973; 1979; Chapters 1 and 15 in this volume; Kiesler, Bernstein, & Anchin, 1976) elaborates several major Sullivanian themes through integrating empirical research on nonverbal communication (e.g., Mehrabian, 1972), communication-oriented psychiatry and psychotherapy (e.g., Beier, 1966; Watzlawick, Beavin, & Jackson, 1967), and interpersonal theories of personality (e.g., Carson, 1969; Leary, 1957; Lorr & McNair, 1963, 1965, 1966; Lorr, Bishop, & McNair, 1965; Newcomb, 1953; Secord & Backman, 1965). Carson (Chapter 4) has undertaken the important task of translating the central Sullivanian concepts of personification and parataxic distortion into the more contemporary terms of expectancies and person schemas, in turn using this formulation to propose a solution to the vexing problem of the neurotic paradox (Mowrer, 1948). This linking of Sullivan's formulations to modern-day theory and research on person cognition is similarly reflected in Golding's (1978) efforts to define such Sullivanian concepts as the self-dynamism and selective inattention from the standpoint of "psychological organizing principles." In explaining this concept, Golding (1979) contends that

we can pursue a scientific understanding of clinical and social interactions only if we conceptualize the relationships between "consensually objective" [stimulus conditions] and the "individually subjective" as being *lawfully organized within the person.* This lawful organization of subjective event structure vis-a-vis objective event structure is what I have called a "psychological organizing principle" (Golding, 1978). The task is one of discovering the principles by which experience, especially in reference to interpersonal interactions, is organized.

More generally, Golding's work reflects a much needed effort to effect a rapprochement between the interpersonalist's endorsement of a phenomenological stance and the need for scientific study of subjective experience (see Laing, Phillipson, & Lee, 1966; cognitive-behavioral assessment is also of interest in this context; Kendall & Hollon, 1981; Kendall & Korgeski, 1979). Still other extensions of Sullivanian theory can be seen in Chrzanowski's (Chapter 2) critique and reformulation of Sullivan's ideas on both individual personality and the self (see Chrzanowski, 1977, 1978), as well as his shift from a therapeutic stance of participant observation to that of relational participation. Further, approaches presented by Wachtel (Chapter 3), Anchin (Chapter 6), McLemore and Hart (Chapter 12), and Coyne and Segal (Chapter 13) explicitly extend Sullivan's emphasis upon clarifying the patient's interpersonal field in the direction of direct, active intervention in the latter's current, day-to-day, interpersonal relationships.

Developments such as these confirm the incomplete, open-ended nature of Sullivan's system (Chrzanowski, Chapter 2), while at the same time underscoring "the enduring strengths of Sullivan's conceptions" (Carson, 1969, p. 54). Further, *recasting Sullivanian theory in terms of constructs associated with such contemporary areas as nonverbal communication and cognitive psychology has the important effect of forging a link to extant and developing research methodologies, in turn enabling more precise operationalization and empirical testing of Sullivan's ideas on human development, personality, abnormality, and psychotherapy.* Given Sullivan's continual insistence on developing a science of psychiatry through operationalizing psychiatric concepts, these contemporary retranslations represent a critical step in the evolution of Sullivanian theory. In this connection, current theory and research in such areas as social cognition and information processing (e.g., Wegner & Vallacher, 1977; Wiggins, 1980), the self (e.g., Lewis & Brooks-Gunn, 1979; Shrauger & Schoeneman, 1979; Wegner & Vallacher, 1980), and nonverbal communication (e.g., Harper, Weins, & Matarazzo, 1978; Siegman & Feldstein, 1978; Weitz, 1979) have much to contribute to the ongoing process of empirically investigating, revising, and expanding the "lines of inquiry" which Sullivan pioneered.

CIRCUMPLEX MODELS OF INTERPERSONAL BEHAVIOR

Chapters by Kiesler (Chapter 1), Carson (Chapter 4), Duke and Nowicki (Chapter 5), Anchin (Chapter 6), Horowitz (Chapter 9), Benjamin (Chapter 10), and McLemore and Hart (Chapter 12) converge in illustrating the value of incorporating circumplex models of interpersonal behavior and their associated measurement methodologies in the practice and scientific study of psychotherapy and behavior change. Circumplex models have proliferated in the 30 years since the development of the Interpersonal Circle by Leary and his colleagues (Freedman, Leary, Ossorio, & Coffey, 1951; Leary, 1957), but virtually all have in common the underlying dimensions of *affiliation* (love-hate) and *status/control* (dominance-submission), although Benjamin's SASB model incorporates the latter within a larger, more inclusive *interdependence* dimension. The reader is urged to consult a paper by Jerry Wiggins (in press) in which he presents a wide-ranging, scholarly review and critique of several of the major circumplex models that have been developed for measuring interpersonal behavior, as well as a discussion of their applications to clinical practice and research. As Wiggins points out, the development of circumplex models reflects an attempt "to provide a systematic language for description of interpersonal transactions and to demonstrate that this language permits the specification of a set of variables that are common to the enterprises of assessment, diagnosis, and treatment."

The rationale for applying circumplex models of interpersonal behavior to the assessment and treatment of clinical problems resides in part in a compelling body of theory and research (Anchin, 1977; Benjamin, in press; Horowitz, 1979, Chapter 9 in this volume; Kiesler & Federman, 1978; Leary, 1957; Lorr, Bishop, & McNair, 1965; McLemore & Benjamin, 1979; Plutchik & Platman, 1977; Schaefer & Plutchik, 1966; Wiggins, in press) demonstrating considerable overlap between traditional psychiatric diagnostic categories and interpersonal behavior. The work of Horowitz and Wiggins is particularly important in suggesting that psychiatric categories are prototypes (Rosch, 1978) containing features that are interpersonal in nature. Circumplex models permit a systematic description of these interpersonal components. In this context, Benjamin, in a large-scale investigation funded by the NIMH, is currently examining both the possibility of systematically integrating interpersonal behavior into traditional psychiatric nosology by using the SASB model to describe both inpatients and outpatients assigned to DSM-III categories, as well as the possibility of developing an entirely new classification system based on interpersonal nomenclature anchored in the SASB model. Inpatient diagnostic categories to be studied include paranoid schizophrenia; schizo-affective disorder, manic type; schizo-affective disorder, depressed type; primary affective disorder-uni-polar depression; primary affective disorder-bi-polar manic; primary affective disorder-bi-polar depressed; borderline personality; and antisocial personality. Psychiatric outpatient categories include dependent personality disorder; compulsive personality disorder; histrionic personality disorder; anxiety disorder-generalized anxiety disorder; and chronic depressive disorder. Clearly, results of this study will have significant implications for further demonstrating the relative salience of interpersonal behavior in psychopathology, as well as for the feasibility of an interpersonal nosology. Formal arguments regarding merits of the latter, including clinical and scientific advantages relative to traditional psychiatric nomenclature, are presented by McLemore and Benjamin (1979).

The logic and utility of applying interpersonal circumplex models to clinical practice is further buttressed by the fact that, as Horowitz (Chapter 9) points out, psychotherapeutic interventions usually target interpersonal problems. Moreover, his research shows that the dimensions underlying interpersonal problems are precisely those which underlie the circumplex models of interpersonal behavior. Horowitz' work thus provides an important bridge between the initial, presenting symptoms and complaints that tend to bring people into therapy and the specific circumplex categories of interpersonal styles. In conjunction with the theory and research cited above, an important implication for clinical assessment emerges: if diagnostic categories are prototypes containing interpersonal features, if interpersonal problems are typically targeted in treatment, and if interpersonal problems may be anchored in the circumplex, it follows that *assessment should take place in the same domain that we treat and that interpersonal styles should therefore be assessed directly from the very outset of treatment.*

In establishing the maladaptive interpersonal style correlates of presenting complaints, the clinician may draw on a variety of self-report and significant other rating instruments having as their underlying structure variations of the affiliation and status/control dimensions. A number of these are reviewed and discussed elsewhere in this volume (Kiesler, Chapter 1; Horowitz, Chapter 9; Benjamin, Chapter 10; and McLemore & Hart, Chapter 12). Self-report instruments include Benjamin's SASB questionnaires, the Interpersonal Check List (LaForge & Suczek, 1955), the Inventory of Interpersonal Problems (Horowitz, 1979), the Fundamental Interpersonal Relations Orientation (FIRO-B; Schutz, 1958), and the Schedule of Interpersonal Responses (Lorr, Suziedelis, & Kinnane, 1969). Instruments that may be completed by the therapist and/or extratherapy significant others on the patient include the Interpersonal Behavior Inventory (Lorr & McNair, 1967), the Impact Message Inventory (Kiesler et al., 1976; Perkins et al., 1979), the Interpersonal Check List, and the SASB questionnaires. Clearly, the latter set of measures might also be completed by the patient at periodic time points during treatment as a way of systematically acquiring information about his perceptions of and reactions to relevant significant others with whom he or she is interpersonally engaged.

Golding and Knudson (1975) highlight an important yet thus far largely neglected line of research in their investigation of the convergent validity of several of these indices. In addition to these paper and pencil instruments, coding of the patient's and/or significant others' behavior according to circumplex-based behavioral observation schemes (e.g., Raush et al., 1959; Shannon & Guerney, 1973) and content analysis systems (e.g., Chance, 1966; Estroff and Benjamin, 1979; Terrill & Terrill, 1965) may be profitably employed in such assessment situations, discussed by Peterson (Chapter 8), as the interview, naturalistic settings, and analogues.

Discussions by Peterson (Chapter 8) and Benjamin (Chapter 10) make it clear that information gathered through assessment and diagnosis should translate directly into implications for treatment. Diagnosing the patient's maladaptive functioning from the standpoint of circumplex-based interpersonal styles leads to clear and systematic treatment implications. For example, goals may be set in terms of fostering increased capacity to enact specific circumplex-based interpersonal styles in which the patient is currently deficient and whose incorporation into his or her repertoire is hypothesized to be associated with clinical improvement (e.g., reduction in symptomatology). Moreover, as discussed by Anchin in Chapter 6, *circumplex categories provide an individual differences system to facilitate assessment and modification of covert processes associated with problematic stylistics.* Importantly, though, since the circumplex categories of interpersonal behavior are themselves atheoretical (Wiggins, in press), the therapist is not bound to any single approach or set of interventions in fostering goal attainment. In addition, *the circumplex enables one to draw inferences about complementary styles which are automatically induced in others and which perpetuate the patient's maladjustment* (i.e., precisely how others become "accomplices" in the patient's neurosis; Wachtel, Chapter 3); this in turn translates directly into styles which the therapist must steadfastly avoid enacting during interactions with the patient. Further, beyond the Rogerian triad, one can define the precise nature of asocial responses and stylistics (Young & Beier, Chapter 14) which may be optimal when enacted at appropriate points in shifting the patient toward more adaptive interpersonal stances. In Chapter 4 and elsewhere (Carson, 1977), Carson alludes to the value of well-timed, planned enactment of particular styles by the therapist in the service of modifying the patient's disordered behavior.

Because Benjamin's (Chapter 10) SASB model is characterized by mathematical logic and a high degree of specificity, it optimizes these and other treatment implications stemming from circumplex-based assessment and diagnosis. For this reason one may expect this model to have an increasing impact upon treatment conducted from a principally interpersonal perspective. As illustrated by Benjamin in Chapter 10 and elsewhere (Benjamin, 1977, 1979a, in press), the principles of opposites, complements, antithesis, and introjection translate into an impressively systematic approach to treatment. For example, in discussing SASB-guided treatment of a family in therapy (Benjamin, 1977),

McLemore and Benjamin (1979) summarize: "the SASB model facilitated (a) explicit charting of the child's behavior disturbance, (b) clear specification of treatment goals, (c) detailed elaboration of the social context of the problem, (d) reconstruction of the developmental history of this context across generations, (e) ongoing monitoring of change over time, and (f) reasonably objective criteria for improvement and success. Benjamin's model also suggested a direction for treatment by specifying the antidote to what was initially happening between mother and son" (p. 29). The SASB model also enables a precise definition for a given case of such clinically rich concepts as double-binding and ambivalence.

More extensive application of circumplex models of interpersonal behavior and related measurement methodologies is warranted not only in the domain of clinical practice, but crucially, in the areas of psychotherapy process and outcome research as well. Horowitz (Chapter 9), for example, notes that despite the emphasis of treatment on interpersonal problems, outcome research has typically focused primarily upon symptoms. Others have similarly pointed to the need for and potential value of investigating therapeutic process and outcome in terms of explicitly interpersonal variables. Thus, nearly a decade ago, Kiesler (1973), following a brief review of Bierman's (1969) paper which cites evidence demonstrating the salience of the affiliation and status/control dimension across a wide range of social interactional situations (e.g., parent-child, teacher-student; see Carson, 1969), recommended that

Future studies of the psychotherapy relationship . . . should begin their conceptualization within this two-dimensional framework or some similar one. This evidence, furthermore, suggests that psychotherapy investigators might reap unusual benefits by serious attempts to apply interpersonal theories of personality and their measurement methodologies (for example, Leary, 1957; Schutz, 1958) to the interpersonal events of psychotherapy. [P. 331.]

Nevertheless, the important and necessary hook-up to interpersonal circumplex methodology has yet to be sufficiently realized. For example, the empirical literature on therapy process and outcome using instruments tied to interpersonal circumplex conceptualizations is relatively small, and the majority of these studies are of the analogue variety. Representative investigations include Anchin (1978), Beery (1970), Benjamin (1977, 1979), Crowder (1972), Cutler (1958), Greenwood (1978), Heller, Myers, and Kline (1963), Mueller (1969), Mueller and Dilling (1968), Reagan and Kallman (1977), and Swensen (1967). Recently, Bergin and Lambert (1978) stated that, "We assume that as the interpersonal dimensions of therapy interactions are more carefully examined, it will become possible to define more clearly which kinds of persons help which kinds of clients most effectively. Such evidence will reduce the importance placed on creating techniques and will increase the emphasis on therapist selection and interpersonal skill development" (p. 180). If we assume that the patient-therapist interaction is but a "special case" of dyadic interaction (see, e.g., Bierman, 1969; Goldstein, Heller, & Sechrest, 1966; Swensen, 1967), then knowledge of these dimensions is already in hand, and therefore it is time to pursue more vigorously than has heretofore been the case the kinds of matching studies implicit in Bergin and Lambert's statement. In this regard, it is notable that Berzins (1977) explicitly recommends that studies of patient-therapist matching should use as a theoretical guide "conceptualizations of therapeutic interactions in terms of the dimensions and categories of the Interpersonal Circle" (p. 245), while proposing Kiesler's (1971) Grid Model, "with its emphasis on studying temporal changes in homogeneous patient-therapist dyads" (p. 245), as a methodological guide. Berzins' inclusion of temporal considerations in matching studies is noteworthy; it points to the possibility that the multiphasic model of interpersonal relationships presented by Duke and Nowicki (Chapter 5) may be an exceedingly rich source of hypotheses in investigating patient-therapist interactions from the standpoint of circumplex conceptualizations.

Circumplex-based measures, particularly those to be completed by significant others, represent an important addition to psychotherapy research from still another vantage point. Though writing from quite different perspectives, both Kazdin (1977) and Strupp (Strupp & Hadley, 1977) have argued for *the value and importance of obtaining judgments of significant others in the patient's life as a necessary aspect of evaluating treatment outcomes.* Kazdin (1977), for example, writes:

> Social validation determines the efficacy of treatment in resolving clinical and social problems more directly than do specific discrete behavioral measures alone. The ultimate question of all treatment is whether it effects clinically important change. For most treatment techniques, this question has not even begun to be addressed. The criteria for evaluating treatment beyond the usual outcome measures may broaden in upcoming years to include such diverse measures as consumer acceptability of treatment, cost effectiveness, ease of implementation and dissemination, and others. Among these is the major concern with isolating treatments that go beyond discrete behavioral changes to affect client functioning in the natural environment. [Pp. 447–448.]

As argued throughout this volume, the natural environment is principally interpersonal and social in character, and therefore the various significant other measures cited above would all appear to be legitimate instruments for empirically assessing the impact of behavior change upon this environment. Indeed, Kazdin (1977) draws a distinction between social comparison and subjective evaluation methods of social validation; the latter method is especially relevant in the present context: "With the subjective evaluation method, the client's behavior is evaluated by individuals who are likely to have contact with him to determine whether the change made during treatment is important. *The question addressed by this method of validation is whether behavior changes have led to qualitative differences in how the client is viewed by others*" (p. 431, emphasis added). The potentiality of circumplex-based significant other measures in operationally anchoring this subjective evaluation method is clear. Moreover, since the distinction between outcome and process is mostly spurious (Kiesler, 1966, 1971), these evaluations would best be conducted on a repeated measures basis, provided that the distinctive methodological considerations attendant upon repeated measurement have been dealt with (see, e.g., Hersen & Barlow, 1976).

In this context, circumplex-based measurement devices would be an interesting addition to behaviorally oriented group and single-case (Hersen & Barlow, 1976) investigations of social skills training. Thus, while behaviorally oriented scientist-practitioners have developed an impressive technology of social skills training and provided numerous group and single-case demonstrations of its efficacy in modifying discrete verbal and nonverbal components of social behavior (see, e.g., Bellack & Hersen, 1979; Curran & Wessberg, in press; Hersen & Bellack, 1976; Trower, Bryant, & Argyle, 1978), these studies have rarely incorporated measures of the reciprocal overt and covert reactions of significant others in the patient's life which would demonstrate that the behavioral changes make a difference. Obtaining repeated measures by significant others with such instruments as the SASB questionnaires or the Impact Message Inventory before, during, and following social skills training is not at all incompatible with obtaining measures indicating changes in the patient's verbal and nonverbal behavior, and indeed would have the advantageous effect of linking what have thus far, unfortunately, been two disparate approaches to interpersonal functioning. A rapprochement of this sort would facilitate demonstrations of precisely what social skill behavioral changes mean in terms of the pervasive affiliation and status/control dimensions of social/interactional behavior.

A final point to be emphasized concerns *the necessity for achieving a consensus as to a standardized battery of circumplex-based interpersonal measures*, a direction currently being pursued by McLemore and Hart (Chapter 12). Bergin and Lambert (1978), for example, express reservations regarding the core battery recommended in Waskow and Parloff (1975) and propose that "several core batteries could be developed and applied to treatment situations where appropriate" (p. 176). Development of a core battery of interpersonal measures is thus highly desirable, although not only from the perspective of psychotherapy process and outcome research, but for other reasons as well: "Agreement as to a standard set of measures would . . . bring continuity and cumulative knowledge to important areas of current research on such topics as interaction sequences in dyadic relationships, affective reactions to interpersonal communications, individual differences in interpersonal construal styles, and interpersonal implications of psychiatric diagnoses" (Wiggins, in press, p. 63).

PROCEDURAL VARIABILITY AMONG INTERPERSONAL THEORISTS

Any attempt to compare and contrast different therapeutic approaches must immediately confront the question of what dimensions to employ in distinguishing among treatments. Thus, does one compare treatment approaches in terms of targets for change? Extent to which technique is operationalized? Duration of therapy? Goals? The answer, of course, is that these and certainly many other dimensions are all appropriate in analyzing psychotherapy systems (see Ford & Urban, 1963). Judicious selection of differentiating dimensions becomes particularly important, however, when approaches are founded upon certain common assumptions, as in the present volume. My intent here is briefly to discuss interpersonal approaches presented in this volume in terms of several of their more salient differentiating characteristics, leaving a more extensive comparative analysis of interpersonal approaches to psychotherapy for another time and place.

One of the most clear-cut dimensions in terms of which these interpersonal treatment systems differ is the extent to which the patient-therapist relationship serves as the explicit focus of therapeutic exploration and intervention. At one extreme are those approaches (Cashdan, Chapter 11; Young & Beier, Chapter 14) which focus almost exclusively throughout the course of treatment upon here and now patient-therapist interactions, emphasizing strategic responding to the patient's maladaptive interpersonal ploys during patient-therapist exchanges. At the other extreme are approaches (Coyne and Segal, Chapter 13; Weissman et al., Chapter 16) which minimize in-therapy examination of the patient-therapist relationship, emphasizing instead intervening in the patient's current extratherapy interpersonal situations. Clearly, the brief, time-limited nature of the latter approaches has much to do with this minimization of in-therapy focus, a point to which I shall return shortly. By far the majority of approaches presented in previous chapters fall between these two extremes, recognizing the crucial importance of explicitly addressing patient-therapist relationship factors which are assessed to be representative of the patient's maladaptive ways of interacting, but at the same time recognizing the need to examine—and when necessary to intervene in—the patient's extratherapy relationships if insights garnered through examination of patient-therapist interactions are to generalize to significant others outside of treatment (Chrzanowski, Chapter 2; Wachtel, Chapter 3; Carson, Chapter 4; Anchin, Chapter 6; Benjamin, Chapter 10; McLemore & Hart, Chapter 12; Kiesler, Chapter 15). In terms of systematizing treatment, an important issue is that of the particular sequencing of these respective foci as a function of stage of treatment, the patient's predominant style, and so on.

When events occurring between the patient and therapist are targeted in the effort to promote change, the overarching commonality entails the interpersonal therapist's strategic use of self as a real-life dyadic partner (as opposed to an exclusively transferential figure), thereby providing an asocial response (Young & Beier, Chapter 14; Beier, 1966) which avoids reinforcing the patient's interpersonal pathology. *Procedural differences, however, are apparent in precisely how and when the therapist addresses the in-therapy interaction.* For example, although Cashdan (Chapter 11) and Kiesler (Chapter 15) both emphasize the value of explicitly feeding back to the patient his or her impact upon the therapist, Cashdan delays these metacommunicative "impact confrontations" until Stage 4 (Adaptive Strategies)—the next to last stage—of his interactional psychotherapy. This is preceded by explicit attempts during Stage 2 (Maladaptive Strategies) first to foster in-therapy manifestation of self-defeating stylistics through direct confrontation and dare ploys in response to the patient's linguistic productions. This is followed by Stage 3, Stripping, in which the therapist refuses to respond as the patient wishes. In contrast, Kiesler views metacommunication about the patient's impact to be an interventional priority throughout the entire course of treatment, and indeed states that exploration of the patient-therapist relationship "is particularly crucial in early sessions with clients, but remains a metacommunication priority throughout therapy." Parenthetically, Kiesler's discussion of the "hooked" and "disengagement" phases with regard to the therapist's internal experiences in relation to the patient would seem to have generality across all interpersonal approaches presented in this volume. Carson (Chapter 4) provides still a third illustration of procedural variability in responding to the patient's maladaptive tactics. Reflecting his cognitive emphasis, Carson recommends a hypothesis testing model, according to which the therapist undertakes "a thorough examination of the evidential bases of the characteristics assigned to him, and repeatedly assert[s] his willingness to be put to *fair* tests, having *explicit* criteria, concerning his personal attitudes." Additional asocial response modes are discussed by Young and Beier (Chapter 14).

Obviously, these and other methods discussed in previous chapters for addressing the patient's self-defeating maneuvers as they emerge during therapeutic interactions are not mutually exclusive. As always, specificity considerations must guide the choice of what form of asocial responding should be employed in any given instance; these considerations include such factors as the precise nature of the patient's maladaptive style, the stage of therapy, the quality of the patient-therapist relationship at that point in treatment, the interpersonal issues thus far examined, and the therapist's own personality characteristics.

Variability in procedures for investigating and modifying the patient's extratherapy relationships is also evident. For example, Wachtel (Chapter 3), reflecting the psychoanalytic elements of his treatment approach, examines internal conflicts as these pertain to significant others, while he integrates behavioral procedures for rehearsing alternative interpersonal responses. Anchin (Chapter 6) similarly emphasizes use of behavioral as well as cognitive interventions to effect changes in extratherapy interpersonal patterns, while also undertaking interpersonal communication analysis of the patient's dysfunctional style as this manifests itself in day-to-day interactions. McLemore and Hart (Chapter 12) bring relevant significant others into treatment as a central component of their Disclosure procedure in the overall effort to increase the patient's capacity to attain intimacy with others. Coyne and Segal (Chapter 13) emphasize the use of homework, direct and indirect suggestion, and paradox as aspects of their brief, strategic therapy approach. A particularly signficant aspect of the latter approach is that, rooted as it is in the family therapy tradition of Bateson, Jackson, Haley, Watzlawick, and others, it suggests systematic ways in which ideas and techniques emphasized by systems-oriented couple and family therapists (e.g., Jackson, 1968a, 1968b; Haley, 1976; Watzlawick, Beavin, & Jackson, 1967; Watzlawick, Weakland, & Fisch, 1974; Watzlawick & Weakland, 1977; Watzlawick, 1978) may be used in treating the individual patient. The potential for cross-fertilizations between individual-interpersonal and couple and family systems approaches has yet to be fully exploited (e.g., see Kantor, 1980, for another family systems approach which has clear utility in treating the individual patient).

The brief, time-limited approach presented by Coyne and Segal, as well as that discussed by Weissman et al. (Chapter 16), represent significant developments within the interpersonal paradigm for several other reasons as well. Not the least of these is the need to develop effective and efficient therapeutic approaches to clinical problems in a time when third-party payments for a delimited number of sessions are emerging as a major source of payment to psychotherapists. Further, Strupp (1978) has presented a number of arguments to the effect that short-term psychotherapy may well be the most practical approach to treatment, leading him to predict "that short-term psychotherapy will receive increasing attention from therapists and researchers in the coming years" (p. 17) and that "we are on the threshold of what may be revolutionary change in therapeutic practice" (p. 18). It is encouraging that the interpersonal approach is meeting this challenge. Further, other therapeutic approaches presented in this volume may profit by explicitly and selectively incorporating features, reviewed by Butcher and Koss (1978), which characterize brief, time-limited therapies. In addition to time limitation, these include such characteristics as limited goals, focused interviewing, activity and directiveness, rapid and early assessment, therapeutic flexibility, and promptness of intervention. While certain of these features are already clearly an element of many of the longer-term approaches presented in previous chapters, continued efforts to monitor one's treatment practices in terms of these parameters and to incorporate them whenever feasible is strongly recommended.

While interpersonal approaches may be differentiated in terms of such factors as therapeutic focus, specific interventional strategies and techniques, and time duration, it is important to balance such considerations with the sobering possibility—discussed by Lakoff (Chapter 7) in her linguistic analysis and by Young and Beier (Chapter 14) in their "asocial theory"—that the factors which are common to all therapies, interpersonal or otherwise, may be more pivotal in producing significant clinical change than those characteristics which differentiate treatments.

CONCLUSION

The interpersonal perspective on personality and psychotherapy is far from new. McLemore (1979) concisely summarizes in noting that its theoretical roots extend back, on the clinical side, to Harry Stack Sullivan and other neo-Freudians, and on the empirical side to Timothy Leary and the landmark investigations conducted by him and his colleagues on multilevel interpersonal diagnosis. Further, volumes by Carson (1969), Swensen (1973),

Danziger (1976), Levinger and Raush (1977), and Hinde (1979) document that an impressive body of theory and research on interpersonal relationships has steadily accumulated over the past 35 to 40 years.

Nevertheless, the theory, practice, and scientific study of individual psychotherapy and behavior change have yet fully and systematically to incorporate the knowledge and measurement methodologies associated with this rich and productive interpersonal tradition. For example, Kiesler, Bernstein, and Anchin (1976) observed that the theoretical and research themes of both interactional and transactional dyadic communication approaches to human behavior, particularly as these pertain to clinical practice and research, have been lying "virtually dormant for decades" (p. 22). More recently, McLemore and Benjamin (1979) have posed a provocative, potentially far-reaching reminder to the field by asking, "Whatever happened to interpersonal diagnosis?": "for some time now behavioral scientists have been in possession of the concepts and methodologies necessary to create a truly psychosocial taxonomy of personality function and dysfunction. Such a creative venture, however, has yet to capture the imagination of either psychologists or psychiatrists." (p. 18). And in a similar vein, Wiggins (in press) has noted that "relatively impassioned pleas for the utility of [interpersonal circumplex approaches] for clinical practice have been issued every five years over the past three decades (e.g., Freedman et al., 1951; Leary, 1957; Foa, 1961; Adams, 1964; Carson, 1969; Benjamin, 1974; McLemore and Benjamin, 1979), suggesting that the approach has not been accorded as prominent a place in the mainstream of clinical thought as its proponents would desire" (p. 1). Carson (1980) has similarly offered comments to the effect that the interpersonal dimension of abnormality has generally not received the attention it merits.

The present volume represents one attempt toward remedying this curious state of affairs. The convergence of theoretical and empirical analyses suggesting that presenting complaints and DSM-III categories are prototypes which have definite interpersonal features underscores the need for and utility of contemporary interpersonal formulations and intervention strategies, as discussed in previous chapters. These conceptualizations and the research traditions to which they are linked can serve as explicit guides for the scientific and clinical study of interpersonal maladjustment. Further, interpersonal treatment strategies are becoming increasingly systematized and operationalized, thereby setting the stage for much needed empirical investigations of outcome efficacy with homogeneously defined patient groups. Importantly, however, it has been shown that many of these intervention strategies for modifying dysfunctional interpersonal processes have been drawn from other treatment paradigms. An interpersonal perspective therefore encourages one to consider how different therapy systems complement one another, an issue at least equally important to that of comparative effectiveness (see Goldfried, 1980). Further, circumplex-based conceptualizations have generated a measurement network which has important implications for expanding the scope of both group and single-case studies of therapeutic process and outcome. These as well as other developments examined throughout this volume clearly demonstrate that the interpersonal paradigm is steadily maturing, and that more concerted attention to its evolving constructs, methodologies, and treatment procedures can considerably enrich the science and practice of individual psychotherapy.

REFERENCES

Adams, H. B. "Mental illness" or interpersonal behavior? *American Psychologist*, 1964, **19**, 191–197.
Anchin, J. C. A communications model of psychotherapy and application to the "obsessive person-

ality." In J. C. Anchin (Chair.), *Communications approaches to psychotherapy*. Symposium presented at the meeting of the Southeastern Psychological Association, Hollywood, Florida, May, 1977.

Anchin, J. C. *The effects of interpersonal stress upon the impact messages generated by the "obsessive personality."* Unpublished doctoral dissertation, Virginia Commonwealth University, Richmond, 1978.

Beery, J. W. Therapists' responses as a function of level of therapist experience and attitude of the patient. *Journal of Consulting and Clinical Psychology*, 1970, **34**, 239–243.

Beier, E. G. *The silent language of psychotherapy: Social reinforcement of unconscious processes*. Chicago: Aldine, 1966.

Bellack, A. S. & Hersen, M. *Research and practice in social skills training*. New York: Plenum Press, 1979.

Benjamin, L. S. Structural analysis of social behavior. *Psychological Review*, 1974, **81**, 392–425.

Benjamin, L. S. Structural analysis of a family in therapy. *Journal of Consulting and Clinical Psychology*, 1977, **45**, 391–406.

Benjamin, L. S. Structural analysis of differentiation failure. *Psychiatry*, 1979, **42**, 1–23. (a)

Benjamin, L. S. Use of structural analysis of social behavior (SASB) and Markov chains to study dyadic interactions. *Journal of Abnormal Psychology*, 1979, **88**, 303–319. (b)

Benjamin, L. S. A psychosocial competence classification system. In J. D. Wine & M. D. Smye (Eds.), *Social competence*. New York: Guilford Press, in press.

Bergin, A. E. & Lambert, M. J. The evaluation of therapeutic outcomes. In S. L. Garfield & A. E. Bergin (Eds.), *Handbook of psychotherapy and behavior change: An empirical analysis*. New York: Wiley, 1978.

Berzins, J. I. Therapist-patient matching. In A. S. Gurman & A. M. Razin (Eds.), *Effective psychotherapy: A handbook of research*. New York: Pergamon, 1977.

Bierman, R. Dimensions of interpersonal facilitation in psychotherapy and child development. *Psychological Bulletin*, 1969, **72**, 338–352.

Butcher, J. N. & Koss, M. P. Research on brief and crisis-oriented psychotherapies. In S. L. Garfield & A. E. Bergin (Eds.), *Handbook of psychotherapy and behavior change: An empirical analysis*. New York: Wiley, 1978.

Carson, R. C. *Interaction concepts of personality*. Chicago: Aldine, 1969.

Carson, R. C. Therapeutic communication in the modification of interpersonal cosmologies. In J. C. Anchin (Chair.), *Communications approaches to psychotherapy*. Symposium presented at the meeting of the Southeastern Psychological Association, Hollywood, Florida, May, 1977.

Carson, R. C. Personality and exchange in developing relationships. In R. L. Burgess & T. L. Houston (Eds.), *Social exchange in developing relationships*. New York: Academic Press, 1979.

Carson, R. C. Personal communication, July 15, 1980.

Chance, E. Content analysis of verbalizations about interpersonal experience. In L. A. Gottschalk & A. H. Auerbach (Eds.), *Methods of research in psychotherapy*. New York: Appleton-Century-Crofts, 1966.

Chrzanowski, G. *Interpersonal approach to psychoanalysis: Contemporary view of Harry Stack Sullivan*. New York: Gardner Press, 1977.

Chrzanowski, G. From ego psychology to a psychology of self. In E. G. Witenberg (Ed.), *Interpersonal psychoanalysis: New directions*. New York: Gardner Press, 1978.

Coyne, J. C. Therapeutic communication with depressives. In J. C. Anchin (Chair.), *Communications approaches to psychotherapy*. Symposium presented at the meeting of the Southeastern Psychological Association, Hollywood, Florida, May, 1977.

Coyne, J. C. Some unnecessary constraints on therapeutic intervention: A transactional perspective. In C. W. McLemore (Chair.), *New frontiers in interpersonal theory, research, and practice*. Symposium presented at the meeting of the American Psychological Association, New York City, September, 1979.

Coyne, J. C. & Lazarus, R. S. *Cognition and depression*. Paper presented at the meeting of the American Psychological Association, Montreal, Canada, September, 1980.

Crowder, J. E. Relationship between therapist and client interpersonal behaviors and psychotherapy outcome. *Journal of Counseling Psychology*, 1972, **19**, 68–75.

Curran, J. P. & Wessberg, H. W. The assessment of social inadequacy. In D. H. Barlow (Ed.), *Behavioral assessment of adult disorders*. New York: Guilford Press, in press.

Cutler, R. L. Countertransference effects in psychotherapy. *Journal of Consulting Psychology*, 1958, **22**, 349–356.

Danziger, K. *Interpersonal communication*. New York: Pergamon, 1976.

Estroff, S. & Benjamin, L. S. *Coding manual for using SASB to rate typescripts*. Unpublished manuscript, University of Wisconsin, Madison, May, 1979.

Foa, U. G. Convergences in the analysis of the structure of interpersonal behavior. *Psychological Review*, 1961, **68**, 341–358.

Ford, D. H. & Urban, H. B. *Systems of psychotherapy: A comparative study*. New York: Wiley, 1963.

Freedman, M. B., Leary, T. F., Ossorio, A. G., & Coffey, H. S. The interpersonal dimension of personality. *Journal of Personality*, 1951, **20**, 143–161.

Goldfried, M. R. Toward the delineation of therapeutic principles. *American Psychologist*, 1980, **35**, 991–999.

Golding, S. L. Individual differences in the construal of interpersonal interactions. In D. Magnussson & N. Endler (Eds.), *Personality at the crossroads: Current issues in interactional psychology*. Hillsdale, N.J.: Erlbaum, 1977.

Golding, S. L. Toward a more adequate theory of personality: Psychological organizing principles. In H. London & N. Hirschberg (Eds.), *Personality: A new look at metatheories*. Washington, D.C.: Hemisphere Press, 1978.

Golding, S. L. Abstract to The clinical relevance of psychological organizing principles. In C. W. McLemore (Chair.), *New frontiers in interpersonal theory, research, and practice*. Symposium presented at the meeting of the American Psychological Association, New York City, September, 1979.

Golding, S. L. & Knudson, R. M. Multivariable-multimethod convergence in the domain of interpersonal behavior. *Multivariate Behavioral Research*, 1975, **10**, 425–448.

Golding, S. L., Valone, K., & Foster, S. W. Interpersonal construal: An individual differences framework. In N. Hirschberg (Ed.), *Multivariate methods in the social sciences: Applications*. Hillsdale, N.J.: Erlbaum, 1980.

Goldstein, A. P., Heller, K., & Sechrest, L. B. *Psychotherapy and the psychology of behavior change*. New York: Wiley, 1966.

Greenwood, V. B. *The effects of the interviewer's status upon the linguistic style and impact messages generated by the "obsessive personality."* Unpublished doctoral dissertation, Virginia Commonwealth University, Richmond, 1978.

Guntrip, H. *Psychoanalytic theory, therapy, and the self*. New York: Basic Books. 1973.

Haley, J. *Problem-solving therapy*. San Francisco: Jossey-Bass, 1976.

Harper, R. G., Wiens, A. N., & Matarazzo, J. D. *Nonverbal communication: The state of the art*. New York: Wiley, 1978.

Heller, K., Myers, R. A., & Kline, L. V. Interviewer behavior as a function of standardized client roles. *Journal of Consulting Psychology*, 1963, **27**, 117–122.

Hersen, M. & Barlow, D. H. *Single-case experimental designs: Strategies for studying behavioral change*. New York: Pergamon, 1976.

Hersen, M. & Bellack, A. S. Social skills training for chronic psychiatric patients: Rationale, research findings, and future directions. *Comprehensive Psychiatry*, 1976, **17**, 559–580.

Hinde, R. A. *Towards understanding relationships*. New York: Academic Press, 1979.

Hollon, S. D. & Kendall, P. C. Cognitive-behavioral interventions: Theory and procedure. In P. C. Kendall & S. D. Hollon (Eds.), *Cognitive-behavioral interventions: Theory, research, and procedures*. New York: Academic Press, 1979.

Horowitz, L. M. On the cognitive structure of interpersonal problems treated in psychotherapy. *Journal of Consulting and Clinical Psychology*, 1979, **47**, 1–15.

Jackson, D. D. (Ed.) *Communication, family, and marriage.* Palo Alto, Calif.: Science and Behavior Books, 1968. (a)

Jackson, D. D. (Ed.). *Therapy, communication, and change.* Palo Alto, Calif.: Science and Behavior Books, 1968. (b)

Kantor, D. Critical identity image: A concept linking individual, couple, and family development. In J. K. Pearce & L. J. Friedman (Eds.), *Family perspectives on psychotherapy.* New York: Grune & Stratton, 1980.

Kazdin, A. Assessing the clinical or applied importance of behavior change through social validation. *Behavior Modification,* 1977, **1**, 427–451.

Kendall, P. C. & Hollon, S. D. (Eds.) *Assessment strategies for cognitive-behavioral interventions.* New York: Academic Press, 1981.

Kendall, P. C. & Korgeski, G. P. Assessment and cognitive-behavioral interventions. *Cognitive Therapy and Research,* 1979, **3**, 1–21.

Kiesler, D. J. Some myths of psychotherapy research and the search for a paradigm. *Psychological Bulletin,* 1966, **65**, 110–136.

Kiesler, D. J. Experimental designs in psychotherapy research. In A. E. Bergin & S. L. Garfield (Eds.), *Handbook of psychotherapy and behavior change: An empirical analysis.* New York: Wiley, 1971.

Kiesler, D. J. *The process of psychotherapy: Empirical foundations and systems of analysis.* Chicago: Aldine, 1973 (a)

Kiesler, D. J. *A communications approach to modification of the "obsessive personality:" An initial formulation.* Unpublished manuscript, Emory University, Atlanta, 1973. (b)

Kiesler, D. J. *Communications assessment of interview behaviors of the "obsessive personality."* Unpublished manuscript, Virginia Commonwealth University, Richmond, 1977.

Kiesler, D. J. An interpersonal communication analysis of relationship in psychotherapy. *Psychiatry,* 1979, **42**, 299–311.

Kiesler, D. J., Anchin, J. C., Perkins, M. J., Chirico, B. M., Kyle, E. M., & Federman, E. J. *The Impact Message Inventory.* Richmond: Virginia Commonwealth University, 1976.

Kiesler, D. J., Bernstein, A. J., & Anchin, J. C. *Interpersonal communication, relationship and the behavior therapies.* Richmond, Virginia Commonwealth University, 1976.

Kiesler, D. J. & Federman, E. J. *Differential effects of obsessive and hysteric personality descriptions on impact messages decoded by judges.* Unpublished manuscript, Virginia Commonwealth University, Richmond, 1978.

Kuhn, T. S. *The structure of scientific revolutions,* 2nd ed. Chicago: University of Chicago Press, 1970.

LaForge, R. & Suczek, R. F. The interpersonal dimension of personality: III. An interpersonal checklist. *Journal of Personality,* 1965, **24**, 94–112.

Laing, R. D., Phillipson, H., & Lee, A. R. *Interpersonal perception: A theory and a method of research.* New York: Springer, 1966.

Leary, T. *Interpersonal diagnosis of personality: A functional theory and methodology for personality evaluation.* New York: Ronald Press, 1957.

Levinger, G. & Raush, H. L. (Eds.) *Close relationships: Perspectives on the meaning of intimacy.* Amherst: University of Massachusetts Press, 1977.

Lewis, M. & Brooks-Gunn, J. *Social cognition and the acquisition of self.* New York: Plenum Press, 1979.

Lorr, M., Bishop, P. R., & McNair, D. Interpersonal types among psychiatric patients. *Journal of Abnormal Psychology,* 1965, **70**, 468–472.

Lorr, M. & McNair, D. M. An interpersonal behavior circle. *Journal of Abnormal and Social Psychology,* 1963, **67**, 68–75.

Lorr, M. & McNair, D. M. Expansion of the interpersonal behavior circle. *Journal of Personality and Social Psychology,* 1965, **2**, 823–830.

Lorr, M. & McNair, D. M. Methods relating to evaluation of therapeutic outcome. In L. A. Gottschalk & A. H. Auerbach (Eds.), *Methods of research in psychotherapy.* New York: Appleton-

Century-Crofts, 1966.

Lorr, M. & McNair, D. M. *The Interpersonal Behavior Inventory* (Form 4). Washington, D.C.: The Catholic University of America, 1967.

Lorr, M., Suziedelis, A., & Kinnane, J. F. Characteristic response modes to interpersonal situations. *Multivariate Behavioral Research*, 1969, **4**, 445–458.

McLemore, C. W. Abstract for C. W. McLemore (Chair.), *New frontiers in interpersonal theory, research, and practice.* Symposium presented at the meeting of the American Psychological Association, New York City, September, 1979.

McLemore, C. W. & Benjamin, L. S. Whatever happened to interpersonal diagnosis? A psychosocial alternative to DSM-III. *American Psychologist*, 1979, **34**, 17–34.

Mehrabian, A. *Nonverbal communication.* Chicago: Aldine, 1972.

Mowrer. O. H. Learning theory and the neurotic paradox. *American Journal of Orthopsychiatry*, 1948, **18**, 571–610.

Mueller, W. J. Patterns of behavior and their reciprocal impact in the family and in psychotherapy. *Journal of Counseling Psychology Monograph*, 1969, **16**, (2, part 2).

Mueller, W. J. & Dilling, C. A. Therapist-client interview behavior and personality characteristics of therapists. *Journal of Projective Techniques and Personality Assessment*, 1968, **32**, 281–288.

Newcomb, T. M. An approach to the study of communicative acts. *Psychological Review*, 1953, **60**, 393–404.

Perkins, M. J., Kiesler, D. J., Anchin, J. C., Chirico, B. M., Kyle, B. M., & Federman, E. J. The Impact Message Inventory: A new measure of relationship in counseling/psychotherapy and other dyads. *Journal of Counseling Psychology*, 1979, **26**, 363–367.

Peterson, D. R. A functional approach to the study of person-person interaction. In D. Magnusson & N. S. Endler (Eds.), *Personality at the cross-roads: Current issues in interactional psychology.* Hillsdale, N.J.: Erlbaum, 1977.

Peterson, D. R. Assessing interpersonal relationships by means of interaction records. *Behavioral Assessment*, 1979, **1**, 221–236. (a)

Peterson, D. R. Assessing interpersonal relationships in natural settings. *New Directions for Methodology of Behavioral Science*, 1979, **2**, 33–54. (b)

Plutchik, R. & Platman, S. R. Personality connotations of psychiatric diagnoses: Implications for a similarity model. *Journal of Nervous and Mental Disease*, 1977, **165**, 418–422.

Raush, H. L., Dittman, A. T., & Taylor, T. J. The interpersonal behavior of children in residential treatment. *Journal of Abnormal and Social Psychology*, 1959, **58**, 9–26.

Reagan, S. A. & Kallman, W. *The Impact Message Inventory: An interpersonal measure of assertive behavior.* Paper presented at the Southeastern Psychological Association Meeting, Hollywood, Florida, May, 1977.

Rosch, E. Principles of categorization. In E. Rosch & D. B. Lloyd (Eds.), *Cognition and categorization.* Hillsdale, N.J.: Erlbaum, 1978.

Schaefer, E. S. & Plutchik, R. Interrelationships of emotions, traits, and diagnostic constructs. *Psychological Reports*, 1966, **18**, 399–410.

Schutz, W. C. *FIRO: A three-dimensional theory of interpersonal behavior.* New York: Holt, Rinehart & Winston, 1958.

Secord, P. F. & Backman, C. W. An interpersonal approach to personality. In B. A. Maher (Ed.), *Progress in experimental personality research*, vol. 2. New York: Academic Press, 1965.

Shannon, J. & Guerney, B., Jr. Interpersonal effects of interpersonal behavior. *Journal of Personality and Social Psychology*, 1973, **26**, 142–150.

Shrauger, J. S. & Schoeneman, T. J. Symbolic interactionist view of self-concept: Through the looking glass darkly. *Psychological Bulletin*, 1979, **86**, 549–573.

Siegman, A. W. & Feldstein, S. (Eds.) *Nonverbal behavior and communication.* Hillsdale, N.J.: Erlbaum, 1978.

Strupp, H. H. Psychotherapy research and practice: An overview. In S. L. Garfield & A. E. Bergin (Eds.), *Handbook of psychotherapy and behavior change: An empirical analysis.* New York: Wiley, 1978.

Sullivan, H. S *Conceptions of modern psychiatry.* New York: Norton, 1940.

Sullivan, H. S. *The interpersonal theory of psychiatry.* New York: Norton, 1953.

Sullivan, H. S. *The psychiatric interview.* New York: Norton, 1954.

Sullivan, H. S. *Clinical studies in psychiatry.* New York: Norton, 1956.

Sullivan, H. S. *Schizophrenia as a human process.* New York: Norton, 1962.

Swensen, C. H., Jr. Psychotherapy as a special case of dyadic interaction: Some suggestions for theory and research. *Psychotherapy: Theory, Research and Practice,* 1967, **4**, 7–13.

Swensen, C. H., Jr. *Introduction to interpersonal relations.* Glenview, Ill.: Scott, Foresman and Company, 1973.

Terrill, J. M. & Terrill, R. E. A method for studying family communication. *Family Process,* 1965, **4**, 259–270.

Trower, P., Bryant, B., & Argyle, M. *Social skills and mental health.* Pittsburgh: University of Pittsburgh Press, 1978.

Wachtel, P. L. Interaction cycles, unconscious processes, and the person-situation issue. In D. Magnusson & N. Endler (Eds.), *Personality at the cross-roads: Current issues in interactional psychology.* Hillsdale, N.J.: Erlbaum, 1977. (a)

Wachtel, P. L. *Psychoanalysis and behavior therapy: Toward an integration.* New York: Basic Books, 1977. (b)

Waskow, I. E. & Parloff, M. B. *Psychotherapy change measures.* Washington, D.C.: DHEW, 1975.

Watzlawick, P. *The language of change.* New York: Basic Books, 1978.

Watzlawick, P., Beavin, J. H., & Jackson, D. D. *Pragmatics of human communication: A study of interactional patterns, pathologies, and paradoxes.* New York: Norton, 1967.

Watzlawick, P. & Weakland, J. H. (Eds.) *The interactional view: Studies at the Mental Research Institute, Palo Alto, 1965–1974.* New York: Basic Books, 1977.

Watzlawick, P., Weakland, J. H., & Fisch, R. *Change: Principles of problem formation and problem resolution.* New York: Norton, 1974.

Wegner, D. M. & Vallacher, R. R. (Eds.) *The self in social psychology.* New York: Oxford University Press, 1980.

Weitz, S. (Ed.) *Nonverbal communication: Readings with commentary,* 2nd ed. New York: Oxford University Press, 1979.

Wiggins, J. S. Circumplex models of interpersonal behavior. In L. Wheeler (Ed.), *Review of personality and social psychology,* vol. 1. Beverly Hills: Sage Publications, 1980.

Wiggins, J. S. Circumplex models of interpersonal behavior in clinical psychology. In P. C. Kendall & J. N. Butcher (Eds.), *Handbook of research methods in clinical psychology.* New York: Wiley Interscience, in press.

Author Index

SUBJECT INDEX

About the Editors
and Contributors

Jack C. Anchin, Ph.D., is Assistant Professor of Psychology at the State University of New York College at Buffalo. He received his B.A. summa cum laude from Adelphi University in 1973 and was awarded his M.S. (1975) and Ph.D. (1978) in Clinical Psychology from Virginia Commonwealth University, Richmond. Upon completion of his clinical internship at Brown University–Butler Hospital in 1978, he served as Research Coordinator and Staff Psychologist at South Shore Mental Health Center, Quincy, Massachusetts. He held this position for three years before moving to the State University College at Buffalo in 1981. His interests include theory and research on cognitive and interpersonal approaches to personality psychopathology, and its treatment, psychotherapy process and outcome research, as well as professional practice and training in adult psychotherapy.

Donald J. Kiesler, Ph.D., is Professor of Clinical Psychology at Virginia Commonwealth University in Richmond. Born in Louisville, Kentucky, he completed his undergraduate work there at Bellarmine College in 1958, and in 1963 was awarded his Ph.D. in Clinical Psychology from the University of Illinois. During 1963–1964 he was first a United States Public Health Service post-doctoral research Fellow and subsequently Director of the psychotherapy research project at the University of Wisconsin Psychiatric Institute in Madison. From 1964–1967 he served as Assistant Professor in psychology at the University of Iowa at Iowa City, and from 1967–1973 as Associate Professor and Professor of psychology at Emory University in Atlanta, Georgia. Coming to Virginia Commonwealth University in 1973, he first held the administrative position of Director of the doctoral program in Clinical Psychology, and in 1976 returned to his duties as Professor in that program. His primary interests are theory, research and training in adult psychotherapy from an interpersonal communication framework.

Ernst G. Beier, Ph.D., is Professor of Psychology at the University of Utah, Salt Lake City. Author of *The Silent Language of Psychotherapy* and *People Reading*, he is Counsel Representative to the American Psychological Association and was APA Convention Chairman (1980) and Chairman of International Relations (1978). His present research interests include theoretical issues in relating psychotherapy to nonverbal behavior, identification of stress states, and disaster prevention and control.

Lorna Smith Benjamin, Ph.D., is Professor of Psychiatry in the Department of Psychiatry at the University Hospitals in Madison, Wisconsin. Favorite teaching duties in-

343

clude a seminar on interviewing skills for psychiatric residents, and a weekly difficult case-conference demonstrating developmental and interpersonal views of in-patients. Major research activity is a National Institute of Mental Health-funded Interpersonal Diagnostic Study wherein there will be an attempt to develop a proposal for systematically adding interpersonal dimensions to DSM-III and/or an alternative interpersonal nosology.

Robert C. Carson, Ph.D., is Professor of Psychology in the Department of Psychology, and Professor of Medical Psychology in the Department of Psychiatry at Duke University, Durham, North Carolina. His interests lie in the study of psychopathology and its treatment, principally from a social/interpersonal perspective.

Sheldon Cashdan, Ph.D., is a member of the clinical training faculty at the University of Massachusetts. He also has a private practice in Amherst where he specializes in the treatment of marital disturbances. The author of *Interactional Psychotherapy*, Professor Cashdan currently is working on a book dealing with "marital identity" and the interactional treatment of couples.

Eve S. Chevron, M.S., is a Ph.D. Candidate in Clinical Psychology in the Yale University Graduate School. As a Psychologist (Project Coordinator) in the Depression Research Unit of Yale's Department of Psychiatry, she is involved in development and administration of a training program in IPT with acutely depressed patients. She is also engaged in individual supervision of clinical trainees at the Connecticut Mental Health Center. Her research interest in IPT includes issues of selection and training of therapists to participate in psychotherapy outcome studies.

Gerard Chrzanowski, M.D., is supervisory and training analyst, as well as a faculty member of the William Alanson White Institute and the Psychoanalytic Division of New York Medical College. Additionally, he is Associate Professor of Clinical Psychiatry at New York Medical College and Medical Director of the Bleuler Psychotherapy Center. His publications include *Interpersonal Approach to Psychoanalysis: Contemporary View of Harry Stack Sullivan*.

James C. Coyne, Ph.D., is Assistant Professor of Psychology at the University of California, Berkeley, as well as Director of Research at the Mental Research Institute, Palo Alto. His research interests include depression, stress, and brief therapy.

Marshall P. Duke, Ph.D., is Associate Professor of Psychology at Emory University, Atlanta, Georgia. In addition to his empirical and theoretical interests in interpersonal psychology, he is studying genetic determinants of personality. A Kaiserian psychotherapist by training, he also is involved in psychotherapy practice and supervision.

Rita deSales French, M.A., is presently working on her doctoral degree in Psychology at Stanford University. Her research interests include the study of interpersonal problem solving skill in lonely people and the study of cognitive processes in personality psychology, as well as investigation of current diagnostic categorization systems viewed from the perspective of "prototypes." She also works with the Bay Area Foster Care Project at the Boys Town Center for the Study of Youth Development at Stanford University.

Phyllis P. Hart, Ph.D., is Assistant Professor of Psychology in the Graduate School of Psychology, Fuller Theological Seminary, Pasadena, California, as well as Director of Training for The Psychological Center sponsored by and affiliated with Fuller. Her research interests include the psychology of women and human sexuality.

Leonard M. Horowitz, Ph.D., is Professor of Psychology at Stanford University, Stanford, California. He has been affiliated with the Mt. Zion Psychiatric Clinic, and he has a private practice in San Francisco. His research concerns the cognitive representation of interpersonal processes and the measurement of change following psychotherapy.

Gerald L. Klerman, M.D., is Director of the Stanley Cobb Psychiatric Research Laboratories, Massachusetts General Hospital, Boston, and Professor of Psychiatry in the Harvard Medical School. Formerly Administrator of the Alcohol, Drug Abuse, and Mental Health Administration, Public Health Service, U.S. Department of Health and Human Services, his current research interests include the study of affective disorders.

Robin Tolmach Lakoff, Ph.D., is Professor of Linguistics at the University of California, Berkeley. She received a Ph.D. in Linguistics in 1967 from Harvard University. She has been at Berkeley since 1972, and was previously (1969-1971) at the University of Michigan, and (1971-1972) at the Center of Advanced Study for the Behavioral Sciences, Stanford. Her current research interests are in the area of pragmatics and sociolinguistics, especially concerning conversational analysis and discourse theory.

Jeffrey S. Lapid, M.A., is now in the Ph.D. program in Clinical Psychology at the University of Colorado, Boulder. His research interests focus on the relationship between psychodiagnosis, interpersonal problems and object relations theory.

Clinton W. McLemore, Ph.D., is Associate Professor of Psychology in the Graduate School of Psychology, Fuller Theological Seminary, Pasadena, California. His research interests include sequence analysis of psychotherapy process, models of interpersonal behavior, and relationships between social behavior and psychopathology.

Carlos Neu, M.D., is Assistant Clinical Professor of Psychiatry, Harvard Medical School at Cambridge Hospital. Additionally, he is a Staff Psychiatrist and Clinical Supervisor of Primary Care Residents at the Harvard Community Health Plan. He also has a private practice in Cambridge, Massachusetts.

Stephen Nowicki, Jr., Ph.D., is Professor of Psychology and Director of the Clinical Psychology Program at Emory University, Atlanta, Georgia. His major research interests are in applications of Rotter's social learning theory.

Donald R. Peterson, Ph.D., is Dean of the Graduate School of Applied and Professional Psychology and Professor of Psychology at Rutgers, the State University of New Jersey. As a clinician and as a researcher, he has been active in the assessment and change of interpersonal behavior for more than 25 years.

Bruce J. Rounsaville, M.D., is Director of Research, Substance Abuse Treatment Unit, Connecticut Mental Health Center, and Assistant Professor of Psychiatry, Yale University School of Medicine, New Haven, Connecticut. His primary research activities involve evaluating the efficacy of psychological and pharmacological treatments of depression and opiate addiction.

Lynn Segal, L.C.S.W., is Research Associate, Mental Research Institute (MRI), Palo Alto, California, as well as a staff member of the MRI Brief Therapy Center. Additionally, he is a Training Consultant and clinical social worker in private practice.

Hans H., Strupp, Ph.D., is Distinguished Professor of Psychology at Vanderbilt University, Nashville, Tennessee. He is a Diplomate in Clinical Psychology, ABPP, and his interests in psychotherapy are in research, training, and professional practice, with particular emphasis on time-limited dynamic psychotherapy.

Paul L. Wachtel, Ph.D., is Professor of Psychology and Associate Director of the Ph.D. Program in Clinical Psychology, City College of the City University of New York. His interests include active intervention in psychotherapy, personality theory, and social implications of psychological ideas.

David A. Weckler, Ph.D., is a post-doctoral Fellow in the multidisciplinary NIMH Research Training Program on Organizations and Mental Health in the Department of Sociology and the Graduate School of Business at Stanford University. His research and practical interests include the institutional and interpersonal factors affecting the delivery of mental health services and cognitive and interpersonal processes in group decision making and performance.

Myrna M. Weissman, Ph.D., is a tenured Associate Professor of Psychiatry and Epidemiology at Yale University School of Medicine, New Haven, CT, and Director of the Depression Research Unit, Connecticut Mental Health Center. Her professional discipline is psychiatric epidemiology of psychiatric disorders in the community, and the treatment and the genetics of affective disorders.

David M. Young, Ph.D., is Associate Professor of Psychological Sciences at Indiana University-Purdue University at Fort Wayne, Indiana. His research interests include communication processes and community psychology. He is also in private practice.